THE GOLD OF ROCK & ROLL
1955–1967

The Gold of Rock & Roll 1955-1967

Edited, with special appreciations, by
H. KANDY ROHDE

with research assistance by Laing Ned Kandel

ARBOR HOUSE

New York

to Stephen,
to Louis and Ewole,
the Hell Gang,
Cool Mary,
to Lois and Ron,
Tina and the Sonises,
to Eacy and Ray,
all the kids on
Central Avenue and McCorkle Avenue
to Rusty and Diane,
Bull and Roschel,
the BookStrap staff,
to Neddy
and everybody at Charleston High

ACKNOWLEDGEMENTS

There is a big gap between loving
rock and roll and getting the
opportunity to publish a book that
can tell the world how much you do.
I truly thank the people who gave
me the help and encouragement to
close that gap, especially
Edward Stephens and Ken Morton who
made me realize I could write, and
Charles Rembar who made me realize
I could sell my writing.

My special thanks to Bob Entley and
WKLC for their help gathering
Top 10 information, to Evelyn Carter
for her background story on
"Rock Around the Clock," and to
Larry Petrowski, Joel Anderson,
Jo Ann Krushevsky, and Don Fine.

CONTENTS

INTRODUCTION

THIS book is meant to carry old time rock and roll fans back to the days of the sock hop—back to the days before we were married and had jobs and the responsibilities of adulthood. Despite our membership in the Pepsi generation, our life has generally become stabilized. We have years and years of memories of play and dating and school days. The years 1955–1967 are our good old days. And playing in the background as we grew from bobby sox to briefcase was rock and roll music.

A stack of records is like a stack of photographs. The song brings back a personal experience—your steady boyfriend, a dance, graduation. And this is a book of cues for each fan's reminiscence.

The bobby-soxer of the fifties and today's teenybopper differ radically in their view of music. The old days put few analytical demands on a fan. We didn't study the structure of our music, the poetry of our lyrics. We were busy being kids and the music was just an accepted part of our lives. Now that we are grown, we find ourselves looking back at the old days and cueing those looks with old rock and roll.

We could analyze the developing chordal structure of rock and roll, but that wouldn't bring back the warm feelings of merely dating a song title to the time that something happened. A general reminiscence that "Finger Poppin' Time" was the song played on the 1960 American Bandstand dance contest triggers for me a web of high school memories that I might not otherwise have recalled, and that no industry analysis could cue.

Aside from my deep conviction that there is a fraternity of ex-bobby-soxers—each with personal memories but all accessible through rock and roll—I have observed objective indications that such a camaraderie of rock and roll is alive.

I found it accidentally. People my age commented that we are part of a bygone era. Today's music isn't fun for us. At parties they don't dance like they used to. Everyone is too busy being deep and committed, sitting on the floor smoking grass instead of having a rocking beer party.

And then conversations about the old music . . . "Remember when Elvis Presley first started? When I heard his voice I thought he was an old man." "Remember the Del Vikings? They played 'Come Go with Me' over and over at my first dance."

The rock and roll revival can also be seen in the success of groups like Sha Na Na or the new demand for the Everly Brothers, whose act is almost all their old hits, or the sales of oldies albums, or most recently in the rock and roll revival concerts.

I was playing old records a few weeks ago and my downstairs neighbor came up, introduced himself and asked if he could stay and listen. We'd grown up in different worlds, economically, geographically, but we were brothers. Each song brought a rush of memories—mostly personal but anchored in general memories of the times.

I have seen groups of old fans sit around and try to remember which group did which song, or what the title of the group's follow-up song was. I know fans who go to record stores to read the Phonolog and try to glean this information.

That is why I hope you will read the texts and lists together. It is the combination that will best evoke your memories. The text is meant to be just enough of a cue to bring back the year. It is vital that this cue be limited. It is not meant to be comprehensive, only to pull you back into your past. As hard as it may be for non-rock and roll fans to understand, we can read the list and hear every song.

We lived it. We—today's young marrieds and young parents—are the kids who wept over Ritchie Valens and squealed at Elvis. We don't need to be told about rock and roll. We could thumb through and through the old Top 10's and through and through our memories.

Other books have been written for people who need an education about rock and roll because they are too old or too young or were outside during the old rock and roll days. These books see rock and roll and today's rock as one music, and I do not.

Rock and roll simply passed away in 1967. As any observer of the arts should have seen, rock and roll stepped from its simplest primitive days of Bill Haley, Buddy Holly, and U. S. Bonds to the perfectly balanced style of the Beatles' "Rubber Soul" and the Mamas and Papas early hits to the self-indulgent preoccupation with technique of "Sargeant Pepper" and "Fresh Cream." And here rigor mortis set in, when lesser technicians were left to execute a music that was more technique than content.

Without the genuine happy quality that had sustained rock and roll, rock after 1967 was left wanting—an exercise in musical technique.

Our music is in the past. And it's great in these troubled times to look back to those simple, happy days.

H. Kandy Rohde,
New York, April, 1970

12

In researching the Top 10's and Top 50's we found numerous discrepancies within and among the sources indicating that some license had been taken in compiling the source lists. The Top 10's in this book were arrived at by weighing the charts of leading trade journals, cooperating radio stations representing regional variations, and our notes and recollections from the rock and roll era.

These lists, therefore, may vary from what the reader recalls or what was broadcast over his local stations. Nevertheless, we believe that, short of asking everyone what his favorite song was, these charts represent as accurate a view of national popularity as is possible and necessary.

FATS DOMINO

January, 1955, may have started with a rare winter hurricane, but the New Year didn't promise to be anything out of the ordinary.

"White Christmas" was the Number 2 song, still hanging on from the holiday season. And, as usual on January 1, there was the Rose Bowl game where Ohio State outsloshed Southern Cal 20 to 7.

Washington, still worrying about the Russians, dismissed three thousand security risks from federal positions, while the Senate voted unanimously to continue the investigation of Communism.

The country's attitude was still left over from the McCarthy era. There was open pride in the West, and you could still say you were anti-Communist with a straight face.

Time's Man of the Year was Harlow Herbert Curtice, president of General Motors, in a tribute to America's competitive expanding economy.

It was our parent's world then. They were excited about the great era of United States prosperity. They could buy longer, lower cars with more horsepower, tubeless tires, wraparound windshields and flashy two-tone paint jobs. They danced the mambo and could travel in less time than ever in the new Viscount prop jets. In sports, they watched All-American Bill Russell lead the University of San Francisco to the NCAA championship. They saw Rocky Marciano twice defend his heavyweight title. And in the World Series they saw the unbeatable Yankees, American League champs six times in the last seven years, beaten in seven games by Brooklyn.

In 1955 they bought black and white television sets to watch the top rated shows like Groucho Marx's "You Bet Your Life" or their little bitty buddy George Gobel or the perennials "Toast of the Town" and "Dragnet." If they could afford compatible color they could see such great

1955

... the rowdy element was represented by "Rock Around the Clock" theme song of the controversial film *The Blackboard Jungle.* The rock 'n roll school in general concentrated on a minimum of melodic line and a maximum of rhythmic noise, deliberately competing with the artistic ideals of the jungle itself.

Yearbook
Encyclopedia Brittanica

ninety-minute spectaculars as Mary Martin in "Peter Pan."

The bulk of us had not yet reached our teens. Our world was at school where we learned the old math, were guinea pigs for the Salk vaccine, and read about the Cold War in our Weekly Readers.

Though we were too grown up to wear Davy Crockett coonskin caps, and we begged our mothers to let us wear straight skirts, lower hemlines and stockings, we weren't too sophisticated to watch Roy and Jimmie and all the Mouseketeers on the "Mickey Mouse Club."

We patterned ourselves after those glamorous high school kids—the girls in their full skirts and crinolines, the boys in their white socks and paratrooper boots with taps on the soles. We watched our older sisters and their girl friends at their slumber parties. We listened to them talk about the dreamiest boys, the strictest teachers and the newest cheers. We spied on them when they experimented with pincurls and strapless prom dresses. We tried on their cinch belts and lipstick.

And we heard the music they were discovering. The music wasn't started by those midfifties teens. It was generally a cross between rhythm and blues and pop, which had remained separate but equal until the end of 1954.

There seemed to be a fear among the adults that pop music was dying. *Billboard* magazine kept writing "Keep pop alive in '55" at the bottom of its Top 10 charts. But what they were calling pop music was really the music that appealed to the adults. It was a remnant of the smooth big band vocal sound of the forties.

Hollywood's music and movies catered to the adults, too. The best song, "Love Is a Many Splendored Thing," made it big on the pop charts though not on the rhythm and blues charts. Incidentally, the Oscar for the best film went to

Marty, and the best actor was its star, Earnest Borgnine. Anna Magnani's performance in *The Rose Tattoo* won her the best actress award.

Rock and roll did have its first hit from a movie in 1955. It was "Rock Around the Clock" from *The Blackboard Jungle.*

It's odd that "Rock Around the Clock" should have been so vital to the development of the new music. It's writers, Friedman and Meyers (who used the name DeKnight on this record) were elderly men and only part time songwriters. Friedman really made his living as a postal employee.

When they wrote "Rock Around the Clock" they never considered it rock and roll. They had one group record it and it sounded so terrible they decided to junk the whole venture. They were embarrassed to take the record to disk jockeys. Months later they had Bill Haley try the song. This time they took it to the d.j.'s and we took it from there. The song was already becoming a hit when the makers of "Blackboard Jungle" asked to use it.

To us, "Rock Around the Clock" was a good song mainly because of the good dance beat. We were less happy with the movie because it just added to the overabundance of publicity kids were getting as juvenile delinquents. A lot of vocal people who saw the movie seemed happy to classify teenagers as a bunch of hoods who thrived on crude behavior and rowdy music. In fact, most of us were doing nothing evil and neither was our music, but we were constantly being misinterpreted by adults who were often exploiting us commercially.

There was a lot of criticism from the adult world about the lyrics of this "hoody" music the kids were adopting. The grown-ups had two rather paradoxical complaints. Sometimes they said they couldn't understand the words. Sometimes they said the words were dirty.

There is no doubt that our lyrics were not the slick, well chosen words of Tin Pan Alley. But the words were used to convey an emotion simply, with little regard to choosing multisyllabic words or making complex rhymes.

The rock and roll lyrics, mostly written by poorer, earthier, blacker writers than the old pop, showed love as a gutsier experience than did the supposedly more sophisticated adult pop.

When Ray Charles sang:

I've got a woman
Way across town
She's good to me

they wondered about his intentions. And when he went on:

She saves her lovin'
Early in the morn
Just for me

they thought they knew.

Maybe it didn't make sense when Bo Diddley chanted:

Bo Diddley bought a nanny goat
To make his pretty baby a Sunday coat
Bo Diddley bought a bearcat
To make his pretty baby a Sunday hat

but the beat was great and the words were for fun. There was a simple spontaneity that sang to our youth. And the words were really not dirty. It was absurd to think the nation's twelve-year-olds would perpetrate such a plot against American decency.

Many of us were even too young to stay up to see "Your Hit Parade," where Snooky Lanson, Russell Arms, Giselle MacKenzie and Dorothy Collins tried to interpret the new rock and roll music. The songs that had roots in rhythm and blues usually didn't work.

Though there were songs like "Unchained Melody" that bridged the gap between pop and rock and roll, the pop charts were dominated by white singers, songs and arrangements that were acceptable to our parents. Some songs like "Ain't That a Shame" and "Sincerely" made it on both charts, but by different artists. Etta James's "Wallflower" was "Dance with Me Henry" as a pop hit.

Yet the songs that actually show the move toward later rock and roll were rhythm and blues. "Poison Ivy," "I've Got a Woman," "Bo Diddley" and "Pledging My Love" were to become the ancestors of the best rock and roll of the sixties. "Earth Angel," which was rhythm and blues and was in the Top 10 the first fifteen weeks of 1955, was to become one of the greatest rock and roll classics, and would be revived to become a hit twice again.

As rock and roll was pulling away from the old pop, the adults were slow to take to the change. They kept writing rock and roll in quotes and passing it off as a teenage fad. And the more our parents told us to turn our noise down, the more we pulled away from them musically. The older kids in their middle and late teens had developed a taste for pop before rock and roll existed. Their musical taste had a split personality.

But those of us who were younger received the new music whole, with little knowledge of what went before. In retrospect we realize rock and roll has not always been around, but, in fact, it has been around as far back as we have been aware.

In a way, a lot of things that were new in 1955 seem to us always to have existed. It is hard to believe it was only 1955 when the United States started supplying direct financial aid to South Vietnam. It was also the year George Meany became president of the AFL–CIO, Sam Rayburn became Speaker of the House and Senator Wayne Morse became a Democrat.

1955 was not only a year of beginnings, traditions were ending that seem not to have existed in our lifetime. Albert Einstein died that year. And though our generation never knew Theda Bara firsthand, it was the end of an era when she died in April. More happily, it was the formal end to the state of war between Russia and Germany.

As 1955 itself drew to an end, rock and roll seemed to us to be moving toward a great new year. It was dominated by solid artists like the Platters, the Drifters, Fats Domino and Laverne Baker. We wanted to believe they were as great as we suspected. We wanted to believe rock and roll was here to stay.

But our elders kept telling us they knew better as they made wise predictions for the coming years: Eisenhower wouldn't run again after his heart attack, schools would desegregate with all deliberate speed, strengthening Germany would threaten world peace, United States prosperity would go on forever, Bermuda shorts would never go out of style—and rock and roll would never last. And they would have cut off our allowances if we had argued.

The Top Fifty

1955

1.	ROCK AROUND THE CLOCK	B. Haley and the Comets
2.	PLEDGING MY LOVE	J. Ace
3.	CHERRY PINK AND APPLE BLOSSOM WHITE	P. Prado
4.	ONLY YOU	The Platters
5.	MAYBELLINE	C. Berry
6.	YELLOW ROSE OF TEXAS	M. Miller
7.	AIN'T THAT a SHAME	F. Domino
8.	EARTH ANGEL	The Penguins
9.	BALLAD OF DAVY CROCKETT	B. Hayes
10.	I'VE GOT A WOMAN	R. Charles
11.	WALLFLOWER	E. James
12.	HEARTS OF STONE	The Charms
13.	TWEEDLE DEE	L. Baker
14.	SINCERELY	The Moonglows
15.	MY BABE	Little Walter
16.	UNCHAINED MELODY	R. Hamilton
17.	STORY UNTOLD	The Nutmegs
18.	BO DIDDLEY	Bo Diddley
19.	SIXTEEN TONS	Tennessee Ernie Ford
20.	SOLDIER BOY	The Four Fellows
21.	LING, TING, TONG	The Five Keys
22.	UNCHAINED MELODY	A. Hibbler
23.	I HEAR YOU KNOCKING	S. Lewis
24.	AT MY FRONT DOOR	The El Dorados
25.	DON'T BE ANGRY	N. Brown
26.	LOVE IS a MANY SPLENDORED THING	D. Cornell
27.	KOKOMO	Gene and Eunice
28.	AS LONG AS I'M MOVING	R. Brown
29.	ALL BY MYSELF	F. Domino
30.	BLOSSOM FELL	Nat (King) Cole
31.	WALKING THE BLUES	J. DuPree
32.	THIRTY DAYS	C. Berry
33.	LEARNIN' THE BLUES	F. Sinatra
34.	CLOSE YOUR EYES	The Five Keys
35.	LET ME GO LOVER	T. Brewer
36.	MR. SANDMAN	The Chordettes
37.	SOMETHING'S GOTTA GIVE	The McGuire Sisters
38.	BOP TING a LING	L. Baker
39.	THAT'S ALL I WANT FROM YOU	D. Washington
40.	AUTUMN LEAVES	R. Williams
41.	MOMENTS TO REMEMBER	The Four Lads
42.	THIS OLE HOUSE	R. Clooney
43.	WITCHCRAFT	The Spiders
44.	IF I MAY	Nat (King) Cole
45.	DOOR IS STILL OPEN	The Cardinals
46.	SEVENTEEN	B. Bennett
47.	TEACH ME TONIGHT	The Moonglows
48.	SHIFTING, WHISPERING SANDS	R. Draper
49.	LING, TING, TONG	The Charms
50.	DANCE WITH ME HENRY	G. Gibbs

January 1

1. **HEARTS OF STONE**
   The Charms
   R. Jackson–E. Ray,   DeLuxe 6062
   (Regent, BMI)

2. **EARTH ANGEL**
   The Penguins
   C. Williams,   Dootone 348
   (Dootsie Williams, BMI)

3. **SINCERELY**
   The Moonglows
   H. Fugua–A. Freed,   Chess 1581
   (Arc, BMI)

4. **WHITE CHRISTMAS**
   The Drifters
   I. Berlin,   Atlantic 1048
   (Berlin, ASCAP)

5. **MR. SANDMAN**
   The Chordettes
   P. Ballard,   Cadence 1247
   (E. H. Morris, ASCAP)

6. **TEACH ME TONIGHT**
   D. Washington
   S. Cahn-G. DePaul,
   Mercury 70497   (Hub, ASCAP)

7. **LING, TING, TONG**
   The Five Keys
   M. Godwin,   Capitol 2945
   (St. Louis, BMI)

8. **HURT**
   R. Hamilton
   J. Crane–A. Jacobs,   Epic 9086
   (Miller, ASCAP)

9. **THIS OLE HOUSE**
   R. Clooney
   S. Hamblen,   Columbia 40266
   (Hamblen, BMI)

10. **MAMBO BABY**
    R. Brown
    C. Singleton-R. M. McCoy,
    Atlantic 1044   (M&M, BMI)

January 8

1. **HEARTS OF STONE**
   The Charms
   R. Jackson–E. Ray,   DeLuxe 6062
   (Regent, BMI)

2. **EARTH ANGEL**
   The Penguins
   C. Williams,   Dootone 348
   (Dootsie Williams, BMI)

3. **WHITE CHRISTMAS**
   The Drifters
   I. Berlin,   Atlantic 1048
   (Berlin, ASCAP)

4. **SINCERELY**
   The Moonglows
   H. Fugua–A. Freed,   Chess 1581
   (Arc, BMI)

5. **TEACH ME TONIGHT**
   D. Washington
   S. Cahn-G. DePaul,
   Mercury 70497   (Hub, ASCAP)

6. **MR. SANDMAN**
   The Chordettes
   P. Ballard,   Cadence 1247
   (E. H. Morris, ASCAP)

7. **LING, TING, TONG**
   The Five Keys
   M. Godwin,   Capitol 2945
   (St. Louis, BMI)

8. **THIS OLE HOUSE**
   R. Clooney
   S. Hamblen,   Columbia 40266
   (Hamblen, BMI)

9. **POISON IVY**
   W. Mabon
   Leiber-Stoller,   Chess 1580
   (Tiger, BMI)

10. **HURT**
    R. Hamilton
    J. Crane-A. Jacobs,   Epic 9086
    (Miller, ASCAP)

January 15

1. **HEARTS OF STONE**
   The Charms
   R. Jackson–E. Ray, DeLuxe 6062
   (Regent, BMI)
2. **SINCERELY**
   The Moonglows
   H. Fugua–A. Freed, Chess 1581
   (Arc, BMI)
3. **LING, TING, TONG**
   The Five Keys
   M. Godwin, Capitol 2945
   (St. Louis, BMI)
4. **TWEEDLE DEE**
   L. Baker
   W. Scott, Atlantic 1047
   (Progressive, BMI)
5. **EARTH ANGEL**
   The Penguins
   C. Williams, Dootone 348
   (Dootsie Williams, BMI)
6. **HURT**
   R. Hamilton
   J. Crane–A. Jacobs, Epic 9086
   (Miller, ASCAP)
7. **MR. SANDMAN**
   The Chordettes
   P. Ballard, Cadence 1247
   (E. H. Morris, ASCAP)
8. **TEACH ME TONIGHT**
   D. Washington
   S. Cahn–G. DePaul,
   Mercury 70497 (Hub, ASCAP)
9. **POISON IVY**
   W. Mabon
   Leiber–Stoller, Chess 1580
   (Tiger, BMI)
10. **THIS OLE HOUSE**
    R. Clooney
    S. Hamblen, Columbia 40266
    (Hamblen, BMI)

January 22

1. **SINCERELY**
   The Moonglows
   H. Fugua–A. Freed, Chess 1581
   (Arc, BMI)
2. **EARTH ANGEL**
   The Penguins
   C. Williams, Dootone 348
   (Dootsie Williams, BMI)
3. **HEARTS OF STONE**
   The Charms
   R. Jackson–E. Ray, DeLuxe 6062
   (Regent, BMI)
4. **LING, TING, TONG**
   The Five Keys
   M. Godwin, Capitol 2945
   (St. Louis, BMI)
5. **TWEEDLE DEE**
   L. Baker
   W. Scott, Atlantic 1047
   (Progressive, BMI)
6. **LING, TING, TONG**
   The Charms
   M. Godwin, DeLuxe 6065
   (St. Louis, BMI)
7. **MR. SANDMAN**
   The Chordettes
   P. Ballard, Cadence 1247
   (E. H. Morris, ASCAP)
8. **TEACH ME TONIGHT**
   D. Washington
   S. Cahn–G. DePaul,
   Mercury 70497 (Hub. ASCAP)
9. **PLEDGING MY LOVE**
   J. ACE
   D. D. Robey–F. Washington,
   Duke 136 (Lion, BMI)
10. **THIS OLE HOUSE**
    R. Clooney
    S. Hamblen, Columbia 40266
    (Hamblen, BMI)

January 29

1. **EARTH ANGEL**
   The Penguins
   C. Williams, Dootone 348
   (Dootsie Willaims, BMI)
2. **SINCERELY**
   The Moonglows
   H. Fugua–A. Freed Chess 1581
   (Arc, BMI)
3. **HEARTS OF STONE**
   The Charms
   R. Jackson–E. Ray, DeLuxe 6062
   (Regent, BMI)
4. **LING, TING, TONG**
   The Charms
   M. Godwin, DeLuxe 6065
   (St. Louis, BMI)
5. **TWEEDLE DEE**
   L. Baker
   W. Scott, Atlantic 1047
   (Progressive, BMI)
6. **PLEDGING MY LOVE**
   J. Ace
   D. D. Robey–F. Washington,
   Duke 136 (Lion, BMI)
7. **LET ME GO LOVER**
   T. Brewer
   J. L. Carson, Coral 61315
   (Hill & Range, BMI)
8. **TEACH ME TONIGHT**
   D. Washington
   S. Cahn–G. DePaul,
   Mercury 70497 (Hub, ASCAP)
9. **MR. SANDMAN**
   The Chordettes
   P. Ballard, Cadence 1247
   (E. H. Morris, ASCAP)
10. **I'VE GOT A WOMAN**
    R. Charles
    R. Charles–R. Richard,
    Atlantic 1050 (Progressive, BMI)

February 5

1. **EARTH ANGEL**
The Penguins
C. Williams, Dootone 348
(Dootsie Williams, BMI)

2. **SINCERELY**
The Moonglows
H. Fugua–A. Freed,
Chess 1581 (Arc, BMI)

3. **PLEDGING MY LOVE**
J. ACE
D. D. Robey–F. Washington,
Duke 136 (Lion, BMI)

4. **HEARTS OF STONE**
The Charms
R. Jackson–E. Ray, DeLuxe 6062
(Regent, BMI)

5. **LING, TING, TONG**
The Charms
M. Godwin, DeLuxe 6065
(St. Louis, BMI)

6. **TWEEDLE DEE**
L. Baker
W. Scott, Atlantic 1047
(Progressive, BMI)

7. **I'VE GOT A WOMAN**
R. Charles
R. Charles–R. Richard, Atlantic
1050
(Progressive, BMI)

8. **LET ME GO LOVER**
T. Brewer
J. L. Carson, Coral 61315
(Hill & Range, BMI)

9. **KOKOMO**
Gene and Eunice
F. Wilson–J. Porter–E. Levy,
Combo 64 (Meridian, BMI)

10. **DIM, DIM THE LIGHTS**
B. Haley
B. Ross–J. Dixon, Decca 29317
(Republic, BMI)

February 12

1. **PLEDGING MY LOVE**
J. ACE
D. D. Robey–F. Washington,
Duke 136 (Lion, BMI)

2. **EARTH ANGEL**
The Penguins
C. Willaims, Dootone 348
(Dootsie Williams, BMI)

3. **SINCERELY**
The Moonglows
H. Fugua–A. Freed, Chess 1581
(Arc, BMI)

4. **I'VE GOT A WOMAN**
R. Charles
R. Charles–R. Richard
Atlantic 1050 (Progressive, BMI)

5. **TWEEDLE DEE**
L. Baker
W. Scott, Atlantic 1047
(Progressive, BMI)

6. **HEARTS OF STONE**
The Charms
R. Jackson–E. Ray, DeLuxe 6062
(Regent, BMI)

7. **LET ME GO LOVER**
T. Brewer
J. L. Carson, Coral 61315
(Hill & Range, BMI)

8. **LING, TING, TONG**
The Charms
M. Godwin, DeLuxe 6065
(St. Louis, BMI)

9. **KOKOMO**
Gene and Eunice
F. Wilson–J. Porter–E. Levy,
Combo 64 (Meridian, BMI)

10. **DIM, DIM THE LIGHTS**
B. Haley
B. Ross–J. Dixon, Decca 29317
(Republic, BMI)

February 19

1. **PLEDGING MY LOVE**
J. Ace
D. D. Robey–F. Washington,
Duke 136 (Lion, BMI)

2. **I'VE GOT A WOMAN**
R. Charles
R. Charles–R. Richard,
Atlantic 1050 (Progressive, BMI)

3. **EARTH ANGEL**
The Penguins
C. Williams, Dootone 348
(Dootsie Williams, BMI)

4. **TWEEDLE DEE**
L. Baker
W. Scott, Atlantic 1047
(Progressive, BMI)

5. **SINCERELY**
The Moonglows
H. Fugua–A. Freed, Chess 1581
(Arc, BMI)

6. **KOKOMO**
Gene and Eunice
F. Wilson–J. Porter–E. Levy,
Combo 64 (Meridian, BMI)

7. **HEARTS OF STONE**
The Charms
R. Jackson–E. Ray, DeLuxe 6062
(Regent, BMI)

8. **LET ME GO LOVER**
T. Brewer
J. L. Carson, Coral 61315
(Hill & Range, BMI)

9. **LING, TING, TONG**
The Charms
M. Godwin, DeLuxe 6065
(St. Louis, BMI)

10. **WALLFLOWER**
E. JAMES
J. E. Rogers–P. Otis, Modern 947
(Modern, BMI)

1955

February 26

1. **PLEDGING MY LOVE**
   J. Ace
   D. D. Robey–F. Washington,
   Duke 136 (Lion, BMI)

2. **I'VE GOT A WOMAN**
   R. Charles
   R. Charles–R. Richard,
   Atlantic 1050 (Progressive, BMI)

3. **EARTH ANGEL**
   The Penguins
   C.Williams, Dootone 348
   (Dootsie Williams, BMI)

4. **TWEEDLE DEE**
   L. Baker
   W. Scott, Atlantic 1047
   (Progressive, BMI)

5. **KOKOMO**
   Gene and Eunice
   F. Wilson–J. Porter–E. Levy,
   Combo 64 (Meridian, BMI)

6. **SINCERELY**
   The Moonglows
   H. Fugua–A. Freed, Chess 1581
   (Arc, BMI)

7. **LET ME GO LOVER**
   T. Brewer
   J. L. Carson, Coral 61315
   (Hill & Range, BMI)

8. **HEARTS OF STONE**
   The Charms
   R. Jackson–E. Ray, DeLuxe 6062
   (Regent, BMI)

9. **WALLFLOWER**
   E. James
   J. E. Rogers–P. Otis, Modern 947
   (Modern, BMI)

10. **LING, TING, TONG**
    The Charms
    M. Godwin, DeLuxe 6065
    (St. Louis, BMI)

March 5

1. **PLEDGING MY LOVE**
   J. Ace
   D. D. Robey–F. Washington,
   Duke 136 (Lion, BMI)

2. **EARTH ANGEL**
   The Penguins
   C. Williams, Dootone 348
   (Dootsie Williams, BMI)

3. **I'VE GOT A WOMAN**
   R. Charles
   R. Charles–R. Richard,
   Atlantic 1050 (Progressive, BMI)

4. **TWEEDLE DEE**
   L. Baker
   W. Scott, Atlantic 1047
   (Progressive, BMI)

5. **KOKOMO**
   Gene and Eunice
   F. Wilson–J. Porter–E. Levy,
   Combo 64 (Meridian, BMI)

6. **WALLFLOWER**
   E. James
   J. E. Rogers–P. Otis, Modern 947
   (Modern, BMI)

7. **SINCERELY**
   The Moonglows
   H. Fugua–A. Freed, Chess 1581
   (Arc, BMI)

8. **LET ME GO LOVER**
   T. Brewer
   J. L. Carson, Coral 61315
   (Hill & Range, BMI)

9. **HEARTS OF STONE**
   The Charms
   R. Jackson–E. Ray, DeLuxe 6062
   (Regent, BMI)

10. **THAT'S ALL I WANT FROM**
    YOU
    D. Washington
    M. Rotha, Mercury 70537
    (Weiss and Barry, BMI)

March 12

1. **PLEDGING MY LOVE**
   J. Ace
   D. D. Robey–F. Washington,
   Duke 136 (Lion, BMI)

2. **I'VE GOT A WOMAN**
   R. Charles
   R. Charles–R. Richard,
   Atlantic 1050 (Progressive, BMI)

3. **EARTH ANGEL**
   The Penguins
   C. Williams, Dootone 348
   (Dootsie Williams, BMI)

4. **TWEEDLE DEE**
   L. Baker
   W. Scott, Atlantic 1047
   (Progressive, BMI)

5. **WALLFLOWER**
   E. James
   J. E. Rogers–P. Otis, Modern 947
   (Modern, BMI)

6. **THAT'S ALL I WANT FROM**
   YOU
   D. Washington
   M. Rotha, Mercury 70537
   (Weiss and Barry, BMI)

7. **KOKOMO**
   Gene and Eunice
   F. Wilson–J. Porter–E. Levy,
   Combo 64 (Meridian, BMI)

8. **SINCERELY**
   The Moonglows
   H. Fugua–A. Freed, Chess 1581
   (Arc, BMI)

9. **MY BABE**
   Little Walter
   W. Dixon–C. Stone, Checker 811
   (Arc, BMI)

10. **BALLAD OF DAVY**
    CROCKETT
    B. Hayes
    T. Blackburn–G. Burns,
    Cadence 1256
    (Wonderland, BMI)

March 19

1. **PLEDGING MY LOVE**
J. Ace
D. D. Robey–F. Washington,
Duke 136 (Lion, BMI)

2. **WALLFLOWER**
E. James
J. E. Rogers–P. Otis, Modern 947
(Modern, BMI)

3. **I'VE GOT A WOMAN**
R. Charles
R. Charles–R. Richard,
Atlantic 1050 (Progressive,BMI)

4. **EARTH ANGEL**
The Penguins
C. Williams, Dootone 348
(Dootsie Williams, BMI)

5. **TWEEDLE DEE**
L. Baker
W. Scott, Atlantic 1047
(Progressive, BMI)

6. **MY BABE**
Little Walter
W. Dixon–C. Stone, Checker 811
(Arc, BMI)

7. **THAT'S ALL I WANT FROM YOU**
D. Washington
M. Rotha, Mercury 70537
(Weiss and Barry, BMI)

8. **KOKOMO**
Gene and Eunice
F. Wilson–J. Porter–E. Levy,
Combo 64 (Meridian, BMI)

9. **BALLAD OF DAVY CROCKETT**
B. Hayes
T. Blackburn–G. Burns,
Cadence 1256
(Wonderland, BMI)

10. **SINCERELY**
The Moonglows
H. Fugua–A. Freed, Chess 1581
(Arc, BMI)

March 26

1. **PLEDGING MY LOVE**
J. Ace
D. D. Robey–F. Washington,
Duke 136 (Lion, BMI)

2. **WALLFLOWER**
E. James
J. E. Rogers–P. Otis, Modern 947
(Modern, BMI)

3. **MY BABE**
Little Walter
W. Dixon–C. Stone, Checker 811
(Arc, BMI)

4. **I'VE GOT A WOMAN**
R. Charles
R. Charles–R. Richard,
Atlantic 1050 (Progressive, BMI)

5. **EARTH ANGEL**
The Penguins
C. Williams, Dootone 348
(Dootsie Williams, BMI)

6. **CLOSE YOUR EYES**
The Five Keys
C.Willis, Capitol 3032
(Tideland, BMI)

7. **TWEEDLE DEE**
L. Baker
W. Scott, Atlantic 1047
(Progressive, BMI)

8. **BALLAD OF DAVY CROCKETT**
B. Hayes
T. Blackburn–G. Burns,
Cadence 1256
(Wonderland, BMI)

9. **THAT'S ALL I WANT FROM YOU**
D. Washington
M. Rotha, Mercury 70537
(Weiss and Barry, BMI)

10. **KOKOMO**
Gene and Eunice
F. Wilson–J. Porter–E. Levy,
Combo 64 (Meridian, BMI)

April 2

1. **PLEDGING MY LOVE**
J. Ace
D. D. Robey–F. Washington,
Duke 136 (Lion, BMI)

2. **WALLFLOWER**
E. James
J. E. Rogers–P. Otis, Modern 947
(Modern, BMI)

3. **MY BABE**
Little Walter
W. Dixon–G. Stone, Checked 811
(Arc, BMI)

4. **I'VE GOT A WOMAN**
R. Charles
R. Charles–R. Richard,
Atlantic 1050 (Progressive, BMI)

5. **CLOSE YOUR EYES**
The Five Keys
C. Willis, Capitol 3032
(Tideland, BMI)

6. **EARTH ANGEL**
The Penguins
C. Williams, Dootone 348
(Dootsie Williams, BMI)

7. **TWEEDLE DEE**
L. Baker
W. Scott, Atlantic 1047
(Progressive, BMI)

8. **BALLAD OF DAVY CROCKETT**
B. Hayes
T. Blackburn–G. Burns,
Cadence 1256
(Wonderland, BMI)

9. **FLIP, FLOP AND FLY**
J. Turner
C. Calhoun–L. W. Turner,
Atlantic 1053 (Progressive, BMI)

10. **THAT'S ALL I WANT FROM YOU**
D. Washington
M. Rotha, Mercury 70537
(Weiss and Barry, BMI)

1955

April 9

1. **PLEDGING MY LOVE**
   J. Ace
   D. D. Robey–F. Washington,
   Duke 136   (Lion, BMI)

2. **WALLFLOWER**
   E. James
   J. E. Rogers–P. Otis,
   Modern 947   (Modern, BMI)

3. **MY BABE**
   Little Walter
   W. Dixon–G. Stone,   Checker 811
   (Arc, BMI)

4. **CLOSE YOUR EYES**
   The Five Keys
   C. Willis,   Capitol 3032
   (Tideland, BMI)

5. **I'VE GOT A WOMAN**
   R. Charles
   R. Charles–R. Richard,
   Atlantic 1050   (Progressive, BMI)

6. **BALLAD OF DAVY CROCKETT**
   B. Hayes
   T. Blackburn–G. Burns,
   Cadence 1256
   (Wonderland, BMI)

7. **EARTH ANGEL**
   The Penguins
   C. Williams,   Dootone 348
   (Dootsie Williams, BMI)

8. **FLIP, FLOP AND FLY**
   J. Turner
   C. Calhoun–L. W. Turner,
   Atlantic 1053   (Progressive, BMI)

9. **TWEEDLE DEE**
   L. Baker
   W. Scott,   Atlantic 1047
   (Progressive, BMI)

10. **THAT'S ALL I WANT FROM YOU**
    D. Washington
    M. Rotha,   Mercury 70537
    (Weiss and Barry, BMI)

April 16

1. **PLEDGING MY LOVE**
   J. Ace
   D. D. Robey–F. Washington,
   Duke 136   (Lion, BMI)

2. **MY BABE**
   Little Walter
   W. Dixon–G. Stone,   Checker 811
   (Arc, BMI)

3. **WALLFLOWER**
   E. James
   J. E. Rogers–P. Otis,   Modern 947
   (Modern, BMI)

4. **CLOSE YOUR EYES**
   The Five Keys
   C. Willis,   Capitol 3032
   (Tideland, BMI)

5. **BALLAD OF DAVY CROCKETT**
   B. Hayes
   T. Blackburn–G. Burns,
   Cadence 1256
   (Wonderland, BMI)

6. **I'VE GOT A WOMAN**
   R. Charles
   R. Charles–R. Richard,
   Atlantic 1050   (Progressive, BMI)

7. **FLIP, FLOY AND FLY**
   J. Turner
   C. Calhoun–L. W. Turner,
   Atlantic 1053   (Progressive, BMI)

8. **CHERRY PINK AND APPLE BLOSSOM WHITE**
   P. Prado
   Louiguy–David,   Victor 20-5965
   (Chappell, ASCAP)

9. **EARTH ANGEL**
   The Penguins
   C. Williams,   Dootone 348
   (Dootsie Williams, BMI)

10. **TWEEDLE DEE**
    L. Baker
    W. Scott,   Atlantic 1047
    (Progressive, BMI)

April 23

1. **MY BABE**
   Little Walter
   W. Dixon–G. Stone,   Checker 811
   (Arc, BMI)

2. **PLEDGING MY LOVE**
   J. Ace
   D. D. Robey–F. Washington,
   Duke 136   (Lion, BMI)

3. **BALLAD OF DAVY CROCKETT**
   B. Hayes
   T. Blackburn–G. Burns
   Cadence 1256
   (Wonderland, BMI)

4. **WALLFLOWER**
   E. James
   J. E. Rogers–P. Otis,   Modern 947
   (Modern, BMI)

5. **CLOSE YOUR EYES**
   The Five Keys
   C. Willis,   Capitol 3032
   (Tideland, BMI)

6. **CHERRY PINK AND APPLE BLOSSOM WHITE**
   P. Prado
   Louiguy–David,   Victor 20-5965
   (Chappell, ASCAP)

7. **I'VE GOT A WOMAN**
   R. Charles
   R. Charles–R. Richard,
   Atlantic 1050   (Progressive, BMI)

8. **FLIP, FLOP AND FLY**
   J. Turner
   C. Calhoun–L. W. Turner,
   Atlantic 1053   (Progressive, BMI)

9. **UNCHAINED MELODY**
   A. Hibbler
   H. Zert–A. North,
   Decca 29441   (Frank, ASCAP)

10. **DON'T BE ANGRY**
    N. Brown
    N. Brown–F. Madison–R. M.
    McCoy,
    Savoy 1151   (Republic, BMI)

25

April 30

1. **MY BABE**
   Little Walter
   W. Dixon–G. Stone, Checker 811 (Arc, BMI)

2. **BALLAD OF DAVY CROCKETT**
   B. Hayes
   T. Blackburn–G. Burns, Cadence 1256 (Wonderland, BMI)

3. **PLEDGING MY LOVE**
   J. Ace
   D. D. Robey–F. Washington, Duke 136 (Lion, BMI)

4. **WALLFLOWER**
   E. James
   J. E. Rogers–P. Otis, Modern 947 (Modern, BMI)

5. **CHERRY PINK AND APPLE BLOSSOM WHITE**
   P. Prado
   Louiguy–David, Victor 20-5965 (Chappell, ASCAP)

6. **CLOSE YOUR EYES**
   The Five Keys
   C. Willis, Capitol 3032 (Tideland, BMI)

7. **UNCHAINED MELODY**
   A. Hibbler
   H. Zert–A. North, Decca 29441 (Frank, ASCAP)

8. **DON'T BE ANGRY**
   N. Brown
   N. Brown–F. Madison–R. M. McCoy, Savoy 1155 (Republic, BMI)

9. **FLIP, FLOP AND FLY**
   J. Turner
   C. Calhoun–L. W. Turner, Atlantic 1053 (Progressive, BMI)

10. **I'VE GOT A WOMAN**
    R. Charles
    R. Charles–R. Richard, Atlantic 1050 (Progressive, BMI)

May 7

1. **BALLAD OF DAVY CROCKETT**
   B. Hayes
   T. Blackburn–G. Burns, Cadence 1256 (Wonderland, BMI)

2. **MY BABE**
   Little Walter
   W. Dixon–G. Stone, Checker 811 (Arc, BMI)

3. **DON'T BE ANGRY**
   N. Brown
   N. Brown–F. Madison–R. M. McCoy, Savoy 1155 (Republic, BMI)

4. **UNCHAINED MELODY**
   A. Hibbler
   H. Zert–A. North, Decca 29441 (Frank, ASCAP)

5. **WALLFLOWER**
   E. James
   J. E. Rogers–P. Otis, Modern 947 (Modern, BMI)

6. **CHERRY PINK AND APPLE BLOSSOM WHITE**
   P. Prado
   Louiguy–David, Victor 20-5965 (Chappell, ASCAP)

7. **PLEDGING MY LOVE**
   J. Ace
   D. D. Robey–F. Washington, Duke 136 (Lion, BMI)

8. **CLOSE YOUR EYES**
   The Five Keys
   C. Willis, Capitol 3032 (Tideland, BMI)

9. **FLIP, FLOP AND FLY**
   J. Turner
   C. Calhoun–L. W. Turner, Atlantic 1053 (Progressive, BMI)

10. **I'VE GOT A WOMAN**
    R. Charles
    R. Charles–R. Richard, Atlantic 1050 (Progressive, BMI)

May 14

1. **BALLAD OF DAVY CROCKETT**
   B. Hayes
   T. Blackburn–G. Burns, Cadence 1256 (Wonderland, BMI)

2. **MY BABE**
   Little Walter
   W. Dixon–G. Stone, Checker 811 (Arc, BMI)

3. **CHERRY PINK AND APPLE BLOSSOM WHITE**
   P. Prado
   Louiguy–David, Victor 20-5965 (Chappell, ASCAP)

4. **DON'T BE ANGRY**
   N. Brown
   N. Brown–F. Madison–R. M. McCoy, Savoy 1155 (Republic, BMI)

5. **UNCHAINED MELODY**
   A. Hibbler
   H. Zert–A. North, Decca 29441 (Frank, ASCAP)

6. **WALLFLOWER**
   E. James
   J. E. Rogers–P. Otis, Modern 947 (Modern, BMI)

7. **UNCHAINED MLODY**
   R. Hamilton
   H. Zert–A. North, Epic 9102 (Frank, ASCAP)

8. **PLEDGING MY LOVE**
   J. Ace
   D. D. Robey–F. Washington, Duke 136 (Lion, BMI)

9. **FLIP, FLOP AND FLY**
   J. Turner
   C. Calhoun–L. W. Turner, Atlantic 1053 (Progressive, BMI)

10. **DOOR IS STILL OPEN**
    The Cardinals
    H. Willis, Atlantic 1054 (Rush, BMI)

1955

May 21

1. **BALLAD OF DAVY CROCKETT**
B. Hayes
T. Blackburn–G. Burns, Cadence 1256 (Wonderland, BMI)

2. **UNCHAINED MELODY**
A. Hibbler
H. Zert–A. North, Decca 29441 (Frank, ASCAP)

3. **MY BABE**
Little Walter
W. Dixon–G. Stone, Checker 811 (Arc, BMI)

4. **CHERRY PINK AND APPLE BLOSSOM WHITE**
P. Prado
Louiguy–David, Victor 20-5965 (Chappell, ASCAP)

5. **DON'T BE ANGRY**
N. Brown
N. Brown–F. Madison–R. M. McCoy, Savoy 1155 (Republic, BMI)

6. **UNCHAINED MELODY**
R. Hamilton
H. Zert–A. North, Epic 9102 (Frank, ASCAP)

7. **WALLFLOWER**
E. James
J. E. Rogers–P. Otis, Modern 947 (Modern, BMI)

8. **BO DIDDLEY**
Bo Diddley
E. McDaniels, Checker 814 (Arc, BMI)

9. **BOP TING A LING**
L. Baker
W. Scott, Atlantic 1057 (Progressive, BMI)

10. **DANCE WITH ME HENRY**
G. Gibbs
J. Taub–J. Josea–S. Ling, Mercury 70572 (Modern, BMI)

May 28

1. **UNCHAINED MELODY**
A. Hibbler
H. Zert–A. North, Decca 29441 (Frank, ASCAP)

2. **BALLAD OF DAVY CROCKET**
B. Hayes
T. Blackburn–G. Burns, Cadence 1256 (Wonderland, BMI)

3. **CHERRY PINK AND APPLE BLOSSOM WHITE**
P. Prado
Louiguy–David, Victor 20-5965 (Chappell, ASCAP)

4. **MY BABE**
Little Walter
W. Dixon–G. Stone, Checker 811 (Arc, BMI)

5. **UNCHAINED MELODY**
R. Hamilton
H. Zert–A. North, Epic 9102 (Frank, ASCAP)

6. **BO DIDDLEY**
Bo Diddley
E. McDaniels, Checker 814 (Arc, BMI)

7. **DON'T BE ANGRY**
N. Brown
N. Brown–F. Madison–R. M. McCoy, Savoy 1155 (Republic, BMI)

8. **BOP TING A LING**
L. Baker
W. Scott, Atlantic 1057 (Progressive, BMI)

9. **WALLFLOWER**
E. James
J. E. Rogers–P. Otis, Modern 947 (Modern, BMI)

10. **AIN'T THAT A SHAME**
F. Domino
D. Bartholomew–A. Domino, Imperial 5348 (Commodore, BMI)

June 4

1. **UNCHAINED MELODY**
A. Hibbler
H. Zert–A. North, Decca 29441 (Frank, ASCAP)

2. **UNCHAINED MELODY**
R. Hamilton
H. Zert–A. North, Epic 9102 (Frank, ASCAP)

3. **CHERRY PINK AND APPLE BLOSSOM WHITE**
P. Prado
Louiguy–David, Victor 20-5965 (Chappell, ASCAP)

4. **MY BABE**
Little Walter
W. Dixon–G. Stone, Checker 811 (Arc, BMI)

5. **BALLAD OF DAVY CROCKETT**
B. Hayes
T. Blackburn–G. Burns, Cadence 1256 (Wonderland, BMI)

6. **BO DIDDLEY**
Bo Diddley
E. McDaniels, Checker 814 (Arc, BMI)

7. **BOP TING A LING**
L. Baker
W. Scott, Atlantic 1057 (Progressive, BMI)

8. **AIN'T THAT A SHAME**
F. Domino
D. Bartholomew–A. Domino, Imperial 5348 (Commodore, BMI)

9. **STORY UNTOLD**
The Nutmegs
L. Griffin, Herald 452 (Rush, BMI)

10. **WALLFLOWER**
E. James
J. E. Rogers–P. Otis, Modern 947 (Modern, BMI)

June 11

1. **UNCHAINED MELODY**
R. Hamilton
*H. Zert–A. North, Epic 9102
(Frank, ASCAP)*

2. **CHERRY PINK AND APPLE BLOSSOM WHITE**
P. Prado
*Louiguy–David, Victor 20-5965
(Chappell, ASCAP)*

3. **UNCHAINED MELODY**
A. Hibbler
*H. Zert–A. North, Decca 29441
(Frank, ASCAP)*

4. **BO DIDDLEY**
Bo Diddley
*E. McDaniels, Checker 814
(Arc, BMI)*

5. **MY BABE**
Little Walter
*W. Dixon–G. Stone, Checker 811
(Arc, BMI)*

6. **BALLAD OF DAVY CROCKETT**
B. Hayes
*T. Blackburn–G. Burns, Cadence
1256 (Wonderland, BMI)*

7. **BOP TING A LING**
L. Baker
*W. Scott, Atlantic 1057
(Progressive, BMI)*

8. **AIN'T THAT A SHAME**
F. Domino
*D. Bartholomew–A. Domino,
Imperial 5448 (Commodore,
BMI)*

9. **STORY UNTOLD**
The Nutmegs
*L. Griffin, Herald 452
(Rush, BMI)*

10. **BLOSSOM FELL**
Nat (King) Cole
*H. Barnes–H. Cornelius–D. John,
Capitol 3095 (Shapiro–
Bernstein, ASCAP)*

June 18

1. **CHERRY PINK AND APPLE BLOSSOM WHITE**
P. Prado
*Louiguy–David, Victor 20-5965
(Chappell, ASCAP)*

2. **UNCHAINED MELODY**
R. Hamilton
*H. Zert–A. North, Epic 9102
(Frank, ASCAP)*

3. **AIN'T THAT A SHAME**
F. Domino
*D. Bartholomew–A. Domino,
Imperial 5348 (Commodore,
BMI)*

4. **BO DIDDLEY**
Bo Diddley
*E. McDaniels, Checker 814
(Arc, BMI)*

5. **UNCHAINED MELODY**
A. Hibbler
*H. Zert–A. North, Decca 29441
(Frank, ASCAP)*

6. **STORY UNTOLD**
The Nutmegs
*L. Griffin, Herald 452
(Rush, BMI)*

7. **BALLAD OF DAVY CROCKETT**
B. Hayes
*T. Blackburn–G. Burns, Cadence
1256 (Wonderland, BMI)*

8. **MY BABE**
Little Walter
*W. Dixon–G. Stone, Checker 811
(Arc, BMI)*

9. **BOP TING A LING**
L. Baker
*W. Scott, Atlantic 1057
(Progressive, BMI)*

10. **BLOSSOM FELL**
Nat (King) Cole
*H. Barnes–H. Cornelius–D. John,
Capitol 3095 (Shapiro–
Bernstein, ASCAP)*

June 25

1. **CHERRY PINK AND APPLE BLOSSOM WHITE**
P. Prado
*Louiguy–David, Victor 20-5965
(Chappell, ASCAP)*

2. **AIN'T THAT A SHAME**
F. Domino
*D. Bartholomew–A. Domino,
Imperial 5348 (Commodore, BMI)*

3. **UNCHAINED MELODY**
R. Hamilton
*H. Zert–A. North, Epic 9102
(Frank, ASCAP)*

4. **BO DIDDLEY**
Bo Diddley
*E. McDaniels, Checker 814
(Arc, BMI)*

5. **STORY UNTOLD**
The Nutmegs
*L. Griffin, Herald 452
(Rush, BMI)*

6. **UNCHAINED MELODY**
A. Hibbler
*H. Zert–A. North, Decca 29441
(Frank, ASCAP)*

7. **BLOSSOM FELL**
Nat (King) Cole
*H. Barnes–H. Cornelius–D. John,
Capitol 3095 (Shapiro–
Bernstein, ASCAP)*

8. **MY BABE**
Little Walter
*W. Dixon–G. Stone, Checker 811
(Arc, BMI)*

9. **BOP TING A LING**
L. Baker
*W. Scott, Atlantic 1057
(Progressive, BMI)*

10. **BALLAD OF DAVY CROCKETT**
B. Hayes
*T. Blackburn–G. Burns, Cadence
1256 (Wonderland, BMI)*

1955

July 2

1. **CHERRY PINK AND APPLE BLOSSOM WHITE**
P. Prado
Louiguy–David, Victor 20-5965 (Chappell, ASCAP)

2. **AIN'T THAT A SHAME**
F. Domino
D. Bartholomew–A. Domino, Imperial 5348 (Commodore, BMI)

3. **BO DIDDLEY**
Bo Diddley
E. McDaniels, Checker 814 (Arc, BMI)

4. **UNCHAINED MELODY**
R. Hamilton
H. Zert–A. North, Epic 9102 (Frank, ASCAP)

5. **STORY UNTOLD**
The Nutmegs
L. Griffin, Herald 452 (Rush, BMI)

6. **SOMETHING'S GOTTA GIVE**
The McGuire Sisters
J. Mercer, Coral 61423 (Robbins, ASCAP)

7. **UNCHAINED MELODY**
A. Hibbler
H. Zert–A. North, Decca 29441 (Frank, ASCAP)

8. **BLOSSOM FELL**
Nat (King) Cole
H. Barnes–H. Cornelius–D. John, Capitol 3095 (Shapiro–Bernstein, ASCAP)

9. **BOP TING A LING**
L. Baker
W. Scott, Atlantic 1057 (Progressive, BMI)

10. **MY BABE**
Little Walter
W. Dixon–G. Stone, Checker 811 (Arc, BMI)

July 9

1. **AIN'T THAT A SHAME**
F. Domino
D. Bartholomew–A. Domino, Imperial 5348 (Commodore, BMI)

2. **CHERRY PINK AND APPLE BLOSSOM WHITE**
P. Prado
Louiguy–David, Victor 20-5965 (Chappell, ASCAP)

3. **BO DIDDLEY**
Bo Diddley
E. McDaniels, Checker 814 (Arc, BMI)

. **STORY UNTOLD**
The Nutmegs
L. Griffin, Herald 452 (Rush, BMI)

5. **UNCHAINED MELODY**
R. Hamilton
H. Zert–A. North, Epic 9102 (Frank, ASCAP)

6. **SOMETHING'S GOTTA GIVE**
The McGuire Sisters
J. Mercer, Coral 61423 (Robbins, ASCAP)

7. **ROCK AROUND THE CLOCK**
B. Haley and the Comets
M. Freedman–J. DeKnight, Decca 29124 (Meyers, ASCAP)

8. **BLOSSOM FELL**
Nat (King) Cole
H. Barnes–H. Cornelius–D. John, Capitol 3095 (Shapiro–Bernstein, ASCAP)

9. **BOP TING A LING**
L. Baker
W. Scott, Atlantic 1057 (Progressive, BMI)

10. **UNCHAINED MELODY**
A. Hibbler
H. Zert–A. North, Epic 9102 (Frank, ASCAP)

July 16

1. **AIN'T THAT A SHAME**
F. Domino
D. Bartholomew–A. Domino, Imperial 5348 (Commodore, BMI)

2. **CHERRY PINK AND APPLE BLOSSOM WHITE**
P. Prado
Louiguy–David, Victor 20-5965 (Chappell, ASCAP)

3. **STORY UNTOLD**
The Nutmegs
L. Griffin, Herald 452 (Rush, BMI)

4. **BO DIDDLEY**
Bo Diddley
E. McDaniels, Checker 814 (Arc, BMI)

5. **ROCK AROUND THE CLOCK**
B. Haley and the Comets
M. Freedman–J. DeKnight, Decca 29124 (Meyers, ASCAP)

6. **SOMETHING'S GOTTA GIVE**
The McGuire Sisters
J. Mercer, Coral 61423 (Robbins, ASCAP)

7. **UNCHAINED MELODY**
R. Hamilton
H. Zert–A. North, Epic 9102 (Frank, ASCAP)

8. **BLOSSOM FELL**
Nat (King) Cole
H. Barnes–H. Cornelius–D. John, Capitol 3095 (Shapiro–Bernstein, ASCAP)

9. **BOP TING A LING**
L. Baker
W. Scott, Atlantic 1057 (Progressive, BMI)

10. **LEARNIN' THE BLUES**
F. Sinatra
Silvers, Capitol 3102 (Barton, ASCAP)

29

July 23

1. **AIN'T THAT A SHAME**
   F. Domino
   *D. Bartholomew–A. Domino,
   Imperial 5348 (Commodore,
   BMI)*

2. **ROCK AROUND THE CLOCK**
   B. Haley and the Comets
   *M. Freedman–J. DeKnight,
   Decca 29124 (Meyers,
   ASCAP)*

3. **STORY UNTOLD**
   The Nutmegs
   *L. Griffin, Herald 452
   (Rush, BMI)*

4. **CHERRY PINK AND APPLE
   BLOSSOM WHITE**
   P. Prado
   *Louiguy–David Victor
   20-5965 (Chappell, ASCAP)*

5. **BO DIDDLEY**
   Bo Diddley
   *E. McDaniels, Checker 814
   (Arc, BMI)*

6. **LEARNIN' THE BLUES**
   F. Sinatra
   *Silvers, Capitol 3102
   (Barton, ASCAP)*

7. **SOMETHING'S GOTTA GIVE**
   The McGuire Sisters
   J.Mercer, Coral 61423

8. **SOLDIER BOY**
   The Four Fellows
   *D. Jones–T. Williams, Glory
   234 (E. B. Marks, BMI)*

9. **AS LONG AS I'M MOVING**
   R. Brown
   *C. E. Calhoun, Atlantic 1059
   (Progressive, BMI)*

10. **UNCHAINED MELODY**
    R. Hamilton
    *H. Zert–A. North, Epic 9102
    (Frank, ASCAP)*

July 30

1. **AIN'T THAT A SHAME**
   F. Domino
   *D. Bartholomew–A. Domino,
   Imperial 5348 (Commodore,
   BMI)*

2. **ROCK AROUND THE CLOCK**
   B. Haley and the Comets
   *M. Freedman–J. DeKnight, Decca
   29124 (Meyers, ASCAP)*

3. **STORY UNTOLD**
   The Nutmegs
   *L. Griffin, Herald 452
   (Rush, BMI)*

4. **LEARNIN' THE BLUES**
   F. Sinatra
   *Silvers, Capitol 3102
   (Barton, ASCAP)*

5. **BO DIDDLEY**
   Bo Diddley
   *E. McDaniels, Checker 814
   (Arc, BMI)*

6. **CHERRY PINK AND APPLE
   BLOSSOM WHITE**
   P. Prado
   *Louiguy–David, Victor
   20-5965 (Chappell, ASCAP)*

7. **SOLDIER BOY**
   The Four Fellows
   *D. Jones–T. Williams, Glory
   234 (E. B. Marks, BMI)*

8. **AS LONG AS I'M MOVING**
   R. Brown
   *C. E. Calhoun, Atlantic 1059
   (Progressive, BMI)*

9. **SOMETHING'S GOTTA GIVE**
   The McGuire Sisters
   *J. Mercer, Coral 61423
   (Robbins, ASCAP)*

10. **UNCHAINED MELODY**
    R. Hamilton
    *H. Zert–A. North, Epic 9102
    (Frank, ASCAP)*

August 6

1. **AIN'T THAT A SHAME**
   F. Domino
   *D. Bartholomew–A. Domino,
   Imperial 5348 (Commodore,
   BMI)*

2. **ROCK AROUND THE CLOCK**
   B. Haley and the Comets
   *M. Freedman–J. DeKnight, Decca
   29124 (Meyers, ASCAP)*

3. **STORY UNTOLD**
   The Nutmegs
   *L. Griffin, Herald 452
   (Rush, BMI)*

4. **SOLDIER BOY**
   The Four Fellows
   *D. Jones–T. Williams,
   Glory 234
   (E. B. Marks, BMI)*

5. **LEARNIN' THE BLUES**
   F. Sinatra
   *Silvers, Capitol 3102
   (Barton, ASCAP)*

6. **BO DIDDLEY**
   Bo Diddley
   *E. McDaniels, Checker 814
   (Arc, BMI)*

7. **AS LONG AS I'M MOVING**
   R. Brown
   *C. E. Calhoun, Atlantic
   1059 (Progressive, BMI)*

8. **CHERRY PINK AND APPLE
   BLOSSOM WHITE**
   P. Prado
   *Louiguy–David, Victor
   20-5965 (Chappell, ASCAP)*

9. **MAYBELLINE**
   C. Berry
   *C. Berry, Chess 1604
   (Arc, BMI)*

10. **SOMETHING'S GOTTA GIVE**
    The McGuire Sisters
    *J. Mercer, Coral 61423
    (Robbins, ASCAP)*

August 13

1. **AIN'T THAT A SHAME**
F. Domino
D. Bartholomew–A. Domino, Imperial 5348 (Commodore, BMI)

2. **ROCK AROUND THE CLOCK**
B. Haley and the Comets
M. Freedman–J. DeKnight, Decca 29124 (Meyers, ASCAP)

3. **STORY UNTOLD**
The Nutmegs
L. Griffin, Herald 452 (Rush, BMI)

4. **AS LONG AS I'M MOVING**
R. Brown
C. E. Calhoun, Atlantic 1059 (Progressive, BMI)

5. **SOLDIER BOY**
The Four Fellows
D. Jones–T. Williams, Glory 234 (E. B. Marks, BMI)

6. **MAYBELLINE**
C. Berry
C. Berry, Chess 1604 (Arc, BMI)

7. **BO DIDDLEY**
Bo Diddley
E. McDaniels, Checker 814 (Arc, BMI)

8. **LEARNIN' THE BLUES**
F. Sinatra
Silvers, Capitol 3102 (Barton, ASCAP)

9. **HUMMINGBIRD**
L. Paul and M. Ford
D. Robertson, Capitol 3165 (Ross Jungnickel, ASCAP)

10. **CHERRY PINK AND APPLE BLOSSOM WHITE**
P. Prado
Louiguy–David, Victor 20-5965 (Chappell, ASCAP)

August 20

1. **ROCK AROUND THE CLOCK**
B. Haley and the Comets
M. Freedman–J. DeKnight, Decca 29124 (Meyers, ASCAP)

2. **AIN'T THAT A SHAME**
F. Domino
D. Bartholomew–A. Domino, Imperial 5348 (Commodore, BMI)

3. **AS LONG AS I'M MOVING**
R. Brown
C. E. Calhoun, Atlantic 1059 (Progressive, BMI)

4. **STORY UNTOLD**
The Nutmegs
L. Griffin, Herald 452 (Rush, BMI)

5. **MAYBELLINE**
C. Berry
C. Berry, Chess 1604 (Arc, BMI)

6. **SOLDIER BOY**
The Four Fellows
D. Jones–T. Williams, Glory 234 (E. B. Marks, BMI)

7. **HUMMINGBIRD**
L. Paul and M. Ford
D. Robertson, Capitol 3165 (Ross Jungnickel, ASCAP)

8. **BO DIDDLEY**
Bo Diddley
E. McDaniels, Checker 814 (Arc, BMI)

9. **LEARNIN' THE BLUES**
F. Sinatra
Silvers, Capitol 3102 (Barton, ASCAP)

10. **IF I MAY**
Nat (King) Cole
C. Singleton–R. M. McCoy, Capitol 3195 (Roosevelt, BMI)

August 27

1. **ROCK AROUND THE CLOCK**
B. Haley and the Comets
M. Freedman–J. DeKnight, Decca 29124 (Meyers, ASCAP)

2. **AIN'T THAT A SHAME**
F. Domino
D. Bartholomew–A. Domino, Imperial 5348 (Commodore, BMI)

3. **MAYBELLINE**
C. Berry
C. Berry, Chess 1604 (Arc, BMI)

4. **AS LONG AS I'M MOVING**
R. Brown
C. E. Calhoun, Atlantic 1059 (Progressive, BMI)

5. **STORY UNTOLD**
The Nutmegs
L. Griffin, Herald 452 (Rush, BMI)

6. **HUMMINGBIRD**
L. Paul and M. Ford
D. Robertson, Capitol 3165 (Ross Jungnickel, ASCAP)

7. **SOLDIER BOY**
The Four Fellows
D. Jones–T. Williams, Glory 234 (E. B. Marks, BMI)

8. **IF I MAY**
Nat (King) Cole
C. Singleton–R. M. McCoy, Capitol 3195 (Roosevelt, BMI)

9. **SEVENTEEN**
B. Bennett
J. F. Young–C. Gorman–B. Bennett, King 1470 (Lois, BMI)

10. **ONLY YOU**
The Platters
B. Ram, Mercury 70633 (Ram, BMI)

September 3

1. **ROCK AROUND THE CLOCK**
B. Haley and the Comets
M. Freedman–J. DeKnight, Decca 29124 (Meyers, ASCAP)

2. **MAYBELLINE**
C. Berry
C. Berry, Chess 1604 (Arc, BMI)

3. **AIN'T THAT A SHAME**
F. Domino
D. Bartholomew–A. Domino, Imperial 5348 (Commodore, BMI)

4. **AS LONG AS I'M MOVING**
R. Brown
C. E. Calhoun, Atlantic 1059 (Progressive, BMI)

5. **SEVENTEEN**
B. Bennett
J. F. Young–C. Gorman–B. Bennett, King 1470 (Lois, BMI)

6. **STORY UNTOLD**
The Nutmegs
L. Griffin, Herald 452 (Rush, BMI)

7. **IF I MAY**
Nat (King) Cole
C. Singleton–R. M. McCoy, Capitol 3195 (Roosevelt, BMI)

8. **ONLY YOU**
The Platters
B. Ram, Mercury 70633 (Ram, BMI)

9. **HUMMINGBIRD**
L. Paul and M. Ford
D. Robertson, Capitol 3165 (Ross Jungnickel, ASCAP)

10. **SOLDIER BOY**
The Four Fellows
D. Jones–T. Williams, Glory 234 (E. B. Marks, BMI)

September 10

1. **ROCK AROUND THE CLOCK**
B. Haley and the Comets
M. Freedman–J. DeKnight, Decca 29124 (Meyers, ASCAP)

2. **MAYBELLINE**
C. Berry
C. Berry, Chess 1604 (Arc, BMI)

3. **AIN'T THAT A SHAME**
F. Domino
D. Bartholomew–A. Domino, Imperial 5348 (Commodore, BMI)

4. **SEVENTEEN**
B. Bennett
J. F. Young–C. Gorman–B. Bennett, King 1470 (Lois, BMI)

5. **AS LONG AS I'M MOVING**
R. Brown
C. E. Calhoun, Atlantic 1059 (Progressive, BMI)

6. **ONLY YOU**
The Platters
B. Ram, Mercury 70633 (Ram, BMI)

7. **IF I MAY**
Nat (King) Cole
C. Singleton–R. M. McCoy, Capitol 3195 (Roosevelt, BMI)

8. **WALKING THE BLUES**
J. DuPree
D. Bartholomew, King 4812 (Commodore, BMI)

9. **STORY UNTOLD**
The Nutmegs
L. Griffin, Herald 452 (Rush, BMI)

10. **SOLDIER BOY**
The Four Fellows
D. Jones–T. Williams, Glory 234 (E. B. Marks, BMI)

September 17

1. **MAYBELLINE**
C. Berry
C. Berry, Chess 1604 (Arc, BMI)

2. **ROCK AROUND THE CLOCK**
B. Haley and the Comets
M. Freedman–J. DeKnight, Decca 29124 (Meyers, ASCAP)

3. **AIN'T THAT A SHAME**
F. Domino
D. Bartholomew–A. Domino, Imperial 5348 (Commodore, BMI)

4. **ONLY YOU**
The Platters
B. Ram, Mercury 70633 (Ram, BMI)

5. **SEVENTEEN**
B. Bennett
J. F. Young–C. Gorman–B. Bennett, King 1470 (Lois, BMI)

6. **WALKING THE BLUES**
J. DuPree
D. Bartholomew, King 4812 (Commodore, BMI)

7. **AS LONG AS I'M MOVING**
R. Brown
C. E. Calhoun, Atlantic 1059 (Progressive, BMI)

8. **YELLOW ROSE OF TEXAS**
M. Miller
D. George, Columbia 40540 (Planetary, ASCAP)

9. **IF I MAY**
Nat (King) Cole
C. Singleton–R. M. McCoy, Capitol 3195 (Roosevelt, BMI)

10. **LOVE IS A MANY SPLENDORED THING**
D. Cornell
S. Webster, Coral 61467 (Miller, ASCAP)

September 24

1. **MAYBELLINE**
C. Berry
C. Berry, Chess 1604
(Arc, BMI)

2. **ROCK AROUND THE CLOCK**
B. Haley and the Comets
M. Freedman–J. DeKnight,
Decca 29124
(Meyers, ASCAP)

3. **ONLY YOU**
The Platters
B. Ram, Mercury 70633
(Ram, BMI)

4. **AIN'T THAT A SHAME**
F. Domino
D. Bartholomew–A. Domino,
Imperial 5348
(Commodore, BMI)

5. **YELLOW ROSE OF TEXAS**
M. Miller
D. George, Columbia 40540
(Planetary, ASCAP)

6. **SEVENTEEN**
B. Bennett
J. F. Young–C. Gorman–
B. Bennett, King 1470
(Lois, BMI)

7. **WALKING THE BLUES**
J. DuPree
D. Bartholomew, King 4812
(Commodore, BMI)

8. **LOVE IS A MANY**
SPLENDORED THING
D. Cornell
S. Webster, Coral 61467
(Miller, ASCAP)

9. **AS LONG AS I'M MOVING**
R. Brown
C. E. Calhoun, Atlantic 1059
(Progressive, BMI)

10. **IF I MAY**
Nat (King) Cole
C. Singleton–R. M. McCoy,
Capitol 3195 (Roosevelt, BMI)

October 1

1. **MAYBELLINE**
C. Berry
C. Berry, Chess 1604
(Arc, BMI)

2. **ONLY YOU**
The Platters
B. Ram, Mercury 70633
(Ram, BMI)

3. **YELLOW ROSE OF TEXAS**
M. Miller
D. George, Columbia 40540
(Planetary, ASCAP)

4. **ROCK AROUND THE CLOCK**
B. Haley and the Comets
M. Freedman–J. DeKnight,
Decca 29124
(Meyers, ASCAP)

5. **AIN'T THAT A SHAME**
F. Domino
D. Bartholomew–A. Domino,
Imperial 5348
(Commodore, BMI)

6. **LOVE IS A MANY**
SPLENDORED THING
D. Cornell
S. Webster, Coral 61467
(Miller, ASCAP)

7. **ALL BY MYSELF**
F. Domino
D. Bartholomew–A. Domino,
Imperial 5357
(Commodore, BMI)

8. **SEVENTEEN**
B. Bennett
J. F. Young–C. Gorman–
B. Bennett, King 1470
(Lois, BMI)

9. **WALKING THE BLUES**
J. DuPree
D. Bartholomew,
King 4812
(Commodore, BMI)

10. **I HEAR YOU KNOCKING**
S. Lewis
D. Bartholomew–P. King,
Imperial 5356
(Commodore, BMI)

October 8

1. **MAYBELLINE**
C. Berry
C. Berry, Chess 1604
(Arc, BMI)

2. **ONLY YOU**
The Platters
B. Ram, Mercury 70633
(Ram, BMI)

3. **YELLOW ROSE OF TEXAS**
M. Miller
D. George, Columbia 40540
(Planetary, ASCAP)

4. **LOVE IS A MANY**
SPLENDORED THING
D. Cornell
S. Webster, Coral 61467
(Miller, ASCAP)

5. **ALL BY MYSELF**
F. Domino
D. Bartholomew–A. Domino,
Imperial 5357
(Commodore, BMI)

6. **AIN'T THAT A SHAME**
F. Domino
D. Bartholomew–A. Domino,
Imperial 5348
(Commodore, BMI)

7. **ROCK AROUND THE CLOCK**
B. Haley and the Comets
M. Freedman–J. DeKnight,
Decca 29124
(Meyers, ASCAP)

8. **I HEAR YOU KNOCKING**
S. Lewis
D. Bartholomew–P. King,
Imperial 5356
(Commodore, BMI)

9. **ALL AROUND THE WORLD**
Little Willie John
D. Craig–D. K. Baker,
King 4818 (Commodore, BMI)

10. **WALKING THE BLUES**
J. DuPree
D. Bartholomew, King 4812
(Commodore, BMI)

October 15

1. **ONLY YOU**
   The Platters
   B. Ram, Mercury 70633
   (Ram, BMI)

2. **MAYBELLINE**
   C. Berry
   C. Berry, Chess 1604
   (Arc, BMI)

3. **YELLOW ROSE OF TEXAS**
   M. Miller
   D. George, Columbia 40540
   (Planetary, ASCAP)

4. **ALL BY MYSELF**
   F. Domino
   D. Bartholomew–A. Domino,
   Imperial 5357
   (Commodore, BMI)

5. **LOVE IS A MANY**
   SPLENDORED THING
   D. Cornell
   S. Webster, Coral 61467
   (Miller, ASCAP)

6. **I HEAR YOU KNOCKING**
   S. Lewis
   D. Bartholomew–P. King,
   Imperial 5356
   (Commodore, BMI)

7. **ALL AROUND THE WORLD**
   Little Willie John
   D. Craig–D. K. Baker,
   King 4818 (Commodore, BMI)

8. **AIN'T THAT A SHAME**
   F. Domino
   D. Bartholomew–A. Domino,
   Imperial 5348
   (Commodore, BMI)

9. **ROCK AROUND THE CLOCK**
   B. Haley and the Comets
   M. Freedman–J. DeKnight,
   Decca 29124
   (Meyers, ASCAP)

10. **AT MY FRONT DOOR**
    The El Dorados
    Moore–Abner, VeeJay 147
    (Tollie, BMI)

October 22

1. **ONLY YOU**
   The Platters
   B. Ram, Mercury 70633
   (Ram, BMI)

2. **YELLOW ROSE OF TEXAS**
   M. Miller
   D. George, Columbia 40540
   (Planetary, ASCAP)

3. **MAYBELLINE**
   C. Berry
   C. Berry, Chess 1604
   (Arc, BMI)

4. **I HEAR YOU KNOCKING**
   S. Lewis
   D. Bartholomew–P. King
   Imperial 5356
   (Commodore, BMI)

5. **ALL BY MYSELF**
   F. Domino
   D. Bartholomew–A. Domino,
   Imperial 5357
   (Commodore, BMI)

6. **LOVE IS A MANY**
   SPLENDORED THING
   D. Cornell
   S. Webster, Coral 61467
   (Miller, ASCAP)

7. **AT MY FRONT DOOR**
   The El Dorados
   Moore–Abner, VeeJay 147
   (Tollie, BMI)

8. **ALL AROUND THE WORLD**
   Little Willie John
   D. Craig–D. K. Baker,
   King 4818 (Commodore, BMI)

9. **AIN'T THAT A SHAME**
   F. Domino
   D. Bartholomew–A. Domino,
   Imperial 5348
   (Commodore, BMI)

10. **MOMENTS TO REMEMBER**
    The Four Lads
    Stillmen–Allen, Columbia
    40539 (Beaver, ASCAP)

October 29

1. **YELLOW ROSE OF TEXAS**
   M. Miller
   D. George, Columbia 40540
   (Planetary, ASCAP)

2. **ONLY YOU**
   The Platters
   B. Ram, Mercury 70633
   (Ram, BMI)

3. **I HEAR YOU KNOCKING**
   S. Lewis
   D. Bartholomew–P. King,
   Imperial 5356
   (Commodore, BMI)

4. **MAYBELLINE**
   C. Berry
   C. Berry, Chess 1604
   (Arc, BMI)

5. **ALL BY MYSELF**
   F. Domino
   D. Bartholomew–A. Domino,
   Imperial 5357
   (Commodore, BMI)

6. **AT MY FRONT DOOR**
   The El Dorados
   Moore–Abner, VeeJay 147
   (Tollie, BMI)

7. **LOVE IS A MANY**
   SPLENDORED THING
   D. Cornell
   S. Webster, Coral 61467
   (Miller, ASCAP)

8. **ALL AROUND THE WORLD**
   Little Willie John
   D. Craig–D. K. Baker,
   King 4818 (Commodore, BMI)

9. **MOMENTS TO REMEMBER**
   The Four Lads
   Stillmen–Allen, Columbia 40539
   (Beaver, ASCAP)

10. **AIN'T THAT A SHAME**
    F. Domino
    D. Bartholomew–A. Domino,
    Imperial 5348
    (Commodore, BMI)

November 5

1. **YELLOW ROSE OF TEXAS**
M. Miller
D. George, Columbia 40540
(Planetary, ASCAP)

2. **ONLY YOU**
The Platters
B. Ram, Mercury 70633
(Ram, BMI)

3. **I HEAR YOU KNOCKING**
S. Lewis
D. Bartholomew–P. King,
Imperial 5356
(Commodore, BMI)

4. **AT MY FRONT DOOR**
The El Dorados
Moore–Abner, VeeJay 147
(Tollie, BMI)

5. **MAYBELLINE**
C. Berry
C. Berry, Chess 1604
(Arc, BMI)

6. **ALL BY MYSELF**
F. Domino
D. Bartholomew–A. Domino,
Imperial 5357
(Commodore, BMI)

7. **MOMENTS TO REMEMBER**
The Four Lads
Stillmen–Allen, Columbia 40539
(Beaver, ASCAP)

8. **LOVE IS A MANY
SPLENDORED THING**
D. Cornell
S. Webster, Coral 61467
(Miller, ASCAP)

9. **ALL AROUND THE WORLD**
Little Willie John
D. Craig–D. K. Baker, King 4818
(Commodore, BMI)

10. **THIRTY DAYS**
C. Berry
C. Berry, Chess 1610
(Arc, BMI)

November 12

1. **YELLOW ROSE OF TEXAS**
M. Miller
D. George, Columbia 40540
(Planetary, ASCAP)

2. **ONLY YOU**
The Platters
B. Ram, Mercury 70633
(Ram, BMI)

3. **AT MY FRONT DOOR**
The El Dorados
Moore–Abner, VeeJay 147
(Tollie, BMI)

4. **I HEAR YOU KNOCKING**
S. Lewis
D. Bartholomew–P. King,
Imperial 5356
(Commodore, BMI)

5. **THIRTY DAYS**
C. Berry
C. Berry, Chess 1610
(Arc, BMI)

6. **ALL BY MYSELF**
F. Domino
D. Bartholomew–A. Domino,
Imperial 5357
(Commodore,BMI)

7. **MOMENTS TO REMEMBER**
The Four Lads
Stillmen–Allen, Columbia
40539 (Beaver, ASCAP)

8. **MAYBELLINE**
C. Berry
C. Berry, Chess 1604
(Arc, BMI)

9. **LOVE IS A MANY SPLEN-
DORED THING**
D. Cornell
S. Webster, Coral 61467
(Miller, ASCAP)

10. **SHIFTING, WHISPERING
SANDS**
R. Draper
M. Gilbert–V. Gilbert, Mercury
70696 (Gallatin, BMI)

November 19

1. **YELLOW ROSE OF TEXAS**
M. Miller
D. George, Columbia 40540
(Planetary, ASCAP)

2. **ONLY YOU**
The Platters
B. Ram, Mercury 70633
(Ram, BMI)

3. **THIRTY DAYS**
C. Berry
C. Berry, Chess 1610
(Arc, BMI)

4. **AT MY FRONT DOOR**
The El Dorados
Moore–Abner, VeeJay 147
(Tollie, BMI)

5. **I HEAR YOU KNOCKING**
S. Lewis
D. Bartholomew–P. King,
Imperial 5356
(Commodore, BMI)

6. **ALL BY MYSELF**
F. Domino
D. Bartholomew–A. Domino,
Imperial 5357
(Commodore, BMI)

7. **SHIFTING, WHISPERING
SANDS**
R. Draper
M. Gilbert–V. Gilbert,
Mercury 70696 (Gallatin, BMI)

8. **MOMENTS TO REMEMBER**
The Four Lads
Stillmen–Allen, Columbia
40539 (Beaver, ASCAP)

9. **ADORABLE**
The Drifters
B. Ram, Atlantic 1078
(Panther, ASCAP)

10. **MAYBELLINE**
C. Berry
C. Berry, Chess 1604
(Arc, BMI)

November 26

1. **YELLOW ROSE OF TEXAS**
   M. Miller
   D. George, Columbia 40540
   (Planetary, ASCAP)
2. **ONLY YOU**
   The Platters
   B. Ram, Mercury 70633
   (Ram, BMI)
3. **THIRTY DAYS**
   C. Berry
   C. Berry, Chess 1610
   (Arc, BMI)
4. **AT MY FRONT DOOR**
   The El Dorados
   Moore–Abner, VeeJay 147
   (Tollie, BMI)
5. **SHIFTING, WHISPERING SANDS**
   R. Draper
   M. Gilbert–V. Gilbert, Mercury 70696 (Gallatin, BMI)
6. **ADORABLE**
   The Drifters
   B. Ram, Atlantic 1078
   (Panther, ASCAP)
7. **I HEAR YOU KNOCKING**
   S. Lewis
   D. Bartholomew–P. King, Imperial 5356 (Commodore, BMI)
8. **ALL BY MYSELF**
   F. Domino
   D. Bartholomew–A. Domino, Imperial 5357 (Commodore, BMI)
9. **HANDS OFF**
   P. Bowman
   J. McShann, VeeJay 155
   (Tollie, BMI)
10. **MOMENTS TO REMEMBER**
   The Four Lads
   Stillmen–Allen, Columbia 40539 (Beaver, ASCAP)

December 3

1. **ADORABLE**
   The Drifters
   B. Ram, Atlantic 1078
   (Panther, ASCAP)
2. **YELLOW ROSE OF TEXAS**
   M. Miller
   D. George, Columbia 40540
   (Planetary, ASCAP)
3. **ONLY YOU**
   The Platters
   B. Ram, Mercury 70633
   (Ram, BMI)
4. **HANDS OFF**
   P. Bowman
   J. McShann, VeeJay 155
   (Tollie, BMI)
5. **SHIFTING, WHISPERING SANDS**
   R. Draper
   M. Gilbert–V. Gilbert, Mercury 70696 (Gallatin, BMI)
6. **THIRTY DAYS**
   C. Berry
   C. Berry, Chess 1610
   (Arc, BMI)
7. **AT MY FRONT DOOR**
   The El Dorados
   Moore–Abner, VeeJay 147
   (Tollie, BMI)
8. **I HEAR YOU KNOCKING**
   S. Lewis
   D. Bartholomew–P. King, Imperial 5356 (Commodore, BMI)
9. **ALL BY MYSELF**
   F. Domino
   D. Bartholomew–A. Domino, Imperial 5357 (Commodore, BMI)
10. **AUTUMN LEAVES**
   R. Williams
   J. Mercer–J. Prevert–J. Kosma, Kapp 116 (Ardmore, ASCAP)

December 10

1. **ADORABLE**
   The Drifters
   B. Ram, Atlantic 1078
   (Panther, ASCAP)
2. **ONLY YOU**
   The Platters
   B. Ram, Mercury 70633
   (Ram, BMI)
3. **HANDS OFF**
   P. Bowman
   J. McShann, VeeJay 155
   (Tollie, BMI)
4. **YELLOW ROSE OF TEXAS**
   M. Miller
   D. George, Columbia 40540
   (Planetary, ASCAP)
5. **SHIFTING, WHISPERING SANDS**
   R. Draper
   M. Gilbert–V. Gilbert, Mercury 70696 (Gallatin, BMI)
6. **AUTUMN LEAVES**
   R. Williams
   J. Mercer–J. Prevert–J. Kosma, Kapp 116 (Ardmore, ASCAP)
7. **SIXTEEN TONS**
   Tennessee Ernie Ford
   M. Travis, Capitol 3262
   (American Music, BMI)
8. **THIRTY DAYS**
   C. Berry
   C. Berry, Chess 1610
   (Arc, BMI)
9. **AT MY FRONT DOOR**
   The El Dorados
   Moore–Abner, VeeJay 147
   (Tollie, BMI)
10. **WITCHCRAFT**
   The Spiders
   D. Bartholomew–P. King, Imperial 5366 (Commodore, BMI)

December 17

1. **HANDS OFF**
P. Bowman
J. McShann,   VeeJay 155
(Tollie, BMI)

2. **ADORABLE**
The Drifters
B. Ram,   Atlantic 1078
(Panther, ASCAP)

3. **ONLY YOU**
The Platters
B. Ram,   Mercury 70633
(Ram, BMI)

4. **SIXTEEN TONS**
Tennessee Ernie Ford
M. Travis,   Capitol 3262
(American Music, BMI)

5. **AUTUMN LEAVES**
R. Williams
J. Mercer–J. Prevert–J. Kosma,
Kapp 116   (Ardmore, ASCAP)

6. **SHIFTING, WHISPERING
SANDS**
R. Draper
M. Gilbert–V. Gilbert,
Mercury 70696   (Gallatin, BMI)

7. **WITCHCRAFT**
The Spiders
D. Bartholomew–P. King,
Imperial 5366
(Commodore, BMI)

8. **YELLOW ROSE OF TEXAS**
M. Miller
D. George,   Columbia 40540
(Planetary, ASCAP)

9. **AT MY FRONT DOOR**
The El Dorados
Moore–Abner,   VeeJay 147,
(Tollie, BMI)

10. **LOVE AND MARRIAGE**
F. Sinatra
S. Cahn–J. VanHeusen,   Capitol
3260   (Barton, ASCAP)

December 24

1. **HANDS OFF**
P. Bowman
J. McShann,   VeeJay 155
(Tollie, BMI)

2. **SIXTEEN TONS**
Tennessee Ernie Ford
M. Travis,   Capitol 3262
(American Music, BMI)

3. **ONLY YOU**
The Platters
B. Ram,   Mercury 70633
(Ram, BMI)

4. **AUTUMN LEAVES**
R. Williams
J. Mercer–J. Prevert–J. Kosma,
Kapp 116   (Ardmore, ASCAP)

5. **ADORABLE**
The Drifters
B. Ram,   Atlantic 1078
(Panther, ASCAP)

6. **LOVE AND MARRIAGE**
F. Sinatra
S. Cahn–J. VanHeusen,
Capitol 3260   (Barton, ASCAP)

7. **SHIFTING, WHISPERING
SANDS**
R. Draper
M. Gilbert–V. Gilbert,
Mercury 70696   (Gallatin, BMI)

8. **WITCHCRAFT**
The Spiders
D. Bartholomew–P. King,
Imperial 5366
(Commodore, BMI)

9. **MEMORIES ARE MADE OF
THIS**
D. Martin
Gillkyson–Dehr–Miller,
Capitol 3295   (Montclare, BMI)

10. **AT MY FRONT DOOR**
The El Dorados
Moore–Abner,   VeeJay 147
(Tollie, BMI)

December 31

1. **HANDS OFF**
P. Bowman
J. McShann,   VeeJay 155
(Tollie, BMI)

2. **LOVE AND MARRIAGE**
F. Sinatra
S. Cahn–J. VanHeusen,
Capitol 3260   (Barton, ASCAP)

3. **ONLY YOU**
The Platters
B. Ram,   Mercury 70633
(Ram, BMI)

4. **MEMORIES ARE MADE OF
THIS**
D. Martin
Gillkyson–Dehr–Miller,
Capitol 3295   (Montclare, BMI)

5. **AUTUMN LEAVES**
R. Williams
J. Mercer–J. Prevert–J. Kosma,
Kapp 116   (Ardmore, ASCAP)

6. **SIXTEEN TONS**
Tennessee Ernie Ford
M. Travis,   Capitol 3262
(American Music, BMI)

7. **ADORABLE**
The Drifters
B. Ram,   Atlantic 1078
(Panther, ASCAP)

8. **TENDER TRAP**
F. Sinatra
S. Cahn–J. VanHeusen,   Capitol
3290   (Barton, ASCAP)

9. **WITCHCRAFT**
The Spiders
D. Bartholomew–P. King,
Imperial 5366
(Commodore, BMI)

10. **SHIFTING, WHISPERING
SANDS**
R. Draper
M. Gilbert–V. Gilbert,
Mercury 70696   (Gallatin, BMI)

ELVIS PRESLEY

The world was in a state of relative calm in early 1956. The United States was hopeful that Ike would recover from his second heart attack in January. No one doubted integration would soon be an established fact if only those stubborn Southerners would realize they must bow to the rulings of the righteous North. Even the biggest problem of recent years, the menacing Russians, seemed to be in check as Khrushchev and Bulganin made goodwill tours to the West to boast of the new de-Stalinized Russia.

America was still boasting its growth and development in the material world. The West raced Russia to have the best air force. There was also great pride in commercial airlines that could fly from New York to Paris in twelve hours and New York to Los Angeles in eight hours. The automobile industry advertised cars for the "superhighway age" and continued the horsepower race. The hardtop caught on for the first time and accounted for nearly one-third of all auto sales. Growing baby-boom families pushed up sales of station wagons in 1956. And Ford Motor Company stock went on sale to the public for the first time.

Generally, the economy was slowing a bit after the early fifties boom, but giant strides in sales were made by the record industry. 1956 record sales were 90 million and topped the old record high of 80 million set in 1955. Ten million of these records were by Elvis Presley. The demand for his recordings was so great that RCA had to engage the pressing facilities of competing manufacturers to produce them. Surprisingly, Elvis was the first RCA recording artist to have 2 million-selling records in a row. There were 856,327 orders for "Love Me Tender" a week before the record was released. Elvis' record earnings were estimated at $450,000. And that was only a fraction of his 1956 income.

1956

. . . a Tennessee youth named Elvis Presley gave spread to a national juvenile mania called rock and roll.

Walter Cronkite
Foreword, Facts on File Yearbook, Vol XVI 1956

39

Hats, T-shirts, bluejeans, kerchiefs, bobby sox, sneakers, skirts, blouses, belts, purses, billfolds, wallets, charm bracelets, necklaces, magazines, gloves, mittens, a statue, book ends, guitars, lipstick, cologne, stuffed hound dogs, stuffed dancing dolls, stationery, greeting cards, sweaters, a soft drink and glow-in-the-dark pictures of Elvis were marketed by a merchandising company in conjunction with Elvis and his manager, Colonel Tom Parker.

And Elvis starred in his first film, a Western called *Love Me Tender.* We all flocked to the movies to see him and hear his speaking voice. It was so neat to see him that many of us couldn't help squealing. But we felt a twinge of disappointment when we found out the film wasn't in color.

Love Me Tender, a quick black-and-white production, was hardly representative of Hollywood, 1956, the year of the spectacle. Mike Todd's *Around the World in 80 days* won the Oscar for the best picture. Yul Brynner in *The King and I* was the best actor, and Ingrid Bergman in *Anastasia* was the best actress.

It was television's tenth year and the nation was wrapped up in the newest TV sensation—the big quiz shows. Perhaps the most familiar melody of 1956 to every age group was the thinking theme (dum dum da da da da dum dum da da da da) on the "$64,000 Question."

In radio, KLAC in Los Angeles introduced the "Top Thirty" and thereby became a pioneer in the staple of rock and roll programming.

Not only was our taste in music encroaching upon radio programming and the pop charts, but our artists and songwriters were beginning to take over. The Teenagers and Patience and Prudence broke into a field that had belonged exclusively to the older generation. Even Elvis and Pat Boone were just a few years older than we were. These young singers could move us. They weren't talking down to us, and they weren't speaking glibly of adult experience. What's more, they implanted the notion in our minds that we could become rock and roll stars, or their girl friends, or their managers. We had had a music with words and rhythms for kids, and now we had our contemporaries writing and singing it.

In 1956 it became possible to trace rock and roll in the pop charts. Adults still weren't ready to acknowledge rock and roll as the dominant popular music, and they kept classifying the rougher rock and roll as rhythm and blues. At this point it was primarily the recording artist that made a song rhythm and blues or pop. Pat Boone, with his clean religious training and white buck shoes, really made it in 1956 by cover recording songs like "I Almost Lost My Mind" and "Long, Tall Sally." Our parents could tolerate these songs by Boone, although they called them suggestive when sung by the original Negro artists, Ivory Joe Hunter and Little Richard. Elvis was really the first white rock and roll singer who could evoke the teenager's love and the parent's condemnation with a quality that was later to be called "soul."

Elvis Presley was the most exciting personality we had ever experienced. He had a special sensual magic about him. He looked kind of "hoody"—not like the clean little boys we knew at school. Adults and kids who were too sophisticated to be swept up by our generation's first idol were so busy attacking his looks and lyrics that they failed to understand he was saying more than:

> You ain't nothin' but a hound dog
> You ain't nothin' but a hound dog
> Cryin' all the time
> You ain't never caught a rabbit
> And you ain't no friend of mine.

And the way Elvis moved was sexy to girls of all ages. Well, not our mothers, who seemed threatened by our preoccupation with the mumbling, gyrating star.

Our parents may not have understood us, our music, or our star, but they understood that you can't argue with success. And in 1956 success was Elvis Presley. On April 14 "Heartbreak Hotel" first showed up in the Top 10. It was Number 1 on May 5.

Some heroes of 1956 other than Elvis caught the interest of both parents and kids. All of us except the Dodgers were thrilled to see Don Larsen of the Yankees pitch the first perfect game in a World Series.

Doctor Albert Sabins became a hero of a different sort when he discovered the oral polio vaccine. And twenty-one-year-old Floyd Patterson knocked out Archie Moore to replace retired heavyweight boxing champ Rocky Marciano.

The FBI even proved heroic by solving the Brinks robbery although they recovered none of the money.

And, until Elvis came along, every girl in America was watching as Grace Kelly, heroine so often in the movies, prepared to become a real live princess.

1956 was a vintage year for romance. Prince Rainier and Grace Kelly may have snatched most of the publicity, but wedding bells also rang for Margaret Truman and Clifton Daniels, Jean Ann Kennedy and Stephen Smith, and Marilyn Monroe and Arthur Miller.

There were tragedies in 1956 that jarred us all: the collision of the *Andrea Doria* and the *Stockholm*; the deaths of H. L. Mencken, Connie Mack and Babe Zaharias; the futile rebellion in Hungary; the crash of two airliners over the Grand Canyon which killed 128 people.

Most of us were still young enough to look on the heavy snows in mid-March as a chance to miss school, go sledding and make snowmen. But the adult world was paralyzed from Maine to West Virginia where about 18 inches of snow was responsible for 164 deaths from auto accidents and heart attacks.

And nearly all of the 167.5 million Americans felt a bit of sadness when Ringling Brothers and Barnum and Bailey announced the death of the tent circus.

To our parents, the biggest issue of 1956 was the election. After long speculation about Eisenhower's health, he announced he would run again, and added some months later that his running mate would be his controversial Vice President Richard Nixon.

The Democrats selected Adlai Stevenson and Estes Kefauver. Though Stevenson cried out against H-bomb testing and extreme anti-Communist views, he was hardly heard as the nation cheered Ike, its only hero who could have topped Elvis in a popularity contest.

Eisenhower carried forty-one states in the November election, leaving only seven deep South and always Democratic states to Stevenson. This would be the last Presidential election before the Democratic rule of the South would be challenged.

A sign of the political change about to stir the South was visible in Montgomery, Alabama, in a movement begun by an unknown minister. It was there that the era of street demonstrations came into being as Doctor Martin Luther King, Jr., came forth to lead the city's Negroes in a boycott of city buses to protest segregated seating.

The University of Alabama was in chaos as Autherine Lucy tried to establish the Negro's right to a college education at the state university. At other United States colleges the issues were not yet civil rights. The University of Kansas expelled fifty-eight students for a panty raid on a sorority house. Harvard raised tuition for September, 1956, from $800 to $1,000. Notre Dame's quarterback Paul Hornung was drafted by the Green Bay Packers.

Rock and roll had not yet made it big on college campuses. College students were more interested in emulating the adults than in clinging to the bobby sox interests of us younger kids.

They may have been listening to rock and roll in the privacy of their rooms, but outwardly their music taste was jazz and pop. Some college-age kids joined with our parents as they continued to discuss the evil in rock and roll and worry where our generation was heading.

But the adults were involved in some strange fads of their own. It was the beginning of the trading stamp boom, and our parents were generally excited about the prospect of getting something for what appeared to be nothing. They were also busy searching for Bridie Murphy after the movie renewed public curiosity about reincarnation. It was the year of "togetherness" too, although there were few areas where we really had anything in common with the grown-ups.

In 1956 our generation took a giant step toward establishing an identity. We finally had reason to believe that our music—rock and roll—was here to stay, no matter how often our parents predicted the return of the ballad and the big band.

Elvis Presley had brought real rock and roll into the white middle-class mainstream by proving that rhythm and blues was not strictly in the black domain.

Economics brought the music industry into line. A year before there were fears that pop music would die and leave a great void. Now rock and roll was selling more records than pop ever had.

And for kids, rock and roll was a great new means of communication. It was a chance for us to talk to each other without the adults eavesdropping.

And as Danny and the Juniors said:

Rock and roll is here to stay
I'll dig it to the end
It'll go down in history
Just you wait my friend
I don't care what people say
Rock and roll is here to stay.

The Top Fifty
1956

1. DON'T BE CRUEL — E. Presley
2. HEARTBREAK HOTEL — E. Presley
3. MEMORIES ARE MADE OF THIS — D. Martin
4. MOONGLOW AND THEME FROM PICNIC — M. Stoloff
5. WAYWARD WIND — G. Grant
6. LISBON ANTIGUA — N. Riddle
7. WHATEVER WILL BE, WILL BE (QUE SERA SERA) — D. Day
8. I WANT YOU, I NEED YOU, I LOVE YOU — E. Presley
9. MY PRAYER — The Platters
10. BLUE SUEDE SHOES — C. Perkins
11. ROCK AND ROLL WALTZ — K. Starr
12. HOUND DOG — E. Presley
13. GREAT PRETENDER — The Platters
14. THE POOR PEOPLE OF PARIS — L. Baxter
15. HONKY TONK — B. Doggett
16. LOVE ME TENDER — E. Presley
17. JUST WALKING IN THE RAIN — J. Ray
18. I'M IN LOVE AGAIN — F. Domino
19. GREEN DOOR — J. Lowe
20. CANADIAN SUNSET — H. Winterhalter and E. Heywood
21. NO, NOT MUCH — The Four Lads
22. I ALMOST LOST MY MIND — P. Boone
23. SIXTEEN TONS — Tennessee Ernie Ford
24. HOT DIGGITY — P. Como
25. ALLEGHENY MOON — P. Page
26. TONIGHT YOU BELONG TO ME — Patience and Prudence
27. BE BOP A LULA — G. Vincent
28. WHY DO FOOLS FALL IN LOVE — The Teen-Agers
29. STANDING ON THE CORNER — The Four Lads
30. FLYING SAUCER — Buchanan and Goodman
31. IVORY TOWER — O. Williams
32. SEE YOU LATER, ALLIGATOR — B. Haley and the Comets
33. ON THE STREET WHERE YOU LIVE — V. Damone
34. MAGIC TOUCH — The Platters
35. BAND OF GOLD — D. Cherry
36. BORN TO BE WITH YOU — The Chordettes
37. SINGING THE BLUES — G. Mitchell
38. BLUEBERRY HILL — F. Domino
39. TRANSFUSION — Nervous Norvous
40. TRUE LOVE — B. Crosby and G. Kelly
41. LONG TALL SALLY — Little Richard
42. IN THE STILL OF THE NIGHT — The Five Satins
43. FEVER — Little Willie John
44. IT ONLY HURTS FOR A LITTLE WHILE — The Ames Brothers
45. LET THE GOOD TIMES ROLL — Shirley and Lee
46. SPEEDO — The Cadillacs
47. TUTTI FRUTTI — Little Richard
48. RIP IT UP — Little Richard
49. EDDIE MY LOVE — The Teen Queens
50. TREASURE OF LOVE — C. McPhatter

January 7

1. **SIXTEEN TONS**
Tennessee Ernie Ford
M. Travis, Capitol 3262
(American, BMI)

2. **MEMORIES ARE MADE OF THIS**
D. Martin
Gillkyson–Dehr–Miller,
Capitol 3295
(Montclare, BMI)

3. **MOMENTS TO REMEMBER**
The Four Lads
Stillmen–Allen, Columbia
40539 (Beaver, ASCAP)

4. **HE**
A. Hibbler
Mullan–Richards, Decca 29660
(Avas, BMI)

5. **I HEAR YOU KNOCKIN'**
S. Lewis
D. Bartholomew, Imperial 5356
(Commodore, BMI)

6. **AUTUMN LEAVES**
R. Williams
J. Mercer–J. Prevert–J. Kosma,
Kapp 116 (Ardmore, ASCAP)

7. **NUTTIN' FOR CHRISTMAS**
Gordon and Mooney
Peppert–Bennett, MGM
12092 (Ross Jungnickel,
ASCAP)

8. **LOVE AND MARRIAGE**
F. Sinatra
S. Cahn–J. VanHeusen, Capitol
3260 (Barton, ASCAP)

9. **IT'S ALMOST TOMORROW**
The Dream Weavers
Adkinson, Decca 29683
(Northern, ASCAP)

10. **ONLY YOU**
The Platters
B. Ram, Mercury 70633
(Wildwood, BMI)

January 14

1. **MEMORIES ARE MADE OF THIS**
D. Martin
Gillkyson–Dehr–Miller, Capitol
3295 (Montclare, BMI)

2. **SIXTEEN TONS**
Tennessee Ernie Ford
M. Travis, Capitol 3262
(American, BMI)

3. **MOMENTS TO REMEMBER**
The Four Lads
Stillmen–Allen, Columbia
40539 (Beaver, ASCAP)

4. **I HEAR YOU KNOCKIN'**
S. Lewis
D. Bartholomew, Imperial 5356
(Commodore, BMI)

5. **HE**
A. Hibbler
Mullan–Richards, Decca 29660
(Avas, BMI)

6. **LOVE AND MARRIAGE**
F. Sinatra
S. Cahn–J. VanHeusen, Capitol
3260 (Barton, ASCAP)

7. **AUTUMN LEAVES**
R. Williams
J. Mercer–J. Prevert–J. Kosma,
Kapp 116 (Ardmore, ASCAP)

8. **ONLY YOU**
The Platters
B. Ram, Mercury 70633
(Wildwood, BMI)

9. **GREAT PRETENDER**
The Platters
B. Ram, Mercury 70753
(Southern, ASCAP)

10. **IT'S ALMOST TOMORROW**
The Dream Weavers
Adkinson, Decca 29683
(Northern, ASCAP)

1956

January 21

1. **SIXTEEN TONS**
Tennessee Ernie Ford
*M. Travis,   Capitol 3262
(American, BMI)*

2. **IT'S ALMOST TOMORROW**
The Dream Weavers
*Adkinson,   Decca 29683
(Northern, ASCAP)*

3. **HE**
A. Hibbler
*Mullan–Richards,   Decca 29660
(Avas, BMI)*

4. **GREAT PRETENDER**
The Platters
*B. Ram,   Mercury 70753
(Southern, ASCAP)*

5. **AUTUMN LEAVES**
R. Williams
*J. Mercer–J. Prevert–J. Kosma,
Kapp 116 (Ardmore, ASCAP)*

6. **I HEAR YOU KNOCKIN'**
S. Lewis
*D. Bartholomew,   Imperial 5356
(Commodore, BMI)*

7. **MOMENTS TO REMEMBER**
The Four Lads
*Stillmen–Allen,   Columbia
40539 (Beaver, ASCAP)*

8. **BAND OF GOLD**
D. Cherry
*Musel–Taylor,   Columbia
40597 (Ludlow, BMI)*

9. **MEMORIES ARE MADE
OF THIS**
D. Martin
*Gillkyson–Dehr–Miller,   Capitol
3295 (Montclare, BMI)*

10. **LOVE AND MARRIAGE**
F. Sinatra
*S. Cahn–J. VanHeusen,   Capitol
3260 (Barton, ASCAP)*

January 28

1. **SIXTEEN TONS**
Tennessee Ernie Ford
*M. Travis,   Capitol 3262
(American, BMI)*

2. **ROCK AND ROLL WALTZ**
K. Starr
*Ware–Allen,   Victor 20–6359
(Sheldon, BMI)*

3. **LISBON ANTIGUA**
N. Riddle
*Galherdo–Vale–Partela,
Capitol 3287 (Southern, ASCAP)*

4. **MEMORIES ARE MADE
OF THIS**
D. Martin
*Gillkyson–Dehr–Miller,   Capitol
3295 (Montclare, BMI)*

5. **GREAT PRETENDER**
The Platters
*B. Ram,   Mercury 70753
(Southern, ASCAP)*

6. **MOMENTS TO REMEMBER**
The Four Lads
*Gillkyson–Dehr–Miller,   Capitol
3295 (Montclare, BMI)*

7. **HE**
A. Hibbler
*Mullan–Richards,   Decca 29660
(Avas, BMI)*

8. **IT'S ALMOST TOMORROW**
The Dream Weavers
*Adkinson,   Decca 29683
(Northern, ASCAP)*

9. **BAND OF GOLD**
D. Cherry
*Musel–Taylor,   Columbia 40597
(Ludlow, BMI)*

10. **DUNGAREE DOLL**
E. Fisher
*Raleigh–Edwards,   Victor
20–6337 (Marks, BMI)*

February 4

1. **SIXTEEN TONS**
Tennessee Ernie Ford
*M. Travis,   Capitol 3262
(American, BMI)*

2. **ROCK AND ROLL WALTZ**
K. Starr
*Ware–Allen,   Victor 20–6359
(Sheldon, BMI)*

3. **LISBON ANTIGUA**
N. Riddle
*Galherde–Vale–Partela,
Capitol 3287 (Southern, ASCAP)*

4. **GREAT PRETENDER**
The Platters
*B. Ram,   Mercury 70753
(Southern, ASCAP)*

5. **MEMORIES ARE MADE
OF THIS**
D. Martin
*Gillkyson–Dehr–Miller,   Capitol
3295 (Montclare, BMI)*

6. **IT'S ALMOST TOMORROW**
The Dream Weavers
*Adkinson,   Decca 29683
(Northern, ASCAP)*

7. **HE**
A. Hibbler
*Mullan–Richards,   Decca 29660
(Avas, BMI)*

8. **TEEN AGE PRAYER**
G. Storm
*Reicher–Love,   Dot 15436
(LaSalle, ASCAP)*

9. **BAND OF GOLD**
D. Cherry
*Musel–Taylor,   Columbia 40597
(Ludlow, BMI)*

10. **DUNGAREE DOLL**
E. Fisher
*Raleigh–Edwards,   Victor
20–6337 (Marks, BMI)*

February 11

1. **GREAT PRETENDER**
The Platters
B. Ram,   Mercury 70753
(Sourthern, ASCAP)

2. **MEMORIES ARE MADE OF THIS**
D. Martin
Gillkyson–Dehr–Miller   Capitol
3295   (Montclare, BMI)

3. **LISBON ANTIGUA**
N. Riddle
Galherdo–Vale–Partela,   Captiol
3287   (Southern, ASCAP)

4. **ROCK AND ROLL WALTZ**
K. Starr
Ware–Allen,   Victor 20–6359
(Sheldon, BMI)

5. **SIXTEEN TONS**
Tennessee Ernie Ford
M. Travis,   Capitol 3262
(American, BMI)

6. **BAND OF GOLD**
D. Cherry
Musel–Taylor,   Columbia 40597
(Ludlow, BMI)

7. **IT'S ALMOST TOMORROW**
The Dream Weavers
Adkinson,   Decca 29683
(Northern, ASCAP)

8. **HE**
A. Hibbler
Mullan–Richards,   Decca 29660
(Avas, BMI)

9. **DUNGAREE DOLL**
E. Fisher
Raleigh–Edwards,   Victor
20–6337   (E. B. Marks, BMI)

10. **SEE YOU LATER, ALLIGATOR**
B. Haley and the Comets
Guidry,   Decca 29791
(Arc, BMI)

February 18

1. **MEMORIES ARE MADE OF THIS**
D. Martin
Gillkyson–Dehr–Miller,   Capitol
3295   (Montclare, BMI)

2. **GREAT PRETENDER**
The Platters
B. Ram,   Mercury 70753
(Southern, ASCAP)

3. **ROCK AND ROLL WALTZ**
K. Starr
Ware–Allen,   Victor 20–6359
(Sheldon, BMI)

4. **LISBON ANTIGUA**
N. Riddle
Galherdo–Vale–Partela,
Capitol 3287   (Southern, ASCAP)

5. **SIXTEEN TONS**
Tennessee Ernie Ford
M. Travis,   Capitol 3262
(American, BMI)

6. **BAND OF GOLD**
D. Cherry
Musel–Taylor,   Columbia 40597
(Ludlow, BMI)

7. **NO, NOT MUCH**
The Four Lads
Stillmen–Allen,   Columbia
40629   (Beaver, ASCAP)

8. **SEE YOU LATER, ALLIGATOR**
B. Haley and the Comets
Guidry,   Decca 29791
(Arc, BMI)

9. **IT'S ALMOST TOMORROW**
The Dream Weavers
Adkinson,   Decca 29683
(Northern, ASCAP)

10. **DUNGAREE DOLL**
E. Fisher
Raleigh–Edwards,   Victor
20–6337   (Marks, BMI)

February 25

1. **ROCK AND ROLL WALTZ**
K. Starr
Ware–Allen,   Victor 20–6359
(Sheldon, BMI)

2. **GREAT PRETENDER**
The Platters
B. Ram,   Mercury 70753
(Southern, ASCAP)

3. **MEMORIES ARE MADE OF THIS**
D. Martin
Gillkyson–Dehr–Miller,   Capitol
3295   (Montclare, BMI)

4. **LISBON ANTIGUA**
N. Riddle
Galherdo–Vale–Partela,   Capitol
3287   (Southern, ASCAP)

5. **NO, NOT MUCH**
The Four Lads
Stillmen–Allen   Columbia
40629   (Beaver, ASCAP)

6. **BAND OF GOLD**
D. Cherry
Musel–Taylor,   Columbia 40597
(Ludlow, BMI)

7. **SEE YOU LATER, ALLIGATOR**
B. Haley and the Comets
Guidry,   Decca 29791
(Arc, BMI)

8. **IT'S ALMOST TOMORROW**
The Dream Weavers
Adkinson,   Decca 29683
(Northern, ASCAP)

9. **THE POOR PEOPLE OF PARIS**
L. Baxter
dePauvre–Monnet–Lawrence,
Capitol 3336
(Reg Connelly, ASCAP)

10. **SIXTEEN TONS**
Tennessee Ernie Ford
M. Travis,   Capitol 3262
(American, BMI)

March 3

1. **ROCK AND ROLL WALTZ**
K. Starr
Ware–Allen, Victor 20–6359
(Sheldon, BMI)

2. **LISBON ANTIGUA**
N. Riddle
Galherdo–Vale–Partela, Capitol
3287 (Southern, ASCAP)

3. **GREAT PRETENDER**
The Platters
B. Ram, Mercury 70753
(Southern, ASCAP)

4. **MEMORIES ARE MADE
OF THIS**
D. Martin
Gillkyson–Dehr–Miller, Capitol
3295 (Montclare, BMI)

5. **NO, NOT MUCH**
The Four Lads
Stillmen–Allen, Columbia
40629 (Beaver, ASCAP)

6. **THE POOR PEOPLE OF PARIS**
L. Baxter
dePauvre–Monnet–Lawrence,
Capitol 3336
(Reg Connelly, ASCAP)

7. **THEME FROM THREE
PENNY OPERA**
D. Hyman
K. Weill–B. Brecht, MGM 12149
(Harms, ASCAP)

8. **IT'S ALMOST TOMORROW**
The Dream Weavers
Adkinson, Decca 29683
(Northern, ASCAP)

9. **BAND OF GOLD**
D. Cherry
Musel–Taylor, Columbia 40597
(Ludlow, BMI)

10. **SEE YOU LATER, ALLIGATOR**
B. Haley and the Comets
Guidry, Decca 29791
(Arc, BMI)

March 10

1. **LISBON ANTIGUA**
N. Riddle
Galherdo–Vale–Partela, Capitol
3287 (Southern, ASCAP)

2. **THE POOR PEOPLE OF PARIS**
L. Baxter
dePauvre–Monnet–Lawrence,
Capitol 3336
(Reg Connelly, ASCAP)

3. **THEME FROM THREE
PENNY OPERA**
D. Hyman
K. Weill–B. Brecht, MGM 12149
(Harms, ASCAP)

4. **NO, NOT MUCH**
The Four Lads
Stillmen–Allen, Columbia
40629 (Beaver, ASCAP)

5. **GREAT PRETENDER**
The Platters
B. Ram, Mercury 70753
(Southern, ASCAP)

6. **ROCK AND ROLL WALTZ**
K. Starr
Ware–Allen, Victor 20–6359
(Sheldon, BMI)

7. **I'LL BE HOME**
P. Boone
Washington–Lewis, Dot 15443
(Arc, BMI)

8. **SEE YOU LATER, ALLIGATOR**
B. Haley and the Comets
Guidry, Decca 29791
(Arc, BMI)

9. **MEMORIES ARE MADE
OF THIS**
D. Martin
Gillkyson–Dehr–Miller, Capitol
3295 (Montclare, BMI)

10. **BAND OF GOLD**
D. Cherry
Musel–Taylor, Columbia 40597
(Ludlow, BMI)

March 17

1. **LISBON ANTIGUA**
N. Riddle
Galherdo–Vale–Partela,
Capitol 3287 (Southern, ASCAP)

2. **NO, NOT MUCH**
The Four Lads
Stillmen–Allen, Columbia
40629 (Beaver, ASCAP)

3. **THE POOR PEOPLE OF PARIS**
L. Baxter
dePauvre–Monnet–Lawrence,
Capitol 3336 (Reg Connelly,
ASCAP)

4. **ROCK AND ROLL WALTZ**
K. Starr
Ware–Allen, Victor 20–6359
(Sheldon, BMI)

5. **GREAT PRETENDER**
The Platters
B. Ram, Mercury 70753
(Southern, ASCAP)

6. **THEME FROM THREE
PENNY OPERA**
D. Hyman
K. Weill–B. Brecht, MGM
12149 (Harms, ASCAP)

7. **MEMORIES ARE MADE
OF THIS**
D. Martin
Gillkyson–Dehr–Miller,
Capitol 3295 (Montclare, BMI)

8. **I'LL BE HOME**
P. Boone
Washington–Lewis, Dot 15443
(Arc, BMI)

9. **WHY DO FOOLS FALL
IN LOVE?**
The Teen Agers
Lyman–Goldner, Bee 1002
(Patricia, BMI)

10. **SEE YOU LATER, ALLIGATOR**
B. Haley and the Comets
Guidry, Decca 29791
(Arc, BMI)

March 24

1. **ROCK AND ROLL WALTZ**
K. Starr
Ware–Allen,   Victor 20–6359
(Sheldon, BMI)

2. **THE POOR PEOPLE OF PARIS**
L. Baxter
dePauvre–Monnet–Lawrence,
Capitol 3336   (Reg Connelly,
ASCAP)

3. **LISBON ANTIGUA**
N. Riddle
Galherdo–Vale–Partela,
Capitol 3287   (Southern, ASCAP)

4. **NO, NOT MUCH**
The Four Lads
Stillmen–Allen, Columbia
40629   (Beaver, ASCAP)

5. **GREAT PRETENDER**
The Platters
B. Ram,   Mercury 70753
(Southern, ASCAP)

6. **THEME FROM THREE
PENNY OPERA**
D. Hyman
K. Weill–B. Brecht, MGM
12149 (Harms, ASCAP)

7. **I'LL BE HOME**
P. Boone
Washington–Lewis,   Dot 15443
(Arc, BMI)

8. **WHY DO FOOLS FALL
IN LOVE?**
The Teen Agers
Lyman–Goldner,   Bee 1002
(Patricia, BMI)

9. **MEMORIES ARE MADE
OF THIS**
D. Martin
Gillykson–Dehr–Miller,
Capitol 3295   (Montclare, BMI)

10. **SEE YOU LATER, ALLIGATOR**
B. Haley and the Comets
Guidry,   Decca 29791
(Arc, BMI)

March 31

1. **THE POOR PEOPLE OF PARIS**
L. Baxter
dePauvre–Monnet–Lawrence,
Capitol 3336   (Reg Connelly,
ASCAP)

2. **LISBON ANTIGUA**
N. Riddle
Galherdo–Vale–Partela,
Capitol 3287   (Southern, ASCAP)

3. **ROCK AND ROLL WALTZ**
K. Starr
Ware–Allen,   Victor 20–6359
(Sheldon, BMI)

4. **NO, NOT MUCH**
The Four Lads
Stillmen–Allen, Columbia
40629   (Beaver, ASCAP)

5. **WHY DO FOOLS FALL
IN LOVE?**
The Teen Agers
Lyman–Goldner,   Bee 1002
(Patricia, BMI)

6. **GREAT PRETENDER**
The Platters
B. Ram,   Mercury 70753
(Southern, ASCAP)

7. **I'LL BE HOME**
P. Boone
Washington–Lewis,   Dot 15443
(Arc, BMI)

8. **THEME FROM THREE
PENNY OPERA**
D. Hyman
K. Weill–B. Brecht, MGM
12149 (Harms, ASCAP)

9. **HOT DIGGITY**
P. Como
A. Hoffman–D. Manning, Victor
20–6427 (Roncom, ASCAP)

10. **EDDIE MY LOVE**
The Teen Queens
Collins–Ling–Davis,   RPM 543
(Modern–Roosevelt, BMI)

April 7

1. **THE POOR PEOPLE OF PARIS**
L. Baxter
dePauvre–Monnet–Lawrence,
Capitol 3336   (Reg Connelly,
ASCAP)

2. **LISBON ANTIGUA**
N. Riddle
Galherdo–Vale–Partela,
Capitol 3287   (Southern, ASCAP)

3. **ROCK AND ROLL WALTZ**
K. Starr
Ware–Allen,   Victor 20–6359
(Sheldon, BMI)

4. **NO, NOT MUCH**
The Four Lads
Stillmen–Allen, Columbia
40629   (Beaver, ASCAP)

5. **WHY DO FOOLS FALL
IN LOVE?**
The Teen Agers
Lyman–Goldner,   Bee 1002
(Patricia, BMI)

6. **I'LL BE HOME**
P. Boone
Washington–Lewis,   Dot 15443
(Arc, BMI)

7. **HOT DIGGITY**
P. Como
A. Hoffman–D. Manning,   Victor
20–6427   (Roncom, ASCAP)

8. **BLUE SUEDE SHOES**
C. Perkins
C. Perkins,   Sun 234
(Hi-Lo-Hill & Range, BMI)

9. **THEME FROM THREE
PENNY OPERA**
D. Hyman
K. Weill–B. Brecht, MGM 12149
(Harms, ASCAP)

10. **GREAT PRETENDER**
The Platters
B. Ram,   Mercury 70753
(Southern, ASCAP)

April 14

1. **HOT DIGGITY**
P. Como
A. Hoffman–D. Manning, Victor 20–6427 (Roncom, ASCAP)

2. **ROCK AND ROLL WALTZ**
K. Starr
Ware–Allen, Victor 20–6359 (Sheldon, BMI)

3. **BLUE SUEDE SHOES**
C. Perkins
C. Perkins, Sun 234 (Hi-Lo-Hill & Range, BMI)

4. **NO, NOT MUCH**
The Four Lads
Stillmen–Allen, Columbia 40629 (Beaver, ASCAP)

5. **WHY DO FOOLS FALL IN LOVE?**
The Teen Agers
Lyman–Goldner, Bee 1002 (Patricia, BMI)

6. **I'LL BE HOME**
P. Boone
Washington–Lewis, Dot 15443 (Arc, BMI)

7. **LISBON ANTIGUA**
N. Riddle
Galherdo–Vale–Partela, Capitol 3287 (Southern, ASCAP)

8. **THE POOR PEOPLE OF PARIS**
L. Baxter
dePauvre–Monnet–Lawrence, Capitol 3336 (Reg Connelly, ASCAP)

9. **EDDIE MY LOVE**
The Teen Queens
Collins–Ling–Davis, RPM 543 (Modern–Roosevelt, BMI)

10. **HEARTBREAK HOTEL**
E. Presley
Axton–Durden–Presley, Victor 20–6420 (Tree, BMI)

April 21

1. **BLUE SUEDE SHOES**
C. Perkins
C. Perkins, Sun 234 (Hi Lo-Hill & Range, BMI)

2. **WHY DO FOOLS FALL IN LOVE?**
The Teen Agers
Lyman–Goldner, Bee 1002 (Patricia, BMI)

3. **HEARTBREAK HOTEL**
E. Presley
Axton–Durden–Presley, Victor 20–6420 (Tree, BMI)

4. **THE POOR PEOPLE OF PARIS**
L. Baxter
dePauvre–Monnet–Lawrence, Capitol 3336 (Reg Connelly, ASCAP)

5. **HOT DOGGITY**
P. Como
A. Hoffman–D. Manning, Victor 20–6427 (Roncom, ASCAP)

6. **LISBON ANTIGUA**
N. Riddle
Galherdo–Vale–Partela, Capitol 3287 (Southern, ASCAP)

7. **NO, NOT MUCH**
The Four Lads
Stillmen–Allen, Columbia 40629 (Beaver, ASCAP)

8. **ROCK AND ROLL WALTZ**
K. Starr
Ware–Allen, Victor 20–6359 (Sheldon, BMI)

9. **I'LL BE HOME**
P. Boone
Washington–Lewis, Dot 15443 (Arc, BMI)

10. **EDDIE MY LOVE**
The Teen Queens
Collins–Ling–Davis, RPM 543 (Modern–Roosevelt, BMI)

April 28

1. **THE POOR PEOPLE OF PARIS**
L. Baxter
dePauvre–Monnet–Lawrence, Capitol 3336 (Reg Connelly, ASCAP)

2. **HEARTBREAK HOTEL**
E. Presley
Axton–Durden–Presley, Victor 20–6420 (Tree, BMI)

3. **HOT DIGGITY**
P. Como
A. Hoffman–D. Manning, Victor 20–6427 (Roncom, ASCAP)

4. **BLUE SUEDE SHOES**
C. Perkins
C. Perkins, Sun 234 (Hi-Lo-Hill & Range, BMI)

5. **LISBON ANTIGUA**
N. Riddle
Galherdo–Vale–Partela, Capitol 3287 (Southern, ASCAP)

6. **WHY DO FOOLS FALL IN LOVE?**
The Teen Agers
Lyman–Goldner, Bee 1002 (Patricia, BMI)

7. **ROCK AND ROLL WALTZ**
K. Starr
Ware–Allen, Victor 20–6359 (Sheldon, BMI)

8. **NO, NOT MUCH**
The Four Lads
Stillmen–Allen, Columbia 40629 (Beaver, ASCAP)

9. **I'LL BE HOME**
P. Boone
Washington–Lewis, Dot 15443 (Arc, BMI)

10. **MAIN TITLE MOLLY-O (MAN WITH THE GOLDEN ARM)**
R. Maltby
S. Fine–E. Bernstein, Vik 0196 (Dena, ASCAP)

May 5

1. **HEARTBREAK HOTEL**
   E. Presley
   *Axton–Durden–Presley, Victor
   20–6420 (Tree, BMI)*

2. **THE POOR PEOPLE OF PARIS**
   L. Baxter
   *dePauvre–Monnet–Lawrence,
   Capitol 3336 (Reg Connelly,
   ASCAP)*

3. **HOT DIGGITY**
   P. Como
   *A. Hoffman–D. Manning, Victor
   20–6427 (Roncom, ASCAP)*

4. **IVORY TOWER**
   O. Williams
   *J. Fulton–L. Steele, DeLuxe
   6093 (E. H. Morris, ASCAP)*

5. **BLUE SUEDE SHOES**
   C. Perkins
   *C. Perkins, Sun 234
   (Hi-Lo-Hill & Range, BMI)*

6. **MAGIC TOUCH**
   The Platters
   *B. Ram, Mercury 70819
   (Panther, ASCAP)*

7. **WHY DO FOOLS FALL
   IN LOVE?**
   The Teen Agers
   *Lyman–Goldner, Bee 1002
   (Patricia, BMI)*

8. **ROCK AND ROLL WALTZ**
   K. Starr
   *Ware–Allen, Victor 20–6359
   (Sheldon, BMI)*

9. **MOONGLOW AND THEME
   FROM PICNIC**
   M. Stoloff
   *Hudson–Delange–Mills, Decca
   29888 (Mills–Columbia Pictures,
   ASCAP)*

10. **LISBON ANTIGUA**
    N. Riddle
    *Galherdo–Vale–Partela,
    Capitol 3287 (Southern, ASCAP)*

May 12

1. **HEARTBREAK HOTEL**
   E. Presley
   *Axton–Durden–Presley, Victor
   20–6420 (Tree, BMI)*

2. **HOT DIGGITY**
   P. Como
   *A. Hoffman–D. Manning, Victor
   20–6427 (Roncom, ASCAP)*

3. **IVORY TOWER**
   O. Williams
   *J. Fulton–L. Steele, DeLuxe
   6093 (E. H. Morris, ASCAP)*

4. **THE POOR PEOPLE OF PARIS**
   L. Baxter
   *dePauvre–Monnet–Lawrence,
   Capitol 3336 (Reg Connelly,
   ASCAP)*

5. **WHY DO FOOLS FALL
   IN LOVE?**
   The Teen Agers
   *Lyman–Goldner, Bee 1002
   (Patricia, BMI)*

6. **BLUE SUEDE SHOES**
   C. Perkins
   *C. Perkins, Sun 234
   (Hi-Lo-Hill & Range, BMI)*

7. **LONG TALL SALLY**
   Little Richard
   *E. Johnson, Specialty 572
   (Venice, BMI)*

8. **MOONGLOW AND THEME
   FROM PICNIC**
   M. Stoloff
   *Hudson–Delange–Mills, Decca
   29888 (Mills–Columbia Pictures,
   ASCAP)*

9. **LISBON ANTIGUA**
   N. Riddle
   *Galherdo–Vale–Partela
   Capitol 3287 (Southern, ASCAP)*

10. **A TEAR FELL**
    Ivory Joe Hunter
    *D. Burton–E. Randolph,
    Atlantic 1086 (Progressive, BMI)*

May 19

1. **HOT DIGGITY**
   P. Como
   *A. Hoffman–D. Manning, Victor
   20–6427 (Roncom, ASCAP)*

2. **IVORY TOWER**
   O. Williams
   *J. Fulton–L. Steele, DeLuxe
   6093 (E. H. Morris, ASCAP)*

3. **MOONGLOW AND THEME
   FROM PICNIC**
   M. Stoloff
   *Hudson–Delange–Mills, Decca
   29888 (Mills–Columbia Pictures,
   ASCAP)*

4. **THE POOR PEOPLE OF PARIS**
   L. Baxter
   *dePauvre–Monnet–Lawrence,
   Capitol 3336 (Reg Connelly,
   ASCAP)*

5. **HEARTBREAK HOTEL**
   E. Presley
   *Axton–Durden–Presley,
   Victor 29–6420 (Tree, BMI)*

6. **BLUE SUEDE SHOES**
   C. Perkins
   *C. Perkins, Sun 234
   (Hi-Lo-Hill & Range, BMI)*

7. **WHY DO FOOLS FALL
   IN LOVE?**
   The Teen Agers
   *Lyman–Goldner, Bee 1002
   (Patricia, BMI)*

8. **MAGIC TOUCH**
   The Platters
   *B. Ram, Mercury 70819
   (Panther, ASCAP)*

9. **A TEAR FELL**
   Ivory Joe Hunter
   *D. Burton–E. Randolph,
   Atlantic 1086 (Progressive, BMI)*

10. **LISBON ANTIGUA**
    N. Riddle
    *Galherdo–Vale–Partela,
    Capitol 3287 (Southern, ASCAP)*

1956

May 26

1. **HEARTBREAK HOTEL**
E. Presley
Axton–Durden–Presley, Victor 20-6420 (Tree, BMI)
2. **MOONGLOW AND THEME FROM PICNIC**
M. Stoloff
Hudson–Delange–Mills, Decca 29888 (Mills–Columbia Pictures, ASCAP)
3. **IVORY TOWER**
O. Williams
J. Fulton–L. Steele, DeLuxe 6093 (E. H. Morris, ASCAP)
4. **HOT DIGGITY**
P. Como
A. Hoffman–D. Manning, Victor 20-6427 (Roncom, ASCAP)
5. **THE POOR PEOPLE OF PARIS**
L. Baxter
dePauvre–Monnet–Lawrence, Capitol 3336 (Reg Connelly, ASCAP)
6. **BLUE SUEDE SHOES**
C. Perkins
C. Perkins, Sun 234 (Hi-Lo–Hill & Range, BMI)
7. **STANDING ON THE CORNER**
The Four Lads
F. Loesser, Columbia 40674 (Frank, ASCAP)
8. **MAGIC TOUCH**
The Platters
B. Ram, Mercury 70819 (Panther, ASCAP)
9. **WHY DO FOOLS FALL IN LOVE?**
The Teen Agers
Lyman–Goldner, Bee 1002 (Patricia, BMI)
10. **WAYWARD WIND**
G. Grant
S. Lebousky–H. Newman, Era 1013 (Warman, BMI)

June 2

1. **MOONGLOW AND THEME FROM PICNIC**
M. Stoloff
Hudson–Delange–Mills, Decca 29888 (Mills–Columbia Pictures, ASCAP)
2. **HEARTBREAK HOTEL**
E. Presley
Axton–Durden–Presley, Victor 20-6420 (Tree, BMI)
3. **IVORY TOWER**
O. Williams
J. Fulton–L. Steele, Deluxe 6093 (E. H. Morris, ASCAP)
4. **HOT DIGGITY**
P. Como
A. Hoffman–D. Manning, Victor 20-6427 (Roncom, ASCAP)
5. **STANDING ON THE CORNER**
The Four Lads
F. Loesser, Columbia 40674 (Frank, ASCAP)
6. **WAYWARD WIND**
G. Grant
S. Lebousky–H. Newman, Era 1013 (Warman, BMI)
7. **BLUE SUEDE SHOES**
C. Perkins
C. Perkins, Sun 234 (Hi-Lo–Hill & Range, BMI)
8. **THE POOR PEOPLE OF PARIS**
L. Baxter
dePauvre–Monnet–Lawrence, Capitol 3336 (Reg Connelly, ASCAP)
9. **MAGIC TOUCH**
The Platters
B. Ram, Mercury 70819 (Panther, ASCAP)
10. **LONG TALL SALLY**
Little Richard
E. Johnson, Specialty 572 (Venice, BMI)

June 9

1. **MOONGLOW AND THEME FROM PICNIC**
M. Stoloff
Hudson–Delange–Mills, Decca 29888 (Mills–Columbia Pictures, ASCAP)
2. **IVORY TOWER**
O. Williams
J. Fulton–L. Steele, DeLuxe 6093 (E. H. Morris, ASCAP)
3. **HEARTBREAK HOTEL**
E. Presley
Axton–Durden–Presley, Victor 20-6420 (Tree, BMI)
4. **WAYWARD WIND**
G. Grant
S. Lebousky–H. Newman, Era 1013 (Warman, BMI)
5. **STANDING ON THE CORNER**
The Four Lads
F. Loesser, Columbia 40674 (Frank, ASCAP)
6. **HOT DIGGITY**
P. Como
A. Hoffman–D. Manning, Victor 20-6427 (Roncom, ASCAP)
7. **BLUE SUEDE SHOES**
C. Perkins
C. Perkins, Sun 234 (Hi-Lo–Hill & Range, BMI)
8. **WALK HAND IN HAND**
T. Martin
J. Cowell, Victor 20-6493 (Republic, BMI)
9. **MAGIC TOUCH**
The Platters
B. Ram, Mercury 70819 (Panther, ASCAP)
10. **THE POOR PEOPLE OF PARIS**
L. Baxter
dePauvre–Monnet–Lawrence, Capitol 3336 (Reg Connelly, ASCAP)

June 16

1. **WAYWARD WIND**
G. Grant
S. Lebousky–H. Newman,
Era 1013 (Warman, BMI)

2. **HEARTBREAK HOTEL**
E. Presley
Axton–Durden–Presley, Victor
20–6420 (Tree, BMI)

3. **IVORY TOWER**
O. Williams
H. Fulton–L. Steele, DeLuxe
6093 (E. H. Morris, ASCAP)

4. **STANDING ON THE CORNER**
The Four Lads
F. Loesser, Columbia 40674
(Frank, ASCAP)

5. **ON THE STREET WHERE**
YOU LIVE
V. Damone
A. J. Lerner–F. Loewe, Columbia
40654 (Chappell, ASCAP)

6. **MOONGLOW AND THEME**
FROM PICNIC
M. Stoloff
Hudson–Delange–Mills, Decca
29888 (Mills–Columbia Pictures,
ASCAP)

7. **HOT DIGGITY**
P. Como
A. Hoffman–D. Manning, Victor
20–6427 (Roncom, ASCAP)

8. **WALK HAND IN HAND**
T. Martin
J. Cowell, Victor 20–6493
(Republic, BMI)

9. **I'M IN LOVE AGAIN**
F. Domino
A. Domino–D. Bartholomew,
Imperial 5386 (Reene, BMI)

10. **PICNIC**
The McGuire Sisters
G. Dunning–S. Allen, Coral
61627 (Shapiro–Bernstein,
ASCAP)

June 23

1. **WAYWARD WIND**
G. Grant
S. Lebousky–H. Newman, Era
1013 (Warman, BMI)

2. **IVORY TOWER**
O. Williams
J. Fulton–L. Steele, DeLuxe
6093 (E. H. Morris, ASCAP)

3. **MOONGLOW AND THEME**
FROM PICNIC
M. Stoloff
Hudson–Delange–Mills, Decca
29888 (Mills–Columbia Pictures,
ASCAP)

4. **HEARTBREAK HOTEL**
E. Presley
Axton–Durden–Presley,
Victor 20–6420 (Tree, BMI)

5. **STANDING ON THE CORNER**
The Four Lads
F. Loesser, Columbia 40674
(Frank, ASCAP)

6. **HOT DOGGITY**
P. Como
A. Hoffman–D. Manning, Victor
20–6427 (Roncom, ASCAP)

7. **ON THE STREET WHERE**
YOU LIVE
V. Damone
A. J. Lerner–F. Loewe, Columbia
40654 (Chappell, ASCAP)

8. **I ALMOST LOST MY MIND**
P. Boone
I. J. Hunter, Dot 15472,
(Hill & Range, BMI)

9. **I'M IN LOVE AGAIN**
F. Domino
A. Domino–D. Bartholomew,
Imperial 5386 (Reene, BMI)

10. **WALK HAND IN HAND**
T. Martin
J. Cowell, Victor 20–6493
(Republic, BMI)

June 30

1. **MOONGLOW AND THEME**
FROM PICNIC
M. Stoloff
Hudson–Delange–Mills, Decca
29888 (Mills–Columbia Pictures,
ASCAP)

2. **WAYWARD WIND**
G. Grant
S. Lebousky–H. Newman, Era
1013 (Warman, BMI)

3. **IVORY TOWER**
O. Williams
J. Fulton–L. Steele, DeLuxe
6093 (E. H. Morris, ASCAP)

4. **STANDING ON THE CORNER**
The Four Lads
F. Loesser, Columbia 40674
(Frank, ASCAP)

5. **ON THE STREET WHERE**
YOU LIVE
V. Damone
A. J. Lerner–F. Loewe, Columbia
40654 (Chappell, ASCAP)

6. **I ALMOST LOST MY MIND**
P. Boone
I. J. Hunter, Dot 15472 (Hill &
Range, BMI)

7. **HEARTBREAK HOTEL**
E. Presley
Axton–Durden–Presley, Victor
20–6420 (Tree, BMI)

8. **I'M IN LOVE AGAIN**
F. Domino
A. Domino–D. Bartholomew,
Imperial 5386 (Reene, BMI)

9. **WALK HAND IN HAND**
T. Martin
J. Cowell, Victor 20–6493
(Republic, BMI)

10. **PICNIC**
The McGuire Sisters
G. Dunning–S. Allen, Coral
61627 (Shapiro–Bernstein,
ASCAP)

July 7

1. **WAYWARD WIND**
G. Grant
S. Lebousky–H. Newman, Era 1013 (Warman, BMI)

2. **MOONGLOW AND THEME FROM PICNIC**
M. Stoloff
Hudson–Delange–Mills, Decca 29888 (Mills–Columbia Pictures, ASCAP)

3. **IVORY TOWER**
O. Williams
J. Fulton–L. Steele, DeLuxe 6093 (E. H. Morris, ASCAP)

4. **I ALMOST LOST MY MIND**
P. Boone
I. J. Hunter, Dot 15472 (Hill & Range, BMI)

5. **STANDING ON THE CORNER**
The Four Lads
F. Loesser, Columbia 40674 (Frank, ASCAP)

6. **ON THE STREET WHERE YOU LIVE**
V. Damone
A. J. Lerner–F. Loewe, Columbia 40654 (Chappell, ASCAP)

7. **I WANT YOU, I NEED YOU, I LOVE YOU**
E. Presley
M. Mysels–I. Kosloff, Victor 20-6540 (Elvis Presley, BMI)

8. **I'M IN LOVE AGAIN**
F. Domino
A. Domino–D. Bartholomew, Imperial 5386 (Reene, BMI)

9. **HEARBREAK HOTEL**
E. Presley
Axton–Durden–Presley, Victor 20-6420 (Tree, BMI)

10. **BORN TO BE WITH YOU**
The Chordettes
D. Robertson, Cadence 1291 (E. H. Morris, ASCAP)

July 14

1. **WAYWARD WIND**
G. Grant
S. Lebousky–H. Newman, Era 1013 (Warman, BMI)

2. **MOONGLOW AND THEME FROM PICNIC**
M. Stoloff
Hudson–Delange–Mills, Decca 29888 (Mills–Columbia Pictures, ASCAP)

3. **I ALMOST LOST MY MIND**
P. Boone
I. J. Hunter, Dot 15472 (Hill & Range, BMI)

4. **IVORY TOWER**
O. Williams
J. Fulton–L. Steele, DeLuxe 6093 (E. H. Morris, ASCAP)

5. **ON THE STREET WHERE YOU LIVE**
V. Damone
A. J. Lerner–F. Loewe, Columbia 40654 (Chappell, ASCAP)

6. **STANDING ON THE CORNER**
The Four Lads
F. Loesser, Columbia 40674 (Frank, ASCAP)

7. **I WANT YOU, I NEED YOU, I LOVE YOU**
E. Presley
M. Mysels–I. Kosloff, Victor 20-6540 (Elvis Presley, BMI)

8. **ALLEGHENY MOON**
P. Page
A. Hoffman–D. Manning, Mercury 70878 (Oxford, ASCAP)

9. **BORN TO BE WITH YOU**
The Chordettes
D. Robertson, Cadence 1291 (E. H. Morris, ASCAP)

10. **I'M IN LOVE AGAIN**
F. Domino
A. Domino–D. Bartholomew, Imperial 5386 (Reene, BMI)

July 21

1. **ON THE STREET WHERE YOU LIVE**
V. Damone
A. J. Lerner–F. Loewe, Columbia 40654 (Chappell, ASCAP)

2. **MOONGLOW AND THEME FROM PICNIC**
M. Stoloff
Hudson–Delange–Mills, Decca 29888 (Mills–Columbia Pictures, ASCAP)

3. **I WANT YOU, I NEED YOU, I LOVE YOU**
E. Presley
M. Mysels–I. Kosloff, Victor 20-6540 (Elvis Presley, BMI)

4. **WAYWARD WIND**
G. Grant
S. Lebousky–H. Newman, Era 1013 (Warman, BMI)

5. **IVORY TOWER**
O. Williams
J. Fulton–L. Steele, DeLuxe 6093 (E. H. Morris, ASCAP)

6. **STANDING ON THE CORNER**
The Four Lads
F. Loesser, Columbia 40674 (Frank, ASCAP)

7. **WHATEVER WILL BE, WILL BE (QUE SERA SERA)**
D. Day
Livingston–Evans, Columbia 40704 (Artists, ASCAP)

8. **I ALMOST LOST MY MIND**
P. Boone
I. J. Hunter, Dot 15472 (Hill & Range, BMI)

9. **ALLEGHENY MOON**
P. Page
A. Hoffman–D. Manning, Mercury 70878 (Oxford, ASCAP)

10. **I'M IN LOVE AGAIN**
F. Domino
A. Domino–D. Bartholomew, Imperial 5386 (Reene, BMI)

July 28

1. **I WANT YOU, I NEED YOU, I LOVE YOU**
E. Presley
M. Mysels–I. Kosloff, Victor 20-6540 (Elvis Presley, BMI)

2. **MOONGLOW AND THEME FROM PICNIC**
M. Stoloff
Hudson–Delange–Mills, Decca 29888 (Mills–Columbia Pictures, ASCAP)

3. **ALLEGHENY MOON**
P. Page
A. Hoffman–D. Manning, Mercury 70878 (Oxford, ASCAP)

4. **I ALMOST LOST MY MIND**
P. Boone
I. J. Hunter, Dot 15472 (Hill & Range, BMI)

5. **WAYWARD WIND**
G. Grant
S. Lebousky–H. Newman, Era 1013 (Warman, BMI)

6. **IVORY TOWER**
O. Williams
J. Fulton–L. Steele, DeLuxe 6093 (E. H. Morris, ASCAP)

7. **ON THE STREET WHERE YOU LIVE**
V. Damone
A. J. Lerner–F. Loewe, Columbia 40654 (Chappell, ASCAP)

8. **MY PRAYER**
The Platters
Boulanger–Kennedy, Mercury 70893 (Skidmore, ASCAP)

9. **WHATEVER WILL BE, WILL BE (QUE SERA SERA)**
D. Day
Livingston–Evans, Columbia 40704 (Artists, ASCAP)

10. **BORN TO BE WITH YOU**
The Chordettes
D. Robertson, Cadence 1291 (E. H. Morris, ASCAP)

54

August 4

1. **WAYWARD WIND**
G. Grant
S. Lebousky–H. Newman, Era 1013 (Warman, BMI)

2. **I ALMOST LOST MY MIND**
P. Boone
I. J. Hunter, Dot 15472 (Hill & Range, BMI)

3. **ALLEGHENY MOON**
P. Page
A. Hoffman–D. Manning, Mercury 70878 (Oxford, ASCAP)

4. **I WANT YOU, I NEED YOU, I LOVE YOU**
E. Presley
M. Mysels–I. Kosloff, Victor 20-6540 (Elvis Presley, BMI)

5. **MY PRAYER**
The Platters
Boulanger–Kennedy, Mercury 70893 (Skidmore, ASCAP)

6. **WHATEVER WILL BE, WILL BE (QUE SERA SERA)**
D. Day
Livingston–Evans, Columbia 40704 (Artists, ASCAP)

7. **MOONGLOW AND THEME FROM PICNIC**
M. Stoloff
Hudson–Delange–Mills, Decca 29888 (Mills–Columbia Pictures, ASCAP)

8. **ON THE STREET WHERE YOU LIVE**
V. Damone
A. J. Lerner–F. Loewe, Columbia 4-654 (Chappell, ASCAP)

9. **BORN TO BE WITH YOU**
The Chordettes
D. Robertson, Cadence 1291 (E. H. Morris, ASCAP)

10. **SWEET OLD-FASHIONED GIRL**
T. Brewer
B. Merrill, Coral 61636 (Valor, ASCAP)

August 11

1. **WAYWARD WIND**
G. Grant
S. Lebousky–H. Newman, Era 1013 (Warman, BMI)

2. **MY PRAYER**
The Platters
Boulanger–Kennedy, Mercury 70893 (Skidmore, ASCAP)

3. **WHATEVER WILL BE, WILL BE (QUE SERA SERA)**
D. Day
Livingston–Evans, Columbia 40704 (Artists, ASCAP)

4. **I ALMOST LOST MY MIND**
P. Boone
I. J. Hunter, Dot 15472 (Hill & Range, BMI)

5. **ALLEGHENY MOON**
P. Page
A. Hoffman–D. Manning, Mercury 70878 (Oxford, ASCAP)

6. **I WANT YOU, I NEED YOU, I LOVE YOU**
E. Presley
M. Mysels–I. Kosloff, Victor 20-6540 (Elvis Presley, BMI)

7. **ON THE STREET WHERE YOU LIVE**
V. Damone
A. J. Lerner–F. Loewe, Columbia 40654 (Chappell, ASCAP)

8. **MOONGLOW AND THEME FROM PICNIC**
M. Stoloff
Hudson–Delange–Mills, Decca 29888 (Mills–Columbia Pictures, ASCAP)

9. **SWEET OLD-FASHIONED GIRL**
T. Brewer
B. Merrill, Coral 61636 (Valor, ASCAP)

10. **HOUND DOG**
E. Presley
J. Lieber–M. Stoller, Victor 20-6604 (Elvis Presley–Lion, BMI)

August 18

1. **MY PRAYER**
The Platters
Boulanger–Kennedy, Mercury 70893 (Skidmore, ASCAP)

2. **WHATEVER WILL BE, WILL BE (QUE SERA SERA)**
D. Day
Livingston–Evans, Columbia 40704 (Artists, ASCAP)

3. **WAYWARD WIND**
G. Grant
S. Lebousky–H. Newman, Era 1013 (Warman, BMI)

4. **I ALMOST LOST MY MIND**
P. Boone
I. J. Hunter, Dot 15472 (Hill & Range, BMI)

5. **HOUND DOG**
E. Presley
J. Lieber–M. Stoller, Victor 20-6604 (Elvis Presley–Lion, BMI)

6. **ALLEGHENY MOON**
P. Page
A. Hoffman–D. Manning, Mercury 70878 (Oxford, ASCAP)

7. **I WANT YOU, I NEED YOU, I LOVE YOU**
E. Presley
M. Mysels–I. Kosloff, Victor 20-6540 (Elvis Presley, BMI)

8. **CANADIAN SUNSET**
H. Winterhalter and E. Heywood
E. Heywood–N. Gimbel, Victor 20-6537 (Meridian, BMI)

9. **ON THE STREET WHERE YOU LIVE**
V. Damone
A. J. Lerner–F. Loewe, Columbia 40654 (Chappell, ASCAP)

10. **SWEET OLD-FASHIONED GIRL**
T. Brewer
B. Merrill, Coral 61636 (Valor, ASCAP)

August 25

1. **HOUND DOG**
E. Presley
J. Leiber–M. Stoller, Victor 20-6604 (Elvis Presley–Lion, BMI)

2. **MY PRAYER**
The Platters
Boulanger–Kennedy, Mercury 70893 (Skidmore, ASCAP)

3. **ALLEGHENY MOON**
P. Page
A. Hoffman–D. Manning, Mercury 70878 (Oxford, ASCAP)

4. **WAYWARD WIND**
G. Grant
S. Lebousky–H. Newman Era 1013 (Warman, BMI)

5. **WHATEVER WILL BE, WILL BE (QUE SERA SERA)**
D. Day
Livingston–Evans, Columbia 40704 (Artists, ASCAP)

6. **I WANT YOU, I NEED YOU, I LOVE YOU**
E. Presley
M. Mysels–I. Kosloff, Victor 20-6540 (Elvis Presley, BMI)

7. **DON'T BE CRUEL**
E. Presley
O. Blackwell, Victor 20-6604 (Elvis Presley–Shalimar, BMI)

8. **CANADIAN SUNSET**
H. Winterhalter and E. Heywood
E. Heywood–N. Gimbel, Victor 20-6537 (Meridian, BMI)

9. **I ALMOST LOST MY MIND**
P. Boone
I. J. Hunter, Dot 15442 (Hill & Range, BMI)

10. **FLYING SAUCER**
Buchanan and Goodman
Buchanan–Goodman, Luniverse 101 (Luniverse, BMI)

September 1

1. **HOUND DOG**
E. Presley
J. Leiber–M. Stoller, Victor 20-6604 (Elvis Presley–Lion, BMI)

2. **WHATEVER WILL BE, WILL BE (QUE SERA SERA)**
D. Day
Livingston–Evans, Columbia 40704 (Artists, ASCAP)

3. **MY PRAYER**
The Platters
Boulanger–Kennedy, Mercury 70893 (Skidmore, ASCAP)

4. **CANADIAN SUNSET**
H. Winterhalter and E. Heywood
E. Heywood–N. Gimbel, Victor 20-6537 (Meridian, BMI)

5. **ALLEGHENY MOON**
P. Page
A. Hoffman–D. Manning, Mercury 70878 (Oxford, ASCAP)

6. **DON'T BE CRUEL**
E. Presley
O. Blackwell, Victor 20-6604 (Elvis Presley–Shalimar, BMI)

7. **WAYWARD WIND**
G. Grant
S. Lebousky–H. Newman, Era 1013 (Warman, BMI)

8. **I ALMOST LOST MY MIND**
P. Boone
I. J. Hunter, Dot 15472 (Hill & Range, BMI)

9. **FLYING SAUCER**
Buchanan and Goodman
Buchanan–Goodman, Luniverse 101 (Luniverse, BMI)

10. **I WANT YOU, I NEED YOU, I LOVE YOU**
E. Presley
M. Mysels–I. Kosloff, Victor 20-6540 (Elvis Presley, BMI)

September 8

1. **MY PRAYER**
The Platters
Boulanger–Kennedy, Mercury 70893 (Skidmore, ASCAP)

2. **WHATEVER WILL BE, WILL BE (QUE SERA SERA)**
D. Day
Livingston–Evans, Columbia 40704 (Artists, ASCAP)

3. **HOUND DOG**
E. Presley
J. Leiber–M. Stoller, Victor 20-6604 (Elvis Presley–Lion, BMI)

4. **DON'T BE CRUEL**
E. Presley
O. Blackwell, Victor 20-6604 (Elvis Presley–Shalimar, BMI)

5. **ALLEGHENY MOON**
P. Page
A. Hoffman–D. Manning, Mercury 70878 (Oxford, ASCAP)

6. **CANADIAN SUNSET**
H. Winterhalter and E. Heywood
E. Heywood–N. Gimbel, Victor 20-6537 (Meridian, BMI)

7. **WAYWARD WIND**
G. Grant
S. Lebousky–H. Newman, Era 1013 (Warman, BMI)

8. **SONG FOR A SUMMER NIGHT**
M. Miller
R. Allen, Columbia 40730 (April, ASCAP)

9. **I ALMOST LOST MY MIND**
P. Boone
I. J. Hunter, Dot 15472 (Hill & Range, BMI)

10. **FLYING SAUCER**
Buchanan and Goodman
Buchanan and Goodman, Luniverse 101 (Luniverse, BMI)

September 15

1. **DON'T BE CRUEL**
E. Presley
O. Blackwell, Victor 20-6604 (Elvis Presley–Shalimar, BMI)

2. **CANADIAN SUNSET**
H. Winterhalter and E. Heywood
E. Heywood–N. Gimbel, Victor 20-6537 (Meridian, BMI)

3. **TONIGHT YOU BELONG TO ME**
Patience and Prudence
B. Rose–L. David, Liberty 55022 (Mills, ASCAP)

4. **MY PRAYER**
The Platters
Boulanger–Kennedy, Mercury 70893 (Skidmore, ASCAP)

5. **ALLEGHENY MOON**
P. Page
A. Hoffman–D. Manning, Mercury 70878 (Oxford, ASCAP)

6. **WHATEVER WILL BE, WILL BE (QUE SERA SERA)**
D. Day
Livingston–Evans, Columbia 40704 (Artists, ASCAP)

7. **HOUND DOG**
E. Presley
J. Leiber–M. Stoller, Victor 20-6604 (Elvis Presley, BMI)

8. **WAYWARD WIND**
G. Grant
S. Lebousky–H. Newman, Era 1013 (Warman, BMI)

9. **FLYING SAUCER**
Buchanan and Goodman
Buchanan–Goodman, Luniverse 101 (Luniverse, BMI)

10. **SONG FOR A SUMMER NIGHT**
M. Miller
R. Allen, Columbia 40730 (April, ASCAP)

September 22

1. **DON'T BE CRUEL**
E. Presley
O. Blackwell, Victor 20-6604 (Elvis Presley–Shalimar, BMI)

2. **CANADIAN SUNSET**
H. Winterhalter and E. Heywood
E. Heywood–N. Gimbel, Victor 20-6537 (Meridian, BMI)

3. **WHATEVER WILL BE, WILL BE (QUE SERA SERA)**
D. Day
Livingston–Evans, Columbia 40704 (Artists, ASCAP)

4. **MY PRAYER**
The Platters
Boulanger–Kennedy, Mercury 70893 (Skidmore, ASCAP)

5. **HOUND DOG**
E. Presley
J. Leiber–M. Stoller, Victor 20-6604 (Elvis Presley–Lion, BMI)

6. **TONIGHT YOU BELONG TO ME**
Patience and Prudence
B. Rose–L. David, Liberty 55022 (Mills, ASCAP)

7. **ALLEGHENY MOON**
P. Page
A. Hoffman–D. Manning, Mercury 70878 (Oxford), ASCAP

8. **HONKY TONK**
B. Doggett
Shepard–Scott–Butler, King 4950 (Bilace, BMI)

9. **SONG FOR A SUMMER NIGHT**
M. Miller
R. Allen, Columbia 40730 (April, ASCAP)

10. **SOFT SUMMER BREEZE**
E. Heywood
E. Heywood–J. Spenser, Mercury 70863 (Regent, BMI)

September 29

1. **DON'T BE CRUEL**
E. Presley
*O. Blackwell, Victor 20-6604
(Elvis Presley–Shalimar, BMI)*

2. **CANADIAN SUNSET**
H. Winterhalter and E. Heywood
E. Heywood–N. Gimbel, Victor 20-6537 (Meridian, BMI)

3. **WHATEVER WILL BE, WILL BE (QUE SERA SERA)**
D. Day
Livingston–Evans, Columbia 40704 (Artists, ASCAP)

4. **MY PRAYER**
The Platters
Boulanger–Kennedy Mercury 70893 (Skidmore, ASCAP)

5. **TONIGHT YOU BELONG TO ME**
Patience and Prudence
B. Rose–L. David, Liberty 55022 (Mills, ASCAP)

6. **HONKY TONK**
B. Doggett
Shepard–Scott–Butler, King 4950 (Bilace, BMI)

7. **HOUND DOG**
E. Presley
J. Leiber–M. Stoller, Victor 20-6604 (Elvis Presley–Lion, BMI)

8. **ALLEGHENY MOON**
P. Page
A. Hoffman–D. Manning, Mercury 70878 (Oxford, ASCAP))

9. **SONG FOR A SUMMER NIGHT**
M. Miller
R. Allen, Columbia 40730 (April, ASCAP)

10. **SOFT SUMMER BREEZE**
E. Heywood
E. Heywood–J. Spenser, Mercury 70863 (Regent, BMI)

October 6

1. **DON'T BE CRUEL**
E. Presley
*O. Blackwell, Victor 20-6604
(Elvis Presley–Shalimar, BMI)*

2. **CANADIAN SUNSET**
H. Winterhalter and E. Heywood
E. Heywood–N. Gimbel, Victor 20-6537 (Meridian, BMI)

3. **WHATEVER WILL BE, WILL BE (QUE SERA SERA)**
D. Day
Livingston–Evans, Columbia 40704 (Artists, ASCAP)

4. **TONIGHT YOU BELONG TO ME**
Patience and Prudence
B. Rose–L. David, Liberty 55022 (Mills, ASCAP)

5. **MY PRAYER**
The Platters
Boulanger–Kennedy, Mercury 70893 (Skidmore, ASCAP)

6. **HOUND DOG**
E. Presley
J. Leiber–M. Stoller, Victor 20-6604 (Elvis Presley–Lion, BMI)

7. **ALLEGHENY MOON**
P. Page
A. Hoffman–D. Manning, Mercury 70863 (Oxford, ASCAP)

8. **HONKY TONK**
B. Doggett
Shepard–Scott–Butler, King 4950 (Bilace, BMI)

9. **GREEN DOOR**
J. Lowe
Davis–Moore, Dot 15486 (Trinity, BMI)

10. **SOFT SUMMER BREEZE**
E. Heywood
E. Heywood–J. Spenser Mercury 70863 (Regent, BMI)

October 13

1. **DON'T BE CRUEL**
E. Presley
*O. Blackwell, Victor 20-6604
(Elvis Presley–Shalimar, BMI)*

2. **CANADIAN SUNSET**
H. Winterhalter and E. Heywood
E. Heywood–N. Gimbel, Victor 20-6537 (Meridian, BMI)

3. **TONIGHT YOU BELONG TO ME**
Patience and Prudence
B. Rose–L. David, Liberty 55022 (Mills, ASCAP)

4. **WHATEVER WILL BE, WILL BE (QUE SERA SERA)**
D. Day
Livingston–Evans, Columbia 40704 (Artists, ASCAP)

5. **GREEN DOOR**
J. Lowe
Davis–Moore, Dot 15486 (Trinity, BMI)

6. **HONKY TONK**
B. Doggett
Shepard–Scott–Butler, King 4950 (Bilace, BMI)

7. **ALLEGHENY MOON**
P. Page
A. Hoffman–D. Manning, Mercury 70863 (Oxford, ASCAP)

8. **HOUND DOG**
E. Presley
J. Leiber–M. Stoller, Victor 20-6604 (Elvis Presley–Lion, BMI)

9. **JUST WALKING IN THE RAIN**
J. Ray
Bragg–Riley, Columbia 40729 (Golden West Melodies, BMI)

10. **MY PRAYER**
The Platters
Boulanger–Kennedy, Mercury 70893 (Skidmore, ASCAP)

1. **TONIGHT YOU BELONG TO ME**
Patience and Prudence
*B. Rose–L. David,   Liberty 55022
(Mills, ASCAP)*

2. **GREEN DOOR**
J. Lowe
*Davis–Moore,   Dot 15486
(Trinity, BMI)*

3. **CANADIAN SUNSET**
H. Winterhalter and E. Heywood
E. Heywood–N. Gimbel,   Victor 20–6537   (Meridian, BMI)

4. **DON'T BE CRUEL**
E. Presley
*O. Blackwell,   Victor 20–6604
(Elvis Presley–Shalimar, BMI)*

5. **HONKY TONK**
B. Doggett
Shepard–Scott–Butler,   King 4950   (Bilace, BMI)

6. **LOVE ME TENDER**
E. Presley
E. Presley–V. Watson,   Victor 20–6643   (Elvis Presley, BMI)

7. **JUST WALKING IN THE RAIN**
J. Ray
Bragg–Riley,   Columbia 40729 (Golden West Melodies, BMI)

8. **WHATEVER WILL BE, WILL BE (QUE SERA SERA)**
D. Day
Livingston–Evans, Columbia 40704 (Artists, ASCAP)

9. **TRUE LOVE**
B. Crosby and G. Kelly
*C. Porter,   Capitol 3507
(Buxton Hill, ASCAP)*

10. **MY PRAYER**
The Platters
Boulanger–Kennedy, Mercury 70893 (Skidmore, ASCAP)

1. **DON'T BE CRUEL**
E. Presley
*O. Blackwell,   Victor 20–6604
(Elvis Presley–Shalimar, BMI)*

2. **CANADIAN SUNSET**
H. Winterhalter and E. Heywood
E. Heywood–N. Gimbel,   Victor 20–6537   (Meridian, BMI)

3. **LOVE ME TENDER**
E. Presley
E. Presley–V. Watson,   Victor 20–6643   (Elvis Presley, BMI)

4. **TONIGHT YOU BELONG TO ME**
Patience and Prudence
B. Rose–L. David,   Liberty 55022   (Mills, ASCAP)

5. **GREEN DOOR**
J. Lowe
*Davis–Moore,   Dot 15486
(Trinity, BMI)*

6. **JUST WALKING IN THE RAIN**
J. Ray
Bragg–Riley,   Columbia 40729 (Golden West Melodies, BMI)

7. **WHATEVER WILL BE, WILL BE (QUE SERA SERA)**
D. Day
Livingston–Evans,   Columbia 40704   (Artists, ASCAP)

8. **HONKY TONK**
B. Doggett
Shepard–Scott–Butler,   King 4950 (Bilace, BMI)

9. **TRUE LOVE**
B. Crosby and G. Kelly
*C. Porter,   Capitol 3507
(Buxton Hill, ASCAP)*

10. **MY PRAYER**
The Platters
Boulanger–Kennedy, Mercury 70893 (Skidmore, ASCAP)

1. **LOVE ME TENDER**
E. Presley
E. Presley–V. Watson,   Victor 20–6643   (Elvis Presley, BMI)

2. **DON'T BE CRUEL**
E. Presley
O. Blackwell,   Victor 20–6604   (Elvis Presley–Shalimar, BMI)

3. **GREEN DOOR**
J. Lowe
*Davis–Moore,   Dot 15486
(Trinity, BMI)*

4. **JUST WALKING IN THE RAIN**
J. Ray
Bragg–Riley,   Columbia 40729 (Golden West Melodies, BMI)

5. **CANADIAN SUNSET**
H. Winterhalter and E. Heywood
E. Heywood–N. Gimbel,   Victor 20–6537   (Meridian, BMI)

6. **TONIGHT YOU BELONG TO ME**
Patience and Prudence
B. Rose–L. David,   Liberty 55022   (Mills, ASCAP)

7. **HONKY TONK**
B. Doggett
Shepard–Scott–Butler,   King 4950   (Bilace, BMI)

8. **TRUE LOVE**
B. Crosby and G. Kelly
*C. Porter,   Capitol 3507
(Buxton Hill, ASCAP)*

9. **WHATEVER WILL BE, WILL BE (QUE SERA SERA)**
D. Day
Livingston–Evans,   Columbia 40704   (Artists, ASCAP)

10. **FRIENDLY PERSUASION**
P. Boone
Webster–Tiomkin,   Dot 15490   (Leo Feist, ASCAP)

November 10

1. **LOVE ME TENDER**
E. Presley
E. Presley–V. Watson, Victor 20–6643 (Elvis Presley, BMI)

2. **GREEN DOOR**
J. Lowe
Davis–Moore, Dot 15486 (Trinity, BMI)

3. **JUST WALKING IN THE RAIN**
J. Ray
Bragg–Riley, Columbia 40729 (Golden West Melodies, BMI)

4. **DON'T BE CRUEL**
E. Presley
O. Blackwell, Victor 20–6604 (Elvis Presley–Shalimar, BMI)

5. **CANADIAN SUNSET**
H. Winterhalter and E. Heywood
E. Heywood–N. Gimbel, Victor 20–6537 (Meridian, BMI)

6. **TRUE LOVE**
B. Crosby and G. Kelly
C. Porter, Capitol 3507 (Buxton Hill, ASCAP)

7. **TONIGHT YOU BELONG TO ME**
Patience and Prudence
B. Rose–L. David, Liberty 55022 (Mills, ASCAP)

8. **BLUEBERRY HILL**
F. Domino
Lewis–Stock–Rose, Imperial 5407 (Chappell, ASCAP)

9. **FRIENDLY PERSUASION**
P. Boone
Webster–Tiomkin, Dot 15490 (Leo Feist, ASCAP)

10. **HONKY TONK**
B. Doggett
Shepard–Scott–Butler, King 4950 (Bilace, BMI)

November 17

1. **JUST WALKING IN THE RAIN**
J. Ray
Bragg–Riley, Columbia 40729 (Golden West Melodies, BMI)

2. **DON'T BE CRUEL**
E. Presley
O. Blackwell, Victor 20–6604 (Elvis Presley, BMI)

3. **LOVE ME TENDER**
E. Presley
E. Presley–V. Watson, Victor 20–6643 (Elvis Presley, BMI)

4. **GREEN DOOR**
J. Lowe
Davis–Moore, Dot 15486 (Trinity, BMI)

5. **SINGING THE BLUES**
G. Mitchell
Endsley, Columbia 40767 (Acuff–Rose, BMI)

6. **TRUE LOVE**
B. Crosby and G. Kelly
C. Porter, Capitol 3507 (Buxton Hill, ASCAP)

7. **CANADIAN SUNSET**
H. Winterhalter and E. Heywood
E. Heywood–N. Gimbel, Victor 20–6537 (Meridian, BMI)

8. **BLUEBERRY HILL**
F. Domino
Lewis–Stock–Rose, Imperial 5407 (Chappell, ASCAP)

9. **TONIGHT YOU BELONG TO ME**
Patience and Prudence
B. Rose–L. David, Liberty 55022 (Mills, ASCAP)

10. **HONKY TONK**
B. Doggett
Shepard–Scott–Butler, King 4950 (Bilace, BMI)

November 24

1. **JUST WALKING IN THE RAIN**
J. Ray
Bragg–Riley, Columbia 40729 (Golden West Melodies, BMI)

2. **SINGING THE BLUES**
G. Mitchell
Endsley, Columbia 40767 (Acuff–Rose, BMI)

3. **GREEN DOOR**
J. Lowe
Davis–Moore, Dot 15486 (Trinity, BMI)

4. **TRUE LOVE**
B. Crosby and G. Kelly
C. Porter, Capitol 3507 (Buxton Hill, ASCAP)

5. **LOVE ME TENDER**
E. Presley
E. Presley–V. Watson, Victor 20–6643 (Elvis Presley, BMI)

6. **DON'T BE CRUEL**
E. Presley
O. Blackwell, Victor 20–6604 (Elvis Presley–Shalimar, BMI)

7. **BLUEBERRY HILL**
F. Domino
Lewis–Stock–Rose, Imperial 5407 (Chappell, ASCAP)

8. **HONKY TONK**
B. Doggett
Shepard–Scott–Butler King 4950 (Bilace, BMI)

9. **CINDY, OH, CINDY**
V. Martin
Barron–Long, Glory 247 (E. B. Marks, BMI)

10. **FRIENDLY PERSUASION**
P. Boone
Webster–Tiomkin, Dot 15490 (Leo Feist, ASCAP)

December 1

1. **LOVE ME TENDER**
E. Presley
E. Presley–V. Watson, Victor 20–6643 (Elvis Presley, BMI)

2. **GREEN DOOR**
J. Lowe
Davis–Moore, Dot 15486 (Trinity, BMI)

3. **SINGING THE BLUES**
G. Mitchell
Endsley, Columbia 40767 (Acuff–Rose, BMI)

4. **JUST WALKING IN THE RAIN**
J. Ray
Bragg–Riley, Columbia 40729 (Golden West Melodies, BMI)

5. **TRUE LOVE**
B. Crosby and G. Kelly
C. Porter, Capitol 3507 (Buxton Hill, ASCAP)

6. **BLUEBERRY HILL**
F. Domino
Lewis–Stock–Rose, Imperial 5407 (Chappell, ASCAP)

7. **DON'T BE CRUEL**
E. Presley
O. Blackwell, Victor 20–6604 (Elvis Presley–Shalimar, BMI)

8. **HONKY TONK**
B. Doggett
Shepard–Scott–Butler, King 4950 (Bilace, BMI)

9. **HEY! JEALOUS LOVER**
F. Sinatra
Cahn–Walker–Twomey, Capitol 3552 (Barton, ASCAP)

10. **CINDY, OH, CINDY**
V. Martin
Barron–Long, Glory 247 (E. B. Marks, BMI)

December 8

1. **GREEN DOOR**
J. Lowe
Davis–Moore, Dot 15486 (Trinity, BMI)

2. **JUST WALKING IN THE RAIN**
J. Ray
Bragg–Riley, Columbia 40729 (Golden West Melodies, BMI)

3. **TRUE LOVE**
B. Crosby and G. Kelly
C. Porter, Capitol 3507 (Buxton Hill, ASCAP)

4. **SINGING THE BLUES**
G. Mitchell
Endsley, Columbia 40767 (Acuff–Rose, BMI)

5. **LOVE ME TENDER**
E. Presley
E. Presley–V. Watson, Victor 20–6643 (Elvis Presley, BMI)

6. **HEY! JEALOUS LOVER**
F. Sinatra
Cahn–Walker–Twomey, Capitol 3552 (Barton, ASCAP)

7. **BLUEBERRY HILL**
F. Domino
Lewis–Stock–Rose, Imperial 5407 (Chappell, ASCAP)

8. **CINDY, OH, CINDY**
V. Martin
Barron–Long, Glory 247 (E. B. Marks, BMI)

9. **FRIENDLY PERSUASION**
P. Boone
Webster–Tiomkin, Dot 15490 (Leo Feist, ASCAP)

10. **HONKY TONK**
B. Doggett
Shepard–Scott–Butler, King 4950 (Bilace, BMI)

December 15

1. **GREEN DOOR**
J. Lowe
Davis–Moore, Dot 15486 (Trinity, BMI)

2. **LOVE ME TENDER**
E. Presley
E. Presley–V. Watson, Victor 20–6643 (Elvis Presley, BMI)

3. **SINGING THE BLUES**
G. Mitchell
Endsley, Columbia 40767 (Acuff–Rose, BMI)

4. **TRUE LOVE**
B. Crosby and G. Kelly
C. Porter, Capitol 3507 (Buxton Hill, ASCAP)

5. **JUST WALKING IN THE RAIN**
J. Ray
Bragg–Riley, Columbia 40729 (Golden West Melodies, BMI)

6. **BLUEBERRY HILL**
F. Domino
Lewis–Stock–Rose, Imperial 5407 (Chappell, ASCAP)

7. **CINDY, OH, CINDY**
V. Martin
Barron–Long, Glory 247 (E. B. Marks, BMI)

8. **HEY! JEALOUS LOVER**
F. Sinatra
Cahn–Walker–Twomey, Capitol 3552 (Barton, ASCAP)

9. **FRIENDLY PERSUASION**
P. Boone
Webster–Tiomkin, Dot 15490 (Leo Feist, ASCAP)

10. **HONKY TONK**
B. Doggett
Shepard–Scott–Butler, King 4950 (Bilace, BMI)

December 22

1. **SINGING THE BLUES**
   G. Mitchell
   Endsley,   Columbia 40767
   (Acuff–Rose, BMI)

2. **LOVE ME TENDER**
   E. Presley
   E. Presley–V. Watson,
   Victor 20–6643   (Elvis Presley,
   BMI)

3. **GREEN DOOR**
   J. Lowe
   Davis–Moore,   Dot 15486
   (Trinity, BMI)

4. **TRUE LOVE**
   B. Crosby and G. Kelly
   C. Porter,   Capitol 3507
   (Buxton Hill, ASCAP)

5. **JUST WALKING IN THE RAIN**
   J. Ray
   Bragg–Riley,   Columbia 40729
   (Golden West Melodies, BMI)

6. **BLUEBERRY HILL**
   F. Domino
   Lewis–Stock–Rose,   Imperial
   5407 (Chappell, ASCAP)

7. **CINDY, OH, CINDY**
   V. Martin
   Barron–Long,   Glory 247
   (E. B. Mark, BMI)

8. **HEY! JEALOUS LOVER**
   F. Sinatra
   Cahn–Walker–Twomey,   Capitol
   3552   (Barton, ASCAP)

9. **LOVE ME**
   E. Presley
   J. Leiber–M. Stoller,   Victor
   45 EPA 992   (Hill & Range,
   BMI)

10. **FRIENDLY PERSUASION**
    P. Boone
    Webster–Tiomkin,   Dot 15490
    (Leo Feist, ASCAP)

December 29

1. **LOVE ME TENDER**
   E. Presley
   E. Presley–V. Watson   Victor
   20–6643   (Acuff–Rose, BMI)

2. **TRUE LOVE**
   B. Crosby and G. Kelly
   C. Porter   Capitol 3507
   (Buxton Hill, ASCAP)

3. **SINGING THE BLUES**
   G. Mitchell
   Endsley   Columbia 40767
   (Acuff–Rose, BMI)

4. **BLUEBERRY HILL**
   F. Domino
   Lewis–Stock–Rose   Imperial
   5407   (Chappell, ASCAP)

5. **GREEN DOOR**
   J. Lowe
   Davis–Moore   Dot 15486
   (Trinity, BMI)

6. **CINDY, OH, CINDY**
   V. Martin
   Barron–Long,   Glory 247
   (E. B. Marks, BMI)

7. **HEY! JEALOUS LOVER**
   F. Sinatra
   Cahn–Walker–Twomey   Capitol
   3552   (Barton, ASCAP)

8. **JUST WALKING IN THE RAIN**
   J. Ray
   Bragg–Riley   Columbia 40729
   (Golden West Melodies, BMI)

9. **LOVE ME**
   E. Presley
   J. Leiber–M. Stoller   Victor
   45 EPA 992   (Hill & Range,
   BMI)

10. **ROSE AND A BABY RUTH**
    G. Hamilton IV
    J. Dee   ABC–Paramount 9765
    (Bentley, BMI)

JERRY LEE LEWIS

For rock and roll it was a year of settling in. Elvis had proved that rock and roll could not be lightly dismissed as a childish fad. But he did not put rock and roll into the ranks of respectable music. The young intelligentsia clung to jazz as the enlightened music, and the adults were temporarily distracted from the 1940's sounds by the cha cha.

The cha cha influence did penetrate the heartbeat of rock and roll, but in rock language it was chalypso, or calypso music with a cha cha beat. Parents were feeling smug in early 1957 when they heard their teenagers playing "all day, all night, Marianne," "Day-O" and "The Banana Boat Song." They were sure this meant a trend toward clearer, more complicated lyrics and away from the Presley slur.

There was also a ripple of influence toward better lyrics from folk music by Jimmie Rodgers with "Honeycomb" and "Kisses Sweeter than Wine." What's more, the adults were pleased to see their kids dancing a heavy-beated cha cha. It looked like teens were finally "coming to their senses."

Rockabilly—hillbilly plus rock and roll—was another force in teen music. Elvis first brought Nashville music from the country-western charts in a big way. And once the door was opened, Furlin Husky, Marty Robbins, George Hamilton IV and Gale Storm moved in with their country style hits, "Gone," "White Sport Coat," "A Rose and a Baby Ruth" and "Dark Moon."

If country-western influenced rock and roll, it was nothing compared with the influence on television. 1957 was without a doubt the year of the Western or, as it was called, the adult Western.

The quiz shows of 1956 had become old hat. After America watched Charles Van Doren win $129,000, and ten-year-old Robert Strom win $192,000, prize money seemed cheap and viewers began to look elsewhere for thrills.

1957

Turn that damn thing down!

Raymond I. Kandel,
Charleston, W. Va.

And as they looked to the West they found what they wanted in "Tombstone Territory," "Sugarfoot," "Colt 45," "Wells Fargo," "Zorro," "Have Gun, Will Travel" and at least a dozen others. "Maverick" was seriously challenging Ed Sullivan's traditional Sunday night audience.

The only other sensation on TV was the "Tonight Show" with Jack Paar. His success was to set the pattern for late-night viewing for the next decade.

Television was so powerfully established by 1957 that the movie industry was afraid it might collapse because of TV's competition. Twelve hundred theaters closed that year as film companies complained that new movies couldn't compete with old movies which were free on TV. Still, it was Hollywood's fiftieth anniversary as the United States film capital and it carried on bravely. Oscars went to *Bridge on the River Kwai* as the best film, its star, Alec Guinness, as best actor and Joanne Woodward from *Three Faces of Eve* as best actress. But the biggest headline came from Hollywood when Mike Todd, the sparkling entrepreneur, won the hand of movie queen Elizabeth Taylor.

Mike Todd was not the only winner in 1957. Lew Burdette won three games in the World Series to make the Milwaukee Braves champions over the New York Yankees. Lester Pearson of Canada won the Nobel Peace Prize, and Albert Camus of France won the Nobel Prize in literature. The Democrats made gains across the nation in local elections and in New York City, Democratic Mayor Robert Wagner was reelected. The Negro community won a victory when the New York City Council passed an open housing law. And despite Strom Thurmond's record filibuster, 24 hours and 13 minutes, the Civil Rights Bill to protect voting rights was passed by Congress.

The South was in and out of chaos throughout the year. About the only good news they got was that Marian Ann McKnight of South Carolina was chosen Miss America 1957.

In late June, Hurricane Audrey and a tidal wave hit the Texas-Louisiana coast, leaving 531 persons dead or missing. In September the Arkansas National Guard blocked Negro students from entering Central High School in Little Rock. Two weeks later, Governor Faubus removed the troops to comply with a federal court injunction. But rioters forced the Negro students to withdraw three days later.

Washington had more trouble than the headaches over school desegregation. The year started out hopefully for the popular administration with the Eisenhower-Nixon inauguration. Among the pictures of the inauguration is one in *Life* magazine that foreshadows a great moment in America's future: little Julie Nixon is standing next to lip-biting, bow-tied, crew-cut David Eisenhower, as the President and the Vice President show off the administration's younger generation.

After the inauguration came the Middle East turmoil. The United States sent the Sixth Fleet into the Mediterranean to protect Jordan from international Communism. And there was the continued fighting in Cuba.

Senator Joseph McCarthy died in 1957 although national distrust of Communism lived on. For the most part, the Russians were busy shifting personnel in the government hierarchy. There was also much back and forth between the United States and the Russians about who would support who in the Middle East conflict, and about who would inspect who in a disarmament agreement.

This was the first year of the great East-West space race. The International Geophysical Year started July 1 with scientists from sixty-seven countries participating; in October, Russia made the other sixty-six countries look Stone Age by launching Sputnik I, the first earth satellite. On November 3 they sent up Sputnik II with a live dog in it. The United States tried to launch a Vanguard rocket with a satellite in it, but it exploded on lift-off at Cape Canaveral. It was suddenly apparent that we were nowhere in our development of rockets and space vehicles. A panic set in that we were slipping into the Number 2 spot on the globe. Even the United States firing of its first successful ICBM was little consolation with Sputnik spinning around overhead.

And on the earth there was a severe economic slump and a rise in the cost of living. And in November, Eisenhower suffered a minor stroke.

The average American even felt the pressure of some of the government's problems. With business doing poorly and prices up. three-fourths of the population was earning less than $7,000. The average factory worker made only $82.50 a week and, after the postwar spending spree, he was feeling the squeeze.

There was a trend toward economy in cars as American finances forced buyers to think more about efficiency than power. The auto industry decided to stop subdidizing stock car races, to stress safety and to cut down on horsepower race advertising. With this new emphasis, foreign cars were beginning to get some attention, especially the ugly little Volkswagen.

Yet this slowing of the economy seemed to be happening faster than Detroit realized. In the United States auto industry everyone was still looking forward, especially Chrysler Corporation when it put sweeping high tailfins on its models to prove that "suddenly it was 1960." Ford was also quite optimistic as it introduced its exciting new Edsel.

More bombs than the Edsel were built in 1957. On January 22, George Metesky, New York's mad bomber, was caught after spreading bombs through the city during the Christmas holidays. In Montgomery, Alabama, there were six bombings of churches and homes following the desegregation of city buses.

Our most direct involvement with the country's problems was at school. Many of us—black and white—were feeling the pressures of the community as our schools were desegregated. Even when it was peaceful, desegregation was a jolting experience. The younger and more naive among us realized what segregation was only when it was so abruptly opposed. For the blacks it was difficult and disorienting to be suddenly an underprepared, unwelcome newcomer in a white school. And yet, for some us, it was the awakening of a racial awareness and a witnessing of injustice that would later enable our generation to march in Selma, to respect Black Power and to move in some way against the apartheid of the fifties.

The Sputnik pressure also reached into the population, and especially hit those of us in school. There was a big push to upgrade our educational system so that we could produce thinkers equal to the Russians. Schools forced math and science down our throats with little regard for our aptitude. Accelerated programs offered algebra and geometry in elementary school. And some schools changed their hours, adding extra periods and cutting into free time. If political propaganda didn't make us hate the Communists, the education race did.

Out of school, Elvis was still our real hero. New rock and roll singers were strumming guitars, growing sideburns and combing their hair in ducks (or ducktails or ducks ass). Rick Nelson, who had grown up with us as Ricky, was the first successful imitation Presley.

Girls even imitated their idol by cutting their hair short, slicking back the sides, combing a limp twist of hair onto their foreheads and cutting improvised sideburns.

Of course, there were still teenagers whose appearances weren't severly altered by rock and roll. Elvis could wear his hair long and greasy, but most boys wore crewcuts or flat tops which they kept waxed up tall.

For girls, the sloppy rolled-up-blue-jean look was starting to go out of style. It was being replaced with neater outfits of Bermudas (or the shorter Jamaicas) and knee socks. The trend toward neatness was obvious as girls began to wear jewelry and to shed heavy saddles and bobby soxs for stockings and T-straps. Loafers and knee socks were also very popular, especially as plaid pleated skirts came in. Girls wore sets of matching pullover and cardigan sweaters with these mid-calf length skirts. Boys wore short-sleeved shirts with a small cuff rolled in the sleeve.

Marty Robbins dressed for the dance in a white sport coat and a pink carnation, and in that he looked fairly typical. Although his parents certainly protested, his socks had to be white and his pants were probably pegged. At school the pegged pants got tighter and tighter (twelve inches, if possible) and were adorned with an Ivy League buckle across the back. Girls had buckles too—on skirts, slacks, Bermudas, and even on the backs of saddle shoes. At some schools kids wore their buckles undone if they were not going with anyone, and buckled them if they were going steady.

Actually, going steady was just becoming a reality, and not just something for the older kids. Rock and roll fans were finally growing up. Many of us had pushed into our teens and rock and roll had become the primary music of high school kids. These kids were old enough to have dances and dates, and out of this grew some important features of the rock and roll era.

One was the sock hop. The name was coined because high school kids held informal dances in the gym where they had to shed their saddle shoes so they wouldn't scratch the gym floor. The term was really institutionalized when Danny and the Juniors sang:

> You can rock it
> You can roll it
> You can bop it
> You can stroll it
> At the hop

Another institution was Johnny Mathis, king of necking music. As much as we loved to be rocked by our music, we found that there were those quiet times when only Mathis would do. Only Johnny Mathis could say those tender things that we were too shy and inexperienced to think of. Things like:

> Chances are that I wear a silly grin
> The moment you step into view
> Chances are you think that I'm in love with you.

Or, after a school dance, as we sat in the living room with the football player we'd had a crush on for weeks, and savored the fact that he was really there and we were holding hands . . .

> Perhaps the glow of love will grow
> With every passing day
> Or we may never meet again
> But then, it's not for me to say.

Even though we were growing up and rock and roll had been around solidly for two years, the adults were not accustomed to the sexy messages. In Boston "Wake Up Little Susie" was banned because it said:

The movie wasn't so hot
It didn't have much of a plot
We fell asleep; our goose is cooked
Our reputation is shot.

The Everly Brothers were justified when they worried what to tell their parents and friends when they said "oo, lah, lah!" Spending the night together, even asleep at the movies, was a sin.

Buddy Knox was even more explicit as he asked a girl to come along and be his party doll, that he'd make love to her, because:

Every man has got to have a party doll
To come along with him when he's feelin' wild
To be ever lovin', true and fair
To run her fingers through his hair.

But, as in the past, Pat Boone kept the reputation of rock and roll out of the gutter with the innocence of "April Love" (all the seven wonders, one little kiss can tell you that it's true).

Pat Boone may have been as American as pizza pie, but his brand of young person was on the way out. We were growing wiser, and maybe wilder, than our parents wanted to know. And this growing would be expressed over and over in our music, pushing parents and censors farther and farther out of power until years later, when the Doors would open and all would be exposed.

In 1957 we not only knew rock and roll would last but also that it would experiment, enlarge and envelop. It didn't stand or fall with one man anymore as it had with Elvis. It had captivated millions of people and dollars. It was moving abroad. It was growing in awareness as we were, and the more dedicated among us were sure it would be the music of our generation as long as we lasted.

The Top Fifty
1957

1.	ALL SHOOK UP	E. Presley	26.	IT'S NOT FOR ME TO SAY	J. Mathis
2.	YOUNG LOVE	S. James	27.	WAKE UP LITTLE SUSIE	The Everly Brothers
3.	ROUND AND ROUND	P. Como			
4.	LITTLE DARLIN'	The Diamonds	28.	WHITE SPORT COAT	M. Robbins
5.	LOVE LETTERS IN THE SAND	P. Boone	29.	OLD CAPE COD	P. Page
6.	TAMMY	D. Reynolds	30.	BUTTERFLY	A. Williams
7.	MARIANNE	The Hilltoppers	31.	BANANA BOAT SONG	The Tarriers
8.	DON'T FORBID ME	P. Boone	32.	WHY BABY WHY	P. Boone
9.	TEDDY BEAR	E. Presley	33.	JAILHOUSE ROCK	E. Presley
10.	SO RARE	J. Dorsey	34.	SILHOUETTES	The Rays
11.	BYE BYE LOVE	The Everly Brothers	35.	YOU SEND ME	S. Cooke
12.	HONEYCOMB	J. Rodgers	36.	SCHOOL DAY	C. Berry
13.	FASCINATION	J. Morgan	37.	THAT'LL BE THE DAY	B. Holly
14.	AROUND THE WORLD	V. Young and B. Crosby	38.	WHOLE LOTTA SHAKIN' GOIN' ON	J. L. Lewis
15.	BANANA BOAT (DAY-O)	H. Belafonte	39.	MELODIE D'AMOUR	The Ames Brothers
16.	SINGING THE BLUES	G. Mitchell	40.	FOUR WALLS	J. Lowe
17.	DIANA	P. Anka	41.	BE-BOP BABY	R. Nelson
18.	WHITE SILVER SANDS	D. Rondo	42.	TEENAGER'S ROMANCE	R. Nelson
19.	PARTY DOLL	B. Knox	43.	SEARCHIN'	The Coasters
20.	CHANCES ARE	J. Mathis	44.	RAINBOW	R. Hamilton
21.	GONE	F. Husky	45.	IN THE MIDDLE OF AN ISLAND	T. Bennett
22.	DARK MOON	G. Storm			
23.	COME GO WITH ME	The Del Vikings	46.	MR. LEE	The Bobbettes
24.	I'M GONNA SIT RIGHT DOWN AND WRITE MYSELF A LETTER	B. Williams	47.	MY HEART REMINDS ME	D. Reese
			48.	I'M WALKIN'	F. Domino
25.	TOO MUCH	E. Presley	49.	LITTLE BITTY PRETTY ONE	T. Harris
			50.	LOVE IS STRANGE	Mickey and Sylvia

1. **SINGING THE BLUES**
   G. Mitchell
   Endsley,   Columbia 40767
   (Acuff–Rose, BMI)

2. **LOVE ME TENDER**
   E. Presley
   E. Presley–V. Watson,
   Victor 20–6643   (Elvis Presley,
   BMI)

3. **GREEN DOOR**
   J. Lowe
   Davis–Moore,   Dot 15486
   (Trinity, BMI)

4. **BLUEBERRY HILL**
   F. Domino
   Stock–Lewis–Rose,   Imperial
   5407   (Chappell, ASCAP)

5. **TRUE LOVE**
   B. Crosby and G. Kelly
   C. Porter,   Capitol 3507
   (Buxton Hill, ASCAP)

6. **JUST WALKING IN THE
   RAIN**
   J. Ray
   Bragg–Riley,   Columbia 40729
   (Golden West Melodies, BMI)

7. **CINDY, OH, CINDY**
   E. Fisher
   Barron–Long,   Victor 20–6677
   (E. B. Marks, BMI)

8. **LOVE ME**
   E. Presley
   J. Leiber–M. Stoller,   Victor
   45 EPA 992   (Hill & Range,
   BMI)

9. **A ROSE AND A BABY RUTH**
   G. Hamilton IV
   Dee,   ABC Paramount 9765
   (Bently, BMI)

10. **HEY! JEALOUS LOVER**
    F. Sinatra
    Cahn–Walker–Twomey,   Capitol
    3532   (Barton, ASCAP)

1. **SINGING THE BLUES**
   G. Mitchell
   Endsley,   Columbia 40767
   (Acuff–Rose, BMI)

2. **LOVE ME TENDER**
   E. Presley
   E. Presley–V. Watson,   Victor
   20–6643   (Elvis Presley, BMI)

3. **BLUEBERRY HILL**
   F. Domino
   Lewis–Stock–Rose,   Imperial
   5407   (Chappell, ASCAP)

4. **GREEN DOOR**
   J. Lowe
   Davis–Moore,   Dot 15486
   (Trinity, BMI)

5. **TRUE LOVE**
   B. Crosby and G. Kelly
   C. Porter,   Capitol 3507
   (Buxton Hill, ASCAP)

6. **BANANA BOAT SONG**
   The Tarriers
   Arkin–Carey–Darling   Glory
   249   (Bryden, BMI)

7. **CINDY, OH, CINDY**
   E. Fisher
   Barron–Long,   Victor 20–6677
   (E. B. Marks, BMI)

8. **JUST WALKING IN THE
   RAIN**
   J. Ray
   Bragg–Riley,   Columbia 40729
   (Golden West Melodies, BMI)

9. **LOVE ME**
   E. Presley
   J. Leiber–M. Stoller,   Victor
   45 EPA 992   (Hill & Range,
   BMI)

10. **HEY! JEALOUS LOVER**
    F. Sinatra
    Cahn–Walker–Twomey,   Capitol
    3532   (Barton, ASCAP)

January 19

1. **SINGING THE BLUES**
G. Mitchell
Endsley, Columbia 40767
(Acuff–Rose, BMI)

2. **BANANA BOAT SONG**
The Tarriers
Arkin–Carey–Darling, Glory
249 (Bryden, BMI)

3. **YOUNG LOVE**
S. James
C. Jayner–R. Carter, Capitol
3602 (Lowery, BMI)

4. **GREEN DOOR**
J. Lowe
Davis–Moore, Dot 15486
(Trinity, BMI)

5. **BLUEBERRY HILL**
F. Domino
Lewis–Stock–Rose, Imperial
5407 (Chappell, ASCAP)

6. **LOVE ME TENDER**
E. Presley
E. Presley–V. Watson, Victor
20–6643 (Elvis Presley, BMI)

7. **TRUE LOVE**
B. Crosby and G. Kelly
C. Porter, Capitol 3507
(Buxton Hill, ASCAP)

8. **DON'T FORBID ME**
P. Boone
Singleton, Dot 15521
(Roosevelt, BMI)

9. **LOVE ME**
E. Presley
J. Leiber–M. Stoller, Victor
EPA 992 (Hill & Range, BMI)

10. **JUST WALKING IN THE
RAIN**
J. Ray
Bragg–Riley, Columbia 40729
(Golden West Melodies, BMI)

January 26

1. **SINGING THE BLUES**
G. Mitchell
Endsley, Columbia 40767
(Acuff–Rose, BMI)

2. **YOUNG LOVE**
S. James
C. Jayner–R. Carter, Capitol
3602 (Lowery, BMI)

3. **BANANA BOAT SONG**
The Tarriers
Arkin–Carey–Darling, Glory
249 (Bryden, BMI)

4. **GREEN DOOR**
J. Lowe
Davis–Moore, Dot 15486
(Trinity, BMI)

5. **BLUEBERRY HILL**
F. Domino
Lewis–Stock–Rose, Imperial
5407 (Chappell, ASCAP)

6. **DON'T FORBID ME**
P. Boone
Singleton, Dot 15521
(Roosevelt, BMI)

7. **LOVE ME TENDER**
E. Presley
E. Presley–V. Watson, Victor
20–6643 (Elvis Presley, BMI)

8. **TRUE LOVE**
B. Crosby and G. Kelly
C. Porter, Capitol 3507
(Buxton Hill, ASCAP)

9. **MOONLIGHT GAMBLER**
F. Laine
Hilliard–Springer, Columbia
40780 (E. H. Morris, ASCAP)

10. **JUST WALKING IN THE
RAIN**
J. Ray
Bragg–Riley, Columbia 40729
(Golden West Melodies, BMI)

February 2

1. **YOUNG LOVE**
S. James
C. Jayner–R. Carter, Capitol
3602 (Lowery, BMI)

2. **SINGING THE BLUES**
G. Mitchell
Endsley, Columbia 40767
(Acuff–Rose, BMI)

3. **DON'T FORBID ME**
P. Boone
Singleton, Dot 15521
(Roosevelt, BMI)

4. **BANANA BOAT SONG**
The Tarriers
Arkin–Carey–Darling, Glory
249 (Bryden, BMI)

5. **BANANA BOAT (DAY-O)**
H. Belafonte
Belafonte–Burgess–Attaway,
Victor 20–6771 (Shari, ASCAP)

6. **BLUEBERRY HILL**
F. Domino
Lewis–Stock–Rose, Imperial
5407 (Chappell, ASCAP)

7. **MOONLIGHT GAMBLER**
F. Laine
Hilliard–Springer, Columbia
40780 (E. H. Morris, ASCAP)

8. **GREEN DOOR**
J. Lowe
Davis–Moore, Dot 15486
(Trinity, BMI)

9. **TRUE LOVE**
B. Crosby and G. Kelly
C. Porter, Capitol 3507
(Buxton Hill, ASCAP)

10. **LOVE ME TENDER**
E. Presley
E. Presley–V. Watson, Victor
20–6643 (Elvis Presley, BMI)

February 9

1. **YOUNG LOVE**
S. James
C. Jayner–R. Carter, Capitol 3602 (Lowery, BMI)

2. **DON'T FORBID ME**
P. Boone
Singleton, Dot 15521 (Roosevelt, BMI)

3. **SINGING THE BLUES**
G. Mitchell
Endsley, Columbia 40767 (Acuff–Rose, BMI)

4. **BANANA BOAT SONG**
The Tarriers
Arkin–Carey–Darling, Glory 249 (Bryden, BMI)

5. **TOO MUCH**
E. Presley
L. Rosenberg–B. Weinman, Victor 20-6800 (Southern Belle–Elvis Presley, BMI)

6. **MOONLIGHT GAMBLER**
F. Laine
Hilliard–Springer, Columbia 40780 (E. H. Morris, ASCAP)

7. **BANANA BOAT (DAY-O)**
H. Belafonte
Belafonte–Burgess–Attaway, Victor 20-6771 (Shari, ASCAP)

8. **BLUEBERRY HILL**
F. Domino
Lewis–Stock–Rose, Imperial 5407 (Chappell, ASCAP)

9. **TRUE LOVE**
B. Crosby and G. Kelly
C. Porter, Capitol 3507 (Buxton Hill, ASCAP)

10. **LOVE ME TENDER**
E. Presley
E. Presley–V. Watson, Victor 20-6643 (Elvis Presley, BMI)

February 16

1. **YOUNG LOVE**
S. James
C. Jayner–R. Carter, Capitol 3602 (Lowery, BMI)

2. **DON'T FORBID ME**
P. Boone
Singleton, Dot 15521 (Roosevelt, BMI)

3. **BANANA BOAT SONG**
The Tarriers
Arkin–Carey–Darling, Glory 249 (Bryden, BMI)

4. **SINGING THE BLUES**
G. Mitchell
Endsley, Columbia 40767 (Acuff–Rose, BMI)

5. **BANANA BOAT (DAY-O)**
H. Belafonte
Belafonte–Burgess–Attaway, Victor 20–6771 (Shari, ASCAP)

6. **MOONLIGHT GAMBLER**
F. Laine
Hilliard–Springer, Columbia 40780 (E. H. Morris, ASCAP)

7. **BLUE MONDAY**
F. Domino
D. Bartholomew–A. Domino, Imperial 5417 (Commodore, BMI)

8. **TOO MUCH**
E. Presley
L. Rosenberg–B. Weinman Victor 20–6800 (Southern Belle–Elvis Presley, BMI)

9. **TRUE LOVE**
B. Crosby and G. Kelly
C. Porter, Capitol 3507 (Buxton Hill, ASCAP)

10. **LOVE ME TENDER**
E. Presley
E. Presley–V. Watson, Victor 20-6643 (Elvis Presley, BMI)

February 23

1. **YOUNG LOVE**
S. James
C. Jayner–R. Carter, Capitol 3602 (Lowery, BMI)

2. **DON'T FORBID ME**
P. Boone
Singleton, Dot 15521 (Roosevelt, BMI)

3. **BANANA BOAT SONG**
The Tarriers
Arkin–Carey–Darling, Glory 249 (Bryden, BMI)

4. **TOO MUCH**
E. Presley
L. Rosenberg–B. Weinman Victor 20–6800 (Southern Belle–Elvis Presley, BMI)

5. **SINGING THE BLUES**
G. Mitchell
Endsley, Columbia 40767 (Acuff–Rose, BMI)

6. **BANANA BOAT (DAY-O)**
H. Belafonte
Belafonte–Burgess–Attaway, Victor 20–6771 (Shari, ASCAP)

7. **MOONLIGHT GAMBLER**
F. Laine
Hilliard–Springer, Columbia 40780 (E. H. Morris, ASCAP)

8. **MARIANNE**
The Hilltoppers
Gillykson–Dehr–Miller, Dot 15537 (Montclare, BMI)

9. **TRUE LOVE**
B. Crosby and G. Kelly
C. Porter, Capitol 3507 (Buxton Hill, ASCAP)

10. **BLUE MONDAY**
F. Domino
D. Bartholomew–A. Domino, Imperial 5417 (Commodore, BMI)

1957

March 2

1. **YOUNG LOVE**
S. James
C. Jayner–R. Carter, Capitol 3602 (Lowery, BMI)

2. **DON'T FORBID ME**
P. Boone
Singleton, Dot 15521 (Roosevelt, BMI)

3. **TOO MUCH**
E. Presley
L. Rosenberg–B. Weinman, Victor 20–6800 (Southern Belle–Elvis Presley, BMI)

4. **BANANA BOAT SONG**
The Tarriers
Arkin–Carey–Darling, Glory 249 (Bryden, BMI)

5. **MARIANNE**
The Hilltoppers
Gillykson–Dehr–Miller, Dot 15537 (Montclare, BMI)

6. **BANANA BOAT DAY-O**
H. Belafonte
Belafonte–Burgess–Attaway, Victor 20–6771 (Shari, ASCAP)

7. **SINGING THE BLUES**
G. Mitchell
Endsley, Columbia 40767 (Acuff–Rose, BMI)

8. **BLUE MONDAY**
F. Domino
D. Bartholomew–A. Domino, Imperial 5417 (Commodore, BMI)

9. **BUTTERFLY**
A. Williams
A. September, Cadence 1308 (Mayland–Presley, BMI)

10. **MOONLIGHT GAMBLER**
F. Laine
Hilliard–Springer, Columbia 40780 (E. H. Morris, ASCAP)

March 9

1. **YOUNG LOVE**
S. James
C. Jayner–R. Carter, Capitol 3602 (Lowery, BMI)

2. **DON'T FORBID ME**
P. Boone
Singleton, Dot 15521 (Roosevelt, BMI)

3. **TOO MUCH**
E. Presley
L. Rosenberg–B. Weinman, Victor 20–6800 (Southern Belle–Elvis Presley, BMI)

4. **MARIANNE**
The Hilltoppers
Gillykson–Dehr–Miller, Dot 15537 (Montclare, BMI)

5. **BANANA BOAT SONG**
The Tarriers
Arkin–Carey–Darling, Glory 249 (Bryden, BMI)

6. **BANANA BOAT (DAY-O)**
H. Belafonte
Belafonte–Burgess–Attaway, Victor 20–6771 (Shari, ASCAP)

7. **BUTTERFLY**
A. Williams
A. September, Cadence 1308 (Mayland–Presley, BMI)

8. **SINGING THE BLUES**
G. Mitchell
Endsley, Columbia 40767 (Acuff–Rose, BMI)

9. **TEENAGE CRUSH**
T. Sands
A. Allison–J. Allison, Capitol F3639 (Central Songs Inc., BMI)

10. **MOONLIGHT GAMBLER**
F. Laine
Hilliard–Springer, Columbia 40780 (E. H. Morris, ASCAP)

March 16

1. **YOUNG LOVE**
S. James
C. Jayner–R. Carter, Capitol 3602 (Lowery, BMI)

2. **MARIANNE**
The Hilltoppers
Gillykson–Dehr–Miller, Dot 15537 (Montclare, BMI)

3. **DON'T FORBID ME**
P. Boone
Singleton, Dot 15521 (Roosevelt, BMI)

4. **TOO MUCH**
E. Presley
L. Rosenberg–B. Weinman, Victor 20–6800 (Southern Belle–Elvis Presley, BMI)

5. **BUTTERFLY**
A. Williams
A. September, Cadence 1308 (Mayland–Presley, BMI)

6. **BANANA BOAT (DAY-O)**
H. Belafonte
Belafonte–Burgess–Attaway, Victor 20–6771 (Shari, ASCAP)

7. **PARTY DOLL**
B. Knox
J. Bowen–B. Knox, Roulette 4002 (Jackie, BMI)

8. **TEENAGE CRUSH**
T. Sands
A. Allison–J. Allison, Capitol F3639 (Central Songs Inc., BMI)

9. **BANANA BOAT SONG**
The Tarriers
Arkin–Carey–Darling, Glory 249 (Bryden, BMI)

10. **ROUND AND ROUND**
P. Como
L. Stallman–J. Shapiro, Victor 20–6815 (Rush, BMI)

March 23

1. **MARIANNE**
The Hilltoppers
Gillkyson–Dehr–Miller, Dot 15537 (Montclare, BMI)

2. **BUTTERFLY**
A. Williams
A. September, Cadence 1308 (Mayland–Presley, BMI)

3. **YOUNG LOVE**
S. James
C. Jayner–R. Carter, Capitol 3602 (Lowery, BMI)

4. **TOO MUCH**
E. Presley
L. Rosenberg–B. Weinman, Victor 20–6800 (Southern Belle–Elvis Presley, BMI)

5. **DON'T FORBID ME**
P. Boone
Singleton, Dot 15521 (Roosevelt, BMI)

6. **PARTY DOLL**
B. Knox
J. Bowen–B. Knox, Roulette 4002 (Jackie, BMI)

7. **TEENAGE CRUSH**
T. Sands
A. Allison–J. Allison, Capitol F3639 (Central Songs Inc., BMI)

8. **BANANA BOAT (DAY-O)**
H. Belafonte
Belafonte–Burgess–Attaway, Victor 20–6815 (Rush, BMI)

9. **BANANA BOAT SONG**
The Tarriers
Arkin–Carey–Darling, Glory 249 (Bryden, BMI)

10. **ROUND AND ROUND**
P. Como
L. Stallman–J. Shapiro, Victor 20–6815 (Rush, BMI)

March 30

1. **MARIANNE**
The Hilltoppers
Gillkyson–Dehr–Miller, Dot 15537 (Montclare, BMI)

2. **BUTTERFLY**
A. Williams
A. September, Cadence 1308 (Mayland–Presley, BMI)

3. **PARTY DOLL**
B. Knox
J. Bowen–B. Knox, Roulette 4002 (Jackie, BMI)

4. **YOUNG LOVE**
S. James
C. Jayner–R. Carter, Capitol 3602 (Lowery, BMI)

5. **ROUND AND ROUND**
P. Como
L. Stallman–J. Shapiro, Victor 20–6815 (Rush, BMI)

6. **DON'T FORBID ME**
P. Boone
Singleton, Dot 15521 (Roosevelt, BMI)

7. **TOO MUCH**
E. Presley
L. Rosenberg–B. Weinman, Victor 20–6800 (Southern Belle–Elvis Presley, BMI)

8. **TEENAGE CRUSH**
T. Sands
A. Allison–J. Allison, Capitol F3639 (Central Songs Inc., BMI)

9. **BANANA BOAT SONG**
The Tarriers
Arkin–Carey–Darling, Glory 249 (Bryden, BMI)

10. **I'M WALKIN'**
F. Domino
A. Domino–D. Bartholomew, Imperial 5428 (Reeve, BMI)

April 6

1. **BUTTERFLY**
A. Williams
A. September, Cadence 1308 (Mayland–Presley, BMI)

2. **YOUNG LOVE**
S. James
C. Jayner–R. Carter, Capitol 3602 (Lowery, BMI)

3. **MARIANNE**
The Hilltoppers
Gillykson–Dehr–Miller, Dot 15537 (Montclare, BMI)

4. **PARTY DOLL**
B. Knox
J. Bowen–B. Knox, Roulette 4002 (Jackie, BMI)

5. **ROUND AND ROUND**
P. Como
L. Stallman–J. Shapiro, Victor 20–6815 (Rush, BMI)

6. **LITTLE DARLIN'**
The Diamonds
M. Williams, Mercury 71060 (Excellorec, BMI)

7. **TEENAGE CRUSH**
T. Sands
A. Allison–J. Allison, Capitol F3639 (Central Songs Inc., BMI)

8. **I'M WALKIN'**
F. Domino
A. Domino–D. Bartholomew, Imperial 5428 (Reeve, BMI)

9. **TOO MUCH**
E. Presley
L. Rosenberg–B. Weinman, Victor 20–6800 (Southern Belle–Elvis Presley, BMI)

10. **DON'T FORBID ME**
P. Boone
Singleton, Dot 15521 (Roosevelt, BMI)

1957

April 13

1. **BUTTERFLY**
A. Williams
*A. September, Cadence 1308
(Mayland–Presley, BMI)*

2. **PARTY DOLL**
B. Knox
*J. Bowen–B. Knox, Roulette
4002 (Jackie, BMI)*

3. **ROUND AND ROUND**
P. Como
*L. Stallman–J. Shapiro,
Victor 20–6815 (Rush, BMI)*

4. **MARIANNE**
The Hilltoppers
*Gillykson–Dehr–Miller, Dot
15537 (Montclare, BMI)*

5. **YOUNG LOVE**
S. James
*C. Jayner–R. Carter, Capitol
3602 (Lowery, BMI)*

6. **ALL SHOOK UP**
E. Presley
*O. Blackwell–E. Presley,
Victor 20-6870 (Presley–
Shalimar, BMI)*

7. **LITTLE DARLIN'**
The Diamonds
*M. Williams, Mercury 71060
(Excellorec, BMI)*

8. **I'M WALKIN'**
F. Domino
*A. Domino–D. Bartholomew,
Imperial 5428 (Reeve, BMI)*

9. **WHY BABY WHY**
P. Boone
*Dixon–Harrison, Dot 15545
(Winneton, BMI)*

10. **GONE**
F. Husky
*S. Rogers, Capitol 3628
(Hill & Range, BMI)*

April 20

1. **ALL SHOOK UP**
E. Presley
*O. Blackwell–E. Presley, Victor
20–6870 (Presley–Shalimar,
BMI)*

2. **BUTTERFLY**
A. Williams
*A. September, Cadence 1308
(Mayland–Presley, BMI)*

3. **LITTLE DARLIN'**
The Diamonds
*M. Williams, Mercury 71060
(Excellorec, BMI)*

4. **ROUND AND ROUND**
P. Como
*L. Stallman–J. Shapiro, Victor
20–6815 (Rush, BMI)*

5. **MARIANNE**
The Hilltoppers
*Gillkyson–Dehr–Miller, Dot
15537 (Montclare, BMI)*

6. **YOUNG LOVE**
S. James
*C. Jayner–R. Carter, Capitol
3602 (Lowery, BMI)*

7. **WHY BABY WHY**
P. Boone
*Dixon–Harrison, Dot 15545
(Winneton, BMI)*

8. **PARTY DOLL**
B. Knox
*J. Bowen–B. Knox, Roulette 4002
(Jackie, BMI)*

9. **SCHOOL DAY**
C. Berry
*C. Berry, Chess 1653
(Arc, BMI)*

10. **GONE**
F. Husky
*S. Rogers, Capitol 3628
(Hill & Range, BMI)*

April 27

1. **ALL SHOOK UP**
E. Presley
*O. Blackwell–E. Presley, Victor
20–6870 (Presley–Shalimar,
BMI)*

2. **LITTLE DARLIN'**
The Diamonds
*M. Williams, Mercury 71060
(Excellorec, BMI)*

3. **BUTTERFLY**
A. Williams
*A. September, Cadence 1308
(Mayland–Presley, BMI)*

4. **ROUND AND ROUND**
P. Como
*L. Stallman–J. Shapiro, Victor
20–6815 (Rush, BMI)*

5. **MARIANNE**
The Hilltoppers
*Gillkyson–Dehr–Miller, Dot
15537 (Montclare, BMI)*

6. **GONE**
F. Husky
*S. Rogers, Capitol 3628
(Hill & Range, BMI)*

7. **WHY BABY WHY**
P. Boone
*Dixon–Harrison, Dot 15545
(Winneton, BMI)*

8. **SCHOOL DAY**
C. Berry
*C. Berry, Chess 1653
(Arc, BMI)*

9. **PARTY DOLL**
B. Knox
*J. Bowen–B. Knox, Roulette
4002 (Jackie, BMI)*

10. **COME GO WITH ME**
The Del Vikings
*C. E. Quick, Dot 15538
(G. I. Fee–Bee, BMI)*

1. **ALL SHOOK UP**
E. Presley
O. Blackwell–E. Presley, Victor 20–6870 (Presley–Shalimar, BMI)

2. **LITTLE DARLIN'**
The Diamonds
M. Williams, Mercury 71060 (Excellorec, BMI)

3. **BUTTERFLY**
A. Williams
A. September, Cadence 1308 (Mayland–Presley, BMI)

4. **ROUND AND ROUND**
P. Como
L. Stallman–J. Shapiro, Victor 20–6815 (Rush, BMI)

5. **GONE**
F. Husky
S. Rogers, Capitol 3628 (Hill & Range, BMI)

6. **MARIANNE**
The Hilltoppers
Gillkyson–Dehr–Miller, Dot 15537 (Montclare, BMI)

7. **SCHOOL DAY**
C. Berry
C. Berry, Chess 1653 (Arc, BMI)

8. **COME GO WITH ME**
The Del Vikings
C. E. Quick, Dot 15538 (G. I. Fee–Bee, BMI)

9. **WHY BABY WHY**
P. Boone
Dixon–Harrison, Dot 15545 (Winneton, BMI)

10. **PARTY DOLL**
B. Knox
J. Bowen–B. Knox, Roulette 4002 (Jackie, BMI)

1. **ALL SHOOK UP**
E. Presley
O. Blackwell–E. Presley, Victor 20–6870 (Presley–Shalimar, BMI)

2. **LITTLE DARLIN'**
The Diamonds
M. Williams, Mercury 71060 (Excellorec, BMI)

3. **GONE**
F. Husky
S. Rogers, Capitol 3628 (Hill & Range, BMI)

4. **ROUND AND ROUND**
P. Como
L. Stallman–J. Shapiro, Victor 20–6815 (Rush, BMI)

5. **DARK MOON**
G. Storm
N. Miller, Dot 15558 (Dandelion, BMI)

6. **COME GO WITH ME**
The Del Vikings
C. E. Quick, Dot 15538 (G. I. Fee–Bee, BMI)

7. **MARIANNE**
The Hilltoppers
Gillkyson–Dehr–Miller, Dot 15537 (Montclare, BMI)

8. **SCHOOL DAY**
C. Berry
C. Berry, Chess 1653 (Arc, BMI)

9. **PARTY DOLL**
B. Knox
J. Bowen–B. Knox, Roulette 4002 (Jackie, BMI)

10. **WHITE SPORT COAT**
M. Robbins
M. Robbins, Columbia 40864 (Acuff–Rose, BMI)

1. **ALL SHOOK UP**
E. Presley
O. Blackwell–E. Presley, Victor 20–6870 (Presley–Shalimar, BMI)

2. **LITTLE DARLIN'**
The Diamonds
M. Williams, Mercury 71060 (Excellorec, BMI)

3. **DARK MOON**
G. Storm
N. Miller, Dot 15558 (Dandelion, BMI)

4. **ROUND AND ROUND**
P. Como
L. Stallman–J. Shapiro, Victor 20–6815 (Rush, BMI)

5. **COME GO WITH ME**
The Del Vikings
C. E. Quick, Dot 15538 (G. I. Fee–Bee, BMI)

6. **WHITE SPORT COAT**
M. Robbins
M. Robbins, Columbia 40864 (Acuff–Rose, BMI)

7. **SCHOOL DAY**
C. Berry
C. Berry, Chess 1653 (Arc, BMI)

8. **GONE**
F. Husky
S. Rogers, Capitol 3628 (Hill & Range, BMI)

9. **LOVE LETTERS IN THE SAND**
P. Boone
N. Kenny–C. Kenny–Coots, Dot 15570 (Bourne, ASCAP)

10. **SO RARE**
J. Dorsey
J. Herst–J. Sharpe, Fraternity 755 (Robbins, ASCAP)

1957

May 27

1. **ALL SHOOK UP**
E. Presley
*O. Blackwell–E. Presley, Victor
20–6870 (Presley–Shalimar,
BMI)*

2. **DARK MOON**
G. Storm
*N. Miller, Dot 15558
(Dandelion, BMI)*

3. **LITTLE DARLIN'**
The Diamonds
*M. Williams, Mercury 71060
(Excellorec, BMI)*

4. **LOVE LETTERS IN THE SAND**
P. Boone
*N. Kenny–C. Kenny–Coots, Dot
15570 (Bourne, ASCAP)*

5. **WHITE SPORT COAT**
M. Robbins
*M. Robbins, Columbia 40864
(Acuff–Rose, BMI)*

6. **ROUND AND ROUND**
P. Como
*L. Stallman–J. Shapiro, Victor
20–6815 (Rush, BMI)*

7. **COME GO WITH ME**
The Del Vikings
*C. E. Quick, Dot 15538
(G. I. Fee–Bee, BMI)*

8. **SCHOOL DAY**
C. Berry
*C. Berry, Chess 1653
(Arc, BMI)*

9. **SO RARE**
J. Dorsey
*J. Herst–J. Sharpe, Fraternity
755 (Robbins, ASCAP)*

10. **FOUR WALLS**
J. Lowe
*M. Moore–G. Campbell, Dot
15569 (Sheldon, BMI)*

June 3

1. **ALL SHOOK UP**
E. Presley
*O. Blackwell–E. Presley
Victor 20–6870
(Presley–Shalimar, BMI)*

2. **DARK MOON**
G. Storm
*N. Miller, Dot 15558
(Dandelion, BMI)*

3. **LOVE LETTERS IN THE SAND**
P. Boone
*N. Kenny–C. Kenny–Coots, Dot
15570 (Bourne, ASCAP)*

4. **LITTLE DARLIN'**
The Diamonds
*M. Williams, Mercury 71060
(Excellorec, BMI)*

5. **WHITE SPORT COAT**
M. Robbins
*M. Robbins, Columbia 40864
(Acuff–Rose, BMI)*

6. **SO RARE**
J. Dorsey
*J. Herst–J. Sharpe, Fraternity
755 (Robbins, ASCAP)*

7. **SCHOOL DAY**
C. Berry
*C. Berry, Chess 1653
(Arc, BMI)*

8. **ROUND AND ROUND**
P. Como
*L. Stallman–J. Shapiro, Victor
20–6815 (Rush, BMI)*

9. **FOUR WALLS**
J. Lowe
*M. Moore–G. Campbell, Dot
15569 (Sheldon, BMI)*

10. **COME GO WITH ME**
The Del Vikings
*C. E. Quick, Dot 15538
(G. I. Fee–Bee, BMI)*

June 10

1. **ALL SHOOK UP**
E. Presley
*O. Blackwell–E. Presley, Victor
20–6870 (Presley–Shalimar,
BMI)*

2. **LOVE LETTERS IN THE SAND**
P. Boone
*N. Kenny–C. Kenny–Coots, Dot
15570 (Bourne, ASCAP)*

3. **DARK MOON**
G. Storm
*N. Miller, Dot 15558
(Dandelion, BMI)*

4. **LITTLE DARLIN'**
The Diamonds
*M. Williams, Mercury 71060
(Excellorec, BMI)*

5. **WHITE SPORT COAT**
M. Robbins
*M. Robbins, Columbia 40864
(Acuff–Rose, BMI)*

6. **SO RARE**
J. Dorsey
*J. Herst–J. Sharpe, Fraternity
755 (Robbins, ASCAP)*

7. **SCHOOL DAY**
C. Berry
*C. Berry, Chess 1653
(Arc, BMI)*

8. **FOUR WALLS**
J. Lowe
*M. Moore–G. Campbell, Dot
15569 (Sheldon, BMI)*

9. **ROUND AND ROUND**
P. Como
*L. Stallman–J. Shapiro, Victor
20–6815 (Rush, BMI)*

10. **COME GO WITH ME**
The Del Vikings
*C. E. Quick, Dot 15538
(G. I. Fee–Bee, BMI)*

June 17

1. **LOVE LETTERS IN THE SAND**
P. Boone
N. Kenny–C. Kenny–Coots, Dot 15570 (Bourne, ASCAP)

2. **ALL SHOOK UP**
E. Presley
O. Blackwell–E. Presley, Victor 20–6870 (Presley–Shalimar, BMI)

3. **DARK MOON**
G. Storm
N. Miller, Dot 15558 (Dandelion, BMI)

4. **SO RARE**
J. Dorsey
J. Herst–J. Sharpe, Fraternity 755 (Robbins, ASCAP)

5. **LITTLE DARLIN'**
The Diamonds
M. Williams, Mercury 71060 (Excellorec, BMI)

6. **WHITE SPORT COAT**
M. Robbins
M. Robbins, Columbia 40864 (Acuff–Rose, BMI)

7. **BYE BYE LOVE**
The Everly Brothers
B. Bryant–F. Bryant, Cadence 1315 (Acuff–Rose, BMI)

8. **SCHOOL DAY**
C. Berry
C. Berry, Chess 1653 (Arc, BMI)

9. **FOUR WALLS**
J. Lowe
M. Moore–G. Campbell, Dot 15569 (Sheldon, BMI)

10 **ROUND AND ROUND**
P. Como
L. Stallman–J. Shapiro, Victor 20–6815 (Rush, BMI)

June 24

1. **LOVE LETTERS IN THE SAND**
P. Boone
N. Kenny–C. Kenny–Coots, Dot 15570 (Bourne, ASCAP)

2. **SO RARE**
J. Dorsey
J. Herst–J. Sharpe, Fraternity 755 (Robbins, ASCAP)

3. **DARK MOON**
G. Storm
N. Miller, Dot 15558 (Dandelion, BMI)

4. **BYE BYE LOVE**
The Everly Brothers
B. Bryant–F. Bryant, Cadence 1315 (Acuff–Rose, BMI)

5. **ALL SHOOK UP**
E. Presley
O. Blackwell–E. Presley, Victor 20–6870 (Presley–Shalimar, BMI)

6. **WHITE SPORT COAT**
M. Robbins
M. Robbins, Columbia 40864 (Acuff–Rose, BMI)

7. **LITTLE DARLIN'**
The Diamonds
M. Williams, Mercury 71060 (Excellorec, BMI)

8. **FOUR WALLS**
J. Lowe
M. Moore–G. Campbell, Dot 15569 (Sheldon, BMI)

9. **VALLEY OF TEARS**
F. Domino
A. Domino–D. Bartholomew, Imperial 5442 (Travis, BMI)

10. **TEENAGER'S ROMANCE**
R. Nelson
Giltam, Verve 10047 (Aztec, ASCAP)

July 1

1. **LOVE LETTERS IN THE SAND**
P. Boone
N. Kenny–C. Kenny–Coots, Dot 15570 (Bourne, ASCAP)

2. **SO RARE**
J. Dorsey
J. Herst–J. Sharpe, Fraternity 755 (Robbins, ASCAP)

3. **DARK MOON**
G. Storm
N. Miller, Dot 15558 (Dandelion, BMI)

4. **BYE BYE LOVE**
The Everly Brothers
B. Bryant–F. Bryant, Cadence 1315 (Acuff–Rose, BMI)

5. **WHITE SPORT COAT**
M. Robbins
M. Robbins, Columbia 40864 (Acuff–Rose, BMI)

6. **TEDDY BEAR**
E. Presley
K. Mann–B. Lowe, Victor 47–700 (Gladys, ASCAP)

7. **ALL SHOOK UP**
E. Presley
O. Blackwell–E. Presley, Victor 20–6870 (Presley–Shalimar, BMI)

8. **SEARCHIN'**
The Coasters
J. Leiber–M. Stoller, Atco 6087 (Tiger, BMI)

9. **OLD CAPE COD**
P. Page
Rogh–Rock–Wakus, Mercury 71101 (Geroge Pinkus and Sons, ASCAP)

10. **IT'S NOT FOR ME TO SAY**
J. Mathis
A. Stillmen–R. Allen, Columbia 40851 (Korwin, ASCAP)

July 8

1. **LOVE LETTERS IN THE SAND**
   P. Boone
   N. Kenny–C. Kenny–Coots, Dot 15570 (Bourne, ASCAP)

2. **SO RARE**
   J. Dorsey
   J. Herst–J. Sharpe, Fraternity 755 (Robbins, ASCAP)

3. **BYE BYE LOVE**
   The Everly Brothers
   B. Bryant–F. Bryant, Cadence 1315 (Acuff–Rose, BMI)

4. **DARK MOON**
   G. Storm
   N. Miller, Dot 15558 (Dandelion, BMI)

5. **TEDDY BEAR**
   E. Presley
   K. Mann–B. Lowe, Victor 47-700 (Gladys, ASCAP)

6. **OLD CAPE COD**
   P. Page
   Rogh–Rock–Wakus, Mercury 71101 (George Pinkus and Sons, ASCAP)

7. **IT'S NOT FOR ME TO SAY**
   J. Mathis
   A. Stillmen–R. Allen, Columbia 40851 (Korwin, ASCAP)

8. **SEARCHIN'**
   The Coasters
   J. Leiber–M. Stoller, Atco 6087 (Tiger, BMI)

9. **WHITE SPORT COAT**
   M. Robbins
   M. Robbins, Columbia 40864 (Acuff–Rose, BMI)

10. **I'M GONNA SIT RIGHT DOWN AND WRITE MYSELF A LETTER**
    B. Williams
    J. Young–F. Ahlert, Coral 61830 (DeSylva–Brown–Henderson, AS-CAP)

July 15

1. **LOVE LETTERS IN THE SAND**
   P. Boone
   N. Kenny–C. Kenny–Coots, Dot 15570 (Bourne, ASCAP)

2. **BYE BYE LOVE**
   The Everly Brothers
   B. Bryant–F. Bryant, Cadence 1315 (Acuff–Rose, BMI)

3. **SO RARE**
   J. Dorsey
   J. Herst–J. Sharpe, Fraternity 755 (Robbins, ASCAP)

4. **TEDDY BEAR**
   E. Presley
   K. Mann–B. Lowe, Victor 47-700 (Gladys, ASCAP)

5. **OLD CAPE COD**
   P. Page
   Rogh–Rock–Wakus, Mercury 71101 (George Pinkus and Sons, ASCAP)

6. **DARK MOON**
   G. Storm
   N. Miller, Dot 15558 (Dandelion, BMI)

7. **IT'S NOT FOR ME TO SAY**
   J. Mathis
   A. Stillmen–R. Allen, Columbia 40851 (Korwin, ASCAP)

8. **I'M GONNA SIT RIGHT DOWN AND WRITE MYSELF A LETTER**
   B. Williams
   J. Young–F. Ahlert, Coral 61830 (DeSylva–Brown–Henderson, AS-CAP)

9. **WHITE SPORT COAT**
   M. Robbins
   M. Robbins, Columbia 40864 (Acuff–Rose, BMI)

10. **AROUND THE WORLD**
    V. Young and B. Crosby
    V. Young, Decca 30262 (Victor Young, ASCAP)

July 22

1. **LOVE LETTERS IN THE SAND**
   Pat Boone
   N. Kenny–C. Kenny–Coots, Dot 15570 (Bourne, ASCAP)

2. **TEDDY BEAR**
   E. Presley
   K. Mann–B. Lowe, Victor 47-700 (Gladys, ASCAP)

3. **BYE BYE LOVE**
   The Everly Brothers
   B. Bryant–F. Bryant, Cadence 1315 (Acuff–Rose, BMI)

4. **SO RARE**
   J. Dorsey
   J. Herst–J. Sharpe, Fraternity 755 (Robbins, ASCAP)

5. **OLD CAPE COD**
   P. Page
   Rogh–Rock–Wakus, Mercury 71101 (George Pinkus and Sons, ASCAP)

6. **I'M GONNA SIT RIGHT DOWN AND WRITE MYSELF A LETTER**
   B. Williams
   J. Young–F. Ahlert, Coral 61830 (DeSylva–Brown–Henderson, AS-CAP)

7. **AROUND THE WORLD**
   V. Young and B. Crosby
   V. Young, Decca 30262 (Victor Young, ASCAP)

8. **IT'S NOT FOR ME TO SAY**
   J. Mathis
   A. Stillmen–R. Allen, Columbia 40851 (Korwin, ASCAP)

9. **DARK MOON**
   G. Storm
   N. Miller, Dot 15558 (Dandelion, BMI)

10. **WHITE SILVER SANDS**
    D. Rondo
    C. Mathews, Jubilee 5288 (Fellow–Peer, BMI)

July 29

1. **LOVE LETTERS IN THE SAND**
   P. Boone
   N. Kenny–C. Kenny–Coots, Dot 15570 (Bourne, ASCAP)

2. **TEDDY BEAR**
   E. Presley
   K. Mann–B. Lowe, Victor 47–700 (Gladys, ASCAP)

3. **SO RARE**
   J. Dorsey
   J. Herst–J. Sharpe, Fraternity 755 (Robbins, ASCAP)

4. **OLD CAPE COD**
   P. Page
   Rogh–Rock–Wakus, Mercury 71101 (George Pinkus and Sons, ASCAP)

5. **BYE BYE LOVE**
   The Everly Brothers
   B. Bryant–F. Bryant, Cadence 1315 (Acuff–Rose, BMI)

6. **I'M GONNA SIT RIGHT DOWN AND WRITE MYSELF A LETTER**
   B. Williams
   J. Young–F. Ahlert, Coral 61830 (DeSylva–Brown–Henderson, AS-CAP)

7. **AROUND THE WORLD**
   V. Young and B. Crosby
   V. Young, Decca 30262 (Victor Young, ASCAP)

8. **IT'S NOT FOR ME TO SAY**
   J. Mathis
   A. Stillmen–R. Allen, Columbia 40851 (Korwin, ASCAP)

9. **TAMMY**
   D. Reynolds
   J. Livingston–R. Evans, Coral 61851 (Northern, ASCAP)

10. **WHITE SILVER SANDS**
    D. Rondo
    C. Mathews, Jubilee 5288 (Fellow–Peer, BMI)

August 5

1. **LOVE LETTERS IN THE SAND**
   P. Boone
   N. Kenny–C. Kenny–Coots, Dot 15570 (Bourne, ASCAP)

2. **TEDDY BEAR**
   E. Presley
   K. Mann–B. Lowe, Victor 47–700 (Gladys, ASCAP)

3. **TAMMY**
   D. Reynolds
   J. Livingston–R. Evans, Coral 61851 (Northern, ASCAP)

4. **BYE BYE LOVE**
   The Everly Brothers
   B. Bryant–F. Bryant, Cadence 1315 (Acuff–Rose, BMI)

5. **I'M GONNA SIT RIGHT DOWN AND WRITE MYSELF A LETTER**
   B. Williams
   J. Young–F. Ahlert, Coral 61830 (DeSylva–Brown–Henderson, AS-CAP)

6. **AROUND THE WORLD**
   V. Young and B. Crosby
   V. Young, Decca 30262 (Victor Young, ASCAP)

7. **OLD CAPE COD**
   P. Page
   Rogh–Rock–Wakus, Mercury 71101 (George Pinkus and Sons, ASCAP)

8. **SO RARE**
   J. Dorsey
   J. Herst–J. Sharpe, Fraternity 755 (Robbins, ASCAP)

9. **IT'S NOT FOR ME TO SAY**
   J. Mathis
   A. Stillmen–R. Allen, Columbia 40851 (Korwin, ASCAP)

10. **WHITE SILVER SANDS**
    D. Rondo
    C. Mathews, Jubilee 5288 (Fellow–Peer, BMI)

August 12

1. **TAMMY**
   D. Reynolds
   J. Livingston–R. Evans, Coral 61851 (Northern, ASCAP)

2. **LOVE LETTERS IN THE SAND**
   P. Boone
   N. Kenny–C. Kenny–Coots, Dot 15570 (Bourne, ASCAP)

3. **I'M GONNA SIT RIGHT DOWN AND WRITE MYSELF A LETTER**
   B. Williams
   J. Young–F. Ahlert, Coral 61830 (DeSylva–Brown–Henderson, AS-CAP)

4. **TEDDY BEAR**
   E. Presley
   K. Mann–B. Lowe, Victor 47–4700 (Gladys, ASCAP)

5. **BYE BYE LOVE**
   The Everly Brothers
   B. Bryant–F. Bryant, Cadence 1315 (Acuff–Rose, BMI)

6. **WHITE SILVER SANDS**
   D. Rondo
   C. Mathews, Jubilee 5288 (Fellow–Peer, BMI)

7. **AROUND THE WORLD**
   V. Young and B. Crosby
   V. Young, Decca 30262 (Victor Young, ASCAP)

8. **OLD CAPE COD**
   P. Page
   Rogh–Rock–Wakus, Mercury 71101 (George Pinkus and Sons, ASCAP)

9. **SO RARE**
   J. Dorsey
   J.Herst–J. Sharpe, Fraternity 755 (Robbins, AS-CAP)

10. **IT'S NOT FOR ME TO SAY**
    J. Mathis
    A. Stillmen–R. Allen, Columbia 40851 (Korwin, ASCAP)

August 19

1. **TAMMY**
D. Reynolds
J. Livingston–R. Evans,
Coral 61851 (Northern, ASCAP)

2. **TEDDY BEAR**
E. Presley
K. Mann–B. Lowe, Victor
47–700 (Gladys, ASCAP)

3. **LOVE LETTERS IN THE SAND**
P. Boone
N. Kenny–C. Kenny–Coots,
Dot 15570 (Bourne, ASCAP)

4. **WHITE SILVER SANDS**
D. Rondo
C. Mathews, Jubilee 5288
(Fellow–Peer, BMI)

5. **I'M GONNA SIT RIGHT DOWN AND WRITE MYSELF A LETTER**
B. Williams
J. Young–F. Ahlert,
Coral 61830 (DeSylva–Brown–
Henderson, ASCAP)

6. **BYE BYE LOVE**
The Everly Brothers
B. Bryant–F. Bryant,
Cadence 1315
(Acuff–Rose, BMI)

7. **AROUND THE WORLD**
V. Young and B. Crosby
V. Young, Decca 30262
(Victor Young, ASCAP)

8. **OLD CAPE COD**
P. Page
Rogh–Rock–Wakus,
Mercury 71101 (George Pinkus
and Sons, ASCAP)

9. **IT'S NOT FOR ME TO SAY**
J. Mathis
A. Stillmen–R. Allen,
Columbia 40851 (Korwin, AS-
CAP)

10. **SO RARE**
J. Dorsey
J. Herst–J. Sharpe,
Fraternity 755 (Robbins, AS-
CAP)

August 26

1. **TAMMY**
D. Reynolds
J. Livingston–R. Evans,
Coral 61851 (Northern, ASCAP)

2. **TEDDY BEAR**
E. Presley
K. Mann–B. Lowe, Victor
47–700 (Gladys, ASCAP)

3. **WHITE SILVER SANDS**
D. Rondo
C. Mathews, Jubilee 5288
(Fellow–Peer, BMI)

4. **AROUND THE WORLD**
V. Young and B. Crosby
V. Young, Decca 30262
(Victor Young, ASCAP)

5. **LOVE LETTERS IN THE SAND**
P. Boone
N. Kenny–C. Kenny–Coots,
Dot 15570 (Bourne, ASCAP)

6. **I'M GONNA SIT RIGHT DOWN AND WRITE MYSELF A LETTER**
B. Williams
J. Young–F. Ahlert, Coral
61830 (DeSylva–Brown–
Henderson, ASCAP)

7. **BYE BYE LOVE**
The Everly Brothers
B. Bryant–F. Bryant,
Cadence 1315
(Acuff–Rose, BMI)

8. **OLD CAPE COD**
P. Page
Rogh–Rock–Wakus, Mercury
71101 (George Pinkus and Sons,

9. **DIANA**
P. Anka
P. Anka, ABC–Paramount
9831 (Pamco, BMI)

10. **RAINBOW**
R. Hamilton
R. Hulme, Kapp 184
(Robbins, ASCAP)

September 2

1. **TAMMY**
D. Reynolds
J. Livingston–R. Evans,
Coral 61851 (Northern,
ASCAP)

2. **TEDDY BEAR**
E. Presley
K. Mann–B. Lowe, Victor
47–700 (Gladys, ASCAP)

3. **AROUND THE WORLD**
V. Young and B. Crosby
V. Young, Decca 30262
(Victor Young, ASCAP)

4. **WHITE SILVER SANDS**
D. Rondo
C. Mathews, Jubilee 5288
(Fellow–Peer, BMI)

5. **DIANA**
P. Anka
P. Anka, ABC–Paramount
9831 (Pamco, BMI)

6. **LOVE LETTERS IN THE SAND**
P. Boone
N. Kenny–C. Kenny–Coots, Dot
15570 (Bourne, ASCAP)

7. **BYE BYE LOVE**
The Everly Brothers
B. Bryant–F. Bryant, Cadence
1315 (Acuff–Rose, BMI)

8. **HONEYCOMB**
J. Rodgers
B. Merrill, Roulette 4015
(Hawthorne, ASCAP)

9. **I'M GONNA SIT RIGHT DOWN AND WRITE MYSELF A LETTER**
B. Williams
J. Young–F. Ahlert, Coral 61830
(DeSylva–Brown–Henderson, AS-
CAP)

10. **THAT'LL BE THE DAY**
B. Holly
J. Allison–B. Holly–N. Petty,
Brunswick 550099 (Nor-Va-Jak,
BMI)

81

September 2

1. **TAMMY**
D. Reynolds
*J. Livingston–R. Evans, Coral
61851 (Northern, ASCAP)*

2. **AROUND THE WORLD**
V. Young and B. Crosby
*V. Young, Decca 30262
(Victor Young, ASCAP)*

3. **DIANA**
P. Anka
*P. Anka, ABC–Paramount 9831
(Pamco, BMI)*

4. **HONEYCOMB**
J. Rodgers
*B. Merrill, Roulette 4015
(Hawthorne, ASCAP)*

5. **TEDDY BEAR**
E. Presley
*K. Mann–B. Lowe, Victor
47-700 (Gladys, ASCAP)*

6. **WHITE SILVER SANDS**
D. Rondo
*C. Mathews, Jubilee 5288
(Fellow–Peer, BMI)*

7. **FASCINATION**
J. Morgan
*S. D. Marchetti–D. Manning,
Kapp 191 (Southern, ASCAP)*

8. **THAT'LL BE THE DAY**
B. Holly
*J. Allison–B. Holly–N. Petty,
Brunswick 55009
(Nor-Va-Jak, BMI)*

9. **WHOLE LOTTA SHAKIN'
GOIN' ON**
J. L. Lewis
*D. Williams–S. David, Sun
267 (Martyn, BMI*

10. **RAINBOW**
R. Hamilton
*R. Hulme, Kapp 184
(Robbins, ASCAP)*

September 16

1. **TAMMY**
D. Reynolds
*J. Livingston–R. Evans, Coral
61851 (Northern, ASCAP)*

2. **DIANA**
P. Anka
*P. Anka, ABC–Paramount 9831
(Pamco, BMI)*

3. **HONEYCOMB**
J. Rodgers
*B. Merrill, Roulette 4015
(Hawthorne, ASCAP)*

4. **FASCINATION**
J. Morgan
*S. D. Marchetti–D. Manning,
Kapp 191 (Southern, ASCAP)*

5. **AROUND THE WORLD**
V. Young and B. Crosby
*V. Young, Decca 30262
(Victor Young, ASCAP)*

6. **THAT'LL BE THE DAY**
B. Holly
*J. Allison–B. Holly–N. Petty,
Brunswick 55009
(Nor-Va-Jak, BMI)*

7. **WHOLE LOTTA SHAKIN'
GOIN' ON**
J. L. Lewis
*D. Williams–S. David, Sun 267
(Martyn, BMI)*

8. **WHITE SILVER SANDS**
D. Rondo
*C. Mathew, Jubilee 5288
(Fellow–Peer, BMI)*

9. **RAINBOW**
R. Hamilton
*R. Hulme, Kapp 184
(Robbins, ASCAP)*

10. **IN THE MIDDLE OF AN IS-
LAND**
T. Bennett
*Varnick–Acquiviva, Columbia
40965 (Mayfair, ASCAP)*

September 23

1. **TAMMY**
D. Reynolds
*J. Livingston–R. Evans, Coral
61851 (Northern, ASCAP)*

2. **HONEYCOMB**
J. Rodgers
*B. Merrill, Roulette 4015
(Hawthorne, ASCAP)*

3. **DIANA**
P. Anka
*P. Anka, ABC–Paramount 9831
(Pamco, BMI)*

4. **THAT'LL BE THE DAY**
B. Holly
*J. Allison–B. Holly–N. Petty,
Brunswick 55009
(Nor-Va-Jak, BMI)*

5. **FASCINATION**
J. Morgan
*S. D. Marchetti–D. Manning,
Kapp 191 (Southern, ASCAP)*

6. **WHOLE LOTTA SHAKIN'
GOIN' ON**
J. L. Lewis
*D. Williams–S. David, Sun 267
(Martyn, BMI)*

7. **IN THE MIDDLE OF AN IS-
LAND**
T. Bennett
*Varnick–Acquiviva, Columbia
40965 (Mayfair, ASCAP)*

8. **AROUND THE WORLD**
V. Young and B. Crosby
*V. Young, Decca 30262
(Victor Young, ASCAP)*

9. **RAINBOW**
R. Hamilton
*R. Hulme, Kapp 184
(Robbins, ASCAP)*

10. **MR. LEE**
The Bobbettes
*The Bobbettes, Atlantic 1144
(Progressive, BMI)*

1957

September 30

1. **TAMMY**
D. Reynolds
*J. Livingston–R. Evans, Coral
61851 (Northern, ASCAP)*

2. **HONEYCOMB**
J. Rodgers
*B. Merrill, Roulette 4015
(Hawthorne, ASCAP)*

3. **DIANA**
P. Anka
*P. Anka, ABC-Paramount 9831
(Pamco, BMI)*

4. **THAT'LL BE THE DAY**
B. Holly
*J. Allison–B. Holly–N. Petty
Brunswick 55009
(Nor-Va-Jak, BMI)*

5. **FASCINATION**
J. Morgan
*S. D. Marchetti–D. Manning,
Kapp 191 (Southern, ASCAP)*

6. **CHANCES ARE**
J. Mathis
*A. Stillmen–R. Allen,
Columbia 40993
(Korwin, ASCAP)*

7. **RAINBOW**
R. Hamilton
*R. Hulme, Kapp 184
(Robbins, ASCAP)*

8. **AROUND THE WORLD**
V. Young and B. Crosby
*V. Young, Decca 30262
(Victor Young, ASCAP)*

9. **IN THE MIDDLE OF AN IS-
LAND**
T. Bennett
*Varnick–Acquiviva, Columbia
40965 (Mayfair, ASCAP)*

10. **WHOLE LOTTA SHAKIN'
GOIN' ON**
J. L. Lewis
*D. Williams–S. David, Sun 267
(Martyn, BMI)*

October 7

1. **HONEYCOMB**
J. Rodgers
*B. Merrill, Roulette 4015
(Hawthorne, ASCAP)*

2. **TAMMY**
D. Reynolds
*J. Livingston–R. Evans, Coral
61851 (Northern, ASCAP)*

3. **DIANA**
P. Anka
*P. Anka, ABC-Paramount 9831
(Pamco, BMI)*

4. **THAT'LL BE THE DAY**
B. Holly
*J. Allison–B. Holly–N. Petty,
Brunswick 55009
(Nor-Va-Jak, BMI)*

5. **FASCINATION**
J. Morgan
*S. D. Marchetti–D. Manning,
Kapp 191 (Southern, ASCAP)*

6. **CHANCES ARE**
J. Mathis
*A. Stillmen–R. Allen, Columbia
40993 (Korwin, ASCAP)*

7. **WAKE UP LITTLE SUSIE**
The Everly Brothers
*F. Bryant–B. Bryant, Cadence
1337 (Acuff–Rose, BMI)*

8. **RAINBOW**
R. Hamilton
*R. Hulme, Kapp 184
(Robbins, ASCAP)*

9. **AROUND THE WORLD**
V. Young and B. Crosby
*V. Young, Decca 30262
(Victor Young, ASCAP)*

10. **WHOLE LOTTA SHAKIN'
GOIN' ON**
J. L. Lewis
*D. Williams–S. David, Sun 267
(Martyn, BMI)*

October 14

1. **WAKE UP LITTLE SUSIE**
The Everly Brothers
*F. Bryant–B. Bryant, Cadence
1337 (Acuff–Rose, BMI)*

2. **HONEYCOMB**
J. Rodgers
*B. Merrill, Roulette 4015
(Hawthorn, ASCAP)*

3. **CHANCES ARE**
J. Mathis
*A. Stillmen–R. Allen, Columbia
40993 (Korwin, ASCAP)*

4. **TAMMY**
D. Reynolds
*J. Livingston–R. Evans, Coral
61851 (Northern, ASCAP)*

5. **FASCINATION**
J. Morgan
*S. D. Marchetti–D. Manning,
Kapp 191 (Southern, ASCAP)*

6. **DIANA**
P. Anka
*P. Anka, ABC-Paramount 9831
(Pamco, BMI)*

7. **THAT'LL BE THE DAY**
B. Holly
*J. Allison–B. Holly–N. Petty,
Brunswick 55009
(Nor-Va-Jak, BMI)*

8. **WHITE SILVER SANDS**
D. Rondo
*C. Mathews, Jubilee 5288
(Fellow–Peer, BMI)*

9. **MY HEART REMINDS ME**
D. Reese
*A. Stillmen–C. Bargoni,
Jubilee 5292
(Symphony House, ASCAP)*

10. **JAILHOUSE ROCK**
E. Presley
*J. Leiber–M. Stoller, Victor 7035
(Elvis Presley, BMI)*

October 21

1. **WAKE UP LITTLE SUSIE**
   The Everly Brothers
   F. Bryant–B. Bryant, Cadence 1337 (Acuff–Rose, BMI)
2. **JAILHOUSE ROCK**
   E. Presley
   J. Leiber–M. Stoller, Victor 7035 (Elvis Presley, BMI)
3. **HONEYCOMB**
   J. Rodgers
   B. Merrill, Roulette 4015 (Hawthorne, ASCAP)
4. **TAMMY**
   D. Reynolds
   J. Livingston–R. Evans, Coral 61851 (Northern, ASCAP)
5. **CHANCES ARE**
   J. Mathis
   A. Stillmen–R. Allen, Columbia 40993 (Korwin, ASCAP)
6. **FASCINATION**
   J. Morgan
   S. D. Marchetti–D. Manning, Kapp 191 (Southern, ASCAP)
7. **DIANA**
   P. Anka
   P. Anka, ABC–Paramount 9831 (Pamco, BMI)
8. **THAT'LL BE THE DAY**
   B. Holly
   J. Allison–B. Holly–N. Petty, Brunswick 55009 (Nor-Va-Jak, BMI)
9. **MY HEART REMINDS ME**
   D. Reese
   A. Stillman–C. Bargoni, Jubilee 5292 (Symphony House, ASCAP)
10. **AROUND THE WORLD**
    V. Young and B. Crosby
    V. Young, Decca 30262 (Victor Young, ASCAP)

October 28

1. **WAKE UP LITTLE SUSIE**
   The Everly Brothers
   F. Bryant–B. Bryant, Cadence 1337 (Acuff–Rose, BMI)
2. **JAILHOUSE ROCK**
   E. Presley
   J. Leiber–M. Stoller, Victor 7035 (Elvis Presley, BMI)
3. **CHANCES ARE**
   J. Mathis
   A. Stillmen–R. Allen Columbia 40993 (Korwin, ASCAP)
4. **TAMMY**
   D. Reynolds
   J. Livingston–R. Evans, Coral 61851 (Northern, ASCAP)
5. **HONEYCOMB**
   J. Rodgers
   B. Merrill, Roulette 4015 (Hawthorne, ASCAP)
6. **FASCINATION**
   J. Morgan
   S. D. Marchetti–D. Manning, Kapp 191 (Southern, ASCAP)
7. **SILHOUETTES**
   The Rays
   Slay–Crewe, Cameo 117 (Regent, BMI)
8. **BE-BOP BABY**
   R. Nelson
   P. Longhurst, Imperial 5463 (Travis, BMI)
9. **MELODIE D'AMOUR**
   The Ames Brothers
   L. Johns–H. Salvador, Victor 7046 (Rayven, BMI)
10. **DIANA**
    P. Anka
    P. Anka ABC–Paramount 9831 (Pamco, BMI)

November 4

1. **JAILHOUSE ROCK**
   E. Presley
   J. Leiber–M. Stoller, Victor 7035 (Elvis Presley, BMI)
2. **CHANCES ARE**
   J. Mathis
   A. Stillmen–R. Allen, Columbia 40993 (Korwin, ASCAP)
3. **WAKE UP LITTLE SUSIE**
   The Everly Brothers
   F. Bryant–B. Bryant, Cadence 1337 (Acuff–Rose, BMI)
4. **TAMMY**
   D. Reynolds
   J. Livingston–R. Evans, Coral 61851 (Northern, ASCAP)
5. **HONEYCOMB**
   J. Rodgers
   B. Merrill, Roulette 4015 (Hawthorne, ASCAP)
6. **FASCINATION**
   J. Morgan
   S. D. Marchetti–D. Manning, Kapp 191 (Southern, ASCAP)
7. **SILHOUETTES**
   The Rays
   Slay–Crewe, Cameo 117 (Regent, BMI)
8. **BE-BOP BABY**
   R. Nelson
   F. Longhurst, Imperial 5463 (Travis, BMI)
9. **MELODIE D'AMOUR**
   The Ames Brothers
   L. Johns–H. Salvador, Victor 7046 (Rayven, BMI)
10. **YOU SEND ME**
    S. Cooke
    L. C. Cooke, Keen 34013 (Highvera, BMI)

1957

November 11	November 18	November 25

November 11

1. **JAILHOUSE ROCK**
E. Presley
J. Leiber–M. Stoller, Victor 7045 (Elvis Presley, BMI)

2. **WAKE UP LITTLE SUSIE**
The Everly Brothers
F. Bryant–B. Bryant, Cadence 1337 (Acuff–Rose, BMI)

3. **CHANCES ARE**
J. Mathis
A. Stillmen–R. Allen, Columbia 40993 (Korwin, ASCAP)

4. **YOU SEND ME**
S. Cooke
L. C. Cooke, Keen 34013 (Highvera, BMI)

5. **SILHOUETTES**
The Rays
Slay–Crewe Cameo 117 (Regent, BMI)

6. **FASCINATION**
J. Morgan
S. D. Marchetti–D. Manning, Kapp 191 (Southern, ASCAP)

7. **APRIL LOVE**
P. Boone
Fain–Webster, Dot 15560 (Leo Feist, ASCAP)

8. **TAMMY**
D. Reynolds
J. Livingston–R. Evans, Coral 61851 (Northern, ASCAP)

9. **MELODIE D'AMOUR**
The Ames Brothers
L. Johns–H. Salvador, Victor 7046 (Rayven, BMI)

10. **HONEYCOMB**
J. Rodgers
B. Merrill, Roulette 4015 (Hawthorne, ASCAP)

November 18

1. **JAILHOUSE ROCK**
E. Presley
J. Leiber–M. Stoller, Victor 7045 (Elvis Presley, BMI)

2. **WAKE UP LITTLE SUSIE**
The Everly Brothers
F. Bryant–B. Bryant, Cadence 1337 (Acuff–Rose, BMI)

3. **SILHOUETTES**
The Rays
Slay–Crewe, Cameo 117 (Regent, BMI)

4. **CHANCES ARE**
J. Mathis
A. Stillmen–R. Allen, Columbia 40993 (Korwin, ASCAP)

5. **YOU SEND ME**
S. Cooke
L. C. Cooke, Keen 34013 (Highvera, BMI)

6. **APRIL LOVE**
P. Boone
Fain–Webster, Dot 15660 (Leo Feist, ASCAP)

7. **FASCINATION**
J. Morgan
S. D. Marchetti–D. Manning, Kapp 191 (Southern, ASCAP)

8. **BE-BOP BABY**
R. Nelson
P. Longhurst, Imperial 5463 (Travis, BMI)

9. **MY SPECIAL ANGEL**
B. Helms
J. Duncan, Decca 30423 (Merge, BMI)

10. **TAMMY**
D. Reynolds
J. Livingston–R. Evans, Coral 61851 (Northern, ASCAP)

November 25

1. **YOU SEND ME**
S. Cooke
L. C. Cooke, Keen 34013 (Highvera, BMI)

2. **JAILHOUSE ROCK**
E. Presley
J. Leiber–M. Stoller, Victor 7045 (Elvis Presley, BMI)

3. **WAKE UP LITTLE SUSIE**
The Everly Brothers
F. Bryant–B. Bryant, Cadence 1337 (Acuff–Rose, BMI)

4. **SILHOUETTES**
The Rays
Slay–Crewe, Cameo 117 (Regent, BMI)

5. **APRIL LOVE**
P. Boone
Fain–Webster, Dot 15660 (Leo Feist, ASCAP)

6. **CHANCES ARE**
J. Mathis
A. Stillmen–R. Allen, Columbia 40993 (Korwin, ASCAP)

7. **FASCINATION**
J. Morgan
S. D. Marchetti–D. Manning, Kapp 191 (Southern, ASCAP)

8. **BE-BOP BABY**
R. Nelson
P. Longhurst, Imperial 5463 (Travis, BMI)

9. **MELODIE D'AMOUR**
The Ames Brothers
L. Johns–H. Salvador, Victor 7046 (Rayven, BMI)

10. **RAUNCHY**
B. Justis
Justis–Manker, Phillips International 3519 (Hi-Lo, BMI)

December 2

1. **YOU SEND ME**
S. Cooke
L. C. Cooke, Keen 34013
(Highvera, BMI)

2. **JAILHOUSE ROCK**
E. Presley
J. Leiber–M. Stoller,
Victor 7045 (Elvis Presley, BMI)

3. **SILHOUETTES**
The Rays
Slay–Crewe, Cameo 117
(Regent, BMI)

4. **APRIL LOVE**
P. Boone
Fain–Webster, Dot 15660
(Leo Feist, ASCAP)

5. **RAUNCHY**
B. Justis
Justis–Manker, Phillips
International 3519
(Hi-Lo, BMI)

6. **WAKE UP LITTLE SUSIE**
The Everly Brothers
F. Bryant–B. Bryant, Cadence
1337 (Acuff–Rose, BMI)

7. **CHANCES ARE**
J. Mathis
A. Stillmen–R. Allen,
Columbia 40993 (Korwin,
ASCAP)

8. **FASCINATION**
J. Morgan
S. D. Marchetti–D. Manning,
Kapp 191 (Southern, ASCAP)

9. **MELODIE D'AMOUR**
The Ames Brothers
L. Johns–H. Salvador, Victor
7046 (Rayven, BMI)

10. **ALL THE WAY**
F. Sinatra
S. Cahn–J. VanHeusen, Capitol
3793 (Maraville, ASCAP)

December 9

1. **APRIL LOVE**
P. Boone
Fain–Webster, Dot 15660
(Leo Feist, ASCAP)

2. **RAUNCHY**
B. Justis
Justis–Manker, Phillips
International 3519
(Hi-Lo, BMI)

3. **YOU SEND ME**
S. Cooke
L. C. Cooke, Keen 34013
(Highvera, BMI)

4. **JAILHOUSE ROCK**
E. Presley
J. Leiber–M. Stoller, Victor
7045 (Elvis Presley, BMI)

5. **ALL THE WAY**
F. Sinatra
S. Cahn–J. VanHeusen, Capitol
3793 (Maraville, ASCAP)

6. **SILHOUETTES**
The Rays
Slay–Crewe, Cameo 117
(Regent, BMI)

7. **CHANCES ARE**
J. Mathis
A. Stillmen–R. Allen, Columbia
40993 (Korwin, ASCAP)

8. **FASCINATION**
J. Morgan
S. D. Marchetti–D. Manning,
Kapp 191 (Southern, ASCAP)

9. **WAKE UP LITTLE SUSIE**
The Everly Brothers
F. Bryant–B. Bryant, Cadence
1337 (Acuff–Rose, BMI)

10. **KISSES SWEETER THAN WINE**
J. Rodgers
P. Campbell–J. Newman,
Roulette
4031 (Folkways, BMI)

December 16

1. **RAUNCHY**
B. Justis
Justis–Manker, Phillips
International 3519
(Hi-Lo, BMI)

2. **APRIL LOVE**
P. Boone
Fain–Webster, Dot 15560
(Leo Feist, ASCAP)

3. **YOU SEND ME**
S. Cooke
L. C. Cooke, Keen 34013
(Highvera, BMI)

4. **ALL THE WAY**
F. Sinatra
S. Cahn–J. VanHeusen, Capitol
3793 (Maraville, ASCAP)

5. **JAILHOUSE ROCK**
E. Presley
J. Leiber–M. Stoller, Victor
7045 (Elvis Presley, BMI)

6. **KISSES SWEETER THAN WINE**
J. Rodgers
P. Campbell–J. Newman,
Roulette 4031 (Folkways, BMI)

7. **SILHOUETTES**
The Rays
Slay–Crewe, Cameo 117
(Regent, BMI)

8. **PEGGY SUE**
B. Holly
J. Allison–N. Petty, Coral
61885 (Nor-Va-Jak, BMI)

9. **CHANCES ARE**
J. Mathis
A. Stillmen–R. Allen,
Columbia 40993
(Korwin, ASCAP)

10. **FASCINATION**
J. Morgan
S. D. Marchetti–D. Manning,
Kapp 191 (Southern, ASCAP)

December 23

1. **RAUNCHY**
B. Justis
Justis–Manker, Phillips
International 3519
(Hi-Lo, BMI)

2. **APRIL LOVE**
P. Boone
Fain–Webster, Dot 15660
(Leo Feist, ASCAP)

3. **YOU SEND ME**
S. Cooke
L. C. Cooke, Keen 34013
(Highvera, BMI)

4. **ALL THE WAY**
F. Sinatra
S. Cahn–J. Van Heusen,
Capitol 3793 (Maraville,
ASCAP)

5. **JAILHOUSE ROCK**
E. Presley
J. Leiber–M. Stoller, Victor
7045 (Elvis Presley, BMI)

6. **KISSES SWEETER THAN
WINE**
J. Rodgers
P. Campbell–J. Newman,
Roulette 4031 (Folkways, BMI)

7. **SILHOUETTES**
The Rays
Slay–Crewe, Cameo 117
(Regent, BMI)

8. **PEGGY SUE**
B. Holly
J. Allison–N. Petty, Coral
61885 (Nor-Va-Jak, BMI)

9. **CHANCES ARE**
J. Mathis
A. Stillmen–R. Allen,
Columbia 40993 (Korwin,
ASCAP)

10. **AT THE HOP**
Danny and the Juniors
Singer–Medora–White, ABC–
Paramount 9871 (Singular,
BMI)

December 30

1. **APRIL LOVE**
P. Boone
Fain–Webster, Dot 15560
(Leo Feist, ASCAP)

2. **RAUNCHY**
B. Justis
Justis–Manker, Phillips
International 3519
(Hi-Lo, BMI)

3. **YOU SEND ME**
S. Cooke
L. C. Cooke, Keen 34013
(Highvera, BMI)

4. **KISSES   SWEETER   THAN
WINE**
J. Rodgers
P. Campbell–J. Newman,
Roulette 4031   (Folkways, BMI)

5. **ALL THE WAY**
F. Sinatra
S. Cahn–J. VanHeusen, Capitol
3793 (Maraville, ASCAP)

6. **PEGGY SUE**
B. Holly
J. Allison–N. Petty, Coral
61885 (Nor-Va-Jak, BMI)

7. **JAILHOUSE ROCK**
E. Presley
J. Leiber–M. Stoller, Victor
7045 (Elvis Presley, BMI)

8. **AT THE HOP**
Danny and the Juniors
Singer–Medora–White, ABC–
Paramount 9871 (Singular,
BMI)

9. **GREAT BALLS OF FIRE**
J. L. Lewis
J. Hammer–O. Blackwell, Sun
281 (BRS, BMI)

10. **SILHOUETTES**
The Rays
Slay–Crewe, Cameo 117
(Regent, BMI)

CHUCK BERRY

We were still bucking the adults in 1958, but ultimately it would prove to be the year that we came into power. By December we would shed our bobby socks, make it on TV and Broadway and see dozens of kids become rock and roll stars, writers and producers.

As usual, there were the constant jabs at rock and roll by the adults. Now the critics said the decline had set in. As evidence they pointed to songs like "It's All in the Game" and "Volare" which they said were not rock and roll. They also gloated over the revival of "Smoke Gets in Your Eyes," saying we had to go back to their music for the big hits. Another victory for the adult world was that lovely young man Van Cliburn, who played fine music and proved to the world that American youth was as cultured as European youth. The twenty-three-year-old Texan was given a ticker-tape parade in New York after winning first prize in the International Tchaikovsky Competition in Moscow. Surely, New Yorkers would have thrown more than ticker tape at rock and roll's favorite Texan, the Big Bopper.

The perennial favorite of our mothers and grandmothers, Pat Boone, was still in the spotlight in 1958. Boone, who counted among his claims to fame a great-great-great-great–grandfather named Daniel, wrote the Number 2 nonfiction best seller of the year, '*Twixt Twelve and Twenty.*' In it he made some comments about morality for teens that only a mother could love. About kissing he said, "Kissing for fun is like playing with a beautiful candle in a roomful of dynamite! . . . I really think it's better to amuse ourselves in some other way . . . I say go bowling, or to a basketball game."

In other sports: The Yankees won the World Series, Ohio State won the Rose Bowl, Sugar Ray regained his title. Silky Sullivan was the horse-racing highlight of the year. He was the horse

1958

It's got a good beat . . . You can dance to it . . . I like the words . . . I'll give it a 98.

Bobby, 14
American Bandstand

that would drop back forty lengths, then sprint and win.

Most girls cared more about the boys who were spectators than about the sports. Our favorite sport was catching boys to go steady. And the trophy was usually a high school ring to wear on a chain around your neck. This custom lasted all through the years of rock and roll. In some neighborhoods, a girl wore her steady's ring on a bracelet or on her finger. There were two popular ways to get the boy's ring small enough to fit: you could wrap the ring with brightly colored angora yarn or wrap it tightly with string and cover the string with clear nail polish.

Elvis sang the greatest tribute to the high school ring:

> Won't you wear my ring
> Around your neck
> To show the world
> I'm yours, by heck!

Parenthetically, his failure to mention that she should hang the ring on a chain makes you think that either he had very fat fingers or she had a very small neck.

Younger kids imitated the going steady rituals by trading friendship rings. In some places steadies traded identification bracelets. But Adults were violently opposed to going steady or even going together. Few even grasped the distinction that "going steadily" or "going together" were less formal than "going steady," which required giving a class ring and could last a whole school year.

Even if we could follow the changing steadies, it was hard to keep up with all the changes in fashion. Almost no girls wore bobby sox to sock hops in 1958. White socks were finally giving way to colored tights. We wore matching bulky sweaters and tights, usually in red or turquoise, with plaid pleated kilts. For dress, it was the sack, and for the less daring of us, the blouson. Most of us were old enough to wear heels in 1958,

and they were getting lower and easier to walk in. For the prom, all the girls had to have balloon skirts and fluffy hairdos. We turned in our bobby pins and pincurls for rollers, so we could set our hair in bubbles and pageboy fluffs. For the special twenties' look, we pulled our headbands down onto our foreheads to make headache bands. On Saturday afternoons we were all wearing pedal pushers or capris, crew neck sweaters and car coats. Some of us even tried low shoe-boots with slacks, although most of us stuck with saddles or loafers.

As in fashion, there was revolution in the record world. Aside from the change in the price of 45 rpm records from 98 cents to 89 cents, there was the introduction of stereo. Previously, stereophonic sound could only be achieved with tape recording but in May, 1958, stereophonic records became available. It wasn't until midsummer that stereo record players were on sale everywhere.

Even with the introduction of stereo, most of us still played our 45's on our $20. portable record players. Very little of our music was taken seriously enough to record on this grand new device.

Television changed as much as the record industry in 1958. Of course, there were still twenty-one adult Westerns left over from the 1957 season. And 11 more were added in 1958. The Olympics said it for the networks that year when they sang:

> To save my soul I can't get a date
> My baby's got it tuned on Channel eight
> Wyatt Earp and big Cheyenne
> Comin' thru the TV; shootin' up this land
> My baby loves the western movies.
> TV had some slick Easterners back from

1957. There was Peter Lawford, The Thin Man, the perennial Perry Como, who also had two Top 10 hits ("Catch a Falling Star" and "Kewpie Doll") and Jack Paar, who was rumored to receive $200,000 in 1958 for doing the "Tonight Show."

"Your Hit Parade" made a last feeble attempt to stay alive with a revamped format starring Johnny Desmond and Dorothy Collins. But it was just too absurd to watch them sing "Splish, Splash" and "Willie and the Hand Jive."

The quiz shows, which were fading in 1957, grew into the great TV scandal of 1958. The last of the quiz shows were quickly taken off the air, and many of the people involved were criminally prosecuted.

On the brighter side for the industry was the first use of videotape, which revolutionized TV by freeing production from slow, staged kinescoping and the often clumsy and embarrassing live broadcasting.

1958 may have been the biggest year for the "Arthur Murray Party," but for us the Murray's smooth ballroom style held no fascination. Every weekday afternoon we watched our own kind of dance show, "American Bandstand."

"Bandstand" had started locally in Philadelphia in 1952. The dancing on camera is supposed to have been the spontaneous idea of the kids in the studio. Dick Clark became the host in 1956, and in 1957, "American Bandstand" was picked up by the ABC network.

By 1958, "American Bandstand" was more popular than the hoola hoop. The 8.5 million kids who watched faithfully made it the Number 1 daytime show. "American Bandstand" became a way of life for many of us. The kids on the show set the styles of dance, clothing, slang and music. Every time Carol changed her hairdo, we rushed to the mirror to experiment. We wanted to know who was friends with who, and which couples

were going steady. We all followed the ups and downs of Arlene and Kenny. And there was Justine (She's supposed to have become a model) and the twins Arlene and Bobby, and little Peggy, who was such a good dancer, and beautiful blonde Fran and Mike with those haunting eyes and Yvette and her sister Carmen with the blonde streak.

Those were the kids all American teens studied. Every day we watched them push to the front line of dancers to be on camera and show off that special "Bandstand" way of bouncing as they danced.

They taught us how to Lindy, and in 1958, how to stroll. In the next few years they would introduce us to the twist, the pony and the fly before the adults ever heard of the Peppermint Twist.

"American Bandstand" also gave us a chance to see our rock and roll heroes perform, or, at least mouth their records. And Dick Clark was great at interviewing them so we could hear them talk and find out that they were real people. Except for the famous Alan Freed shows at the Brooklyn Fox Theater in New York, "American Bandstand" was as close as we could get to the sources of rock and roll.

Dick Clark's Saturday night show started in February, 1958. It was a rock and roll stage show with all the big stars on to mouth their latest records. On the first Saturday show were Pat Boone, Chuck Willis, Jerry Lee Lewis, Connie Francis and the Royal Teens. Incidentally, the Royal Teens featured Al Kooper, who was later to play with the Blues Project, Blood, Sweat and Tears and eventually would make it on his own.

At the first Dick Clark nighttime show, he filled a few front rows with regulars from the daytime show to show the endorsement of our friends from "Bandstand." Dick Clark also had a

Sunday evening panel show called "Take a Good Look," but it never was as popular as his other two shows.

The Broadway theater was naturally slower to respond to teenagers than television. Generally it was still dominated by such adult-type entertainment as *Flower Drum Song,* which had advance sales of $1 million before it opened in New York. But there was some indication that the theater might become sensitive to the interests of kids when *Blue Denim* opened. It was a teenager's love story and starred sixteen-year-old Carol Lynley. Unfortunately, it would be about the only Broadway play to reach our age group until we grew into *Barefoot in the Park.*

It was the first year of transistor radios. Actually, we had the new space program to thank for this great step toward twenty-four-hour-a-day rock and roll. The space program had to miniaturize electronic equipment so that spacecraft could be small and light enough to be lifted out of of the atmosphere. In 1958 there was still a great deal of doubt as to whether the United States could build rockets with the thrust to carry great weight enormous distances. And for this the transistor was perfected.

Transistor radios kept us in constant contact with the world. About every thirty minutes our favorite deejay was rudely interrupted by the most up-to-the-minute news and headlines.

Most of us didn't care very much about the news, but in five–minute doses we became well aware that in the Soviet Union Khrushchev succeeded Bulganin as premier, that Tito of Yugolavia was taking a stand for independence from Moscow, that the USS *Nautilus* completed the first crossing of the North Pole under the polar icecap, that Pope Pius XII died and Pope John XXIII was elected as his successor, that the Fifth French Republic was established and DeGaulle

was elected president and that last year's glamor man Mike Todd was killed in a plane crash.

And there was other news that droned on for weeks between records and raucous disc jockeys: the continuing recession, the Sherman Adams scandal, the stoning of Nixon during his South American tour, the dual between the federal government and local Southern governments over desegregation.

Throughout the year the news was full of the ups and downs of the United States space program from Explorer I, the first American satellite, through two Pioneer moon probes that didn't get halfway to the moon, to the Atlas communications satellite that transmitted Eisenhower's Christmas peace message around the world.

A worldwide peace was still a crazy dream in 1958, with the continued fighting in the Middle East and Cuba, the continuing Cold War, the West's refusal to end the occupation of Berlin as the Russian's had proposed, and the United States announcement that Quemoy and Matsu would be defended if there were fighting there between the Chinese Communists and Nationalists.

The news story that grabbed us came in April, when Elvis Presley was drafted into the Army. We all ached suitably when his beautiful hair was barbered, but happily his songs were still coming out. And by now there were enough other performers to keep us fairly satisfied.

Some of the greatest names in rock and roll were sprinkled through the charts in 1958 . . . names like the Everly Brothers, the Platters, Rick Nelson, the Coasters, Jerry Lee Lewis, the Kingston Trio, Bobby Darin, Buddy Holly, Sam Cooke, Chuck Berry, Duane Eddy and Elvis Presley. Rock and roll was beginning to have a true, lasting aristocracy. The old crack that rock and roll singers were no-talent-flashes-in-the-pan was being disproved.

And perhaps the greatest rock and roll mogul got started in 1958. Phil Spector, eighteen years old and a student at Fairfax High School in Los Angeles, wanted to be a court reporter but instead became a singer, writer, producer and millionaire. Spector joined with a few kids from high school to become the Teddy Bears, the group that recorded "To Know Him Is To Love Him." That title is said to have been Spector's father's epitaph.

With success, rock and roll moved to the city. Until 1958 the big-city recording talent was mostly concentrating on "good" music. But after Nashville and the small companies proved that rock and roll could be lucrative, the powerful city slickers moved in. The capital was Philadelphia. It is hard to say whether "American Bandstand" or Philadelphia music came first, but there is no doubt that it was the powerful influence of "American Bandstand" and Dick Clark that made the young Philadelphians our idols in 1958.

We were very susceptible to these dark handsome young men. They were just like the boys we wished we were dating—sexy, but not rough like Elvis. We didn't really care if Fabian, Bobby Rydell, Freddy Cannon or Frankie Avalon could sing. Some could, others were hopeless. But their songs were so simple it was hard to lose the tune, and it was their presence, not their singing, that we adored. Their rise would peak in 1959, and they would be, as our parents predicted, flashes in the pan. Many deserted the rolls of rock singers and courted the adult audiences. Few met with much success. And those of us who had been their fans would remember them with a flush of embarrassment because our squeals were so childish, because their singing was so pat and because, for a moment, we were taken in the purest commercialism.

It was a step away from innocence, but nothing like the one we would take in 1959 when the payola scandals would rock us but would prove that our music was solid enough to survive.

The Top Fifty
1958

1. **ALL I HAVE TO DO IS DREAM** — The Everly Brothers
2. **WITCH DOCTOR** — D. Seville
3. **PATRICIA** — P. Prado
4. **VOLARE** — D. Modugno
5. **TEQUILA** — The Champs
6. **IT'S ALL IN THE GAME** — T. Edwards
7. **RETURN TO ME** — D. Martin
8. **DON'T/I BEG OF YOU** — E. Presley
9. **GET A JOB** — The Silhouettes
10. **LITTLE STAR** — The Elegants
11. **TWILIGHT TIME** — The Platters
12. **HE'S GOT THE WHOLE WORLD IN HIS HANDS** — L. London
13. **AT THE HOP** — Danny and the Juniors
14. **RAUNCHY** — B. Justis
15. **APRIL LOVE** — P. Boone
16. **GREAT BALLS OF FIRE** — J. L. Lewis
17. **THE PURPLE PEOPLE EATER** — S. Wooley
18. **CATCH A FALLING STAR** — P. Como
19. **SAIL ALONG SILVERY MOON** — B. Vaughn
20. **ROCK-IN ROBIN** — B. Day
21. **POOR LITTLE FOOL** — R. Nelson
22. **YAKETY YAK** — The Coasters
23. **IT'S ONLY MAKE BELIEVE** — C. Twitty
24. **BIRD DOG** — The Everly Brothers
25. **STOOD UP** — R. Nelson
26. **SECRETLY** — J. Rodgers
27. **WEAR MY RING AROUND YOUR NECK** — E. Presley
28. **SUGARTIME** — The McGuire Sisters
29. **THE STROLL** — The Diamonds
30. **SPLISH SPLASH** — B. Darin
31. **LOLLIPOP** — The Chordettes
32. **SHORT SHORTS** — The Royal Teens
33. **TEARS ON MY PILLOW** — Little Anthony and the Imperials
34. **BOOK OF LOVE** — The Monotones
35. **TOPSY II** — C. Cole
36. **TOM DOOLEY** — The Kingston Trio
37. **SWEET LITTLE SIXTEEN** — C. Berry
38. **JUST A DREAM** — J. Clanton
39. **DO YOU WANT TO DANCE** — B. Freeman
40. **WHO'S SORRY NOW?** — C. Francis
41. **OH, JULIE** — The Crescendos
42. **REBEL-ROUSER** — D. Eddy
43. **MY TRUE LOVE** — J. Scott
44. **WHEN** — The Kalin Twins
45. **TO KNOW HIM IS TO LOVE HIM** — The Teddy Bears
46. **LOOKING BACK** — Nat (King) Cole
47. **TEA FOR TWO CHA CHA** — Tommy Dorsey Orchestra
48. **ENDLESS SLEEP** — J. Reynolds
49. **OH, LONESOME ME** — D. Gibson
50. **HARD HEADED WOMAN** — E. Presley

January 6

1. **APRIL LOVE**
P. Boone
*Fain–Webster, Dot 15660
(Leo Feist, ASCAP)*

2. **RAUNCHY**
B. Justis
*Justis–Manker, Phillips
International 3519
(Hi-Lo, BMI)*

3. **YOU SEND ME**
S. Cooke
*L. C. Cooke, Keen 34013
(Highvera, BMI)*

4. **KISSES SWEETER THAN
WINE**
J. Rodgers
*P. Campbell–J. Newman,
Roulette 4031 (Folkways, BMI)*

5. **ALL THE WAY**
F. Sinatra
*S. Cahn–J. VanHeusen,
Capitol 3793 (Maraville,
ASCAP)*

6. **PEGGY SUE**
B. Holly
*J. Allison–N. Petty, Coral
61885 (Nor-Va-Jak, BMI)*

7. **AT THE HOP**
Danny and the Juniors
*Singer–Medora–White, ABC–
Paramount 9871 (Singular, BMI)*

8. **GREAT BALLS OF FIRE**
J. L. Lewis
*J. Hammer–O. Blackwell, Sun
281 (BRS, BMI)*

9. **JINGLE BELL ROCK**
B. Helms
*J. Beal–J. Boothe, Decca
35013 (Cornell, BMI)*

10. **JAILHOUSE ROCK**
E. Presley
*J. Leiber–M. Stoller, Victor
7035 (Elvis Presley, BMI)*

January 13

1. **AT THE HOP**
Danny and the Juniors
*Singer–Medora–White, ABC–
Paramount 9871 (Singular,
BMI)*

2. **APRIL LOVE**
P. Boone
*Fain–Webster, Dot 15560
(Leo Feist, ASCAP)*

3. **RAUNCHY**
B. Justis
*Justis–Manker, Phillips
International 3519
(Hi-Lo, BMI)*

4. **PEGGY SUE**
B. Holly
*J. Allison–N. Petty,
Coral 61885 (Nor-Va-Jak, BMI)*

5. **KISSES SWEETER THAN
WINE**
J. Rodgers
*P. Campbell–J. Newman,
Roulette 4031 (Folkways, BMI)*

6. **GREAT BALLS OF FIRE**
J. L. Lewis
*J. Hammer–O. Blackwell,
Sun 281 (BRS, BMI)*

7. **ALL THE WAY**
F. Sinatra
*S. Cahn–J. VanHeusen, Capitol
3793 (Maraville, ASCAP)*

8. **JINGLE BELL ROCK**
B. Helms
*J. Beal–J. Boothe, Decca 30513
(Cornell, ASCAP)*

9. **WHY DON'T THEY UNDER-
STAND**
G. Hamilton IV
*J. Henderson–J. Fishman, ABC–
Paramount 9862 (Hollis, BMI)*

10. **YOU SEND ME**
S. Cooke
*L. C. Cooke, Keen 34013
(Highvera, BMI)*

January 20

1. **AT THE HOP**
Danny and the Juniors
Singer–Medora–White, ABC–
Paramount 9871 (Singular,
BMI)

2. **APRIL LOVE**
P. Boone
Fain–Webster, Dot 15660
(Leo Feist, ASCAP)

3. **RAUNCHY**
B. Justis
Justis–Manker, Phillips
International 3519
(Hi-Lo, BMI)

4. **PEGGY SUE**
B. Holly
J. Allison–M. Petty, Coral
61885 (Nor-Va-Jak, BMI)

5. **KISSES SWEETER THAN WINE**
J. Rodgers
P. Campbell–J. Newman,
Roulette 4031 (Folkways, BMI)

6. **SUGARTIME**
The McGuire Sisters
C. Phillips–O. Echols, Coral
61924 (Nor-Va-Jak, BMI)

7. **ALL THE WAY**
F. Sinatra
S. Cahn–J. VanHeusen, Capitol
3793 (Maraville, ASCAP)

8. **GREAT BALLS OF FIRE**
J. L. Lewis
J. Hammer–O. Blackwell, Sun
281 (BRS, BMI)

9. **WHY DON'T THEY UNDERSTAND**
G. Hamilton IV
J. Henderson–J. Fishman, ABC–
Paramount 9862 (Hollis, BMI)

10. **YOU SEND ME**
S. Cooke
L. C. Cooke, Keen 34013
(Highvera, BMI)

January 27

1. **AT THE HOP**
Danny and the Juniors
Singer–Medora–White, ABC–
Paramount 9871 (Singular,
BMI)

2. **APRIL LOVE**
P. Boone
Fain–Webster, Dot 15660
(Leo Feist, ASCAP)

3. **RAUNCHY**
B. Justis
Justis–Manker, Phillips
International 3519
(Hi-Lo, BMI)

4. **PEGGY SUE**
B. Holly
J. Allison–N. Petty, Coral
61885 (Nor-Va-Jak, BMI)

5. **KISSES SWEETER THAN WINE**
J. Rodgers
P. Campbell–J. Newman,
Roulette 4031 (Folkways, BMI)

6. **SUGARTIME**
The McGuire Sisters
C. Phillips–O. Echols, Coral
61924 (Nor-Va-Jak, BMI)

7. **ALL THE WAY**
F. Sinatra
S. Cahn–J. VanHeusen, Capitol
3793 (Maraville, ASCAP)

8. **WHY DON'T THEY UNDERSTAND**
G. Hamilton IV
J. Henderson–J. Fishman, ABC–
Paramount 9862 (Hollis, BMI)

9. **GREAT BALLS OF FIRE**
J. L. Lewis
J. Hammer–O. Blackwell, Sun
281 (BRS, BMI)

10. **THE STROLL**
The Diamonds
C.Otis–N. Lee, Mercury
71242 (Meridian, BMI)

February 3

1. **AT THE HOP**
Danny and the Juniors
Singer–Medora–White, ABC–
Paramount 9871 (Singular,
BMI)

2. **SUGARTIME**
The McGuire Sisters
C. Phillips–O. Echols, Coral
61924 (Nor-Va-Jak, BMI)

3. **APRIL LOVE**
P. Boone
Fain–Webster, Dot 15660
(Leo Feist, ASCAP)

4. **RAUNCHY**
B. Justis
Justis–Manker, Phillips
International 3519
(Hi-Lo, BMI)

5. **GET A JOB**
The Silhouettes
Ulyses–Bagby, Ember 1029
(Wildcat, BMI)

6. **PEGGY SUE**
B. Holly
J. Allison–N. Petty, Coral
61885 (Nor-Va-Jak, BMI)

7. **THE STROLL**
The Diamonds
C. Otis–N. Lee, Mercury 71242
(Meridian, BMI)

8. **SAIL ALONG SILVERY MOON**
B. Vaughn
Wenrich–Tobias, Dot 15661
(Jay, ASCAP)

9. **KISSES SWEETER THAN WINE**
J. Rodgers
P. Campbell–J. Newman,
Roulette 4031 (Folkways, BMI)

10. **ALL THE WAY**
F. Sinatra
S. Cahn–J. VanHeusen,
Capitol 3793 (Maraville,
ASCAP)

97

February 10

1. **AT THE HOP**
Danny and the Juniors
Singer–Medora–White, ABC–Paramount 9871 (Singular, BMI)

2. **SUGARTIME**
The McGuire Sisters
C. Phillips–O. Echols, Coral 61924 (Nor-Va-Jak, BMI)

3. **GET A JOB**
The Silhouettes
Ulyses–Bagby, Ember 1029 (Wildcat, BMI)

4. **APRIL LOVE**
P. Boone
Fain–Webster, Dot 15660 (Leo Feist, ASCAP)

5. **SAIL ALONG SILVERY MOON**
B. Vaughn
Wenrich–Tobias, Dot 15661 (Jay, ASCAP)

6. **DON'T**
E. Presley
J. Leiber–M. Stoller, Victor 7150 (Elvis Presley, BMI)

7. **THE STROLL**
The Diamonds
C. Otis–N. Lee, Mercury 71242 (Meridian, BMI)

8. **CATCH A FALLING STAR**
P. Como
P. Vance–L. Pockris, Victor 7128 (Marvin, ASCAP)

9. **PEGGY SUE**
B. Holly
J. Allison–N. Petty, Coral 61885 (Nor-Va-Jak, BMI)

10. **ALL THE WAY**
F. Sinatra
S. Cahn–J. VanHeusen, Capitol 3793 (Maraville, ASCAP)

February 17

1. **SUGARTIME**
The McGuire Sisters
C. Phillips–O. Echols, Coral 61924 (Nor-Va-Jak, BMI)

2. **AT THE HOP**
Danny and the Juniors
Singer–Medora–White, ABC–Paramount 9871 (Singular, BMI)

3. **CATCH A FALLING STAR**
P. Como
P. Vance–L. Pockris, Victor 7128 (Marvin, ASCAP)

4. **GET A JOB**
The Silhouettes
Ulyses–Bagby, Ember 1029 (Wildcat, BMI)

5. **DON'T**
E. Presley
J. Leiber–M. Stoller, Victor 7150 (Elvis Presley, BMI)

6. **YOU ARE MY DESTINY**
P. Anka
P. Anka, ABC–Paramount 9880 (Pamco, BMI)

7. **APRIL LOVE**
P. Boone
Fain–Webster, Dot 15560 (Leo Feist, ASCAP)

8. **THE STROLL**
The Diamonds
C. Otis–N. Lee, Mercury 71242 (Meridian, BMI)

9. **SAIL ALONG SILVERY MOON**
B. Vaughn
Wenrich–Tobias, Dot 15661 (Jay, ASCAP)

10. **WITCHCRAFT**
F. Sinatra
C. Coleman–C. Leigh, Capitol 3859 (E. H. Morris Inc., ASCAP)

February 24

1. **CATCH A FALLING STAR**
P. Como
P. Vance–L. Pockris, Victor 7128 (Marvin, ASCAP)

2. **SUGARTIME**
The McGuire Sisters
C. Phillips–O. Echols, Coral 61924 (Nor-Va-Jak, BMI)

3. **AT THE HOP**
Danny and the Juniors
Singer–Medora–White, ABC–Paramount 9871 (Singular, BMI)

4. **SAIL ALONG SILVERY MOON**
B. Vaughn
Wenrich–Tobias, Dot 15661 (Jay, ASCAP)

5. **GET A JOB**
The Silhouettes
Ulyses–Bagby, Ember 1029 (Wildcat, BMI)

6. **DON'T**
E. Presley
J. Leiber–M. Stoller, Victor 7150 (Elvis Presley, BMI)

7. **SHORT SHORTS**
The Royal Teens
T. Austin–B. Gaudio, ABC–Paramount 9882 (Admiration, BMI)

8. **MAGIC MOMENTS**
P. Como
H. David–B. Bacharach, Victor 7128 (Famous, ASCAP)

9. **OH, JULIE**
The Crescendos
Moffet–Ball, Nasco 6005 (Excellorec, BMI)

10. **YOU ARE MY DESTINY**
P. Anka
P. Anka, ABC–Paramount 9880 (Pamco, BMI)

1958

March 3

1. **SUGARTIME**
   The McGuire Sisters
   C. Phillips–O. Echols, Coral 61924 (Nor-Va-Jak, BMI)

2. **CATCH A FALLING STAR**
   P. Como
   P. Vance–L. Pockris, Victor 7128 (Marvin, ASCAP)

3. **DON'T**
   E. Presley
   J. Leiber–M. Stoller, Victor 7150 (Elvis Presley, BMI)

4. **SAIL ALONG SILVERY MOON**
   B. Vaughn
   Wenrich–Tobias, Dot 15661 (Jay, ASCAP)

5. **GET A JOB**
   The Silhouettes
   Ulyses–Bagby, Ember 1029 (Wildcat, BMI)

6. **AT THE HOP**
   Danny and the Juniors
   Singer–Medora–White, ABC–Paramount 9871 (Singular, BMI)

7. **TWENTY-SIX MILES**
   The Four Preps
   G. Larsen–B. Belland, Capitol 3845 (Beechwood, BMI)

8. **SHORT-SHORTS**
   The Royal Teens
   T. Austin–B. Gaudio, ABC–Paramount 9882 (Admiration, BMI)

9. **YOU ARE MY DESTINY**
   P. Anka
   P. Anka, ABC–Paramount 9880 (Pamco, BMI)

10. **OH, JULIE**
    The Crescendos
    Moffet–Ball, Nasco 6005 (Excellorec, BMI)

March 10

1. **DON'T**
   E. Presley
   J. Leiber–M. Stoller, Victor 7150 (Elvis Presley, BMI)

2. **CATCH A FALLING STAR**
   P. Como
   P. Vance–L. Pockris, Victor 7128 (Marvin, ASCAP)

3. **SUGARTIME**
   The McGuire Sisters
   C. Phillips–O. Echols, Coral 61924 (Nor-Va-Jak, BMI)

4. **SAIL ALONG SILVERY MOON**
   B. Vaughn
   Wenrich–Tobias, Dot 15661 (Jay, ASCAP)

5. **SWEET LITTLE SIXTEEN**
   C. Berry
   C. Berry, Chess 1683 (Arc, BMI)

6. **SHORT SHORTS**
   The Royal Teens
   T. Austin–B. Gaudio, ABC–Paramount 9882 (Admiration, BMI)

7. **TWENTY-SIX MILES**
   The Four Preps
   G. Larsen–B. Belland, Capitol 3845 (Beechwood, BMI)

8. **GET A JOB**
   The Silhouettes
   Ulyses–Bagby, Ember 1029 (Wildcat BMI)

9. **SWINGING SHEPHERD BLUES**
   M. Koffmann Quartet
   M. Koffman, Jubilee 5311 (Benell, BMI)

10. **OH, JULIE**
    The Crescendos
    Moffet–Ball, Nasco 6005 (Excellorec, BMI)

March 17

1. **DON'T**
   E. Presley
   J. Leiber–M. Stoller, Victor 7150 (Elvis Presley, BMI)

2. **SUGARTIME**
   The McGuire Sisters
   C. Phillips–O. Echols, Coral 61924 (Nor-Va-Jak, BMI)

3. **TWENTY-SIX MILES**
   The Four Preps
   G. Larsen–B. Belland, Capitol 3845 (Beechwood, BMI)

4. **TEQUILA**
   The Champs
   C. Rio, Challenge 1016 (Jat, BMI)

5. **SWEET LITTLE SIXTEEN**
   C. Berry
   C. Berry, Chess 1683 (Arc, BMI)

6. **SAIL ALONG SILVERY MOON**
   B. Vaughn
   Wenrich–Tobias, Dot 15661 (Jay, ASCAP)

7. **DON'T**
   E. Presley
   J. Leiber–M. Stoller, Victor 7150 (Elvis Presley, BMI)

8. **WHO'S SORRY NOW?**
   C. Francis
   Snyder–Calmar–Ruby, M-G-M 12588 (Mills, ASCAP)

9. **GET A JOB**
   The Silhouettes
   Ulyses–Bagby, Ember 1029 (Wildcat, BMI)

10. **SWINGING SHEPHERD BLUES**
    M. Koffmann Quartet
    M. Koffmann, Jubilee 5311 (Benell, BMI)

March 24

1. **TEQUILA**
   The Champs
   C. Rio, Challenge 1016
   (Jat, BMI)

2. **CATCH A FALLING STAR**
   P. Como
   P. Vance–L. Pockris, Victor
   7128 (Marvin, ASCAP)

3. **SUGARTIME**
   The McGuire Sisters
   C. Phillips–O. Echols, Coral
   61924 (Nor-Va-Jak, BMI)

4. **TWENTY-SIX MILES**
   The Four Preps
   G. Larsen–B. Belland, Capitol
   3845 (Beechwood, BMI)

5. **LOLLIPOP**
   The Chordettes
   J. Dickson–B. Ross, Cadence
   1345 (E. B. Marks, BMI)

6. **SWEET LITTLE SIXTEEN**
   C. Berry
   C. Berry, Chess 1683
   (Arc, BMI)

7. **WHO'S SORRY NOW?**
   C. Francis
   Snyder–Calmar–Ruby, M-G-M
   12588 (Mills, ASCAP)

8. **DON'T**
   E. Presley
   J. Leiber–M. Stoller, Victor
   7150 (Elvis Presley, BMI)

9. **ARE YOU SINCERE?**
   A. Williams
   W. Walker, Cadence 1340
   (Cedarwood, BMI)

10. **SAIL ALONG SILVERY MOON**
    B. Vaughn
    Wenrich–Tobias, Dot 15661
    (Jay, ASCAP)

March 31

1. **TEQUILA**
   The Champs
   C. Rio, Challenge 1016
   (Jat, BMI)

2. **LOLLIPOP**
   The Chordettes
   J. Dickson–B. Ross,
   Cadence 1345
   (E. B. Marks, BMI)

3. **CATCH A FALLING STAR**
   P. Como
   P. Vance–L. Pockris, Victor
   7128 (Marvin, ASCAP)

4. **SUGARTIME**
   The McGuire Sisters
   C. Phillips–O. Echols, Coral
   61924 (Nor-Va-Jak, BMI)

5. **ARE YOU SINCERE?**
   A. Williams
   W. Walker, Cadence 1340
   (Cedarwood, BMI)

6. **SWEET LITTLE SIXTEEN**
   C. Berry
   C. Berry, Chess 1683
   (Arc, BMI)

7. **WHO'S SORRY NOW?**
   C. Francis
   Snyder–Calmar–Ruby, M-G-M
   12588 (Mills, ASCAP)

8. **TWENTY-SIX MILES**
   The Four Preps
   G. Larsen–B. Belland, Capitol
   3845 (Beechwood, BMI)

9. **TWILIGHT TIME**
   The Platters
   B. Ram–M. & A. Nevins–A. Dunn,
   Mercury 71289 (Porgie, BMI)

10. **SAIL ALONG SILVERY MOON**
    B. Vaughn
    Wenrich–Tobias, Dot 15661
    (Jay, ASCAP)

April 7

1. **LOLLIPOP**
   The Chordettes
   J. Dickson–B. Ross, Cadence
   1345 (E. B. Marks, BMI)

2. **TEQUILA**
   The Champs
   C. Rio, Challenge 1016
   (Jat, BMI)

3. **CATCH A FALLING STAR**
   P. Como
   P. Vance–L. Pockris, Victor
   7128 (Marvin, ASCAP)

4. **HE'S GOT THE WHOLE WORLD IN HIS HANDS**
   L. London
   Linden–Henry, Capitol 3891
   (Chappell, ASCAP)

5. **ARE YOU SINCERE?**
   A. Williams
   W. Walker, Cadence 1340
   (Cedarwood BMI)

6. **SUGARTIME**
   The McGuire Sisters
   C. Phillips–O. Echols, Coral
   61924 (Nor-Va-Jak, BMI)

7. **WHO'S SORRY NOW?**
   C. Francis
   Snyder–Calmar–Ruby, M-G-M
   12588 (Mills, ASCAP)

8. **SWEET LITTLE SIXTEEN**
   C. Berry
   C. Berry, Chess 1683
   (Arc, BMI)

9. **TWENTY-SIX MILES**
   The Four Preps
   G. Larsen–B. Belland, Capitol
   3845 (Beechwood, BMI)

10. **SAIL ALONG SILVERY MOON**
    B. Vaughn
    Wenrich–Tobias, Dot 15661
    (Jay, ASCAP)

April 14	*April 21*	*April 28*

April 14

1. **HE'S GOT THE WHOLE WORLD IN HIS HANDS**
L. London
Linden–Henry, Capitol 3891 (Chappell ASCAP)

2. **TWILIGHT TIME**
The Platters
B. Ram–M. & A. Nevins–A. Dunn, Mercury 71289 (Porgie, BMI)

3. **ARE YOU SINCERE?**
A. Williams
W. Walker, Cadence 1340 (Cedarwood, BMI)

4. **TEQUILA**
The Champs
C. Rio, Challenge 1016 (Jat, BMI)

5. **LOLLIPOP**
The Chordettes
J. Dickson–B. Ross, Cadence 1345 (E. B. Marks, BMI)

6. **WHO'S SORRY NOW?**
C. Francis
Snyder–Calmar–Ruby, M-G-M 12588 (Mills, ASCAP)

7. **SUGARTIME**
The McGuire Sisters
C. Phillips–O. Echols, Coral 61924 (Nor-Va-Jak, BMI)

8. **CATCH A FALLING STAR**
P. Como
P. Vance–L. Pockris, Victor 7128 (Marvin, ASCAP)

9. **SWEET LITTLE SIXTEEN**
C. Berry
C. Berry, Chess 1683 (Arc, BMI)

10. **SAIL ALONG SILVERY MOON**
B. Vaughn
Wenrich–Tobias, Dot 15661 (Jay, ASCAP)

April 21

1. **HE'S GOT THE WHOLE WORLD IN HIS HANDS**
L. London
Linden–Henry, Capitol 3891 (Chappell, ASCAP)

2. **TWILIGHT TIME**
The Platters
B. Ram–A. & M. Nevins–A. Dunn, Mercury 71289 (Porgie, BMI)

3. **TEQUILA**
The Champs
C. Rio, Challenge 1016 (Jat, BMI)

4. **LOLLIPOP**
The Chordettes
J. Dickson–B. Ross, Cadence 1345 (E. B. Marks, BMI)

5. **WHO'S SORRY NOW?**
C. Francis
Snyder–Calmar–Ruby, M-G-M 12588 (Mills, ASCAP)

6. **CATCH A FALLING STAR**
P. Como
P. Vance–L. Pockris, Victor 7128 (Marvin, ASCAP)

7. **SUGARTIME**
The McGuire Sisters
C. Phillips–O. Echols, Coral 61294 (Nor-Va-Jak, BMI)

8. **WITCH DOCTOR**
D. Seville
R. Bagdasarian, Liberty 55132 (Monarch, ASCAP)

9. **ARE YOU SINCERE?**
A. Williams
W. Walker, Cadence 1340 (Cedarwood, BMI)

10. **A WONDERFUL TIME UP THERE**
P. Boone
Abernathy, Dot 15690 (Fowler, BMI)

April 28

1. **HE'S GOT THE WHOLE WORLD IN HIS HANDS**
L. London
Linden–Henry, Capitol 3891 (Chappell, ASCAP)

2. **TWILIGHT TIME**
The Platters
B. Ram–A. & M. Nevins–A. Dunn, Mercury 71289 (Porgie, BMI)

3. **WITCH DOCTOR**
D. Seville
R. Bagdasarian, Liberty 55132 (Monarch, ASCAP)

4. **WEAR MY RING AROUND YOUR NECK**
E. Presley
Carroll–Moody, Victor 7240 (Rush–Elvis Presley, BMI)

5. **TEQUILA**
The Champs
C. Rio, Challenge 1016 (Jat, BMI)

6. **CATCH A FALLING STAR**
P. Como
P. Vance–L. Pockris, Victor 7128 (Marvin, ASCAP)

7. **LOLLIPOP**
The Chordettes
J. Dickson–B. Ross, Cadence 1345 (E. B. Marks, BMI)

8. **WHO'S SORRY NOW?**
C. Francis
Snyder–Calmar–Ruby, M-G-M 12588 (Mills, ASCAP)

9. **ALL I HAVE TO DO IS DREAM**
The Everly Brothers
B. Bryant, Cadence 1348 (Acuff–Rose, BMI)

10. **SUGARTIME**
The McGuire Sisters
C. Phillips–O. Echols, Coral 61924 (Nor-Va-Jak, BMI)

1. **HE'S GOT THE WHOLE WORLD IN HIS HANDS**
   L. London
   Linden–Henry, Capitol 3891 (Chappell, ASCAP)

2. **WITCH DOCTOR**
   D. Seville
   R. Bagdasarian, Liberty 55132 (Monarch, ASCAP)

3. **TWILIGHT TIME**
   The Platters
   B. Ram–A. & M. Nevins–A. Dunn, Mercury 71289 (Porgie, BMI)

4. **WEAR MY RING AROUND YOUR NECK**
   E. Presley
   Carroll–Moody, Victor 7240 (Rush–Elvis Presley, BMI)

5. **ALL I HAVE TO DO IS DREAM**
   The Everly Brothers
   B. Bryant, Cadence 1348 (Acuff–Rose, BMI)

6. **CHANSON D'AMOUR**
   A. Todd and D. Todd
   Shanklin, Era 1064 (Meadowlark, ASCAP)

7. **RETURN TO ME**
   D. Martin
   C. Lombardo–D. Minno, Capitol 3894 (Sourthern, ASCAP)

8. **LOLLIPOP**
   The Chordettes
   J. Dickson–B. Ross, Cadence 1345 (Marks, BMI)

9. **WHO'S SORRY NOW?**
   C. Francis
   Snyder–Calmar–Ruby, M-G-M 12588 (Mills, ASCAP)

10. **TEQUILA**
    The Champs
    C. Rio, Challenge 1016 (Jat, BMI)

1. **ALL I HAVE TO DO IS DREAM**
   The Everly Brothers
   B. Bryant, Cadence 1348 (Acuff–Rose, BMI)

2. **WITCH DOCTOR**
   D. Seville
   R. Bagdasarian, Liberty 55132 (Monarch, ASCAP)

3. **TWILIGHT TIME**
   The Platters
   B. Ram–A. & M. Nevins–A. Dunn, Mercury 71289 (Porgie, BMI)

4. **HE'S GOT THE WHOLE WORLD IN HIS HANDS**
   L. London
   Linden–Henry, Capitol 3891 (Chappell, ASCAP)

5. **WEAR MY RING AROUND YOUR NECK**
   E. Presley
   Carroll–Moody, Victor 7240 (Rush–Elvis Presley, BMI)

6. **CHANSON D'AMOUR**
   A. Todd and D. Todd
   Shanklin, Era 1064 (Meadowlark, ASCAP)

7. **RETURN TO ME**
   D. Martin
   C. Lombardo–D. Minno, Capitol 3894 (Southern, ASCAP)

8. **KEWPIE DOLL**
   P. Como
   S. Tepper–R. Bennet, Victor 7202 (Leeds, ASCAP)

9. **LOLLIPOP**
   The Chordettes
   J. Dickson–B. Ross Cadence 1345 (Marks, BMI)

10. **LOOKING BACK**
    Nat (King) Cole
    Otis–Benton–Hendricks, Capitol3939 (Eden-Sweco, BMI)

1. **ALL I HAVE TO DO IS DREAM**
   The Everly Brothers
   B. Bryant, Cadence 1348 (Acuff–Rose, BMI)

2. **WITCH DOCTOR**
   D. Seville
   R. Bagdasarian, Liberty 55132 (Monarch, ASCAP)

3. **TWILIGHT TIME**
   The Platters
   B. Ram–A. & M. Nevins–A. Dunn, Mercury 71289 (Porgie, BMI)

4. **HE'S GOT THE WHOLE WORLD IN HIS HANDS**
   L. London
   Linden–Henry, Capitol 3891 (Chappell, ASCAP)

5. **WEAR MY RING AROUND YOUR NECK**
   E. Presley
   Carroll–Moody, Victor 7240 (Rush–Elvis Presley, BMI)

6. **CHANSON D'AMOUR**
   A. Todd and D. Todd
   Shanklin, Era 1064 (Meadowlark, ASCAP)

7. **RETURN TO ME**
   D. Martin
   C. Lombardo–D. Minno, Capitol 3894 (Southern, ASCAP)

8. **KEWPIE DOLL**
   P. Como
   S. Tepper–R. Bennett, Victor 7202 (Leeds, ASCAP)

9. **LOOKING BACK**
   Nat (King) Cole
   Otis–Benton–Hendricks, Capitol 3939 (Eden-Sweco, BMI)

10. **BOOK OF LOVE**
    The Monotones
    W. Davis–G. Malone–C. Patrick, Argo 5290 (Arc-Keel, BMI)

May 26

1. **ALL I HAVE TO DO IS DREAM**
The Everly Brothers
*B. Bryant, Cadence 1348
(Acuff–Rose, BMI)*

2. **WITCH DOCTOR**
D. Seville
*R. Bagdasarian, Liberty 55132
(Monarch, ASCAP)*

3. **TWILIGHT TIME**
The Platters
*B. Ram–A. & M. Nevins–A. Dunn,
Mercury 71289 (Porgie, BMI)*

4. **HE'S GOT THE WHOLE WORLD IN HIS HANDS**
L. London
*Linden–Henry, Capitol 3891
(Chappell, ASCAP)*

5. **WEAR MY RING AROUND YOUR NECK**
E. Presley
*Carroll–Moody, Victor 7240
(Rush–Elvis Presley, BMI)*

6. **RETURN TO ME**
D. Martin
*C. Lombardo–D. Minno, Capitol
3894 (Southern, ASCAP)*

7. **CHANSON D'AMOUR**
A. Todd and D. Todd
*Shanklin, Era 1064
(Meadowlark, ASCAP)*

8. **KEWPIE DOLL**
P. Como
*S. Tepper–R. Bennett, Victor
7202 (Leeds, ASCAP)*

9. **BIG MAN**
The Four Preps
*G. Larsen–B. Belland, Capitol
3960 (Beechwood, BMI)*

10. **LOOKING BACK**
Nat (King) Cole
*Benton–Otis–Hendricks, Capitol
3939 (Eden–Sweco, BMI)*

June 2

1. **ALL I HAVE TO DO IS DREAM**
The Everly Brothers
*B. Bryant, Cadence 1348
(Acuff–Rose, BMI)*

2. **WITCH DOCTOR**
D. Seville
*R. Bagdasarian, Liberty 55132
(Monarch, ASCAP)*

3. **TWILIGHT TIME**
The Platters
*B. Ram–A. & M. Nevins–A.
Dunn, Mercury 71289
(Porgie, BMI)*

4. **RETURN TO ME**
D. Martin
*C. Lombardo–D. Minno, Capitol
3894 (Southern, ASCAP)*

5. **HE'S GOT THE WHOLE WORLD IN HIS HANDS**
L. London
*Linden–Henry, Capitol 3891
(Chappell, ASCAP)*

6. **WEAR MY RING AROUND YOUR NECK**
E. Presley
*Carroll–Moody, Victor 7240
(Rush–Elvis Presley, BMI)*

7. **CHANSON D'AMOUR**
A. Todd and D. Todd
*Shanklin, Era 1064
(Meadowlark, ASCAP)*

8. **SUGAR MOON**
P. Boone
*D. Wolfe, Dot 15750
(Gallatin, BMI)*

9. **BIG MAN**
The Four Preps
*G. Larsen–B. Belland, Capitol
3960 (Beechwood, BMI)*

10. **KEWPIE DOLL**
P. Como
*S. Tepper–R. Bennett, Victor
7202 (Leeds, ASCAP)*

June 9

1. **ALL I HAVE TO DO IS DREAM**
The Everly Brothers
*B. Bryant, Cadence 1348
(Acuff–Rose, BMI)*

2. **RETURN TO ME**
D. Martin
*C. Lombardo–D. Minno, Capitol
3894 (Southern, ASCAP)*

3. **WITCH DOCTOR**
D. Seville
*R. Bagdasarian, Liberty 55132
(Monarch, ASCAP)*

4. **THE PURPLE PEOPLE EATER**
S. Wooley
*S. Wooley, M-G-M 12651
(Cordeal, BMI)*

5. **SECRETLY**
J. Rodgers
*Hoffman–Manning–Maxwell,
Roulette 4070
(Planetary, ASCAP)*

6. **TWILIGHT TIME**
The Platters
*B. Ram–A. & M. Nevins–A.
Dunn, Mercury 71289
(Porgie, BMI)*

7. **CHANSON D' AMOUR**
A. Todd and D. Todd
*Shanklin, Era 1064
(Meadowlark, ASCAP)*

8. **SUGAR MOON**
P. Boone
*D. Wolfe, Dot 15750
(Gallatin, BMI)*

9. **BIG MAN**
The Four Preps
*G. Larsen–B. Belland, Capitol
3960 (Beechwood, BMI)*

10. **HE'S GOT THE WHOLE WORLD IN HIS HANDS**
L. London
*Linden–Henry, Capitol 3891
(Chappell, ASCAP)*

June 16

1. **ALL I HAVE TO DO IS DREAM**
The Everly Brothers
B. Bryant, Cadence 1348 (Acuff–Rose, BMI)

2. **RETURN TO ME**
D. Martin
C. Lombardo–D. Minno, Captiol 3894 (Southern, ASCAP)

3. **THE PURPLE PEOPLE EATER**
S. Wooley
S. Wooley, M-G-M 12651 (Cordeal, BMI)

4. **SECRETLY**
J. Rodgers
Hoffmann–Manning–Markwell, Roulette 4070 (Planetary, ASCAP

5. **WITCH DOCTOR**
D. Seville
R. Bagdasarian, Liberty 55132 (Monarch, ASCAP)

6. **TWILIGHT TIME**
The Platters
B. Ram–A. & M. Nevins–A. Dunn, Mercury 71289 (Porgie, BMI)

7. **SUGAR MOON**
P. Boone
D. Wolfe, Dot 15750 (Gallatin, BMI)

8. **CHANSON D' AMOUR**
A. Todd and D. Todd
Shanklin, Era 1064 (Meadowlark, ASCAP)

9. **BIG MAN**
The Four Preps
G. Larsen–B. Belland, Capitol 3960 (Beechwood, BMI)

10. **HE'S GOT THE WHOLE WORLD IN HIS HANDS**
L. London
Linden–Henry, Capitol 3891 (Chappell, ASCAP)

June 23

1. **THE PURPLE PEOPLE EATER**
S. Wooley
S. Wooley, M-G-M 12651 (Cordeal, BMI)

2. **ALL I HAVE TO DO IS DREAM**
The Everly Brothers
B. Bryant, Cadence 1348 (Acuff–Rose, BMI)

3. **RETURN TO ME**
D. Martin
C. Lombardo–D. Minno, Capitol 3894 (Southern, ASCAP)

4. **SECRETLY**
J. Rodgers
Hoffman–Manning–Markwell, Roulette 4070 (Planetary, ASCAP)

5. **WITCH DOCTOR**
D. Seville
R. Bagdasarian, Liberty 55132 (Monarch, ASCAP)

6. **BIG MAN**
The Four Preps
G. Larsen–B. Belland, Capitol 3960 (Beechwood, BMI)

7. **SUGAR MOON**
P. Boone
D. Wolfe, Dot 15750 (Gallatin, BMI)

8. **TWILIGHT TIME**
The Platters
B. Ram–A. & M. Nevins–A. Dunn, Mercury 71289 (Porgie, BMI)

9. **YAKETY YAK**
The Coasters
J. Leiber–M. Stoller, Atco 6116 (Tiger, BMI)

10. **CHANSON D' AMOUR**
A. Todd and D. Todd
Shanklin, Era 1064 (Meadowlark, ASCAP)

June 30

1. **THE PURPLE PEOPLE EATER**
S. Wooley
S. Wooley, ,M-G-M 12651 (Cordeal, BMI)

2. **ALL I HAVE TO DO IS DREAM**
The Everly Brothers
B. Bryant, Cadence 1348 (Acuff–Rose, BMI)

3. **SECRETLY**
J. Rodgers
Hoffman–Manning–Markwell, Roulette 4070 (Planetary, ASCAP)

4. **RETURN TO ME**
D. Martin
C. Lombardo–D. Minno, Capitol 3894 (Southern, ASCAP)

5. **YAKETY YAK**
The Coasters
J. Leiber–M. Stoller, Atco 6116 (Tiger, BMI)

6. **BIG MAN**
The Four Preps
G. Larsen–B. Belland, Capitol 3960 (Beechwood, BMI)

7. **WITCH DOCTOR**
D. Seville
R. Bagdasarian, Liberty 55132 (Monarch, ASCAP)

8. **SUGAR MOON**
P. Boone
D. Wolfe, Dot 15750 (Gallatin, BMI)

9. **ENDLESS SLEEP**
J. Reynolds
J. Reyonds–D. Nance, Demon 1507 (Johnston–Montei–Elizabeth, BMI)

10. **TWILIGHT TIME**
The Platters
B. Ram–A. & M. Nevins–A. Dunn, Mercury 71289 (Porgie, BMI)

JULY 7

1. **SECRETLY**
J. Rodgers
*Hoffman–Manning–Markwell,
Roulette 4070
(Planetary, ASCAP)*

2. **THE PURPLE PEOPLE EATER**
S. Wooley
*S. Wooley, M-G-M 12651
(Cordeal, BMI)*

3. **ALL I HAVE TO DO IS DREAM**
The Everly Brothers
*B. Bryant, Cadence 1348
(Acuff–Rose, BMI)*

4. **YAKETY YAK**
The Coasters
*J. Leiber–M. Stoller, Atco 6116
(Tiger, BMI)*

5. **HARD HEADED WOMAN**
E. Presley
*Metruis, Victor 7280
(Gladys, ASCAP)*

6. **RETURN TO ME**
D. Martin
*C. Lombardo–D. Minno, Capitol
3894 (Southern, ASCAP)*

7. **PATRICIA**
P. Prado
*P. Prado, Victor 7245
(L. Foster, BMI)*

8. **SUGAR MOON**
P. Boone
*D. Wolfe, Dot 15750
(Gallatin, BMI)*

9. **ENDLESS SLEEP**
J. Reynolds
*J. Reynolds–D. Nance, Demon
1507 (Johnston–Montei–
Elizabeth, BMI)*

10. **TWILIGHT TIME**
The Platters
*B. Ram–A & M. Nevins–A. Dunn,
Mercury 71289
(Porgie, BMI)*

July 14

1. **YAKETY YAK**
The Coasters
*J. Leiber–M. Stoller, Atco
6116 (Tiger, BMI)*

2. **HARD HEADED WOMAN**
E. Presley
*Metruis, Victor 7280
(Gladys, ASCAP)*

3. **SECRETLY**
J. Rodgers
*Hoffman–Manning–Markwell,
Roulette 4070
(Planetary, ASCAP)*

4. **PATRICIA**
P. Prado
*P. Prado, Victor 7245
(L. Foster, BMI)*

5. **THE PURPLE PEOPLE EATER**
S. Wooley
*S. Wooley, M-G-M 12651
(Cordeal, BMI)*

6. **ALL I HAVE TO DO IS DREAM**
The Everly Brothers
*B. Bryant, Cadence 1348
(Acuff–Rose, BMI)*

7. **POOR LITTLE FOOL**
R. Nelson
*S. Sheeley, Imperial 5528
(Eric, BMI)*

8. **RETURN TO ME**
D. Martin
*C. Lombardo–D. Minno,
Captiol 3894
(Southern, ASCAP)*

9. **PADRE**
T. Arden
*A. Romans–P. Webster, Decca
30628 (Ross Jungnickel,
ASCAP)*

10. **SPLISH SPLASH**
B. Darin
*Darin–Murray, Atco 6117
(Portrait, BMI)*

July 21

1. **HARD HEADED WOMAN**
E. Presley
*Metruis, Victor 7280
(Gladys, ASCAP)*

2. **YAKITY YAK**
The Coasters
*J. Leiber–,M. Stoller, Atco
6116 (Tiger, BMI)*

3. **THE PURPLE PEOPLE EATER**
S. Wooley
*S. Wooley, M-G-M 12651
(Cordeal, BMI)*

4. **PATRICIA**
P. Prado
*P. Prado, Victor 7245
(L. Foster, BMI)*

5. **SPLISH SPLASH**
B. Darin
*Darin–Murray, Atco 6117
(Portrait, BMI)*

6. **POOR LITTLE FOOL**
R. Nelson
*S. Sheeley, Imperial 5528
(Eric, BMI)*

7. **WHEN**
The Kalin Twins
*J. Reardon–P. Evans, Decca
30642 (Sounds and Michelle,
ASCAP)*

8. **SECRETLY**
J. Rodgers
*Hoffmann–Manning–Markwell,
Roulette 4070
(Planetary, ASCAP)*

9. **IF DREAMS CAME TRUE**
P. Boone
*Allen–Stillmen, Dot 15785
(Korwin, ASCAP)*

10. **ALL I HAVE TO DO IS DREAM**
Everly Brothers
*B. Bryant, Cadence 1348
(Acuff–Rose, BMI)*

July 28	*August 4*	*August 11*

July 28

1. **PATRICIA**
P. Prado
P. Prado, Victor 7245
(L. Foster, BMI)

2. **HARD HEADED WOMAN**
E. Presley
Metruis, Victor 7280
(Gladys, ASCAP)

3. **POOR LITTLE FOOL**
R. Nelson
S. Sheeley, Imperial 5528
(Eric, BMI)

4. **YAKETY YAK**
The Coasters
J. Leiber–M. Stoller, Atco
6116 (Tiger, BMI)

5. **SPLISH SPLASH**
B. Darin
Darin–Murray, Atco 6117
(Portrait, BMI)

6. **THE PURPLE PEOPLE EATER**
S. Wooley
S. Wooley, M-G-M 12651
(Cordeal, BMI)

7. **WHEN**
The Kalin Twins
J. Reardon–P. Evans, Decca
30642 (Sounds and Michelle,
ASCAP)

8. **SECRETLY**
J. Rodgers
Hoffman–Manning–Markwell,
Roulette 4070
(Planetary, ASCAP)

9. **LEFT RIGHT OUT OF YOUR HEART**
P. Page
M. Garson–E. Shuman, Mercury
71331 (Shapiro–Bernstein,
ASCAP)

10. **ALL I HAVE TO DO IS DREAM**
The Everly Brothers
B. Bryant, Cadence 1348
(Acuff–Rose, BMI)

August 4

1. **POOR LITTLE FOOL**
R. Nelson
S. Sheeley, Imperial 5528
(Eric, BMI)

2. **PATRICIA**
P. Prado
P. Prado, Victor 7245
(L. Foster, BMI)

3. **SPLISH SPLASH**
B. Darin
Darin–Murray, Atco 6117
(Portrait, BMI)

4. **HARD HEADED WOMAN**
E. Presley
Metruis, Victor 7280
(Gladys, ASCAP)

5. **WHEN**
The Kalin Twins
J. Reardon–P. Evans, Decca
30642 (Sounds and Michelle,
ASCAP)

6. **REBEL-ROUSER**
D. Eddy
D. Eddy–Hazelwood, Jamie
4104 (Gregmark, BMI)

7. **YAKETY YAK**
The Coasters
J. Leiber–M. Stoller, Atco
6116 (Tiger, BMI)

8. **FEVER**
P. Lee
Davenport–Cooley, Capitol
3998 (Lois, BMI)

9. **MY TRUE LOVE**
J. Scott
J. Scott, Carlton 462
(Starfire–Peer International, BMI)

10. **WILLIE AND THE HAND JIVE**
The Johnny Otis Show
J. Otis, Capitol 3966
(El Dorado, BMI)

August 11

1. **POOR LITTLE FOOL**
R. Nelson
S. Sheeley, Imperial 5528
(Eric, BMI)

2. **PATRICIA**
P. Prado
P. Prado, Victor 7245
(L. Foster, BMI)

3. **WHEN**
The Kalin Twins
J. Reardon–P. Evans, Decca
30642
(Sounds and Michele, ASCAP)

4. **SPLISH SPLASH**
B. Darin
Darin–Murray, Atco 6117
(Portrait, BMI)

5. **MY TRUE LOVE**
J. Scott
J. Scott, Carlton 462
(Starfire–Peer International, BMI)

6. **VOLARE**
D. Modugno
D. Modugno, Decca 30677
(Robbins, ASCAP)

7. **HARD HEADED WOMAN**
E. Presley
Metruis, Victor 7280
(Gladys, ASCAP)

8. **WILLIE AND THE HAND JIVE**
The Johnny Otis Show
J. Otis, Capitol 3966
(El Dorado, BMI)

9. **JUST A DREAM**
J. Clanton
Clanton–Matassa, Ace 546
(Ace, BMI)

10. **REBEL-ROUSER**
D. Eddy
D. Eddy–L. Hazelwood, Jamie
4104 (Gregmark, BMI)

August 18

1. **POOR LITTLE FOOL**
R. Nelson
S. Sheeley, Imperial 5528
(Eric, BMI)

2. **PATRICIA**
P. Prado
P. Prado, Victor 7245
(L. Foster, BMI)

3. **VOLARE**
D. Modugno
D.Modugno, Decca 30677
(Robbins, ASCAP)

4. **MY TRUE LOVE**
J. Scott
J. Scott, Carlton 462
(Starfire–Peer International, BMI)

5. **LITTLE STAR**
The Elegants
Venosa–Picone, Apt. 25005
(Keel, BMI)

6. **JUST A DREAM**
J. Clanton
Clanton–Matassa, Ace 546
(Ace, BMI)

7. **WHEN**
The Kalin Twins
J. Reardon–P. Evans, Decca
30642 (Sounds and Michelle,
ASCAP)

8. **REBEL-ROUSER**
D. Eddy
D. Eddy–L. Hazelwood, Jamie
4104 (Gregmark, BMI)

9. **FEVER**
P. Lee
Davenport–Cooley, Capitol
3998 (Lois, BMI)

10. **SPLISH SPLASH**
B. Darin
Darin–Murray, Atco 6117
(Portrait, BMI)

August 25

1. **LITTLE STAR**
The Elegants
Venosa–Picone, Apt. 25005
(Keel, BMI)

2. **VOLARE**
D. Modugno
D. Modugno, Decca 30677
(Robbins, ASCAP)

3. **BIRD DOG**
The Everly Brothers
B. Bryant, Cadence 1350
(Acuff–Rose, BMI)

4. **JUST A DREAM**
J. Clanton
Clanton–Matassa, Ace 546
(Ace, BMI)

5. **MY TRUE LOVE**
J. Scott
J. Scott, Carlton 462
(Starfire–Peer International, BMI)

6. **POOR LITTLE FOOL**
R. Nelson
S. Sheeley, Imperial 5528
(Eric, BMI)

7. **PATRICIA**
P. Prado
P. Prado, Victor 7245
(L. Foster, BMI)

8. **FEVER**
P. Lee
Davenport–Cooley, Capitol
3998 (Lois, BMI)

9. **BORN TOO LATE**
The Pony Tails
S. Tobias–C. Strouse,
ABC–Paramount 9934
(Mansion, ASCAP)

10. **WHEN**
The Kalin Twins
J. Reardon–P. Evans, Decca
30642 (Sounds and Michele,
ASCAP)

September 1

1. **VOLARE**
D. Modugno
D. Modugno, Decca 30677
(Robbins, ASCAP)

2. **LITTLE STAR**
The Elegants
Venosa–Picone, Apt. 25005
(Keel, BMI)

3. **BIRD DOG**
The Everly Brothers
B. Bryant, Cadence 1350
(Acuff–Rose, BMI)

4. **JUST A DREAM**
J. Clanton
Clanton–Matassa, Ace 546
(Ace, BMI)

5. **POOR LITTLE FOOL**
R. Nelson
S. Sheeley, Imperial 5528
(Eric, BMI)

6. **PATRICIA**
P. Prado
P. Prado, Victor 7245
(L. Foster, BMI)

7. **MY TRUE LOVE**
J. Scott
J. Scott, Carlton 462
(Starfire–Peer International, BMI)

8. **WHEN**
The Kalin Twins
J. Reardon–P. Evans, Decca
30642 (Sounds and Michele,
ASCAP)

9. **GINGER BREAD**
F. Avalon
C. Ballard–H. Hunter,
Chancellor 1021
(Rambed, BMI)

10. **ARE YOU REALLY MINE?**
J. Rodgers
Hoffman–Manning–Markwell
Roulette 4090
(Planetary, ASCAP)

September 8

1. **VOLARE**
D. Modugno
D. Modugno, Decca 30677
(Robbins, ASCAP)

2. **BIRD DOG**
The Everly Brothers
B. Bryant, Cadence 1350
(Acuff–Rose, BMI)

3. **LITTLE STAR**
The Elegants
Venosa–Picone, Apt. 25005
(Keel, BMI)

4. **PATRICIA**
P. Prado
P. Prado, Victor 7245
(L. Foster, BMI)

5. **JUST A DREAM**
J. Clanton
Clanton–Matassa, Ace 546
(Ace, BMI)

6. **MY TRUE LOVE**
J. Scott
J. Scott, Carlton 462
(Starfire–Peer International, BMI)

7. **GINGER BREAD**
F. Avalon
C. Ballard–H. Hunter,
Chancellor 1021
(Rambed, BMI)

8. **WESTERN MOVIES**
The Olympics
P. Smith–C. Goldsmith,
Demon 1508
(Elizabeth–Aries, BMI)

9. **ROCK-IN' ROBIN**
B. Day
J. Thomas, Class 229
(Recordo, BMI)

10. **POOR LITTLE FOOL**
R. Nelson
S. Sheeley, Imperial 5528
(Eric, BMI)

September 15

1. **VOLARE**
D. Modugno
D. Modugno, Decca 30677
(Robbins, ASCAP)

2. **BIRD DOG**
The Everly Brothers
B. Bryant, Cadence 1350
(Acuff–Rose, BMI)

3. **GINGER BREAD**
F. Avalon
C. Ballard–H. Hunter,
Chancellor 1021
(Rambed, BMI)

4. **LITTLE STAR**
The Elegants
Venosa–Picone, Apt. 25005
(Keel, BMI)

5. **ROCK-IN' ROBIN**
B. Day
J. Thomas, Class 229
(Recordo, BMI)

6. **BORN TOO LATE**
The Poni-Tails
S. Tobias-C. Strouse,
ABC–Paramount 9934
(Mansion, ASCAP)

7. **WESTERN MOVIES**
The Olympics
P. Smith–C. Goldsmith, Demon
1508 Elizabeth–Aries, BMI)

8. **TEARS ON MY PILLOW**
Little Anthony and the Imperials
S. Bradford–A. Lewis, End
1027 (Vanderbilt–Boonie, BMI)

9. **JUST A DREAM**
J. Clanton
Clanton–Matassa, Ace 546
(Ace, BMI)

10. **IT'S ALL IN THE GAME**
T. Edwards
Daves–Sigman, M-G-M 12688
(Remick, ASCAP)

September 22

1. **VOLARE**
D. Modugno
D. Modugno, Decca 30677
(Robbins, ASCAP)

2. **BIRD DOG**
The Everly Brothers
B. Bryant, Cadance
1350 (Acuff–Rose, BMI)

3. **IT'S ALL IN THE GAME**
T. Edwards
Daves–Sigman, M-G-M 12688
(Remick, ASCAP)

4. **LITTLE STAR**
The Elegants
Venosa–Picone, Apt. 25005
(Keel, BMI)

5. **ROCK-IN' ROBIN**
B. Day
J. Thomas, Class 229
(Recordo, BMI)

6. **JUST A DREAM**
J. Clanton
Clanton–Matassa, Ace 546
(Ace, BMI)

7. **TEARS ON MY PILLOW**
Little Anthony and the Imperials
S. Bradford–A. Lewis, End
1027 (Vanderbilt–Boonie, BMI)

8. **SUSIE DARLIN'**
R. Luke
R. Luke, Dot 15781
(Congressional, ASCAP)

9. **BORN TOO LATE**
The Poni-Tails
S. Tobias–C. Strouse,
ABC–Paramount 9934
(Mansion, ASCAP)

10. **DEVOTED TO YOU**
The Everly Brothers
B. Bryant, Cadence
1350 (Acuff–Rose, BMI)

September 29

1. **VOLARE**
D. Modugno
D. Modugno, Decca 30677
(Robbins, ASCAP)

2. **BIRD DOG**
The Everly Brothers
B. Bryant, Cadence
1350 (Acuff–Rose, BMI)

3. **IT'S ALL IN THE GAME**
T. Edwards
Daves–Sigman, M-G-M 12688
(Remick, ASCAP)

4. **LITTLE STAR**
The Elegants
Venosa–Picone, Apt. 25005
(Keel, BMI)

5. **ROCK-IN' ROBIN**
B. Day
J. Thomas, Class 229
(Recordo, BMI)

6. **TEARS ON MY PILLOW**
Little Anthony and the Imperials
S. Bradford–A. Lewis, End
1027 (Vanderbilt-Boonie, BMI)

7. **SUSIE DARLIN'**
R. Luke
R. Luke, Dot 15781
(Congressional, ASCAP)

8. **SUMMERTIME BLUES**
E. Cochran
E. Cochran–J. Capeheart,
Liberty 55144 (American, BMI)

9. **JUST A DREAM**
J. Clanton
Clanton–Matassa, Ace 546
(Ace, BMI)

10. **NEAR YOU**
R. Williams
C. Goell, Kapp 233
(Supreme, ASCAP)

October 6

1. **IT'S ALL IN THE GAME**
T. Edwards
Daves–Sigman, M-G-M 12688
(Remick, ASCAP)

2. **BIRD DOG**
The Everly Brothers
B. Bryant, Cadence
1350 (Acuff–Rose, BMI)

3. **ROCK-IN' ROBIN**
B. Day
J. Thomas, Class 229
(Recordo, BMI)

4. **VOLARE**
D. Modugno
D. Modugno, Decca 30677
(Robbins, ASCAP)

5. **LITTLE STAR**
The Elegants
Venosa–Picone, Apt. 25005
(Keel, BMI)

6. **TEARS ON MY PILLOW**
Little Anthony and the Imperials
S. Bradford–A. Lewis, End
1027 (Vanderbilt–Boonie, BMI)

7. **SUSIE DARLIN'**
R. Luke
R. Luke, Dot 15781
(Congressional, , ASCAP)

8. **NEAR YOU**
R. Williams
C. Goell, Kapp 233
(Supreme, ASCAP)

9. **TEA FOR TWO CHA CHA**
Tommy Dorsey Orchestra
V. Youmans–I. Caeser, Decca
30704 (Harms, ASCAP)

10. **SUMMERTIME BLUES**
E. Cochran
E. Cochran–J. Capeheart,
Liberty 55144
(American, BMI)

October 13

1. **IT'S ALL IN THE GAME**
T. Edwards
Daves–Sigman, M-G-M 12688
(Remick, ASCAP)

2. **BIRD DOG**
The Everly Brothers
B. Bryant, Cadence 1350
(Acuff–Rose, BMI)

3. **ROCK-IN' ROBIN**
B. Day
J. Thomas, Class 229
(Recordo, BMI)

4. **TEARS ON MY PILLOW**
Little Anthony and the Imperials
S. Bradford–A. Lewis, End 1027
(Vanderbilt–Boonie, BMI)

5. **VOLARE**
D. Modugno
D. Modugno, Decca 30677
(Robbins, ASCAP)

6. **THE END**
E. Grant
J. Krondes–S. Jacobson,
Decca 30719 (Criterion, ASCAP)

7. **SUSIE DARLIN'**
R. Luke
R. Luke, Dot 15781
(Congressional, ASCAP)

8. **NEAR YOU**
R. Williams
C. Goell, Kapp 233
(Supreme, ASCAP)

9. **TEA FOR TWO CHA CHA**
Tommy Dorsey Orchestra
V. Youmans–I. Caeser, Decca
30704 (Harms, ASCAP)

10. **IT'S ONLY MAKE BELIEVE**
C. Twitty
Twitty–Nance, M-G-M 12677
(Marielle, BMI)

October 20

1. **IT'S ALL IN THE GAME**
   T. Edwards
   Daves–Sigman,   M-G-M 12688
   (Remick, ASCAP)

2. **BIRD DOG**
   The Everly Brothers
   B. Bryant,   Cadence 1350
   (Acuff–Rose, BMI)

3. **IT'S ONLY MAKE BELIEVE**
   C. Twitty
   Twitty–Nance,   M-G-M 12677
   (Marielle, BMI)

4. **TOPSY II**
   C. Cole
   Battle–Durham,   Love 50034
   (Cosmopolitan, BMI)

5. **ROCK-IN' ROBIN**
   B. Day
   J. Thomas,   Class 229
   (Recordo, BMI)

6. **SUSIE DARLIN'**
   R. Luke
   R. Luke,   Dot 15781
   (Congressional, ASCAP)

7. **TEARS ON MY PILLOW**
   Little Anthony and the Imperials
   S. Bradford–A. Lewis,   End
   1027   (Vanderbilt-Boonie, BMI)

8. **TOM DOOLEY**
   The Kingston Trio
   D. Guard,   Capitol 4049
   (Beechwood, BMI)

9. **TEA FOR TWO CHA CHA**
   Tommy Dorsey Orchestra
   V. Youmans–I. Caeser,   Decca
   30704   (Harms, ASCAP)

10. **CHANTILLY LACE**
    The Big Bopper
    J. Richardson,   Mercury 71343
    (Glad, BMI)

October 27

1. **IT'S ALL IN THE GAME**
   T. Edwards
   Daves–Sigman,   M-G-M 12688
   (Remick, ASCAP)

2. **IT'S ONLY MAKE BELIEVE**
   C. Twitty
   Twitty–Nance,   M-G-M 12677
   (Marielle, BMI)

3. **TOM DOOLEY**
   The Kingston Trio
   D. Guard,   Capitol 4049
   (Beechwood, BMI)

4. **TOPSY II**
   C. Cole
   Battle–Durham,   Love 50034
   (Cosmopolitan, BMI)

5. **ROCK-IN' ROBIN**
   B. Day
   J. Thomas,   Class 229
   (Recordo, BMI)

6. **TEARS ON MY PILLOW**
   Little Anthony and the Imperials
   S. Bradford–A. Lewis,   End
   1027   (Vanderbilt-Boonie, BMI)

7. **BIRD DOG**
   The Everly Brothers
   B. Bryant,   Cadence
   1350   (Acuff–Rose, BMI)

8. **TEA FOR TWO CHA CHA**
   Tommy Dorsey Orchestra
   V. Youmans–I. Caeser,   Decca
   30704   (Harms, ASCAP)

9. **SUSIE DARLIN'**
   R. Luke
   R. Luke,   Dot 15781
   (Congressional, ASCAP)

10. **CHANTILLY LACE**
    The Big Bopper
    J. Richardson,   Mercury 71343
    (Glad, BMI)

November 3

1. **IT'S ALL IN THE GAME**
   T. Edwards
   Daves–Sigman,   M-G-M 12688
   (Remick, ASCAP)

2. **IT'S ONLY MAKE BELIEVE**
   C. Twitty
   Twitty–Nance,   M-G-M 12677
   (Marielle, BMI)

3. **TOPSY II**
   C. Cole
   Battle–Durham,   Love 50034
   (Cosmoplitan, BMI)

4. **TO KNOW HIM IS TO LOVE HIM**
   The Teddy Bears
   P. Spector,   Dore 503
   (Warman, BMI)

5. **TOM DOOLEY**
   The Kingston Trio
   D. Guard,   Capitol 4049
   (Beechwood, BMI)

6. **ROCK-IN' ROBIN**
   B. Day
   J. Thomas,   Class 229
   (Recordo, BMI)

7. **CHANTILLY LACE**
   The Big Bopper
   J. Richardson,   Mercury 71343
   (Glad, BMI)

8. **TEA FOR TWO CHA CHA**
   Tommy Dorsey Orchestra
   V. Youmans–I. Caeser,   Decca
   30704   (Harms, ASCAP)

9. **THE END**
   E. Grant
   J. Krondes–S. Jacobson,   Decca
   30719   (Criterion, ASCAP)

10. **BIRD DOG**
    The Everly Brothers
    B. Bryant,   Cadence
    1350   (Acuff–Rose, BMI)

1958

November 10

1. **IT'S ONLY MAKE BELIEVE**
C. Twitty
*Twitty–Nance, M-G-M 12677
(Marielle, BMI)*

2. **TOM DOOLEY**
The Kingston Trio
*D. Guard, Capitol 4049
(Beechwood, BMI)*

3. **IT'S ALL IN THE GAME**
T. Edwards
*Daves–Sigman, M-G-M 12688
(Remick, ASCAP)*

4. **TOPSY II**
C. Cole
*Battle–Durham, Love 50034
(Cosmopolitan, BMI)*

5. **TO KNOW HIM IS TO LOVE HIM**
The Teddy Bears
*P. Spector, Dore 503
(Warman, BMI)*

6. **THE END**
E. Grant
*J. Krondes–S. Jacobson, Decca
30719 (Criterion, ASCAP)*

7. **CHANTILLY LACE**
The Big Bopper
*J. Richardson, Mercury 71343
(Glad, BMI)*

8. **TEA FOR TWO CHA CHA**
Tommy Dorsey Orchestra
*V. Youmans–I. Caeser, Decca
30704 (Harms, ASCAP)*

9. **I GOT A FEELING**
R. Nelson
*B. Knight, Imperial 5545
(Eric, BMI)*

10. **ROCK-IN' ROBIN**
B. Day
*J. Thomas, Class 229
(Recordo, BMI)*

November 17

1. **IT'S ONLY MAKE BELIEVE**
C. Twitty
*Twitty–Nance, M-G-M 12677
(Marielle, BMI)*

2. **TO KNOW HIM IS TO LOVE HIM**
The Teddy Bears
*P. Spector, Dore 503
(Warman, BMI)*

3. **TOM DOOLEY**
The Kingston Trio
*D. Guard, Capitol 4049
(Beechwood, BMI)*

4. **TOPSY II**
C. Cole
*Battle–Durham, Love 50034
(Cosmopolitan, BMI)*

5. **IT'S ALL IN THE GAME**
T. Edwards
*Daves–Sigman, M-G-M 12688
(Remick, ASCAP)*

6. **CHANTILLY LACE**
The Big Bopper
*J. Richardson, Mercury 71343
(Glad, BMI)*

7. **BEEP BEEP**
The Playmates
*Donny–Morey–Chic, Roulette
4115 (H. and L., BMI)*

8. **QUEEN OF THE HOP**
B. Darin
*W. Harris–B– Darin, Atco
6127 (Walden–Tweed, ASCAP)*

9. **I GOT A FEELING**
R. Nelson
*B. Knight, Imperial 5545
(Eric, BMI)*

10. **LONESOME TOWN**
R. Nelson
*B. Knight, Imperial 5545
(Eric, BMI)*

November 24

1. **IT'S ONLY MAKE BELIEVE**
C. Twitty
*Twitty–Nance, M-G-M 12677
(Marielle, BMI)*

2. **TOM DOOLEY**
The Kingston Trio
*D. Guard, Capitol 4049
(Beechwood, BMI)*

3. **TO KNOW HIM IS TO LOVE HIM**
The Teddy Bears
*P. Spector, Dore 503
(Warman, BMI)*

4. **TOPSY II**
C. Cole
*Battle–Durham, Love 50034
(Cosmopolitan, BMI)*

5. **IT'S ALL IN THE GAME**
T. Edwards
*Daves–Sigman, M-G-M 12688
(Remick, ASCAP)*

6. **BEEP BEEP**
The Playmates
*Donny–Morey–Chic, Roulette
4115 (H. and L., BMI)*

7. **ONE NIGHT**
E. Presley
*D. Bartholomew–P. King,
Victor 7210 (Travis–Presley,
BMI)*

8. **I GOT STUNG**
E. Presley
*A. Schroeder–D. Hill,
Victor 7410 (Gladys, ASCAP)*

9. **LONESOME TOWN**
R. Nelson
*B. Knight, Imperial 5545
(Eric, BMI)*

10. **QUEEN OF THE HOP**
B. Darin
*W. Harris–B. Darin, Atco 6127
(Walden–Tweed, ASCAP)*

December 1

1. **TO KNOW HIM IS TO LOVE HIM**
The Teddy Bears
P. Spector, Dore 503
(Warman, BMI)

2. **TOM DOOLEY**
The Kingston Trio
D. Guard, Capitol 4049
(Beechwood, BMI)

3. **IT'S ONLY MAKE BELIEVE**
C. Twitty
Twitty–Nance, M-G-M 12677
(Marielle, BMI)

4. **BEEP BEEP**
The Playmates
Donny–Morey–Chic, Roulette
4115 (H. and L., BMI)

5. **ONE NIGHT**
E. Presley
D. Bartholomew–P. King,
Victor 7210 (Travis–Presley,
BMI)

6. **TOPSY II**
C. Cole
Battle–Durham, Love 50034
(Cosmopolitan, BMI)

7. **LONESOME TOWN**
R. Nelson
B. Knight, Imperial 5545
(Eric, BMI)

8. **PROBLEMS**
The Everly Brothers
F. Bryant–B. Bryant, Cadence
1355 (Acuff–Rose, BMI)

9. **I GOT STUNG**
E. Presley
A. Schroeder–D. Hill,
Victor 7410 (Gladys, ASCAP)

10. **IT'S ALL IN THE GAME**
T. Edwards
Daves–Sigman, M-G-M 12688
(Remick, ASCAP)

December 8

1. **TO KNOW HIM IS TO LOVE HIM**
The Teddy Bears
P. Spector, Dore 503
(Warman, BMI)

2. **TOM DOOLEY**
The Kingston Trio
D. Guard, Capitol 4049
(Beechwood, BMI)

3. **IT'S ONLY MAKE BELIEVE**
C. Twitty
Twitty–Nance, M-G-M 12677
(Marielle, BMI)

4. **BEEP BEEP**
The Playmates
Donny–Morey–Chic, Roulette
4115 (H. and L., BMI)

5. **ONE NIGHT**
E. Presley
D. Bartholomew–P. King,
Victor 7210 (Travis–Presley,
BMI)

6. **PROBLEMS**
The Everly Brothers
F. Bryant–B. Bryant, Cadence
1355 (Acuff–Rose, BMI)

7. **LONESOME TOWN**
R. Nelson
B. Knight, Imperial 5545
(Eric, BMI)

8. **SMOKE GETS IN YOUR EYES**
The Platters
Harbach–Kearns, Mercury
71353 (Harms, ASCAP)

9. **TOPSY II**
C. Cole
Battle–Durham, Love 50034
(Cosmopolitan, BMI)

10. **I GOT STUNG**
E. Presley
A. Schroeder–D. Hill,
Victor 7410 (Gladys, ASCAP)

December 15

1. **TOM DOOLEY**
The Kingston Trio
D. Guard, Capitol 4049
(Beechwood, BMI)

2. **PROBLEMS**
The Everly Brothers
F. Bryant–B. Bryant, Cadence
1355 (Acuff–Rose, BMI)

3. **TO KNOW HIM IS TO LOVE HIM**
The Teddy Bears
P. Spector, Dore 503
(Warman, BMI)

4. **BEEP BEEP**
The Playmates
Donny–Morey–Chic, Roulette
4115 (H. and L., BMI)

5. **ONE NIGHT**
E. Presley
D. Bartholomew–P. King,
Victor 7210 (Travis–Presley,
BMI)

6. **IT'S ONLY MAKE BELIEVE**
C. Twitty
Twitty–Nance, M-G-M 12677
(Marielle, BMI)

7. **SMOKE GETS IN YOUR EYES**
The Platters
Harbach–Kearns, Mercury
71353 (Harms, ASCAP)

8. **I GOT STUNG**
E. Presley
A. Schroeder–D. Hill,
Victor 7410 (Gladys, ASCAP)

9. **THE CHIPMUNK SONG**
D. Seville and the Chipmunks
R. Bagdasarian, Liberty 55168
(Monarch, ASCAP)

10. **LONESOME TOWN**
R. Nelson
B. Knight, Imperial 5545
(Eric, BMI)

December 22

1. **SMOKE GETS IN YOUR EYES**
The Platters
Harbach–Kearns, Mercury 71353 (Harms, ASCAP)

2. **TOM DOOLEY**
The Kingston Trio
D. Guard, Capitol 4049 (Beechwood, BMI)

3. **TO KNOW HIM IS TO LOVE HIM**
The Teddy Bears
P. Spector, Dore 503 (Warman, BMI)

4. **THE CHIPMUNK SONG**
D. Seville and the Chipmunks
R. Bagdasarian, Liberty 55168 (Monarch, ASCAP)

5. **PROBLEMS**
The Everly Brothers
F. Bryant–B. Bryant, Cadence 1355 (Acuff–Rose, BMI)

6. **ONE NIGHT**
E. Presley
D. Bartholomew–P. King, Victor 7210 (Travis–Presley, BMI)

7. **BEEP BEEP**
The Playmates
Donny–Morey–Chic, Roulette 4115 (H. and L., BMI)

8. **LONESOME TOWN**
R. Nelson
B. Knight, Imperial 5545 (Eric, BMI)

9. **IT'S ONLY MAKE BELIEVE**
C. Twitty
Twitty–Nance, M-G-M 12677 (Marielle, BMI)

10. **A LOVER'S QUESTION**
C. McPhatter
B. Benton–J. Williams, Atlantic 1199 (Eden–Progressive, BMI)

December 29

1. **THE CHIPMUNK SONG**
D. Seville and the Chipmunks
R. Bagdasarian, Liberty 55168 (Monarch, ASCAP)

2. **SMOKE GETS IN YOUR EYES**
The Platters
Harbach–Kearns, Mercury 71353 (Harms, ASCAP)

3. **TO KNOW HIM IS TO LOVE HIM**
The Teddy Bears
P. Spector, Dore 503 (Warman, BMI)

4. **ONE NIGHT**
E. Presley
D. Bartholomew–P. King, Victor 7210 (Travis–Presley, BMI)

5. **PROBLEMS**
The Everly Brothers
F. Bryant–B. Bryant, Cadence 1355 (Acuff–Rose, BMI)

6. **TOM DOOLEY**
The Kingston Trio
D. Guard, Capitol 4049 (Beechwood, BMI)

7. **LONESOME TOWN**
R. Nelson
B. Knight, Imperial 5545 (Eric, BMI)

8. **BEEP BEEP**
The Playmates
Donny–Morey–Chic, Roulette 4115 (H. and L., BMI)

9. **A LOVER'S QUESTION**
C. McPhatter
B. Benton–J. Williams, Atlantic 1199 (Eden–Progressive, BMI)

10. **WHOLE LOTTA LOVING**
F. Domino
A. Domino–D. Bartholomew, Imperial 5533 (Marquis, BMI)

113

RICK NELSON

In 1959, rock and roll blossomed with roots firmly in 1958. "American Bandstand" was still the Number 1 daytime show and the national center of teen music and styles. We had all grown a year older with "Bandstand" regulars like Billy Cook, Pat Mollitari, Myrna Horowitz, Ed Kelly and Charlie "Rubber Legs."

Elvis was still in the Army and his popularity had definitely slipped. He did have a few Top 10 hits in 1959 ("A Fool Such As I," "I Need Your Love Tonite," "A Big Hunk of Love"), but the focus of rock and roll had moved beyond him.

There was a new pack of heroes on the move. Most were already making it in 1958, some with the help of excessive promotion and payola, some because they could really sing. Among the best were Bobby Darin and Paul Anka. Darin wrote and sang "Dream Lover," one of the best songs of the year, which stayed in the Top 10 for nine weeks. It was a follow-up to "Splish Splash" which would prove to be a rock and roll classic. At the time, the song that won the most acclaim was Darin's recording of "Mack the Knife" which was selected by the record industry as the best record of the year. In retrospect it seems obvious that that song was the most praised because it was the least rock and roll. The success of a rock and roll singer was measured by his success doing non-rock and roll music.

Paul Anka was short and not sexy looking like Fabian, but he wrote his own songs and they were consistently good. He had already had one big hit with "Diana" and in 1959 he did "Lonely Boy" and "Put Your Head on My Shoulder."

Near the end of the year Bobby Rydell, or Robert Ridarelli, came to our attention when he recorded "We Got Love." Though he didn't write his hits, he was one of the better singers and more pleasing entertainers of the year.

On the other end of the talent spectrum was

1959

Doom doo-be-doo,
Dahm dahm da-ahm boo da-ahm
   oo-doo-be-doo,
Dahm dahm da-ahm doo da-ahm
   oo-doo-be-doo,
Dahm dahm da-ahm doo da-ahm
   oo-doo-be-doo,
Dahm dahm da-ahm boo da-ahm
   oo-doo-be-doo . . .

"Come Softly to Me"
The Fleetwoods

Fabian. He was all looks and no voice. Even those of us who loved him most knew in our heart of hearts that he couldn't carry a tune. But he was music to watch, and it was worth 89 cents to buy his picture and get the 45 record that came inside. He had a sort of Elvis Presley appeal with a crooked mouth, sly twinkling eyes and that long swept-back slicked hair.

There was another group of girls who swooned over Frankie Avalon. He and Fabian recorded for Chancellor Records and they must have both been sold to us by the same press agent. A mild rivalry was built between Frankie Avalon and Fabian, or rather between their fans, about who was the best (or best-looking). There is little doubt that Frankie Avalon was the better singer and "Venus" and "Why" did have melodies. So, by the end of the year when Fabian was moaning

> Hound dog man
> Hound dog man
> I wanna be your hound dog man

his appeal was growing as flat as his singing voice and he was "going to become an actor."

Up to this time, rock and roll was dominated by male singers, but now Connie Francis and Annette Funicello came into the spotlight. Both had that corny, whining style and their songs had a slight country twang with little rocking and rolling. Annette was the female counterpart of Fabian or Frankie Avalon. She was just the pert mouseketeer grown buxom.

Even with this wealth of new stars, rock and roll felt the impact of its greatest loss—the plane crash that killed three of the most promising, innovative and popular stars, Buddy Holly, Ritchie Valens and Texas deejay J. P. Richardson, the Big Bopper. Although Ritchie Valens and the Big Bopper contributed to rock and roll's greatest

classics with "Oh Donna," "La Bamba" and "Chantilly Lace," it was the contribution of Buddy Holly that would make its mark on rock and roll in the next decade. His style would be evident in the music of the early Beatles and through them would be spread to every corner of mid-sixties rock and roll.

Meanwhile, the American flag was adding stars as fast as rock and roll. On January 3 Ike signed the proclamation making Alaska the forty-ninth state. And on August 21 Hawaii was made the fiftieth state.

Toward the end of 1959, rock and roll became bigger news than the addition of states—even for the adults who were generally waiting like vultures for rock and roll's demise. It was the quiz show scandal that brought rock and roll to everyone's attention. The House of Representatives set up a committee to investigate and, within a few months, confessions were pouring out of Washington. After a year's denial of any rigging, Charles Van Doren confessed to the House that he had received answers in advance and had been coached on how to act in the isolation booth. Almost immediately his resignation from his post as English professor was accepted by Columbia University. And soon after Van Doren lost his $50,000 a year job at NBC as a consultant and regular guest on the "Today Show."

Patty Duke, the twelve-year-old actress who "won" $32,000 on the "$64,000 Challenge," admitted to the House that she had recited answers given to her minutes before the show. An Allentown, Pennsylvania department store owner admitted he paid $10,000 to get one of his employees on the "$64,000 Question" for store publicity.

As more and more confessions came out, the TV networks beat their breasts, ending all the big quiz shows, swearing the ones still on the air were honest, stopping the use of canned applause and laughter, even announcing that interview shows were rehearsed.

The House investigation moved swiftly through quiz shows to other areas of TV and radio and suddenly the word "payola" swept across the nation. Our favorite disk jockeys were called before the House to find out who was being paid to play certain records and who had other financial interest in seeing certain records or artists become popular.

Dick Clark was questioned and was finally ordered by ABC to get rid of his holdings in a record company and in music publishing houses or to leave ABC. With "American Bandstand" the top daytime show we had felt sure no one would threaten Dick Clark's position, but this ABC ultimatum let us know just how deeply rock and roll's establishment was threatened.

We had grown accustomed to the adult world's predictions that rock and roll was teetering, but this time it really was. Radio deejays and local TV record hop hosts were dropping like flies. We even began to doubt our own taste. Had we been sold rock and roll by the same adult world that criticized it? Were all the hits chosen by greedy businessmen instead of us? Were our favorite stars being used? Or were they exploiting us, too? Rock and roll was looking uglier and uglier as the investigation continued. Alan Freed was fired from his radio show and then lost his TV show. Stations were afraid to call their programming "rock and roll" because it was so tied to dishonesty that it scared away advertisers.

There was talk both that the payola scandal would end rock and roll altogether and that it could never exist without payoffs. Traditional musicians and deejays who were put out of work by rock and roll kept insisting that no one would have ever liked rock and roll if they had had a full free choice of music.

We listened to all this with fear in our hearts. We didn't want to lose rock and roll as we had lost the best radio and TV personalities. Even if we had been duped, we liked rock and roll. And no other music being played could take its place. It was hard to believe that the adult world was being fair in so zealously prosecuting the payoffs. Hadn't payola existed in the industry before rock and roll? Adults acted like their hits had been spontaneous and honorable and we were too young to challenge their record morality.

So, even with payola thrown up to us and even with our embarrassment over being taken in, we couldn't stop buying rock and roll. It was in our blood. How it got there was not of major importance. Record sales soared. We bought 20 per cent more records in 1959 than we had in 1958.

There was a magic in the music that was keeping it alive. Enough great music made its way to the air, either despite payola or perhaps partly because of it, to make 1959 rock and roll some of the best to that date. Every time we turned on the radio we knew we would hear the newest, most exciting, inventive delights that rock and roll had ever offered. Each new record was an adventure; each new Top 10 an intoxicating experience. The joy was being sung out in such strong doses that we simply couldn't resist it. Dancing burst from us. And the bond of rock and roll and youth and happiness poured through us and formed a special camaraderie that would last longer than rock and roll itself.

Because of this magic, rock and roll would live on, and 1959 would be remembered for things other than payola. For instance, it was the year the St. Lawrence Seaway was opened and dedicated by President Eisenhower and Queen Elizabeth on her Canadian tour.

Besides the meeting of Queen Elizabeth and President Eisenhower it was a year for meetings between many heads of state. There was the Big Four meeting in Geneva and Khrushchev's meeting with Ike at Camp David where they agreed on new Berlin talks and an expanded U.S.– U.S.S.R. exchange program. Khrushchev also met with Red Chinese leaders when he visited Peking for the Chinese Communist's tenth anniversary celebration.

Among traveling dignitaries was Cuban President Batista who fled Cuba on New Year's Day. And President Eisenhower made a 23,370-mile goodwill tour of Europe, North Africa and the middle East. But the best publicized trip was that of Vice President Nixon to Russia. There he dedicated the American National Exhibition in Moscow, debated with Premier Khrushchev and bid Khrushchev to direct energy toward home improvement instead of communist expansion. It was videotaped and broadcast coast to coast in this country.

Beside TV's quiz show problems and its splashy coverage of the Nixon-Khrushchev debate, there was little action in telecasting that made headlines. 1959 was the last year of the thirty-year-old "Voice of Firestone," seven-year-old "Omnibus" and the long running "Sgt. Bilko Show." It was also the final season for "Your Hit Parade" which just couldn't survive the rock and roll onslaught. Edward R. Murrow took the year off to travel and reflect, and TV also lost the services of Arthur Godfrey, who was off the air for six months while recuperating from a cancer operation. After his illness he returned only to do his morning radio show.

Television was back in the good graces of the movie industry when Hollywood realized it could make shows and commercials for TV and that it could even buy stations and compete directly.

As the film industry started to get back on its feet, so did the national economy. The United States did have to overcome the setback from the strike of half a million steel workers which lasted from July till the Supreme Court stopped it in November by upholding an injunction against the strike. The sting of the recession was still paining the automobile industry. Ford made a last attempt to keep the Edsel alive by dropping the highest priced models and selling it as a low-priced car. But it just couldn't make it because of all the new American compacts—Corvair, Falcon and the like—and the imported economy cars.

If we slowed down to save money on the highway, we made up for it in the sky. The new Boeing 707 began its commercial flights in January, cutting the flying time from New York to Los Angeles to four and a half hours. The United States military was racing Russia for dominance of the skies and beyond. The Russians were maintaining their lead as they sent up Luniks I, II and III, the last of which took the first pictures of the dark side of the moon. The United States missed the moon with Pioneer IV and otherwise count not produce the thrust to beat the Russians in outer space.

All in all the world situation wasn't much different than it had been in 1958. Washington was without John Foster Dulles, who died in May and was succeeded by Christian Herter as Secretary of State. The fighting in Laos had become more intense. And seven astronauts had been chosen for Project Mercury.

We looked about the same, dressing up the 1958 styles with scarab bracelets, circle pins and racoon-collared coats. A few of the brave tried patterned hose, but how could anyone take such a style seriously? The really daring among us bought bikinis although most never had the nerve to wear them. We felt very avant-garde trying two-piece bathing suits—two very big pieces. We also felt very sore when our newly exposed stomachs felt their first scorches of the sun.

Aside from the sunburn it was a wonderful summer. Maybe it was because we were growing up enough to enjoy a new kind of freedom. Our older friends were getting their drivers' licenses and we were discovering the joys of cruising the main drags of town and spending balmy evenings flirting at the drive-in restaurants. For the price of a Coke and french fries we had a whole evening's entertainment watching who drove through together and in whose car. The car radio was the constant source of entertainment. With no parents around, we could turn it up loud and sing. The music would blare through the drive-in and make us feel open—like talking to the kids in the next car. Songs like "The Battle of New Orleans," "Personality" and "Waterloo" became themes of the summer. Jerry Keller really said it all in "Here Comes Summer":

It's summer, drive-in movies every day
Here comes summer
Meet the gang at Joe's Cafe
If she's willing, we'll go steady right away
And let the sun shine bright on my happy
    summer home

Rock and roll was marking the highlights of each year, making it easy to relive a great summer as we daydreamed in geometry. It might have been dragged mercilessly over the coals in 1959, but it was so vital and spontaneous that the exposure of commercialization and dishonesty could not end it. Rather it cleared the least dedicated from the ranks of rock and rollers. And it gave us a perspective on our old idols that would stop us from giving our souls so completely and innocently again until the irresistible Beatles.

The Top Fifty
1959

1. **THE BATTLE OF NEW ORLEANS** — J. Horton
2. **MACK THE KNIFE** — B. Darin
3. **VENUS** — F. Avalon
4. **COME SOFTLY TO ME** — The Fleetwoods
5. **SMOKE GETS IN YOUR EYES** — The Platters
6. **MY HAPPINESS** — C. Francis
7. **STAGGER LEE** — L. Price
8. **TIGER** — Fabian
9. **THE THREE BELLS** — The Browns
10. **SLEEP WALK** — Santo and Johnny
11. **THE HAPPY ORGAN** — D. Cortez
12. **PERSONALITY** — L. Price
13. **QUIET VILLAGE** — M. Denny
14. **LIPSTICK ON YOUR COLLAR** — C. Francis
15. **LONELY BOY** — P. Anka
16. **PINK SHOELACES** — D. Stevens
17. **DONNA** — R. Valens
18. **TO KNOW HIM IS TO LOVE HIM** — The Teddy Bears
19. **PUT YOUR HEAD ON MY SHOULDER** — P. Anka
20. **MR. BLUE** — The Fleetwoods
21. **(TIL) I KISSED YOU** — The Everly Brothers
22. **EL PASO** — M. Robbins
23. **SORRY, I RAN ALL THE WAY HOME** — The Impalas
24. **KANSAS CITY** — W. Harrison
25. **A TEENAGER IN LOVE** — Dion and the Belmonts
26. **DREAM LOVER** — B. Darin
27. **CHARLIE BROWN** — The Coasters
28. **SIXTEEN CANDLES** — The Crests
29. **LAVENDER BLUE** — S. Turner
30. **SEA OF LOVE** — P. Phillips
31. **POISON IVY** — The Coasters
32. **TRAGEDY** — T. Wayne
33. **ALONG CAME JONES** — The Coasters
34. **WATERLOO** — S. Jackson
35. **MY HEART IS AN OPEN BOOK** — C. Dobkins, Jr.
36. **TEEN BEAT** — S. Nelson
37. **IN THE MOOD** — E. Fields
38. **DON'T YOU KNOW** — D. Reese
39. **THERE GOES MY BABY** — The Drifters
40. **A BIG HUNK O' LOVE** — E. Presley
41. **LONELY TEARDROPS** — J. Wilson
42. **GOTTA TRAVEL ON** — R. Nelson
43. **A FOOL SUCH AS I** — E. Presley
44. **TALLAHASSIE LASSIE** — F. Cannon
45. **WHAT'D I SAY** — R. Charles
46. **I'VE HAD IT** — The Bell Notes
47. **KOOKIE KOOKIE (LEND ME YOUR COMB)** — E. Byrnes with C. Stevens
48. **HEARTACHES BY THE NUMBER** — G. Mitchell
49. **BROKEN HEARTED MELODY** — S. Vaughn
50. **BABY TALK** — Jan and Dean

January 5

1. **THE CHIPMUNK SONG**
   D. Seville and the Chip-
   munks
   R. Bagdasarian, Liberty 55168
   (Monarch, ASCAP)

2. **SMOKE GETS IN YOUR
   EYES**
   The Platters
   Harbach–Kearns, Mercury
   71353 (Harms, ASCAP)

3. **TO KNOW HIM IS TO LOVE
   HIM**
   The Teddy Bears
   P. Spector, Dore 503
   (Warman, BMI)

4. **PROBLEMS**
   The Everly Brothers
   F. Bryant–B. Bryant, Cadence
   1355 (Acuff–Rose, BMI)

5. **ONE NIGHT**
   E. Presley
   D. Bartholomew–P. King
   Victor 7210 (Travis-Presley,
   BMI)

6. **MY HAPPINESS**
   C. Francis
   Peterson–Bergentine, M-G-M
   12738 (Happiness, ASCAP)

7. **TOM DOOLEY**
   The Kingston Trio
   D. Guard, Capitol 4049
   (Beechwood, BMI)

8. **A LOVER'S QUESTION**
   C. McPhatter
   B. Benton–T. Williams,
   Atlantic 1199 (Eden-
   Progressive, BMI)

9. **GOTTA TRAVEL ON**
   B. Grammar
   P. Clayton, Monument 400
   (Sanga, BMI)

10. **WHOLE LOTTA LOVING**
    F. Domino
    A. Domino–D. Bartholomew,
    Imperial 5553 (Marquis, BMI)

January 12

1. **SMOKE GETS IN YOUR
   EYES**
   The Platters
   Harbach–Kearns, Mercury
   71353 (Harms, ASCAP)

2. **MY HAPPINESS**
   C. Francis
   Peterson–Bergentine, M-G-M
   12738 (Happiness, ASCAP)

3. **GOTTA TRAVEL ON**
   B. Grammar
   P. Clayton, Monument 400
   (Sanga, BMI)

4. **THE CHIPMUNK SONG**
   D. Seville and the Chip-
   munks
   R. Bagdasarian, Liberty 55168
   (Monarch, ASCAP)

5. **WHOLE LOTTA LOVING**
   F. Domino
   A. Domino–D. Bartholomew,
   Imperial 5553
   (Marquis, BMI)

6. **TO KNOW HIM IS TO LOVE
   HIM**
   The Teddy Bears
   P. Spector, Dore 503
   (Warman, BMI)

7. **ONE NIGHT**
   E. Presley
   D. Bartholomew–P. King,
   Victor 7210 (Travis-Presley,
   BMI)

8. **A LOVER'S QUESTION**
   C. McPhatter
   B. Benton–T. Williams, Atlantic
   1199 (Eden-Progressive, BMI)

9. **PROBLEMS**
   The Everly Brothers
   F. Bryant–B. Bryant, Cadence
   1355 (Acuff–Rose, BMI)

10. **LONESOME TOWN**
    R. Nelson
    B. Knight, Imperial 5545
    (Eric, BMI)

1959

January 19

1. **SMOKE GETS IN YOUR EYES**
The Platters
Harbach–Kearns, Mercury 71353 (Harms, ASCAP)

2. **MY HAPPINESS**
C. Francis
Peterson–Bergentine, M-G-M 12738 (Happiness, ASCAP)

3. **DONNA**
R. Valens
R. Valens, Del-Fi 4110 (Kemo, BMI)

4. **SIXTEEN CANDLES**
The Crests
Dicson–Khent, Coed 506 (January, BMI)

5. **THE CHIPMUNK SONG**
D. Seville and the Chipmunks
R. Bagdasarian, Liberty 55168 (Monarch, ASCAP)

6. **STAGGER LEE**
L. Price
Archibald–Price–Logan, ABC-Paramount 9927 (Sheldon, BMI)

7. **TO KNOW HIM IS TO LOVE HIM**
The Teddy Bears
P. Spector, Dore 503 (Warman, BMI)

8. **A LOVER'S QUESTION**
C. McPhatter
B. Benton–T. Williams, Atlantic 1199 (Eden–Progressive, BMI)

9. **LONELY TEARDROPS**
J. Wilson
B. Gordy–T. Carlo, Brunswick 55105 (Pearl, BMI)

10. **GOODBYE BABY**
J. Scott
J. Scott, Carlton 493 (Starfire, BMI)

January 26

1. **SMOKE GETS IN YOUR EYES**
The Platters
Harbach–Kearns, Mercury 71353 (Harms, ASCAP)

2. **MY HAPPINESS**
C. Francis
Peterson–Bergentine, M-G-M 12738 (Happiness, ASCAP)

3. **DONNA**
R. Valens
R. Valens, Del-Fi 4110 (Kemo, BMI)

4. **SIXTEEN CANDLES**
The Crests
Dicson–Khent, Coed 506 (January, BMI)

5. **STAGGER LEE**
L. Price
Archibald–Price–Logan, ABC-Paramount 9927 (Sheldon, BMI)

6. **GOTTA TRAVEL ON**
B. Grammar
P. Clayton, Monument 400 (Sanga, BMI)

7. **A LOVER'S QUESTION**
C. McPhatter
B. Benton–T. Williams, Atlantic 1199 (Eden–Progressive, BMI)

8. **LONELY TEARDROPS**
J. Wilson
B. Gordy–T. Carlo, Brunswick 55105 (Pearl, BMI)

9. **GOODBYE BABY**
J. Scott
J. Scott, Carlton 493 (Starfire, BMI)

10. **WHOLE LOTTA LOVING**
F. Domino
A. Domino–D. Bartholomew, Imperial 5553 (Marquis, BMI)

February 2

1. **SMOKE GETS IN YOUR EYES**
The Platters
Harbach–Kearns, Mercury 71353 (Harms, ASCAP)

2. **ALL-AMERICAN BOY**
B. Parsons
B. Parsons–O. Lunsford, Fraternity 835 (Buckeye, ASCAP)

3. **DONNA**
R. Valens
R. Valens, Del-Fi 4110 (Kemo, BMI)

4. **SIXTEEN CANDLES**
The Crests
Dicson–Khent, Coed 506 (January, BMI)

5. **STAGGER LEE**
L. Price
Archibald–Price–Logan, ABC-Paramount 9927 (Sheldon, BMI)

6. **MY HAPPINESS**
C. Francis
Peterson–Bergentine, M-G-M 12738 (Happiness, ASCAP)

7. **GOTTA TRAVEL ON**
B. Grammar
P. Clayton, Monument 400 (Sanga, BMI)

8. **LONELY TEARDROPS**
J. Wilson
B. Gordy–T. Carlo, Brunswick 55105 (Pearl, BMI)

9. **A LOVER'S QUESTION**
C. McPhatter
B.Benton–T. Williams, Atlantic 1199 (Eden–Progressive, BMI)

10. **GOODBYE BABY**
J. Scott
J. Scott, Carlton 493 (Starfire, BMI)

February 9

1. **STAGGER LEE**
L. Price
Archibald–Price–Logan,
ABC–Paramount 9927
(Sheldon, BMI)

2. **SIXTEEN CANDLES**
The Crests
Dicson–Khent, Coed 506
(January, BMI)

3. **DONNA**
R. Valens
R. Valens, Del-Fi 4110
(Kemo, BMI)

4. **SMOKE GETS IN YOUR EYES**
The Platters
Harbach–Kearns, Mercury 71353
(Harms, ASCAP)

5. **ALL-AMERICAN BOY**
B. Parsons
B. Parsons–O. Lunsford,
Fraternity 835
(Buckeye, ASCAP)

6. **MY HAPPINESS**
C. Francis
Peterson–Bergentine, M-G-M
12738 (Happiness, ASCAP)

7. **GOODBYE BABY**
J. Scott
J. Scott, Carlton 493
(Starfire, BMI)

8. **LONELY TEARDROPS**
J. Wilson
B. Gordy–T. Carlo, Brunswick
55105 (Pearl, BMI)

9. **MANHATTAN SPIRITUAL**
Reg Owen Orchestra
B. Naxted, Palette 5005
(Zodiac, BMI)

10. **GOTTA TRAVEL ON**
B. Grammar
P. Clayton, Monument 400
(Sanga, BMI)

February 16

1. **STAGGER LEE**
L. Price
Archibald–Logan–Price,
ABC–Paramount 9927
(Sheldon, BMI)

2. **SIXTEEN CANDLES**
The Crests
Dicson–Khent, Coed 506
(January, BMI)

3. **DONNA**
R. Valens
R. Valens, Del-Fi 4110
(Kemo, BMI)

4. **SMOKE GETS IN YOUR EYES**
The Platters
Harbach–Kearns, Mercury
71353 (Harms, ASCAP)

5. **MANHATTAN SPIRITUAL**
Reg Owen Orchestra
B. Naxted, Palette 5005
(Zodiac, BMI)

6. **MY HAPPINESS**
C. Francis
Peterson–Bergentine, M-G-M
12738 (Happiness, ASCAP)

7. **ALL-AMERICAN BOY**
B. Parsons
B. Parsons–O. Lunsford,
Fraternity 835 (Buckeye,
ASCAP)

8. **LONELY TEARDROPS**
J. Wilson
B. Gordy–T. Carlo, Brunswick
55105 (Pearl, BMI)

9. **GOODBYE BABY**
J. Scott
J. Scott, Carlton 493
(Starfire, BMI)

10. **GOTTA TRAVEL ON**
B. Grammar
P. Carlton, Monument 400
(Sanga, BMI)

February 23

1. **STAGGER LEE**
L. Price
Archibald–Logan–Price, ABC–
Paramount 9927 (Sheldon, BMI)

2. **SIXTEEN CANDLES**
The Crests
Dicson–Khent, Coed 506
(January, BMI)

3. **DONNA**
R. Valens
R. Valens, Del-Fi 4110
(Kemo, BMI)

4. **ALL-AMERICAN BOY**
B. Parsons
B. Parsons–O. Lunsford,
Fraternity 835 (Buckeye,
ASCAP)

5. **CHARLIE BROWN**
The Coasters
J. Leiber–M. Stoller, Atco
6132 (Tiger, BMI)

6. **I CRIED A TEAR**
L. Baker
A. Julia, Atlantic 2007
(Progressive, BMI)

7. **TALL PAUL**
Annette
B. Roberts–B. & D. Sherman,
Disneyland 118 (Music World,
BMI)

8. **PETITE FLEUR**
Chris Barber's Jazz Band
S. Bechet, Laurie 3022
(Hill & Range, BMI)

9. **LONELY TEARDROPS**
J. Wilson
B. Gordy–T. Carlo, Brunswick
55105 (Pearl, BMI)

10. **PETER GUNN THEME**
R. Anthony
H. Mancini, Capitol 4041
(Northridge, ASCAP)

1959

March 2

1. **STAGGER LEE**
L. Price
Archibald–Price–Logan, ABC–Paramount 9927 (Sheldon, BMI)

2. **DONNA**
R. Valens
R. Valens, Del-Fi 4110 (Kemo, BMI)

3. **CHARLIE BROWN**
The Coasters
J. Leiber–M. Stoller, Atco 6132 (Tiger, BMI)

4. **SIXTEEN CANDLES**
The Crests
Dicson–Khent, Coed 506 (January, BMI)

5. **PETITE FLEUR**
Chris Barber's Jazz Band
S. Bechet, Laurie 3022 (Hill & Range, BMI)

6. **I CRIED A TEAR**
L. Baker
A. Julia, Atlantic 2007 (Progressive, BMI)

7. **VENUS**
F. Avalon
Marshall, Chancellor 1031 (Rambed–Jimskip, BMI)

8. **PETER GUNN THEME**
R. Anthony
H. Mancini, Capitol 4041 (Northridge, ASCAP)

9. **ALL-AMERICAN BOY**
B. Parsons
B. Parsons–O. Lunsford, Fraternity 835 (Buckeye, ASCAP)

10. **ALVIN'S HARMONICA**
D. Seville and the Chipmunks
R. Bagdasarian, Liberty 55179 (Monarch, ASCAP)

March 9

1. **VENUS**
F. Avalon
Marshall, Chancellor 1031 (Rambed–Jimskip, BMI)

2. **CHARLIE BROWN**
The Coasters
J. Leiber–M. Stoller, Atco 6132 (Tiger, BMI)

3. **STAGGER LEE**
L. Price
Archibald–Price–Logan, ABC–Paramount 9927 (Sheldon, BMI)

4. **DONNA**
R. Valens
R. Valens, Del-Fi 4110 (Kemo, BMI)

5. **ALVIN'S HARMONICA**
D. Seville and the Chipmunks
R. Bagdasarian, Liberty 55179 (Monarch, ASCAP)

6. **I'VE HAD IT**
The Bell Notes
C. Boumura–R. Ceroni, Time 1004 (Brent, BMI)

7. **IT'S JUST A MATTER OF TIME**
B. Benton
B. Benton–H. Otis, Mercury 71394 (Eden, BMI)

8. **PETITE FLEUR**
Chris Barber's Jazz Band
S. Bechet, Laurie 3022 (Hill & Range, BMI)

9. **I CRIED A TEAR**
L. Baker
A. Julia, Atlantic 2007 (Progressive, BMI)

10. **SIXTEEN CANDLES**
The Crests
Dicson–Khent, Coed 506 (January, BMI)

March 16

1. **VENUS**
F. Avalon
Marshall, Chancellor 1031 (Rambed–Jimskip, BMI)

2. **CHARLIE BROWN**
The Coasters
J. Leiber–M. Stoller, Atco 6132 (Tiger, BMI)

3. **STAGGER LEE**
L. Price
Archibald–Logan–Price, ABC–Paramount 9927 (Sheldon, BMI)

4. **IT'S JUST A MATTER OF TIME**
B. Benton
B. Benton–H. Otis, Mercury 71394 (Eden, BMI)

5. **ALVIN'S HARMONICA**
D. Seville and the Chipmunks
R. Bagdasarian, Liberty 55179 (Monarch, ASCAP)

6. **TRAGEDY**
T. Wayne
Burch–Nelson, Fernwood 109 (Bluff City, BMI)

7. **NEVER BE ANYONE ELSE BUT YOU**
R. Nelson
B. Knight, Capitol 4041 (Eric, BMI)

8. **I'VE HAD IT**
The Bell Notes
C. Boumura–R. Ceroni Time 1004 (Brent, BMI)

9. **DONNA**
R. Valens
R. Valens, Del-Fi 4110 (Kemo, BMI)

10. **PETER GUNN THEME**
R. Anthony
H. Mancini, Capitol 4041 (Northridge, ASCAP)

125

March 23

1. **VENUS**
F. Avalon
Marshall, Chancellor 1031
(Rambed–Jimskip, BMI)

2. **CHARLIE BROWN**
The Coasters
J. Leiber–M. Stoller,
Atco 6132 (Tiger, BMI)

3. **ALVIN'S HARMONICA**
D. Seville and the Chip-
munks
R. Bagdasarian, Liberty 55179
(Monarch, ASCAP)

4. **IT'S JUST A MATTER OF
TIME**
B. Benton
B. Benton–H. Otis, Mercury
71394 (Eden, BMI)

5. **TRAGEDY**
T. Wayne
Burch–Nelson, Fernwood 109
(Bluff City, BMI)

6. **I'VE HAD IT**
The Bell Notes
C. Boumura–R. Ceroni,
Time 1004 (Brent, BMI)

7. **STAGGER LEE**
L. Price
Archibald–Logan–Price,
ABC–Paramount 9927
(Sheldon, BMI)

8. **COME SOFTLY TO ME**
The Fleetwoods
Troxel–Christopher–Ellis,
Dolphin 1 (Cornerstone, BMI)

9. **DONNA**
R. Valens
R. Valens, Del-Fi 4110
(Kemo, BMI)

10. **NEVER BE ANYONE ELSE
BUT YOU**
R. Nelson
B. Knight, Imperial 5565
(Eric, BMI)

March 30

1. **VENUS**
F. Avalon
Marshall, Chancellor 1031
(Rambed–Jimskip, BMI)

2. **COME SOFTLY TO ME**
The Fleetwoods
Troxel–Cristopher–Ellis,
Dolphin 1 (Cornerstone, BMI)

3. **CHARLIE BROWN**
The Coasters
J. Leiber–M. Stoller,
Atco 6132 (Tiger, BMI)

4. **IT'S JUST A MATTER OF
TIME**
B. Benton
B. Benton–H. Otis,
Mercury 71394 (Eden, BMI)

5. **TRAGEDY**
T. Wayne
Burch–Nelson, Fernwood 109
(Bluff City, BMI)

6. **ALVIN'S HARMONICA**
D. Seville and the Chip-
munks
R. Bagdasarian, Liberty 55179
(Monarch, ASCAP)

7. **NEVER BE ANYONE ELSE
BUT YOU**
R. Nelson
B. Knight, Imperial 5565
(Eric, BMI)

8. **PINK SHOELACES**
D. Stevens
M. Brant, Crystalette 724
(Pioneer, BMI)

9. **I'VE HAD IT**
The Bell Notes
C. Boumura–R. Ceroni,
Time 1004 (Brent, BMI)

10. **IT'S LATE**
R. Nelson
D. Burnette, Imperial 5565
(Eric, BMI)

April 6

1. **VENUS**
F. Avalon
Marshall, Chancellor 1031
(Rambed–Jimskip, BMI)

2. **COME SOFTLY TO ME**
The Fleetwoods
Troxel–Cristopher–Ellis,
Dolphin 1 (Cornerstone, BMI)

3. **IT'S JUST A MATTER OF
TIME**
B. Benton
B. Benton–H. Otis,
Mercury 71394 (Eden, BMI)

4. **PINK SHOELACES**
D. Stevens
M. Brant, Crystalette 724
(Pioneer, BMI)

5. **TRAGEDY**
T. Wayne
Burch–Nelson, Fernwood 109
(Bluff City, BMI)

6. **NEVER BE ANYONE ELSE
BUT YOU**
R. Nelson
B. Knight, Imperial 5565
(Eric, BMI)

7. **CHARLIE BROWN**
The Coasters
J. Leiber–M. Stoller,
Atco 6132 (Tiger, BMI)

8. **ALVIN'S HARMONICA**
D. Seville and the Chip-
munks
R. Bagdasarian, Liberty 55179
(Monarch, ASCAP)

9. **IT'S LATE**
R. Nelson
D. Burnette, Imperial 5565
(Eric, BMI)

10. **GUITAR BOOGIE SHUFFLE**
The Virtues
Smith Hunt 324
(Shapiro–Bernstein, ASCAP)

April 13

1. **COME SOFTLY TO ME**
The Fleetwoods
*Troxel–Cristopher–Ellis,
Dolphin 1 (Cornerstone, BMI)*
2. **VENUS**
F. Avalon
*Marshall, Chancellor 1031
(Rambed–Jimskip, BMI)*
3. **PINK SHOELACES**
D. Stevens
*M. Brant, Crystalette 724
(Pioneer, BMI)*
4. **IT'S JUST A MATTER OF TIME**
B. Benton
*B. Benton–H. Otis, Mercury
71394 (Eden, BMI)*
5. **TRAGEDY**
T. Wayne
*Burch–Nelson, Fernwood 109
(Bluff City, BMI)*
6. **NEVER BE ANYONE ELSE BUT YOU**
R. Nelson
*B. Knight, Imperial 5565
(Eric, BMI)*
7. **I NEED YOUR LOVE TONIGHT**
E. Presley
*S. Wayne–V. Reichner,
Victor 7506 (Gladys, ASCAP)*
8. **GUITAR BOOGIE SHUFFLE**
The Virtues
*Smith, Hunt 324
(Shapiro–Bernstein, ASCAP)*
9. **CHARLIE BROWN**
The Coasters
*J. Leiber–M. Stoller, Atco 6132
(Tiger, BMI)*
10. **A FOOL SUCH AS I**
E. Presley
*Trader, Victor 7506
(Leeds, ASCAP)*

April 20

1. **COME SOFTLY TO ME**
The Fleetwoods
*Troxel–Christopher–Ellis,
Dolphin 1 (Cornerstone, BMI)*
2. **VENUS**
F. Avalon
*Marshall, Chancellor 1031
(Rambed–Jimskip, BMI)*
3. **PINK SHOELACES**
D. Stevens
*M. Brant, Crystalette 724
(Pioneer, BMI)*
4. **GUITAR BOOGIE SHUFFLE**
The Virtues
*Smith, Hunt 324
(Shapiro–Bernstein, ASCAP)*
5. **I NEED YOUR LOVE TONIGHT**
E. Presley
*S. Wayne–V. Reichner,
Victor 7506 (Gladys, ASCAP)*
6. **IT'S JUST A MATTER OF TIME**
B. Benton
*B. Benton–H. Otis,
Mercury 71394 (Eden, BMI)*
7. **NEVER BY ANYONE ELSE BUT YOU**
R. Nelson
*B. Knight, Imperial 5565
(Eric, BMI)*
8. **TRAGEDY**
T. Wayne
*Burch–Nelson, Fernwood 109
(Bluff City, BMI)*
9. **A FOOL SUCH AS I**
E. Presley
*Trader, Victor 7506
(Leeds, ASCAP)*
10. **TURN ME LOOSE**
Fabian
*D. Tomas–M. Shuman,
Chancellor 1033 (Avalon, BMI)*

April 27

1. **COME SOFTLY TO ME**
The Fleetwoods
*Troxel–Cristopher–Ellis,
Dolphin 1 (Cornerstone, BMI)*
2. **GUITAR BOOGIE SHUFFLE**
The Virtues
*Smith, Hunt 324
(Shapiro–Bernstein, ASCAP)*
3. **PINK SHOELACES**
D. Stevens
*M. Brant, Crystallette 724
(Pioneer, BMI)*
4. **VENUS**
F. Avalon
*Marshall, Chancellor 1031
(Rambed–Jimskip, BMI)*
5. **A FOOL SUCH AS I**
E. Presley
*Trader, Victor 7506
(Leeds, ASCAP)*
6. **THE HAPPY ORGAN**
D. Cortez
*Woods–Clowny–Kriegsman,
Clock 1009 (Lowell, BMI)*
7. **I NEED YOUR LOVE TONIGHT**
E. Presley
*S. Wayne–V. Reichner,
Victor 7506 (Gladys, ASCAP)*
8. **TELL HIM NO**
Travis and Bob
*T. Pritchett, Sandy 1017
(Burnt–Oak–Lowell, BMI)*
9. **SORRY, I RAN ALL THE WAY HOME**
The Impalas
*Zwirn–Giosasi, Cub 9022
(Figure, BMI)*
10. **TURN ME LOOSE**
Fabian
*D. Tomas–M. Shuman,
Chancellor 1033 (Avalon, BMI)*

May 4

1. **COME SOFTLY TO ME**
The Fleetwoods
Troxel–Cristopher–Ellis,
Dolphin 1 (Cornerstone, BMI)

2. **THE HAPPY ORGAN**
D. Cortez
Woods–Clowny–Kriegsman,
Clock 1009 (Lowell, BMI)

3. **SORRY, I RAN ALL THE WAY HOME**
The Impalas
Zwirn–Giosasi, Cub 9022
(Figure, BMI)

4. **PINK SHOELACES**
D. Stevens
M. Brant, Crystalette 724
(Pioneer, BMI)

5. **GUITAR BOOGIE SHUFFLE**
The Virtues
Smith, Hunt 324
(Shapiro–Bernstein, ASCAP)

6. **A FOOL SUCH AS I**
E. Presley
Trader, Victor 7506
(Leeds, ASCAP)

7. **I NEED YOUR LOVE TONIGHT**
E. Presley
S. Wayne–V. Reichner,
Victor 7506 (Gladys, ASCAP)

8. **TELL HIM NO**
Travis and Bob
T. Pritchett, Sandy 1017
(Burnt–Oak–Lowell, BMI)

9. **VENUS**
F. Avalon
Marshall, Chancellor 1031
(Rambed–Jimskip, BMI)

10. **TURN ME LOOSE**
Fabian
D. Tomas–M. Shuman,
Chancellor 1033 (Avalon, BMI)

May 11

1. **THE HAPPY ORGAN**
D. Cortez
Woods–Clowny–Kriegsman,
Clock 1009 (Lowell, BMI)

2. **SORRY, I RAN ALL THE WAY HOME**
The Impalas
Zwirn–Giosasi, Cub 9022
(Figure, BMI)

3. **COME SOFTLY TO ME**
The Fleetwoods
Troxel–Cristopher–Ellis,
Dolphin 1 (Cornerstone, BMI)

4. **KOOKIE, KOOKIE (LEND ME YOUR COMB)**
E. Byrnes with C. Stevens
I. Taylor, Warner Brothers
5047 (Witmark, ASCAP)

5. **A FOOL SUCH AS I**
E. Presley
Trader, Victor 7506
(Leeds, ASCAP)

6. **KANSAS CITY**
W. Harrison
J. Leiber–M. Stoller,
Fury 1023 (Fire, BMI)

7. **GUITAR BOOGIE SHUFFLE**
The Virtues
Smith, Hunt 324
(Shapiro–Bernstein, ASCAP)

8. **PINK SHOELACES**
D. Stevens
M. Brant, Crystalette 724
(Pioneer, BMI)

9. **TURN ME LOOSE**
Fabian
D. Tomas–M. Shuman,
Chancellor 1033 (Avalon, BMI)

10. **I NEED YOUR LOVE TONIGHT**
E. Presley
S. Wayne–V. Reichner,
Victor 7506 (Gladys, ASCAP)

May 18

1. **SORRY, I RAN ALL THE WAY HOME**
The Impalas
Zwirn–Giosasi, Cub 9022
(Figure, BMI)

2. **THE HAPPY ORGAN**
D. Cortez
Woods–Clowny–Kriegsman,
Clock 1009 (Lowell, BMI)

3. **KANSAS CITY**
W. Harrison
J. Leiber–M. Stoller,
Fury 1023 (Fire, BMI)

4. **A TEENAGER IN LOVE**
Dion and the Belmonts
D. Pomus–M. Shuman, Laurie
3627 (Rumbalero, BMI)

5. **KOOKIE, KOOKIE (LEND ME YOUR COMB)**
E. Byrnes with C. Stevens
I. Taylor, Warner Brothers
5047 (Witmark, ASCAP)

6. **QUIET VILLAGE**
M. Denny
L. Baxter, Liberty 55162
(Wright, BMI)

7. **TURN ME LOOSE**
Fabian
D. Tomas–M. Shuman,
Chancellor 1033 (Avalon, BMI)

8. **DREAM LOVER**
B. Darin
B. Darin, Atco 6140
(Progressive–Fern–Trinity, BMI)

9. **PINK SHOELACES**
D. Stevens
M. Brant, Crystallette 724
(Pioneer, BMI)

10. **THE BATTLE OF NEW ORLEANS**
J. Horton
J. Driftwood, Columbia
41339 (Warden, BMI)

May 25

1. **SORRY, I RAN ALL THE WAY HOME**
The Impalas
Zwirn–Giosasi, Cub 9022 (Figure, BMI)

2. **KANSAS CITY**
W. Harrison
J. Leiber–M. Stoller, Fury 1009 (Fire, BMI)

3. **THE BATTLE OF NEW ORLEANS**
J. Horton
J. Driftwood, Columbia 41339 (Warden, BMI)

4. **QUIET VILLAGE**
M. Denny
L. Baxter, Liberty 55162 (Baxter–Wright, BMI)

5. **A TEENAGER IN LOVE**
Dion and the Belmonts
D. Pomus–M. Shuman, Laurie 3627 (Rumbalero, BMI)

6. **KOOKIE, KOOKIE (LEND ME YOUR COMB)**
E. Byrnes with C. Stevens
I. Taylor, Warner Brothers 5047 (Witmark, ASCAP)

7. **PERSONALITY**
L. Price
Logan–Price, ABC–Paramount 10018 (Lloyd–Logan, BMI)

8. **DREAM LOVER**
B. Darin
B. Darin, Atco 6140 (Progressive–Fern–Trinity, BMI)

9. **THE HAPPY ORGAN**
D. Cortez
Woods–Clowny–Kriegsman, Clock 1009 (Lowell, BMI)

10. **ONLY YOU**
F. Pourcel
Ram–Rand, Capitol 4165 (Wildwood, BMI)

June 1

1. **THE BATTLE OF NEW ORLEANS**
J. Horton
J. Driftwood, Columbia 41339 (Warden, BMI)

2. **KANSAS CITY**
W. Harrison
J. Leiber–M. Stoller, Fury 1023 (Fire, BMI)

3. **DREAM LOVER**
B. Darin
B. Darin, Atco 6140 (Progressive–Fern–Trinity, BMI)

4. **QUIET VILLAGE**
M. Denny
L. Baxter, Liberty 55162 (Baxter–Wright, BMI)

5. **PERSONALITY**
L. Price
Logan–Price, ABC–Paramount 10018 (Lloyd–Logan, BMI)

6. **A TEENAGER IN LOVE**
Dion and the Belmonts
D. Pomus–M. Shuman, Laurie 3627 (Rumbalero, BMI)

7. **KOOKIE, KOOKIE (LEND ME YOUR COMB)**
E. Byrnes with C. Stevens
I. Taylor, Warner Brothers 5047 (Witmark, ASCAP)

8. **SORRY, I RAN ALL THE WAY HOME**
The Impalas
Zwirn–Giosasi, Cub 9022 (Figure, BMI)

9. **ONLY YOU**
F. Pourcel
Ram–Rand, Capitol 4165 (Wildwood, BMI)

10. **THE HAPPY ORGAN**
D. Cortez
Woods–Clowny–Kriegsman, Clock 1009 (Lowell, BMI)

June 8

1. **THE BATTLE OF NEW ORLEANS**
J. Horton
J. Driftwood, Columbia 41339 (Warden, BMI)

2. **DREAM LOVER**
B. Darin
B. Darin, Atco 6140 (Progressive–Fern–Trinity, BMI)

3. **PERSONALITY**
L. Price
Logan–Price, ABC–Paramount 10018 (Lloyd–Logan, BMI)

4. **KANSAS CITY**
W. Harrison
J. Leiber–M. Stoller, Fury 1023 (Fire, BMI)

5. **QUIET VILLAGE**
M. Denny
L. Baxter, Liberty 55162 (Baxter–Wright, BMI)

6. **A TEENAGER IN LOVE**
Dion and the Belmonts
D. Pomus–M. Shuman, Laurie 3627 (Rumbalero, BMI)

7. **KOOKIE, KOOKIE (LEND ME YOUR COMB)**
E. Byrnes with C. Stevens
I. Taylor, Warner Brothers 5047 (Witmark, ASCAP)

8. **SORRY, I RAN ALL THE WAY HOME**
The Impalas
Zwirn–Giosasi, Cub 9022 (Figure, BMI)

9. **ONLY YOU**
F. Pourcel
Ram–Rand, Capitol 4165 (Wildwood, BMI)

10. **THE HAPPY ORGAN**
D. Cortez
Woods–Clowny–Kriegsman, Clock 1009 (Lowell, BMI)

June 15

1. **THE BATTLE OF NEW OR-
   LEANS**
   J. Horton
   *J. Driftwood, Columbia 41339
   (Warden, BMI)*

2. **PERSONALITY**
   L. Price
   *Logan–Price, ABC–Paramount
   10018 (Lloyd–Logan, BMI)*

3. **DREAM LOVER**
   B. Darin
   *B. Darin, Atco 6140
   (Progressive–Fern–Trinity, BMI)*

4. **QUIET VILLAGE**
   M. Denny
   *L. Baxter, Liberty 55162
   (Baxter–Wright, BMI)*

5. **KANSAS CITY**
   W. Harrison
   *J. Leiber–M. Stoller,
   Fury 1023 (Fire, BMI)*

6. **A TEENAGER IN LOVE**
   Dion and the Belmonts
   *D. Pomus–M. Shuman, Laurie
   3627 (Rumbalero, BMI)*

7. **KOOKIE, KOOKIE (LEND
   ME YOUR COMB)**
   E. Byrnes with C. Stevens
   *I. Taylor, Warner Brothers
   5047 (Witmark, ASCAP)*

8. **LONELY BOY**
   P. Anka
   *P. Anka, ABC–Paramount
   10022 (Spanka, BMI)*

9. **ONLY YOU**
   F. Pourcel
   *Ram–Rand, Capitol 4165
   (Wildwood, BMI)*

10. **TALLAHASSEE LASSIE**
    F. Cannon
    *Slay–Crewe–Picariello,
    Swan 4031 (Conley, BMI)*

June 22

1. **THE BATTLE OF NEW OR-
   LEANS**
   J. Horton
   *J. Driftwood, Columbia
   41339 (Warden, BMI)*

2. **PERSONALITY**
   L. Price
   *Logan–Price, ABC–Paramount
   10018 (Lloyd–Logan, BMI)*

3. **LONELY BOY**
   P. Anka
   *P. Anka, ABC–Paramount 10022
   (Spanka, BMI)*

4. **LIPSTICK ON YOUR COLLAR**
   C. Francis
   *Lewis–Goehring, M-G-M 12793
   (Joy, ASCAP)*

5. **DREAM LOVER**
   B. Darin
   *B. Darin, Atco 6140
   (Progressive–Fern–Trinity, BMI)*

6. **KANSAS CITY**
   W. Harrison
   *J. Leiber–M. Stoller,
   Fury 1023 (Fire, BMI)*

7. **QUIET VILLAGE**
   M. Denny
   *L. Baxter, Liberty 55162
   (Baxter–Wright, BMI)*

8. **TALLAHASSEE LASSIE**
   F. Cannon
   *Slay–Crewe–Picariello,
   Swan 4031 (Conley, BMI)*

9. **A TEENAGER IN LOVE**
   Dion and the Belmonts
   *D. Pomus–M. Shuman, Laurie
   3627 (Rumbalero, BMI)*

10. **ALONG CAME JONES**
    The Coasters
    *J. Leiber–M. Stoller,
    Atco 6141 (Tiger, BMI)*

June 29

1. **THE BATTLE OF NEW OR-
   LEANS**
   J. Horton
   *J. Driftwood, Columbia 41339
   (Warden, BMI)*

2. **PERSONALITY**
   L. Price
   *Logan–Price, ABC–Paramount
   10018 (Lloyd–Logan, BMI)*

3. **LONELY BOY**
   P. Anka
   *P. Anka, ABC–Paramount 10022
   (Spanka, BMI)*

4. **LIPSTICK ON YOUR COLLAR**
   C. Francis
   *Lewis–Goehring, M-G-M 12793
   (Joy, ASCAP)*

5. **DREAM LOVER**
   B. Darin
   *B. Darin, Atco 6140
   (Progressive–Fern–Trinity, BMI)*

6. **KANSAS CITY**
   W. Harrison
   *J. Leiber–M. Stoller,
   Fury 1023 (Fire, BMI)*

7. **QUIET VILLAGE**
   M. Denny
   *L. Baxter, Liberty 55162
   (Baxter–Wright, BMI)*

8. **TALLAHASSEE LASSIE**
   F. Cannon
   *Slay–Crewe–Picariello,
   Swan 4031 (Conley, BMI)*

9. **FRANKIE**
   C. Francis
   *Sedaka–Greenfield, M-G-M
   12793 (Aldon, BMI)*

10. **TIGER**
    Fabian
    *O. Jones, Chancellor 1037
    (Roosevelt, BMI)*

1959

July 6

1. **THE BATTLE OF NEW OR-LEANS**
J. Horton
J. Driftwood, Columbia 41339 (Warden, BMI)

2. **LONELY BOY**
P. Anka
P. Anka, ABC–Paramount 10022 (Spanka, BMI)

3. **PERSONALITY**
L. Price
Logan–Price, ABC–Paramount 10018 (Lloyd–Logan, BMI)

4. **DREAM LOVER**
B. Darin
B. Darin, Atco 6140 (Progressive–Fern–Trinity, BMI)

5. **LIPSTICK ON YOUR COLLAR**
C. Francis
Lewis–Goehring, M-G-M 12793 (Joy, ASCAP)

6. **WATERLOO**
S. Jackson
Wilkin–Loudermilk, Columbia 41393 (Cedarwood, BMI)

7. **TALLAHASSEE LASSIE**
F. Cannon
Slay–Crewe–Picariello, Swan 4031 (Conley, BMI)

8. **BOBBY SOX TO STOCKINGS**
F. Avalon
Faith–DiCicco, Chancellor 1036 (Debmar, ASCAP)

9. **FRANKIE**
C. Francis
Sedaka–Greenfield, M-G-M 12793 (Aldon, BMI)

10. **TIGER**
Fabian
O. Jones, Chancellor 1037 (Roosevelt, BMI)

July 13

1. **THE BATTLE OF NEW OR-LEANS**
J. Horton
J. Driftwood, Columbia 41339 (Warden BMI)

2. **LONELY BOY**
P. Anka
P. Anka, ABC–Paramount 10022 (Spanka, BMI)

3. **PERSONALITY**
L. Price
Logan–Price, ABC–Paramount 10018 (Lloyd–Logan, BMI)

4. **LIPSTICK ON YOUR COLLAR**
C. Francis
Lewis–Goehring, M-G-M 12793 (Joy, ASCAP)

5. **WATERLOO**
S. Jackson
Wilkin–Loudermilk, Columbia 41393 (Cedarwood, BMI)

6. **TALLAHASSEE LASSIE**
F. Cannon
Slay–Crewe–Picariello, Swan 4031 (Conley, BMI)

7. **MY HEART IS AN OPEN BOOK**
C. Dobkins, Jr.
H. David–L. Pockris, Decca 30803 (Sequence, BMI)

8. **A BOY WITHOUT A GIRL**
F. Avalon
S. Jacobsen–R. Sexter, Chancellor 1036 (Arch, ASCAP)

9. **DREAM LOVER**
B. Darin
B. Darin, Atco 6140 (Progressive–Fern–Trinity, BMI)

10. **TIGER**
Fabian
O. Jones, Chancellor 1037 (Roosevelt, BMI)

July 20

1. **THE BATTLE OF NEW OR-LEANS**
J. Horton
J. Driftwood, Columbia 41339 (Warden, BMI)

2. **LONELY BOY**
P. Anka
P. Anka, ABC–Paramount 10022 (Spanka, BMI)

3. **WATERLOO**
S. Jackson
Wilkin–Loudermilk, Columbia 41393 (Cedarwood, BMI)

4. **TIGER**
Fabian
O. Jones, Chancellor 1037 (Roosevelt, BMI)

5. **MY HEART IS AN OPEN BOOK**
C. Dobkins, Jr.
H. David–L. Pockris, Decca 30803 (Sequence, BMI)

6. **TALLAHASSEE LASSIE**
F. Cannon
Slay–Crewe–Picariello, Swan 4031 (Conley, BMI)

7. **PERSONALITY**
L. Price
Logan–Price, ABC–Paramount 10018 (Lloyd–Logan, BMI)

8. **A BIG HUNK O'LOVE**
E. Presley
Schroeder–Wyche, Victor 7600 (Elvis Presley, BMI)

9. **A BOY WITHOUT A GIRL**
F. Avalon
S. Jacobsen–R. Sexter, Chancellor 1036 (Arch, ASCAP)

10. **LIPSTICK ON YOUR COLLAR**
C. Francis
Lewis–Goehring, M-G-M 12793 (Joy, ASCAP)

July 27

1. **LONELY BOY**
P. Anka
P. Anka, ABC–Paramount 10022 (Spanka, BMI)

2. **THE BATTLE OF NEW OR- LEANS**
J. Horton
J. Driftwood, Columbia 41339 (Warden, BMI)

3. **TIGER**
Fabian
O. Jones, Chancellor 1037 (Roosevelt, BMI)

4. **WATERLOO**
S. Jackson
Wilten–Loudermilk, Columbia 41393 (Cedarwood, BMI)

5. **A BIG HUNK O' LOVE**
E. Presley
Schroeder–Wyche, Victor 7600 (Elvis Presley, BMI)

6. **MY HEART IS AN OPEN BOOK**
C. Dobkins, Jr.
H. David–L. Pockris, Decca 30803 (Sequence, BMI)

7. **THERE GOES MY BABY**
The Drifters
Patterson–Treadwell, Atlantic 2025 (Jat–Progressive, BMI)

8. **LIPSTICK ON YOUR COLLAR**
C. Francis
Lewis–Goehring, M-G-M 12793 (Joy, ASCAP)

9. **FORTY MILES OF BAD ROAD**
D. Eddy
D. Eddy–A. Casey, Jamie 1126 (Gregmark, BMI)

10. **PERSONALITY**
L. Price
Logan–Price, ABC–Paramount 10018 (Lloyd–Logan, BMI)

August 3

1. **LONELY BOY**
P. Anka
P. Anka, ABC–Paramount 10022 (Spanka, BMI)

2. **A BIG HUNK O' LOVE**
E. Presley
Schroeder–Wyche, Victor 7600 (Elvis Presley, BMI)

3. **MY HEART IS AN OPEN BOOK**
C. Dobkins, Jr.
H. David–L. Pockris, Decca 30803 (Sequence, BMI)

4. **THE BATTLE OF NEW OR- LEANS**
J. Horton
J. Driftwood, Columbia 41339 (Warden, BMI)

5. **TIGER**
Fabian
O. Jones, Chancellor 1037 (Roosevelt, BMI)

6. **THERE GOES BY BABY**
The Drifters
Patterson–Treadwell, Atlantic 2025 (Jat–Progressive, BMI)

7. **WATERLOO**
S. Jackson
Wilten–Loudermilk, Columbia 41393 (Cedarwood, BMI)

8. **LAVENDER BLUE**
S. Turner
L. Morey–E. David, Big Top 3016 (Joy, ASCAP)

9. **SWEETER THAN YOU**
R. Nelson
B. Knight, Imperial 5595 (Hilliard, BMI)

10. **FORTY MILES OF BAD ROAD**
D. Eddy
D. Eddy–A. Casey, Jamie 1126 (Gregmark, BMI)

August 10

1. **A BIG HUNK O' LOVE**
E. Presley
Schroeder–Wyche, Voctor 7600 (Elvis Presley, BMI)

2. **LONELY BOY**
P. Anka
P. Anka, ABC–Paramount 10022 (Spanka, BMI)

3. **MY HEART IS AN OPEN BOOK**
C. Dobkins, Jr.
H. David–L. Pockris, Decca 30803 (Sequence, BMI)

4. **THERE GOES MY BABY**
The Drifters
Patterson–Treadwell, Atlantic 2025 (Jat–Progressive, BMI)

5. **LAVENDER BLUE**
S. Turner
L. Morey–E. David, Big Top 3016 (Joy, ASCAP)

6. **TIGER**
Fabian
O. Jones, Chancellor 1037 (Roosevelt, BMI)

7. **WHAT A DIFFERENCE A DAY MAKES**
D. Washington
Grever–Adams, Mercury 71345 (E. B. Marks, BMI)

8. **WHAT'D I SAY**
R. Charles
R. Charles, Atlantic 2031 (Progressive, BMI)

9. **WATERLOO**
S. Jackson
Wilten–Loudermilk, Columbia 41393 (Cedarwood, BMI)

10. **THE BATTLE OF NEW OR- LEANS**
J. Horton
J. Driftwood, Columbia 41339 (Warden, BMI)

August 17

1. **THERE GOES MY BABY**
   The Drifters
   Patterson–Treadwell, Atlantic 2025 (Jat–Progressive, BMI)
2. **A BIG HUNK O' LOVE**
   E. Presley
   Schroeder–Wyche, Victor 7600 (Elvis Presley, BMI)
3. **LAVENDER BLUE**
   S. Turner
   L. Morey–E. David, Big Top 3016 (Joy, ASCAP)
4. **THE THREE BELLS**
   The Browns
   D. Manning–J. Villard, RCA Victor 7555 (Harris, ASCAP)
5. **MY HEART IS AN OPEN BOOK**
   C. Dobkins, Jr.
   H. David–L. Pockris, Decca 30803 (Sequence, BMI)
6. **WHAT A DIFFERENCE A DAY MAKES**
   D. Washington
   Grever–Adams, Mercury 71345 (E. B. Marks, BMI)
7. **WHAT'D I SAY**
   R. Charles
   R. Charles, Atlantic 2031 (Progressive, BMI)
8. **LONELY BOY**
   P. Anka
   P. Anka, ABC–Paramount 10022 (Spanka, BMI)
9. **FORTY MILES OF BAD ROAD**
   D. Eddy
   D. Eddy–A. Casey, Jamie 1126 (Gregmark, BMI)
10. **JUST A LITTLE TOO MUCH**
    R. Nelson
    J. Burnette, Imperial 5595 (Hilliard, BMI)

August 24

1. **LAVENDER BLUE**
   S. Turner
   L. Morey–E. David, Big Top 3016 (Joy, ASCAP)
2. **A BIG HUNK O' LOVE**
   E. Presley
   Schroeder–Wyche, Victor 7600 (Elvis Presley, BMI)
3. **THE THREE BELLS**
   The Browns
   D. Manning–J. Villard, Victor 7555 (Harris, ASCAP)
4. **SEA OF LOVE**
   P. Phillips
   G. Khary–P. Battiste, Mercury 71465 (Kamar, BMI)
5. **MY HEART IS AN OPEN BOOK**
   C. Dobkins, Jr.
   H. David–L. Pockris, Decca 30803 (Sequence, BMI)
6. **WHAT'D I SAY**
   R. Charles
   R. Charles, Atlantic 2031 (Progressive, BMI)
7. **THERE GOES BY BABY**
   The Drifters
   Patterson–Treadwell, Atlantic 2025 (Jat–Progressive, BMI)
8. **SLEEP WALK**
   Santo and Johnny
   Farine–Farine–Farine, Canadian–American 103 (Trinity, BMI)
9. **WHAT A DIFFERENCE A DAY MAKES**
   D. Washington
   Grever–Adams, Mercury 71345 (E. B. Marks, BMI)
10. **I WANT TO WALK YOU HOME**
    F. Domino
    A. Domino, Imperial 5606 (Alan–Edwards, BMI)

August 31

1. **THE THREE BELLS**
   The Browns
   D. Manning–J. Villard, Victor 7555 (Harris, ASCAP)
2. **SEA OF LOVE**
   P. Phillips
   G. Khary–P. Battiste, Mercury 71645 (Kamar, BMI)
3. **SLEEP WALK**
   Santo and Johnny
   Farine–Farine–Farine, Canadian–American 103 (Trinity, BMI)
4. **LAVENDER BLUE**
   S. Turner
   L. Morey–E. David, Big Top 3016 (Joy, ASCAP)
5. **I'M GONNA GET MARRIED**
   L. Price
   H. Logan–L. Price, ABC–Paramount 10032 (Lloyd–Logan, BMI)
6. **WHAT'D I SAY**
   R. Charles
   R. Charles, Atlantic 2031 (Progressive, BMI)
7. **A BIG HUNK O' LOVE**
   E. Presley
   Schroeder–Wyche, Victor 7600 (Elvis Presley, BMI)
8. **THERE GOES MY BABY**
   The Drifters
   Patterson–Treadwell, Atlantic 2025 (Jat–Progressive, BMI)
9. **RED RIVER ROCK**
   Johnny and the Hurricanes
   King–Mack–Mendelsohn, Warwick 509 (Vicki, BMI)
10. **I WANT TO WALK YOU HOME**
    F. Domino
    A. Domino, Imperial 5606 (Alan–Edwards, BMI)

133

September 7

1. **THE THREE BELLS**
   The Browns
   D. Manning–J. Villard,
   Victor 7555 (Harris, ASCAP)
2. **SLEEP WALK**
   Santo and Johnny
   Farine–Farine–Farine,
   Canadian–American 103
   (Trinity, BMI)
3. **SEA OF LOVE**
   P. Phillips
   G. Khary–P. Battiste, Mercury
   71465 (Kamar, BMI)
4. **I'M GONNA GET MARRIED**
   L. Price
   H. Logan–L. Price, ABC–
   Paramount 10032 (Lloyd–
   Logan, BMI)
5. **RED RIVER ROCK**
   Johnny and the Hur-
   ricanes
   King–Mack–Mendelsohn,
   Warwick 509 (Vicki, BMI)
6. **(TIL) I KISSED YOU**
   The Everly Brothers
   D. Everly, Cadence 1369
   (Acuff–Rose, BMI)
7. **BROKEN HEARTED MELODY**
   S. Vaughn
   H. David–S. Edwards, Mercury
   71477 (Mansion, ASCAP)
8. **LAVENDER BLUE**
   S. Turner
   L. Morey–E. David, Big Top
   3016 (Joy, ASCAP)
9. **WHAT'D I SAY**
   R. Charles
   R. Charles, Atlantic 2031
   (Progressive, BMI)
10. **I WANT TO WALK YOU**
    HOME
    F. Domino
    A. Domino, Imperial 5606
    (Alan–Edwards, BMI)

134

September 14

1. **SLEEP WALK**
   Santo and Johnny
   Farine–Farine–Farine,
   Canadian–American 103
   (Trinity, BMI)
2. **I'M GONNA GET MARRIED**
   L. Price
   H. Logan–L. Price, ABC–
   Paramount 10032 (Lloyd–
   Logan, BMI)
3. **THE THREE BELLS**
   The Browns
   D. Manning–J. Villard,
   Victor 7555 (Harris, ASCAP)
4. **SEA OF LOVE**
   P. Phillips
   G. Khary–P. Battiste, Mercury
   71465 (Kamar, BMI)
5. **(TIL) I KISSED YOU**
   The Everly Brothers
   D. Everly, Cadence 1369
   (Acuff–Rose, BMI)
6. **I WANT TO WALK YOU**
   HOME
   F. Domino
   A. Domino, Imperial 5606
   (Alan–Edwards, BMI)
7. **MACK THE KNIFE**
   B. Darin
   Weill–Brecht–Blizstein,
   Atco 6147 (Harms, ASCAP)
8. **BABY TALK**
   Jan and Dean
   M. Schwartz, Dore 522
   (Hilliary–Ultia–Admiration, BMI)
9. **BROKEN HEARTED MELODY**
   S. Vaughn
   H. David–S. Edwards,
   Mercury 71477 (Mansion,
   ASCAP)
10. **RED RIVER ROCK**
    Johnny and the Hur-
    ricanes
    King–Mack–Mendelsohn,
    Warwick 509 (Vicki, BMI)

September 21

1. **SLEEP WALK**
   Santo and Johnny
   Farine–Farine–Farine,
   Canadian–American 103
   (Trinity, BMI)
2. **I'M GONNA GET MARRIED**
   L. Price
   H. Logan–L. Price, ABC–
   Paramount 10032 (Lloyd–
   Logan, BMI)
3. **THE THREE BELLS**
   The Browns
   D. Manning–J. Villard,
   Victor 7555 (Harris, ASCAP)
4. **(TIL) I KISSED YOU**
   The Everly Brothers
   D. Everly, Cadence 1369
   (Acuff–Rose, BMI)
5. **MACK THE KNIFE**
   B. Darin
   Weill–Brecht–Blizstein,
   Atco 6147 (Harms, ASCAP)
6. **SEA OF LOVE**
   P. Phillips
   G. Khary–P. Battiste,
   Mercury 71465 (Kamar, BMI)
7. **I WANT TO WALK YOU**
   HOME
   F. Domino
   A. Domino, Imperial 5606
   (Alan–Edwards, BMI)
8. **BROKEN HEARTED MELODY**
   S. Vaughn
   H. David–S. Edwards, Mercury
   71477 (Mansion, ASCAP)
9. **PUT YOUR HEAD ON MY**
   SHOULDER
   P. Anka
   P. Anka, ABC–Paramount 10040
   (Spanka, BMI)
10. **RED RIVER ROCK**
    Johnny and the Hur-
    ricanes
    King–Mack–Mendelsohn,
    Warwick 509 (Vicki, BMI)

1959

September 28

1. **SLEEP WALK**
Santo and Johnny
Farine–Farine–Farine,
Canadian–American 103
(Trinity, BMI)

2. **MACK THE KNIFE**
B. Darin
Weill–Brecht–Blizstein,
Atco 7147 (Harms, ASCAP)

3. **THE THREE BELLS**
The Browns
D. Manning–J. Villard,
Victor 7555 (Harris, ASCAP)

4. **(TIL) I KISSED YOU**
The Everly Brothers
D. Everly, Cadence 1369
(Acuff–Rose, BMI)

5. **I'M GONNA GET MARRIED**
L. Price
H. Logan–L. Price, ABC–
Paramount 10032 (Lloyd–
Logan, BMI)

6. **SEA OF LOVE**
P. Phillips
G. Khary–P. Battiste,
Mercury 71645 (Kamar, BMI)

7. **PUT YOUR HEAD ON MY**
SHOULDER
P. Anka
P. Anka, ABC–Paramount
10040 (Spanka, BMI)

8. **RED RIVER ROCK**
Johnny and the Hur-
ricanes
King–Mack–Mendelsohn,
Warwick 509 (Vicki, BMI)

9. **TEEN BEAT**
S. Nelson
Nelson–Egnolan, Original
Sound 5 (Drive-In, BMI)

10. **BROKEN HEARTED MELODY**
S. Vaughn
H. David–S. Edwards, Mercury
71477 (Mansion, ASCAP)

October 5

1. **MACK THE KNIFE**
B. Darin
Weill–Brecht–Blizstein,
Atco 7147 (Harms, ASCAP)

2. **PUT YOUR HEAD ON MY**
SHOULDER
P. Anka
P. Anka, ABC–Paramount 10040
(Spanka, BMI)

3. **SLEEP WALK**
Santo and Johnny
Farine–Farine–Farine,
Canadian–American 103
(Trinity, BMI)

4. **(TIL) I KISSED YOU**
The Everly Brothers
D. Everly, Cadence 1369
(Acuff–Rose, BMI)

5. **THE THREE BELLS**
The Browns
D. Manning–J. Villard,
Victor 7555 (Harris, ASCAP)

6. **TEEN BEAT**
S. Nelson
Nelson–Egnolan, Original
Sound 5 (Drive-In, BMI)

7. **I'M GONNA GET MARRIED**
L. Price
H. Logan–L. Price, ABC–
Paramount 10032 (Lloyd–
Logan, BMI)

8. **MR. BLUE**
Fleetwoods
D. Blackwell, Dolphin 5
(Cornerstone, BMI)

9. **RED RIVER ROCK**
Johnny and the Hur-
ricanes
King–Mack–Mendelsohn,
Warwick 509 (Vicki, BMI)

10. **POISON IVY**
The Coasters
J. Leiber–M. Stoller,
Atco 6146 (Tiger, BMI)

October 12

1. **MACK THE KNIFE**
B. Darin
Weill–Brecht–Blizstein,
Atco 7147 (Harms, ASCAP)

2. **PUT YOUR HEAD ON MY**
SHOULDER
P. Anka
P. Anka, ABC–Paramount
10040 (Spanka, BMI)

3. **MR. BLUE**
Fleetwoods
D. Blackwell, Dolphin 5
(Cornerstone, BMI)

4. **SLEEPWALK**
Santo and Johnny
Farine–Farine–Farine,
Canadian–American 103
(Trinity, BMI)

5. **(TIL) I KISSED YOU**
The Everly Brothers
D. Everly, Cadence 1369
(Acuff–Rose, BMI)

6. **TEEN BEAT**
S. Nelson
Nelson–Egnolan, Original
Sound 5 (Drive-In, BMI)

7. **THE THREE BELLS**
The Browns
D. Manning–J. Villard,
Victor 7555 (Harris, ASCAP)

8. **JUST ASK YOUR HEART**
F. Avalon
DeNota–Ricci–Damata,
Chancellor 1040 (Rambed, BMI)

9. **LONELY STREET**
A. Williams
Souder–Stevenson–Belew,
Cadence 1370 (Four Star, BMI)

10. **POISON IVY**
The Coasters
J. Leiber–M. Stoller, Atco 6146
(Tiger, BMI)

October 19

1. **MACK THE KNIFE**
B. Darin
Weill–Brecht–Blizstein,
Atco 7147 (Harms, ASCAP)

2. **MR. BLUE**
The Fleetwoods
D. Blackwell, Dolphin 5
(Cornerstone, BMI)

3. **PUT YOUR HEAD ON MY SHOULDER**
P. Anka
P. Anka, ABC–Paramount 10040
(Spanka, BMI)

4. **TEEN BEAT**
S. Nelson
Nelson–Egnolan, Original
Sound 5 (Drive-In, BMI)

5. **(TIL) I KISSED YOU**
The Everly Brothers
D. Everly, Cadence 1369
(Acuff–Rose, BMI)

6. **LONELY STREET**
A. Williams
Souder–Stevenson–Belew,
Cadence 1370 (Four Star, BMI)

7. **POISON IVY**
The Coasters
J. Leiber–M. Stoller,
Atco 6146 (Tiger, BMI)

8. **JUST ASK YOUR HEART**
F. Avalon
DeNota–Ricci–Damata,
Chancellor 1040 (Rambed, BMI)

9. **THE THREE BELLS**
The Browns
D. Manning–J. Villard,
Victor 7555 (Harris, ASCAP)

10. **SLEEPWALK**
Santo and Johnny
Farine–Farine–Farine,
Canadian–American 103
(Trinity, BMI)

October 26

1. **MACK THE KNIFE**
B. Darin
Weill–Brecht–Blizstein,
Atco 7147 (Harms, ASCAP)

2. **MR. BLUE**
The Fleetwoods
D. Blackwell, Dolphin 5
(Cornerstone, BMI)

3. **PUT YOUR HEAD ON MY SHOULDER**
P. Anka
P. Anka, ABC–Paramount
10040 (Spanka, BMI)

4. **TEEN BEAT**
S. Nelson
Nelson–Egnolan, Original
Sound 5 (Drive-In, BMI)

5. **DON'T YOU KNOW**
D. Reese
B. Worth, Victor 7591
(Alexis, ASCAP)

6. **LONELY STREET**
A. Williams
Souder–Stevenson–Belew,
Cadence 1370 (Four Star, BMI)

7. **JUST ASK YOUR HEART**
F. Avalon
DeNota–Ricci–Damata,
Chancellor 1040 (Rambed, BMI)

8. **PRIMROSE LANE**
J. Wallace
Callender–Shanlin,
Challenge 59047
(Music Productions, ASCAP)

9. **POISON IVY**
The Coasters
J. Leiber–M. Stoller,
Atco 6146 (Tiger, BMI)

10. **DECK OF CARDS**
W. Martindale
I. T. Tyler, Dot 15968
(American, BMI)

November 2

1. **MACK THE KNIFE**
B. Darin
Weill–Brecht–Blizstein,
Atco 7147 (Harms, ASCAP)

2. **MR. BLUE**
The Fleetwoods
D. Blackwell, Dolphin 5
(Cornerstone, BMI)

3. **PUT YOUR HEAD ON MY SHOULDER**
P. Anka
P. Anka, ABC–Paramount
10040 (Spanka, BMI)

4. **DON'T YOU KNOW**
D. Reese
B. Worth, Victor 7591
(Alexis, ASCAP)

5. **TEEN BEAT**
S. Nelson
Nelson–Egnolan, Original
Sound 5 (Drive-In, BMI)

6. **LONELY STREET**
A. Williams
Souder–Stevenson–Belew,
Cadence 1370 (Four Star, BMI)

7. **DECK OF CARDS**
W. Martindale
I. T. Tyler, Dot 15968
(American, BMI)

8. **PRIMROSE LANE**
J. Wallace
Callender–Shanlin, Challenge
59047 (Music Productions, AS-
CAP)

9. **POISON IVY**
The Coasters
J. Leiber–M. Stoller,
Atco 6146 (Tiger, BMI)

10. **JUST ASK YOUR HEART**
F. Avalon
DeNota–Ricci–Damata,
Chancellor 1040 (Rambed, BMI)

November 9

1. **MACK THE KNIFE**
B. Darin
Weill–Brecht–Blizstein,
Atco 7147 (Harms, ASCAP)

2. **MR. BLUE**
The Fleetwoods
D. Blackwell, Dolphin 5
(Cornerstone, BMI)

3. **PUT YOUR HEAD ON MY SHOULDER**
P. Anka
P. Anka, ABC–Paramount
10040 (Spanka, BMI)

4. **DON'T YOU KNOW**
D. Reese
B. Worth, Victor 7591
(Alexis, ASCAP)

5. **LONELY STREET**
A. Williams
Souder–Stevenson–Belew,
Cadence 1370 (Four Star, BMI)

6. **TEEN BEAT**
S. Nelson
Nelson–Egnolan, Original
Sound 5 (Drive-In, BMI)

7. **DECK OF CARDS**
W. Martindale
I. T. Tyler, Dot 15698
(American, BMI)

8. **PRIMROSE LANE**
J. Wallace
Callender–Shanlin,
Challenge 59047
(Music Productions, ASCAP)

9. **SEVEN LITTLE GIRLS (SITTIN' IN THE BACK SEAT)**
P. Evans and Curls
Hilliard–Pockriss, Guaranteed
200 (Sequence, ASCAP)

10. **HEARTACHES BY THE NUMBER**
G. Mitchell
H. Howard, Columbia 41476
(Pamper, BMI)

November 16

1. **MACK THE KNIFE**
B. Darin
Weill–Brecht–Blizstein,
Atco 7147 (Harms, ASCAP)

2. **MR. BLUE**
The Fleetwoods
D. Blackwell, Dolphin 5
(Cornerstone, BMI)

3. **PUT YOUR HEAD ON MY SHOULDER**
P. Anka
P. Anka, ABC–Paramount
10040 (Spanka, BMI)

4. **HEARTACHES BY THE NUMBER**
G. Mitchell
H. Howard, Columbia 41476
(Pamper, BMI)

5. **DON'T YOU KNOW**
D. Reese
B. Worth, Victor 7591
(Alexis, ASCAP)

6. **SO MANY WAYS**
B. Benton
B. Stevenson, Mercury 71512
(Brenda, BMI)

7. **PRIMROSE LANE**
J. Wallace
Callender–Shanlin, Challenge
59047 (Music Productions,
ASCAP)

8. **TEEN BEAT**
S. Nelson
Nelson–Egnolan, Original
Sound 5 (Drive-In, BMI)

9. **DECK OF CARDS**
W. Martindale
I. T. Tyler, Dot 15698
(American, BMI)

10. **LONELY STREET**
A. Williams
Souder–Stevenson–Belew,
Cadence 1370 (Four Star, BMI)

November 23

1. **MACK THE KNIFE**
B. Darin
Weill–Brecht–Blizstein,
Atco 7147 (Harms, ASCAP)

2. **MR. BLUE**
The Fleetwoods
D. Blackwell, Dolphin 5
(Cornerstone, BMI)

3. **DON'T YOU KNOW**
D. Reese
B. Worth, Victor 7591
(Alexis, ASCAP)

4. **HEARTACHES BY THE NUMBER**
G. Mitchell
H. Howard, Columbia 41476
(Pamper, BMI)

5. **SO MANY WAYS**
B. Benton
B. Stevenson, Mercury 71512
(Brenda, BMI)

6. **PUT YOUR HEAD ON MY SHOULDER**
P. Anka
P. Anka, ABC–Paramount 1040
(Spanka, BMI)

7. **IN THE MOOD**
E. Fields
J. Garland–A. Razas,
Rendezvous 110
(Shapiro–Bernstein, ASCAP)

8. **BE BY GUEST**
F. Domino
Domino–Marascalco–Boyce,
Imperial 5629 (Travis, BMI)

9. **WE GOT LOVE**
B. Rydell
K. Davis–B. Lowe, Cameo 169
(Kaimana–Lowe, ASCAP)

10. **PRIMROSE LANE**
J. Wallace
Callender–Shanlin, Challenge
59047 (Music Productions,
ASCAP)

1. **MACK THE KNIFE**
B. Darin
Weill–Brecht–Blizstein,
Atco 7147 (Harms, ASCAP)

2. **DON'T YOU KNOW**
D. Reese
B. Worth, Victor 7591
(Alexis, ASCAP)

3. **MR. BLUE**
The Fleetwoods
D. Blackwell, Dolphin 5
(Cedarwood, BMI)

4. **HEARTACHES BY THE NUMBER**
G. Mitchell
H. Howard, Columbia 41476
(Pamper, BMI)

5. **IN THE MOOD**
E. Fields
J. Garland–A. Razas,
Rendezvous 110
(Shapiro–Bernstein, ASCAP)

6. **SO MANY WAYS**
B. Benton
B. Stevenson, Mercury 71512
(Brenda, BMI)

7. **PUT YOUR HEAD ON MY SHOULDER**
P. Anka
P. Anka, ABC–Paramount
10040 (Spanka, BMI)

8. **WE GOT LOVE**
B. Rydell
K. Davis–B. Lowe, Cameo 169
(Kaimana–Lowe, ASCAP)

9. **BE MY GUEST**
F. Domino
Domino–Marascalco–Boyce,
Imperial 5629 (Travis, BMI)

10. **SEVEN LITTLE GIRLS (SITTIN' IN THE BACK SEAT)**
P. Evans and Curls
Hilliard–Pockriss, Guaranteed
200 (Sequence, ASCAP)

1. **MACK THE KNIFE**
B. Darin
Weill–Brecht–Blizstein,
Atco 7147 (Harms, ASCAP)

2. **HEARTACHES BY THE NUMBER**
G. Mitchell
H. Howard, Columbia 41476
(Pamper, BMI)

3. **MR. BLUE**
The Fleetwoods
D. Blackwell, Dolphin 5
(Cornerstone, BMI)

4. **DON'T YOU KNOW**
D. Reese
B. Worth, Victor 7591
(Alexis, ASCAP)

5. **IN THE MOOD**
E. Fields
J. Garland–A. Razas,
Rendezvous 110
(Shapiro–Bernstein, ASCAP)

6. **WE GOT LOVE**
B. Rydell
K. Davis–B. Lowe, Cameo 169
(Kaimana–Lowe, ASCAP)

7. **SO MANY WAYS**
B. Benton
B. Stevenson, Mercury 71512
(Brenda, BMI)

8. **BE MY GUEST**
F. Domino
Domino–Marascalco–Boyce,
Imperial 5629 (Travis, BMI)

9. **OH, CAROL**
N. Sedaka
N. Sedaka–H. Greenfield,
Victor 7595 (Aldon, BMI)

10. **DANNY BOY**
C. Twitty
Weatherly, M-G-M 12820
(Bossey and Hawkes, ASCAP)

1. **HEARTACHES BY THE NUMBER**
G. Mitchell
H. Howard, Columbia 41476
(Pamper, BMI)

2. **MR. BLUE**
The Fleetwoods
D. Blackwell, Dolphin 5
(Cornerstone, BMI)

3. **MACK THE KNIFE**
B. Darin
Weill–Brecht–Blizstein,
Atco 7147 (Harms, ASCAP)

4. **IN THE MOOD**
E. Fields
J. Garland–A. Razas,
Rendezvous 110
(Shapiro–Bernstein, ASCAP)

5. **WHY**
F. Avalon
Marcucci–DeAngelis,
Chancellor 1045 (Debmar,
ASCAP)

6. **WE GOT LOVE**
B. Rydell
K. Davis–B. Lowe, Cameo 169
(Kaimana–Lowe, ASCAP)

7. **SO MANY WAYS**
B. Benton
B. Stevenson, Mercury 71512
(Brenda, BMI)

8. **DON'T YOU KNOW**
D. Reese
B. Worth, Victor 7591
(Alexis, ASCAP)

9. **THE BIG HURT**
T. Fisher
W. Shanklin, Signet 275
(Music Productions, ASCAP)

10. **IT'S TIME TO CRY**
P. Anka
P. Anka, ABC–Paramount 10064
(Spanka, BMI)

December 21

1. **HEARTACHES BY THE NUMBER**
G. Mitchell
H. Howard, Columbia 41476
(Pamper, BMI)

2. **EL PASO**
M. Robbins
M. Robbins, Columbia 41511
(Marty's, BMI)

3. **WHY**
F. Avalon
Marcucci–DeAngelis,
Chancellor 1045 (Debmar,
ASCAP)

4. **IT'S TIME TO CRY**
P. Anka
P. Anka, ABC-Paramount 10064
(Spanka, BMI)

5. **WE GOT LOVE**
B. Rydell
K. Davis–B. Lowe, Cameo 169
(Kaimana-Lowe, ASCAP)

6. **THE BIG HURT**
T. Fisher
W. Shanklin, Signet 275
(Music Productions, ASCAP)

7. **WAY DOWN YONDER IN NEW ORLEANS**
F. Cannon
Cramer-Layton, Swan 4043
(Shapiro-Bernstein, ASCAP)

8. **MACK THE KNIFE**
B. Darin
Weill–Brecht–Blizstein,
Atco 7147 (Harms, ASCAP)

9. **HOUND DOG MAN**
Fabian
Pomus-Shuman, Chancellor
1044 (Fabulous, BMI)

10. **AMONG MY SOUVENIRS**
C. Francis
Leslie-Nicholls, M-G-M 12841
(DeSylva-Brown-Henderson,
ASCAP)

December 28

1. **EL PASO**
M. Robbins
M. Robbins, Columbia 41511
(Marty's, BMI)

2. **THE BIG HURT**
T. Fisher
W. Shanklin, Signet 275
(Music Productions, ASCAP)

3. **WHY**
F. Avalon
Marcucci–DeAngelis,
Chancellor 1045 (Debmar,
ASCAP)

4. **WAY DOWN YONDER IN NEW ORLEANS**
F. Cannon
Cramer-Layton, Swan 4043
(Shapiro-Bernstein, ASCAP)

5. **IT'S TIME TO CRY**
P. Anka
P. Anka, ABC-Paramount
10064 (Spanka, BMI)

6. **HEARTACHES BY THE NUMBER**
G. Mitchell
H. Howard, Columbia 41476
(Pamper, BMI)

7. **AMONG MY SOUVENIRS**
C. Francis
Leslie-Nicholls, M-G-M 12841
(DeSylva-Brown-Henderson,
ASCAP)

8. **MACK THE KNIFE**
B. Darin
Weill–Brecht–Blizstein,
Atco 7147 (Harms, ASCAP)

9. **HOUND DOG MAN**
Fabian
Pomus-Shuman, Chancellor
1044 (Fabulous, BMI)

10. **PRETTY BLUE EYES**
S. Lawrence
Randazzo-Weinstein, ABC-
Paramount 10058 (Almimo,
BMI)

PAUL ANKA

The FCC payola hearings that had started in December, 1959, were still going on, and the turmoil was apparent in early 1960. As the adults had predicted, the voiceless heroes of pre-payola were going. Fabian was now an actor of sorts. And except for a "Pineapple Princess' relapse, Annette was forgotten as a singer, and she even began to regain her status in our memories as the star of the Walt Disney "Annette" serial.

The best of the Philadelphian American Bandstand style singers kept pumping out hits. Anka, Rydell, Darin and Avalon were again frequent names in the Top 10. And now they were joined by Neil Sedaka, Jimmy Clanton and Freddy Cannon. Sedaka's music, which he wrote himself, was certainly fun to listen to, bouncing over itself and bright. The problem was that "Stairway to Heaven" sounded like "Calendar Girl," which sounded like "Happy Birthday Sweet Sixteen," and it was soon too much of a good thing.

Jimmy Clanton was one of those decent-looking kids with a big smile who was fair as a singer. Most of his records were worth about a 75 rating, yet he was able to slip into the Top 10 with "Go Jimmy, Go." Freddy Cannon was another one who was billed as a star, yet it was hard to find a fan of his except Carmen from "American Bandstand."

Sadly there was a monotony about all these singers. That is not to say that their music wasn't enjoyable. Rather, it was too smooth and Tin Pan Alley; the singers were too well coached, too white and they lacked the dynamite qualities of Elvis Presley, Little Richard or even the Everlys.

In 1960 a lot of songs made it to the Top 10 because they had a gimmick. The biggest gimmick of the year was the answer song. Though they were called "answers," the only question apparent in their parent songs was "Why write an answer?" Using the melody of the original song, the

1960

SO MUCH (Jackie Wilson; Brunswick, mono and stereo) Singer Wilson, who bears a startling physical resemblance to Sammy Davis, Jr., is presented to his fans as "Mr. Excitement." The excitement consists of a bludgeoning Neanderthal style, and the package should be labeled "For Unregenerate Rock and Rollers Only."

Time review, Feb. 8, 1960

parasitic answer song was easy to write and had a ready-made audience of first song fans.

Although most of these songs failed miserably, two were big successes: Damita Jo's "I'm Saving the Last Dance for You" and Jeanne Black's "He'll Have to Stay," obviously the answers to the Drifters' "Save the Last Dance for Me" and Jim Reeves' "He'll Have to Go":

Should I hang up
Or will you tell him
He'll have to go . . .

to which she answers he'll have to stay.

Lesser answers were "I Can't Help You, I'm Falling, Too" to "Please Help Me I'm Falling," and "Poor Begonia Caught Pneumonia" to "Itsy Bitsy Teenie Weenie . . ." To "You Talk Too Much" songwriters ran off at the pen with "I Talk Too Much," "Who Talks Too Much" and "I Don't Talk Too Much."

And last was "Tell Tommy I Miss Him," the wail of the left-behind girl friend of a boy who died in a stock car race trying to win the money to buy her a wedding ring. The original song was "Tell Laura I Love Her" a sample of the story song, a gimmick that had shown up in the Top 10's of 1959 with the Browns' "Three Bells" and would live into the mid sixties. The other prominent tear jerker of 1960 was "Teen Angel" a song about a girl who, one fateful night, was hit by a train as she ran back to get her steady's high school ring from his car which was stuck on the railroad tracks. And so he sings:

Teen angel can you hear me
Teen angel can you see-ee me
Are you somewhere up above
And am I still your o-own true love.

Happily, Teen Angel doesn't answer him.

Though we sang of tragedy in 1960, the mood of the country was bright. It was a new decade in every way. We were about to be awakened and thrust into a new era of intellectualism and humanitarianism by the best-loved youth hero since Elvis Presley. Senator John F. Kennedy was older than many of our parents and yet he was closer to us in spirit than Dick Clark. Maybe it was because he was married to a lady as young looking and lovely as a *Seventeen* model, or because they had such a young attractive little girl, or because he was better looking than Rock Hudson and so untarnished by the cynicism of our parents that there were tears in his eyes when he met the poor of Appalachia. But whatever his magic, he was as fresh and exhilarating as rock and roll. He belonged to us and his spirit carried all America to a time of youth and optimism.

It was not the kind of year that might attract so spellbinding a leader.

The country was dragging through a recession in mid-1960. A U-2 reconnaisance plane had been shot down in Russia and its pilot, Gary Francis Powers, was convicted three months later. This proved embarrassing internationally as the President tried to squirm out of the accusation that we were spying.

The spring summit talks in Paris ended when Khrushchev denounced the United States over the U-2 incident; President Eisenhower accused him of sabotaging the talks and declared that the United States had stopped the flights. The other three powers then met without Khrushchev who was now threatening retaliations against United States bases because of the U-2 flights. Two months later, another American plane was shot down over the Barents Sea by the Russians, showing the world clearly that the United States had lied.

If all this wasn't enough, Eisenhower had to cancel a stop in Japan on his goodwill tour because of the anti-American demonstrations there and the United States got itself locked into a confrontation with the Russians over Cuba.

Eisenhower cut Cuba's sugar quota by 95 per cent because of Cuba's hostility toward the United States. He then invoked the Monroe Doctrine (a concept most of us believed was restricted to high school history class) to keep the Russian Communists out of Cuba. Khrushchev countered that the U.S.S.R. would use rockets against the United States if it intervened militarily in Cuba and Castro announced the forcible expropriation of American firms in Cuba.

This would all fall into the lap of the new President, not to mention the pressure of the "missile gap." It was a time of acute nuclear lust as we strove for more and more overkill. In 1960, the United States was reported to have 400 B-52 bombers ready to go—each with nuclear explosives equal to 1000 Hiroshimas. The Russians, too, aggressively stocked nuclear overkill, and, in February, 1960, France joined the bomb race by exploding its first atomic device.

The logic of the times led us into the bomb shelter craze. The federal government spent $500 million to seek out and mark all potential shelter areas—caves, basements and other protected areas. And private citizens spent unmeasured dollars digging out their basements, swimming pools and backyards to put in lead-walled shelters with air and water purificatiion systems, pantries, battery powered generators—all to prolong their molelike existence in a new world without air, water or communists.

With all the problems it was no wonder President Eisenhower was ready to step down. Besides, the oldest United States President hoped to pass his responsibilities to the flamboyant young Vice President, Richard Nixon.

In February it looked as if Ike would get his wish. Nixon led JFK—the most popular Democrat—53 to 47 per cent in a Gallup poll. And to make Ike even happier it looked like the Democrats would probably run one of their older and easier-to-beat stalwarts like Humphrey or Johnson. By May, JFK had the West Virginia victory and even the old pros believed he might be nominated. We were starting to turn up our radios to hear the half-hour headlines so we could keep up with JFK's progress. He hypnotized us. Maybe he used his good looks and his sense of humor, but we were willing prey. We were sick of the old fears that had dominated 1950's politics, and Kennedy talked as if we could fight the problems of the new decade, as if with our youth and our vigor we could make a world without poverty and without war. Most of us had never even thought about these things, but instead of making us feel dumb and young and powerless Kennedy promised that the future was ours, and ours to make beautiful.

When he accepted the Democratic nomination in July he said "the world is changing; the old era is dying; the old ways will not do . . ." And although he based his 75,000-mile campaign on beating Communism, he saw the victory in terms of winning the world's allegiance with our help and kindness and interest and sacrifices, ideas far more appealing to us than overkill.

By the TV debates in the fall we were awake politically as a generation. Just about all of us were too young to vote, and the majority of us were too young to work on a campaign, but our opinions were formed. Nixon was everything that had bored us in the past. Our parents might have liked Ike and some of them liked Dick, but we disagreed. JFK belonged to us and the future.

Jack and Jackie were our new stars. There

was so much to watch about them—the clan, the New England language, bouffant hairdos, pillbox hats, the new baby. When JFK won, we won. The charges against him of immaturity were laid to rest and the decade of youth began. It looked as if the next eight years would be glorious.

We memorized the names of the new Kennedy Cabinet. We daydreamed about sacrifice and pictured ourselves in the new Peace Corps. The Beatniks could keep their alienation. Our time had come.

Even rock and roll had a reawakening in late 1960. The well-marketed music of the early part of the year was still represented by Connie Francis bleating that her heart had a mind of its own and Annette's precious "Pineapple Princess." But finally, rock and roll of classic proportion was making its way again into the Top 10's with Sam Cooke's "Chain Gang," "Stay" by Maurice Williams and the Zodiacs, U. S. Bond's "New Orleans," "Save the Last Dance . . ." "Georgia . . ." The music of late 1960 would pull rock and roll out of a sad recession.

And the return of Elvis Presley from the Army gave rock and roll a boost. He never regained his mid-fifties dominance, but his 1960 recordings of "Stuck on You" and "Are You Lonesome Tonight?" were tremendous hits. And his album "GI Blues" was one of the sixteen LP's that got Gold Album awards. Only two of the other Top LP's were even marginal rock and roll, a Johnny Mathis album and one by Pat Boone.

Some greedy adults were still after our allowances. There was a nineteen-year-old singer named Rod Lauren whose real name was Roger Strunk. "Discovered" by RCA, he recorded "If I had a Girl" and RCA spent $50,000 promoting his sullen good looks. This latter-day Fabian never made it, which proved that a record company could not make us buy just anyone.

The rock and roll of late 1960 had regenerated itself after rock and roll's worst crisis. The payola scandal did little more to rock and roll than drive away the leeches. The music that the slick promoters had taken away from us was dropped back into our hands. And our idealism revived it.

We were riding high as 1960 came to an end. Elvis Presley was back in the Number 1 spot and John Kennedy's inauguration was twenty days away. 1961 had to be a year of the young, a year "for Unregenerate Rock and Rollers Only."

THE TOP FIFTY
1960

1. THEME FROM A SUMMER PLACE   P. Faith
2. RUNNING BEAR   J. Preston
3. EL PASO   M. Robbins
4. TEEN ANGEL   M. Dinning
5. ARE YOU LONESOME TONIGHT?   E. Presley
6. WHY   F. Avalon
7. WILD ONE   B. Rydell
8. STUCK ON YOU   E. Presley
9. GREENFIELDS   The Brothers Four
10. CATHY'S CLOWN   The Everly Brothers
11. EVERYBODY'S SOMEBODY'S FOOL   C. Francis
12. ALLEY OOP   The Hollywood Argyles
13. GOOD TIMIN'   J. Jones
14. HE'LL HAVE TO GO   J. Reeves
15. I'M SORRY   B. Lee
16. HANDY MAN   J. Jones
17. ITSY BITSY TEENIE WEENIE
    YELLOW POLKA DOT BIKINI   B. Hyland
18. IT'S NOW OR NEVER   E. Presley
19. THE TWIST   C. Checker
20. MY HEART HAS A MIND
    OF ITS OWN   C. Francis
21. CHAIN GANG   S. Cooke
22. MR. CUSTER   L. Verne
23. SAVE THE LAST
    DANCE FOR ME   The Drifters
24. POETRY IN MOTION   J. Tillotson
25. STAY   M. Williams and the Zodiacs

26. ONLY THE LONELY   R. Orbison
27. WALK, DON'T RUN   The Ventures
28. A THOUSAND STARS   K. Young
    and the Innocents
29. LAST DATE   F. Cramer
30. GEORGIA ON MY MIND   R. Charles
31. I WANT TO BE WANTED   B. Lee
32. NORTH TO ALASKA   J. Horton
33. THE BIG HURT   T. Fisher
34. PUPPY LOVE   P. Anka
35. SINK THE BISMARK   J. Horton
36. SIXTEEN REASONS   C. Stevens
37. BEYOND THE SEA   B. Darin
38. BURNING BRIDGES   J. Scott
39. MULE SKINNER BLUES   The Fendermen
40. YOU TALK TOO MUCH   J. Jones
41. FINGER POPPIN' TIME   H. Ballard
42. WHAT IN THE WORLD'S
    COME OVER YOU   J. Scott
43. SWEET NOTHIN'S   B. Lee
44. BECAUSE THEY'RE YOUNG   D. Eddy
45. A MILLION TO ONE   J. Charles
46. TELL LAURA I LOVE HER   R. Peterson
47. NIGHT   J. Wilson
48. VOLARE   B. Rydell
49. YOU'VE GOT WHAT IT TAKES   M. Johnson
50. DEVIL OR ANGEL   B. Vee

January 4

1. **WHY**
F. Avalon
Marcucci–DeAngelis,
Chancellor 1045 (Debmar,
ASCAP)

2. **THE BIG HURT**
T. Fisher
W. Shanklin, Signet 275
(Music Productions, ASCAP)

3. **EL PASO**
M. Robbins
M. Robbins, Columbia 41511
(Marty's, BMI)

4. **WAY DOWN YONDER IN NEW ORLEANS**
F. Cannon
Cramer–Layton, Swan 4043
(Shapiro–Bernstein, ASCAP)

5. **RUNNING BEAR**
J. Preston
J. P. Richardson, Mercury
71474 (Big Bopper, BMI)

6. **AMONG MY SOUVENIRS**
C. Francis
Leslie–Nicholls, M-G-M 12841
(Brown–Henderson, ASCAP)

7. **IT'S TIME TO CRY**
P. Anka
P. Anka, ABC–Paramount
10064 (Spanka, BMI)

8. **HEARTACHES BY THE NUMBER**
G. Mitchell
H. Howard, Columbia 41476
(Pamper, BMI)

9. **GO, JIMMY, GO**
J. Clanton
Pomus–Shuman, Ace 575
(Wills–Ace, BMI)

10. **PRETTY BLUE EYES**
S. Lawrence
Randazzo–Weinstein, ABC-
Paramount 10058 (Almino,
BMI)

January 11

1. **EL PASO**
M. Robbins
M. Robbins, Columbia 41511
(Marty's, BMI)

2. **WAY DOWN YONDER IN NEW ORLEANS**
F. Cannon
Cramer–Layton, Swan 4043
(Shapiro–Bernstein, ASCAP)

3. **WHY**
F. Avalon
Marcucci–DeAngelis,
Chancellor 1045 (Debmar,
ASCAP)

4. **THE BIG HURT**
T. Fisher
W. Shanklin, Signet 275
(Music Productions, ASCAP)

5. **RUNNING BEAR**
J. Preston
J. P. Richardson, Mercury 71474
(Big Bopper, BMI)

6. **GO, JIMMY, GO**
J. Clanton
Pomus–Shuman, Ace 575
(Wills–Ace, BMI)

7. **IT'S TIME TO CRY**
P. Anka
P. Anka, ABC–Paramount 10064
(Spanka, BMI)

8. **AMONG MY SOUVENIRS**
C. Francis
Leslie–Nicholls, M-G-M 12841
(Brown–Henderson, ASCAP)

9. **PRETTY BLUE EYES**
S. Lawrence
Randazzo–Weinstein, ABC-
Paramount 10058 (Almimo,
BMI)

10. **HEARTACHES BY THE NUMBER**
G. Mitchell
H. Howard, Columbia 41476
(Pamper, BMI)

1960

January 18

1. **RUNNING BEAR**
J. Preston
J. P. Richardson, Mercury 71474 (Big Bopper, BMI)
2. **WHY**
F. Avalon
Marcucci–DeAngelis, Chancellor 1045 (Debmar, ASCAP)
3. **EL PASO**
M. Robbins
M. Robbins, Columbia 41511 (Marty's, BMI)
4. **THE BIG HURT**
T. Fisher
W. Shanklin, Signet 275 (Music Productions, ASCAP)
5. **WAY DOWN YONDER IN NEW ORLEANS**
F. Cannon
Cramer–Layton, Swan 4043 (Shapiro–Bernstein, ASCAP)
6. **GO, JIMMY, GO**
J. Clanton
Pomus–Shuman, Ace 575 (Wills–Ace, BMI)
7. **TEEN ANGEL**
M. Dinning
JNR–Surrey, M-G-M 12845 (Acuff–Rose, BMI)
8. **THE VILLAGE OF ST. BERNADETTE**
A. Williams
Eula–Parker, Cadence 1374 (Ludlow, BMI)
9. **PRETTY BLUE EYES**
S. Lawrence
Randazzo–Weinstein, ABC Paramount 10058 (Almimo, BMI)
10. **AMONG MY SOUVENIRS**
C. Francis
Leslie–Nicholls, M-G-M 12841 (Brown–Henderson, ASCAP)

January 25

1. **RUNNING BEAR**
J. Preston
J. P. Richardson, Mercury 71474 (Big Bopper, BMI)
2. **EL PASO**
M. Robbins
M. Robbins, Columbia 41511 (Marty's, BMI)
3. **WHY**
F. Avalon
Marcucci–DeAngelis, Chancellor 1045 (Debmar, ASCAP)
4. **TEEN ANGEL**
M. Dinning
JNR–Surrey, M-G-M 12845 (Acuff–Rose, BMI)
5. **WAY DOWN YONDER IN NEW ORLEANS**
F. Cannon
Cramer–Layton, Swan 4043 (Shapiro–Bernstein, ASCAP)
6. **THE BIG HURT**
T. Fisher
W. Shanklin, Signet 275 (Music Productiions, ASCAP)
7. **THE VILLAGE OF ST. BERNADETTE**
A. Williams
Eula–Parker, Cadence 1374 (Ludlow, BMI)
8. **GO, JIMMY, GO**
J. Clanton
Pomus–Shuman, Ace 575 (Wills–Ace, BMI)
9. **PRETTY BLUE EYES**
S. Lawrence
Randazzo–Weinstein, ABC–Paramount 10058 (Almimo, BMI)
10. **WHERE OR WHEN**
Dion and the Belmonts
Rodgers–Hart, Laurie 3044 (Chappell, ASCAP)

February 1

1. **RUNNING BEAR**
J. Preston
J. P. Richardson, Mercury 71474 (Big Bopper, BMI)
2. **TEEN ANGEL**
M. Dinning
JNR–Surrey, M-G-M 12845 (Acuff–Rose, BMI)
3. **EL PASO**
M. Robbins
M. Robbins, Columbia 41511 (Marty's, BMI)
4. **GO, JIMMY, GO**
J. Clanton
Pomus–Shuman, Ace 575 (Wills–Ace, BMI)
5. **WHERE OR WHEN**
Dion and the Belmonts
Rodgers–Hart, Laurie 3044 (Chappell, ASCAP)
6. **HANDY MAN**
J. Jones
Blackwell–Jones, Cub 9049 (Sheldon, BMI)
7. **WAY DOWN YONDER IN NEW ORLEANS**
F. Cannon
Cramer–Layton, Swan 4043 (Shapiro–Bernstein, ASCAP)
8. **WHY**
F. Avalon
Marcucci–DeAngelis, Chancellor 1045 (Debmar, ASCAP)
9. **PRETTY BLUE EYES**
S. Lawrence
Randazzo–Weinstein, ABC–Paramount 10058 (Almimo, BMI)
10. **THE BIG HURT**
T. Fisher
W. Shanklin, Signet 275 (Music Productions, ASCAP)

Feburary 8

1. **TEEN ANGEL**
M. Dinning
JNR–Surrey, M-G-M 12845
(Acuff–Rose, BMI)

2. **RUNNING BEAR**
J. Preston
J. P. Richardson, Mercury 71474
(Big Bopper, BMI)

3. **HANDY MAN**
J. Jones
Blackwell–Jones, Cub 9049
(Sheldon, BMI)

4. **WHERE OR WHEN**
Dion and the Belmonts
Rodgers–Hart, Laurie 3044
(Chappell, ASCAP)

5. **LONELY BLUE BOY**
C. Twitty
Weisman–Wyse, M-G-M 12857
(May, ASCAP)

6. **EL PASO**
M. Robbins
M. Robbins, Columbia 41511
(Marty's, BMI)

7. **YOU'VE GOT WHAT IT TAKES**
M. Johnson
Gordy–Davis–Gordy, United Artists 185 (Fidelity, BMI)

8. **WHAT IN THE WORLD'S COME OVER YOU**
J. Scott
J. Scott, Top Rank 2028
(Peer International–Star Fire, BMI)

9. **HE'LL HAVE TO GO**
J. Reeves
J. Allison–A. Allison, Victor 7643 (Central Songs, BMI)

10. **WHY**
F. Avalon
Marcucci–DeAngelis, Chancellor 1045 (Debmar, ASCAP)

February 15

1. **TEEN ANGEL**
M. Dinning
JNR–Surrey, M-G-M 12845
(Acuff–Rose, BMI)

2. **RUNNING BEAR**
J. Preston
J. P. Richardson, Mercury 71474 (Big Bopper, BMI)

3. **HANDY MAN**
J. Jones
Blackwell–Jones, Cub 9049
(Sheldon, BMI)

4. **HE'LL HAVE TO GO**
J. Reeves
J. Allison–A. Allison, Victor 7643 (Central Songs, BMI)

5. **WHERE OR WHEN**
Dion and the Belmonts
Rodgers–Hart, Laurie 3044
(Chappell, ASCAP)

6. **THEME FROM A SUMMER PLACE**
P. Faith
Steiner, Columbia 40490
(Witmark, ASCAP)

7. **WHAT IN THE WORLD'S COME OVER YOU**
J. Scott
J. Scott, Top Rank 2028
(Peer International–Star Fire, BMI)

8. **LONELY BLUE BOY**
C. Twitty
Weisman–Wyse, M-G-M 12857
(May, ASCAP)

9. **LET IT BE ME**
The Everly Brothers
Curtis–Defano–Becaud, Cadence 9359 (Leeds, ASCAP)

10. **EL PASO**
M. Robbins
M. Robbins, Columbia 41511
(Marty's, BMI)

February 22

1. **THEME FROM A SUMMER PLACE**
P. Faith
Steiner, Columbia 40490
(Witmark, ASCAP)

2. **TEEN ANGEL**
M. Dinning
JNR–Surrey, M-G-M 12845
(Acuff–Rose, BMI)

3. **HANDY MAN**
J. Jones
Blackwell–Jones, Cub 9049
(Sheldon, BMI)

4. **RUNNING BEAR**
J. Preston
J. P. Richardson, Mercury 71474
(Big Bopper, BMI)

5. **HE'LL HAVE TO GO**
J. Reeves
J. Allison–A. Allison, Victor 7643 (Central Songs, BMI)

6. **WHAT IN THE WORLD'S COME OVER YOU**
J. Scott
J. Scott, Top Rank 2028
(Peer International–Star Fire, BMI)

7. **BEYOND THE SEA**
B. Darin
Trenet–Lawrence, Atco 6158
(Harms, ASCAP)

8. **WHERE OR WHEN**
Dion and the Belmonts
Rodgers–Hart, Laurie 3044
(Chappell, ASCAP)

9. **LET IT BE ME**
The Everly Brothers
Curtis–Defano–Becaud, Cadence 9359 (Leeds, ASCAP)

10. **LONELY BLUE BOY**
C. Twitty
Weisman–Wyse, M-G-M 12857
(May, ASCAP)

1960

February 29

1. **THEME FROM A SUMMER PLACE**
P. Faith
Steiner, Columbia 40490 (Witmark, ASCAP)

2. **HANDY MAN**
J. Jones
Blackwell–Jones, Cub 9049 (Sheldon, BMI)

3. **BEYOND THE SEA**
B. Darin
Trenet–Lawrence, Atco 6158 (Harms, ASCAP)

4. **HE'LL HAVE TO GO**
J. Reeves
J. Allison–A. Allison, Victor 7643 (Central Songs, BMI)

5. **TEEN ANGEL**
M. Dinning
JNR–Surrey, M-G-M 12845 (Acuff–Rose, BMI)

6. **WHAT IN THE WORLD'S COME OVER YOU**
J. Scott
J. Scott, Top Rank 2028 (Peer International–Star Fire, BMI)

7. **LET IT BE ME**
The Everly Brothers
Curtis–Defano–Becaud, Cadence 9359 (Leeds, ASCAP)

8. **WILD ONE**
B. Rydell
F. Tobias, Cameo 171 (Lowe, ASCAP)

9. **RUNNING BEAR**
J. Preston
J. P. Richardson, Mercury 71474 (Big Bopper, BMI)

10. **BABY**
B. Benton and D. Washington
C.Otis–M. Stein, Mercury 71565 (Meridian–Play, BMI)

March 7

1. **THEME FROM A SUMMER PLACE**
P. Faith
Steiner, Columbia 40490 (Witmark, ASCAP)

2. **HE'LL HAVE TO GO**
J. Reeves
J. Allison–A. Allison, Victor 7643 (Central Songs, BMI)

3. **HANDY MAN**
J. Jones
Blackwell–Jones, Cub 9049 (Sheldon, BMI)

4. **WILD ONE**
B. Rydell
F. Tobias, Cameo 171 (Lowe, ASCAP)

5. **WHAT INTHE WORLD'S COME OVER YOU**
J. Scott
J. Scott, Top Rank 2028 (Peer International–Star Fire, BMI)

6. **TEEN ANGEL**
M. Dinning
JNR–Surrey, M-G-M 12845 (Acuff–Rose, BMI)

7. **BEYOND THE SEA**
B. Darin
Trenet–Lawrence, Atco 6158 (Harms, ASCAP)

8. **BABY**
B. Benton and D. Washington
C. Otis–M. Stein, Mercury 71565 (Meridian–Play, BMI)

9. **LET IT BE ME**
The Everly Brothers
Curtis–Defano–Becaud, Cadence 9359 (Leeds, ASCAP)

10. **RUNNING BEAR**
J. Preston
J. P. Richardson, Mercury 71474 (Big Bopper, BMI)

March 14

1. **THEME FROM A SUMMER PLACE**
P. Faith
Steiner, Columbia 40490 (Witmark, ASCAP)

2. **HE'LL HAVE TO GO**
J. Reeves
A. Allison–J. Allison, Victor 7643 (Harms, ASCAP)

3. **WILD ONE**
B. Rydell
F. Tobias, Cameo 171 (Lowe, ASCAP)

4. **HANDY MAN**
J. Jones
Blackwell–Jones, Cub 9049 (Sheldon, BMI)

5. **WHAT IN THE WORLD'S COME OVER YOU**
J. Scott
J. Scott, Top Rank 2028 (Peer International–Star Fire, BMI)

6. **BABY**
B. Benton and D. Washington
C. Otis–M. Stein, Mercury 71565 (Meridian–Play, BMI)

7. **TEEN ANGEL**
M. Dinning
JNR–Surrey, M-G-M 12845 (Acuff–Rose, BMI)

8. **BEYOND THE SEA**
B. Darin
Trenet–Lawrence, Atco 6158 (Harms, ASCAP)

9. **PUPPY LOVE**
P. Anka
P. Anka, ABC–Paramount 10082 (Spanka, BMI)

10. **HARBOR LIGHTS**
The Platters
H. Williams–J. Kennedy, Mercury 71563 (Chappell, ASCAP)

149

March 21

1. **THEME FROM A SUMMER PLACE**
   P. Faith
   Steiner, Columbia 40490 (Witmark, ASCAP)
2. **HE'LL HAVE TO GO**
   J. Reeves
   J. Allison–A. Allison, Victor 7643 (Harms, ASCAP)
3. **WILD ONE**
   B. Rydell
   F. Tobias, Cameo 171 (Lowe, ASCAP)
4. **HANDY MAN**
   J. Jones
   Blackwell–Jones, Cub 9049 (Sheldon, BMI)
5. **BABY**
   B. Benton and D. Washington
   C. Otis–M. Stein, Mercury 71565 (Meridian–Play, BMI)
6. **WHAT IN THE WORLD'S COME OVER YOU**
   J. Scott
   J. Scott, Top Rank 2028 (Peer International–Star Fire, BMI)
7. **PUPPY LOVE**
   P. Anka
   P. Anka, ABC–Paramount 10082 (Spanka, BMI)
8. **SWEET NOTHIN'S**
   B. Lee
   R. Self, Decca 30967 (Champion, BMI)
9. **TEEN ANGEL**
   M. Dinning
   JNR–Surrey, M-G-M 12845 (Acuff–Rose, BMI)
10. **HARBOR LIGHTS**
    The Platters
    H. Williams–J. Kennedy, Mercury 71563 (Chappell, ASCAP)

March 28

1. **THEME FROM A SUMMER PLACE**
   P. Faith
   Steiner, Columbia 40490 (Witmark, ASCAP)
2. **PUPPY LOVE**
   P. Anka
   P. Anka, ABC–Paramount 10082 (Spanka, BMI)
3. **WILD ONE**
   B. Rydell
   F. Tobias, Cameo 171 (Lowe, ASCAP)
4. **HE'LL HAVE TO GO**
   J. Reeves
   J. Allison–A. Allison, Victor 7643 (Harms, ASCAP)
5. **HARBOR LIGHTS**
   The Platters
   H. Williams–J. Kennedy, Mercury 71563 (Chappell, ASCAP)
6. **HANDY MAN**
   J. Jones
   Blackwell–Jones, Cub 9049 (Sheldon, BMI)
7. **SWEET NOTHIN'S**
   B. Lee
   R. Self, Decca 30967 (Champion, BMI)
8. **BABY**
   B. Benton and D. Washington
   C. Otis–M. Stein, Mercury 71565 (Meridian–Play, BMI)
9. **O, DIO MIO**
   Annette
   A. Hoffman–D. Manning, Vista 354 (Topper, ASCAP)
10. **FOREVER**
    The Little Dippers
    B. Killen, University 210 (Tree, BMI)

April 4

1. **THEME FROM A SUMMER PLACE**
   P. Faith
   Steiner, Columbia 40490 (Witmark, ASCAP)
2. **WILD ONE**
   B. Rydell
   F. Tobias, Cameo 171 (Lowe, ASCAP)
3. **PUPPY LOVE**
   P. Anka
   P. Anka, ABC–Paramount 10082 (Spanka, BMI)
4. **HE'LL HAVE TO GO**
   J. Reeves
   J. Allison–A. Allison, Victor 7643 (Harms, ASCAP)
5. **SINK THE BISMARK**
   J. Horton
   J. Horton–T. Franks, Columbia 41568 (Cajun, BMI)
6. **SWEET NOTHIN'S**
   B. Lee
   R. Self, Decca 30967 (Champion, BMI)
7. **HARBOR LIGHTS**
   The Platters
   H. Williams–J. Kennedy, Mercury 71563 (Chappell, ASCAP)
8. **FOOTSTEPS**
   S. Lawrence
   B. Mann–H. Hunter, ABC–Paramount 10085 (Aldon, BMI)
9. **MAMA**
   C. Francis
   Bixio–Cherubini–Barlow–Brito, M-G-M 12878 (Southern, ASCAP)
10. **BABY**
    B. Benton and D. Washington
    C. Otis–M. Stein, Mercury 71565 (Meridian–Play, BMI)

1960

April 11

1. **THEME FROM A SUMMER PLACE**
P. Faith
Steiner, Columbia 40490 (Witmark, ASCAP)

2. **PUPPY LOVE**
P. Anka
P. Anka, ABC–Paramount 10082 (Spanka, BMI)

3. **HE'LL HAVE TO GO**
J. Reeves
J. Allison–A. Allison, Victor 7643 (Harms, ASCAP)

4. **WILD ONE**
B. Rydell
F. Tobias, Cameo 171 (Lowe, ASCAP)

5. **GREENFIELDS**
The Brothers Four
T. Gillkyson–R. Dehr–F. Miller, Columbia 41571 (Montclare, BMI)

6. **SWEET NOTHIN'S**
B. Lee
R. Self, Decca 30967 (Champion, BMI)

7. **SINK THE BISMARK**
J. Horton
J. Horton–T. Franks, Columbia 41568 (Cajun, BMI)

8. **MAMA**
C. Francis
Bixio–Cherubini–Barlow–Brito, M-G-M 12878 (Southern, ASCAP)

9. **I LOVE THE WAY YOU LOVE**
M. Johnson
Gordy–Mikaljon, United Artists 208 (Jobete, BMI)

10. **FOOTSTEPS**
S. Lawrence
B. Mann–H. Hunter, ABC–Paramount 10085 (Aldon, BMI)

April 18

1. **THEME FROM A SUMMER PLACE**
P. Faith
Steiner, Columbia 40490 (Witmark, ASCAP)

2. **GREENFIELDS**
The Brothers Four
T. Gillkyson–R. Dehr–F. Miller, Columbia 41571 (Montclare, BMI)

3. **PUPPY LOVE**
P. Anka
P. Anka, ABC–Paramount 10082 (Spanka, BMI)

4. **SWEET NOTHIN'S**
B. Lee
R. Self, Decca 30967 (Champion, BMI)

5. **SINK THE BISMARK**
J. Horton
J. Horton–T. Franks, Columbia 41568 (Cajun, BMI)

6. **STUCK ON YOU**
E. Presley
A. Schroeder–J. L. MacFarland, Victor 7740 (Gladys, ASCAP)

7. **WILD ONE**
B. Rydell
F. Tobias, Cameo 171 (Lowe, ASCAP)

8. **HE'LL HAVE TO GO**
J. Reeves
J. Allison–A. Allison, Victor 7643 (Harms, ASCAP)

9. **SIXTEEN REASONS**
C. Stevens
B. Post–D. Post, Warner Brothers 5137 (American, BMI)

10. **MAMA**
C. Francis
Bixio–Cherubini–Barlow–Brito, M-G-M 12878 (Southern, ASCAP)

April 25

1. **STUCK ON YOU**
E. Presley
A. Schroeder–J. L. MacFarland, Victor 7740 (Gladys, ASCAP)

2. **GREENFIELDS**
The Brothers Four
T. Gillkyson–R. Dehr–F. Miller, Columbia 41571 (Montclare, BMI)

3. **SINK THE BISMARK**
J. Horton
J. Horton–T. Franks, Columbia 41568 (Cajun, BMI)

4. **SIXTEEN REASONS**
C. Stevens
B. Post–D. Post, Warner Brothers 5137 (American, BMI)

5. **THEME FROM A SUMMER PLACE**
P. Faith
Steiner, Columbia 40490 (Witmark, ASCAP)

6. **SWEET NOTHIN'S**
B. Lee
R. Self, Decca 30967 (Champion, BMI)

7. **THE OLD LAMPLIGHTER**
The Browns
C. Tobias–N. Simon, Victor 7700 (Shapiro–Bernstein, ASCAP)

8. **PUPPY LOVE**
P. Anka
P. Anka, ABC–Paramount 10082 (Spanka, BMI)

9. **HE'LL HAVE TO GO**
J. Reeves
J. Allison–A. Allison, Victor 7643 (Harms, ASCAP)

10. **WHITE SILVER SANDS**
Bill Black's Combo
C. G. Mathews–G. Reinhart, Hi 2021 (Sharina, BMI)

May 2

1. **STUCK ON YOU**
   E. Presley
   A. Schroeder–J. L. MacFarland, Victor 7740 (Gladys, ASCAP)

2. **SIXTEEN REASONS**
   C. Stevens
   B. Post–D. Post, Warner Brothers 5137 (American, BMI)

3. **SINK THE BISMARK**
   J. Horton
   J. Horton–T. Franks, Columbia 41568 (Cajun, BMI)

4. **GREENFIELDS**
   The Brothers Four
   T. Gillkyson–R. Dehr–F. Miller, Columbia 41571 (Montclare, BMI)

5. **THE OLD LAMPLIGHTER**
   The Browns
   C. Tobias–N. Simon, Victor 7700 (Shapiro–Bernstein, ASCAP)

6. **LET THE LITTLE GIRL DANCE**
   B. Bland
   H. Glover, Old Town 1076 (Glover, BMI)

7. **NIGHT**
   J. Wilson
   J. Lehman–H. Miller, Brunswick 55166 (Pearl, BMI)

8. **SWEET NOTHIN'S**
   B. Lee
   R. Self, Decca 30967 (Champion, BMI)

9. **CRADLE OF LOVE**
   J. Preston
   Fautheree–Gray, Mercury 71598 (Big Bopper–Tree, BMI)

10. **THEME FROM A SUMMER PLACE**
    P. Faith
    Steiner, Columbia 40490 (Witmark, ASCAP)

May 9

1. **STUCK ON YOU**
   E. Presley
   A. Schroeder–J. L. MacFarland, Victor 7740 (Gladys, ASCAP)

2. **GREENFIELDS**
   The Brothers Four
   T. Gillkyson–R. Dehr–F. Miller, Columbia 41571 (Montclare, BMI)

3. **CATHY'S CLOWN**
   The Everly Brothers
   D. Everly–P. Everly, Warner Brothers 5051 (Acuff–Rose, BMI)

4. **NIGHT**
   J. Wilson
   J. Lehman–H. Miller, Brunswick 55166 (Pearl, BMI)

5. **SIXTEEN REASONS**
   C. Stevens
   B. Post–D. Post, Warner Brothers 5137 (American, BMI)

6. **SINK THE BISMARK**
   J. Horton
   J. Horton–T. Franks, Columbia 41568 (Cajun, BMI)

7. **THE OLD LAMPLIGHTER**
   The Browns
   C. Tobias–N. Simon, Victor 7700 (Shapiro–Bernstein, ASCAP)

8. **CRADLE OF LOVE**
   J. Preston
   Fautheree–Gray, Mercury 71598 (Big Bopper–Tree, BMI)

9. **STAIRWAY TO HEAVEN**
   N. Sedaka
   N. Sedaka–H. Greenfield, Victor 7709 (Aldon, BMI)

10. **LET THE LITTLE GIRL DANCE**
    B. Bland
    H. Glover, Old Town 1076 (Glover, GMI)

May 16

1. **STUCK ON YOU**
   E. Presley
   A. Schroeder–J. L. MacFarland, Victor 7740 (Gladys, ASCAP)

2. **CATHY'S CLOWN**
   The Everly Brothers
   D. Everly–P. Everly, Warner Brothers 5051 (Acuff–Rose, BMI)

3. **GREENFIELDS**
   The Brothers Four
   T. Gillkyson–R. Dehr–F. Miller, Columbia 41571 (Montclare, BMI)

4. **NIGHT**
   J. Wilson
   J. Lehman–H. Miller, Brunswick 55166 (Pearl, BMI)

5. **GOOD TIMIN'**
   J. Jones
   Tobias–Ballard, Cub 9076 (Sequence, ASCAP)

6. **SIXTEEN REASONS**
   C. Stevens
   B. Post–D. Post, Warner Brothers 5137 (American, BMI)

7. **LET THE LITTLE GIRL DANCE**
   B. Bland
   H. Glover, Old Town 1076 (Glover, BMI)

8. **CRADLE OF LOVE**
   J. Preston
   Fautheree–Gray, Mercury 71598 (Big Bopper–Tree, BMI)

9. **SINK THE BISMARK**
   J. Horton
   J. Horton–T. Franks, Columbia 41568 (Cajun, BMI)

10. **HE'LL HAVE TO STAY**
    J. Black
    C. Grean–J. Allison–A. Allison, Capitol 4368 (Central Songs, BMI)

1960

May 23

1. **CATHY'S CLOWN**
   The Everly Brothers
   D. Everly–P. Everly, Warner Brothers 5051 (Acuff–Rose, BMI)

2. **STUCK ON YOU**
   E. Presley
   A. Schroeder–J. L. MacFarland, Victor 7740 (Gladys, ASCAP)

3. **GOOD TIMIN'**
   J. Jones
   Tobias–Ballard, Cub 9076 (Sequence, ASCAP)

4. **GREENFIELDS**
   The Brothers Four
   T. Gillkyson–R. Dehr–F. Miller, Columbia 41571 (Montclare, BMI)

5. **NIGHT**
   J. Wilson
   J. Lehman–H. Miller, Brunswick 55166 (Pearl, BMI)

6. **SIXTEEN REASONS**
   C. Stevens
   B. Post–D. Post, Warner Brothers 5137 (American, BMI)

7. **CRADLE OF LOVE**
   J. Preston
   Fautheree–Gray, Mercury 71598 (Big Bopper–Tree, BMI)

8. **HE'LL HAVE TO STAY**
   J. Black
   C. Grean–J. Allison–A. Allison, Capitol 4368 (Central Songs, BMI)

9. **LET THE LITTLE GIRL DANCE**
   B. Bland
   H. Glover, Old Town 1076 (Glover, BMI)

10. **PAPER ROSES**
    A. Bryant
    Spielman–Torre, Carlton 528 (Pambill, ASCAP)

May 30

1. **CATHY'S CLOWN**
   The Everly Brothers
   D. Everly–P. Everly, Warner Brothers 5051 (Acuff–Rose, BMI)

2. **GOOD TIMIN'**
   J. Jones
   Tobias–Ballard, Cub 9076 (Sequence, ASCAP)

3. **STUCK ON YOU**
   E. Presley
   A. Schroeder–J. L. MacFarland, Victor 7740 (Gladys, ASCAP)

4. **GREENFIELDS**
   The Brothers Four
   T. Gillkyson–R. Dehr–F. Miller, Columbia 41571 (Montclare, BMI)

5. **NIGHT**
   J. Wilson
   J. Lehman–H. Miller, Brunswick 55166 (Pearl, BMI)

6. **SIXTEEN REASONS**
   C. Stevens
   B. Post–D. Post, Warner Brothers 5137 (American, BMI)

7. **HE'LL HAVE TO STAY**
   J. Black
   C. Grean–J. Allison–A. Allison, Capitol 4368 (Central Songs, BMI)

8. **PAPER ROSES**
   A. Bryant
   Spielman–Torre, Carlton 528 (Pambill, ASCAP)

9. **CRADLE OF LOVE**
   J. Preston
   Fautheree–Gray, Mercury 71598 (Big Bopper–Tree, BMI)

10. **BURNING BRIDGES**
    J. Scott
    J. Scott, Top Rank 2041 (Sage and Sand, SESAC)

June 6

1. **CATHY'S CLOWN**
   The Everly Brothers
   D. Everly–P. Everly, Warner Brothers 5051 (Acuff–Rose, BMI)

2. **GOOD TIMIN'**
   J. Jones
   Tobias–Ballard, Cub 9076 (Sequence, ASCAP)

3. **STUCK ON YOU**
   E. Presley
   A. Schroeder–J. L. MacFarland, Victor 7740 (Gladys, ASCAP)

4. **SIXTEEN REASONS**
   C. Stevens
   B. Post–D. Post, Warner Brothers 5137 (American, BMI)

5. **HE'LL HAVE TO STAY**
   J. Black
   C. Grean–J. Allison–A. Allison, Capitol 4368 (Central Songs, BMI)

6. **BURNING BRIDGES**
   J. Scott
   J. Scott, Top Rank 2041 (Sage and Sand, SESAC)

7. **PAPER ROSES**
   A. Bryant
   Spileman–Torre, Carlton 528 (Pambill, ASCAP)

8. **NIGHT**
   J. Wilson
   J. Lehman–H. Miller, Brunswick 55166 (Pearl, BMI)

9. **EVERYBODY'S SOMEBODY'S FOOL**
   C. Francis
   Keller–Greenfield, M-G-M 12899 (Aldon, BMI)

10. **LOVE YOU SO**
    R. Holden
    R. Holden, Donna 1315 (Maravilla, BMI)

153

June 13

1. **CATHY'S CLOWN**
   The Everly Brothers
   D. Everly–P. Everly, Warner Brothers 5051 (Acuff–Rose, BMI)

2. **EVERYBODY'S SOMEBODY'S FOOL**
   C. Francis
   Keller–Greenfield, M-G-M 12899 (Aldon, BMI)

3. **BURNING BRIDGES**
   J. Scott
   J. Scott, Top Rank 2041 (Sage and Sand, SESAC)

4. **GOOD TIMIN'**
   J. Jones
   Tobias–Ballard, Cub 9076 (Sequence, ASCAP)

5. **PAPER ROSES**
   A. Bryant
   Spielman–Torre, Carlton 528 (Pambill, ASCAP)

6. **HE'LL HAVE TO STAY**
   J. Black
   C. Grean–J. Allison–A. Allison, Capitol 4368 (Central Songs, BMI)

7. **LOVE YOU SO**
   R. Holden
   R. Holden, Donna 1315 (Maravilla, BMI)

8. **STUCK ON YOU**
   E. Presley
   A. Schroeder–J. L. MacFarland, Victor 7740 (Gladys, ASCAP)

9. **SWINGING SCHOOL**
   B. Rydell
   Lowe–Appell–Mann, Cameo 175 (Columbia, ASCAP)

10. **HAPPY-GO-LUCKY ME**
    P. Evans
    Evans–Byron, Guaranteed 208 (Pambill–Lyle, ASCAP)

June 20

1. **CATHY'S CLOWN**
   The Everly Brothers
   D. Everly–P. Everly, Warner Brothers 5051 (Acuff–Rose, BMI)

2. **EVERYBODY'S SOMEBODY'S FOOL**
   C. Francis
   Keller–Greenfield, M-G-M 12899 (Aldon, BMI)

3. **BURNING BRIDGES**
   J. Scott
   J. Scott, Top Rank 2041 (Sage and Sand, SESAC)

4. **GOOD TIMIN'**
   J. Jones
   Tobias–Ballard, Cub 9076 (Sequence, ASCAP)

5. **SWINGING SCHOOL**
   B. Rydell
   Lowe–Appell–Mann, Cameo 175 (Columbia, ASCAP)

6. **ALLEY-OOP**
   The Hollywood Argyles
   Fraizer, Lute 5905 (Kavelin–Maverick, BMI)

7. **PAPER ROSES**
   A. Bryant
   Spielman–Torre, Carlton 528 (Pambill, ASCAP)

8. **LOVE YOU SO**
   R. Holden
   R. Holden, Donna 1315 (Maravilla, BMI)

9. **HE'LL HAVE TO STAY**
   J. Black
   C. Grean–J. Allison–A. Allison, Capitol 4368 (Central Songs, BMI)

10. **STUCK ON YOU**
    E. Presley
    A. Schroeder–J. L. MacFarland, Victor 7740 (Gladys, ASCAP)

June 27

1. **EVERYBODY'S SOMEBODY'S FOOL**
   C. Francis
   Keller–Greenfield, M-G-M 12899 (Aldon, BMI)

2. **CATHY'S CLOWN**
   The Everly Brothers
   D. Everly–P. Everly, Warner Brothers 5051 (Acuff–Rose, BMI)

3. **ALLEY-OOP**
   The Hollywood Argyles
   Frazier, Lute 5905 (Kavelin–Maverick BMI)

4. **BURNING BRIDGES**
   J. Scott
   J. Scott, Top Rank 2041 (Sage and Sand, SESAC)

5. **BECAUSE THEY'RE YOUNG**
   D. Eddy
   Schroeder–God–Costa, Jamie 1156 (Columbia Pictures, ASCAP)

6. **PAPER ROSES**
   A. Bryant
   Spielman–Torre, Carlton 528 (Pambill, ASCAP)

7. **I'M SORRY**
   B. Lee
   R. Self, Decca 31093 (Champion, BMI)

8. **A ROCKIN' GOOD WAY**
   D. Washington and B. Benton
   B. Benton, Mercury 71629 (Eden, BMI)

9. **GOOD TIMIN'**
   J. Jones
   Tobias–Ballard, Cub 9076 (Sequence, ASCAP)

10. **SWINGING SCHOOL**
    B. Rydell
    Lowe–Appell–Mann, Cameo 175 (Columbia, ASCAP)

1960

July 4

1. **EVERYBODY'S SOMEBODY'S FOOL**
C. Francis
Keller–Greenfield, M-G-M 12899 (Aldon, BMI)

2. **ALLEY-OOP**
The Hollywood Argyles
Fraizer, Lute 5905 (Kavelin–Maverick, BMI)

3. **I'M SORRY**
B. Lee
R. Self, Decca 31093 (Champion, BMI)

4. **BECAUSE THEY'RE YOUNG**
D. Eddy
Schroeder–God–Costa, Jamie 1156 (Columbia Pictures, ASCAP)

5. **CATHY'S CLOWN**
The Everly Brothers
D. Everly–P. Everly, Warner Brothers 5051 (Acuff–Rose, BMI)

6. **THAT'S ALL YOU GOTTA DO**
B. Lee
J. Reed, Decca 31093 (Lowery, BMI)

7. **BURNING BRIDGES**
J. Scott
J. Scott, Top Rank 2041 (Sage and Sand, SESAC)

8. **MY HOME TOWN**
P. Anka
P. Anka, ABC–Paramount 10106 (Spanka, BMI)

9. **MULE SKINNER BLUES**
The Fendermen
J. Rodgers, Soma 1137 (Peer–International, BMI)

10. **A ROCKIN' GOOD WAY**
D. Washington and B. Benton
B. Benton, Mercury 71629 (Eden, BMI)

July 11

1. **I'M SORRY**
B. Lee
R, Self, Decca 31093 (Champion, BMI)

2. **ALLEY-OOP**
The Hollywood Argyles
Fraizer, Lute 5905 (Kavelin–Maverick, BMI)

3. **EVERYBODY'S SOMEBODY'S FOOL**
C. Francis
Keller–Greenfield, M-G-M 12899 (Aldon, BMI)

4. **MULE SKINNER BLUES**
The Fendermen
J. Rodgers, Soma 1137 (Peer–International, BMI)

5. **ONLY THE LONELY**
R. Orbison
R. Orbison–Melson, Monument 421 (Acuff–Rose, BMI)

6. **BECAUSE THEY'RE YOUNG**
D. Eddy
Schroeder–God–Costa, Jamie 1156 (Columbia Pictures, ASCAP)

7. **A ROCKIN' GOOD WAY**
D. Washington and B. Benton
B. Benton, Mercury 71629 (Eden, BMI)

8. **THAT'S ALL YOU GOTTA DO**
B. Lee
J. Reed, Decca 31093 (Lowery, BMI)

9. **WHEN WILL I BE LOVED?**
The Everly Brothers
Everly, Cadence 1380 (Acuff–Rose, BMI)

10. **MY HOME TOWN**
P. Anka
P. Anka, ABC–Paramount 10106 (Spanka, BMI)

July 18

1. **ALLEY-OOP**
The Hollywood Argyles
Fraizer, Lute 5905 (Kavelin–Maverick, BMI)

2. **I'M SORRY**
B. Lee
R. Self, Decca 31093 (Champion, BMI)

3. **EVERYBODY'S SOMEBODY'S FOOL**
C. Francis
Keller–Greenfield, M-G-M 12899 (Aldon, BMI)

4. **THAT'S ALL YOU GOTTA DO**
B. Lee
J. Reed, Decca 31093 (Lowery, BMI)

5. **ONLY THE LONELY**
R. Orbison
R. Orbison–Melson, Monument 421 (Acuff–Rose, BMI)

6. **BECAUSE THEY'RE YOUNG**
D. Eddy
Schroeder–God–Costa, Jamie 1156 (Columbia Pictures, ASCAP)

7. **WHEN WILL I BE LOVED?**
The Everly Brothers
Everly, Cadence 1380 (Acuff–Rose, BMI)

8. **MULE SKINNER BLUES**
The Fendermen
J. Rodgers, Soma 1137 (Peer–International, BMI)

9. **TELL LAURA I LOVE HER**
R. Peterson
Bany–Raleigh, Victor 7745 (Marks, BMI)

10. **ITSY BITSY TEENIE WEENIE YELLOW POLKA DOT BIKINI**
B. Hyland
Vance–Pockriss, Leader 805 (Pincus, ASCAP)

July 25

1. **I'M SORRY**
B. Lee
R. Self, Decca 31093
(Champion, BMI)

2. **ONLY THE LONELY**
R. Orbison
R. Orbison–Melson, Monument 421 (Acuff–Rose, BMI)

3. **ALLEY-OOP**
The Hollywood Argyles
Fraizer, Lute 5905
(Kavelin-Maverick, BMI)

4. **EVERYBODY'S SOMEBODY'S FOOL**
C. Francis
Keller–Greenfield, M-G-M 12899 (Aldon, BMI)

5. **ITSY BITSY TEENIE WEENIE POLKA DOT BIKINI**
B. Hyland
Vance–Pockriss, Leader 805
(Pincus, ASCAP)

6. **MULE SKINNER BLUES**
The Fendermen
J. Rodgers, Soma 1137
(Peer–International, BMI)

7. **IMAGE OF A GIRL**
The Safaris
Clasky–Rosenberg, Eldo 101
(Eldorado, BMI)

8. **TELL LAURA I LOVE HER**
R. Peterson
Bany–Raleigh, Victor 7745
(Marks, BMI)

9. **PLEASE HELP ME, I'M FALLING**
H. Locklin
H. Locklin, Victor 7692
(Ross Jungnickel, ASCAP)

10. **THAT'S ALL YOU GOTTA DO**
B. Lee
J. Reed, Decca 31093
(Lowery, BMI)

August 1

1. **ITSY BITSY TEENIE WEENIE YELLOW POLKA DOT BIKINI**
B. Hyland
Vance–Pockriss, Leader 805
(Pincus, ASCAP)

2. **I'M SORRY**
B. Lee
R. Self, Decca 31093
(Champion, BMI)

3. **ONLY THE LONELY**
R. Orbison
R. Orbison–Melson, Monument 421 (Acuff–Rose, BMI)

4. **ALLEY-OOP**
The Hollywood Argyles
Fraizer, Lute 5905
(Kavelin-Maverick, BMI)

5. **IT'S NOW OR NEVER**
E. Presley
Gold–Schroeder, Victor 7777
(Gladys, ASCAP)

6. **MULE SKINNER BLUES**
The Fendermen
J. Rodgers, Soma 1137
(Peer–International, BMI)

7. **IMAGE OF A GIRL**
The Safaris
Clasky–Rosenberg, Eldo 101
(Eldorado, BMI)

8. **TELL LAURA I LOVE HER**
R. Peterson
Bany–Raleigh, Victor 7745
(E. B. Marks, BMI)

9. **PLEASE HELP ME, I'M FALLING**
H. Locklin
H. Locklin, Victor 7692
(Ross Jungnickel, ASCAP)

10. **WALKIN' TO NEW ORLEANS**
F. Domino
A. Domino–D. Bartholomew–Guiery, Imperial 5675
(Travis, BMI)

August 8

1. **ITSY BITSY TEENIE WEENIE YELLOW POLKA DOT BIKINI**
B. Hyland
Vance–Pockriss, Leader 805
(Pincus, ASCAP)

2. **IT'S NOW OR NEVER**
E. Presley
Gold–Schroeder, Victor 7777
(Gladys, ASCAP)

3. **I'M SORRY**
B. Lee
R. Self, Decca 31093
(Champion, BMI)

4. **ONLY THE LONELY**
R. Orbison
R. Orbison–Melson, Monument 421 (Acuff–Rose, BMI)

5. **IMAGE OF A GIRL**
The Safaris
Clasky–Rosenberg, Eldo 101
(Eldorado, BMI)

6. **WALK, DON'T RUN**
The Ventures
Smith, Dolton 25
(Electron, BMI)

7. **ALLEY-OOP**
The Hollywood Argyles
Fraizer, Lute 5905
(Kavelin-Maverick BMI)

8. **TELL LAURA I LOVE HER**
R. Peterson
Bany–Raleigh, Victor 7745
(E. B. Marks, BMI)

9. **PLEASE HELP ME, I'M FALLING**
H. Locklin
H. Locklin, Victor 7692
(Ross Jungnickel, ASCAP)

10. **WALKIN' TO NEW ORLEANS**
F. Domino
A. Domino–D. Bartholomew–Guiery, Imperial 5675
(Travis, BMI)

August 15

1. **IT'S NOW OR NEVER**
E. Presley
*Gold–Schroeder, Victor 7777
(Gladys, ASCAP)*

2. **ITSY BITSY TEENIE
WEENIE YELLOW POLKA
DOT BIKINI**
B. Hyland
*Vance–Pockriss, Leader 805
(Pincus, ASCAP)*

3. **I'M SORRY**
B. Lee
*R. Self, Decca 31093
(Champion, BMI)*

4. **ONLY THE LONELY**
R. Orbison
*R. Orbison–Melson, Monument
421 (Acuff–Rose, BMI)*

5. **WALK, DON'T RUN**
The Ventures
*Smith, Dolton 25
(Electron, BMI)*

6. **WALKIN' TO NEW ORLEANS**
F. Domino
*A. Domino–D. Bartholomew–
Guiery, Imperial 5675
(Travis, BMI)*

7. **FINGER POPPIN' TIME**
H. Ballard and the
Midnighters
*H. Ballard, King 8341
(Wisto, BMI)*

8. **THE TWIST**
C. Checker
*H. Ballard, Parkway 811
(Jay and Cee–Armo, BMI)*

9. **IMAGE OF A GIRL**
The Safaris
*Clasky–Rosenberg, Eldo 101
(Eldorado, BMI)*

10. **TELL LAURA I LOVE HER**
R. Peterson
*Bany–Raleigh, Victor 7745
(E. B. Marks, BMI)*

August 22

1. **IT'S NOW OR NEVER**
E. Presley
*Gold–Schroeder, Victor 7777
(Gladys, ASCAP)*

2. **ITSY BITSY TEENIE
WEENIE YELLOW POLKA
DOT BIKINI**
B. Hyland
*Vance–Pockriss, Leader 805
(Pincus, ASCAP)*

3. **WALK, DON'T RUN**
The Ventures
*Smith, Dolton 25
(Electron, BMI)*

4. **THE TWIST**
C. Checker
*H. Ballard, Parkway 811
(Jay and Cee–Armo, BMI)*

5. **I'M SORRY**
B. Lee
*R. Self, Decca 31093
(Champion, BMI)*

6. **ONLY THE LONELY**
R. Orbison
*R. Orbison–Melson, Monument
421 (Acuff–Rose, BMI)*

7. **VOLARE**
B. Rydell
*Moduno–Parish, Cameo 179
(Robbins, ASCAP)*

8. **FINGER POPPIN' TIME**
H. Ballard and the
Midnighters
*H. Ballard, King 8341
(Wisto, BMI)*

9. **MISSION BELL**
D. Brooks
*Michael, Era 3018
(Bamboo, BMI)*

10. **IMAGE OF A GIRL**
The Safaris
*Clasky–Rosenberg, Eldo 101
(Eldorado, BMI)*

August 29

1. **IT'S NOW OR NEVER**
E. Presley
*Gold–Schroeder, Victor 7777
(Gladys, ASCAP)*

2. **WALK, DON'T RUN**
The Ventures
*Smith, Dolton 25 (Electron,
BMI)*

3. **THE TWIST**
C. Checker
*H. Ballard, Parkway 811
(Jay and Cee–Armo, BMI)*

4. **VOLARE**
B. Rydell
*Modugno–Parish, Cameo 179
(Robbins, ASCAP)*

5. **I'M SORRY**
B. Lee
*R. Self, Decca 31093
(Champion, BMI)*

6. **FINGER POPPIN'TIME**
H. Ballard and the
Midnighters
*H. Ballard, King 8341
(Wisto, BMI)*

7. **ITSY BITSY TEENIE
WEENIE YELLOW POLKA
DOT BIKINI**
B. Hyland
*Vance–Pockriss, Leader 805
(Pincus, ASCAP)*

8. **MISSION BELL**
D. Brooks
*Michael, Era 3018
(Bamboo, BMI)*

9. **IN MY LITTLE CORNER OF
THE WORLD**
A. Bryant
*Pockriss–Hilliard, Carlton 530
(Shapiro–Bernstein, ASCAP)*

10. **ONLY THE LONELY**
R. Orbison
*R. Orbison–Melson, Monument
421 (Acuff–Rose, BMI)*

September 5

1. **IT'S NOW OR NEVER**
   E. Presley
   Gold–Schroeder, Victor 7777 (Gladys, ASCAP)

2. **WALK, DON'T RUN**
   The Ventures
   Smith, Dolton 25 (Electron, BMI)

3. **THE TWIST**
   C. Checker
   H. Ballard, Parkway 811 (Jay and Cee–Armo, BMI)

4. **I'M SORRY**
   B. Lee
   R. Self, Decca 31093 (Champion, BMI)

5. **MISSION BELL**
   D. Brooks
   Michael, Era 3018 (Bamboo, BMI)

6. **FINGER POPPIN' TIME**
   H. Ballard and the Midnighters
   H. Ballard, King 8341 (Wisto, BMI)

7. **ITSY BITSY TEENIE WEENIE YELLOW POLKA DOT BIKINI**
   B. Hyland
   Vance–Pockriss, Leader 805 (Pincus, ASCAP)

8. **VOLARE**
   B. Rydell
   Modugno–Parish, Cameo 179 (Robbins, ASCAP)

9. **THEME FROM THE APARTMENT**
   Ferrante and Teicher
   C. Williams, United Artists 231 (Mills, ASCAP)

10. **IN MY LITTLE CORNER OF THE WORLD**
    A. Bryant
    Pockriss–Hilliard, Carlton 530 (Shapiro–Bernstein, ASCAP)

September 12

1. **THE TWIST**
   C. Checker
   H. Ballard, Parkway 811 (Jay and Cee–Armo, BMI)

2. **IT'S NOW OR NEVER**
   E. Presley
   Gold–Schroeder, Victor 7777 (Gladys, ASCAP)

3. **MY HEART HAS A MIND OF ITS OWN**
   C. Francis
   Greenfield–Keller, M-G-M 12923 (Aldon, BMI)

4. **MR. CUSTER**
   L. Verne
   F. Darien–A. DeLory–J. Van Winkle, Era 3024 (Pattern, ASCAP)

5. **WALK, DON'T RUN**
   The Ventures
   Smith, Dolton 25 (Electron, BMI)

6. **CHAIN GANG**
   S. Cooke
   S. Cooke, Victor 7783 (Kags, BMI)

7. **VOLARE**
   B. Rydell
   Moduno–Parish, Cameo 179 (Robbins, ASCAP)

8. **KIDDIO**
   B. Benton
   B. Benton–C. Otis, Mercury 71652 (Eden–Brookville, BMI)

9. **YOGI**
   The Ivory Three
   Jacobson–Stallman–Kottelman, Shell 720 (Saxon, BMI)

10. **MISSION BELL**
    D. Brooks
    Michael, Era 3018 (Bamboo, BMI)

September 19

1. **THE TWIST**
   C. Checker
   H. Ballard, Parkway 811 (Jay and Cee–Armo, BMI)

2. **MY HEART HAS A MIND OF ITS OWN**
   C. Francis
   Greenfield–Keller, M-G-M 12923 (Aldon, BMI)

3. **IT'S NOW OR NEVER**
   E. Presley
   Gold–Schroeder, Victor 7777 (Gladys, ASCAP)

4. **MR. CUSTER**
   L. Verne
   F. Darien–A. DeLory–J. Van Winkle, Era 3024 (Pattern, ASCAP)

5. **CHAIN GANG**
   S. Cooke
   S. Cooke, Victor 7783 (Kags, BMI)

6. **KIDDIO**
   B. Benton
   B. Benton–C. Otis, Mercury 71652 (Eden–Brookville, BMI)

7. **WALK, DON'T RUN**
   The Ventures
   Smith, Dolton 25 (Electron, BMI)

8. **A MILLION TO ONE**
   J. Charles
   P. Medley, Promo 1002 (Starflower, BMI)

9. **VOLARE**
   B. Rydell
   Modugno–Parish, Cameo 179 (Robbins, ASCAP)

10. **YOGI**
    The Ivory Three
    Jacobson–Stallman–Kottelman, Shell 720 (Saxon, BMI)

September 26

1. **CHAIN GANG**
S. Cooke
S. Cooke, Victor 7783
(Kags, BMI)

2. **MY HEART HAS A MIND OF ITS OWN**
C. Francis
Greenfield–Keller, M-G-M 12923 (Aldon, BMI)

3. **MR. CUSTER**
L. Verne
F. Darien–A. DeLoy–J. VanWinkle, Era 3024 (Patterson, ASCAP)

4. **THE TWIST**
C. Checker
H. Ballard, Parkway 811 (Jay and Cee–Armo, BMI)

5. **IT'S NOW OR NEVER**
E. Presley
Gold–Schroeder, Victor 7777 (Gladys, ASCAP)

6. **A MILLION TO ONE**
J. Charles
P. Medley, Promo 1002 (Starflower, BMI)

7. **SAVE THE LAST DANCE FOR ME**
The Drifters
Pomus–Shuman, Atlantic 2071 (Rumbalero–Progressive, BMI)

8. **WALK, DON'T RUN**
The Ventures
Smith, Dolton 25 (Electron, BMI)

9. **PINEAPPLE PRINCESS**
Annette
B. Sherman–D. Sherman, Vista 362 (Music World, BMI)

10. **KIDDIO**
B. Benton
B. Benton–C. Otis, Mercury 71652 (Eden-Brookville, BMI)

October 3

1. **CHAIN GANG**
S. Cooke
S. Cooke, Victor 7783 (Kags, BMI)

2. **MR. CUSTER**
L. Verne
F. Darien–A. DeLory–J. VanWinkle, Era 3024 (Pattern, ASCAP)

3. **MY HEART HAS A MIND OF ITS OWN**
C. Francis
Greenfield–Keller, M-G-M 12923 (Aldon, BMI)

4. **THE TWIST**
C. Checker
H. Ballard, Parkway 811 (Jay and Cee–Armo, BMI)

5. **A MILLION TO ONE**
J. Charles
P. Medley, Promo 1002 (Starflower, BMI)

6. **SAVE THE LAST FOR ME**
The Drifters
Pomus–Shuman, Atlantic 2071 (Rumbalero–Progressive, BMI)

7. **IT'S NOW OR NEVER**
E. Presley
Gold–Schroeder, Victor 7777 (Gladys, ASCAP)

8. **WALK, DON'T RUN**
The Ventures
Smith, Dolton 25 (Electron, BMI)

9. **SO SAD**
The Everly Brothers
D. Everly, Warner Brothers 5163 (Acuff-Rose, BMI)

10. **THEME FROM THE APARTMENT**
Ferrante and Teicher
C. Williams, United Artists 231 (Mills, ASCAP)

October 10

1. **MR. CUSTER**
L. Verne
F. Darien–A. DeLory–J. Van Winkle, Era 3024 (Pattern, ASCAP)

2. **CHAIN GANG**
S. Cooke
S. Cooke, Victor 7783 (Kags, BMI)

3. **MY HEART HAS A MIND OF ITS OWN**
C. Francis
Greenfield-Keller, M-G-M 12923 (Aldon, BMI)

4. **SAVE THE LAST DANCE FOR ME**
The Drifters
Pomus-Shuman, Atlantic 2071 (Rumbalero-Progressive, BMI)

5. **THE TWIST**
C. Checker
H. Ballard, Parkway 811 (Jay and Cee–Armo, BMI)

6. **I WANT TO BE WANTED**
B. Lee
Gannon-Spotti-Testa, Decca 31149 (Leeds, ASCAP)

7. **A MILLION TO ONE**
J. Charles
P. Medley, Promo 1002 (Starflower, BMI)

8. **DEVIL OR ANGEL**
B. Vee
B. Carter, Liberty 55270 (Progressive, BMI)

9. **KIDDIO**
B. Benton
B. Benton-C, Otis, Mercury 71652 (Eden-Brookville, BMI)

10. **SO SAD**
The Everly Brothers
D. Everly, Warner Brothers 5163 (Acuff-Rose, BMI)

October 17

1. **SAVE THE LAST DANCE FOR ME**
   The Drifters
   Pomus-Shuman,   Atlantic 2071 (Rumbalero-Progressive, BMI)

2. **CHAIN GANG**
   S. Cooke
   S. Cooke,   Victor 7783 (Kags, BMI)

3. **I WANT TO BE WANTED**
   B. Lee
   Gannon-Spotti-Testa, Decca 31149   (Leeds, ASCAP)

4. **DEVIL OR ANGEL**
   B. Vee
   B. Carter,   Liberty 55270 (Progressive, BMI)

5. **MY HEART HAS A MIND OF ITS OWN**
   C. Francis
   Greenfield-Keller, M-G-M 12923   (Aldon, BMI)

6. **THE TWIST**
   C. Checker
   H. Ballard,   Parkway 811 (Jay and Cee-Armo, BMI)

7. **A MILLION TO ONE**
   J. Charles
   P. Medley,   Promo 1002 (Starflower, BMI)

8. **MR. CUSTER**
   L. Verne
   F. Darien-A. DeLory-J. Van Winkle,   Era 3024   (Pattern, ASCAP)

9. **IT'S NOW OR NEVER**
   E. Presley
   Gold-Schroeder,   Victor 7777 (Gladys, ASCAP)

10. **LET'S THINK ABOUT LIVING'**
    B. Luman
    Bryant,   Warner Brothers 5172 (Acuff-Rose, BMI)

October 24

1. **SAVE THE LAST DANCE FOR ME**
   The Drifters
   Pomus-Shuman,   Atlantic 2071 (Rumbalero-Progressive, BMI)

2. **THE TWIST**
   C. Checker
   H. Ballard,   Parkway 811 (Jay and Cee-Armo, BMI)

3. **I WANT TO BE WANTED**
   B. Lee
   Gannon-Spotti-Testa,   Decca 31149   (Leeds, ASCAP)

4. **MY HEART HAS A MIND OF ITS OWN**
   C. Francis
   Greenfield-Keller,   M-G-M 12923   (Aldon, BMI)

5. **CHAIN GANG**
   S. Cooke
   S..Cooke,   Victor 7783 (Kags, BMI)

6. **DEVIL OR ANGEL**
   B. Vee
   B. Carter,   Liberty 55270 (Progressive, BMI)

7. **LET'S THINK ABOUT LIVIN'**
   B. Luman
   Bryant,   Warner Brothers 5172 (Acuff-Rose, BMI)

8. **SO SAD**
   The Everly Brothers
   D. Everly,   Warner Brothers 5163   (Acuff-Rose, BMI)

9. **MR. CUSTER**
   L. Verne
   F. Darien-A. DeLory-J. Van Winkle,   Era 3024   (Pattern, ASCAP)

10. **THEME FROM THE APARTMENT**
    Ferrante and Teicher
    C. Williams,   United Artists 231 (Mills, ASCAP)

October 31

1. **SAVE THE LAST DANCE FOR ME**
   The Drifters
   Pomus-Shuman,   Atlantic 2071 (Rumbalero-Progressive, BMI)

2. **I WANT TO BE WANTED**
   B. Lee
   Gannon-Spotti-Testa, Decca 31149   (Leeds, ASCAP)

3. **MY HEART HAS A MIND OF ITS OWN**
   C. Francis
   Greenfield-Keller,   M-G-M 12923   (Aldon, BMI)

4. **THE TWIST**
   C. Checker
   H. Ballard,   Parkway 811 (Jay and Cee-Armo, BMI)

5. **CHAIN GANG**
   S. Cooke
   S. Cooke,   Victor 7783 (Kags, BMI)

6. **DEVIL OR ANGEL**
   B. Vee
   B. Carter,   Liberty 55270   (Progressive, BMI)

7. **POETRY IN MOTION**
   J. Tillotson
   Kaufman-Anthony,   Cadence 1384   (Meridian, BMI)

8. **GEORGIA ON MY MIND**
   R. Charles
   H. Carmichael-S. Gorrell, ABC-Paramount 10135 (Peer-International, BMI)

9. **YOU TALK TOO MUCH**
   J. Jones
   J. Jones-R. Hall,   Roulette 4304 (Kahl, BMI)

10. **LET'S THINK ABOUT LIVIN**
    B. Luman
    Bryant,   Warner Brothers 5172 (Acuff-Rose, BMI)

1960

November 7

1. **SAVE THE LAST DANCE FOR ME**
   The Drifters
   Pomus–Shuman, Atlantic 2071 (Rumbalero–Progressive, BMI)

2. **POETRY IN MOTION**
   J. Tillotson
   Kaufman–Anthony, Cadence 1384 (Meridian, BMI)

3. **GEORGIA ON MY MIND**
   R. Charles
   H. Carmichael–S. Gorrell, ABC–Paramount 10135 (Peer–International, BMI)

4. **I WANT TO BE WANTED**
   B. Lee
   Gannon–Spotti–Testa, Decca 31149 (Leeds, ASCAP)

5. **STAY**
   M. Willaims and the Zodiacs
   M. Williams, Herald 552 (Windsong, BMI)

6. **YOU TALK TOO MUCH**
   J. Jones
   J. Jones–R. Hall, Roulette 4304 (Kahl, BMI)

7. **MY HEART HAS A MIND OF ITS OWN**
   C. Francis
   Greenfield–Keller, M-G-M 12923 (Aldon, BMI)

8. **DEVIL OR ANGEL**
   B. Vee
   B. Carter, Liberty 55270 (Progressive, BMI)

9. **LET'S GO, LET'S GO, LET'S GO**
   H. Ballard and the Midnighters
   H. Ballard, King 5400 (Lois, BMI)

10. **LAST DATE**
    F. Cramer
    F. Cramer, Victor 7775 (Acuff–Rose, BMI)

November 14

1. **POETRY IN MOTION**
   J. Tillotson
   Kaufman–Anthony, Cadence 1384 (Meridian, BMI)

2. **GEORGIA ON MY MIND**
   R. Charles
   H. Carmichael–S. Gorrell, ABC–Paramount 10135 (Peer–International, BMI)

3. **YOU TALK TOO MUCH**
   J. Jones
   J. Jones–R. Hall, Roulette 4304 (Kahl, BMI)

4. **I WANT TO BE WANTED**
   B. Lee
   Gannon–Spotti–Testa, Decca 31149 (Leeds, ASCAP)

5. **SAVE THE LAST DANCE FOR ME**
   The Drifters
   Pomus–Shuman, Atlantic 2071 (Rumbalero–Progressive, BMI)

6. **STAY**
   M. Williams and the Zodiacs
   M. Williams, Herald 552 (Windsong, BMI)

7. **LET'S GO, LET'S GO, LET'S GO**
   H. Ballard and the Midnighters
   H. Ballard, King 5400 (Lois, BMI)

8. **LAST DATE**
   F. Cramer
   F. Cramer, Victor 7775 (Acuff–Rose, BMI)

9. **A THOUSAND STARS**
   K. Young and the Innocents
   Pearson, Indigo 108 (Bryden, BMI)

10. **BLUE ANGEL**
    R. Orbison
    R. Orbison–Melson, Monument 425 (Acuff–Rose, BMI)

November 21

1. **STAY**
   M. Williams and the Zodiacs
   M. Williams, Herald 552 (Windsong, BMI)

2. **ARE YOU LONESOME TONIGHT?**
   E. Presley
   P. Evans–M. Williams, Victor 7810 (Bourne–Cromwell, ASCAP)

3. **POETRY IN MOTION**
   J. Tillotson
   Kaufman–Anthony, Cadence 1384 (Meridian, BMI)

4. **LAST DATE**
   F. Cramer
   F. Cramer, Victor 7775 (Acuff–Rose, BMI)

5. **GEORGIA ON MY MIND**
   R. Charles
   H. Carmichael–S. Gorrell, ABC–Paramount 10135 (Peer–International, BMI)

6. **A THOUSAND STARS**
   K. Young and the Innocents
   Pearson, Indigo 108 (Bryden, BMI)

7. **LET'S GO, LET'S GO, LET'S GO**
   H. Ballard and the Midnighters
   H. Ballard, King 5400 (Lois, BMI)

8. **YOU TALK TOO MUCH**
   J. Jones
   J. Jones–R. Hall, Roulette 4304 (Kahl, BMI)

9. **SAVE THE LAST DANCE FOR ME**
   The Drifters
   Pomus–Shuman, Atlantic 2071 (Rumbalero–Progressive, BMI)

10. **NEW ORLEANS**
    U.S. Bonds
    Guida–Royster, Legrand 819 (Pope, BMI)

November 28

1. **STAY**
M. Williams and the
Zodiacs
M. Williams, Herald 552
(Windsong, BMI)

2. **ARE YOU LONESOME
TONIGHT?**
E. Presley
P. Evans–M. Williams, Victor
7810 (Bourne–Cromwell,
ASCAP)

3. **LAST DATE**
F. Cramer
F. Cramer, Victor 7775
(Acuff–Rose, BMI)

4. **A THOUSAND STARS**
K. Young and the
Innocents
Pearson, Indigo 108
(Bryden, BMI)

5. **POETRY IN MOTION**
J. Tillotson
Kaufman–Anthony,
Cadence 1384 (Meridian, BMI)

6. **GEORGIA ON MY MIND**
R. Charles
H. Carmichael–S. Gorrell,
ABC–Paramount 10135
(Peer–International, BMI)

7. **NEW ORLEANS**
U.S. Bonds
Guida–Royster, Legrand 819
(Pope, BMI)

8. **LET'S GO, LET'S GO,
LET'S GO**
H. Ballard and the
Midnighters
H. Ballard, King 5400
(Lois, BMI)

9. **NORTH TO ALASKA**
J. Horton
Phillips, Columbia 41782
(Robbins, ASCAP)

10. **ALONE AT LAST**
J. Wilson
Lehman, Brunswick 55170
(Pearl, BMI)

December 5

1. **ARE YOU LONESOME
TONIGHT?**
E. Presley
P. Evans–M. Williams, Victor
7810 (Bourne–Cromwell,
ASCAP)

2. **POETRY IN MOTION**
J. Tillotson
Kaufman–Anthony, Cadence
1384 (Meridian, BMI)

3. **LAST DATE**
F. Cramer
F. Cramer, Victor 7775
(Acuff–Rose, BMI)

4. **STAY**
M. Williams and the
Zodiacs
M. Williams, Herald 552
(Windsong, BMI)

5. **A THOUSAND STARS**
K. Young and the
Innocents
Pearson, Indigo 108
(Bryden, BMI)

6. **NORTH TO ALASKA**
J. Horton
Phillips, Columbia 41782
(Robbins, ASCAP)

7. **HE WILL BREAK YOUR
HEART**
J. Butler
J. Butler–C. Mayfield–Carter,
VeeJay 354 (Conrad, BMI)

8. **NEW ORLEANS**
U.S. Bonds
Guida–Royster, Legrand 819
(Pope, BMI)

9. **SAILOR (YOUR HOME IS IN
THE SEA)**
Lolita
Scharfenburger–Busch, Kapp
349 (Garland, ASCAP)

10. **LET'S GO, LET'S GO,
LET'S GO**
H. Ballard
H. Ballard, King 5400
(Lois, BMI)

December 12

1. **ARE YOU LONESOME
TONIGHT?**
E. Presley
P. Evans–M. Williams, Victor
7810 (Bourne–Cromwell,
ASCAP)

2. **LAST DATE**
F. Cramer
F. Cramer, Victor 7775
(Acuff–Rose, BMI)

3. **A THOUSAND STARS**
K. Young and the
Innocents
Pearson, Indigo 108
(Bryden, BMI)

4. **WONDERLAND BY NIGHT**
B. Kaempfert
B. Kaempfert, Decca 31141
(Roosevelt, BMI)

5. **NORTH TO ALASKA**
J. Horton
Phillips, Columbia 41782
(Robbins, ASCAP)

6. **HE WILL BREAK YOUR
HEART**
J. Butler
J. Butler–C. Mayfield–Carter,
VeeJay 354 (Conrad, BMI)

7. **POETRY IN MOTION**
J. Tillotson
Kaufman–Anthony, Cadence
1384 (Meridian, BMI)

8. **SAILOR (YOUR HOME IS IN
THE SEA)**
Lolita
Scharfenburger–Busch, Kapp
349 (Garland, ASCAP)

9. **EXODUS**
Ferrante and Teicher
Gold, United Artists 274
(Chappell, ASCAP)

10. **YOU'RE SIXTEEN**
J. Burnette
Sherman–Sherman, Liberty
55285 (Blue Grass, GMI)

1960

December 19

1. **ARE YOU LONESOME TONIGHT?**
E. Presley
P. Evans–M. Williams, Victor 7810 (Bourne–Cromwell, ASCAP)

2. **LAST DATE**
F. Cramer
F. Cramer, Victor 7775 (Acuff–Rose, BMI)

3. **NORTH TO ALASKA**
J. Horton
Phillips, Columbia 41782 (Robbins, ASCAP)

4. **WONDERLAND BY NIGHT**
B. Kaempfert
B. Kaempfert, Decca 31141 (Roosevelt, BMI)

5. **EXODUS**
Ferrante and Teicher
Gold, United Artists 274 (Chappell, ASCAP)

6. **A THOUSAND STARS**
K. Young and the Innocents
Pearson, Indigo 108 (Bryden, BMI)

7. **YOU'RE SIXTEEN**
J. Burnette
Sherman–Sherman, Liberty 55285 (Blue Grass, BMI)

8. **HE WILL BREAK YOUR HEART**
J. Butler
J. Butler–C. Mayfield–Carter, VeeJay 354 (Conrad, BMI)

9. **SAILOR (YOUR HOME IS IN THE SEA)**
Lolita
Scharfenburger–Busch, Kapp 349 (Garland, ASCAP)

10. **MANY TEARS AGO**
C. Francis
Scott, M-G-M 12964 (Roosevelt, BMI)

December 26

1. **ARE YOU LONESOME TONIGHT?**
E. Presley
P. Evans–M. Williams, Victor 7810 (Bourne–Cromwell, ASCAP)

2. **LAST DATE**
F. Cramer
F. Cramer, Victor 7775 (Acuff–Rose, BMI)

3. **A THOUSAND STARS**
K. Young and the Innocents
Pearson, Indigo 108 (Bryden, BMI)

4. **WONDERLAND BY NIGHT**
B. Kaempfert
B. Kaempfert, Decca 31141 (Roosevelt, BMI)

5. **EXODUS**
Ferrante and Teicher
Gold, United Artists 274 (Chappell, ASCAP)

6. **YOU'RE SIXTEEN**
J. Burnette
Sherman–Sherman, Liberty 55285 (Blue Grass, BMI)

7. **NORTH TO ALASKA**
J. Horton
Phillips, Columbia 41782 (Robbins, ASCAP)

8. **MANY TEARS AGO**
C. Francis
Scott, M-G-M 12964 (Roosevelt, BMI)

9. **CORRINA, CORRINA**
R. Peterson
Parish–Chapman–Williams, Dunes 2002 (Mills, ASCAP)

10. **SAILOR (YOUR HOME IS IN THE SEA)**
Lolita
Scharfenburger–Busch, Kapp 349 (Garland, ASCAP)

CONNIE FRANCIS

Things were different in this new decade. We didn't have to scream that we were old enough to stay out late, to drive the car, to fall in love, to understand.

The older pioneers of rock and roll were out of high school—some giving up their Harleys for jobs as clerks and shoe salesmen, and some going on to college taking our barbarous music behind the hallowed walls of ivy.

Jack Kennedy had turned the national kleig lights on us. He was telling the world we were vital and idealistic, and it sounded so good we decided to become just that. We chucked our "Archie" comics and *Hit Parader* magazines and picked up *The Ugly American, The Wastemakers, Catcher in the Rye,* and *Conscience of a Conservative.* If we had preferred the issue of the big allowance to foreign aid in 1959, we couldn't admit it in this thrilling new day of commitment. College kids pondered race relations, the bomb, capital punishment, and the poor of Appalachia. They denounced their older brothers and sisters who were concerned with security, material wealth and pleasure.

The only major lapse in this new moral fitness came at Easter when the colleges released hordes of spring vacationers to Fort Lauderdale, an orgy of beer, blankets, and bodies that outdid any self-indulgences of the 50's.

We were turning away from heroes like Fabian who was having trouble getting enough credits to get out of South Philadelphia High School with a diploma. Now we were vowing to carry on the work in Laos of Doctor Tom Dooley, who had died that year. And, if high school would ever end, we could join the Peace Corps. We swelled with pride at the thought of turning our highly touted courage and energy into technology for the undeveloped nations.

We followed the Freedom Riders as they

1961

Let the word go forth
from this time and place,
to friend and foe alike,
that the torch has been
passed to a new generation
of Americans . . .

John F. Kennedy
Inaugural Address, January 20, 1961

toured the South to protest bus segregation. We felt envy, awe, and moral indignation as they faced the white mobs in Alabama. We began to believe that we were inheriting a badly balanced world that the purity of our youth would have to cleanse.

A lot of adults wanted to be in on this new dawn and, entrapped in the old anti-Communist rhetoric, they rededicated themselves to saving the universe. The most concentrated crusades were in Laos, Berlin, Cuba, and suborbital outer space. In Laos, the civil war was blazing as the United States called out for an end to the fighting. Dean Rusk went to the SEATO meeting in Bangkok to make the fateful plea to the free world that it aid Southeast Asia against Communist aggression. By April the Laotian government accepted a cease fire proposed by the United States and Russia. And in October, neutralist Prince Souvanna Phouma became the premier of the new Laotian coalition government, a choice acceptable to East and West to quiet the troublesome Peasants' War.

The Cubans were blowing up whatever bridges were joining them with the United States. In January, diplomatic relations were severed. By spring, pro-American rebels attacked southern Cuba to irritate the American-Russian antagonism. Khrushchev demanded that the United States stop the invasion, saying Russia would step in and help Castro. Kennedy responded that the United States would not allow a Russian military intervention. Luckily, they were never held to their words, since Cuba stopped the rebels in less than three days. In the last days of 1961 Castro cut the United States out of Cuba's world by declaring himself a Marxist-Leninist and forming a party to bring Communism to Cuba.

East-West tension clamped down on Berlin in midsummer, just after the Cuban hotspot cooled a bit. The Russians closed the border between East and West Berlin to stop immigration to the West. In the postwar years the United States had poured money into West Berlin, making it one of the most properous cities in the world. So many East Berliners had flocked to the boom city to rebuild their lives that the eastern city was becoming a ghost town. The West protested the closing of the border and the United States sent fifteen-hundred troops to West Berlin to stop what we all believed to be an act of intimidation by the evil Russians.

With our troops poised in Berlin and President Kennedy asking for two-hundred thousand more men to be readied to stop the worldwide Soviet threat, the Russians announced that they were going to resume nuclear testing. Their gall was staggering. John F. Kennedy and England's Harold Macmillan protested the fallout threat. But it didn't phase the Russians, who made fifty tests in late 1961 including a whopping 50-megaton bomb, which they tested in the Artic while the United Nations begged them to stop. The United States made some underground tests which, of course, were morally acceptable because there was no fallout.

We were still racing with Russia to stake our claim on the as yet uncontaminated moon. In February Russia sent an unmanned probe toward Venus. And two months later Yuri Gagarin orbited the earth for 108 minutes, the first man to experience outer space. The world was awed, but finally the United States began to grab the headlines. In May, Alan Shepard became the first American in space with his fifteen minute suborbital flight in the Mercury capsule. And in July, Gus Grissom made the second American shot. It looked like things were A-OK for an American space victory when, in August, a Russian cosmonaut made a seventeen orbit, twenty-five hour flight. Once again they made the United States look like monkeys, which were, in fact, the only animals we were able to put into earth orbit by the end of 1961.

And yet, as bad as things looked, the charm and style of the new administration made us feel that we must be doing the fine and honorable thing. It was almost a pleasure to follow current events for government class. And we gladly watched the inauguration to see America's new prince, tousled by the wind, promise the future to us.

Jackie, too, was a joy to follow. She was the Number 1 best-dressed woman, and the simple, loose-fitting clothes she chose set the styles for the rest of the sixties. We weren't too young in 1961 to wish for a dress by Oleg Cassini or to save our money for a haircut by Mr. Kenneth. We wished they could make us look like our new First Lady. Those of us with limp or frizzy hair might have resented her perfect bouffant, but if we had big feet she was a savior. Now we could wear our size 10's with stacked heels and be comfortable with no worries about being ugly because we didn't teeter on tiny feet and spike heels.

The Kennedys were changing so many of our ideas. They were giving the nation another chance at being young. The new President stressed physical fitness. And our schools joined in the effort. If Jackie could play touch football, so could we. They were getting us out of the bleachers and onto the field.

And if the Kennedys weren't getting new people active in athletics, the professional leagues were. 1961 was the year the American and National Baseball Leagues grew to ten teams apiece, adding the Twins and the Angels and the Mets and the Astros. It was a new era for baseball with the 162-game season giving Mantle and Maris a chance to pound away at Babe Ruth's home run record. In professional football, too, a new era

was begun when the Green Bay Packers rose to rule the game, a reign that would last deep into the decade.

Our new leaders were as American as football, and yet they were without doubt citizens of the world. In 1961 President Kennedy met with Macmillan, Khrushchev, deGaulle, and Adenauer. He set up the Alliance for Progress to aid Latin America. Everywhere he went he was shown more affection then any recent American leader. And if the world was impressed by the President, it was enchanted by his First Lady. She spoke softly to the crowds, and in their own languages, something, American officialdom rarely had done.

Even though we were entering a rougher time of world politics, the Kennedys gave us hope that the United States would grow in stature in the eyes of the world. America was now without Speaker Rayburn and the world was without Dag Hammarskjold. The East and West were in a stalemate with an ideological wall between them as clear as the one going up in Berlin.

President Kennedy had decided not to send combat troops into VietNam, but we were already so entrenched in defending selected Southeast Asian regimes that it seemed we might slip into a quicksand of endless fighting. And there were twenty-five nonaligned nations to be courted, most of them less then a year old. The Middle East was still simmering, although the Eichmann trial and conviction was a bigger story than the endless border skirmishes.

And as out interests were maturing under the new era of youth, the adults were slipping backward. It centered around a tiny nightclub in New York City called the Peppermint Lounge. The club featured a run-of-the-mill rock and roll group, Joey Dee and the Starlighters. They were one of the thousands of groups that played the day's big hits for the crowd to dance to instead of to listen to. But it was for them that lighting struck, and by late 1961 they had a Top 10 hit with "The Peppermint Twist." The Peppermint Lounge became the busiest spot in town. It was packed by the nation's elite—Senator Javits, Garbo, Arthur Murray—socialites, grandmothers, politicians, hipsters.

Everyone but the kids fought to get in. No one thought he was too old or dignified or fat to yield to the call of the twist. And if there was ever a group that could be stereotyped by lack of natural rhythm, this was it. Twist teachers replaced the old masters of the mambo and cha cha. Adults everywhere were practicing "boxing" or "drying their behinds with an imaginary towel" as they were instructed by their twist-dissecting mentors.

Chubby Checker was selling them a million records of "The Twist" left over from 1959. Since we had adopted the twist, he had already sung the pony and the fly to fame. We chuckled smugly as our parents struggled to keep up with the passe dance. If they were going to make fools of themselves they might at least do so with the pony or the Bristol stomp. We wished they would go back to worrying about cholesterol and heart disease.

As much as we had wanted our parents' acceptance of rock and roll, this was not what we had envisioned. Their interest now was only an absurd attempt to keep up with the newest country club fad. They still expected rock and roll to mature into Benny Goodman.

There was really nothing to indicate that this would ever happen. If anything, rock and roll was moving back to the rauchier rhythm and blues sound. "American Bandstand" was starting to lose its grip. And with it, the pretty white singers of the last few years were losing their source of publicity. Of course it wasn't all over, and Dion's

Number 1 record, "Runaround Sue," a classic "Bandstand" style song, got such an ovation when he performed it there that he had to sing it twice in a row to quiet the kids.

The newer sounds were by black singers. But the new records didn't sound like the old Charms or Chords or Five Keys. Now the groups had bigger backing financially and orchestrally. Some even tried string sections, an innovation that would become the staple of Motown arrangers.

This was the year that the Detroit sound started to be heard nationwide. Berry Gordy and Smokey Robinson's great "Shop Around" was a tremendous hit, and so was the Marvelettes record of "Please, Mr. Postman."

Songs of similar style were making it from a variety of sources. U. S.Bond's (who many people thought was a group), Chris Kenner, Dee Clark, Ernie K. Doe, and Bobby Lewis had hits that laid the groundwork for the mid-sixties melodic Negro music, which would popularly be called Motown, Detroit, or soul.

Ben E. King, now singing without the Drifters, had hits with "Spanish Harlem" and "Stand by Me." The Drifters, one of the longest surviving rock and roll groups, also made their mark on the 1961 charts with "Please Stay" a song they should have dedicated to Ben E. King.

Dedications ran rampant during these years. Shrieking disk jockeys wound up and fired off lists of kids who requested that songs be played for them, their steadies, their friends, rivals or enemies—depending on the words to the song. The Shirelles (the only girl group to really join rock and roll's elite until the Supremes would take away the spotlight) made the super-dedication of all rock and roll:

Each night befo-ore you go to bed,
  my baby

Whisper a little pra-ayer for me, my
   baby
And te-ell all the stars abo-ove
This is dedicated to the one I LOVE.

As sentimental as our dedications might be,
they couldn't touch the sticky sweetness of our
reminiscences of bygone rock and roll. Whether
your first true love caught fire in 1955 to the
sounds of Johnny Ace or in 1960 to Kathy Young
and the Innocents, there was one song in 1961 that
could move you to reverie. Dear old Little Caesar
and the Romans knew what made us mellow:

Those oldies but goodies reminds me of you
The songs of the past bring back memories
   old and new
Forever they will haunt me but what can
   I do
Those oldies but, goodies remi-i-nds me
   of you.

THE TOP FIFTY
1961

1. **I FALL TO PIECES** — P. Cline
2. **TOSSIN' AND TURNIN'** — B. Lewis
3. **CRYIN'** — R. Orbison
4. **ON THE REBOUND** — F. Cramer
5. **MICHAEL** — The Highwaymen
6. **WHEELS** — The String-A-Longs
7. **MY TRUE STORY** — The Jive Five
8. **PONY TIME** — C. Checker
9. **CALCUTTA** — L. Welk
10. **RAINDROPS** — D. Clark
11. **WOODEN HEART** — J. Dowell
12. **DEDICATED TO THE ONE I LOVE** — The Shirelles
13. **RUNNIN' SCARED** — R. Orbison
14. **LAST NIGHT** — The Mar Keys
15. **TAKE GOOD CARE OF MY BABY** — B. Vee
16. **(WILL YOU LOVE ME) TOMORROW** — The Shirelles
17. **HIT THE ROAD JACK** — R. Charles
18. **EXODUS** — Ferrante and Teicher
19. **SAD MOVIES (MAKE ME CRY)** — S. Thompson
20. **WHERE THE BOYS ARE** — C. Francis
21. **MOTHER-IN-LAW** — E. K. Doe
22. **SHOP AROUND** — The Miracles
23. **BOLL WEEVIL SONG** — B. Benton
24. **BRISTOL STOMP** — The Dovells
25. **ONE HUNDRED POUNDS OF CLAY** — G. McDaniels

26. **TRAVELIN' MAN** — R. Nelson
27. **QUARTER TO THREE** — U. S. Bonds
28. **I LIKE IT LIKE THAT** — C. Kenner
29. **THE MOUNTAIN'S HIGH** — Dick and Deedee
30. **CALENDAR GIRL** — N. Sedaka
31. **PORTRAIT OF MY LOVE** — S. Lawrence
32. **WINGS OF A DOVE** — F. Husky
33. **BLUE MOON** — The Marcels
34. **WHO PUT THE BOMP (IN THE BOMP, BOMP, BOMP)** — B. Mann
35. **RUNAWAY** — D. Shannon
36. **DADDY'S HOME** — Shep and the Limelights
37. **DON'T WORRY (LIKE ALL THE OTHER TIMES)** — M. Robbins
38. **APACHE** — J. Ingman
39. **THIS TIME** — T. Shondell
40. **DON'T BET MONEY HONEY** — L. Scott
41. **RUNAROUND SUE** — Dion
42. **HURT** — T. Yuro
43. **THERE'S A MOON OUT TONIGHT** — The Capris
44. **WITHOUT YOU** — J. Tillotson
45. **LITTLE SISTER** — E. Presley
46. **HELLO MARY LOU** — R. Nelson
47. **HELLO WALLS** — F. Young
48. **ASIA MINOR** — Kokomo
49. **BUT I DO** — C. Henry
50. **YELLOW BIRD** — A. Lyman

January 2

1. **ARE YOU LONESOME TONIGHT?**
E. Presley
P. Evans–M. Williams, Victor 7810 (Bourne–Cromwell, ASCAP)

2. **LAST DATE**
F. Cramer
F. Cramer, Victor 7775 (Acuff–Rose, BMI)

3. **WONDERLAND BY NIGHT**
B. Kaempfert
B. Kaempfert, Decca 31141 (Roosevelt, BMI)

4. **EXODUS**
Ferrante and Teicher
Gold, United Artists 274 Chappell, ASCAP)

5. **NORTH TO ALASKA**
J. Horton
Phillips, Columbia 41782 (Robbins, ASCAP)

6. **A THOUSAND STARS**
K. Young and the Innocents
Pearson, Indigo 108 (Bryden, BMI)

7. **CORRINA, CORRINA**
R. Peterson
Parish–Chapman–Williams, Dunes 2002 (Mills, ASCAP)

8. **ANGEL BABY**
Rosie and the Originals
R. Hamlin, Highland 1011 (Figure, BMI)

9. **MANY TEARS AGO**
C. Francis
Scott, M-G-M 12964 (Roosevelt, BMI)

10. **YOU'RE SIXTEEN**
J. Burnette
Sherman–Sherman, Liberty 55285 (Blue Grass, BMI)

January 9

1. **WONDERLAND BY NIGHT**
B. Kaempfert
B. Kaempfert, Decca 31141 (Roosevelt, BMI)

2. **EXODUS**
Ferrante and Teicher
Gold, United Artists 274 (Chappell, ASCAP)

3. **ARE YOU LONESOME TONIGHT?**
E. Presley
P. Evans–M. Williams, Victor 7810 (Bourne-Cromwell, ASCAP)

4. **(WILL YOU LOVE ME) TOMORROW**
The Shirelles
C. King–J. Goffin, Scepter 1211 (Aldon, BMI)

5. **LAST DATE**
F. Cramer
F. Cramer, Victor 7775 (Acuff-Rose, BMI)

6. **ANGEL BABY**
Rosie and the Originals
R. Hamlin, Highland 1011 (Figure, BMI)

7. **CORRINA, CORRINA**
R. Peterson
Parish–Chapman–Williams, Dunes 2002 (Mills, ASCAP)

8. **RUBBER BALL**
B. Vee
A. Schroeder–A. Orlowski, Liberty 55287 (Arch, ASCAP)

9. **NORTH TO ALASKA**
J. Horton
Phillips, Columbia 41782 (Robbins, ASCAP)

10. **YOU'RE SIXTEEN**
J. Burnette
Sherman–Sherman, Liberty 55285 (Blue Grass, BMI)

January 16

1. **WONDERLAND BY NIGHT**
B. Kaempfert
B. Kaempfert,   Decca 31141
(Roosevelt, BMI)

2. **ARE YOU LONESOME TONIGHT?**
E. Presley
P. Evans–M. Williams,   Victor 7810 (Bourne–Cromwell, ASCAP)

3. **EXODUS**
Ferrante and Teicher
Gold,   United Artists 274
(Chappell, ASCAP)

4. **(WILL YOU LOVE ME) TOMORROW**
The Shirelles
C. King–J. Goffin,   Scepter 1211   (Aldon, BMI)

5. **CALCUTTA**
L. Welk
Gaze–Bradtke,   Dot 16161
(Pincus–Symphony House, ASCAP)

6. **ANGEL BABY**
Rosie and the Originals
R. Hamlin,   Highland 1011
(Figure, BMI)

7. **RUBBER BALL**
B. Vee
A. Schroeder–A. Orlowski,
Liberty 55287   (Arch, ASCAP)

8. **LAST DATE**
F. Cramer
F. Cramer,   Victor 7775
(Acuff–Rose, BMI)

9. **NORTH TO ALASKA**
J. Horton
Phillips,   Columbia 41782
(Robbins, ASCAP)

10. **CORRINA, CORRINA**
R. Peterson
Parish–Chapman–Williams,
Dunes 2002   (Mills, ASCAP)

January 23

1. **EXODUS**
Ferrante and Teicher
Gold,   United Artists 274
(Chappell, ASCAP)

2. **WONDERLAND BY NIGHT**
B. Kaempfert
B. Kaempfert,   Decca 31141
(Roosevelt, BMI)

3. **(WILL YOU LOVE ME) TOMORROW**
The Shirelles
C. King–J. Goffin,   Scepter 1211   (Aldon, BMI)

4. **ANGEL BABY**
Rosie and the Originals
R. Hamlin,   Highland 1011
(Figure, BMI)

5. **CALCUTTA**
L. Welk
Gaze–Bradtke,   Dot 16161
(Pincus–Symphony House, ASCAP)

6. **SHOP AROUND**
The Miracles
B. Gordy–W. Robinson,   Tamla 54034   (Jobbett, BMI)

7. **ARE YOU LONESOME TONIGHT?**
E. Presley
P. Evans–M. Williams,   Victor 7810 (Bourne–Cromwell, ASCAP)

8. **RUBBER BALL**
B. Vee
A. Schroeder–A. Orlowski,
Liberty 55287   (Arch, ASCAP)

9. **CORRINA, CORRINA**
R. Peterson
Parish–Chapman–Williams,
Dunes 2002   (Mills, ASCAP)

10. **CALENDAR GIRL**
N. Sedaka
H. Greenfield–N. Sedaka,   Victor 7829   (Aldon, BMI)

January 30

1. **(WILL YOU LOVE ME) TOMORROW**
The Shirelles
C. King–J. Goffin,   Scepter 1211   (Aldon, BMI)

2. **EXODUS**
Ferrante and Teicher
Gold,   United Artists 274
(Chappell, ASCAP)

3. **CALCUTTA**
L. Welk
Gaze–Bradtke,   Dot 16161
(Pincus–Symphony House, ASCAP)

4. **SHOP AROUND**
The Miracles
B. Gordy–W. Robinson,   Tamla 54034   (Jobbett, BMI)

5. **WONDERLAND BY NIGHT**
B. Kaempfert
B. Kaempfert,   Decca 31141
(Roosevelt, BMI)

6. **RUBBER BALL**
B. Vee
A. Schroeder–A. Orlowski,
Liberty 55287   (Arch, ASCAP)

7. **ANGEL BABY**
Rosie and the Originals
R. Hamlin,   Highland 1011
(Figure, BMI)

8. **CALENDAR GIRL**
N. Sedaka
H. Greenfield–N. Sedaka,   Victor 7829   (Aldon, BMI)

9. **EMOTIONS**
B. Lee
Tillis–Ramsey–Kearney,   Decca 31195   (Cedarwood, BMI)

10. **ARE YOU LONESOME TONIGHT?**
E. Presley
P. Evans–M. Williams,   Victor 7810   (Bourne–Cromwell, ASCAP)

February 6

1. **(WILL YOU LOVE ME) TOMORROW**
   The Shirelles
   C. King–J. Goffin, Scepter 1211 (Aldon, BMI)

2. **CALCUTTA**
   L. Welk
   Gaze–Bradtke, Dot 16161 (Pincus–Symphony House, ASCAP)

3. **EXODUS**
   Ferrante and Teicher
   Gold, United Artists 274 (Chappell, ASCAP)

4. **SHOP AROUND**
   The Miracles
   B. Gordy–W. Robinson, Tamla 54034 (Jobbett, BMI)

5. **CALENDAR GIRL**
   N. Sedaka
   H. Greenfield–N. Sedaka, Victor 7829 (Aldon, BMI)

6. **WONDERLAND BY NIGHT**
   B. Kaempfert
   B. Kaempfert, Decca 31141 (Roosevelt,BMI)

7. **ANGEL BABY**
   Rosie and the Originals
   R. Hamlin, Highland 1011 (Figure, BMI)

8. **EMOTIONS**
   B. Lee
   Tillis–Ramsey–Kearney, Decca 31195 (Cedarwood, BMI)

9. **RUBBER BALL**
   B. Vee
   A. Schroeder–A. Orlowski, Liberty 55287 (Arch, ASCAP)

10. **MY EMPTY ARMS**
    J. Wilson
    A. Kasha–H. Hunter, Brunswick 44201 (Merimac, BMI)

February 13

1. **(WILL YOU LOVE ME) TOMORROW**
   The Shirelles
   C. King–J. Goffin, Scepter 1211 (Aldon, BMI)

2. **CALCUTTA**
   L. Welk
   Gaze–Bradtke, Dot 16161 (Pincus–Symphony House, ASCAP)

3. **SHOP AROUND**
   The Miracles
   B. Gordy–W. Robinson, Tamla 54034 (Jobbett, BMI)

4. **CALENDAR GIRL**
   N. Sedaka
   H. Greenfield–N. Sedaka, Victor 7829 (Aldon, BMI)

5. **PONY TIME**
   C. Checker
   D. Covay–J. Berry, Parkway 818 (Alank, BMI)

6. **EMOTIONS**
   B. Lee
   Tillis–Ramsey–Kearney, Decca 31195 (Cedarwood, BMI)

7. **EXODUS**
   Ferrante and Teicher
   Gold, United Artists 274 (Chappell, ASCAP)

8. **ANGEL BABY**
   Rosie and the Originals
   R. Hamlin, Highland 1011 (Figure, BMI)

9. **WONDERLAND BY NIGHT**
   B. Kaempfert
   B. Kaempfert, Decca 31141 (Roosevelt, BMI)

10. **THERE' A MOON OUT TONIGHT**
    The Capris
    Stiano–Luccisano–Gentile, Old Town 1094 (Rob-Ann, BMI)

February 20

1. **CALCUTTA**
   L. Welk
   Gaze–Bradtke, Dot 16161 (Pincus–Symphony House, ASCAP)

2. **(WILL YOU LOVE ME) TOMORROW**
   The Shirelles
   C. King–J. Goffin, Sceptor 1211 (Aldon, BMI)

3. **SHOP AROUND**
   The Miracles
   B. Gordy–W. Robinson, Tamla 54034 (Jobbett, BMI)

4. **THERE'S A MOON OUT TONIGHT**
   The Capris
   Stiano–Luccisano–Gentile, Old Town 1094 (Rob-Ann, BMI)

5. **PONY TIME**
   C. Checker
   D. Covay–J. Berry, Parkway 818 (Alank, BMI)

6. **EMOTIONS**
   B. Lee
   Tillis–Ramsey–Kearney, Decca 31195 (Cedarwood, BMI)

7. **CALENDAR GIRL**
   N. Sedaka
   H. Greenfield–N. Sedaka, Victor 7829 (Aldon, BMI)

8. **EXODUS**
   Ferrante and Teicher
   Gold, United Artists 274 (Chappell, ASCAP)

9. **DEDICATED TO THE ONE I LOVE**
   The Shirelles
   Pauling–Bass, Scepter 1203 (Armo, BMI)

10. **WHEELS**
    The String-A-Longs
    Torres–Stephens, Warwick 603 (Dundee, BMI)

1961

February 27

1. **PONY TIME**
C. Checker
D. Covay–J. Berry, Parkway 818 (Alank, BMI)

2. **CALCUTTA**
L. Welk
Gaze–Bradtke, Dot 16161 (Pincus–Symphony House, ASCAP)

3. **THERE'S A MOON OUT TONIGHT**
The Capris
Stiano–Luccisano–Gentile, Old Town 1094 (Rob–Ann, BMI)

4. **SURRENDER**
E. Presley
D. Pomus–M. Shuman, Victor 7850 (Elvis Presley, BMI)

5. **DON'T WORRY (LIKE ALL THE OTHER TIMES)**
M. Robbins
M. Robbins, Columbia 41992 (Marty's, BMI)

6. **DEDICATED TO THE ONE I LOVE**
The Shirelles
Pauling–Bass, Scepter 1203 (Armo, BMI)

7. **SHOP AROUND**
The Miracles
B. Gordon–W. Robinson, Tamla 54034 (Jobbett, BMI)

8. **EBONY EYES**
The Everly Brothers
J. D. Loudermilk, Warner Brothers 5199 (Acuff–Rose, BMI)

9. **WHEELS**
The String-A-Longs
Torres–Stephens, Warwick 603 (Dundee, BMI)

10. **WHERE THE BOYS ARE**
C. Francis
H. Greenfield–N. Sedaka, M-G-M 12071 (Aldon, BMI)

March 6

1. **PONY TIME**
C. Checker
D. Covay–J. Berry, Parkway 818 (Alank, BMI)

2. **WHEELS**
The String-A-Longs
Torres–Stephens, Warwick 603 (Dundee, BMI)

3. **SURRENDER**
E. Presley
D. Pomus–M. Shuman, Victor 7850 (Elvis Presley, BMI)

4. **DON'T WORRY (LIKE ALL THE OTHER TIMES)**
M. Robbins
M. Robbins, Columbia 41922 (Marty's, BMI)

5. **THERE'S A MOON OUT TONIGHT**
The Capris
Stiano–Lucciasano–Gentile, Old Town 1094 (Rob–Ann, BMI)

6. **EBONY EYES**
The Everly Brothers
J. D. Loudermilk, Warner Brothers 5199 (Acuff–Rose, BMI)

7. **WHERE THE BOYS ARE**
C. Francis
H. Greenfield–N. Sedaka, M-G-M 12071 (Aldon, BMI)

8. **CALCUTTA**
L. Welk
Gaze–Bradtke, Dot 16161 (Pincus–Symphony House, ASCAP)

9. **BABY SITTIN' BOOGIE**
B. Clifford
J. Parker, Columbia 41876 (Reis, BMI)

10. **DEDICATED TO THE ONE I LOVE**
The Shirelles
Pauling–Bass, Scepter 1203 (Armo, BMI)

March 13

1. **SURRENDER**
E. Presley
D. Pomus–Shuman, Victor 7850 (Elvis Presley, BMI)

2. **PONY TIME**
C. Checker
D. Covay–J. Berry, Parkway 818 (Alank, BMI)

3. **WHEELS**
The String-A-Longs
Torres–Stephens, Warwick 603 (Dundee, BMI)

4. **BABY SITTIN' BOOGIE**
B. Clifford
J. Parker, Columbia 41876 (Reis, BMI)

5. **DON'T WORRY (LIKE ALL THE OTHER TIMES)**
M. Robbins
M. Robbins, Columbia 41922 (Marty's, BMI)

6. **WHERE THE BOYS ARE**
C. Francis
H. Greenfield–N. Sedaka, M-G-M 12071 (Aldon, BMI)

7. **DEDICATED TO THE ONE I LOVE**
The Shirelles
Pauling–Bass, Scepter 1203 (Armo, BMI)

8. **CALCUTTA**
L. Welk
Gaze–Bradtke, Dot 16161 (Pincus–Symphony House, ASCAP)

9. **EBONY EYES**
The Everly Brothers
J. D. Loudermilk, Warner Brothers 5199 (Acuff–Rose, BMI)

10. **SPANISH HARLEM**
B. E. King
J. Leiber–P. Spector, Atco 6185 (Progressive–Trio, BMI)

March 20

1. **SURRENDER**
E. Presley
D. Pomus–Shuman, Victor 7850 (Presley, BMI)

2. **PONY TIME**
C. Checker
D. Covay–J. Berry, Parkway 818 (Alank, BMI)

3. **DON'T WORRY (LIKE ALL THE OTHER TIMES)**
M. Robbins
M. Robbins, Columbia 41922 (Marty's BMI)

4. **WHERE THE BOYS ARE**
C. Francis
H. Greenfield–N. Sedaka, M-G-M 12071 (Aldon, BMI)

5. **DEDICATED TO THE ONE I LOVE**
The Shirelles
Pauling–Bass, Scepter 1203 (Armo, BMI)

6. **APACHE**
J. Ingmann
Lordan, Atco 6184 (Regent, BMI)

7. **WHEELS**
The String-A-Longs
Torres–Stephens, Warwick 603 (Dundee, BMI)

8. **WALK RIGHT BACK**
The Everly Brothers
S. Curtis, Warner Brothers 5199 (Crickett, BMI)

9. **BABY SITTIN' BOOGIE**
B. Clifford
J. Parker, Columbia 41876 (Reis, BMI)

10. **SPANISH HARLEM**
B. E. King
J. Lieber–P. Spector, Atco 6185 (Progressive–Trio, BMI)

March 27

1. **SURRENDER**
E. Presley
D. Pomus–M. Shuman, Victor 7850 (Presley, BMI)

2. **DEDICATED TO THE ONE I LOVE**
The Shirelles
Pauling–Bass, Scepter 1203 (Armo, BMI)

3. **PONY TIME**
C. Checker
D. Covay–J. Berry, Parkway 818 (Alank, BMI)

4. **DON'T WORRY (LIKE ALL THE OTHER TIMES)**
M. Robbins
M. Robbins, Columbia 41922 (Marty's, BMI)

5. **APACHE**
J. Ingmann
Lordan, Atco 6184 (Regent, BMI)

6. **WALK RIGHT BACK**
The Everly Brothers
S. Curtis, Warner Brothers 5199 (Crickett, BMI)

7. **BLUE MOON**
The Marcels
R. Rodgers–L. Hart, Colpix 186 (Robbins, BMI)

8. **GEE WHIZ (LOOK AT HIS EYES)**
C. Thomas
C. Thomas, Atlantic 2086 (East, BMI)

9. **WHEELS**
The String-A-Longs
Torres–Stephens, Warwick 603 (Dundee, BMI)

10. **WHERE THE BOYS ARE**
C. Francis
H. Greenfield–Sedaka, M-G-M 12071 (Aldon, BMI)

April 3

1. **BLUE MOON**
The Marcels
R. Rodgers–L. Hart, Colpix 186 (Robbins, ASCAP)

2. **SURRENDER**
E. Presley
D. Pomus–M. Shuman, Victor 7850 (Presley, BMI)

3. **PONY TIME**
C. Checker
D. Covay–J. Berry, Parkway 818 (Alank, BMI)

4. **DEDICATED TO THE ONE I LOVE**
The Shirelles
Pauling–Bass, Scepter 1203 (Armo, BMI)

5. **APACHE**
J. Ingmann
Lordan, Atco 6184 (Regent, BMI)

6. **WALK RIGHT BACK**
The Everly Brothers
S. Curtis, Warner Brothers 5199 (Crickett, BMI)

7. **DON'T WORRY (LIKE ALL THE OTHER TIMES)**
M. Robbins
M. Robbins, Columbia 41922 (Marty's BMI)

8. **ON THE REBOUND**
F. Cramer
F. Cramer, Victor 7840 (Cigma, BMI)

9. **RUNAWAY**
D. Shannon
M. Crook–C. Westover, Big Top 1067 (Vickie, BMI)

10. **BUT I DO**
C. (Frogman) Henry
R. Guidry–P. Gayten, Argo 5378 (Arc, BMI)

April 10

1. **BLUE MOON**
The Marcels
R. Rodgers–L. Hart, Colpix 186
(Robbins, ASCAP)

2. **APACHE**
J. Ingmann
Lordan, Atco 6184
(Regent, BMI)

3. **DEDICATED TO THE ONE I LOVE**
The Shirelles
Pauling–Bass, Scepter 1203
(Armo, BMI)

4. **RUNAWAY**
D. Shannon
M. Crook–C. Westover, Big Top 1067 (Vickie, BMI)

5. **ON THE REBOUND**
F. Cramer
F. Cramer, Victor 7840
(Cigma, BMI)

6. **BUT I DO**
C. (Frogman) Henry
R. Guidry–P. Gayten, Argo 5378 (Arc, BMI)

7. **SURRENDER**
E. Presley
D. Pomus–M. Shuman, Victor 7850 (Presley, BMI)

8. **MOTHER-IN-LAW**
E. K. Doe
A. Toussaint, Minit 623
(Minit, BMI)

9. **WALK RIGHT BACK**
The Everly Brothers
S. Curtis, Warner Brothers 5199 (Crickett, BMI)

10. **DON'T WORRY (LIKE ALL THE OTHER TIMES)**
M. Robbins
M. Robbins, Columbia 40992
(Marty's, BMI)

April 17

1. **BLUE MOON**
The Marcels
R. Rodgers–L. Hart, Colpix 186
(Robbins, ASCAP)

2. **MOTHER-IN-LAW**
E. K. Doe
A. Toussaint, Minit 623
(Minit, BMI)

3. **RUNAWAY**
D. Shannon
M. Crook–C. Westover, Big Top 1067 (Vickie, BMI)

4. **ON THE REBOUND**
F. Cramer
F. Cramer, Victor 7840
(Cigma, BMI)

5. **DEDICATED TO THE ONE I LOVE**
The Shirelles
Pauling–Bass, Scepter 1203
(Armo, BMI)

6. **BUT I DO**
C. (Frogman) Henry
R. Guidry–P. Gayten, Argo 5378
(Arc, BMI)

7. **APACHE**
J. Ingmann
Lordan, Atco 6184
(Regent, BMI)

8. **ONE HUNDRED POUNDS OF CLAY**
G. McDaniels
Elgin–Dixon–Rogers, Liberty 55308 (Gil, BMI)

9. **SURRENDER**
E. Presley
D. Pomus–M. Shuman, Victor 7850
(Presley, BMI)

10. **ASIA MINOR**
Kokomo
J. Wisner, Felsted 8612
(Barbrab, ASCAP)

April 24

1. **RUNAWAY**
D. Shannon
M. Crook–C. Westover, Big Top 1067 (Vickie, BMI)

2. **MOTHER-IN-LAW**
E. K. Doe
A. Toussaint, Minit 623
(Minit, BMI)

3. **BLUE MOON**
The Marcels
R. Rodgers–L. Hart, Colpix 186
(Robbins, ASCAP)

4. **ONE HUNDRED POUNDS OF CLAY**
G. McDaniels
Elgin–Dixon–Rogers, Liberty 55308 (Gil, BMI)

5. **BUT I DO**
C. (Frogman) Henry
R. Guidry–P. Gayten, Argo 5378 (Arc, BMI)

6. **ON THE REBOUND**
F. Cramer
F. Cramer, Victor 7840
(Cigma, BMI)

7. **I'VE TOLD EVERY LITTLE STAR**
L. Scott
J. Kern–O. Hammerstein II, Canadian–American 123 (Harms, ASCAP)

8. **YOU CAN DEPEND ON ME**
B. Lee
C. Carpenter–L. Dunlap–E. Hines, Decca 31231 (Peer-International, BMI)

9. **TAKE GOOD CARE OF HER**
A. Wade
Kent–Warren, Coed 546
(Recherche-Paxton, ASCAP)

10. **ONE MINT JULEP**
R. Charles
R. Toombs, Impulse 200
(Progressive-Regent, BMI)

May 1

1. **RUNAWAY**
   D. Shannon
   M. Crook–C. Westover, Big Top
   1067 (Vickie, BMI)
2. **MOTHER-IN-LAW**
   E. K. Doe
   A. Toussaint, Minit 623
   (Minit, BMI)
3. **I'VE TOLD EVERY LITTLE STAR**
   L. Scott
   J. Kern–O. Hammerstein II,
   Canadian–American 123
   (Harms, ASCAP)
4. **ONE HUNDRED POUNDS OF CLAY**
   G. McDaniels
   Elgin–Dixon–Rogers, Liberty
   55308 (Gil, BMI)
5. **BLUE MOON**
   The Marcels
   R. Rodgers–L. Hart, Colpix 186
   (Robbins, ASCAP)
6. **BUT I DO**
   C. (Frogman) Henry
   R. Guidry–P. Gayten, Argo
   5378 (Arc, BMI)
7. **TAKE GOOD CARE OF HER**
   A. Wade
   Kent–Warren, Coed 546
   (Recherche–Paxton, ASCAP)
8. **ONE MINT JULEP**
   R. Charles
   R. Toombs, Impulse 200
   (Progressive–Regent, BMI)
9. **ON THE REBOUND**
   F. Cramer
   F. Cramer, Victor 7840
   (Cigma, BMI)
10. **YOU CAN DEPEND ON ME**
    B. Lee
    C. Carpenter–L. Dunlap–E. Hines
    Decca 31231 (Peer-
    International, BMI)

May 8

1. **RUNAWAY**
   D. Shannon
   M. Crook–C. Westover, Big Top
   1067 (Vickie, BMI)
2. **MOTHER-IN-LAW**
   E. K. Doe
   A. Toussaint, Minit 623
   (Minit, BMI)
3. **I'VE TOLD EVERY LITTLE STAR**
   L. Scott
   J. Kern–O. Hammerstein II,
   Canadian–American 123
   (Harms, ASCAP)
4. **ONE HUNDRED POUNDS OF CLAY**
   G. McDaniels
   Elgin–Dixon–Rogers Liberty
   55308 (Gil, BMI)
5. **YOU CAN DEPEND ON ME**
   B. Lee
   C. Carpenter–L. Dunlap–E. Hines,
   Decca 31231
   (Peer–International, BMI)
6. **BLUE MOON**
   The Marcels
   R. Rodgers–L. Hart, Colpix 186
   (Robbins, ASCAP)
7. **PORTRAIT OF MY LOVE**
   S. Lawrence
   C. Ornadel–D. West, United
   Artists 291 (Picadilly, BMI)
8. **TAKE GOOD CARE OF HER**
   A. Wade
   Kent–Warren, Coed 546
   (Recherche–Paxton, ASCAP)
9. **ONE MINT JULIP**
   R. Charles
   R. Toombs, Impulse 200
   (Progressive–Regent, BMI)
10. **ON THE REBOUND**
    F. Cramer
    F. Cramer, Victor 7840
    (Cigma, BMI)

May 15

1. **MOTHER-IIN-LAW**
   E. K. Doe
   A. Toussaint, Minit 623
   (Minit, BMI)
2. **ONE HUNDRED POUNDS OF CLAY**
   G. McDaniels
   Elgin–Dixon–Roger, Liberty
   55308 (Gil, BMI)
3. **RUNAWAY**
   D. Shannon
   M. Crook–C. Westover, Big Top
   1067 (Vickie, BMI)
4. **DADDY'S HOME**
   Shep and the Limelights
   J. Sheppard–C. Basset–C. Baker,
   Hull 740 (Keel, BMI)
5. **I'VE TOLD EVERY LITTLE STAR**
   L. Scott
   J. Kern–O. Hammerstein II,
   Canadian–American 123
   (Harms, ASCAP)
6. **MAMA SAID**
   The Shirelles
   Dixon–Dennison, Scepter 1217
   (Ludix–Betalbin, BMI)
7. **YOU CAN DEPEND ON ME**
   B. Lee
   C. Carpenter–L. Dunlap–E. Hines,
   Decca 31231
   (Peer–International, BMI)
8. **BLUE MOON**
   The Marcels
   R. Rodgers–L. Hart, Colpix 186
   (Robbins, ASCAP)
9. **TRAVELIN' MAN**
   R. Nelson
   J. Fuller, Imperial 5741
   (Four Star Sales, BMI)
10. **TAKE GOOD CARE OF HER**
    A. Wade
    Kent–Warren, Coed 546
    (Recherche–Paxton, ASCAP)

1961

May 22

1. **MOTHER-IN-LAW**
E. K. Doe
A. Toussaint,   Minit 623
(Minit, BMI)
2. **RUNAWAY**
D. Shannon
M. Crook–C. Westover, Big Top
1067 (Vickie, BMI)
3. **DADDY'S HOME**
Shep and the Limelights
J. Sheppard–C. Basset–C. Baker,
Hull 740 (Keel, BMI)
4. **ONE HUNDRED POUNDS
OF CLAY**
G. McDaniels
Elgin–Dixon–Rogers, Liberty
55308 (Gil, BMI)
5. **TRAVELIN' MAN**
R. Nelson
J. Fuller, Imperial 5741
(Four Star Sales, BMI)
6. **MAMA SAID**
The Shirelles
Dixon–Dennison, Scepter 1217
(Ludix–Betalbin, BMI)
7. **RUNNING SCARED**
R. Orbison
R. Orbison–J. Melson,
Monument 328 (Acuff–Rose,
BMI)
8. **HELLO MARY LOU**
R. Nelson
G. Pitney, Imperial 5741
(January, BMI)
9. **I'VE TOLD EVERY LITTLE
STAR**
L. Scott
J. Kern–O. Hammerstein II,
Canadian–American 123
(Harms, ASCAP)
10. **BREAKIN' IN A NEW
BROKEN HEART**
C. Francis
H. Greenfield–Keller, M-G-M
12995 (Aldon, BMI)

May 29

1. **DADDY'S HOME**
Shep and the Limelights
J. Sheppard–C. Basset–C. Baker,
Hull 740 (Keel, BMI)
2. **TRAVELIN' MAN**
R. Nelson
J. Fuller, Imerial 5741
(Four Stars Sales, BMI)
3. **MAMA SAID**
The Shirelles
Dixon–Dennison, Scepter 1217
(Ludix–Betalbin, BMI)
4. **RUNNING SCARED**
R. Orbison
R. Orbison–J. Melson, Monu-
ment 328 (Acuff–Rose, BMI)
5. **MOTHER-IN-LAW**
E. K. Doe
A. Toussaint, Minit 623
(Minit, BMI)
6. **ONE HUNDRED POUNDS OF
CLAY**
G. McDaniels
Elgin–Dixon–Rogers, Liberty
55308 (Gil, BMI)
7. **RUNAWAY**
D. Shannon
M. Crook–C. Westover, Big Top
1607 (Vickie, BMI)
8. **TRAGEDY**
The Fleetwoods
Nelson–Burch, Dolton 40
(Bluff–City, BMI)
9. **BREAKIN' IN A BRAND NEW
BROKEN HEART**
C. Francis
H. Greenfield–Keller, M-G-M
12995 (Aldon, BMI)
10. **I FEEL SO BAD**
E. Presley
C. Willis, Victor 7880
(Berkshire,BMI)

June 5

1. **RUNNING SCARED**
R. Orbison
R. Orbison–J. Melson, Monu-
ment 328 (Acuff–Rose, BMI)
2. **TRAVELIN' MAN**
R. Nelson
J. Fuller, Imperial 5471
(Four Star Sales, BMI)
3. **MAMA SAID**
The Shirelles
Dixon–Dennison, Scepter 1217
(Ludix–Betalbin, BMI)
4. **DADDY'S HOME**
Shep and the Limelights
J.Sheppard–C. Basset–C. Baker,
Hull 740 (Keel, BMI)
5. **RAINDROPS**
D. Clark
D. Clark, VeeJay 383
(Conrad, BMI)
6. **I FEEL SO BAD**
E. Presley
C. Willis, Victor 7880
(Berkshire, BMI)
7. **STAND BY ME**
B.E. King
King–Glick, Atco 6194
(Progressive–Trio, BMI)
8. **MOODY RIVER**
P. Boone
G. Bruce, Dot 16209
(Kava, BMI)
9. **ONE HUNDRED POUNDS OF
CLAY**
G. McDaniels
Elgin–Dixon–Rogers, Liberty
55308 (Gil, BMI)
10. **BREAKIN' IN A BRAND NEW
BROKEN HEART**
C. Francis
H. Greenfield–Keller, M-G-M
12995 (Aldon, BMI)

June 12

1. **TRAVELIN' MAN**
   R. Nelson
   J. Fuller, Imperial 5471
   (Four Star Sales, BMI)
2. **MOODY RIVER**
   P. Boone
   G. Bruce, Dot 16209
   (Kava, BMI)
3. **RUNNING SCARED**
   R. Orbison
   R. Orbison–J. Melson, Monu-
   ment 328 (Acuff–Rose, BMI)
4. **STAND BY ME**
   B. E. King
   King–Glick, Atco 6194
   (Progressive–Trio, BMI)
5. **RAINDROPS**
   D. Clark
   D. Clark, VeeJay 383
   (Conrad, BMI)
6. **THE WRITING ON THE WALL**
   A. Wade
   Barken–Baron–Eddy, Coed 550
   (Winneton–Glenville, BMI)
7. **EVERY BEAT OF MY HEART**
   The Pips
   J. Otis, VeeJay 386
   (Valjo, BMI)
8. **QUARTER TO THREE**
   U.S. Bonds
   Barge–Guida–Anderson–Rayster,
   Le Grand 1008 (Pepe, BMI)
9. **BOLL WEEVIL**
   B. Benton
   C. Otis–B. Benton, Mercury
   71820 (Play, BMI)
10. **I FEEL SO BAD**
    E. Presley
    C. Willis, Victor 7880
    (Berkshire, BMI)

June 19

1. **TRAVELIN' MAN**
   R. Nelson
   J. Fuller, Imperial 5741
   (Four Star Sales, BMI)
2. **MOODY RIVER**
   P. Boone
   G. Bruce, Dot 16209
   (Kava, BMI)
3. **RAINDROPS**
   D. Clark
   D. Clark, VeeJay 383
   (Conrad, BMI)
4. **QUARTER TO THREE**
   U.S. Bonds
   Barge–Guida–Anderson–Rayster
   LeGrand 1008 (Pepe, BMI)
5. **STAND BY ME**
   B.E. King
   King–Glick, Atco 6194
   (Progressive–Trio, BMI)
6. **TOSSIN' AND TURNIN'**
   B. Lewis
   Adams–Rene, Beltone 1002
   (Steven, BMI)
7. **THE WRITING ON THE WALL**
   A. Wade
   Barkan–Baron–Eddy, Coed 550
   (Winneton–Glenville, BMI)
8. **EVERY BEAT OF MY HEART**
   The Pips
   J. Otis, VeeJay 386
   (Valjo, BMI)
9. **BOLL WEEVIL**
   B. Benton
   C. Otis–B. Benton, Mercury
   71820 (Play, BMI)
10. **THOSE OLDIES BUT GOODIES**
    Little Caesar and the Romans
    P. Politi–N. Curinga, DelFi
    4158 (Maravilla, BMI)

June 26

1. **QUARTER TO THREE**
   U.S. Bonds
   Barge–Guida–Anderson–Rayster,
   LeGrand 1008 (Pepe, BMI)
2. **MOODY RIVER**
   P. Boone
   G. Bruce, Dot 16209
   (Kava, BMI)
3. **RAINDROPS**
   D. Clark
   D. Clark, VeeJay 383
   (Conrad, BMI)
4. **TRAVELIN' MAN**
   R. Nelson
   J. Fuller, Imperial 5741
   (Four Star Sales, BMI)
5. **THE WRITING ON THE WALL**
   A. Wade
   Barkan–Baron–Eddy, Coed 550
   (Winneton–Glenville, BMI)
6. **TOSSIN' AND TURNIN'**
   B. Lewis
   Adams–Rene, Beltone 1002
   (Steven, BMI)
7. **BOLL WEEVIL**
   B. Benton
   C. Otis–B. Benton, Mercury
   71820 (Play, BMI)
8. **EVERY BEAT OF MY HEART**
   The Pips
   J. Otis, VeeJay 386
   (Valjo, BMI)
9. **THOSE OLDIES BUT GOODIES**
   Little Caesar and the Romans
   P. Politi–N. Curinga, DelFi
   4158 (Maravilla, BMI)
10. **STAND BY ME**
    B. E. King
    King–Glick, Atco 6194
    (Progressive–Trio, BMI)

July 3

1. **QUARTER TO THREE**
U.S. Bonds
Barge–Guida–Anderson–Rayster,
Le Grand 1008 (Pepe, BMI)

2. **TOSSIN' AND TURNIN'**
B. Lewis
Adams–Rene, Beltone 1002
(Steven, BMI)

3. **BOLL WEEVIL**
B. Benton
C. Otis–B. Benton, Mercury
71820 (Play, BMI)

4. **RAINDROPS**
D. Clark
D. Clark, VeeJay 383
(Conrad, BMI)

5. **THE WRITING ON THE WALL**
A. Wade
Barkan–Baron–Eddy, Coed 550
(Winneton–Glenville, BMI)

6. **MOODY RIVER**
P. Boone
G. Bruce, Dot 16209
(Kava, BMI)

7. **TRAVELIN' MAN**
R. Nelson
J. Fuller, Imperial 5741
(Four Star Sales, BMI)

8. **EVERY BEAT OF MY HEART**
The Pips
J. Otis, VeeJay 386
(Valjo, BMI)

9. **THOSE OLDIES BUT GOODIES**
Little Caesar and the Romans
P. Politi–N. Curinga, DelFi
4858 (Maravilla, BMI)

10. **STAND BY ME**
B.E. King
King–Glick, Atco 6194
(Progressive–Trio, BMI)

July 10

1. **QUARTER TO THREE**
U.S. Bonds
Barge–Guida–Anderson–Rayster,
LeGrand 1008 (Pepe, BMI)

2. **TOSSIN' AND TURNIN'**
B. Lewis
Adams–Rene, Beltone 1002
(Steven, BMI)

3. **BOLL WEEVIL**
B. Benton
C. Otis–B. Benton, Mercury
71820 (Play, BMI)

4. **RAINDROPS**
D. Clark
D. Clark, VeeJay 383
(Conrad, BMI)

5. **EVERY BEAT OF MY HEART**
The Pips
J. Otis, VeeJay 386
(Valjo, BMI)

6. **HATS OFF TO LARRY**
D. Shannon
D. Shannon, Big Top 3075
(Vicki–McLaughlin, BMI)

7. **YELLOW BIRD**
A. Lyman
Luboff–Keith, HiFi 5024
(Frank, ASCAP)

8. **MOODY RIVER**
P. Boone
G. Bruce, Dot 16209
(Kava, BMI)

9. **THE WRITING ON THE WALL**
A. Wade
Barkan–Baron–Eddy, Coed
550 (Winneton–Glenville, BMI)

10. **DANCE ON LITTLE GIRL**
P. Anka
P. Anka, ABC–Paramount
1022
(Spanka, BMI)

July 17

1. **TOSSIN' AND TURNIN'**
B. Lewis
Adams–Rene, Beltone 1002
(Steven, BMI)

2. **QUARTER TO THREE**
U.S. Bonds
Barge–Guida–Anderson–Rayster,
LeGrand 1008 (Pepe, BMI)

3. **BOLL WEEVIL**
B. Benton
C. Otis–B. Benton, Mercury
71820 (Play, BMI)

4. **YELLOW BIRD**
A. Lyman
Luboff–Keith HiFi 5024
(Frank, ASCAP)

5. **EVERY BEAT OF MY HEART**
The Pips
J. Otis, VeeJay 386
(Valjo, BMI)

6. **RAINDROPS**
D. Clark
D. Clark, VeeJay 383
(Conrad, BMI)

7. **HATS OFF TO LARRY**
D. Shannon
D. Shannon, Big Top 3075
(Vicki–McLaughlin, BMI)

8. **SAN ANTONIO ROSE**
F. Cramer
B. Willis, Victor 7893
(Bourne, ASCAP)

9. **I LIKE IT LIKE THAT**
C. Kenner
C. Kenner, Instant 3229
(Tune-Kel, BMI)

10. **DUM DUM**
B. Lee
S. Sheeley–J. DeShannon,
Decca 31272 (Metric, BMI)

July 24

1. **TOSSIN' AND TURNIN'**
   B. Lewis
   *Adams–Rene, Beltone 1002
   (Steven, BMI)*

2. **BOLL WEEVIL**
   B. Benton
   *C. Otis–B. Benton, Mercury
   71820 (Play, BMI)*

3. **QUARTER TO THREE**
   U.S. Bonds
   *Barge–Guida–Anderson–Rayster,
   Le Grand 1008 (Pepe, BMI)*

4. **YELLOW BIRD**
   A. Lyman
   *Luboff–Keith, HiFi 5024
   (Frank, ASCAP)*

5. **I LIKE IT LIKE THAT**
   C. Kenner
   *C. Kenner, Instant 3229
   (Tune–Kel, BMI)*

6. **HATS OFF TO LARRY**
   D. Shannon
   *D. Shannon, Big Top 3075
   (Vicki–McLaughlin. BMI)*

7. **DUM DUM**
   B. Lee
   *S. Sheeley–J. DeShannon,
   Decca 31272 (Metric, BMI)*

8. **TOGETHER**
   C. Francis
   *DeSylva–Brown,–Henderson,
   M-G-M 13019 (DeSylva–Brown–
   Henderson, ASCAP)*

9. **LET'S TWIST AGAIN**
   C. Checker
   *K. Mann–Appel, Parkway 824
   (Kalmann, ASCAP)*

10. **RAINDROPS**
    D. Clark
    *D. Clark, VeeJay 383
    (Conrad, BMI)*

July 31

1. **TOSSIN' AND TURNIN'**
   B. Lewis
   *Adams–Rene, Beltone 1002
   (Steven, BMI)*

2. **BOLL WEEVIL**
   B. Benton
   *C. Otis–B. Benton, Mercury
   71820 (Play, BMI)*

3. **I LIKE IT LIKE THAT**
   C. Kenner
   *C. Kenner, Instant 3229
   (Tune–Kel, BMI)*

4. **QUARTER TO THREE**
   U.S. Bonds
   *Barge–Guida–Anderson–Rayster,
   LeGrand 1008 (Pepe, BMI)*

5. **DUM DUM**
   B. Lee
   *S. Sheeley–J. DeShannon, Decca
   31272 (Metric, BMI)*

6. **HATS OFF TO LARRY**
   D. Shannon
   *D. Shannon, Big Top 3075
   (Vicki–McLaughlin, BMI)*

7. **TOGETHER**
   C. Francis
   *DeSylva–Brown–Henderson,
   M-G-M 13019 (DeSylva–
   Brown–Henderson, ASCAP)*

8. **LAST NIGHT**
   The Mar Keys
   *The Mar Keys, Satellite 107
   (East–Bais, BMI)*

9. **LET'S TWIST AGAIN**
   C. Checker
   *K. Mann–Appel, Parkway 824
   (Kalmann, ASCAP)*

10. **PRETTY LITTLE ANGEL
    EYES**
    C. Lee
    *C. Lee–T. Boyce, Dunes 2007
    (S-P-R, BMI)*

August 7

1. **TOSSIN' AND TURNIN'**
   B. Lewis
   *Adams–Rene, Beltone 1002
   (Steven, BMI)*

2. **I LIKE IT LIKE THAT**
   C. Kenner
   *C. Kenner, Instant 3229
   (Tune–Kel, BMI)*

3. **DUM DUM**
   B. Lee
   *S. Sheeley–J. DeShannon, Decca
   31272 (Metric, BMI)*

4. **LAST NIGHT**
   The Mar Keys
   *The Mar Keys, Satellite 107
   (East–Bais, BMI)*

5. **PRETTY LITTLE ANGEL
   EYES**
   C. Lee
   *C. Lee–T. Boyce, Dunes 2007
   (S-P-R-, BMI)*

6. **HATS OFF TO LARRY**
   D. Shannon
   *D. Shannon, Big Top 3075
   (Vicki–McLaughlin, BMI)*

7. **TOGETHER**
   C. Francis
   *DeSylva–Brown–Henderson,
   M-G-M 13019 (DeSylva–
   Brown–Henderson, ASCAP)*

8. **LET' TWIST AGAIN**
   C. Checker
   *K. Mann–Appel, Parkway 824
   (Kalmann, ASCAP)*

9. **WOODEN HEART**
   J. Dowell
   *Wise–Weisman–Twomey–
   Kaempfert,
   Smash 1708 (Gladys, ASCAP)*

10. **MICHAEL**
    The Highwaymen
    *D. Fisher, United Artists 258
    (United Artists, ASCAP)*

August 14

1. **TOSSIN' AND TURNIN'**
B. Lewis
*Adams–Rene, Beltone 1002
(Steven, BMI)*

2. **I LIKE IT LIKE THAT**
C. Kenner
*C. Kenner, Instant 3229
(Tune-Kel, BMI)*

3. **LAST NIGHT**
The Mar Keys
*The Mar Keys, Satellite 107
(East –Bais, BMI)*

4. **DUM DUM**
B. Lee
*S. Sheeley–J. DeShannon,
Decca 31272 (Metric, BMI)*

4. **WOODEN HEART**
J. Dowell
*Wise–Weisman–Twomey–
Kaempfert, Smash 1708
(Gladys, ASCAP)*

6. **MICHAEL**
The Highwaymen
*D. Fisher, United Artists 258
(United Artists, ASCAP)*

7. **PRETTY LITTLE ANGEL
EYES**
C. Lee
*C. Lee–T. Boyce, Dunes 2007
(S-P-R, BMI)*

8. **LET'S TWIST AGAIN**
C. Checker
*K. Mann–Appel, Parkway 824
(Kalmann, ASCAP)*

9. **SCHOOL IS OUT**
U.S. Bonds
*Anderson–Barge, Le Grand
1009 (Pepe, BMI)*

10. **HATS OFF TO LARRY**
D. Shannon
*D. Shannon, Big Top 3075
(Vicki–McLaughlin, BMI)*

August 21

1. **WOODEN HEART**
J. Dowell
*Wise–Weisman–Twomey–
Kaempfert,
Smash 1708 (Gladys, ASCAP)*

2. **TOSSIN' AND TURNIN'**
B. Lewis
*Adams–Rene, Beltone 1002
(Steven, BMI)*

3. **MICHAEL**
The Highwaymen
*D. Fisher, United Artists 258
(United Artists, ASCAP)*

4. **I LIKE IT LIKE THAT**
C. Kenner
*C. Kenner, Instant 3229
(Tune-Kel, BMI)*

5. **LAST NIGHT**
The Mar Keys
*The Mar Keys, Satellite 107
(East–Bais, BMI)*

6. **DUM DUM**
B. Lee
*S. Sheeley–J. DeShannon, Decca
31272 (Metric, BMI)*

7. **PRETTY LITTLE ANGEL
EYES**
C. Lee
*C. Lee–T. Boyce, Dunes 2007
(S-P-R, BMI)*

8. **YOU DON'T KNOW WHAT
YOU'VE
GOT (UNTIL YOU
LOSE IT)**
R. Donner
*P. Hampton–D. Burton, Gone
5108 (Sequence, ASCAP)*

9. **SCHOOL IS OUT**
U.S. Bonds
*Anderson–Barge, LeGrand 1009
(Pepe, BMI)*

10. **LET'S TWIST AGAIN**
C. Checker
*K. Mann–Appell, Parkway 824
(Kalmann, ASCAP)*

August 28

1. **WOODEN HEART**
*Wise–Weisman–Twomey–
Kaempfert, Smash 1708
(Gladys, ASCAP)*

2. **MICHAEL**
The Highwaymen
*D. Fisher, United Artists 258
(United Artists, ASCAP)*

3. **TOSSIN' AND TURNIN'**
B. Lewis
*Adams–Rene, Beltone 1002
(Steven, BMI)*

4. **I LIKE IT LIKE THAT**
C. Kenner
*C. Kenner, Instant 3229
(Tune-Kel, BMI)*

5. **SCHOOL IS OUT**
U.S. Bonds
*Anderson–Barge, LeGrand 1009
(Pepe, BMI)*

6. **LAST NIGHT**
The Mar Keys
*The Mar Keys, Satellite 107
(East–Bais, BMI)*

7. **YOU DON'T KNOW WHAT
YOU'VE GOT (UNTIL YOU
LOSE IT)**
R. Donner
*P. Hampton–D. Burton, Gone
5108 (Sequence, ASCAP)*

8. **DON'T BET MONEY HONEY**
L. Scott
*L. Scott, Canadian–American
427 (Figure, BMI)*

9. **PRETTY LITTLE ANGEL
EYES**
C. Lee
*C. Lee–T. Boyce, Dunes 2007
(S-P-R, BMI)*

10. **HURT**
T. Yuro
*J. Crane–A. Jacobs, Liberty
55343 (Miller, ASCAP)*

September 4

1. **MICHAEL**
The Highwaymen
*D. Fisher, United Artists 258
(United Artists, ASCAP)*

2. **WOODEN HEART**
J. Dowell
*Wise–Weisman–Twomey–
Kaempfert, Smash 1708
(Gladys, ASCAP)*

3. **TOSSIN' AND TURNIN'**
B. Lewis
*Adams–Rene, Beltone 1002
(Steven, BMI)*

4. **YOU DON'T KNOW WHAT
YOU'VE GOT (UNTIL YOU
LOSE IT)**
R. Donner
*P. Hampton–D. Burton, Gone
5108 (Sequence, ASCAP)*

5. **SCHOOL IS OUT**
U.S. Bonds
*Anderson–Barge, LeGrand
1009 (Pepe, BMI)*

6. **TAKE GOOD CARE OF MY
BABY**
B. Vee
*C. King–J. Goffin, Liberty 55354
(Aldon, BMI)*

7. **MY TRUE STORY**
The Jive Five
*Adams–Rene, Beltone 1006
(Lescay, BMI)*

8. **HURT**
T. Yuro
*J. Crane–A. Jacobs, Liberty
55343 (Miller, ASCAP)*

9. **DON'T BET MONEY HONEY**
L. Scott
*L. Scott, Canadian–American
427 (Figure, BMI)*

10. **PRETTY LITTLE ANGEL
EYES**
C. Lee
*C. Lee–T. Boyce, Dunes 2007
(S-P-R, BMI)*

September 11

1. **MICHAEL**
The Highwaymen
*D. Fisher, United Artists 258
(United Artists, ASCAP)*

2. **YOU DON'T KNOW WHAT
YOU'VE GOT (UNTIL YOU
LOSE IT)**
R. Donner
*P. Hampton–D. Burton, Gone
5108 (Sequence, ASCAP)*

3. **WOODEN HEART**
J. Dowell
*Wise–Weisman–Twomey–
Kaempfert, Smash 1708
(Gladys, ASCAP)*

4. **TAKE GOOD CARE OF MY
BABY**
B. Vee
*C. King–J. Goffin, Liberty 55354
(Aldon, BMI)*

5. **HURT**
T. Yuro
*J. Crane–A. Jacobs, Liberty
55343 (Miller, ASCAP)*

6. **MY TRUE STORY**
The Jive Five
*Adams–Rene, Beltone 1006
(Lescay, BMI)*

7. **WHO PUT THE BOMP (IN
THE BOMP, BOMP, BOMP)**
B. Mann
*B. Mann–J. Goffin,
ABC–Paramount 10237
(Aldon, BMI)*

8. **DOES YOUR CHEWING GUM
LOSE ITS FLAVOR (ON THE
BEDPOST OVER NIGHT)?**
L. Donegan
*Rose–Bloom–Breuer, Dot 15911
(Mills, ASCAP)*

9. **AS IF I DIDN'T KNOW**
A. Wade
*K. David, Coed 563
(Winneton–Glenville, BMI)*

10. **LITTLE SISTER**
E. Presley
*D. Pomus–M. Shuman, Victor
7908 (Elvis Presley, BMI)*

September 18

1. **TAKE GOOD CARE OF MY
BABY**
B. Vee
*C. King–J. Goffin, Liberty 55354
(Aldon, BMI)*

2. **MY TRUE STORY**
The Jive Five
*Adams–Rene, Beltone 1006
(Lescay, BMI)*

3. **(MARIE'S THE NAME) HIS
LATEST FLAME**
E. Presley
*D. Pomus–M. Shuman, Victor
7908 (Elvis Presley, BMI)*

4. **CRYIN'**
R. Orbison
*R. Orbison–J. Melson, Monu-
ment 447 (Acuff–Rose, BMI)*

5. **DOES YOUR CHEWING GUM
LOSE ITS FLAVOR (ON THE
BEDPOST OVER NIGHT)?**
L. Donegan
*Rose–Bloom–Breuer, Dot 15911
(Mills, ASCAP)*

6. **(MARIE'S THE NAME) HIS
LATEST FLAME**
E. Presley
*D. Pomus–M. Shuman, Victor
7908 (Elvis Presley, BMI)*

7. **WITHOUT YOU**
J. Tillotson
*J. Tillotson, Cadence 1404
(Ridge, BMI)*

8. **WOODEN HEART**
J. Dowell
*Wise–Weisman–Twomey–
Kaempfert, Smash 1708
(Gladys, ASCAP)*

9. **ONE TRACK MIND**
B. Lewis
*M. Rene–B. Lewis, Beltone
1012 (Lescay, BMI)*

10. **WHEN WE GET MARRIED**
The Dreamlovers
*D. Hogan, Heritage 102
(Elsher, BMI)*

1961

September 25

1. **TAKE GOOD CARE OF MY BABY**
B. Vee
C. King–J. Goffin, Liberty 55354 (Aldon, BMI)

2. **THE MOUNTAIN'S HIGH**
Dick and Deedee
St. John, Liberty 55350 (Odin, ASCAP)

3. **MICHAEL**
The Highwaymen
D. Fisher, United Artists 258 (United Artists, ASCAP)

4. **CRYIN'**
R. Orbison
R. Orbison–J. Melson, Monument 447 (Acuff–Rose, BMI)

5. **DOES YOUR CHEWING GUM LOSE ITS FLAVOR (ON THE BEDPOST OVER NIGHT)?**
L. Donegan
Rose–Bloom–Breuer, Dot 15911 (Mills, ASCAP)

6. **LITTLE SISTER**
E. Presley
D. Pomus–M. Shuman, Victor 7908 (Elvis Presley, BMI)

7. **WHO PUT THE BOMP (IN THE BOMP, BOMP, BOMP)**
B. Mann
B. Mann–J. Goffin, ABC–Paramount 10237 (Aldon, BMI)

8. **MY TRUE STORY**
The Jive Five
Adams–Rene, Beltone 1006 (Lescay, BMI)

9. **WITHOUT YOU**
J. Tillotson
J. Tillotson, Cadence 1404 (Ridge, BMI)

10. **BRISTOL STOMP**
The Dovells
K. Mann–Appell, Parkway 827 (Kalmann, ASCAP)

October 2

1. **THE MOUNTAIN'S HIGH**
Dick and Deedee
St. John, Liberty 55350 (Odin, ASCAP)

2. **TAKE GOOD CARE OF MY BABY**
B. Vee
C. King–J. Goffin, Liberty 55354 (Aldon, BMI)

3. **HIT THE ROAD JACK**
R. Charles
P. Mayfield, ABC–Paramount 10244 (Tangerine, BMI)

4. **CRYIN'**
R. Orbison
R. Orbison–J. Melson, Monument 447 (Acuff–Rose, BMI)

5. **LITTLE SISTER**
E. Presley
D. Pomus–M. Shuman, Victor 7908 (Elvis Presley, BMI)

6. **YOU MUST HAVE BEEN A BEAUTIFUL BABY**
B. Darin
Warren–Mercer, Atco 6206 (Remick, ASCAP)

7. **MICHAEL**
The Highwaymen
D. Fisher, United Artists 258 (United Artists, ASCAP)

8. **BRISTOL STOMP**
The Dovells
K. Mann–Appell, Parkway 827 (Kalmann, ASCAP)

9. **MEXICO**
B. Moore
B. Bryant, Monument 446 (Acuff–Rose, BMI)

10. **DOES YOUR CHEWING GUM LOSE ITS FLAVOR (ON THE BEDPOST OVER NIGHT)?**
L. Donegan
Rose–Bloom–Breuer, Dot 15911 (Mills, ASCAP)

October 9

1. **HIT THE ROAD JACK**
R. Charles
P. Mayfield, ABC–Paramount 10244 (Tangerine, BMI)

2. **TAKE GOOD CARE OF MY BABY**
B. Vee
C. King–J. Goffin, Liberty 55354 (Aldon, BMI)

3. **CRYIN'**
R. Orbison
R. Orbison–J. Melson, Monument 447 (Acuff–Rose, BMI)

4. **BRISTOL STOMP**
The Dovells
K. Mann–Appell, Parkway 827 (Kalmann, ASCAP)

5. **RUNAROUND SUE**
Dion
E. Maresca–D. DiMucci, Laurie 3110 (Just–Mubon, BMI)

6. **THE MOUNTAIN'S HIGH**
Dick and Deedee
St. John, Liberty 55350 (Odin, ASCAP)

7. **YOU MUST HAVE BEEN A BEAUTIFUL BABY**
B. Darin
Warren–Mercer, Atco 6206 (Remick, ASCAP)

8. **LITTLE SISTER**
E. Presley
D. Pomus–M. Shuman, Victor 7908 (Elvis Presley, BMI)

9. **LET'S GET TOGETHER**
H. Mills
R. M. Sherman–R. B. Sherman, Vista 385 (Wonderland, BMI)

10. **MEXICO**
B. Moore
B. Bryant, Monument 446 (Acuff–Rose, BMI)

185

October 16

1. **HIT THE ROAD JACK**
R. Charles
P. Mayfield, ABC–Paramount 10244 (Tangerine, BMI)

2. **RUNAROUND SUE**
Dion
E. Maresca–D. DiMucci, Laurie 3110 (Just–Mubon, BMI)

3. **BRISTOL STOMP**
The Dovells
Mann–Appell, Parkway 827 (Kalmann, ASCAP)

4. **CRYIN'**
R. Orbison
R. Orbison–J. Melson, Monument 447 (Acuff–Rose, BMI)

5. **YOU MUST HAVE BEEN A BEAUTIFUL BABY**
B. Darin
Warren–Mercer, Atco 6206 (Remick, ASCAP)

6. **TAKE GOOD CARE OF MY BABY**
B. Vee
C. King–J. Goffin, Liberty 55354 (Aldon, BMI)

7. **SAD MOVIES (MAKE ME CRY)**
S. Thompson
J. D. Loudermilk, Hickory 1153 (Acuff–Rose, BMI)

8. **BIG BAD JOHN**
J. Dean
J. Dean, Columbia 42175 (Cigma, BMI)

9. **YAYA**
L. Dorsey
L. Dorsey–W. Robinson, Fury 1053 (Fast–Barich, BMI)

10. **LET'S GET TOGETHER**
H. Mills
R. M. Sherman–R. B. Sherman, Vista 385 (Wonderland, BMI)

October 23

1. **RUNAROUND SUE**
Dion
E. Maresca–D. DiMucci, Laurie 3110 (Just–Mubon, BMI)

2. **HIT THE ROAD JACK**
R. Charles
P. Mayfield, ABC–Paramount 10244 (Tangerine, BMI)

3. **BRISTOL STOMP**
The Dovells
K. Mann–Appell, Parkway 827 (Kalmann, ASCAP)

4. **BIG BAD JOHN**
J. Dean
J. Dean, Columbia 42175 (Cigma, BMI)

5. **I LOVE HOW YOU LOVE ME**
The Paris Sisters
B. Mann–Kolber, Gregmark 6 (Aldon, BMI)

6. **SAD MOVIES (MAKE ME CRY)**
S. Thompson
J. D. Loudermilk, Hickory 1153 (Acuff–Rose, BMI)

7. **THIS TIME**
T. Shondell
C. Moman, Liberty 55353 (Tree, BMI)

8. **YAYA**
L. Dorsey
L. Dorsey–W. Robinson, Fury 1053 (Fast–Barich, BMI)

9. **LET'S GET TOGETHER**
H. Mills
R. M. Sherman–R. B. Sherman, Vista 385 (Wonderland, BMI)

10. **THE FLY**
C. Checker
Madora–White, Parkway 830 (Woodcrest–Mured, BMI)

October 30

1. **RUNAROUND SUE**
Dion
E. Maresca–D. DiMucci, Laurie 3110 (Just–Mubon, BMI)

2. **BRISTOL STOMP**
The Dovells
K. Mann–Appell, Parkway 827 (Kalmann, ASCAP)

3. **HIT THE ROAD JACK**
R. Charles
P. Mayfield, ABC–Paramount 10244 (Tangerine, BMI)

4. **BIG BAD JOHN**
J. Dean
J. Dean, Columbia 42175 (Cigma, BMI)

5. **SAD MOVIES (MAKE ME CRY)**
S. Thompson
J. D. Loudermilk, Hickory 1153 (Acuff–Rose, BMI)

6. **I LOVE HOW YOU LOVE ME**
The Paris Sisters
B. Mann–Kolber, Gregmark 6 (Aldon, BMI)

7. **YAYA**
L. Dorsey
L. Dorsey–W. Robinson, Fury 1053 (Fast–Barich, BMI)

8. **LET'S GET TOGEHTER**
H. Mills
R. M. Sherman–R. B. Sherman, Vista 385 (Wonderland, BMI)

9. **THE FLY**
C. Checker
Madora–White, Parkway 830 (Woodcrest–Mured, BMI)

10. **THIS TIME**
T. Shondell
C. Moman, Liberty 55353 (Tree, BMI)

November 6

1. **BIG BAD JOHN**
J. Dean
*J. Dean, Columbia 42175
(Cigma, BMI)*

2. **RUNAROUND SUE**
Dion
*E. Maresca–D. DiMucci, Laurie
3110 (Just–Mubon, BMI)*

3. **BRISTOL STOMP**
The Dovells
*K. Mann–Appell, Parkway 827
(Kalmann, ASCAP)*

4. **HIT THE ROAD JACK**
R. Charles
*P. Mayfield, ABC–Paramount
10244 (Tangerine, BMI)*

5. **FOOL   1**
B. Lee
*K. Fulton, Decca 31309
(Sure Fire, BMI)*

6. **SAD MOVIES (MAKE ME CRY)**
S. Thompson
*J. D. Loudermilk, Hickory 1153
(Acuff–Rose, BMI)*

7. **THIS TIME**
T. Shondell
*C. Moman, Liberty 55353
(Tree, BMI)*

8. **THE FLY**
C. Checker
*Madora–White, Parkway 830
(Woodcrest–Mured, BMI)*

9. **TOWER OF STRENGTH**
G. McDaniels
*B. Hilliard–B. Bacharach,
Liberty 55371 (Famous,
ASCAP)*

10. **I LOVE HOW YOU LOVE ME**
The Paris Sisters
*B. Mann–Kolber, Gregmark 6
(Aldon, BMI)*

November 13

1. **BIG BAD JOHN**
J. Dean
*J. Dean, Columbia 42175
(Cigma, BMI)*

2. **RUNAROUND SUE**
Dion
*E. Maresca–D. DiMucci, Laurie
3110 (Just–Mubon, BMI)*

3. **BRISTOL STOMP**
The Dovells
*K. Mann–Appell, Parkway 827
(Kalmann, ASCAP)*

4. **FOOL   1**
B. Lee
*K. Fulton, Decca 31309
(Sure Fire, BMI)*

5. **HIT THE ROAD JACK**
R. Charles
*P. Mayfield, ABC–Paramount
10244 (Tangerine, BMI)*

6. **TOWER OF STRENGTH**
G. McDaniels
*B. Hilliard–B. Bacharach,
Liberty 55371 (Famous,
ASCAP)*

7. **THIS TIME**
T. Shondell
*C. Moman, Liberty 55353
(Tree, BMI)*

8. **PLEASE MR. POSTMAN**
The Marvelettes
*Dobbins–Garrett–Brianbert,
Tamla 54046 (Jobete, BMI)*

9. **THE FLY**
C. Checker
*Madora–White, Parkway 830
(Woodcrest–Mured, BMI)*

10. **SAD MOVIES (MAKE ME CRY)**
S. Thompson
*J.D. Loudermilk, Hickory 1153
(Acuff–Rose, BMI)*

November 20

1. **BIG BAD JOHN**
J. Dean
*J. Dean, Columbis 42175
(Cigma, BMI)*

2. **RUNAROUND SUE**
Dion
*E. Maresca–D. DiMucci, Laurie
3110 (Just–Mubon, BMI)*

3. **FOOL   1**
B. Lee
*K. Fulton, Decca 31309
(Sure Fire, BMI)*

4. **BRISTOL STOMP**
The Dovells
*K. Mann–Appell, Parkway 827
(Kalmann, ASCAP)*

4. **TOWER OF STRENGTH**
G. McDaniels
*B. Hilliard–B. Bacharach,
Liberty 55371 (Famous,
ASCAP)*

6. **GOODBYE CRUEL WORLD**
J. Darren
*Shayne, Colpix 609
(Aldon, BMI)*

7. **HIT THE ROAD JACK**
R. Charles
*P. Mayfield, ABC–Paramount
10244 (Tangerine, BMI)*

8. **PLEASE MR. POSTMAN**
The Marvelettes
*Dobbins–Garrett–Brianbert,
Tamala 54046 (Jobete, BMI)*

9. **THIS TIME**
T. Shondell
*C. Moman, Liberty 55353
(Tree, BMI)*

10. **THE FLY**
C. Checker
*Madora–White, Parkway 830
(Woodcrest–Mured, BMI)*

November 27

1. **BIG BAD JOHN**
J. Dean
J. Dean, Columbia 42175
(Cigma, BMI)

2. **RUNAROUND SUE**
Dion
E. Maresca–D. DiMucci, Laurie
3110 (Just–Mubon, BMI)

3. **PLEASE MR. POSTMAN**
The Marvelettes
Dobbins–Garrett–Brianbert,
Tamla 54046 (Jobete, BMI)

4. **GOODBYE CRUEL WORLD**
J. Darren
Shayne, Colpix 609
(Aldon, BMI)

5. **FOOL   1**
B. Lee
K. Fulton, Decca 31309
(Sure Fire, BMI)

6. **BRISTOL STOMP**
The Dovells
K. Mann–Appel, Parkway 827
(Kalmann, ASCAP)

7. **HEARTACHES**
The Marcels
Klenner–Hoffman, Colpix 612
(Leeds, ASCAP)

8. **TOWER OF STRENGTH**
G. McDaniels
B. Hilliard–B. Bacharach,
Liberty 55371 (Famous,
ASCAP)

9. **THIS TIME**
T. Shondell
C. Moman, Liberty 55353
(Tree, BMI)

10. **I UNDERSTAND (JUST HOW YOU FEEL)**
G. Cleffs
P. Best, Terrace 7500
(Jubilee, ASCAP)

December 4

1. **PLEASE MR. POSTMAN**
The Marvelettes
Dobbins–Garrett–Brianbert,
Tamala 54046 (Jobete, BMI)

2. **BIG BAD JOHN**
J. Dean
J. Dean, Columbia 42175
(Cigma, BMI)

3. **GOODBY CRUEL WORLD**
J. Darren
Shayne, Colpix 609
(Aldon, BMI)

4. **FOOL   1**
B. Lee
K. Fulton, Decca 31309
(Sure Fire, BMI)

5. **RUNAROUND SUE**
Dion
E. Maresca–D. DiMucci, Laurie
3110 (Just–Mubon, BMI)

6. **WALK ON BY**
L. VanDyke
Hayes, Mercury 71834
(Lowery, BMI)

7. **I UNDERSTAND(JUST HOW YOU FEEL)**
G Cleffs
P. Best, Terrace 7500
(Jubilee, ASCAP)

8. **THE TWIST**
C. Checker
H. Ballard, Parkway 811
(Jay and Cee–Armo, BMI)

9. **TOWER OF STRENGTH**
G. McDaniels
B. Hilliard–B. Bacharach,
Liberty 55371 (Famous,
ASCAP)

10. **CRAZY**
P. Cline
W. Nelson, Decca 31317
(Pamper, BMI)

December 11

1. **PLEASE MR. POSTMAN**
The Marvelettes
Dobbins–Garrett–Brianbert,
Talma 54046 (Jobete, BMI)

2. **GOODBY CRUEL WORLD**
J. Darren
Shayne, Colpix 609
(Aldon, BMI)

3. **BIG BAD JOHN**
J. Dean
J. Dean, Columbia
42175 (Cigma, BMI)

4. **WALK ON BY**
L. VanDyke
Hayes, Mercury 71834
(Lowery, BMI)

5. **THE TWIST**
C. Checker
H. Ballard, Parkway 811
(Jay and Cee–Armo, BMI)

6. **RUN TO HIM**
B. Vee
Keller–J. Goffin, Liberty 55388
(Aldon, BMI)

7. **THE LION SLEEPS TONIGHT**
The Tokens
Weiss–Pereti–Creatore, Victor
7954 (Folkways, BMI)

8. **TONIGHT**
Ferrante and Teicher
S. Sandheim–L. Bernstein,
United Artists 373
(Schirmer, ASCAP)

9. **LET THERE BE DRUMS**
S. Nelson
S. Nelson–Podoler, Imperial
5775 (Travis, BMI)

10. **HAPPY BIRTHDAY, SWEET SIXTEEN**
N. Sedaka
H. Greenfield–N. Sedaka,
Victor 7957 (Aldon, BMI)

December 18

1. **THE LION SLEEPS TONIGHT**
The Tokens
Weiss–Pereti–Creatore,
Victor 7954 (Folkways, BMI)

2. **PLEASE MR. POSTMAN**
The Marvelettes
Dobbins–Garrett–Brianbert,
Tamla 54046 (Jobete, BMI)

3. **RUN TO HIM**
B. Vee
Keller–J. Goffin, Liberty
55388 (Aldon, BMI)

4. **WALK ON BY**
L. VanDyke
Hayes, Mercury 71834
(Lowery, BMI)

5. **THE TWIST**
C. Checker
H. Ballard, Parkway 811
(Jay and Cee–Armo, BMI)

6. **BIG BAD JOHN**
J. Dean
J. Dean, Columbia 42175
(Cigma, BMI)

7. **GOODBYE CRUEL WORLD**
J. Darren
Shayne, Colpix 609
(Aldon, BMI)

8. **LET THERE BE DRUMS**
S. Nelson
S. Nelson–Podoler, Imperial
5775 (Travis, BMI)

9. **PEPPERMINT TWIST**
J. Dee and the Star-
lighters
J. Dee–H. Glovers, Roulette
4401 (Impact–Ware, BMI)

10. **HAPPY BIRTHDAY, SWEET
SIXTEEN**
N. Sedaka
H. Greenfield–N. Sedaka, Victor
7957 (Aldon, BMI)

December 25

1. **THE LION SLEEPS TONIGHT**
The Tokens
Weiss–Pereti–Creatore, Victor
7954 (Folkways, BMI)

2. **THE TWIST**
C. Checker
H. Ballard, Parkway 811
(Jay and Cee–Armo, BMI)

3. **GOODBYE CRUEL WORLD**
J. Darren
Shayne, Colpix 609
(Aldon, BMI)

4. **RUN TO HIM**
B. Vee
Keller–J. Goffin, Liberty 55388
(Aldon, BMI)

5. **PEPPERMINT TWIST**
J. Dee and the Star-
lighters
J. Dee–H. Glovers, Roulette
4401 (Impact–Ware, BMI)

6. **PLEASE MR. POSTMAN**
The Marvelettes
Dobbins–Garrett–Brianbert,
Tamla 54046 (Jobette, BMI)

7. **WALK ON BY**
L. VanDyke
Hayes, Mercury 71834
(Lowery, BMI)

8. **HAPPY BIRTHDAY, SWEET
SIXTEEN**
N. Sedaka
H. Greenfield–N. Sedaka, Victor
7957 (Aldon, BMI)

9. **CAN'T HELP FALLING IN
LOVE**
E. Presley
Weiss–Pereti–Creatore, Victor
7968 (Gladys, ASCAP)

10. **LET THERE BE DRUMS**
S. Nelson
S. Nelson–Podoler, Imperial
5775 (Travis, BMI)

JOEY DEE

There was really no landmark between the music of 1961 and 1962 and yet at some moment rock and roll rose out of mediocrity into one of its finest years.

The twist was still holding the adult's enthusiasm and Joey Dee and Chubby Checker were joined by U.S. Bonds in exploiting the craze. U.S., or as we were finally told, Gary Bonds had the sort of mock heroic view of twisting that most of us had. Dear Lady was fully two years behind since she'd never twisted and U.S. Bonds was courteously giving her a cram course:

"Get up off of your chair . . . Dear Lady" and about the twist: "It's really not new, but something you've missed." and of course he held out the carrot that was drawing so many dear ladies onto the dance floor: "Do the twist and you'll never grow old."

As silly as the adult twisting was, it was the first move toward reconciling the rock and roll and swing generations. And for that we owe Chubby Checker and Hank Ballard a debt. Adults were finally seeing how much fun rock and roll could be, how great it felt to dance the silliest dance without intellectualizing the life out of it. Naturally, the harmony wasn't complete, but the seven-year-old myth that rock and roll would never last was dying under the stampede to the dance floor.

The twist made its contribution in public relations but there were other songs in 1962 that were as superb as any rock and roll would ever be. The March Top 10's were dominated by "Let Me In," "Hey! Baby," "What's Your Name?" "Dream Baby," "Twistin' the Night Away"—and one of the greatest folk heroes of rock and roll, the "Duke of Earl." It's hard to believe we could ever leave our radios with that kind of ecstasy being broadcast.

But we could leave the music because we

1962

It's been a blast sitting next to you in history class. I'll always remember Miss Hansford's tests. Hope I get to know you better next year. Best of luck to a grate guy.

Love ya, Nancy

191

trusted it to be there always. It wasn't something we analyzed or made predictions about. It had grown secure since the early years. Now there were more stations playing rock and roll and they were the top rated stations in town. And there were more singers and labels and the future looked so secure that it wasn't worth considering.

Dancing grabbed much of our attention now because we wanted to know the pony, the Bristol stomp, the bird, and the mashed potatoes and Watusi. Dances changed from month to month as singers tried to follow Chubby Checker and become associated with a new dance craze. The early rock and roll generation, now married and part of the adult world, had done the chicken and even the stroll and the continental, but never had rock and roll so demanded that we not sit still.

For many of us these were graduation years. The senior privileges varied from high school to high school, but whether it was an extra study hall, senior day, the front seats in the auditorium, or the favored lunch period, we knew a kind of heady feeling at finally being the biggest. And so the dances and the dates and the music took on the extra glow of senior year nostalgia almost immediately.

Sock hop had become an out-of-date expression since only cheerleaders wore socks in 1962, but we were still dancing barefoot on the gym floor. High school assemblies for the yearbook or the Junior Red Cross were now rock and roll assemblies and talent show awards now went to rock and roll singers instead of accordian players and baton twirlers. Stomping and clapping would shake the school auditorium and the stage and aisles would be filled with dancers.

It was a loud, confident year. Rock and roll was no longer underdog or underground. We weren't the squealing twelve-year-olds, the motorcycle hoods or the ragtag followers of the old Alan Freed days. Everybody knew rock and roll and everybody under twenty was at least willing to learn its dances. The young jazz buffs of the fifties drifted deeper into oblivion. Some would become the hard-core folkies of the early sixties. These kids were quickly distinguishable by the guitars they carried and their readiness to put down the words of Ahab the Arab for the meaningful messages of Seeger, White, Odetta, and the like. They took themselves very seriously and looked to the great rock and rolling mass as the intellectual wasteland of the generation. In retrospect it is interesting to note how familiar many former folkies are with the rock and roll of the early sixties. It seems apparent that the underground's underground must have been tuned to a Top 40 station.

At the time we paid little attention to the folk music crowds and listened only to the most commercial of their songs—usually Peter, Paul and Mary or the Kingston Trio. The folk crowd was certainly more committed than we were, but we were still vaguely interested in saving the world. Jack Kennedy's alarms had not wholly been sounded in vain though most of us were too weak to ignore the call of beer parties, Ben Casey, or a cruise through the drive-in. We did care that there was fighting in Laos, counter rebellion in Cuba, and a wasteland on television but we didn't think it touched our particular high school world. We left those worries, those problems of alienation, to the Beatniks, the folk singers, the adults.

We knew that telestar was a great step forward in communication but it was the song "Telestar" that really held our attention. And as horrible as the Thalidomide birth defects were, we loved the new sick jokes.

Even as our dedication to the Kennedy goals waned, our fascination with the Kennedy glamor held strong. We followed Jackie's trip through Rome, India, Pakistan, and England, watching her ride an elephant, play in the sea, and make another part of the world her oyster.

Yet even Jackie Kennedy would never replace the great lady we lost when Eleanor Roosevelt died in November, 1962. In 1960 politics had been entertaining, but with the great new victories of liberalism there was little we wanted to change. We were all satisfied with the over-twenty-one crowd's choices: Ted Kennedy, George Romney, Pat Brown. With Nixon's final defeat in California, we Kennedy kids were so sure of our political security that we could turn our attention to fun.

Even with our grand senior status at school most of us still had to contend with curfews on weeknights. But on weekends, we shoved our books into our lockers and set out to prowl the main drag, to cheer our school's team, to see the latest double feature, to get tickets to Dick Clark's "Caravan of Stars" rock and roll show, or to get one of the eighteen-year-olds to buy 3.2 beer for a party.

The motion picture business knew we were coming, so in addition to turning out such first-rate films as Oscar winners *Lawrence of Arabia, The Miracle Worker, To Kill a Mockingbird* and *Sweet Bird of Youth,* they began to throw together motorcycle dragster and teenie bikini movies. Nearly all of these movies were a gross insult to our intelligence but they nicely filled the second spot on a double feature or were perfect for a six-in-a-row drive-in special. Few of us looked up at the screen long enough to see our old friends from the "Mickey Mouse Club" or the "Donna Reed Show" now matured into beach boppers.

We were really at the drive-in to make-out or more specifically in pre-revolution terms, to neck, to pet, heavy pet, or do It. In 1962, when there were still standards like fast and slow, good and bad reputations, when virginity was posited good

and when we still lived at home, these were vital distinctions. Everyone except Dear Abby thought kissing was all right, but not on the first date. There was some mystical relationship between necking and respect that could be burst if necking was begun before the optimum platonic incubation period was up. And even if the girl enforced the waiting period, the boy might lie to his friends and lower her respect rating anyway.

Needless to say there was great uneasiness between the sexes, since boys had to act like they wanted to do It and girls had to act suitably appalled and no one could be trusted or satisfied. Generally, parents and teachers were the only ones who enjoyed the challenge of our abstinence.

The interesting thing is that *no* girls seemed to do It. There were stories about girls who did It in cars or behind the gym or in phone booths, but it was always a third person who knew the girl.

There was, however, one loophole in all this sex etiquette. If you were going steady, the boy's respect for you was beyond question. Therefore you could neck, pet (above and below the waist), and in the more advanced communities, do It. This ruling was such a boon for going steady that it is surprising that class ring salesmen didn't put it in their ads.

Sports was a less taboo-laden outlet for red-blooded American boys. It was the longest baseball season in history with the expanded leagues plus a National League playoff that put the San Francisco Giants into the World Series where they were defeated in the seventh game by the Yankees.

Heavyweight boxing champ Floyd Patterson was quickly brought to his knees by powerful challenger Sonny Liston. And school sports were always fun, even if your favorite part was the pep assembly or the half-time show.

A lot of fun in 1962 was wrapped in Madras.

Long before kids turned to India for the spiritual, they went for the material. Shirtwaists, hats, Bermudas, slacks, jackets, belts, hair bows, watchbands, headbands, scarves, blouses, skirts, book covers, lamp shades, bedspreads—everything had to be Madras, genuine bleeding Madras.

It was, no doubt, the biggest sensation of the year. Although we might forget it was the year of Glenn, Carpenter, and Schirra's space flights: the death year of Marilyn Monroe, and the year of the discovery of the laser beam, we would remember Madras pictured on page after page of our high school yearbook.

Those Madras-covered yearbooks were filled with faces and fashions that seemed impossible to forget. The picture-taking, ordering and signing rituals were such an important part of those years. We were all busy reserving the big blank pages for the most special friends, signing on the face of our pictures if they were ugly, or taken before we changed our hair or had our braces taken off.

There was a certain rivalry to see how many signers you could get and how many long inscriptions you rated. Personal notes from teachers and principals were a touch of status, as were chummy messages from beauty queens, Student Council presidents, cheerleaders, and athletes of note. Kids who were going on to college vied for the most memberships in language clubs, pep clubs, service clubs, social clubs, and any other activity that would show the desired college how well-rounded they were. Because of this competition these college-prep students strove for the most pictures and the longest listing in the index.

The surest way to make your yearbook an acceptable tribute to you was to work on the staff or date the editor. This guaranteed many pictures and a very knowing intimate caption under your name. But no matter how carefully you set up for a memorable yearbook, there was always the inscription meant for the kid sitting next to you, or the clod who signed on your steady's page, or your name being printed under the janitor's picture.

As absurd as these planned memories may seem now, they are deep in the traditions of the rock and roll generation. Bobby Vinton sang a song about meeting his high school girl friend many years later and recalling what he wrote in her yearbook.

Is that your little girl?
She looks a lot like you
Someday some boy will write in her
    book, too.
Roses are red my love
Violets are blue
Sugar is sweet, my love
Good luck, may God bless you.

The songs were always there, hand-in-hand with the customs. And so our memories are stored in our music almost better than in our yearbooks.

THE TOP FIFTY
1962

1. **SHERRY** — The Four Seasons
2. **JOHNNY ANGEL** — S. Fabares
3. **PEPPERMINT TWIST** — J. Dee and the Starlighters
4. **SOLDIER BOY** — The Shirelles
5. **BREAKING UP IS HARD TO DO** — N. Sedaka
6. **SHEILA** — T. Roe
7. **LOCO-MOTION** — Little Eva
8. **RAMBLIN' ROSE** — Nat (King) Cole
9. **BIG GIRLS DON'T CRY** — The Four Seasons
10. **HEY! BABY** — B. Channel
11. **DUKE OF EARL** — G. Chandler
12. **MASHED POTATO TIME** — D. Sharp
13. **THE STRIPPER** — D. Rose
14. **THE WAH-WATUSI** — The Orlons
15. **CAN'T HELP FALLING IN LOVE** — E. Presley
16. **LET ME IN** — The Sensations
17. **MIDNIGHT IN MOSCOW** — K. Ball
18. **ROSES ARE RED** — B. Vinton
19. **GREEN ONIONS** — Booker T and the MG's
20. **RETURN TO SENDER** — E. Presley
21. **STRANGER ON THE SHORE** — A. Bilk
22. **I CAN'T STOP LOVING YOU** — R. Charles
23. **PALISADES PARK** — F. Cannon
24. **NORMAN** — S. Thompson
25. **HE'S A REBEL** — The Crystals
26. **SEALED WITH A KISS** — B. Hyland
27. **WHAT'S YOUR NAME** — Don and Juan
28. **LOVE LETTERS** — K. Lester
29. **THE MAN WHO SHOT LIBERTY VALANCE** — G. Pitney
30. **THE WANDER** — Dion
31. **CRYING IN THE RAIN** — The Everly Brothers
32. **BABY, IT'S YOU** — The Shirelles
33. **PARTY LIGHTS** — C. Clark
34. **MONSTER MASH** — B. (Boris) Pickett and the Crypt Kickers
35. **DO YOU LOVE ME** — The Contours
36. **PATCHES** — D. Lee
37. **TELESTAR** — The Tornadoes
38. **BOBBY'S GIRL** — M. Blane
39. **SLOW TWISTIN'** — D. Sharp
40. **CINDY'S BIRTHDAY** — J. Crawford
41. **GOOD LUCK CHARM** — E. Presley
42. **DREAM BABY** — R. Orbison
43. **LOVER, PLEASE** — C. McPhatter
44. **SHE CRIED** — Jay and the Americans
45. **YOU DON'T KNOW ME** — R. Charles
46. **SHOUT** — J. Dee and the Starlighters
47. **PLAYBOY** — The Marvelettes
48. **THE ONE WHO REALLY LOVES YOU** — M. Wells
49. **LIMBO ROCK** — C. Checker
50. **ONLY LOVE CAN BREAK A HEART** — G. Pitney

January 6

1. **THE TWIST**
C. Checker
*H. Ballard, Parkway 811
(Jay and Cee–Armo, BMI)*

2. **RUN TO HIM**
B. Vee
*Keller–G. Goffin, Liberty 55388
(Aldon, BMI)*

3. **CAN'T HELP FALLING IN
LOVE**
E. Presley
*Weiss–Peretti–Creatore,
Victor 7968 (Gladys, ASCAP)*

4. **THE LION SLEEPS TONIGHT**
The Tokens
*Weiss–Peretti–Creatore,
Victor 7954 (Folkways, BMI)*

5. **PEPPERMINT TWIST**
J. Dee and the Star-
lighters
*J. Dee–H. Glovers, Roulette
4401 (Impact–Ware, BMI)*

6. **GOODBYE CRUEL WORLD**
J. Darren
*Shayne, Colpix 609
(Aldon, BMI)*

7. **WALK ON BY**
L. Van Dyke
*Hayes, Mercury 71834
(Lowery, BMI)*

8. **HAPPY BIRTHDAY, SWEET
SIXTEEN**
N. Sedaka
*H. Greenfield–N. Sedaka,
Victor 7957 (Aldon, BMI)*

9. **WHEN I FALL IN LOVE**
The Lettermen
*V. Young–E. Heyman, Capitol
4658 (Northern, ASCAP)*

10. **UNCHAIN MY HEART**
R. Charles
*A. Jones–F. James, ABC–
Paramount 10266 (TeePee,
ASCAP)*

January 13

1. **THE TWIST**
C. Checker
*H. Ballard, Parkway 811
(Jay and Cee–Armo, BMI)*

2. **PEPPERMINT TWIST**
J. Dee and the Star-
lighters
*J. Dee–H. Glovers, Roulette
4401 (Impact–Ware, BMI)*

3. **THE LION SLEEPS TONIGHT**
The Tokens
*Weiss–Peretti–Creatore,
Victor 7954 (Folkways, BMI)*

4. **CAN'T HELP FALLING IN
LOVE**
E. Presley
*Weiss–Peretti–Creatore,
Victor 7968 (Gladys, ASCAP)*

5. **RUN TO HIM**
B. Vee
*Keller–G. Goffin, Liberty 55388
(Aldon, BMI)*

6. **HAPPY BIRTHDAY, SWEET
SIXTEEN**
N. Sedaka
*H. Greenfield–N. Sedaka,
Victor 7957 (Aldon, BMI)*

7. **WALK ON BY**
L. VanDyke
*Hayes, Mercury 71834
(Lowery, BMI)*

8. **UNCHAIN MY HEART**
R. Charles
*A. Jones–F. James, ABC–
Paramount 10266 (TeePee,
ASCAP)*

9. **WHEN THE BOY IN YOUR
ARMS**
C. Francis
*Tepper–Bennett, M-G-M 10351
(Pickwick, ASCAP)*

10. **I KNOW**
B. George
*B. George, AFO 302
(Saturn–At Last, BMI)*

1962

January 20

1. **THE TWIST**
C. Checker
*H. Ballard, Parkway 811
(Jay and Cee–Armo, BMI)*

2. **PEPPERMINT TWIST**
J. Dee and the Star-
lighters
*J. Dee–H. Glovers, Roulette
4401 (Impact–Ware, BMI)*

3. **THE LION SLEEPS
TONIGHT**
The Tokens
*Weiss–Peretti–Creatore,
Victor 7954 (Folkways, BMI)*

4. **CAN'T HELP FALLING IN
LOVE**
E. Presley
*Weiss–Peretti–Creatore,
Victor 7968 (Gladys, ASCAP)*

5. **I KNOW**
B. George
*B. George, AFO 302
(Saturn–At Last, BMI)*

6. **HAPPY BIRTHDAY, SWEET
SIXTEEN**
N. Sedaka
*H. Greenfield–N. Sedaka,
Victor 7957 (Aldon, BMI)*

7. **WALK ON BY**
L. VanDyke
*Hayes, Mercury 71834
(Lowery, BMI)*

8. **RUN TO HIM**
B. Vee
*Keller–G. Goffin, Liberty 55388
(Aldon, BMI)*

9. **WHEN I FALL IN LOVE**
The Lettermen
*V. Young–E. Heyman, Capitol
4658 (Northern , ASCAP)*

10. **NORMAN**
S. Thompson
*J. D. Loudermilk, Hickory
1159 (Acuff–Rose, BMI)*

January 27

1. **PEPPERMINT TWIST**
J. Dee and the Star-
lighters
*J. Dee–H. Glovers, Roulette
4401 (Impact–Ware, BMI)*

2. **THE TWIST**
C. Checker
*H. Ballard, Parkway 811
(Jay and Cee–Armo, BMI)*

3. **I KNOW**
B. George
*B. George, AFO 302
(Saturn–At Last, BMI)*

4. **CAN'T HELP FALLING IN
LOVE**
E. Presley
*Weiss–Peretti–Creatore,
Victor 7968 (Gladys, ASCAP)*

5. **NORMAN**
S. Thompson
*J. D. Loudermilk, Hickory
1159 (Acuff–Rose, BMI)*

6. **THE LION SLEEPS TONIGHT**
The Tokens
*Weiss–Peretti–Creatore,
Victor 7954 (Folkways, BMI)*

7. **WHEN I FALL IN LOVE**
The Lettermen
*V. Young–E. Heyman, Capitol
4658 (Northern, ASCAP)*

8. **THE WANDERER**
Dion
*E. Maresca, Laurie 3115
(Schwartz–Disal, ASCAP)*

9. **BABY, IT'S YOU**
The Shirelles
*M. David–B. Williams–B.
Bacharach, Scepter 1227
(Dolfi, ASCAP)*

10. **WALK ON BY**
L. VanDyke
*Hayes, Mercury 71834
(Lowery, BMI)*

February 3

1. **PEPPERMINT TWIST**
J. Dee and the Star-
lighters
*J. Dee–H. Glovers, Roulette
4401 (Impact–Ware, BMI)*

2. **CAN'T HELP FALLING IN
LOVE**
E. Presley
*Weiss–Peretti–Creatore,
Victor 7968 (Gladys, ASCAP)*

3. **THE TWIST**
C. Checker
*H. Ballard, Parkway 811
(Jay and Cee–Armo, BMI)*

4. **NORMAN**
S. Thompson
*J. D. Loudermilk, Hickory
1159 (Acuff–Rose, BMI)*

5. **I KNOW**
B. George
*B. George, AFO 302
(Saturn–At Last, BMI)*

6. **THE WANDERER**
Dion
*E. Maresca, Laurie 3115
(Schwartz–Disal, ASCAP)*

7. **DUKE OF EARL**
G. Chandler
*Williams–Edwards–Dixon,
VeeJay 416 (Conrad, BMI)*

8. **BABY, IT'S YOU**
The Shirelles
*M. David–B. Williams–B.
Bacharach, Scepter 1227
(Dolfi, ASCAP)*

9. **BREAK IT TO ME GENTLY**
B. Lee
*Lampert–Seneca, Decca 31348
(Northern, ASCAP)*

10. **THE LION SLEEPS TONIGHT**
The Tokens
*Weiss–Peretti–Creatore,
Victor 7954 (Folkways, BMI)*

February 10

1. **PEPPERMINT TWIST**
   J. Dee and the Star-
   lighters
   J. Dee–H. Glovers, Roulette
   4401 (Impact–Ware, BMI)
2. **DUKE OF EARL**
   G. Chandler
   Williams–Edwards–Dixon,
   VeeJay 416 (Conrad, BMI)
3. **THE TWIST**
   C. Checker
   H. Ballard, Parkway 811
   (Jay and Cee–Armo, BMI)
4. **CAN'T HELP FALLING IN**
   LOVE
   E. Presley
   Weiss–Peretti–Creatore,
   Victor 7968 (Gladys, ASCAP)
5. **I KNOW**
   B. George
   B. George, AFO 302
   (Saturn–At Last, BMI)
6. **NORMAN**
   S. Thompson
   J. D. Loudermilk, Hickory
   1159 (Acuff–Rose, BMI)
7. **BREAK IT TO ME GENTLY**
   B. Lee
   Lampert–Seneca, Decca 31348
   (Northern, ASCAP)
8. **A LITTLE BITTY TEAR**
   B. Ives
   H. Cochran, Decca 31330
   (Pamper, BMI)
9. **DEAR LADY TWIST**
   G. (U.S.) Bonds
   Guida, LeGrand 1015
   (Pepe, BMI)
10. **THE WANDERER**
    Dion
    E. Maresca, Laurie 3115
    (Schwartz–Disal, ASCAP)

February 17

1. **NORMAN**
   S. Thompson
   J. D. Loudermilk, Hickory
   1159 (Acuff–Rose, BMI)
2. **DUKE OF EARL**
   G. Chandler
   Williams–Edwards–Dixon,
   VeeJay 416 (Conrad, BMI)
3. **PEPPERMINT TWIST**
   J. Dee and the Star-
   lighters
   J. Dee–H. Glovers, Roulette
   4401 (Impact–Ware, BMI)
4. **THE TWIST**
   C. Checker
   H. Ballard, Parkway 811
   (Jay and Cee–Armo, BMI)
5. **BREAK IT TO ME GENTLY**
   B. Lee
   Lampert–Seneca, Decca 31348
   (Northern, ASCAP)
6. **I KNOW**
   B. George
   B. George, AFO 302
   (Saturn–At Last, BMI)
7. **CRYING IN THE RAIN**
   The Everly Brothers
   H. Greenfield–C. King, Warner
   Brothers 5250 (Aldon, BMI)
8. **CAN'T HELP FALLING IN**
   LOVE
   E. Presley
   Weiss–Peretti–Creatore
   Victor 7968 (Gladys, ASCAP)
9. **THE WANDERER**
   Dion
   E. Maresca, Laurie 3115
   (Schwartz–Disal, ASCAP)
10. **DEAR LADY TWIST**
    G. (U.S.) Bonds
    Guida, LeGrand 1015
    (Pepe, BMI)

February 24

1. **NORMAN**
   S. Thompson
   J. D. Loudermilk, Hickory 1159
   (Acuff–Rose, BMI)
2. **DUKE OF EARL**
   G. Chandler
   Williams–Dixon–Edwards,
   VeeJay 416 (Conrad, BMI)
3. **HEY! BABY**
   B. Channel
   Cobb–B. Channel, Smash 1731
   (LeBill, BMI)
4. **THE TWIST**
   C. Checker
   H. Ballard, Parkway 811
   (Jay and Cee–Armo, BMI)
5. **THE WANDERER**
   Dion
   E. Maresca, Laurie 3115
   (Schwartz–Disal, ASCAP)
6. **BREAK IT TO ME GENTLY**
   B. Lee
   Lampert–Seneca, Decca 31348
   (Northern, ASCAP)
7. **PEPPERMINT TWIST**
   J. Dee and the Star-
   lighters
   J. Dee–H. Glovers, Roulette
   4401 (Impact–Ware, BMI)
8. **CRYING IN THE RAIN**
   The Everly Brothers
   H. Greenfield–C. King, Warner
   Brothers 5250 (Aldon, BMI)
9. **DEAR LADY TWIST**
   G. (U.S.) Bonds
   Guida, LeGrand 1015
   (Pepe, BMI)
10. **A LITTLE BITTY TEAR**
    B. Ives
    H. Cochran, Decca 31330
    (Pamper, BMI)

1962

March 3

1. **DUKE OF EARL**
   G. Chandler
   Williams–Edwards–Dixon,
   VeeJay 416   (Conrad, BMI)

2. **HEY! BABY**
   B. Channel
   Cobb–B. Channel,   Smash 1731
   (LeBill, BMI)

3. **THE WANDERER**
   Dion
   E. Maresca,   Laurie 3115
   (Schwartz–Disal, ASCAP)

4. **BREAK IT TO ME GENTLY**
   B. Lee
   Lampert–Seneca,   Decca 31348
   (Northern, ASCAP)

5. **THE TWIST**
   C. Checker
   H. Ballard,   Parkway 811
   (Jay and Cee–Armo, BMI)

6. **CRYING IN THE RAIN**
   The Everly Brothers
   H. Greenfield–C. King,   Warner
   Brothers 5250   (Aldon, BMI)

7. **NORMAN**
   S. Thompson
   J. D. Loudermilk,   Hickory
   1159   (Acuff–Rose, BMI)

8. **MIDNIGHT IN MOSCOW**
   K. Ball
   Saloviev–Sedoi–Matusovosky–
   Ball,   Kapp 442   (Melody
   Trails, BMI)

9. **PEPPERMINT TWIST**
   J. Dee and the Star-
   lighters
   J. Dee–H. Glovers,   Roulette
   4401   (Impact–Ware, BMI)

10. **CHIP CHIP**
    G. McDaniels
    Barry–Crofford–Resnick,
    Liberty 55405   (Glo-Mac, BMI)

March 10

1. **HEY! BABY**
   B. Channel
   Cobb–B. Channel,   Smash 1731
   (LeBill, BMI)

2. **DUKE OF EARL**
   G. Chandler
   Williams–Edwards–Dixon,
   Vee Jay 416   (Conrad, BMI)

3. **MIDNIGHT IN MOSCOW**
   K. Ball
   Saloviev–Sedoi–Matusovosky–
   Ball, Kapp 442   (Melody
   Trails, BMI)

4. **DON'T BREAK THE HEART**
   THAT LOVES YOU
   C. Francis
   David–Murray,   M-G-M 13059
   (Francon, ASCAP)

5. **LET ME IN**
   The Sensations
   Y. Baker,   Argo 5405
   (Arc–Kae Williams, BMI)

6. **CRYING IN THE RAIN**
   The Everly Brothers
   H. Greenfield–C. King,   Warner
   Brothers 5250   (Aldon, BMI)

7. **BREAK IT TO ME GENTLY**
   B. Lee
   Lampert–Seneca,   Decca 31348
   (Northern, ASCAP)

8. **HER ROYAL MAJESTY**
   J. Darren
   G. Goffin–C. King,   Colpix 622
   (Aldon, BMI)

9. **THE WANDERER**
   Dion
   E. Maresca,   Laurie 3115
   (Schwartz–Disal, ASCAP)

10. **WHAT'S YOUR NAME?**
    Don and Juan
    C. Johnson,   Big Top 3079
    (Hill & Range, BMI)

March 17

1. **MIDNIGHT IN MOSCOW**
   K. Ball
   Saloviev–Sedoi–Matusovosky–
   Ball
   Kapp 442   (Melody Trails, BMI)

2. **DON'T BREAK THE HEART**
   THAT LOVES YOU
   C. Francis
   David–Murray,   M-G-M 13059
   (Francon, ASCAP)

3. **HEY! BABY**
   B. Channel
   Cobb–B. Channel,   Smash 1731
   (LeBill, BMI)

4. **DUKE OF EARL**
   G. Chandler
   Williams–Edwards–Dixon,
   VeeJay 416   (Conrad, BMI)

5. **LET ME IN**
   The Sensations
   Y. Baker,   Argo 5405
   (Arc–Kae Williams, BMI)

6. **CRYING IN THE RAIN**
   The Everly Brothers
   H. Greenfield–C. King.   Warner
   Brothers 5250   (Aldon, BMI)

7. **HER ROYAL MAJESTY**
   J. Darren
   G. Goffin–C. King,   Colpix 622
   (Aldon, BMI)

8. **PERCOLATOR (TWIST)**
   Billy Joe and the Check-
   mates
   Bidev–Freeman,   Dore 620
   (Meadowlark, ASCAP)

9. **WHAT'S YOUR NAME?**
   Don and Juan
   C. Johnson,   Big Top 3079
   (Hill & Range, BMI)

10. **BREAK IT TO ME GENTLY**
    B. Lee
    Lampert–Seneca,   Decca 31348
    (Northern, ASCAP)

March 24

1. **LET ME IN**
   The Sensations
   Y. Baker,   Argo 5405
   (Arc–Kae Williams, BMI)

2. **DON'T BREAK THE HEART THAT LOVES YOU**
   C. Francis
   David–Murray,   M-G-M 13059
   (Francon, ASCAP)

3. **HEY! BABY**
   B. Channel
   Cobb–B. Channel,   Smash 1731
   (LeBill, BMI)

4. **MIDNIGHT IN MOSCOW**
   K. Ball
   Saloviev–Sedoi–Matusovosky–
   Ball, Kapp 442   (Melody Trails,
   BMI)

5. **DREAM BABY**
   R. Orbison
   C. Walker,   Monument 456
   (Combine, BMI)

6. **SLOW TWISTIN'**
   C. Checker
   J. Sheldon,   Parkway 835
   (Woodcrest, BMI)

7. **WHAT'S YOUR NAME?**
   Don and Juan
   C. Johnson,   Big Top 3079
   (Hill & Range, BMI)

8. **TWISTIN' THE NIGHT AWAY**
   S. Cooke
   S. Cooke,   Victor 7893
   (Kags, BMI)

9. **HER ROYAL MAJESTY**
   J. Darren
   G. Goffin–C. King,   Colpix 622
   (Aldon, BMI)

10. **DUKE OF EARL**
    G. Chandler
    Williams–Edwards–Dixon,
    VeeJay 416   (Conrad, BMI)

March 31

1. **DON'T BREAK THE HEART THAT LOVES YOU**
   C. Francis
   David–Murray,   M-G-M 13059
   (Francon, AS CAP)

2. **HEY! BABY**
   B. Channel
   Cobb–B. Channel,   Smash 1731
   (LeBill, BMI)

3. **JOHNNY ANGEL**
   S. Fabares
   Pockriss–Dundy,   Colpix 621
   (Post, ASCAP)

4. **DREAM BABY**
   R. Orbison
   C. Walker,   Monument 456
   (Combine, BMI)

5. **MIDNIGHT IN MOSCOW**
   K. Ball
   Saloviev–Sedoi–Matusovosky–
   Ball, Kapp 442   (Melody Trails,
   BMI)

6. **SLOW TWISTIN'**
   C. Checker
   J. Sheldon,   Parkway 835
   (Woodcrest, BMI)

7. **WHAT'S YOUR NAME?**
   Don and Juan
   C. Johnson,   Big Top 3079
   (Hill & Range, BMI)

8. **LET ME IN**
   The Sensations
   Y. Baker,   Argo 5405
   (Arc–Kae Williams, BMI)

9. **GOOD LUCK CHARM**
   E. Presley
   A. Schroeder–W. Gold,
   Victor 7992   (Gladys, ASCAP)

10. **TWISTIN' THE NIGHT AWAY**
    S. Cooke
    S. Cooke,   Victor 7893
    (Kags, BMI)

April 7

1. **JOHNNY ANGEL**
   S. Fabares
   Pockriss–Dundy,   Colpix 621
   (Post, ASCAP)

2. **DON'T BREAK THE HEART THAT LOVES YOU**
   C. Francis
   David–Murray, M-G-M 13059
   (Francon, ASCAP)

3. **GOOD LUCK CHARM**
   E. Presley
   A. Schroeder–W. Gold,   Victor
   7992   (Gladys, ASCAP)

4. **SLOW TWISTIN'**
   C. Checker
   J. Sheldon,   Parkway 835
   (Woodcrest, BMI)

5. **DREAM BABY**
   R. Orbison
   C. Walker,   Monument 456
   (Combine, BMI)

6. **HEY! BABY**
   B. Channel
   Cobb–B. Channel,   Smash 1731
   (LeBill, BMI)

7. **MIDNIGHT IN MOSCOW**
   K. Ball
   Saloviev–Sedoi–Matusovosky–
   Ball, Kapp 442   (Melody Trails,
   BMI)

8. **YOUNG WORLD**
   R. Nelson
   J. Fuller,   Imperial 5805
   (Four Star Sales, BMI)

9. **LOVE LETTERS**
   K. Lester
   V. Young–E. Heyman,   Era 3068
   (Famous, ASCAP)

10. **MASHED POTATO TIME**
    D. Sharp
    K. Mann–Lowe,   Cameo 212
    (Rice–Mill, BMI)

April 14

1. **JOHNNY ANGEL**
S. Fabares
Pockriss–Dundy, Colpix 621
(Post, ASCAP)

2. **GOOD LUCK CHARM**
E. Presley
A. Schroeder–W. Gold, Victor
7992 (Glady, ASCAP)

3. **SLOW TWISTIN'**
C. Checker
J. Sheldon, Parkway 835
(Woodcrest, BMI)

4. **MASHED POTATO TIME**
D. Sharp
K. Mann–Lowe, Cameo 212
(Rice–Mill, BMI)

5. **LOVE LETTERS**
K. Lester
V. Young–E. Heyman, Era
3068 (Famous, ASCAP)

6. **YOUNG WORLD**
R. Nelson,
J. Fuller, Imperial 5805
(Four Star Sales, BMI)

7. **MIDNIGHT IN MOSCOW**
K. Ball
Saloviev–Sedoi–Matusovosky–
Ball, Kapp 442 (Melody Trails,
BMI)

8. **HEY! BABY**
B. Channel
Cobb–B. Channel, Smash 1731
(Le Bill, BMI)

9. **LOVER, PLEASE**
C. McPhatter
B. Swan, Mercury 71941
(Lyn–Lou, BMI)

10. **DON'T BREAK THE
HEART THAT LOVES YOU**
C. Francis
David–Murray, M-G-M 13059
(Francon, ASCAP)

April 21

1. **JOHNNY ANGEL**
S. Fabares
Pockris–Dundy, Colpix 621
(Post, ASCAP)

2. **MASHED POTATO TIME**
D. Sharp
K. Mann–Lowe, Cameo 212
(Rice–Mill, BMI)

3. **GOOD LUCK CHARM**
E. Presley
A. Schroeder–W. Gold, Victor
7992 (Gladys, ASCAP)

4. **SLOW TWISTIN'**
C. Checker
J. Sheldon, Parkway 835
(Woodcrest, BMI)

5. **SOLDIER BOY**
The Shirelles
L. Dixon–F. Green, Scepter
1228 (Ludix, BMI)

6. **LOVE LETTERS**
K. Lester
V. Young–E. Heyman, Era 3068
(Famous, ASCAP)

7. **SHOUT**
J. Dee and the Star-
lighters
The Isley Brothers, Roulette
4416 (Wemar-Nom, BMI)

8. **LOVER, PLEASE**
C. McPhatter
B. Swan, Mercury 71941
(Lyn–Lou, BMI)

9. **STRANGER ON THE SHORE**
A. Bilk
A. Bilk–V. Young, Atco 6217
(Mellin, BMI)

10. **YOUNG WORLD**
R. Nelson
J. Fuller, Imperial 5805
(Four Star Sales, BMI)

April 28

1. **JOHNNY ANGEL**
S. Fabares
Pockriss–Dundy, Colpix 621
(Post, ASCAP)

2. **MASHED POTATO TIME**
D. Sharp
K. Mann–Lowe, Cameo 212
(Rice–Mill, BMI)

3. **GOOD LUCK CHARM**
E. Presley
A. Schroeder–W. Gold, Victor
7992 (Gladys, ASCAP)

4. **SLOW TWISTIN'**
C. Checker
J. Sheldon, Parkway 835
(Woodcrest, BMI)

5. **SOLDIER BOY**
The Shirelles
L. Dixon–F. Green, Scepter
1228 (Ludix, BMI)

6. **YOUNG WORLD**
R. Nelson
J. Fuller, Imperial 5805
(Four Star Sales BMI)

7. **STRANGER ON THE SHORE**
A. Bilk
A. Bilk–V. Young, Atco 6271
(Mellin, BMI)

8. **LOVER, PLEASE**
C. McPhatter
B. Swan, Mercury 71941
(Lyn–Lou, BMI)

9. **SHOUT**
J. Dee and the Star-
lighters
The Isley Brothers, Roulette
4416 (Wemar-Nom, BMI)

10. **TWIST, TWIST SENORA**
G. (U.S.) Bonds
Guida–Barge–Royster, LeGrand
1018 (Rock Masters, BMI)

May 5

1. **SOLDIER BOY**
   The Shirelles
   L. Dixon–F. Green, Scepter 1228 (Ludix, BMI)

2. **MASHED POTATO TIME**
   D. Sharp
   K. Mann–Lowe, Cameo 212 (Rice– Mill, BMI)

3. **JOHNNY ANGEL**
   S. Fabares
   Pockriss–Dundy, Colpix 621 (Post, ASCAP)

4. **STRANGER ON THE SHORE**
   A. Bilk
   Bilk–Young, Atco 6217 (Mellin, BMI)

5. **GOOD LUCK CHARM**
   E. Presley
   A. Schroeder–W. Gold, Victor 7992 (Glady, ASCAP)

6. **SHOUT**
   J. Dee and the Star-lighters
   The Isley Brothers, Roulette 4416 (Wemar–Nom, BMI)

7. **LOVER, PLEASE**
   C. McPhatter
   B. Swan, Mercury 71941 (Lyn–Lou, BMI)

8. **SLOW TWISTIN'**
   C. Checker
   J. Sheldon, Parkway 835 (Woodcrest, BMI)

9. **P. T. 109**
   J. Dean
   Wilkin–Burch, Columbia 42338 (Cedarwood, BMI)

10. **TWIST, TWIST, SENORA**
    G. (U.S.) Bonds
    Guida–Barge–Royster, Le Grand 1018 (Rock Masters, BMI)

May 12

1. **SOLDIER BOY**
   The Shirelles
   L. Dixon–F. Green, Scepter 1229 (Ludix, BMI)

2. **MASHED POTATO TIME**
   D. Sharp
   K. Mann–Lowe, Cameo 212 (Rice–Mill, BMI)

3. **STRANGER ON THE SHORE**
   A. Bilk
   A. Bilk,–V. Young, Atco 621 (Rice–Mill, BMI)

4. **JOHNNY ANGEL**
   S. Fabares
   Pockriss–Dundy, Colpix 621 (Post, ASCAP)

5. **GOOD LUCK CHARM**
   E. Presley
   A. Schroeder–W. Gold, Victor 7992 (Gladys, ASCAP)

6. **SHE CRIED**
   Jay and the Americans
   G. Richards–T. Daryll, United Artists 415 (Trio, BMI)

7. **OLD RIVERS**
   W. Brennan
   Crofford, Liberty 55436 (Glo-mac-Metric, BMI)

8. **SHOUT! SHOUT! (KNOCK YOURSELF OUT)**
   E. Maresca
   E. Maresca–T. E. Bogdany, Saville 117 (Broadway, ASCAP)

9. **TWIST, TWIST, SENORA**
   G. (U.S. Bonds) Bonds
   Guida–Barge–Royster, Le Grand 1018 (Rock Masters, BMI)

10. **SHOUT**
    J. Dee and the Star-lighters
    The Isley Brothers, Roulette 4416 (Wemar–Nom, BMI)

May 19

1. **STRANGER ON THE SHORE**
   A. Bilk
   A. Bilk–V. Young, Atco 6217 (Mellin, BMI)

2. **SOLDIER BOY**
   The Shirelles
   L. Dixon–F. Green, Scepter 1228 (Ludix, BMI)

3. **JOHNNY ANGEL**
   S. Fabares
   Pockriss–Dundy, Colpix 621 (Post, ASCAP)

4. **SHE CRIED**
   Jay and the Americans
   G. Richards–T. Daryll, United Artists 415 (Trio, BMI)

5. **MASHED POTATO TIME**
   D. Sharp
   K. Mann–Lowe, Cameo 212 (Rice–Mill, BMI)

6. **OLD RIVERS**
   W. Brennan
   Crofford, Liberty 55436 (Glo-Mac-Metric, BMI)

7. **P. T. 109**
   J. Dean
   Wilkin–Burch, Columbia 42338 (Cedarwood, BMI)

8. **SHOUT! SHOUT! (KNOCK YOURSELF OUT)**
   E. Maresca
   E. Maresca–T. E. Bogdany, Seville 117 Broadway, ASCAP)

9. **FUNNY WAY OF LAUGHIN'**
   B. Ives
   Cochran, Decca 31371 (Pamper, BMI)

10. **EVERYBODY LOVES ME BUT YOU**
    B. Lee
    R. Self, Decca 31379 (Champion, BMI)

May 26

1. **SOLDIER BOY**
The Shirelles
L. Dixon–F. Green,
Scepter 1228 (Ludix, BMI)

2. **I CAN'T STOP LOVING YOU**
R. Charles
D. Gibson, ABC–Paramount
10330 (Acuff–Rose, BMI)

3. **STRANGER ON THE SHORE**
A. Bilk
A. Bilk–V. Young, Atco 6217
(Mellin, BMI)

4. **MASHED POTATO TIME**
D. Sharp
Lowe–K. Mann, Cameo 212
(Rice–Mill, BMI)

5. **EVERYBODY LOVES ME**
BUT YOU
B. Lee
R. Self, Decca 31379
(Champion, BMI)

6. **P. T. 109**
J. Dean
Wilkin–Burch, Columbia 42338
(Cedarwood, BMI)

7. **OLD RIVERS**
W. Brennan
Crofford, Liberty 55436
(Glo-Mac–Metric, BMI)

8. **SHE CRIED**
Jay and the Americans
G. Richards–T. Daryll, United
Artists 415 (Trio, BMI)

9. **LOVERS WHO WANDER**
Dion
D. DeMucci–E. Maresca,
Laurie 3123 (Disal, ASCAP)

10. **JOHNNY ANGEL**
S. Fabares
Pockriss–Dundy, Colpix 621
(Post, ASCAP)

June 2

1. **I CAN'T STOP LOVING YOU**
R. Charles
D. Gibson, ABC–Paramount
10330 (Acuff–Rose, BMI)

2. **STRANGER ON THE SHORE**
A. Bilk
A. Bilk–V. Young, Atco 6217
(Mellin, BMI)

3. **SOLDIER BOY**
The Shirelles
L. Dixon–F. Green, Scepter
1228 (Ludix, BMI)

4. **LOVERS WHO WANDER**
Dion
D. DiMucci–E. Maresca,
Laurie 3123 (Disal, ASCAP)

5. **MASHED POTATO TIME**
D. Sharp
K. Mann–Lowe, Cameo 212
(Rice–Mill, BMI)

6. **EVERYBODY LOVES ME BUT**
YOU
B. Lee
R. Self, Decca 31379
(Champion, BMI)

7. **SHOUT! SHOUT! (KNOCK**
YOURSELF OUT)
E. Maresca
E. Maresca–T. E. Bogdany,
Saville 117 (Broadway, ASCAP)

8. **OLD RIVERS**
W. Brennan
Crofford, Liberty 55436
(Glo-Mac–Metric, BMI)

9. **THE ONE WHO REALLY**
LOVES YOU
M. Wells
W. Robinson, Motown 1024
(Jobete, BMI)

10. **THE MAN WHO SHOT**
LIBERTY VALANCE
G. Pitney
B. Bacharach–H. David,
Musicor 1020 (Famous, ASCAP)

June 9

1. **I CAN'T STOP LOVING YOU**
R. Charles
D. Gibson, ABC–Paramount
10330 (Acuff–Rose, BMI)

2. **STRANGER ON THE SHORE**
A. Bilk
A. Bilk–V. Young, Atco 6217
(Mellin, BMI)

3. **LOVERS WHO WANDER**
Dion
D. DiMucci–E. Maresca,
Laurie 3123 (Disal, ASCAP)

4. **SOLDIER BOY**
The Shirelles
L. Dixon–F. Green, Scepter
1228 (Ludix, BMI)

5. **THE MAN WHO SHOT**
LIBERTY VALANCE
G. Pitney
B. Bacharach–H. David,
Musicor 1020 (Famous, ASCAP)

6. **MASHED POTATO TIME**
D. Sharp
K. Mann–Lowe, Cameo 212
(Rice–Mill, BMI)

7. **SECOND HAND LOVE**
C. Francis
Hunter–Spector, M-G-M 13074
(Merna, BMI)

8. **THE ONE WHO REALLY**
LOVES YOU
M. Wells
W. Robinson, Motown 1024
(Jobete, BMI)

9. **PALISADES PARK**
F. Cannon
Barris, Swan 4106
(Claridge, ASCAP)

10. **PLAYBOY**
The Marvelettes
Holland–Baleman–Horton–
Stevenson,
Tamla 54060 (Jobete, BMI)

June 16

1. **I CAN'T STOP LOVING YOU**
R. Charles
*D. Gibson, ABC–Paramount
10330 (Acuff–Rose, BMI)*

2. **STRANGER ON THE SHORE**
A. Bilk
*A. Bilk–V. Young, Atco 6217
(Mellin, BMI)*

3. **CINDY'S BIRTHDAY**
J. Crawford
*Winn–Hoover, DiFi 4178
(Maravilla, BMI)*

4. **THE MAN WHO SHOT
LIBERTY VALANCE**
G. Pitney
*B. Bacharach–H. David,
Musicor 1020 (Famous, ASCAP)*

5. **PALISADES PARK**
F. Cannon
*Barris, Swan 4106
(Claridge, ASCAP)*

6. **LOVERS WHO WANDER**
Dion
*D. DiMucci–E. Maresco,
Laurie 3123 (Disal, ASCAP)*

7. **PLAYBOY**
The Marvelettes
*Holland–Baleman–Horton–
Stevenson,
Tamla 54060 (Jobete, BMI)*

8. **THE ONE WHO REALLY
LOVES YOU**
M. Wells
*W. Robinson, Motown 1024
(Jobete, BMI)*

9. **SECOND HAND LOVE**
C. Francis
*Hunter–Spector, M-G-M 13074
(Merna, BMI)*

10. **THE STRIPPER**
D. Rose
*D. Rose, M-G-M K13064
(Rose, ASCAP)*

June 23

1. **PALISADES PARK**
F. Cannon
*Barris, Swan 4106
(Claridge, ASCAP)*

2. **I CAN'T STOP LOVING YOU**
R. Charles
*D. Gibson, ABC–Paramount
10330 (Acuff–Rose, BMI)*

3. **THE STRIPPER**
D. Rose
*D. Rose, M-G-M K 13064
(Rose, ASCAP)*

4. **THE MAN WHO SHOT
LIBERTY VALANCE**
G. Pitney
*B. Bacharach–H. David,
Musicor 1020 (Famous, ASCAP)*

5. **CINDY'S BIRTHDAY**
J. Crawford
*Winn–Hoover, DiFi 4178
(Maravilla, BMI)*

6. **ROSES ARE RED**
B. Vinton
*P. Evans–A. Byron, Epic 9509
(Lyle, ASCAP)*

7. **STRANGER ON THE SHORE**
A. Bilk
*A. Bilk–V. Young, Atco 6217
(Mellin, BMI)*

8. **PLAYBOY**
The Marvelettes
*Holland–Baleman–Horton–
Stevenson,
Tamla 54060 (Jobete, BMI)*

9. **THE ONE WHO REALLY
LOVES YOU**
M. Wells
*W. Robinson, Motown 1024
(Jobete, BMI)*

10. **THAT'S OLD FASHIONED**
The Everly Brothers
*Giant–Baum–Kaye, Warner
Brothers 5273 (Aberbach, BMI)*

June 30

1. **THE STRIPPER**
D. Rose
*D. Rose, M-G-M K 13064
(Rose, ASCAP)*

2. **I CAN'T STOP LOVING YOU**
R. Charles
*D. Gibson, ABC–Paramount
10330 (Acuff–Rose, BMI)*

3. **PALISADES PARK**
F. Cannon
*Barris, Swan 4106
(Claridge, ASCAP)*

4. **ROSES ARE RED**
B. Vinton
*P. Evans–A. Byron, Epic 9509
(Lyle, ASCAP)*

5. **CINDY'S BIRTHDAY**
J. Crawford
*Winn–Hoover, DiFi 4178
(Maravilla, BMI)*

6. **THE MAN WHO SHOT
LIBERTY VALANCE**
G. Pitney
*B. Bacharach–H. Davis,
Musicor 1020 (Famous,
ASCAP)*

7. **PLAYBOY**
The Marvelettes
*Holland–Baleman–Horton–
Stevenson,
Tamla 54060 (Jobete, BMI)*

8. **STRANGER ON THE SHORE**
A. Bilk
*A. Bilk–V. Young, Atco 6217
(Mellin, BMI)*

9. **AL DI LA**
E. Pericoli
*Mogul–Donida–Drake, Warner
Brothers 5259 (Witmark,
ASCAP)*

10. **JOHNNY GET ANGRY**
J. Sommers
*Edwards–David, Warner
Brothers 5275 (Tod,
ASCAP)*

1962

July 7

1. **THE STRIPPER**
D. Rose
*D. Rose M-G-M K13064
(Rose, ASCAP)*

2. **ROSES ARE RED**
B. Vinton
*P. Evans–A. Byron, Epic 9509
(Lyle, ASCAP)*

3. **I CAN'T STOP LOVING YOU**
R. Charles
*D. Gibson, ABC–Paramount
10330 (Acuff–Rose, BMI)*

4. **PALISADES PARK**
F. Cannon
*Barris, Swan 4106
(Claridge, ASCAP)*

5. **CINDY'S BIRTHDAY**
J. Crawford
*Winn–Hoover, DiFi 4178
(Maravilla, BMI)*

6. **AL DI LA**
E. Pericoli
*Mongul–Donida–Drake, Warner
Brothers 5259 (Witmark,
ASCAP)*

7. **WOLVERTON MOUNTAIN**
C. King
*M. Kilgore–C. King, Columbia
42352 (Painted Desert, BMI)*

8. **SNAP YOUR FINGERS**
J. Henderson
*G. Martin–A. Zinetis, Tod
1072 (Cigma, BMI)*

9. **JOHNNY GET ANGRY**
J. Sommers
*Edwards–David, Warner
Brothers 5275 (Tod, ASCAP)*

10. **PLAYBOY**
The Marvelettes
*Holland–Baleman–Horton–
Stevenson,
Tamla 54060 (Jobete, BMI)*

July 14

1. **ROSES ARE RED**
B. Vinton
*P. Evans–A. Byron, Epic 9509
(Lyle, ASCAP)*

2. **THE STRIPPER**
D. Rose
*D. Rose, M-G-M 13064
(Rose, ASCAP)*

3. **I CAN'T STOP LOVING YOU**
R. Charles
*D. Gibson, ABC–Paramount
10330 (Acuff–Rose, BMI)*

4. **THE WAH-WATUSI**
The Orlons
*K. Mann–Appel, Cameo 218
(Kalmann–Lowe, ASCAP)*

5. **SEALED WITH A KISS**
B. Hyland
*Udell–Geld, ABC–Paramount
10336 (Pogo, ASCAP)*

6. **PALISADES PARK**
F. Cannon
*Barris, Swan 4106
(Claridge, ASCAP)*

7. **WOLVERTON MOUNTAIN**
C. King
*M. Kilgore–C. King, Columbia
42352 (Painted Desert, BMI)*

8. **JOHNNY GET ANGRY**
J. Sommers
*Edwards–David, Warner
Brothers 5275 (Tod, ASCAP)*

9. **GRAVY**
D. Sharp
*K. Mann–Appell, Cameo 219
(Kalmann, ASCAP)*

10. **AL DI LA**
E. Pericoli
*Mongul–Donida–Drake, Warner
Brothers 5259 (Witmark,
ASCAP)*

July 21

1. **ROSES ARE RED**
B. Vinton
*P. Evans–A. Byron, Epic 9509
(Lyle, ASCAP)*

2. **I CAN'T STOP LOVING YOU**
R. Charles
*D. Gibson, ABC–Paramount
10330 (Acuff–Rose, BMI)*

3. **THE WAH-WATUSI**
The Orlons
*K. Mann–Appell, Cameo 218
(Kalmann–Lowe, ASCAP)*

4. **SEALED WITH A KISS**
B. Hyland
*Udell–Geld, ABC–Paramount
10336 (Pogo, ASCAP)*

5. **THE STRIPPER**
D. Rose
*Rose, M-G-M K13064
(Rose, ASCAP)*

6. **SPEEDY GONZALES**
P. Boone
*Kaye–Hill–Lee, Dot 16368
(Budd, ASCAP)*

7. **JOHNNY GET ANGRY**
J. Sommers
*Edwards–David Warner
Brothers 5275 (Tod, ASCAP)*

8. **WOLVERTON MOUNTAIN**
C. King
*M. Kilgore–C. King, Columbia
42352 (Painted Desert, BMI)*

9. **PALISADES PARK**
F. Cannon
*Barris, Swan 4106
(Claridge, ASCAP)*

10. **GRAVY**
D. Sharp
*K. Mann–Appell, Cameo 219
(Kalmann, ASCAP)*

1. **ROSES ARE RED**
B. Vinton
P. Evans–A. Byron, Epic 9509
(Lyle, ASCAP)

2. **SEALED WITH A KISS**
B. Hyland
Udell–Gold, ABC–Paramount
10336 (Pogo, ASCAP)

3. **I CAN'T STOP LOVING YOU**
R. Charles
D. Gibson, ABC–Paramount
10330 (Acuff–Rose, BMI)

4. **THE WAH-WATUSI**
The Orlons
K. Mann–Appell, Cameo 218
(Kalmann–Lowe, ASCAP)

5. **THE STRIPPER**
D. Rose
D. Rose, M-G-M K 13064
(Rose, ASCAP)

6. **SPEEDY GONZALES**
P. Boone
Kaye–Hill–Lee, Dot 16368
(Budd, ASCAP)

7. **BREAKING UP IS HARD TO DO**
N. Sedaka
N. Sedaka–H. Greenfield, Victor
8046 (Aldon, BMI)

8. **AHAB THE ARAB**
R. Stevens
R. Stevens, Mercury 71966
(Lowery, ASCAP)

9. **WOLVERTON MOUNTAIN**
C. King
M. Kilgore–C. King, Columbia
42352 (Painted Desert, BMI)

10. **GRAVY**
D. Sharp
K. Mann–Appell, Cameo 219
(Kalmann, ASCAP)

1. **ROSES ARE RED**
B. Vinton
P. Evans–A. Byron, Epic 9509
(Lyle, ASCAP)

2. **BREAKING UP IS HARD TO DO**
N. Sedaka
N. Sedaka–H. Greenfield, Victor
8046 (Aldon, BMI)

3. **SEALED WITH A KISS**
B. Hyland
Udell–Gold, ABC–Paramount
10336 (Pogo, ASCAP)

4. **THE WAH-WATUSI**
The Orlons
K. Mann–Appell, Cameo 218
(Kalmann–Lowe, ASCAP)

5. **AHAB THE ARAB**
R. Stevens
R. Stevens, Mercury 71966
(Lowery, ASCAP)

6. **SPEEDY GONZALES**
P. Boone
Kaye–Hill–Lee, Dot 16368
(Budd, ASCAP)

7. **I CAN'T STOP LOVING YOU**
R. Charles
D. Gibson, ABC–Paramount
10330 (Acuff–Rose, BMI)

8. **LOCO-MOTION**
Little Eva
G. Goffin–C. King, Dimension
1000 (Aldon, BMI)

9. **THE STRIPPER**
D. Rose
D. Rose, M-G-M K13064
(Rose , ASCAP)

10. **THEME FROM DR. KILDARE**
R. Chamberalin
Goldsmith–Winn–Rugulo, M-G-M
13075 (Hastings, BMI)

1. **BREAKING UP IS HARD TO DO**
N. Sedaka
N. Sedaka–H. Greenfield, Victor
8046 (Aldon, BMI)

2. **ROSES ARE RED**
B. Vinton
P. Evans–A. Byron, Epic 9509
(Lyle, ASCAP)

3. **THE WAH-WATUSI**
The Orlons
K. Mann–Appell, Cameo 218
(Kalmann–Lowe, ASCAP)

4. **LOCO-MOTION**
Little Eva
G. Goffin–C. King,
Dimension 1000 (Aldon, BMI)

5. **AHAB THE ARAB**
R. Stevens
R. Stevens, Mercury 71966
(Lowery, ASCAP)

6. **SPEEDY GONZALES**
P. Boone
Kaye–Hill–Lee, Dot 16368
(Budd, ASCAP)

7. **SEALED WITH A KISS**
B. Hyland
Udell–Gold, ABC–Paramount
10336 (Budd, ASCAP)

8. **YOU'LL LOSE A GOOD THING**
B. Lynn
B. L. Ozen, Jamie 1220
(David–Crazy Cajun–Jamie, BMI)

9. **THINGS**
B. Darin
B. Darin, Atco 6229
(Adaris, BMI)

10. **THE STRIPPER**
D. Rose
D. Rose, M-G-M K13064
(Rose, ASCAP)

August 18

1. **BREAKING UP IS HARD TO DO**
N. Sedaka
N. Sedaka–H. Greenfield,
Victor 8046
(Aldon, BMI)

2. **LOCO-MOTION**
Little Eva
G. Goffin–C. King, Dimension
1000 (Aldon, BMI)

3. **ROSES ARE RED**
B. Vinton
P. Evans–A. Byron, Epic 9509
(Lyle, ASCAP)

4. **THE WAH-WATUSI**
The Orlons
K. Mann–Appell, Cameo 218
(Kalmann–Love, ASCAP)

5. **YOU DON'T KNOW ME**
R. Charles
C. Walker–E. Arnold, ABC
Paramount 10345
(Hill & Range, BMI)

6. **THINGS**
B. Darin
B. Darin, Atco 6229
(Adaris, BMI)

7. **LITTLE DIANE**
Dion
D. DiMucci, Laurie 3134
(Discal, ASCAP)

8. **SPEEDY GONZALES**
P. Boone
Kaye–Hill–Lee Dot 16368
(Budd, ASCAP)

9. **SEALED WITH A KISS**
B. Hyland
Udell–Gold, ABC–Paramount
10336 (Pogo, ASCAP)

10. **AHAB THE ARAB**
R. Stevens
R. Stevens, Mercury 71966
(Lowery, ASCAP)

August 25

1. **BREAKING UP IS HARD TO DO**
N. Sedaka
N. Sedaka–H. Greenfield, Victor
8046 (Aldon, BMI)

2. **SHIELA**
T. Roe
T. Roe ABC–Paramount 10329
(Eager–Nitetime, BMI)

3. **THINGS**
B. Darin
B. Darin, Atco 6229
(Adaris, BMI)

4. **LOCO-MOTION**
Little Eva
G. Goffin–C. King,
Dimension 1000 (Aldon, BMI)

5. **PARTY LIGHTS**
C. Clark
C. Clark Chancellor 1113
(Rambed, BMI)

6. **YOU DON'T KNOW ME**
R. Charles
C. Walker–E. Arnold, ABC–
Paramount 10345(Hill & Range,
BMI)

7. **ROSES ARE RED**
B. Vinton
P. Evans–A. Byron, Epic 9509
(Lyle, ASCAP)

8. **LITTLE DIANE**
Dion
D. DiMucci, Laurie 3134
(Disal, ASCAP)

9. **SHE'S NOT YOU**
E. Presley
D. Pomus–H. Stoller–J. Leiber,
Victor 8041
(Elvis Presley, BMI)

10. **AHAB THE ARAB**
R. Stevens
R. Stevens, Mercury 71966
(Lowery, ASCAP)

September 1

1. **BREAKING UP IS HARD TO DO**
N. Sedaka
N. Sedaka–H. Greenfield,
Victor 8046
(Aldon, BMI)

2. **SHEILA**
T. Roe
T. Roe, ABC–Paramount 10329
(Eager–Nitetime, BMI)

3. **LOCO-MOTION**
Little Eva
G. Goffin–C. King,
Dimension 1000
(Aldon, BMI)

4. **PARTY LIGHTS**
C. Clark
C. Clark Chancellor 1113
(Rambed, BMI)

5. **YOU DON'T KNOW ME**
R. Charles
C. Walker–E. Arnold,
ABC–Paramount 10345
(Hill & Range, BMI)

6. **SHE'S NOT YOU**
E. Presley
D. Pomus–H. Stoller–J. Leiber,
Victor 8041 (Elvis Presley, BMI)

7. **THINGS**
B. Darin
B. Darin, Atco 6229
(Adaris, BMI)

8. **ROSES ARE RED**
B. Vinton
P. Evans–A. Byron, Epic 9509
(Lyle, ASCAP)

9. **VACATION**
C. Francis
Hunter–Francis–Weston, M-G-M
13087 (Merna, BMI)

10. **LITTLE DIANE**
Dion
D. DiMucci, Laurie 3134
(Disal, ASCAP)

September 8

1. **SHIELA**
   T. Roe
   T. Roe, ABC–Paramount 10329
   (Eager–Nitetime, BMI)

2. **YOU DON'T KNOW ME**
   R. Charles
   C. Walker–E. Arnold,
   ABC–Paramount 10345
   (Hill & Range, BMI)

3. **LOCO-MOTION**
   Little Eva
   G. Goffin–C. King, Dimension
   1000 (Aldon, BMI)

4. **RAMBLIN' ROSE**
   Nat (King) Cole
   J. Sherman–N. Sherman, Capital
   4804 (Comet, ASCAP)

5. **SHE'S NOT YOU**
   E. Presley
   D. Pomus–H. Stoller–J. Leiber,
   Victor 8041 (Elvis Presley, BMI)

6. **BREAKING UP IS HARD TO DO**
   N. Sedaka
   N. Sedaka–H. Greenfield, Victor
   8046 (Aldon, BMI)

7. **PARTY LIGHTS**
   C. Clark
   C. Clark, Chancellor 113
   (Rambed, BMI)

8. **THINGS**
   B. Darin
   B. Darin, Atco 6229
   (Adaris, BMI)

9. **TEEN AGE IDOL**
   R. Nelson
   J. Lewis, Imperial 5864
   (Nelson, ASCAP)

10. **VACATION**
    C. Francis
    Hunter–Francis–Weston,
    M-G-M 13087
    (Merna, BMI)

September 15

1. **SHERRY**
   The Four Seasons
   B. Guadio, VeeJay 456
   (Bobob, ASCAP)

2. **SHEILA**
   T. Roe
   T. Roe, ABC–Paramount 10329
   (Eager–Nitetime, BMI)

3. **RAMBLIN' ROSE**
   Nat (King) Cole
   J. Sherman–N. Sherman,
   Capitol 4804 (Comet, ASCAP)

4. **LOCO-MOTION**
   Little Eva
   G. Goffin–C. King, Dimension
   1000 (Aldon, BMI)

5. **GREEN ONIONS**
   Booker T and the MG's
   Jones–Cropper–Steinberg–Johnson,
   Stax 127 (East, BMI)

6. **SHE' NOT YOU**
   E. Presley
   D. Pomus–H. Stoller–J. Leiber,
   Victor 8041 (Elvis Presley, BMI)

7. **TEEN AGE IDOL**
   R. Nelson
   J. Lewis, Imperial 5864
   (Nelson, ASCAP)

8. **YOU DON'T KNOW ME**
   R. Charles
   C. Walker–E. Arnold, ABC–
   Paramount 10345 (Hill & Range,
   BMI)

9. **PATCHES**
   D. Lee
   B. Mann–L. Kolber, Smash 1758
   (Aldon, BMI)

10. **RINKY DINK**
    C. (Baby) Cortez
    Clowney–Winley, Chess 1829
    (Arc-Cortez, BMI)

September 22

1. **SHERRY**
   The Four Seasons
   B. Gaudio, VeeJay 456
   (Bobob, ASCAP)

2. **SHEILA**
   T. Roe
   T. Roe, ABC–Paramount 10329
   (Eager–Nitetime, BMI)

3. **RAMBLIN' ROSE**
   Nat (King) Cole
   J. Sherman–N. Sherman, Capitol
   4804 (Comet, ASCAP)

4. **LET'S DANCE**
   C. Montez
   Lee, Monogram 505
   (Rondell and Sherman–DeVorzon,
   BMI)

5. **GREEN ONIONS**
   Booker T and the MG's
   Jones–Cropper–Steinberg–Johnson,
   Stax 127 (East, BMI)

6. **TEEN AGE IDOL**
   R. Nelson
   J. Lewis, Imperial 5864
   (Nelson, ASCAP)

7. **PATCHES**
   D. Lee
   B. Mann–L. Kolber, Smash 1758
   (Aldon, BMI)

8. **YOU BEAT ME TO THE PUNCH**
   M. Wells
   W. Robinson–R. White, Motown
   1032 (Jobete, BMI)

9. **SHE'S NOT YOU**
   E. Presley
   D. Pomus–M. Stoller–J. Leiber,
   Victor 8041 (Elvis Presley, BMI)

10. **YOU BELONG TO ME**
    The Duprees
    P. King–R. Stewart–C. Pierce,
    Coed 569 (Highway, BMI)

September 29

1. **SHERRY**
The Four Seasons
*B. Guadio, VeeJay 456
(Bobob, ASCAP)*

2. **GREEN ONIONS**
Booker T and the MG's
*Jones–Cropper–Steinberg–Johnson,
Stax 127 (East, BMI)*

3. **RAMBLIN' ROSE**
Nat (King) Cole
*J. Sherman–N. Sherman, Capitol
4804 (Comet, ASCAP)*

4. **LET'S DANCE**
C. Montez
*Lee, Monogram 505
(Rondell and Sherman–DeVorzon,
BMI)*

5. **MONSTER MASH**
B. (Boris) Pickett and the
Crypt Kickers
*B. Pickett–L. Capizzi, Garpax
44167 (Garpax. BMI)*

6. **ALLEY CAT**
B. Fabric
*Bjora, Atco 6226
(Meterion, BMI)*

7. **SHEILA**
T. Roe
*T. Roe, ABC–Paramount 10329
(Eager–Nitetime, BMI)*

8. **TEEN AGE IDOL**
R. Nelson
*J. Lewis, Imperial 5864
(Nelson, ASCAP)*

9. **YOU BELONG TO ME**
The Duprees
*P. King–R. Stewart–C. Pierce,
Coed 569 (Highway, BMI)*

10. **YOU BEAT ME TO THE
PUNCH**
M. Wells
*W. Robinson–R. White, Motown
1032 (Jobete, BMI)*

October 6

1. **SHERRY**
The Four Seasons
*B. Gaudio, VeeJay 456
(Bobob, ASCAP)*

2. **MONSTER MASH**
B. (Boris) Pickett and the
Crypt Kickers
*B. Pickett–L. Capizzi, Garpax
44167 (Garpax, BMI)*

3. **RAMBLIN' ROSE**
Nat (King) Cole
*J. Sherman–N. Sherman,
Capitol 4804
(Comet, ASCAP)*

4. **LET'S DANCE**
C. Montez
*Lee, Monogram 505
(Rondell and Sherman–DeVorzon,
BMI)*

5. **GREEN ONIONS**
Booker T and the MG's
*Jones–Cropper–Steinberg–Johnson,
Stax 127 (East, BMI)*

6. **PATCHES**
D. Lee
*B. Mann–L. Kolber, Smash 1758
(Aldon, BMI)*

7. **VENUS IN BLUE JEANS**
J. Clanton
*H. Greenfield–Keller, Ace 8001
(Aldon, BMI)*

8. **I REMEMBER YOU**
F. Ifield
*Mercer–Schertzinger, VeeJay
457 (Paramount, ASCAP)*

9. **ALLEY CAT**
B. Fabric
*Bjora, Atco 6226
(Metorion, BMI)*

10. **YOU BEAT ME TO THE
PUNCH**
M. Wells
*W. Robinson–R. White,
Motown 1032 (Jobete, BMI)*

October 13

1. **SHERRY**
The Four Seasons
*B. Gaudio, VeeJay 456
(Bobob, ASCAP)*

2. **MONSTER MASH**
B. (Boris) Pickett and the
Crypt Kickers
*B. Pickett–L. Capizzi,
Garpax 44167 (Garpax, BMI)*

3. **RAMBLIN' ROSE**
Nat (King) Cole
*J. Sherman–N. Sherman, Capitol
4804 (Comet, ASCAP)*

4. **LET'S DANCE**
C. Montez
*Lee, Monogram 505
(Rondell and Sherman–DeVorzon,
BMI)*

5. **I REMEMBER YOU**
F. Ifield
*Mercor–Schertzinger, VeeJay
457 (Paramount, ASCAP)*

6. **GREEN ONIONS**
Booker T and the MG's
*Jones–Cropper–Steinberg–
Stax 127 (East, BMI)*

7. **DO YOU LOVE ME**
The Contours
*B. Gordy, Jr., Gordy 7005
(Jobete, BMI)*

8. **PATCHES**
D. Lee
*B. Mann–L. Kolber, Smash 1758
(Aldon, BMI)*

9. **ALLEY CAT**
B. Fabric
*Bjora, Atco 6226
(Metorion, BMI)*

10. **IF I HAD A HAMMER**
Peter, Paul and Mary
*P. Seeger–Hays, Warner Brothers
5296 (Ludlow, BMI)*

October 20

1. **MONSTER MASH**
B. (Boris) Pickett and the
Crypt Kickers
*B. Pickett–L. Capizzi, Garpax
44167 (Garpax, BMI)*

2. **SHERRY**
The Four Seasons
*B. Gaudio, VeeJay 456
(Bobob, ASCAP)*

3. **DO YOU LOVE ME?**
The Contours
*B. Gordy, Jr., Gordy 7005
(Jobete, BMI)*

4. **HE'S A REBEL**
The Crystals
*G. Piney, Philles 106
(January, BMI)*

5. **I REMEMBER YOU**
F. Ifield
*Mercor–Schertzinger, VeeJay
457 (Paramount, ASCAP)*

6. **PATCHES**
D. Lee
*B. Mann–L. Kolber, Smash 1758
(Aldon, BMI)*

7. **ONLY LOVE CAN BREAK A
HEART**
G. Pitney
*H. David–B. Bacharach,
Musicor 1022
(Arch, ASCAP)*

8. **GREEN ONIONS**
Booker T and the MG's
*Jones–Cropper–Steinberg–Johnson,
Stax 127 (East, BMI)*

9. **RAMBLIN' ROSE**
Nat (King) Cole
*J. Sherman–N. Sherman,
Capitol 4804 (Comet, ASCAP)*

10. **LET'S DANCE**
C. Montez
*Lee, Monogram 505
(Rondell and Sherman–DeVorzon,
BMI)*

October 27

1. **HE'S A REBEL**
The Crystals
*G. Pitney, Philles 106
(January, BMI)*

2. **DO YOU LOVE ME?**
The Contours
*B. Gordy, Jr., Gordy 7005
(Jobete, BMI)*

3. **MONSTER MASH**
B. (Boris) Pickett and the
Crypt Kickers
*B. Pickett–L. Capizzi, Garpax
44167 (Garpax, BMI)*

4. **SHERRY**
The Four Seasons
*B. Gaudio, VeeJay 456
(Bobob, ASCAP)*

5. **ALL ALONE AM I**
B. Lee
*Hadjidakis–Altman, Decca
31424 (Duchess, BMI)*

6. **ONLY LOVE CAN BREAK A
HEART**
G. Pitney
*H. David–B. Bacharach,
Musicor 1022 (Arch, ASCAP)*

7. **GINA**
J. Mathis
*P. Vance–L. Carr, Columbia
42582 (Elm Drive, ASCAP)*

8. **I REMEMBER YOU**
F. Ifield
*Mercer–Schertzinger, VeeJay
457 (Paramount, ASCAP)*

9. **RAMBLIN' ROSE**
Nat (King) Cole
*J. Sherman–N. Sherman, Capitol
4804 (Comet, ASCAP)*

10. **PATCHES**
D. Lee
*B. Mann–L. Kolber, Smash 1758
(Aldon, BMI)*

November 3

1. **HE'S A REBEL**
The Crystals
*G. Pitney, Philles 106
(January, BMI)*

2. **ONLY LOVE CAN BREAK A
HEART**
G. Pitney
*H. David–B. Bacharach,
Musicor 1022 (Arch, ASCAP)*

3. **DO YOU LOVE ME?**
The Contours
*B. Gordy, Jr., Gordy 7005
(Jobete, BMI)*

4. **ALL ALONE AM I**
B. Lee
*Hadjidakis–Altman,
Decca 31424
(Duchess, BMI)*

5. **MONSTER MASH**
B. (Boris) Pickett and the
Crypt–Kickers
*B. Pickett–G. Capizzi,
Garpax 44167 (Garpax, BMI)*

6. **BIG GIRLS DON'T CRY**
The Four Seasons
*B. Crewe–B. Gaudio, VeeJay
465 (Bobob, ASCAP)*

7. **GINA**
J. Mathis
*P. Vance–L. Carr, Columbia
42582 (Elm Drive, ASCAP)*

8. **LIMBO ROCK**
C. Checker
*W. Strange, Parkway 849
(Four Star–Twist, BMI)*

9. **NEXT DOOR TO AN ANGEL**
N. Sedaka
*H. Greenfield–N. Sedaka,
Victor 8086 (Aldon, BMI)*

10. **RETURN TO SENDER**
E. Presley
*O. Blackwell–W. Scott, Victor
8100 (Elvis Presley, BMI)*

November 10

1. **HE'S A REBEL**
The Crystals
G. Pitney, Philles 106
(January, BMI)

2. **BIG GIRLS DON'T CRY**
The Four Seasons
B. Crewe–B. Gaudio, VeeJay
465 (Bobob, ASCAP)

3. **ALL ALONE AM I**
B. Lee
Hadjidakis–Altman, Decca
31424 (Duchess, BMI)

4. **RETURN TO SENDER**
E. Presley
O. Blackwell–W. Scott, Victor
8100 (Elvis Presley, BMI)

5. **ONLY LOVE CAN BREAK A HEART**
G. Pitney
H. David–B. Bacharach,
Musicor 1022 (Arch, ASCAP)

6. **NEXT DOOR TO AN ANGEL**
N. Sedaka
H. Greenfield–N. Sedaka, Victor
8086 (Aldon, BMI)

7. **GINA**
J. Mathis
P. Vance–L. Carr, Columbia
42582 (Elm Drive, ASCAP)

8. **MONSTER MASH**
B. (Boris) Pickett and the Crypt Kickers
B. Pickett–L. Capizzi,
Garpax 44167 (Garpax, BMI)

9. **DO YOU LOVE ME?**
The Contours
B. Gordy, Jr., Gordy 7005
(Jobete, BMI)

10. **POPEYE THE HITCH-HIKER**
C. Checker
K. Appell–Mann, Parkway 849
(Kalmann, ASCAP)

November 17

1. **BIG GIRLS DON'T CRY**
The Four Seasons
B. Crewe–B. Gaudio,
VeeJay 465 (Bobob, ASCAP)

2. **RETURN TO SENDER**
E. Presley
O. Blackwell–W. Scott,
Victor 8100 (Elvis Presley, BMI)

3. **HE'S A REBEL**
The Crystals
G. Pitney, Philles 106
(January, BMI)

4. **ALL ALONE AM I**
B. Lee
Hadjidakis–Altman,
Decca 31424 (Duchess, BMI)

5. **NEXT DOOR TO AN ANGEL**
N. Sedaka
H. Greenfield–N. Sedaka,
Victor 8086 (Aldon, BMI)

6. **GINA**
J. Mathis
P. Vance–L. Carr, Columbia
42582 (Elm Drive, ASCAP)

7. **BOBBY'S GIRL**
M. Blane
Hoffman–Klein, Seville 120
(A.M.E., BMI)

8. **DON'T HANG UP**
The Orlons
Mann–Appell, Cameo 231
(Kalmann, ASCAP)

9. **LIMBO ROCK**
C. Checker
W. Strange, Parkway 849
(Four Star–Twist, BMI)

10. **THE CHA CHA CHA**
B. Rydell
Mann–Appell, Cameo 228
(Kalmann, ASCAP)

November 24

1. **BIG GIRLS DON'T CRY**
The Four Seasons
B. Crewe–B. Gaudio, VeeJay
465 (Bobob, ASCAP)

2. **RETURN TO SENDER**
E. Presley
O. Blackwell–W. Scott,
Victor 8100 (Elvis Presley, BMI)

3. **NEXT DOOR TO AN ANGEL**
N. Sedaka
H. Greenfield–N. Sedaka,
Victor 8086 (Aldon, BMI)

4. **ALL ALONE AM I**
B. Lee
Hadjidakis–Altman, Decca
31424 (Duchess, BMI)

5. **BOBBY'S GIRL**
M. Blane
Hoffman–Klein, Seville 120
(A.M.E., BMI)

6. **LIMBO ROCK**
C. Checker
W. Strange, Parkway 849
(Four Star–Twist, BMI)

7. **HE'S A REBEL**
The Crystals
G. Pitney, Philles 106
(January, BMI)

8. **RIDE!**
D. Sharp
Sheldon–Leon, Cameo 230
(Woodcrest–Check–Colt, BMI)

9. **GINA**
J. Mathis
P. Vance–L. Carr, Columbia
42582 (Elm Drive, ASCAP)

10. **DON'T HANG UP**
The Orlons
K. Mann–Appell, Cameo 231
(Kalmann, ASCAP)

December 1

1. **BIG GIRLS DON'T CRY**
The Four Seasons
B. Crewe–B. Gaudio, VeeJay
465 (Bobob, ASCAP)

2. **RETURN TO SENDER**
E. Presley
O. Blackwell–W. Scott, Victor
8100 (Elvis Presley, BMI)

3. **LIMBO ROCK**
C. Checker
W. Strange, Parkway 849
(Four Star–Twist, BMI)

4. **BOBBY'S GIRL**
M. Blane
Hoffman–Klein, Seville 120
(A.M.E., BMI)

5. **RIDE!**
D. Sharp
Sheldon–Leon, Cameo 230
(Woodcrest–Check–Colt, BMI)

6. **ALL ALONE AM I**
B. Lee
Hadjidakis–Altman, Decca
31424 (Duchess, BMI)

7. **HE'S A REBEL**
The Crystals
G. Pitney, Philles 106
(January, BMI)

8. **THE LONELY BULL**
The Tijuana Brass
S. Lake, A. and M. 703
(Almo, ASCAP)

9. **NEXT DOOR TO AN ANGEL**
N. Sedaka
H. Greenfield–N. Sedaka,
Victor 8086 (Aldon, BMI)

10. **DON'T HANG UP**
The Orlons
K. Mann–Appell, Cameo 231
(Kalmann, ASCAP)

December 8

1. **BIG GIRLS DON'T CRY**
The Four Seasons
B. Crewe–B. Gaudio, VeeJay
465 (Bobob, ASCAP)

2. **RETURN TO SENDER**
E. Presley
O. Blackwell–W. Scott,
Victor 8100 (Elvis Presley, BMI)

3. **BOBBY'S GIRL**
M. Blane
Hoffman–Klein, Seville 120
(A.M.E., BMI)

4. **LIMBO ROCK**
C. Checker
W. Strange, Parkway 849
(Four Star–Twist, BMI)

5. **RIDE!**
D. Sharp
Sheldon–Leon, Cameo 230
(Woodcrest–Check–Colt, BMI)

6. **THE LONELY BULL**
The Tijuana Brass
S. Lake, A. and M. 703
(Almo, ASCAP)

7. **TELSTAR**
Tornadoes
Meek, London 9561
(Campbell Conelly, ASCAP)

8. **HE'S A REBEL**
The Crystals
G. Pitney, Philles 106
(January, BMI)

9. **ALL ALONE AM I**
B. Lee
Hadjidakis–Altman, Decca
31424 (Duchess, BMI)

10. **RELEASE ME**
"Little Esther" Phillips
Miller–Williams–Yount, Lenox
5555 (Four Star Sales, BMI)

December 15

1. **BIG GIRLS DON'T CRY**
The Four Seasons
B. Crewe–B. Gaudio, VeeJay
465 (Bobob, ASCAP)

2. **RETURN TO SENDER**
E. Presley
O. Blackwell–W. Scott, Victor
8100 (Elvis Presley, BMI)

3. **BOBBY'S GIRL**
M. Blane
Hoffman–Klein, Seville 120
(A.M.E., BMI)

4. **LIMBO ROCK**
C. Checker
W. Strange, Parkway 849
(Four Star–Twist, BMI)

5. **TELSTAR**
Tornadoes
Meek, London 9561
(Campbell Conelly, ASCAP)

6. **LONELY BULL**
The Tijuana Brass
S. Lake, A. and M. 703
(Almo, ASCAP)

7. **RIDE!**
D. Sharp
Sheldon–Leon, Cameo 230
(Woodcrest–Check–Colt, BMI)

8. **RELEASE ME**
"Little Esther" Phillips
Miller–Williams–Yount, Lenox
5555 (Four Star Sales, BMI)

9. **GO AWAY LITTLE GIRL**
S. Lawrence
G. Goffin–C. King, Columbia
42601 (Aldon, BMI)

10. **YOU ARE MY SUNSHINE**
R. Charles
J.Davis–C. Mitchell, ABC-
Paramount 10375 (Peer-
International, BMI)

December 22

1. **TELSTAR**
The Tornadoes
Meek, London 9561 (Campbell Conelly, ASCAP)

2. **LIMBO ROCK**
C. Checker
W. Strange, Parkway 849 (Four Star–Twist, BMI)

3. **RETURN TO SENDER**
E. Presley
O. Blackwell–W. Scott, Victor 8100 (Elvis Presley, BMI)

4. **BOBBY'S GIRL**
M. Blane
Hoffman–Klein, Seville 120 (A.M.E., BMI)

5. **BIG GIRLS DON'T CRY**
The Four Seasons
B. Crewe–B. Gaudio, VeeJay 465 (Bobob, ASCAP)

6. **LONELY BULL**
The Tijuana Brass
S. Lake, A. and M. 703 (Almo, ASCAP)

7. **GO AWAY LITTLE GIRL**
S. Lawrence
G. Goffin–C. King, Columbia 42601 (Aldon, BMI)

8. **RELEASE ME**
"Little Esther" Phillips
Miller–Williams–Yount, Lenox 5555 (Four Star Sales, BMI)

9. **YOU ARE MY SUNSHINE**
R. Charles
J. Davis–C. Mitchell, ABC–Paramount 10375 (Peer–International, BMI)

10. **LOVE CAME TO ME**
Dion
D. DiMucci–J. Falbo, Laurie 3145 (Schwartz–Disal, ASCAP)

December 29

1. **TELSTAR**
The Tornadoes
Meek, London 9561 (Campbell Conelly, ASCAP)

2. **LIMBO ROCK**
C. Checker
W. Strange, Parkway 849 (Four Star–Twist, BMI)

3. **BOBBY'S GIRL**
M. Blane
Hoffman–Klein, Seville 120 (A.M.E., BMI)

4. **GO AWAY LITTLE GIRL**
S. Lawrence
G. Goffin–C. King, Columbia 42601 (Aldon, BMI)

5. **BIG GIRLS DON'T CRY**
The Four Seasons
B. Crewe–B. Gaudio, VeeJay 465 (Bobob, ASCAP)

6. **RETURN TO SENDER**
E. Presley
O. Blackwell–W. Scott, Victor 8100 (Elvis Presley, BMI)

7. **YOU ARE MY SUNSHINE**
R. Charles
J. Davis–C. Mitchell, ABC–Paramount 10375 (Peer–International, BMI)

8. **RELEASE ME**
"Little Esther" Phillips
Miller–Williams–Yount, Lenox 5555 (Four Star, BMI)

9. **ZIP-A-DEE-DOO-DAH**
B. Soxx and the Blue Jeans
R. Gilbert–A. Wrubel, Philles 107 (Joy, ASCAP)

10. **HOTEL HAPPINESS**
B. Benton
L. Carr–E. Shuman, Mercury 72055 (Dayben-Mansion, ASCAP)

THE FOUR SEASONS

We rocked into 1963 on the momentum we had built up in the last great year. The music was as wonderful as we had expected. And now it was developing new depths with the incorporation of folk, surf, Motown, and Bossa Nova into the simpler rock and roll of the old days.

We were developing, too. By 1963 more of us had finished high school than hadn't. We were going out into the world now, finding jobs, getting married, going to trade schools and to college. We were moving out of our parents' homes and were shedding our fears of their criticism. And as we began to feel the joys of this new independence, the adults also became aware of us as the living future. President Kennedy had first made us aware of our potential, but it was hard at sixteen to feel like we could really change the world.

Suddenly now, with our diplomas in hand, we were ready to believe that we were the generation that would turn history around. Adults who had never taken us seriously were suddenly studying our dances, language, dress, and ideas. The advertising world focused on the magic of youth. Fashion ranging from Paris to the new discount stores emphasized the youth look—loose fitting, short, free, with high boots, stretch pants, ski sweaters, textured stockings.

It was youth in politics, too. Not only the handsome young Kennedy men, but an egalitarian liberal young outlook. The new word was civil liberties, the new emphasis was human dignity for the black man, a living wage for the poor man, health care for the old man. The first great freedom march on Washington was mobilized in August with two hundred thousand marchers there to impress on a balky Congress the need for the Kennedy Civil Rights bill. Though the bill never even got to the floor of the House, it was clear the administration had enough popular support to end the legal barriers to voting, housing, and educational freedom.

1963

SUNNNDAY! At beautiful U.S. 20 Dragway . . .

See Danny Darmin in his record-holding jet engine Dragon Dragster . . .

Floyd Fenster in his fuel-injected multi-color Mad, Mad Maverick . . .

And straight from the world's finals, the California turbine dragster XZ 2000!

See them all . . . Danny Darmin, Floyd Fenster, the XZ 2000 . . . plus funny cars, bikes, hot rods and Miss Arizona A-Go-Go!

Sunday . . . 2 P.M. at U.S. 20 Dragway

The Supreme Court was also ready to break with the past. Their ruling to end prayer in the public schools would cause as much controversy as any decision since their order to desegregate schools in 1954.

The Vatican, too, took a step out of the past when Pope John struck the reference to "perifidious Jews" from a Roman Catholic prayer and lifted the blame for Jesus' crucifixion from the Jews to all mankind.

Even the music of youth was catching the ear of the adults. Since their discovery of the twist they were ready to try any new dances we had to offer. And in 1963 we had plenty. Chubby Checker, in the tradition of the twist, pony and fly, was now singing the praises of the limbo. This dance was more of a novelty or a party game than a dance that everyone could do. But the bird and the hitchhiker were everything that the twist had been. Once you caught the movement in the hips you were home free. And your arms could do anything, so each of us had a little area of self-expression. All of this hip-swiveling would eventually fall into the general category of the frug which would dominate our dancing into 1964 and the adults dancing for the rest of the decade.

For the set that still paid for dancing lessons, the Bossa Nova was the latest. But for us it was mostly listening music—we had given up the Latin beats with the decline of the chalypso.

New sounds were making the Top 10 in 1963. The heretofore esoteric folk sound had filled out into the soaring happy group sing, or hootenanny. Television encouraged this good, clean, often idealistic singing. And the Kingston Trio, Peter, Paul and Mary, Joan Baez, Pete Seeger and the Christie Minstrels did a booming business at college homecomings and the like.

The Motown sound also came into its own in 1963. Berry Gordy, Smokey Robinson *et al.* had been making some headway into the Top 10's with some records by Martha and the Vandellas and the Miracles. But in 1963 their labels hit time after time—"Two Lovers," "You've Really Got a Hold on Me," "Come and Get These Memories," "Fingertips," "Heatwave," "Mickey's Monkey," "Quicksand." Mary Wells, Stevie Wonder, Holland, Dozier and Holland staked their claims on the leading positions in the newest successful soul movement.

Girls, too, took a big step forward in rock and roll. In addition to Mary Wells and Martha Reeves, it was the year for Leslie Gore, Little Peggy March, Deedee Sharp and Skeeter Davis. Just a few years ago the only girls who had any success were Annette and Connie Francis and possibly Linda Scott. Of course there were the Shirelles who had had hit after hit since the late fifties and made the Top 10 in 1963 with "Foolish Little Girl."

But now they were joined by a barrage of new girl groups all with the charm and excitement of the Shirelles or the old Bobbettes. The Chiffons, the Angels, the Coolies, the Jaynettes, the Crystals and the Ronnettes all added a fresh new sound, a new solid dancable dimension to rock and roll. Sadly, these groups would fade into oblivion with the coming British invasion, but songs like "He's So Fine", "DaDoo Ron Ron," "My Boyfriend's Back" and "Be My Baby" would be remembered as rock and roll classics even after the Britons had fallen into decay.

There was another new sound budding on the West Coast—the surf sound of the Beach Boys and Jan and Dean. The year 'round sun and sea had gone to the blond heads of the Southern Californians and they began to view the Los Angeles basin as the center of the world. It was in the great Southwest that the car culture, too, began to boom. Not since the '51 Ford with mud flaps and a raccoon tail on the aerial had the automobile been so important a status symbol. In the West, with almost no public transportation, the automobile was such a necessity that kids commonly had their own cars and weren't dependent on the family station wagon. To these car cultists their vehicles were more than a way of getting places, they were a way of life. Naturally some cars were more desirable than others. The 1955, 1956 and 1957 Chevy hardtop was the general favorite—the two-door, built up with mags or chrome wheels, oversized tires and a taxicab yellow paint job. It's hard to understand the beauty in so grotesquely distorted an automobile, but it was more desirable that a 1963 Cadillac. Only a flashy new Corvette or XKE could compete.

Boys threw around talk about overhead cams, fuel injection, wheel bases, turbines, intake, exotic fuels. It put a lot of pressure on girls to learn to love the hum of a well-tuned engine and to give up picnics and movies for dates at the drag strip or cruising the town's main drag. A girl had to appreciate her date's need to blast away from the drive-in, leaving a cloud of dust and ten feet of rubber.

So we added car talk to that generally dull fund of knowledge we girls had to acquire if we didn't want to be left talking to each other on double dates. Now we not only knew that Koufax, Drysdale and Podres pitched the Dodgers to victory over the Yankees, and that those Yankees so completely dominated the American League that we only had to pay attention to the National League race, and that Ara Parseghian was leaving Northwestern for Notre Dame, and that Sonny Liston knocked out Floyd Patterson again and would fight Cassius Clay in 1964. Now we knew about funny cars, and where to find the midnight

drags and when to take out shocks and put in roll bars.

Those of us who left home to go to college found tons of another kind of new information to digest. It was shock enough to eat dorm food and share a bathroom with twenty other kids, but we also had to learn enough about the issues of the day to keep up with all the endless discussions. Those of us who had gossiped about cheerleader tryouts over French fries were now talking about world events over black coffee. Was there really an easing of tension between the United States and Russia? Had the Cuban crisis been handled well? Was the new Hot Line of any value?

We joined the campus political clubs—young Democrats, Republicans and at the most avant-garde schools, SDS. We debated the crisis in Southeast Asia, the impact of the Buddhists burning themselves, the overthrow of the Diem regime.

We questioned the survival of the Republican party and half laughed at the rash of "AuH$_2$O 1964" stickers.

We followed JFK's trip to Europe and applauded him as he charmed the Irish and the West Berliners.

We couldn't help being amazed by the birth of the Fischer quintuplets in South Dakota and couldn't help being amused as Christine Keeler became an overnight celebrity in England.

And yet with all the serious debate on campus, all the differences between roommates, fraternities, political groups, hometowns, we were joined by a common bond of rock and roll. Music poured through the dorms and the most popular rooms were those with the stereos. Dancing styles from different high schools melded together. Surfers, folk fans and devotees of soul found their tastes mingling in this new communal setting.

Suddenly, as we were laughing at elephant jokes, learning the monkey, considering the

Surgeon-General's report and looking forward to Thanksgiving vacation, the whole world seemed to crash. The Top 40 was interrupted. There was a strange ripple through the cafeteria. Strangers questioned strangers on the street. Curiosity, tension, shock hung heavily in the air.

The President has been shot.

The President has been shot.

We collected around radios, televisions. We had to know—to see. God, don't let it be true. Let him live, please. But we saw their faces. The men who had told us about his election. The men of the networks whom we trusted to tell us what was going on in the world, the men who always kept their wits, their perspective. They were crying.

There was no chance. A priest had been called in.

Don't tell us he's dead.

We tried to concentrate on the drone from the television—Parkland Hospital, the book depository—they were words that would be with us forever. And assassination. It belonged in a history book, not here, in this country, to this president.

Our minds rejected it. But our tears repeated what the television kept insisting—President Kennedy is dead.

It hurt so terribly. He was ours, not some old gray-haired politician. We had watched him every day on the news, at press conferences, so sweet with his children, so full of grace and humor. He meant so much to us—our President—young and inspiring and in love with humanity.

We all sat in front of our televisions those next few days. And through our tears we saw a melodrama that seems, in retrospect, a painful gray dream.

We listened as they tracked Lee Harvey Oswald, as the Stock Exchange was closed, as the dead President was flown back to Washington.

While we waited solemnly for the lulling rituals of the funeral, we saw on all three networks a man push through the crowd and murder the suspected assassin. We were one hundred million people, too numb to understand the horror of witnessing this second murder in three days.

In the next days we sat, hollow and aching, as Mrs. Kennedy and the dead President's family moved through the ceremonies of burial with quiet dignity. We felt the grandeur of the Mass, the procession and the imposing spectacle of the world's leaders gathered together to comfort our nation's sorrow.

When these days of pomp and ritual came to an end the country was somehow able to keep going. President Johnson's strength and dignity carried the government along.

1963 came quietly to an end. It hurt too much to think about what had happened in Dallas and it hurt too much to forget it. The Kennedy sparkle was gone. All the joy of the first eleven months of the year was forgotten. The year would be remembered for its weekend of tragedy, a tragedy that was ours especially. Ours because we were the young—the future that he had loved and believed in.

THE TOP FIFTY
1963

1. LOUIE, LOUIE — The Kingsmen
2. FINGERTIPS (PART II) — Little Stevie Wonder
3. MY BOYFRIEND'S BACK — The Angels
4. SUKIYAKI — K. Sakamoto
5. SUGAR SHACK — J. Gilmer and the Fireballs
6. SURFIN' USA — The Beach Boys
7. I WILL FOLLOW HIM — Little Peggy March
8. CAN'T GET USED TO LOSING YOU — A. Williams
9. OUR DAY WILL COME — Ruby and the Romantics
10. HE'S SO FINE — The Chiffons
11. WALK LIKE A MAN — The Four Seasons
12. WALK RIGHT IN — The Rooftop Singers
13. HEY PAULA — Paul and Paula
14. GO AWAY LITTLE GIRL — S. Lawrence
15. TELSTAR — The Tornadoes
16. THE END OF THE WORLD — S. Davis
17. DO DOO RON RON — The Crystals
18. BLUE VELVET — B. Vinton
19. HELLO STRANGER — B. Lewis
20. SO MUCH IN LOVE — The Tymes
21. CANDY GIRL — The Four Seasons
22. UP ON THE ROOF — The Drifters
23. YOU'VE REALLY GOT A HOLD ON ME — The Miracles
24. RHYTHM OF THE RAIN — The Cascades
25. IT'S MY PARTY — Leslie Gore
26. EASIER SAID THAN DONE — The Essex
27. HELLO MUDDAH, HELLO FADDUH — A. Sherman
28. IF YOU WANNA BE HAPPY — J. Soul
29. TWO LOVERS — M. Wells
30. MAMA DIDN'T LIE — J. Bradley
31. THE GYPSY CRIED — L. Christie
32. PUFF (THE MAGIC DRAGON) — Peter, Paul and Mary
33. PIPELINE — The Chantays
34. YOU CAN'T SIT DOWN — The Dovells
35. DOMINIQUE — The Singing Nun
36. DEEP PURPLE — A. Stevens and N. Tempo
37. SINCE I FELL FOR YOU — L. Welsh
38. MONKEY TIME — M. Lance
39. HEAT WAVE — Martha and the Vandellas
40. SURF CITY — Jan and Dean
41. TELL HIM — The Exciters
42. IF I HAD A HAMMER — T. Lopez
43. SALLY GO 'ROUND THE ROSES — The Jaynettes
44. BE MY BABY — The Ronettes
45. JUST ONE LOOK — D. Troy
46. TIE ME KANGAROO DOWN, SPORT — R. Harris
47. THE NIGHT HAS A THOUSAND EYES — B. Vee
48. SOUTH STREET — The Orlons
49. TWO FACES HAVE I — L. Christie
50. ON BROADWAY — The Drifters

January 5

1. **TELSTAR**
   The Tornadoes
   Meek, London 9561 (Campbell Conelly, ASCAP)

2. **GO AWAY LITTLE GIRL**
   S. Lawrence
   G. Goffin–C. King. Columbia 42601 (Aldon, BMI)

3. **LIMBO ROCK**
   C. Checker
   W. Strange, Parkway 849 (Four Star–Twist, BMI)

4. **BOBBY'S GIRL**
   M. Blane
   Hoffman–Klein, Seville 120 (A.M.E., BMI)

5. **BIG GIRLS DON'T CRY**
   The Four Seasons
   B. Crewe–B. Gaudio, VeeJay 465 (Bobob, ASCAP)

6. **HOTEL HAPPINESS**
   B. Benton
   L. Carr–E. Shuman, Mercury 72055 (Dahben–Mansion, ASCAP)

7. **PEPINO THE ITALIAN MOUSE**
   L. Monte
   Allen–Merrell, Reprise 20106 (Romance–Ding Dong, BMI)

8. **RETURN TO SENDER**
   E. Presley
   O. Blackwell–W. Scott, Victor 8100 (Elvis Presley, BMI)

9. **ZIP-A-DEE-DOO-DAH**
   B. Soxx and the Blue Jeans
   R. Gilbert–A. Wrubel, Philles 107 (Joy, ASCAP)

10. **TELL HIM**
    The Exciters
    B. Russell, United Artists 544 (Mellin, BMI)

January 12

1. **GO AWAY LITTLE GIRL**
   S. Lawrence
   G. Goffin–C. King. Columbia 42601 (Aldon, BMI)

2. **TELSTAR**
   The Tornadoes
   Meek, London 9561 (Campbell Conelly, ASCAP)

3. **LIMBO ROCK**
   C. Checker
   W. Strange, Parkway 849 (Four Star–Twist, BMI)

4. **HOTEL HAPPINESS**
   B. Benton
   L. Carr–E. Shuman, Mercury 72055 (Dayben–Mansion, ASCAP)

5. **PEPINO THE ITALIAN MOUSE**
   L. Monte
   Allen–Merrell, Reprise 20106 (Romance–Ding Dong, BMI)

6. **TELL HIM**
   The Exciters
   B. Russell, United Artists 544 (Mellin, BMI)

7. **THE NIGHT HAS A THOUSAND EYES**
   B. Vee
   Weisman–Wayne–Garrett, Liberty 55521 (Blen–Mabs, ASCAP)

8. **ZIP-A-DEE-DOO-DAH**
   B. Soxx and the Blue Jeans
   R. Gilbert–A. Wrubel, Philles 107 (Joy, ASCAP)

9. **TWO LOVERS**
   M. Wells
   W. Robinson, Motown 1035 (Jobete, BMI)

10. **MY DAD**
    P. Peterson
    B. Mann–Weil, Colpix 663 (Aldon, BMI)

January 19

1. GO AWAY LITTLE GIRL
S. Lawrence
G. Goffin–C. King, Columbia 42601 (Aldon, BMI)

2. TELSTAR
The Tornadoes
Meek, London 9561 (Campbell Conelly, ASCAP)

3. HOTEL HAPPINESS
B. Benton
L. Carr–E. Shuman, Mercury 72055 (Dayben–Mansion, ASCAP)

4. LIMBO ROCK
C. Checker
W. Strange, Parkway 849 (Four Star–Twist, BMI)

5. TELL HIM
The Exciters
B. Russell, United Artists 544 (Mellin, BMI)

6. THE NIGHT HAS A THOUSAND EYES
B. Vee
Weisman–Wayne–Garrett, Liberty 55521 (Blen–Mabs, ASCAP)

7. TWO LOVERS
M. Wells
W. Robinson, Motown 1035 (Jobete, BMI)

8. PEPINO THE ITALIAN MOUSE
L. Monte
Allen–Merrell, Reprise 20106 (Romance–Ding Dong, BMI)

9. MY DAD
P. Peterson
B. Mann–Weil, Colpix 663 (Aldon, BMI)

10. WALK RIGHT IN
The Rooftop Singers
Darling–Suanoe, Era 3099 (Ryerson, BMI)

January 26

1. GO AWAY LITTLE GIRL
S. Lawrence
G. Goffin–C. King, Columbia 42601 (Aldon, BMI)

2. TELL HIM
The Exciters
B. Russell, United Artists 544 (Mellin, BMI)

3. WALK RIGHT IN
The Rooftop Singers
Darling–Suance, Era 3099 (Ryerson, BMI)

4. THE NIGHT HAS A THOUSAND EYES
B. Vee
Weisman–Wayne–Garrett, Liberty 55521 (Blen–Mabs, ASCAP)

5. TWO LOVERS
M. Wells
W. Robinson, Motown 1035 (Jobete, BMI)

6. TELSTAR
The Tornadoes
Meek, London 9561 (Campbell Conelly, ASCAP)

7. HEY PAULA
Paul and Paula
R. Hildebrand, Philips 40084 (LeBill–Marbill, BMI)

8. MY DAD
P. Peterson
B. Mann–Weil, Colpix 663 (Aldon, BMI)

9. LIMBO ROCK
C. Checker
W. Strange, Parkway 849 (Four Star–Twist, BMI)

10. LOOP DE LOOP
J. Thunder
Vann–Dong, Diamond 129 (Tobi-Ann and Vann, BMI)

February 2

1. WALK RIGHT IN
The Rooftop Singers
Darling–Suance, Era 3099 (Ryerson, BMI)

2. GO AWAY LITTLE GIRL
S. Lawrence
G. Goffin–C. King, Columbia 42601 (Aldon, BMI)

3. HEY PAULA
Paul and Paula
R. Hildebrand, Phillips 40084 (LeBill–Marbill, BMI)

4. LOOP DE LOOP
J. Thunder
Vann–Dong, Diamond 129 (Tobi-Ann and Vann, BMI)

5. THE NIGHT HAS A THOUSAND EYES
B. Vee
Weisman–Wayne–Garrett, Liberty 55521 (Blen–Mabs, ASCAP)

6. IT'S UP TO YOU
R. Nelson
J. Fuller, Imperial 5901 (Four Star, BMI)

7. UP ON THE ROOF
The Drifters
G. Goffin–C. King, Atlantic 2162 (Aldon, BMI)

8. TELL HIM
The Exciters
B. Russell, United Artists 544 (Mellin, BMI)

9. TWO LOVERS
M. Wells
W. Robinson, Motown 1035 (Jobete, BMI)

10. MY DAD
P. Peterson
B. Mann–Weil, Colpix 663 (Aldon, BMI)

February 9

1. **HEY PAULA**
Paul and Paula
R. Hildebrand, Philips 40084
(LeBill–Marbill, BMI)

2. **WALK RIGHT IN**
The Rooftop Singers
Darling–Suance, Era 3099
(Ryerson, BMI)

3. **THE NIGHT HAS A THOUSAND EYES**
B. Vee
Weisman–Wayne–Garrett,
Liberty 55521 (Blen–Mabs,
ASCAP)

4. **LOOP DE LOOP**
J. Thunder
Vann–Dong, Diamond 129
(Tobi-Ann and Vann, BMI)

5. **UP ON THE ROOF**
The Drifters
G. Goffin–C. King, Atlantic 2162
(Aldon, BMI)

6. **WALK LIKE A MAN**
The Four Seasons
B. Crewe–B. Gaudio, VeeJay 485
(Saturday–Gavadima, ASCAP)

7. **RUBY BABY**
Dion
J. Leiber–M. Stoller, Columbia
42662 (Tiger, BMI)

8. **YOU'VE REALLY GOT A HOLD ON ME**
The Miracles
W. Robinson, Tamla 54073
(Jobete, BMI)

9. **RHYTHM OF THE RAIN**
The Cascades
J. Gummoe, Valiant 6026
(Sherman–DeVorzon, BMI)

10. **GO AWAY LITTLE GIRL**
S. Lawrence
G. Goffin–C. King, Columbia
42601 (Aldon, BMI)

February 16

1. **HEY PAULA**
Paul and Paula
R. Hildebrand, Philips 40084
(LeBill–Marbill, BMI)

2. **WALK RIGHT IN**
The Rooftop Singers
Darling–Suance, Era 3099
(Ryerson, BMI)

3. **THE NIGHT HAS A THOUSAND EYES**
B. Vee
Weisman–Wayne–Garrett,
Liberty 55521 (Blen–Mabs,
ASCAP)

4. **LOOP DE LOOP**
J. Thunder
Vann–Dong, Diamond 129
(Tobi-Ann and Vann, BMI)

5. **UP ON THE ROOF**
The Drifters
G. Goffin–C. King. Atlantic 2162
(Aldon, BMI)

6. **RUBY BABY**
Dion
J. Leiber–M. Stoller, Columbia
42662 (Tiger, BMI)

7. **WALK LIKE A MAN**
The Four Seasons
B. Crewe–B. Gaudio, VeeJay 485
(Saturday–Gavadima, ASCAP)

8. **FROM A JACK TO A KING**
N. Miller
N. Miller, Fabor 114
(Dandelion, BMI)

9. **RHYTHM OF THE RAIN**
The Cascades
J. Gummoe, Valiant 6026
(Sherman–DeVorzon, BMI)

10. **YOU'VE REALLY GOT A HOLD ON ME**
The Miracles
W. Robinson, Tamla 54073
(Jobete, BMI)

February 23

1. **HEY PAULA**
Paul and Paula
R. Hildebrand, Philips 40084
(LeBill–Marbill, BMI)

2. **RUBY BABY**
Dion
J. Leiber–M. Stoller, Columbia
42662 (Tiger, BMI)

3. **WALK LIKE A MAN**
The Four Seasons
B. Crewe–B. Gaudio, VeeJay 485
(Saturday–Gavadima, ASCAP)

4. **WALK RIGHT IN**
The Rooftop Singers
Darling–Suance, Era 3099
(Ryerson, BMI)

5. **RHYTHM OF THE RAIN**
The Cascades
J. Gummoe, Valiant 6026
(Sherman–DeVorzon, BMI)

6. **FROM A JACK TO A KING**
N. Miller
N. Miller, Fabor 114
(Dandelion, BMI)

7. **YOU'RE THE REASON I'M LIVING**
B. Darin
B. Darin, Capitol 4897
(Adaris, BMI)

8. **BLAME IT ON THE BOSSA NOVA**
E. Gorme
B. Mann–Weill, Columbia 42661
(Aldon, BMI)

9. **YOU'VE REALLY GOT A HOLD ON ME**
The Miracles
W. Robinson, Tamla 54073
(Jobete, BMI)

10. **WILD WEEKEND**
The Rebels
Shannon–Todar, Swan 4125
(Shan–Todd–Tupper, BMI)

March 2

1. **WALK LIKE A MAN**
   The Four Seasons
   *B. Crewe–B. Gaudio, VeeJay 485
   (Saturday–Gavadima, ASCAP)*

2. **RUBY BABY**
   Dion
   *J. Leiber–M. Stoller, Columbia
   42662 (Tiger, BMI)*

3. **HEY PAULA**
   Paul and Paula
   *R. Hildebrand, Philips 40084
   (LeBill–Marbille, BMI)*

4. **RYTHM OF THE RAIN**
   The Cascades
   *J. Gummoe, Valiant 6026
   (Sherman–DeVorzon, BMI)*

5. **WALK RIGHT IN**
   The Rooftop Singers
   *Darling–Suance, Era 3099
   (Ryerson, BMI)*

6. **YOU'RE THE REASON
   I'M LIVING**
   B. Darin
   *B. Darin, Capitol 4897
   (Adaris, BMI)*

7. **BLAME IT ON THE BOSSA
   NOVA**
   E. Gorme
   *B. Mann–Weil, Columbia 42661
   (Aldon, BMI)*

8. **FROM A JACK TO A KING**
   N. Miller
   *N. Miller, Fabor 114
   (Dandelion, BMI)*

9. **YOU'VE REALLY GOT A
   HOLD ON ME**
   The Miracles
   *W. Robinson, Tamla 54073
   (Jobete, BMI)*

10. **WILD WEEKEND**
    The Rebels
    *Shannon–Todar, Swan 4125
    (Shan–Todd–Tupper, BMI)*

March 9

1. **RHYTHM OF THE RAIN**
   The Cascades
   *J. Gummoe, Valiant 6026
   (Sherman–DeVorzon, BMI)*

2. **RUBY BABY**
   Dion
   *J. Leiber–M. Stoller, Columbia
   42662 (Tiger, BMI)*

3. **WALK LIKE A MAN**
   The Four Seasons
   *B. Crewe–B. Gaudio, VeeJay 485
   (Saturday–Gavadima, ASCAP)*

4. **HEY PAULA**
   Paul and Paula
   *R. Hildebrand, Philips 40084
   (LeBill–Marbill, BMI)*

5. **OUR DAY WILL COME**
   Ruby and the Romantics
   *B. Hilliard–Garson, Kapp 501
   (Rosewood, ASCAP)*

6. **THE GYPSY CRIED**
   L. Christie
   *Herbert–Sacco, Roulette 4457
   (Painted Desert, BMI)*

7. **THE END OF THE WORLD**
   S. Davis
   *Dee–Kent, Victor 8098
   (Summit, ASCAP)*

8. **YOU'RE THE REASON**
   B. Darin
   *B. Darin, Capitol 4897
   (Adaris, BMI)*

9. **WILD WEEKEND**
   The Rebels
   *Shannon–Todar, Swan 4125
   (Shan–Todd–Tupper, BMI)*

10. **HE'S SO FINE**
    The Chiffons
    *R. Mack, Laurie 3152
    (Bright–Tunes, BMI)*

March 16

1. **OUR DAY WILL COME**
   Ruby and the Romantics
   *B. Hilliard–Garson, Kapp 501
   (Rosewood, ASCAP)*

2. **RHYTHM OF THE RAIN**
   The Cascades
   *J. Gummoe, Valiant 6026
   (Sherman–DeVorzon, BMI)*

3. **WALK LIKE A MAN**
   The Four Seasons
   *B. Gaudio–B. Crewe, VeeJay
   485 (Saturday–Gavadima, ASCAP)*

4. **THE END OF THE WORLD**
   S. Davis
   *B. Dee–Kent, Victor 8098
   (Summit, ASCAP)*

5. **YOU'RE THE REASON**
   B. Darin
   *B. Darin, Capitol 4897
   (Adaris, BMI)*

6. **RUBY BABY**
   Dion
   *J. Leiber–M. Stoller, Columbia
   42662 (Tiger, BMI)*

7. **BLAME IT ON THE BOSSA
   NOVA**
   E. Gorme
   *B. Mann–Weil,
   Columbia 42661 (Aldon, BMI)*

8. **HEY PAULA**
   Paul and Paula
   *R. Hildebrand, Phillips 40084
   (LeBill–Marbill, BMI)*

9. **HE'S SO FINE**
   The Chiffons
   *R. Mack, Laurie 3152
   (Bright–Tunes, BMI)*

10. **WHAT WILL MARY SAY?**
    J. Mathis
    *Vance–Snyder, Columbia 42666
    (Elm Drive, ASCAP)*

March 23

1. **OUR DAY WILL COME**
Ruby and the Romantics
*B. Hilliard–Garson, Kapp 501
(Rosewood, ASCAP)*

2. **YOU'RE THE REASON**
B. Darin
*B. Darin, Capitol 4897
(Adaris, BMI)*

3. **THE END OF THE WORLD**
S. Davis
*Dee–Kent, Victor 8098
(Summit, ASCAP)*

4. **WALK LIKE A MAN**
The Four Seasons
*B. Crewe–B. Gaudio, VeeJay 485
(Saturday–Gavadima, ASCAP)*

5. **HE'S SO FINE**
The Chiffons
*R. Mack, Laurie 3152
(Bright–Tunes, BMI)*

6. **SOUTH STREET**
The Orlons
*K. Mann–Appell, Cameo 243
(Kalmann, ASCAP)*

7. **RHYTHM OF THE RAIN**
The Cascades
*J. Gummoe, Valiant 6026
(Sherman–DeVorzon, BMI)*

8. **MAMA DIDN'T LIE**
J. Bradley
*C. Mayfield, Chess 1845
(Curtom, BMI)*

9. **BLAME IT ON THE BOSSA NOVA**
E. Gorme
*Mann–Weil, Columbia 42666
(Elm Drive, ASCAP)*

10. **IN DREAMS**
R. Orbison
*R. Orbison, Monument 806
(Acuff–Rose, BMI)*

March 30

1. **HE'S SO FINE**
The Chiffons
*R. Mack, Laurie 3152
(Bright–Tunes, BMI)*

2. **THE END OF THE WORLD**
S. Davis
*Dee–Kent, Victor 8098
(Summit, ASCAP)*

3. **OUR DAY WILL COME**
Ruby and the Romantics
*B. Hilliard–Garson, Kapp 501
(Rosewood, ASCAP)*

4. **SOUTH STREET**
The Orlons
*K. Mann–Appell, Cameo 243
(Kalmann, ASCAP)*

5. **YOU'RE THE REASON**
B. Darin,
*B. Darin, Capitol 4897
(Adaris, BMI)*

6. **RHYTHM OF THE RAIN**
The Cascades
*J. Gummoe, Valiant 6026
(Sherman–DeVorzon, BMI)*

7. **BABY WORKOUT**
J. Wilson
*J. Wilson–Tucker, Brunswick
55239 (Merrimac, BMI)*

8. **IN DREAMS**
R. Orbison
*R. Orbison, Monument 806
(Acuff–Rose, BMI)*

9. **OUR WINTER LOVE**
B. Purnell
*Cavell, Columbia 42619
(Cramart, BMI)*

10. **BLAME IT ON THE BOSSA NOVA**
E. Gorme
*Mann–Weil, Columbia 42666
(Elm Drive, ASCAP)*

April 6

1. **THE END OF THE WORLD**
S. Davis
*Dee–Kent, Victor 8098
(Summit, ASCAP)*

2. **HE'S SO FINE**
The Chiffons
*R. Mack, Laurie 3152
(Bright–Tunes, BMI)*

3. **OUR DAY WILL COME**
Ruby and the Romantics
*B. Hilliard–Garson, Kapp 501
(Rosewood, ASCAP)*

4. **CAN'T GET USED TO LOSING YOU**
A. Williams
*D. Pomus–M. Shuman,
Columbia 42674 (Brenner, BMI)*

5. **SOUTH STREET**
The Orlons
*K. Mann–Appell, Cameo 243
(Kalmann, ASCAP)*

6. **IN DREAMS**
R. Orbison
*R. Orbison, Monument 806
(Acuff–Rose, BMI)*

7. **BABY WORKOUT**
J. Wilson
*J. Wilson–Turner,
Brunswick 55239
(Merrimac, BMI)*

8. **RHYTHM OF THE RAIN**
The Cascades
*J. Gummoe, Valiant 6026
(Shannan–DeVorzon, BMI)*

9. **YOUNG LOVERS**
Paul and Paula
*R. Hildebrand–Jackson,
Philips 40096
(LeBill–Marbill, BMI)*

10. **YOU'RE THE REASON**
B. Darin
*B. Darin, Capitol 4897
(Adaris, BMI)*

April 13

1. **CAN'T GET USED TO LOSING YOU**
A. Williams
D. Pomus–M. Shuman,
Columbia 42674 (Brenner, BMI)

2. **HE'S SO FINE**
The Chiffons
R. Mack, Laurie 3152
(Bright–Tunes, BMI)

3. **THE END OF THE WORLD**
S. Davis
Dee–Kent, Victor 8098
(Summit, ASCAP)

4. **BABY WORKOUT**
J. Wilson
J. Wilson–Tucker,
Brunswick 55239
(Merrimac, BMI)

5. **SOUTH STREET**
The Orlons
K. Mann–Appell, Cameo 243
(Kalmann, ASCAP)

6. **OUR DAY WILL COME**
Ruby and the Romantics
B. Hilliard–Garson, Kapp 501
(Rosewood, ASCAP)

7. **I WILL FOLLOW HIM**
Little Peggy March
Altman–Gimbel–Stole–Roma,
Victor 8139 (Leeds, ASCAP)

8. **YOUNG LOVERS**
Paul and Paula
R. Hildebrand–Jackson,
Phillips 40096
(LeBill–Marbill, BMI)

9. **DO THE BIRD**
D. Sharp
K. Mann–Appell, Cameo 244
(Kalmann, ASCAP)

10. **MR. BASS MAN**
J. Cymbal
J. Cymbal, Kapp 503
(Jalo, BMI)

April 20

1. **I WILL FOLLOW HIM**
Little Peggy March
Altman–Gimbel–Stole–Roma,
Victor 8139 (Leeds, ASCAP)

2. **CAN'T GET USED TO LOSING YOU**
A. Williams
D. Pomus–M. Shuman,
Columbia 42674 (Brenner, BMI)

3. **HE'S SO FINE**
The Chiffons
R. Mack, Laurie 3152
(Bright–Tunes, BMI)

4. **YOUNG LOVERS**
Paul and Paula
R. Hildebrand–Jackson,
Phillips 40096
(LeBill–Marbill, BMI)

5. **PUFF (THE MAGIC DRAGON)**
Peter, Paul and Mary
P. Yarrow–Lipton,
Warner Brothers 5348
(Pepamar, BMI)

6. **BABY WORKOUT**
J. Wilson
J. Wilson–Turner,
Brunswick 55239
(Merrimac, BMI)

7. **SOUTH STREET**
The Orlons
K. Mann–Appell, Cameo 243
(Kalmann, ASCAP)

8. **DON'T SAY NOTHIN' BAD ABOUT MY BABY**
The Cookies
C. King–Goffin, Dimension 1008
(Aldon, BMI)

9. **MR. BASS MAN**
J. Cymbal
J. Cymbal, Kapp 503
(Jalo, BMI)

10. **PIPELINE**
The Chantays
Spickard–Carmen, Dot 16440
(Downey, BMI)

April 27

1. **I WILL FOLLOW HIM**
Little Peggy March
Atlman–Gimbel–Stole–Roma,
Victor 8139 (Leeds, ASCAP)

2. **CAN'T GET USED TO LOSING YOU**
A. Williams
D. Pomus–M. Shuman,
Columbia 42674 (Brenner, BMI)

3. **HE'S SO FINE**
The Chiffons
R. Mack Laurie 3152
(Bright–Tunes, BMI)

4. **PIPELINE**
The Chantays
Spickard–Carmen, Dot 16440
(Downey, BMI)

5. **PUFF (THE MAGIC DRAGON)**
Peter, Paul and Mary
P. Yarrow–Lipton,
Warner Brothers 5348
(Pepamar, BMI)

6. **BABY WORKOUT**
J. Wilson
J. Wilson–Turner,
Brunswick 55239
(Merrimac, BMI)

7. **YOUNG LOVERS**
Paul and Paula
R. Hildebrand–Jackson,
Phillips 40096
(LeBill–Marbill, BMI)

8. **DON'T SAY NOTHIN' BAD ABOUT MY BABY**
The Cookies
C. King–G. Goffin,
Dimension 1008 (Aldon, BMI)

9. **WATERMELON MAN**
M. Santamaria
Hancock, Battle 45909
(Aries, BMI)

10. **ON BROADWAY**
The Drifters
Weill–B. Mann–J. Leiber–
M. Stoller, Atlantic 2182
(Aldon, BMI)

225

May 4

1. **I WILL FOLLOW HIM**
   Little Peggy March
   Altman–Gimbel–Stole–Roma,
   Victor 8139   (Leeds, ASCAP)
2. **PUFF (THE MAGIC DRAGON)**
   Peter, Paul and Mary
   P. Yarrow–Lipton,
   Warner Brothers 5348
   (Pepamar, BMI)
3. **CAN'T GET USED TO LOSING YOU**
   A. Williams
   D. Pomus–M. Shuman,
   Columbia 42674 (Brenner, BMI)
4. **PIPELINE**
   The Chantays
   Spickard–Carmen, Dot 16440
   (Downey, BMI)
5. **HE'S SO FINE**
   The Chiffons
   R. Mack, Laurie 3152
   (Bright–Tunes, BMI)
6. **IF YOU WANNA BE HAPPY**
   J. Soul
   Guida–Royster, SPQR 3305
   (Rockmasters, BMI)
7. **SURFIN' USA**
   The Beach Boys
   B. Wilson, Capitol 4932
   (Arc, BMI)
8. **ON BROADWAY**
   The Drifters
   Weil–B. Mann–J. Leiber–
   M. Stoller, Atlantic 2182
   (Aldon, BMI)
9. **WATERMELON MAN**
   M. Santamaria
   Hancock, Battle 45909
   (Aries, BMI)
10. **DON'T SAY NOTHIN' BAD ABOUT MY BABY**
    The Cookies
    C. King–G. Goffin,
    Dimension 1008   (Aldon, BMI)

May 11

1. **IF YOU WANNA BE HAPPY**
   J. Soul
   Guida–Royster, SPQR 3305
   (Rockmasters, BMI)
2. **I WILL FOLLOW HIM**
   Little Peggy March
   Altman–Gimbel–Stole–Roma,
   Victor 8139(Leeds, ASCAP)
3. **PUFF (THE MAGIC DRAGON)**
   Peter, Paul and Mary
   P. Yarrow–Lipton,
   Warner Brothers 5348
   (Pepamar, BMI)
4. **FOOLISH LITTLE GIRL**
   The Shirelles
   Miller–H. Greenfield,
   Scepter 1248   (Aldon, BMI)
5. **CAN'T GET USED TO LOSING YOU**
   A. Williams
   D. Pomus–M. Shuman
6. **HE'S SO FINE**
   The Chiffons
   R. Mack, Laurie 3152
   (Bright–Tunes, BMI)
7. **SURFIN' USA**
   The Beach Boys
   B. Wilson, Capitol 4932
   (Arc, BMI)
8. **REVEREND MR. BLACK**
   The Kingston Trio
   Wheeler–Peters, Capitol 4951
   (Quartet–Butterfield, BMI)
9. **ON BROADWAY**
   The Drifters
   Weil–B. Mann–J. Leiber–M. Stoller,
   Atlantic 2182 (Aldon, BMI)
10. **I LOVE YOU BECAUSE**
    A. Martino
    Payne, Capitol 4930   (Rose, BMI)

May 18

1. **IF YOU WANNA BE HAPPY**
   J. Soul
   Guida–Royster, SPQR 3305
   (Rockmasters, BMI)
2. **PUFF (THE MAGIC DRAGON)**
   Peter, Paul and Mary
   P. Yarrow–Lipton,
   Warner Brothers 5348 (Pepamar, B
3. **I WILL FOLLOW HIM**
   Little Peggy March
   Altman–Gimbel–Stole–Roma
   Victor 8139 (Leeds, ASCAP)
4. **SURFIN' USA**
   The Beach Boys
   B. Wilson, Capitol 4932
   (Arc, BMI)
5. **PIPELINE**
   The Chantays
   Spickard–Carmen Dot 16440
   (Downey, BMI)
6. **FOOLISH LITTLE GIRL**
   The Shirelles
   Miller–H. Greenfield, Scepter
   1248 (Aldon, BMI)
7. **CAN'T GET USED TO LOSING YOU**
   A. Williams
   D. Pomus–M. Shuman,
   Columbia 42674 (Brenner, BMI)
8. **REVEREND MR. BLACK**
   The Kingston Trio
   Wheeler–Peters, Capitol 4951
   (Quartet–Butterfield, BMI)
9. **I LOVE YOU BECAUSE**
   A. Martino
   Payne, Capitol 4930   (Rose, BMI)
10. **MECCA**
    G. Pitney
    Nader–Gluck, Musicor 1028
    (January, BMI)

1963

May 25

1. **IF YOU WANNA BE HAPPY**
J. Soul
*Guida–Royster, SPQR
(Rockmasters, BMI)*

2. **SURFIN' USA**
The Beach Boys
*B. Wilson, Capitol 4932
(Arc, BMI)*

3. **I WILL FOLLOW HIM**
Little Peggy March
*Altman–Gimbel–Stole–Roma,
Victor 8139 (Leeds, ASCAP)*

4. **I LOVE YOU BECAUSE**
A. Martino
*Payne, Capitol 4930
(Rose, BMI)*

5. **TWO FACES HAVE I**
L. Christie
*Herbert–L. Christie, Roulette 4481
(Painted Desert–RTD, BMI)*

6. **FOOLISH LITTLE GIRL**
The Shirelles
*Miller–H. Greenfield,
Scepter 1248 (Aldon, BMI)*

7. **TAKE THESE CHAINS FROM MY HEART**
R. Charles
*Rose–Heath, ABC 10435
(Milene, ASCAP)*

8. **IT'S MY PARTY**
L. Gore
*Weiner–Gluck–Gold,
Mercury 72119
(Arch, ASCAP)*

9. **ANOTHER SATURDAY NIGHT**
S. Cooke
*S. Cooke, Victor 8164
(Kags, BMI)*

10. **MECCA**
G. Pitney
*Nader–Gluck, Musicor 1028
(January, BMI)*

June 1

1. **IT'S MY PARTY**
L. Gore
*Weiner–Gluck–Gold,
Mercury 72119
(Arch, ASCAP)*

2. **SURFIN' USA**
The Beach Boys
*B. Wilson, Capitol 4932
(Arc, BMI)*

3. **DA DOO RON RON**
The Crystals
*P. Spector–E. Greenwich–J. Barry,
Philles 112
(Mother Bertha–Trio, BMI)*

4. **I LOVE YOU BECAUSE**
A. Martino
*Payne, Capitol 4930
(Rose, BMI)*

5. **IF YOU WANNA BE HAPPY**
J. Soul
*Guida–Royster, SPQR 3305
(Rockmasters, BMI)*

6. **TWO FACES HAVE I**
L. Christie
*Herbert–L. Christie, Roulette 4481
(Painted Desert–RTD, BMI)*

7. **I WILL FOLLOW HIM**
Little Peggy March
*Altman–Gimbel–Stole–Roma,
Victor 8139 (Leeds, ASCAP)*

8. **SUKIYAKI**
K. Sakamoto
*Ei-Nakamura, Capitol 4945
(Beechwood, BMI)*

9. **YOU CAN'T SIT DOWN**
The Dovells
*Upchurch–Clark–Muldraw–
Sheldon, Parkway 867
(Conrad–Dasler, BMI)*

10. **KILLER JOE**
The Rocky Fellers
*Russell–Elgin–Medley,
Scepter 1246
(Mellin–White–Castle, BMI)*

June 8

1. **IT'S MY PARTY**
L. Gore
*Weiner–Gluck–Gold,
Mercury 72119
(Arch, ASCAP)*

2. **DA DOO RON RON**
The Crystals
*P. Spector–E. Greenwich–J. Barry,
Philles 112
(Mother Bertha–Trio, BMI)*

3. **SUKIYAKI**
K. Sakamota
*Ei-Nakamura, Capitol 4945
(Beechwood, BMI)*

4. **YOU CAN'T SIT DOWN**
The Dovells
*Upchurch–Clark–Muldraw–
Sheldon, Parkway 867
(Conrad–Dasler, BMI)*

5. **I LOVE YOU BECAUSE**
A. Martino
*Payne, Capitol 4930
(Rose, BMI)*

6. **BLUE ON BLUE**
B. Vinton
*H. David–B. Bacharach, Epic 9593
(Famous, ASCAP)*

7. **STILL**
B. Anderson
*B. Anderson, Decca 31458
(Moss–Rose, BMI)*

8. **TWO FACES HAVE I**
L. Christie
*Herbert–L. Christie, Roulette
4481 (Painted Desert–RTD,
BMI)*

9. **SURFIN' USA**
The Beach Boys
*B. Wilson, Capitol 4932
(Arc, BMI)*

10. **THOSE LAZY HAZY CRAZY DAYS OF SUMMER**
Nat (King) Cole
*Tobias–Carste, Capitol 4965
(Comet, ASCAP)*

227

June 15

1. **DA DOO RON RON**
   The Crystals
   P. Spector–E. Greenwich–J. Barry,
   Philles 112
   (Mother Bertha–Trio, BMI)

2. **IT'S MY PARTY**
   L. Gore
   Weiner–Gluck–Gold, Mercury
   72119 (Arch, ASCAP)

3. **SUKIYAKI**
   K. Sakamoto
   Ei-Nakamura, Captiol 4945
   (Beechwood, BMI)

4. **BLUE ON BLUE**
   B. Vinton
   H. David–B. Bacharach,
   Epic 9593 (Famous, ASCAP)

5. **I LOVE YOU BECAUSE**
   A. Martino
   Payne, Capitol 4930
   (Rose, BMI)

6. **YOU CAN'T SIT DOWN**
   The Dovells
   Upchurch–Clark–Muldraw–
   Sheldon, Parkway 867
   (Conrad–Dasler, BMI)

7. **THOSE LAZY HAZY CRAZY DAYS OF SUMMER**
   Nat (King) Cole
   Tobias–Carste, Captiol 4965
   (Comet, ASCAP)

8. **HELLO STRANGER**
   B. Lewis
   B. Lewis, Atlantic 2184
   (McLaughlin, BMI)

9. **STILL**
   B. Anderson
   B. Anderson, Decca 31458
   (Moss-Rose, BMI)

10. **18 YELLOW ROSES**
    B. Darin
    B. Darin, Capitol 4970
    (T. M., BMI)

June 22

1. **SUKIYAKI**
   K. Sakamoto
   Ei-Nakamura, Captiol 4945
   (Beechwood, BMI)

2. **IT'S MY PARTY**
   L. Gore
   Weiner–Gluck–Gold, Mercury
   72119 (Arch, ASCAP)

3. **YOU CAN'T SIT DOWN**
   The Dovells
   Upchurch–Clark–Muldraw–
   Sheldon, Parkway 867
   (Conrad–Dasler, BMI)

4. **DA DOO RON RON**
   The Crystals
   P. Spector–E. Greenwich–J. Barry
   Philles 112
   (Mother Bertha–Trio, BMI)

5. **HELLO STRANGER**
   B. Lewis
   B. Lewis, Atlantic 2184
   (McLaughlin, BMI)

6. **BLUE ON BLUE**
   B. Vinton
   H. David–B. Bacharach,
   Epic 9593 (Famous, ASCAP)

7. **THOSE LAZY HAZY CRAZY DAYS OF SUMMER**
   Nat (King) Cole
   Tobias–Carste, Captiol 4965
   (Comet, ASCAP)

8. **STILL**
   B. Anderson
   B. Anderson, Decca 31458
   (Moss-Rose, BMI)

9. **I LOVE YOU BECAUSE**
   A. Martino
   Payne, Capitol 4930
   (Rose, BMI)

10. **ONE FINE DAY**
    The Chiffons
    C. King–G. Goffin, Laurie 3179
    (Screen Gems–Columbia, BMI)

June 29

1. **SUKIYAKI**
   K. Sakamoto
   Ei-Nakamura, Captiol 4945
   (Beechwood, BMI)

2. **IT'S MY PARTY**
   L. Gore
   Weiner–Gluck–Gole Mercury
   72119 (Arch, ASCAP)

3. **BLUE ON BLUE**
   B. Vinton
   H. David–B. Bacharach,
   Epic 9593 (Famous, ASCAP)

4. **HELLO STRANGER**
   B. Lewis
   B. Lewis, Atlantic 2184
   (McLaughlin, BMI)

5. **EASIER SAID THAN DONE**
   The Essex
   W. Linton Roulette 4494
   (Nom, BMI)

6. **ONE FINE DAY**
   The Chiffons
   C. King–G. Goffin, Laurie 3179
   (Screen Gems–Columbia, BMI)

7. **YOU CAN'T SIT DOWN**
   The Dovells
   Upchurch–Clark–Muldraw–
   Sheldon, Parkway 867
   (Conrad–Dasler, BMI)

8. **MEMPHIS**
   L. Mack
   C. Berry, Fraternity 906
   (Arc, BMI)

9. **SURF CITY**
   Jan and Dean
   Berry–Wilson, Liberty 55580
   (Screen Gems–Columbia, BMI)

10. **THOSE LAZY HAZY CRAZY DAYS OF SUMMER**
    Nat (King) Cole
    Tobias–Carste, Capitol 4965
    (Comet, ASCAP)

July 6

1. **HELLO STRANGER**
B. Lewis
B. Lewis, Atlantic 2184
(McLaughlin, BMI)

2. **SUKIYAKI**
K. Sakamoto
Ei-Nakamura, Captiol 4945
(Beechwood, BMI)

3. **BLUE ON BLUE**
B. Vinton
H. David–B. Bacharach,
Epic 9593 (Famous, ASCAP)

4. **EASIER SAID THAN DONE**
The Essex
W. Linton, Roulette 4494
(Nom, BMI)

5. **ONE FINE DAY**
The Chiffons
C. King–G. Goffin, Laurie 3179
(Screen Gems–Columbia, BMI)

6. **SURF CITY**
Jan and Dean
Berry–Wilson, Liberty 55580
(Screen Gems–Columbia, BMI)

7. **COME AND GET THESE MEMORIES**
Martha and the Vandellas
Holland–Dozier–Holland, Gordy
7014 (Jobete, BMI)

8. **SO MUCH IN LOVE**
The Tymes
Jackson–Joseph–Williams,
Parkway 781 (Cameo–Parkway,
BMI)

9. **TIE ME KANGAROO DOWN, SPORT**
R. Harris
R. Harris, Epic 9596
(Beechwood, BMI)

10. **IT'S MY PARTY**
L. Gore
Weiner–Gluck–Gold, Mercury
72119 (Arch, ASCAP)

July 13

1. **EASIER SAID THAN DONE**
The Essex
W. Linton, Roulette 4494
(Nom, BMI)

2. **SO MUCH IN LOVE**
The Tymes
Jackson–Joseph–Williams,
Parkway 781 (Cameo–Parkway,
BMI)

3. **TIE ME KANGAROO DOWN, SPORT**
R. Harris
R. Harris, Epic 9596
(Beechwood, BMI)

4. **HELLO STRANGER**
B. Lewis
B. Lewis, Atlantic 2184
(McLauglin, BMI)

5. **SURF CITY**
Jan and Dean
Berry–Wilson, Liberty
55580 (Screen Gems–Columbia,
BMI)

6. **MEMPHIS**
L. Mack
C. Berry, Fraternity 906
(Arc, BMI)

7. **ONE FINE DAY**
The Chiffons
C. King–G. Goffin, Laurie 3179
(Screen Gems–Columbia, BMI)

8. **BLUE ON BLUE**
B. Vinton
H. David–B. Bacharach,
Epic 9593 (Famous, ASCAP)

9. **BLOWIN' IN THE WIND**
Peter, Paul and Mary
B. Dylan, Warner Brothers 5368
(Witmark, ASCAP)

10. **SUKIYAKI**
K. Sakamoto
Ei-Nakamura, Capitol 4945
(Beechwood, BMI)

July 20

1. **EASIER SAID THAN DONE**
The Essex
W. Linton, Roulette 4494
(Nom, BMI)

2. **SURF CITY**
Jan and Dean
Berry–Wilson, Liberty 55580
(Sceen Gems–Columbia, BMI)

3. **SO MUCH IN LOVE**
The Tymes
Jackson–Joseph–Williams,
Parkway 781
(Cameo–Parkway, BMI)

4. **TIE ME KANGAROO DOWN, SPORT**
R. Harris
R. Harris, Epic 9596
(Beechwood, BMI)

5. **MEMPHIS**
L. Mack
C. Berry, Fraternity 906
(Arc, BMI)

6. **BLOWIN' IN THE WIND**
Peter, Paul and Mary
B. Dylan, Warner Brothers 5368
(Witmark, ASCAP)

7. **JUST ONE LOOK**
D. Troy
Carroll–Payne, Atlantic 2118
(Premier, BMI)

8. **(YOU'RE THE) DEVIL IN DISGUISE**
E. Presley
Giant–Baum–Kaye, Victor 8188
(Elvis Presley, BMI)

9. **ON TOP OF SPAGHETTI**
T. Glazer and the Children's Chorus
T. Glazer, Kapp 526
(Songs, ASCAP)

10. **WIPE OUT**
The Surfaris
The Surfaris, Dot 16479
(Miraleste–Robin Hood, BMI)

230

August 17

1. **FINGERTIPS (PART II)**
Little Stevie Wonder
*Paul–Cosby, Tamla 54080
(Jobete, BMI)*

2. **BLOWIN' IN THE WIND**
Peter, Paul and Mary
*B. Dylan, Warner Brothers 5368
(Witmark, ASCAP)*

3. **WIPE OUT**
The Surfaris
*The Surfaris, Dot 16479
(Miraleste–Robin Hood, BMI)*

4. **(YOU'RE THE) DEVIL IN DISGUISE**
E. Presley
*Giant–Baum–Kaye, Victor 8188
(Elvis Presley, BMI)*

5. **CANDY GIRL**
The Four Seasons
*L. Santos, VeeJay 539
(Saturday–Gavadima, ASCAP)*

6. **SO MUCH IN LOVE**
The Tymes
*Jacison–Joseph–Williams,
Parkway 781
(Cameo–Parkway, BMI)*

7. **JUDY'S TURN TO CRY**
L. Gore
*Ross–Lewis, Mercury 72143
(Glamorous, BMI)*

8. **MORE**
K. Winding
*Ortoiani–Olivero, Verve 10925
(E.B. Marks, BMI)*

9. **MY BOYFRIEND'S BACK**
The Angels
*Feldman–Goldstein–Gotteher,
Smash 1834 (Blackwood, BMI)*

10. **EASIER SAID THAN DONE**
The Essex
*W. Linton Roulette 4494
(Nom, BMI)*

August 24

1. **FINGERTIPS (PART II)**
Little Stevie Wonder
*Paul–Cosby, Tamla 54080
(Jobete, BMI)*

2. **BLOWIN' IN THE WIND**
Peter, Paul and Mary
*B. Dylan, Warner Brothers
5368 (Witmark, ASCAP)*

4. **MY BOYFRIEND'S BACK**
The Angels
*Feldman–Goldstein–Gotteher,
Smash 1834 (Blackwood, BMI)*

5. **WIPE OUT**
The Surfaris
*The Surfaris, Dot 16479
(Miraleste–Robin Hood, BMI)*

6. **JUDY'S TURN TO CRY**
L. Gore
*Ross–Lewis, Mercury 72143
(Glamorous, BMI)*

7. **HELLO MUDDAH, HELLO FUDDUH**
A. Sherman
*A. Sherman–Busch,
Warner Brothers 5378
(Curtain Call, BMI)*

8. **DENISE**
Randy and the Rainbows
*Levenson, Rust 5059
(Bright–Tunes, BMI)*

9. **MORE**
K. Winding
*Ortoiani–Olivero,
Verve 10925 (E.B. Marks, BMI)*

10. **MOCKINGBIRD**
I. Foxx
*C. Foxx–I. Foxx, Symbol 919
(Saturn, BMI)*

August 31

1. **MY BOYFRIEND'S BACK**
The Angels
*Feldman–Goldstein–Gotteher,
Smash 1834 (Blackwood, BMI)*

2. **BLOWIN' IN THE WIND**
Peter, Paul and Mary
*B. Dylan, Warner Brothers 5368
(Witmark, ASCAP)*

3. **CANDY GIRL**
The Four Seasons
*L. Santos, VeeJay 539
(Saturday–Gavadima, ASCAP)*

4. **FINGERTIPS (PART II)**
Little Stevie Wonder
*Paul–Cosby, Tamla
54080 (Jobete, BMI)*

5. **HELLO MUDDAH, HELLO FUDDUH**
A. Sherman
*A. Sherman–Busch,
Warner Brothers 5378
(Curtain Call, BMI)*

6. **IF I HAD A HAMMER**
T. Lopez
*Hays–P. Seeger, Reprise 20198
(Ludlow, BMI)*

7. **JUDY'S TURN TO CRY**
L. Gore
*Ross–Lewis, Mercury 72143
(Glamorous, BMI)*

8. **DENISE**
Randy and the Rainbows
*Levenson, Rust 5059
(Bright–Tunes, BMI)*

9. **DANKE SHOEN**
W. Newton
*B. Kaempfert–Hene,
Capitol 4989 (Roosevelt, BMI)*

10. **MOCKINGBIRD**
I. Foxx
*C. Foxx–I. Foxx, Symbol 919
(Saturn, BMI)*

1. **CANDY GIRL**
The Four Seasons
L. Santos,   VeeJay 539
(Saturday–Gavadima, ASCAP)

2. **MY BOYFRIEND'S BACK**
The Angels
Feldman–Goldstein–Gotteher,
Smash 1834   (Blackwood, BMI)

3. **HELLO MUDDAH, HELLO FADDUH**
A. Sherman
A. Sherman–Busch,
Warner Brothers 5378
(Curtain, Call, BMI)

4. **IF I HAD A HAMMER**
T. Lopez
Hays–P. Seeger,   Reprise 20198
(Ludlow, BMI)

5. **BLUE VELVET**
B. Vinton
Wayne–Morris, Epic 9614
(Vogue, BMI)

6. **HEAT WAVE**
Martha and the Vandellas
Holland–Dozier–Holland Gordy
7022 (Jobete, BMI)

7. **MONKEY TIME**
Major Lance
C. Mayfield,   Okeh 7175
(Curtom–Poliro, BMI)

8. **MOCKINGBIRD**
I. Foxx
C. Foxx–I. Foxx,   Symbol 919
(Saturn, BMI)

9. **BLOWIN' IN THE WIND**
Peter, Paul and Mary
B. Dylan,   Warner Brothers 5368
(Witmark, ASCAP)

10. **HEY GIRL**
F. Scott
C. King–G. Goffin,   Colpix 692
(Screen Gems–Columbia, BMI)

1. **BLUE VELVET**
B. Vinton
Wayne–Morris,   Epic 9614
(Vogue, BMI)

2. **MY BOYFRIEND'S BACK**
The Angels
Feldman–Goldstein–Gotteher,
Smash 1834   (Blackwood, BMI)

3. **IF I HAD A HAMMER**
T. Lopez
Hays–P. Seeger,   Reprise 20198
(Ludlow, BMI)

4. **HELLO MUDDUH, HELLO FADDUH**
A. Sherman
A. Sherman–Busch,
Warner Brothers 5378
(Curtain Call, BMI)

5. **SURFER GIRL**
The Beach Boys
B. Wilson,   Capitol 5009
(Guild, BMI)

6. **THEN HE KISSED ME**
The Crystals
P. Spector–E. Greenwich–J. Barry,
Philles 115   (Mother Bertha–
Trio, BMI)

7. **MONKEY TIME**
M. Lance
C. Mayfield,   Okeh 7175
(Curtom–Poliro, BMI)

8. **HEAT WAVE**
Martha and the Vandellas
Holland–Dozier–Holland,   Gordy
7022 (Jobete, BMI)

9. **SALLY, GO 'ROUND THE ROSES**
The Jaynettes
Sander–Stevens,   Tuff 369
(Winlyn, BMI)

10. **THE KIND OF BOY YOU CAN'T FORGET**
The Raindrops
E. Greenwich–J. Barry,
Jubilee 5455   (Trio, BMI)

1. **BLUE VELVET**
B. Vinton
Wayne–Morris,   Epic 9614
(Vogue, BMI)

2. **MY BOYFRIEND'S BACK**
The Angels
Feldman–Goldstein–Gotteher,
Smash 1834   (Blackwood, BMI)

3. **HEAT WAVE**
Martha and the Vandellas
Holland–Dozier–Holland,   Gordy
7022   (Jobete, BMI)

4. **IF I HAD A HAMMER**
T. Lopez
Hays–P. Seeger,   Reprise 20198
(Ludlow, BMI)

5. **THEN HE KISSED ME**
The Crystals
P. Spector–E. Greenwich–J. Barry,
Philles 115   (Mother Bertha–
Trio, BMI)

6. **SALLY, GO 'ROUND THE ROSES**
The Jaynettes
Sanders–Stevens,   Tuff 369
(Winly, BMI)

7. **SURFER GIRL**
The Beach Boys
B. Wilson,   Capitol 5009
(Guild, BMI)

8. **MONKEY TIME**
M. Lance
C. Mayfield,   Okeh 7175
(Curtom–Poliro, BMI)

9. **MICKEY'S MONKEY**
The Miracles
Holland–Dozier,   Tamla 54083
(Jobete, BMI)

10. **CRY BABY**
G. Mimms and the Enchanters
Russell–Meade,   United Artists
629 (Rittenhouse–Mellin, BMI)

1963

September 28

1. **SALLY, GO 'ROUND THE ROSES**
The Jaynettes
Sanders–Stevens, Tuff 369 (Winly, BMI)

2. **BLUE VELVET**
B. Vinton
Wayne–Morris, Epic 9614 (Vogue, BMI)

3. **HEAT WAVE**
Martha and the Vandellas
Holland–Dozier–Holland, Gordy 7022 (Jobete, BMI)

4. **BE MY BABY**
The Ronettes
P. Spector–E. Greenwich–J. Barry, Philles 116 (Mother Bertha–Trio, BMI)

5. **MY BOYFRIEND'S BACK**
The Angels
Feldman–Goldstein–Gotteher, Smash 1834 (Blackwood, BMI)

6. **THEN HE KISSED ME**
The Crystals
P. Spector–E. Greenwich–J. Barry, Philles 115 (Mother Bertha–Trio, BMI)

7. **MICKEY'S MONKEY**
The Miracles
Holland–Dozier, Tamla 54083 (Jobete, BMI)

8. **WONDERFUL! WONDERFUL!**
The Tymes
Raleigh–Edwards, Parkway 884 (E.B. Marks, BMI)

9. **CRY BABY**
G. Mimms and the Enchanters
Russell–Meade United Artists 629 (Rittenhouse–Mellin, BMI)

10. **WALKIN' MIRACLE**
The Essex
Hugo–Luigi–Weiss–Levy, Roulette 4515 (Planetary, ASCAP)

October 5

1. **BE MY BABY**
The Ronettes
P. Spector–E. Greenwich–J. Barry, Philles 116 (Mother Bertha–Trio, BMI)

2. **SALLY, GO 'ROUND THE ROSES**
The Jaynettes
Sanders–Stevens, Tuff 369 (Winlyn, BMI)

3. **BLUE VELVET**
B. Vinton
Wayne–Morris, Epic 9614 (Vogue, BMI)

4. **WONDERFUL! WONDERFUL!**
The Tymes
Raleigh–Edwards, Parkway 884 (E.B. Marks, BMI)

5. **HEAT WAVE**
Martha and the Vandellas
Holland–Dozier–Holland, Gordy 7022 (Jobete, BMI)

6. **CRY BABY**
G. Mimms and the Enchanters
Russell–Meade, United Artists 629 (Rittenhouse–Mellin, BMI)

7. **SUGAR SHACK**
J. Gilmer and the Fireballs
McCormick–Voss, Dot 16487 (Dundee, BMI)

8. **MY BOYFRIEND'S BACK**
The Angels
Feldman–Goldstein–Gotteher, Smash 1834 (Blackwood, BMI)

9. **LITTLE DEUCE COUPE**
The Beach Boys
B. Wilson–Christian, Capitol 5009 (Sea of Tunes, BMI)

10. **WALKIN' MIRACLE**
The Essex
Hugo–Luigi–Weiss–Levy, Roulette 4515 (Planetary, ASCAP)

October 12

1. **BE MY BABY**
The Ronettes
P. Spector–E. Greenwich–J. Barry, Philles 116 (Mother Bertha–Trio, BMI)

2. **SALLY, GO ROUND' THE ROSES**
The Jaynettes
Sanders–Stevens, Tuff 369 (Winlyn, BMI)

3. **CRY BABY**
G. Mimms and the Enchanters
Russell–Meade, United Artists 629 (Rittenhouse–Mellin, BMI)

4. **BLUE VELVET**
B. Vinton
Wayne–Morris, Epic 9614 (Vogue, BMI)

5. **SUGAR SHACK**
J. Gilmer and the Fireballs
McCormick–Voss, Dot 16487 (Dundee, BMI)

6. **LITTLE DEUCE COUPE**
The Beach Boys
B. Wilson–Christian, Capitol 5009 (Sea of Tunes, BMI)

7. **BUSTED**
R. Charles
Howard, ABC 10481 (E.B. Marks, BMI)

8. **MY BOYFIREND'S BACK**
The Angels
Feldman–Goldstein–Gotteher, Smash 1834 (Blackwood, BMI)

9, **HEAT WAVE**
Martha and the Vandellas
Holland–Dozier–Holland, Gordy 7022 (Jobete, BMI)

10. **DONNA THE PRIMA DONNA**
D. DiMucci
D. DiMucci–E. Maresca, Columbia 42852 (Disal, ASCAP)

233

October 19

1. **SUGAR SHACK**
J. Gilmer and the Fireballs
McCormick–Voss, Dot 16487
(Dundee, BMI)

2. **BE MY BABY**
The Ronettes
P. Spector–E. Greenwich–J. Barry
Philles 116 (Mother Bertha–Trio,
BMI)

3. **BUSTED**
R. Charles
Howard, ABC 10481
(E.B. Marks BMI)

4. **BLUE VELVET**
B. Vinton
Wayne–Morris, Epic 9614
(Vogue, BMI)

5. **SALLY, GO 'ROUND THE ROSES**
The Jaynettes
Sanders–Stevens, Tuff 369
(Winlyn, BMI)

6. **CRY BABY**
G. Mimms and the Enchanters
Russell–Meade, United Artists
629 (Rittenhouse–Mellin, BMI)

7. **MEAN WOMAN BLUES**
R. Orbison
DeMetrius, Monument 824
(Glady, ASCAP)

8. **DEEP PURPLE**
N. Tempo–A. Stevens
Parrish–Rose, Atco 6273
(Robbins, ASCAP)

9. **DONNA THE PRIMA DONNA**
D. DiMucci
D. DiMucci–E. Maresca,
Columbia 42852 (Disal, ASCAP)

10. **DON'T THINK TWICE IT'S ALL RIGHT**
Peter, Paul and Mary
B. Dylan, Warner Brothers 5385
(Witmark, ASCAP)

October 26

1. **SUGAR SHACK**
J. Gilmer and the Fireball
McCormick–Voss, Dot 16487
(Dundee, BMI)

2. **DEEP PURPLE**
N. Tempo and A. Stevens
Parrish–Rose, Atco 6273
(Robbins, ASCAP)

3. **BE MY BABY**
The Ronettes
P. Spector–E. Greenwich–J. Barry,
Philles 116 (Mother Bertha–
Trio, BMI)

4. **BUSTED**
R. Charles
Howard, ABC 10481
(E. B. Marks, BMI)

5. **DONNA THE PRIMA DONNA**
D. DiMucci
D. DiMucci–E. Maresca,
Columbia 42852 (Disal, ASCAP)

6. **BLUE VELVET**
B. Vinton
Wayne–Morris, Epic 9614
(Vogue, BMI)

7. **DON'T THINK TWICE IT'S ALL RIGHT**
Peter, Paul and Mary
B. Dylan, Warner Brothers 5385
(Witmark, ASCAP)

8. **MEAN WOMAN BLUES**
R. Orbison
DeMetrius, Monument 824
(Gladys, ASCAP)

9. **CRY BABY**
G. Mimms and the Enchanters
Russell–Meade, United Artists
(Rittenhouse–Mellin, BMI)

10. **WASHINGTON SQUARE**
The Village Stompers
Goldstein, Epic 9617
(Rayven, BMI)

November 2

1. **DEEP PURPLE**
N. Tempo and A. Stevens
Parrish–Rose, Atco 6273
(Robbins, ASCAP)

2. **SUGAR SHACK**
J. Gilmer and the Fireballs
McCormick–Voss, Dot 16487
(Dundee, BMI)

3. **WASHINGTON SQUARE**
The Village Stompers
Goldstein, Epic 9617
(Rayven, BMI)

4. **MEAN WOMAN BLUES**
R. Orbison
DeMetrius, Monument 824
(Gladys, ASCAP)

5. **BUSTED**
R. Charles
Howard, ABC 10481
(Marks, BMI)

6. **I CAN'T STAY MAD AT YOU**
S. Davis
C. King–G. Goffin, Victor 8219
(Screen Gems–Columbia, BMI)

7. **DONNA THE PRIMA DONNA**
D. DiMucci
D. DiMucci–E. Maresca,
Columbia 42852 (Disal, ASCAP)

8. **BE MY BABY**
The Ronettes
P. Spector–E. Greenwich–J. Barry,
Philles 116 (Mother Bertha–Trio,
BMI)

9. **TALK TO ME**
Sunny and the Sunglows
Seneca, Tear Drop 3014
(Jay and the Cee, BMI)

10. **IT'S ALL RIGHT**
Impressions
C. Mayfield, ABC 10487
(Curtom, BMI)

1963

November 9

1. **DEEP PURPLE**
N. Tempo and A. Stevens
Parrish–Rose, Atco 6273
(Robbins, ASCAP)

2. **SUGAR SHACK**
J. Gilmer and the Fireballs
McCormick–Voss, Dot 16487
(Dundee, BMI)

3. **WASHINGTON SQUARE**
The Village Stompers
Goldstein, Epic 9617
(Rayven, BMI)

4. **MEAN WOMAN BLUES**
R. Orbison
DeMetrius, Monument 824
(Gladys, ASCAP)

5. **IT'S ALL RIGHT**
The Impressions
C. Mayfield, ABC 10487
(Curtom, BMI)

6. **MARIA ELANA**
Los Indios Tabajaras
Barcelaca, Victor 8216
(Peer–International, BMI)

7. **BOSSA NOVA BABY**
E. Presley
J. Leiber–M. Stoller, Victor 8243
(Elvis Presley, BMI)

8. **I CAN'T STAY MAD AT YOU**
S. Davis
C. King–G. Goffin, Victor 8219
(Screen Gems–Columbia, BMI)

9. **BUSTED**
R. Charles
Howard, ABC 10481
(Marks, BMI)

10. **I'M LEAVING IT UP TO YOU**
Dale and Grace
Terry, Jr.–Harris, Montel
Michelle 921 (Venice, BMI)

November 16

1. **DEEP PURPLE**
N. Tempo and A. Stevens
Parrish–Rose, Atco 6273
(Robbins, ASCAP)

2. **IT'S ALL RIGHT**
The Impressions
C. Mayfield, ABC 10487
(Curtom, BMI)

3. **SUGAR SHACK**
J. Gilmer and the Fireballs
McCormick–Voss, Dot 16487
(Dundee, BMI)

4. **WASHINGTON SQUARE**
The Village Stompers
Goldstein, Epic 9617
(Rayven, BMI)

5. **I'M LEAVING IT UP TO YOU**
Dale and Grace
Terry, Jr.–Harris, Montel
Michelle 921 (Venice, BMI)

6. **EVERYBODY**
T. Toe
T. Roe, ABC 10478
(Low–Twi, BMI)

7. **SHE'S A FOOL**
L. Gore
Barkan–Raleigh, Mercury
72180 (Helios–MCR, BMI)

8. **BOSSA NOVA BABY**
E. Presley
J. Leiber–M. Stoller, Victor 8243
(Elvis Presley, BMI)

9. **500 MILES AWAY FROM HOME**
B. Bare
B. Bare–Williams, Victor 8238
(Central Songs, BMI)

10. **MARIA ELANA**
Los Indios Tabajaras
Barcelaca, Victor 8216
(Peer–International, BMI)

November 23

1. **I'M LEAVING IT UP TO YOU**
Dale and Grace
Terry, Jr.–Harris, Montel
Michelle 921 (Venice, BMI)

2. **IT'S ALL RIGHT**
The Impressions
C. Mayfield, ABC 10487
(Curtom, BMI)

3. **DEEP PURPLE**
N. Tempo and A. Stevens
Parrish–Rose, Atco 6273
(Robbins, ASCAP)

4. **SUGAR SHACK**
J. Gilmer and the Fireballs
McCormick–Voss, Dot 16487
(Dundee, BMI)

5. **WASHINGTON SQUARE**
The Village Stompers
Goldstein, Epic 9617
(Rayven, BMI)

6. **BOSSA NOVA BABY**
E. Presley
J. Leiber–M. Stoller, Victor 8243
(Elvis Presley, BMI)

7. **SHE'S A FOOL**
L. Gore
Barkan–Raleigh, Mercury 72180
(Helios–MRC, BMI)

8. **DOMINIQUE**
The Singing Nun
Soeur Sourire, Philips 40152
(General, ASCAP)

9. **EVERYBODY**
T. Roe
T. Roe, ABC 10478
(Low–Twi, BMI)

10. **MARIA ELANA**
Los Indios Tabajaras
Barcelaca, Victor 8216
(Peer–International, BMI)

November 30

1. **DOMINIQUE**
The Singing Nun
Soeur Sourire, Philips 40152
(General, ASCAP)

2. **I'M LEAVING IT UP TO YOU**
Dale and Grace
Terry, Jr.–Harris, Montel
Michelle 921 (Venice, BMI)

3 **SUGAR SHACK**
J. Gilmer and the Fireballs
McCormick–Voss, Dot 16487
(Dundee, BMI)

4. **IT'S ALL RIGHT**
The Impressions
C. Mayfield, ABC 10487
(Curtom, BMI)

5. **WASHINGTON SQUARE**
The Village Stompers
Goldstein, Epic 9617
(Rayven, BMI)

6. **EVERYBODY**
T. Roe
T. Roe, ABC 10478
(Low–Twi, BMI)

7. **SHE'S A FOOL**
L. Gore
Barkan–Raleigh, Mercury 72180
(Helios–MCR, BMI)

8. **(DOWN AT) PAPA JOE'S**
The Dixie Bells
Smith, Sound Stage 7 2507
(Tuneville, BMI)

9. **HEY LITTLE GIRL**
M. Lance
C. Mayfield, Okeh 7181
(Curtom–Jalynee, BMI)

10. **DEEP PURPLE**
N. Tempo and A. Stevens
Parrish–Rose, Atco 6273
(Robbins, ASCAP)

December 7

1. **DOMINIQUE**
The Singing Nun
Soeur Sourire, Philips 40152
(General, ASCAP)

2. **EVERYBODY**
T. Roe
T. Roe, ABC 10478
(Low–Twi, BMI)

3. **LOUIE LOUIE**
The Kingsmen
R. Berry, Wand 143
(Limax, BMI)

4. **I'M LEAVING IT UP TO YOU**
Dale and Grace
Terry, Jr.–Harris, Montel
Michelle 921 (Venice, BMI)

5. **SUGAR SHACK**
J. Gilmer and the Fireballs
McCormick–Voss, Dot 16487
(Dundee, BMI)

6. **SHE'S A FOOL**
L. Gore
Barkan–Taleigh, Mercury 72180
(Helios–MRC, BMI)

7. **YOU DON'T HAVE TO BE A
BABY TO CRY**
The Caravelles
Merrill–Shand, Smash 1852
(RFD, ASCAP)

8. **WASHINGTON SQUARE**
The Village Stompers
Goldstein, Epic 9617
(Rayven, BMI)

9. **BE TRUE TO YOUR SCHOOL**
The Beach Boys
B. Wilson, Capitol 5069
(Sea of Tunes, BMI)

10. **WALKING THE DOG**
R. Thomas
R. Thomas, Stax 140
(East, BMI)

December 14

1. **DOMINIQUE**
The Singing Nun
Soeur Sourire, Philips 40152
(General, ASCAP)

2. **LOUIE, LOUIE**
The Kingsmen
R. Berry, Wand 143
(Limax, BMI)

3. **EVERYBODY**
T. Roe
T. Roe, ABC 10478
(Low–Twi, BMI)

4. **SINCE I FELL FOR YOU**
L. Welsh
B. Johnson, Cadence 1439
(Advanced, ASCAP)

5. **I'M LEAVING IT UP TO YOU**
Dale and Grace
Terry, Jr.–Harris Montel
Michelle 921 (Venice, BMI)

6. **YOU DON'T HAVE TO BE A
BABY TO CRY**
The Caravelles
Merrill–Shand, Smash 1852
(RFD, ASCAP)

7. **WONDERFUL SUMMER**
R. Ward
Garfield–Botkin, Dot 1653
(Rock Music, BMI)

8. **BE TRUE TO YOUR SCHOOL**
The Beach Boys
B. Wilson, Capitol 5069
(Sea of Tunes, BMI)

9. **DRIP DROP**
D. DiMucci
J. Leiber–M. Stoller, Columbia
42917 (Tiger, BMI)

10. **POPSICLES ICICLES**
The Murmaids
D. Gates, Chattahoochee 428
(Gates–Dragonwyck, BMI)

1963

December 21

1. **DOMINIQUE**
The Singing Nun
Soeur Soruire, Philips 40152
(General, ASCAP)

2. **SINCE I FELL FOR YOU**
L. Welsh
B. Johnson, Cadence 1439
(Advanced, ASCAP)

3. **LOUIE, LOUIE**
The Kingsmen
R. Berry, Wand 143
(Limax, BMI)

4. **YOU DON'T HAVE TO BE A BABY TO CRY**
The Caravelles
Merrill–Shand, Smash 1852
(RFD, BMI)

5. **WONDERFUL SUMMER**
R. Ward
Garfield–Botkin, Dot 16530
(Rock Music, BMI)

6. **I'M LEAVING IT UP TO YOU**
Dale and Grace
Soeur Sourire, Philips 40152
(General, ASCAP)

7. **THERE! I'VE SAID IT AGAIN**
B. Vinton
Evans–Mann, Epic 9638
(Valiant, ASCAP)

8. **BE TRUE TO YOUR SCHOOL**
The Beach Boys
B. Wilson, Capitol 5069
(Sea of Tunes, BMI)

9. **DRIP DROP**
D. DiMucci
J. Leiber–M. Stoller, Columbia 42917 (Tiger, BMI)

10. **POPSICLES ICICLES**
The Murmaids
D. Gates, Chattahoochee 438
(Gates–Dragonwyck, BMI)

December 28

1. **DOMINIQUE**
The Singing Nun
Terry, Jr.–Harris, Montel
Michelle 921 (Venice, BMI)

2. **LOUIE, LOUIE**
The Kingsmen
R. Berry, Wand 143
(Limax, BMI)

3. **THERE! I'VE SAID IT AGAIN**
B. Vinton
Evans–Mann, Epic 9638
(Valiant, ASCAP)

4. **SINCE I FELL FOR YOU**
L. Welsh,
B. Johnson
Cadence 1439
(Advanced, ASCAP)

5. **YOU DON'T HAVE TO BE A BABY TO CRY**
The Caravelles
Merrill–Shand, Smash 1852
(RFD, ASCAP)

6. **FORGET HIM**
B. Rydell
M. Anthony–T. Hatch,
Cameo 280 (Leeds, ASCAP)

7. **POPSICLES ICICLES**
The Murmaids
D. Gates, Chattahoochee
438 (Gates–Dragonwyck, BMI)

8. **DRIP DROP**
D. DiMucci
J. Leiber–M. Stoller, Columbia 42917 (Tiger, BMI)

9. **BE TRUE TO YOUR SCHOOL**
The Beach Boys
B. Wilson, Capitol 5069
(Sea of Tunes, BMI)

10. **QUICKSAND**
Martha and the Vandellas
B. Gordy, Gordy 7823
(Jobete, BMI)

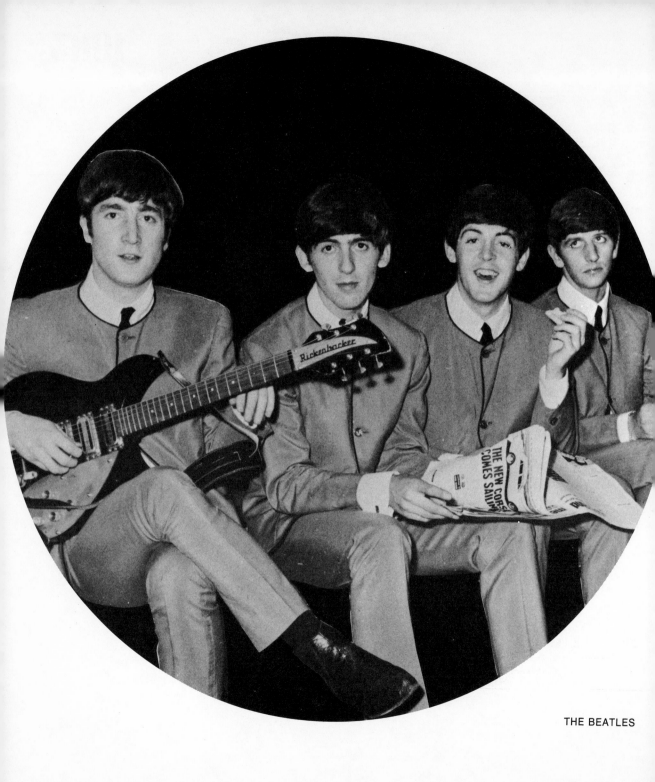

THE BEATLES

1964 slipped in quietly while most of the nation was still numbed by the assassination of President Kennedy. We knew things were happening in Washington, but we just weren't ready to pay attention.

When Barry Goldwater announced his candidacy for the Presidency in January, it wasn't much of a surprise or a promise. Would anyone capture our devotion like JFK had during the past three years? We could hardly imagine it. There seemed to be no more glamor in the world.

Bobby Vinton whined over the Top 40 stations. At least the Kingsmen were good to dance to. Everyone speculated on what was really said in the background of "Louie, Louie," but it was so garbled that it wasn't even banned by the most backward broadcasters. If "Louie, Louie" offended, then rock and roll fans redeemed themselves by making the Singing Nun's "Dominique" a Top 10 hit the first three weeks in 1964.

But we were still looking for some excitement—in music, in anything. Then, at the end of January, we heard confused rumors about a new kind of rock and roll. There was a song out by some singers in England about holding your hand or something. It was hard to believe that England could do more than imitate our sounds. Their top singer, Cliff Richards, was only a crooning copy of what we had in Elvis Presley, Rick Nelson, Ral Donner and Roy Orbison.

February brought the Twenty-Fourth Amendment, the first of the Jack Ruby trial and Cassius Clay's first heavyweight title, but none of these headlines could compare with the one being made in the rock and roll world.

On February 1 the Beatles, that English group we had been hearing about, had the Number 1 song, "I Want To Hold Your Hand." It was to become the Number 1 song of the year and the

1964

You've read about them in *Time, Newsweek, The New York Times.* Here's the big beat sound of that fantastic, phenominal foursome: Meet the Beatles!

"Meet the Beatles"
The first album by "England's phenominal pop combo"

beginning of a rock and roll renaissance. The Beatles weren't just a new group or a new sound. They were a whole new concept in music, dress and manner, and they were to hold this place in the pop culture as they led our tastes from England to India, skifle to electric blues, Edwardian suits to wire rimmed glasses.

The nation moved toward spring and Beatlemania blossomed into a mysterious and exciting subculture. In the ugly world there were race riots in Florida and Jack Ruby was found guilty of first degree murder. But in the world of rock and roll there was nothing but beauty. From the Mecca Liverpool came the music magic that brought life again to rock and roll.

All over the United States things were starting to go-go. We watched girls in cages do the newest dances at the discotheques that were springing up everywhere. Dances changed constantly. By now the twist was completely out of it, and the clumsier rock and roll fans longed for the old days when you could get by if you could "fast dance" and "slow dance." It was socially vital that you know the bird, the monkey, the U.T., the frug, the jerk, and in the West, something akin to the old slop.

This year, in fact, the West Coast drew itself away from the rest of the country in an all out effort to find its own identity. Though its identity crisis started a few years earlier, in 1964 the West gave itself completely to the Surf and all that that implied—long blond hair parted in the center, woodies, skateboards, striped T-shirts, cords, the ocean, and of course, the mighty spokesmen of the movement, the Beach Boys. There were others who tried to sing the glories of the Pacific—Jan and Dean, the Trashmen—but none were born to sing "surf's up" like Brian Wilson, backbone of the Beach Boys, who with a variety of assistants wrote all the major anthems of the surf set.

The new Western image of wind and waves posed problems for the kids who lives west of the Continental Divde. Those of New Mexico, Arizona, Nevada were really more familiar with desert sands than the seashore. And yet they could never declare an allegiance with the alien East.

And so the dry-land surfer sprang up, complete with the dress, hair and language of real surfdom. They would surf in rivers, swimming pools and irrigation canals, but even with such dedication they were scorned by surfers who had gotten their jams wet.

Though the inland Westerners couldn't make it with the wet set, their flat open country was perfect for the West's second true love—the car. All genuine and imitation Californians who weren't speeding across the waves were speeding across the wide new highways. There was plenty of road and room in every western state, and soon the surfing songwriters were writing about the wonders of the dragstrip. The Hondells, Ronny and the Daytonas, Jan and Dean and, most of all, the Beach Boys sang odes to their Hondas, GTO's, T-Birds and to Dead Man's Curve and the Little Old Lady from Pasadena.

On the East Coast there was still a lot of loyalty to New Jersey's own Frankie Valli and the Four Seasons. Their records of "Ronnie," "Rag Doll," "Dawn" and "Save It for Me" were all Top 10 hits in 1964. The East also gave us the Broadway music that made the Top 10. *Hello Dolly* and *Funny Girl* opened that year and produced "Hello Dolly" and "People", the biggest non-rock-and-roll songs of the year. The East still clung to its traditional love of soul, which was well-nourished by the booming Motown labels from Detroit.

Still, it is amazing to note that a year which saw music like this, plus the rise of superstars like the Supremes and Dionne Warwick, seemed at the time to be dominated totally by the Liverpool sound.

In April the Beatles had the top five recordings in the United States. A taste of the Beatles made our appetite for the British beat insatiable. The Dave Clark Five, the Kinks, Gerry and the Pacemakers, Peter and Gordon, Billy J. Kramer and the Zombies added a limey flavor to our rock and roll music. The DC 5 was really the first of these groups to spread the Mersey beat through the charts. Their first bit hit, "Glad All Over," set them up as possible challenge to the Beatles. Radio d.j.'s tried to encourage a rivalry between their fans, but in the end it was no contest. The Beatles were the musical wonder of the decade. They started the brilliant new trend in music.

This new rock and roll was written, played and sung by the members of the group. Each group was a tight portable unit that was perfect for concert performances. Maybe it was the availability of transportation or the money to back groups, or maybe it was because these were the first rock and roll stars who could sing well enough to perform live and could provide their own accompaniment, but suddenly concerts were the thing. Presley had had almost no live exposure. The singers of the early sixties had traveled in piecemeal caravans. But now rock groups traveled first class around the world and performed in the biggest and acoustically best auditoriums available.

The summer of 1964 saw huge excited gatherings of all sorts: the Republicans to nominate Barry Goldwater on the first ballot; the Democrats to pick Lyndon Johnson and Hubert Humphrey. But the largest attraction of all, even overshadowing the World's Fair in New York, were the Beatle concerts. In 1964 the Beatles traveled with the Righteous Brothers, Jackie De-Shannon and the Exciters. Coast to coast in a dozen or so lucky cities the Beatles arrived protected in armored cars and locked in hotel rooms. In every city they performed to screaming mobs who pelted them with jelly babies.

During the same summer crowds were congregating, frenzied by the frustration and futility of their lives rather than the presence of their heroes. These mobs had no more faith in heroes. They filled the streets of Philadelphia and of Harlem. They burned and looted in Rochester until Governor Rockefeller called out the National Guard. And then, to add to their anguish, the murdered bodies of three civil rights workers were found in Mississippi.

The only bright spot in the racial conflict was the passage and signing of the first meaningful Civil Rights Bill. And perhaps the winning of the Oscar for best actor by Sidney Poitier, the first black man so honored by the Academy. Poitier starred in *Lilies of the Field,* one of the nominees for best picture that was beaten out by *Tom Jones.*

But many of us had our own nominee for best movie, the Beatles' first film, *A Hard Day's Night.* As soon as it was released the Beatles were movie stars. We wanted to look at them up close, to study their styles, their mannerisms, their accents. On the large screen, boys could examine their Edwardian clothes and bowl haircuts so they could copy. Girls were looking to England for styles, too. Long straight hair, patterned stockings and most of all—or least of all—the miniskirt. If the Beatles liked them, they must be good.

We were infatuated with every aspect of the Beatle personality. We sat through *A Hard Day's Night* over and over to catch every word they spoke in Liverpudlian. The Liverpool accents didn't really show up when they sang, since they were singing like the older Nashville stars who influenced them.

A Hard Day's Night was a special victory for

all of us who had defended rock through the days of Bill Haley, Elvis Presley and U.S. Bonds. Our music enemies—parents, hard-core folkies, Frank Sinatra buffs, and those who called non-rock radio "good music stations"—were beginning to come around. The Beatles wrote melodies. You could understand the words. The words were worth understanding. The Beatles were called poets in this year of literary famine, which was otherwise highlighted by *Candy* and the *Warren Report,* and in which no Pulitzer Prizes were given.

Television gave us another chance to see the Beatles perform. Ed Sullivan scooped the nation with a Beatle telecast that broke all rating records, and reportedly stopped hubcap thefts across the country during that hour. This was also the year in which "Shindig" was conceived—a show which offered us the most exposure to rock stars since the old Dick Clark nighttime show. This show, later followed by "Hullabaloo," was set in a sort of discotheque while maintaining the adult variety-show presentation. The networks seemed a little afraid that the rock audience was still an underdog, too-young-to-fall-in-love group, since the host of "Shindig" closed the show each week with this touch of paranoia: "No matter what anybody says, rock on!"

We did rock on, into fall when there was more action in the political ranks than in the pop charts. Strom Thurmond left the Democratic Party to join the GOP. And Robert Kennedy left Washington to run for the Senate from New York. New York may have won Bobby Kennedy, but its Yankees lost the World Series to St. Louis in seven games.

Then, on November 3, Lyndon Johnson was elected President by the largest plurality ever, carrying with him Democratic victories in senatorial, gubernatorial and congressional races. People spoke of the death of the Republican party,

and it looked like Democratic-Liberal politics held an unshakable position in American government.

It also looked like the Supremes held an unshakable position with their Number 1 song, "Baby Love." The Supremes were the newest powerhouse from Motown. It was apparent they had fallen heir—or heiress—to our affection for the now faded girl groups of 1963. Three other girls were making it big in late 1964—the Shangri-Las with their song about the demise of their motorcycling hero, the "Leader of the Pack." Another morbid epic, and perhaps the last in the tearful tradition of "Teen Angel" and "Tell Laura I Love Her," was on the rise. It was J. Frank Wilson and the Cavalliers' eloquent tear-jerker, "Last Kiss."

Most of the hits in late 1964 had only been able to push their way into the Top 10 because the Beatles hadn't recorded new songs fast enough to fill the charts. So, after a late autumn digression into pre-Beatle days, our favorite Britons gave us a great Christmas present with their album "Beatles '65." From it came "I Feel Fine/"She's a Woman"—the Number 1 single as the year came to a close.

And "Beatles '65" turned out to be a good prediction. Their new, fuller, more melodic style was to dominate rock and roll music all through the new year.

THE TOP FIFTY
1964

1. **I WANT TO HOLD YOUR HAND**   The Beatles
2. **SHE LOVES YOU**   The Beatles
3. **LAST KISS**   J. Frank Wilson and the Cavaliers
4. **WHERE DID OUR LOVE GO**   The Supremes
5. **HELLO DOLLY**   L. Armstrong
6. **OH, PRETTY WOMAN**   R. Orbison
7. **MY GUY**   M. Wells
8. **LOVE ME DO**   The Beatles
9. **PLEASE, PLEASE ME**   The Beatles
10. **LITTLE CHILDREN**   B. J. Kramer
11. **PEOPLE**   B. Streisand
12. **UNDER THE BOARDWALK**   The Drifters
13. **RAG DOLL**   The Four Seasons
14. **BABY LOVE**   The Supremes
15. **WALK ON BY**   D. Warwick
16. **G.T.O.**   Ronnie and the Daytonas
17. **SHOOP SHOOP SONG**   B. Everett
18. **UM UM UM UM UM**   M. Lance
19. **DON'T LET THE SUN CATCH YOU CRYING**   Gerry and the Pacemakers
20. **A SUMMER SONG**   C. Stuart and J. Clyde
21. **DEAD MAN'S CURVE**   Jan and Dean
22. **I GET AROUND**   The Beach Boys
23. **EVERYBODY LOVES SOMEBODY**   D. Martin
24. **A HARD DAY'S NIGHT**   The Beatles
25. **CHAPEL OF LOVE**   The Dixiecups
26. **WE'LL SING IN THE SUNSHINE**   G. Garnett
27. **JAVA**   A. Hirt
28. **BREAD AND BUTTER**   The Newbeats
29. **WISHIN' AND HOPIN'**   D. Springfield
30. **SUSPICION**   T. Stafford
31. **LET IT BE ME**   J. Butler and B. Everett
32. **MY BOY LOLLIPOP**   M. Small
33. **DO WAH DIDDY DIDDY**   M. Mann
34. **DANCING IN THE STREETS**   Martha and the Vandellas
35. **GIRL FROM IPANEMA**   S. Getz/A. Gilberto
36. **NAVY BLUE**   D. Renay
37. **BABY I NEED YOUR LOVING**   The Four Tops
38. **DO YOU WANT TO KNOW A SECRET?**   The Beatles
39. **(JUST LIKE) ROMEO AND JULIET**   The Reflections
40. **LEADER OF THE PACK**   The Shangri-Las
41. **HOW DO YOU DO IT?**   Gerry and the Pacemakers
42. **BAD TO ME**   B. J. Kramer
43. **LITTLE HONDA**   The Hondells
44. **CAN'T BUY ME LOVE**   The Beatles
45. **REMEMBER (WALKIN' IN THE SAND)**   The Sangri-Las
46. **SEE THE FUNNY LITTLE CLOWN**   B. Goldsboro
47. **GLAD ALL OVER**   The Dave Clark Five
48. **HAVE I THE RIGHT?**   The Honeycombs
49. **WHITE ON WHITE**   D. Williams
50. **BITS AND PIECES**   D. Clark Five

January 4

1. **LOUIE, LOUIS**
The Kingsmen
R. Berry, Wand 143
(Limax, BMI)

2. **THERE! I'VE SAID IT AGAIN**
B. Vinton
Evans–Mann, Epic 9638
(Valiant, ASCAP)

3. **DOMINIQUE**
The Singing Nun
Soeur Sourire, Philips 40163
(General, ASCAP)

4. **QUICKSAND**
Martha and the Vandellas
B. Gordy, Gordy 7823
(Jobete, BMI)

5. **SINCE I FELL FOR YOU**
L. Welsh
B. Johnson, Cadence 1439
(Advanced, ASCAP)

6. **FORGET HIM**
B. Rydell
*M. Anthony–T. Hatch, Cameo
280 (Leeds, ASCAP)*

7. **THE NITTY GRITTY**
S. Ellis
L.Chase, Congress 283
(Gallice, BMI)

8. **POPSICLES ICICLES**
The Murmaids
D. Gates, Chattahoochee 438
(Gates–Dragonwyck, BMI)

9. **TALK BACK WITH TREM-
BLIN' LIPS**
J. Tillotson
J. Loudermilk, MGM 13181
(Acuff–Rose, BMI)

10. **YOU DON'T HAVE TO BE A
BABY TO CRY**
The Caravelles
Merrill–Shand, Smash 1852–
(RFD, ASCAP)

January 11

1. **LOUIE, LOUIE**
The Kingsmen
R. Berry, Wand 143
(Limax, BMI)

2. **QUICKSAND**
Martha and the Vandellas
B. Gordy, Gordy 7823
(Jobete, BMI)

3. **THERE! I'VE SAID IT AGAIN**
B. Vinton
Evans–Mann, Epic 9638
(Valiant, ASCAP)

4. **FORGET HIM**
B. Rydell
*M. Anthony–T. Hatch, Cameo
280 (Leeds, ASCAP)*

5. **DOMINIQUE**
The Singing Nun
*Soeur Sourire, Philips
40163 (General, ASCAP)*

6. **THE NITTY GRITTY**
S. Ellis
L. Chase, Congress 283
(Gallice, BMI)

7. **SINCE I FELL FOR YOU**
L. Welsh
B. Johnson, Cadence 1439
(Advanced, ASCAP)

8. **SURFIN' BIRD**
The Trashmen
S. Wahrer, Garrett 4002
(Willong, BMI)

9. **MIDNIGHT MARY**
J. Powers
Wayne–Raleigh, Amy 982
(Jimskip, BMI)

10. **TALK BACK WITH TREM-
BLIN' LIPS**
J. Tillotson
J. Loudermilk, M-G-M 13181
(Acuff–Rose, BMI)

1964

January 18

1. **LOUIE, LOUIE**
The Kingsmen
R. Berry, Wand 143
(Limax, BMI)

2. **FORGET HIM**
B. Rydell
M. Anthony–T. Hatch, Cameo 280 (Leeds, ASCAP)

3. **THERE! I'VE SAID IT AGAIN**
B. Vinton
Evans–Mann, Epic 9638 (Valiant, ASCAP)

4. **SURFIN' BIRD**
The Trashmen
S. Wahrer, Garrett 4002 (Willong, BMI)

5. **THE NITTY GRITTY**
S. Ellis
L. Chase, Congress 283 (Gallice, BMI)

6. **QUICKSAND**
Martha and the Vandellas
B. Gordy, Gordy 7823 (Jobete, BMI)

7. **OUT OF LIMITS**
The Marketts
M. Gordon, Warner Brothers 5391 (Wrist, BMI)

8. **DRAG CITY**
Jan and Dean
J. Berry–R. Christian–B. Wilson, Liberty 55641 (Screen Gems–Columbia, BMI)

9. **DOMINIQUE**
The Singing Nun
Soeur Sourire, Philips 40163 (General, ASCAP)

10. **HEY LITTLE COBRA**
The Rip Chords
C. Conners–M. H. Conners, Columbia 42921 (Vadim, BMI)

January 25

1. **THERE! I'VE SAID IT AGAIN**
B. Vinton
Evans–Mann, Epic 9638 (Valiant, ASCAP)

2. **LOUIE, LOUIE**
The Kingsmen
R. Berry, Wand 143 (Limax, BMI)

3. **SURFIN' BIRD**
The Trashmen
S. Wahrer, Garrett 4002 (Willong, BMI)

4. **OUT OF LIMITS**
The Marketts
M. Gordon, Warner Brothers 5391 (Wrist, BMI)

5. **I WANT TO HOLD YOUR HAND**
The Beatles
J. Lennon–P. McCartney, Capitol 5112 (Duchess, BMI)

6. **THE NITTY GRITTY**
S. Ellis
L. Chase Congress 283 (Gallice, BMI)

7. **HEY LITTLE COBRA**
The Rip Chords
C. Conners–M. H. Conners, Columbia 42921 (Vadim, BMI)

8. **FORGET HIM**
B. Rydell
M. Anthony–T. Hatch, Cameo 280 (Leeds, ASCAP)

9. **UM UM UM UM UM**
M. Lance
C. Mayfield, Okeh 7187 (Curtom–Jalynne, BMI)

10. **DRAG CITY**
Jan and Dean
J. Berry–R. Christian–B. Wilson, Liberty 55641 (Screen Gems–Columbia, BMI)

February 1

1. **I WANT TO HOLD YOUR HAND**
The Beatles
J. Lennon–P. McCartney, Capitol 5112 (Duchess, BMI)

2. **YOU DON'T OWN ME**
L. Gore
Madora–White, Mercury 72206 (Merjoda, BMI)

3. **OUT OF LIMITS**
The Marketts
M. Gordon, Warner Brothers 5391 (Wrist, BMI)

4. **SURFIN' BIRD**
The Trashmen
S. Wahrer, Garrett 4002 (Willong, BMI)

5. **HEY LITTLE COBRA**
The Rip Chords
C. Conners–M. H. Conners, Columbia 42921 (Vadim, BMI)

6. **LOUIE, LOUIE**
The Kingsmen
R. Berry, Wand 143 (Limax, BMI)

7. **THERE! I'VE SAID IT AGAIN**
B. Vinton
Evans–Mann, Epic 9638 (Valiant, ASCAP)

8. **UM UM UM UM UM**
M. Lance
C. Mayfield, Okeh 7187 (Curtom–Jalynne, BMI)

9. **ANYONE WHO HAD A HEART**
D. Warwick
B. Bacharach–H. David, Scepter 1262 (U.S. Songs, ASCAP)

10. **FOR YOU**
R. Nelson
J. Burke–A. Dubin, Decca 31574 (Witmark, ASCAP)

245

February 8

1. **I WANT TO HOLD YOUR HAND**
The Beatles
J. Lennon–P. McCartney,
Capitol 5112 (Duchess, BMI)

2. **YOU DON'T OWN ME**
L. Gore
Madora–White, Mercury 72206
(Merjoda, BMI)

3. **OUT OF LIMITS**
The Marketts
M. Gordon, Warner Brothers
5391 (Wrist, BMI)

4. **UM UM UM UM UM**
M. Lance
C. Mayfield, Okeh 7187
(Curtom–Jalynne, BMI)

5. **HEY LITTLE COBRA**
The Rip Chords
C. Conners–M. H. Conners,
Columbia 42921 (Vadim, BMI)

6. **SHE LOVES YOU**
The Beatles
J. Lennon–P. McCartney,
Swan 4152 (Gil, BMI)

7. **FOR YOU**
R. Nelson
J. Burke–A. Dubin, Decca 31574
(Witmark, ASCAP)

8. **SURFIN' BIRD**
The Trashmen
S. Wahrer, Garrett 4002
(Willong, BMI)

9. **ANYONE WHO HAD A HEART**
D. Warwick
B. Bacharach–H. David, Scepter
1262 (U.S. Songs, ASCAP)

10. **JAVA**
A. Hirt
A. Toussaint–Tyler–Friday,
Victor 8280 (Tideland, BMI)

February 15

1. **I WANT TO HOLD YOUR HAND**
J. Lennon–P. McCartney, Capitol
5112 (Duchess, BMI)

2. **SHE LOVES YOU**
The Beatles
J. Lennon–P. McCartney, Swan
4152 (Gil, BMI)

3. **YOU DON'T OWN ME**
L. Gore
Madora–White, Mercury 72206
(Merjoda, BMI)

4. **UM UM UM UM UM**
M. Lance
C. Mayfield, Okeh 7187
(Curtom–Jalynne, BMI)

5. **HEY LITTLE COBRA**
The Rip Chords
C. Conners–M. H. Conners,
Columbia 42921 (Vadim, BMI)

6. **FOR YOU**
R. Nelson
J. Burke–A. Dubin, Decca 31574
(Witmark, ASCAP)

7. **ANYONE WHO HAD A HEART**
D. Warwick
B. Bacharach–H. David, Scepter
1262 (U.S. Songs, ASCAP)

8. **JAVA**
A. Hirt
A. Toussaint–Tyler–Friday,
Victor 8280 (Tideland, BMI)

9. **CALIFORNIA SUN**
The Rivieras
H. Glover, Riviera 1401
(Lloyd & Lagan, BMI)

10. **OUT OF LIMITS**
The Marketts
M. Gordon, Warner Brothers
5391 (Wrist, BMI)

February 22

1. **I WANT TO HOLD YOUR HAND**
The Beatles
J. Lennon–P. McCartney,
Capitol 5112 (Duchess, BMI)

2. **SHE LOVES YOU**
The Beatles
J. Lennon–P. McCartney, Swan
4252 (Gil, BMI)

3. **DAWN (GO AWAY)**
The Four Seasons
B. Gaudio, Philips 40166
(Saturday–Gavadima, ASCAP)

4. **YOU DON'T OWN ME**
L. Gore
Madora–White, Mercury 72206
(Merjoda, BMI)

5. **JAVA**
A. Hirt
A. Toussaint–Tyler–Friday,
Victor 8280 (Tideland, BMI)

6. **UM UM UM UM UM**
M. Lance
C. Mayfield, Okeh 7187
(Curtom–Jalynne, BMI)

7. **HEY LITTLE COBRA**
The Rip Chords
C. Conners–M. H. Conners,
Columbia 42921 (Vadim, BMI)

8. **CALIFORNIA SUN**
The Rivieras
H. Glover, Riviera 1401
(Lloyd& Lagan, BMI)

9. **WHAT KIND OF FOOL (DO YOU THINK I AM)?**
The Tams
R. Whitlay, ABC–Paramount
10502 (Low-Tri, BMI)

10. **NAVY BLUE**
D. Renay
B. Crewe–E. Rambeau, 20th Century Fox 456 (Saturday, ASCAP

1964

February 29

1. **I WANT TO HOLD YOUR HAND**
The Beatles
J. Lennon–P. McCartney,
Capitol 5112   (Duchess, BMI)

2. **SHE LOVES YOU**
The Beatles
J. Lennon–P. McCartney,
Swan 4152   (Gil, BMI)

3. **DAWN (GO AWAY)**
The Four Seasons
B. Gaudio,   Philips 40166
(Saturday–Gavadima, ASCAP)

4. **JAVA**
A. Hirt
A. Toussaint–Tyler–Friday,
Victor 8280   (Tideland, BMI)

5. **CALIFORNIA SUN**
The Rivieras
H. Glover,   Riviera 1401
(Lloyd & Lagan, BMI)

6. **PLEASE, PLEASE ME**
The Beatles
J. Lennon–P. McCartney,
VeeJay 581 (Concertone, AS-
CAP)

7. **YOU DON'T OWN ME**
L. Gore
Madora–White,   Mercury 72206
(Merjoda, BMI)

8. **UM UM UM UM UM**
M. Lance
C. Mayfield,   Okeh 7187
(Curtom–Jalynne, BMI)

9. **NAVY BLUE**
D. Renay
B. Crewe–E. Rambeau,   20th Cen-
tury Fox 456   (Saturday, ASCAP)

10. **STOP AND THINK IT OVER**
Dale and Grace
J. Graffiano,   Montel 922
(Crazy Cajun–Red Sticy, BMI)

March 7

1. **SHE LOVES YOU**
The Beatles
J. Lennon–P. McCartney,
Swan 4152   (Gil, BMI)

2. **I WANT TO HOLD YOUR HAND**
The Beatles
J. Lennon–P. McCartney,
Capitol 5112   (Duchess, BMI)

3. **PLEASE, PLEASE ME**
The Beatles
J. Lennon–P. McCartney,
VeeJay 581 (Concertone, AS-
CAP)

4. **JAVA**
A. Hirt
A. Toussaint–Tyler–Friday,
Victor 8280   (Tideland, BMI)

5. **DAWN (GO AWAY)**
The Four Seasons
B. Gaudio,   Philips 40166
(Saturday–Gavadima, ASCAP)

6. **NAVY BLUE**
D. Renay
B. Crew–E. Rambeau,
20th Century Fox 456
(Saturday, ASCAP)

7. **SEE THE FUNNY LITTLE CLOWN**
B. Goldsboro
B. Goldsboro,   United Artists
672   (Unart, BMI)

8. **FUN, FUN, FUN**
The Beach Boys
B. Wilson–M. Love,   Capitol
5118   (Sea of Tunes, BMI)

9. **STOP AND THINK IT OVER**
Dale and Grace
J. Graffiano,   Montel 922
(Crazy Cajun–Red Sticy, BMI)

10. **CALIFORNIA SUN**
The Rivieras
H. Glover,   Riviera 1401
(Lloyd & Lagan, BMI)

March 14

1. **PLEASE, PLEASE ME**
The Beatles
J. Lennon–P. McCartney,
VeeJay 581 (Concertone, AS-
CAP)

2. **I WANT TO HOLD YOUR HAND**
The Beatles
J. Lennon–P. McCartney,
Capitol 5112   (Duchess, BMI)

3. **SHE LOVES YOU**
The Beatles
J. Lennon–P. McCartney,
Swan 4152   (Gil, BMI)

4. **DAWN (GO AWAY)**
The Four Seasons
B. Gaudio,   Philips 40166
(Saturday–Gavadima, ASCAP)

5. **JAVA**
A. Hirt
A. Toussaint–Tyler–Friday,
Victor 8280   (Tideland, BMI)

6. **NAVY BLUE**
D. Renay
B. Crewe–E. Rambeau,
20th Century Fox 456
(Saturday, ASCAP)

7. **FUN, FUN, FUN**
The Beach Boys
B. Wilson–M. Love,   Capitol
5118   (Sea of Tunes, BMI)

8. **CALIFORNIA SUN**
The Rivieras
H. Glover,   Riviera 1401
(Lloyd & Lagan, BMI)

9. **SEE THE FUNNY LITTLE CLOWN**
B. Goldsboro
B. Goldsboro,   United Artists
672   (Unart, BMI)

10. **I LOVE YOU MORE AND MORE EVERY DAY**
A. Martino
D. Robertson,   Capitol 5104
(Robertson, ASCAP)

March 21

1. **SHE LOVES YOU**
   The Beatles
   J. Lennon–P. McCartney,
   Swan 4152 (Gil, BMI)

2. **I WANT TO HOLD YOUR HAND**
   The Beatles
   J. Lennon–P. McCartney,
   Capitol 5112 (Duchess, BMI)

3. **PLEASE, PLEASE ME**
   The Beatles
   J. Lennon–P. McCartney,
   VeeJay 581 (Concertone, AS-
   CAP)

4. **DAWN (GO AWAY)**
   The Four Seasons
   B. Gaudio, Philips 40166
   (Saturday–Gavadima, ASCAP)

5. **FUN, FUN, FUN**
   The Beach Boys
   B. Wilson–M. Love, Capitol
   5118 (Sea of Tunes, BMI)

6. **NAVY BLUE**
   D. Renay
   B. Crewe–E. Rambeau,
   20th Century Fox 456
   (Saturday, ASCAP)

7. **TWIST AND SHOUT**
   The Beatles
   P. Medley–B. Russell, Tollie 9001
   (Mellin–Progressive, BMI)

8. **JAVA**
   A. Hirt
   A. Toussaint–Tyler–Friday,
   Victor 8280 (Tideland, BMI)

9. **I LOVE YOU MORE AND MORE EVERY DAY**
   A. Martino
   D. Robertson, Capitol 5104
   (Robertson, ASCAP)

10. **HELLO DOLLY**
    L. Armstrong
    J. Herman, Kapp 573
    (Morris, ASCAP)

March 28

1. **SHE LOVES YOU**
   The Beatles
   J. Lennon–P. McCartney,
   Swan 4152 (Gil, BMI)

2. **TWIST AND SHOUT**
   The Beatles
   P. Medley–B. Russell, Tollie 9001
   (Mellin–Progressive, BMI)

3. **PLEASE, PLEASE ME**
   The Beatles
   J. Lennon–P. McCartney, VeeJay
   581 (Concertone, ASCAP)

4. **I WANT TO HOLD YOUR HAND**
   The Beatles
   J. Lennon–P. McCartney,
   Capitol 5112 (Duchess, BMI)

5. **SUSPICION**
   T. Stafford
   D. Pomus–D. Daniels, Crusader
   101 (Elvis Presley, BMI)

6. **HELLO DOLLY**
   L. Armstrong
   J. Herman, Kapp 573
   (Morris, ASCAP)

7. **FUN, FUN, FUN**
   The Beach Boys
   B. Wilson–M. Love, Capitol
   5118 (Sea of Tunes, BMI)

8. **GLAD ALL OVER**
   The Dave Clark Five
   D. Clark–M. Smith, Epic 9656
   (Campbell Conelly, ASCAP)

9. **DAWN (GO AWAY)**
   The Four Seasons
   B. Gaudio, Philips 40166
   (Saturday–Gavadima, ASCAP)

10. **MY HEART BELONGS TO ONLY YOU**
    B. Vinton
    F. Daniels–D. Daniels,
    Epic 9662 (Regent, BMI)

April 4

1. **TWIST AND SHOUT**
   The Beatles
   P. Medley–B. Russell, Tollie 9001
   (Mellin–Progressive, BMI)

2. **CAN'T BUY ME LOVE**
   The Beatles
   J. Lennon–P. McCartney,
   Capitol 5150 (Northern, ASCAP)

3. **PLEASE, PLEASE ME**
   The Beatles
   J. Lennon–P. McCartney,
   VeeJay 581 (Concertone, AS-
   CAP)

4. **SHE LOVES YOU**
   The Beatles
   J. Lennon–P. McCartney,
   Swan 4152 (Gil, BMI)

5. **I WANT TO HOLD YOUR HAND**
   The Beatles
   J. Lennon–P. McCartney,
   Capitol 5112 (Duchess, BMI)

6. **SHOOP SHOOP SONG**
   B. Everett
   R. Clark, VeeJay 585
   (T.M., BMI)

7. **SUSPICION**
   T. Stafford
   D. Pomus–D. Daniels, Crusader
   101 (Elvis Presley, BMI)

8. **HELLO DOLLY**
   L. Armstrong
   J. Herman, Kapp 573
   (Morris, ASCAP)

9. **MY HEART BELONGS TO ONLY YOU**
   B. Vinton
   F. Daniels–D. Daniels, Epic
   9662 (Regent, BMI)

10. **GLAD ALL OVER**
    The Dave Clark Five
    D. Clark–M. Smith, Epic 9656
    (Campbell Conelly, ASCAP)

1964

April 11

1. **CAN'T BUY ME LOVE**
   The Beatles
   J. Lennon–P. McCartney,
   Capitol 5150 (Northern, ASCAP)

2. **TWIST AND SHOUT**
   The Beatles
   P. Medley–B. Russell, Tollie 9001
   (Mellin–Progressive, BMI)

3. **SUSPICION**
   T. Stafford
   D. Pomus–D. Daniels, Crusader
   101 (Elvis Presley, BMI)

4. **SHE LOVES YOU**
   The Beatles
   J. Lennon–P. McCartney,
   Swan 4152 (Gil, BMI)

5. **HELLO DOLLY**
   L. Armstrong
   J. Herman, Kapp 573
   (Morris, ASCAP)

6. **SHOOP SHOOP SONG**
   B. Everett
   R. Clark, VeeJay 585
   (T.M., BMI)

7. **I WANT TO HOLD YOUR HAND**
   The Beatles
   J. Lennon–P. McCartney,
   Capitol 5112 (Duchess, BMI)

8. **GLAD ALL OVER**
   The Dave Clark Five
   D. Clark–M. Smith, Epic 9656
   (Campbell Conelly, ASCAP)

9. **PLEASE, PLEASE ME**
   The Beatles
   J. Lennon–P. McCartney,
   VeeJay 581 (Concertone, AS-
   CAP)

10. **DON'T LET THE RAIN COME DOWN (CROOKED LITTLE MAN)**
    The Serendipity Singers
    Bowers–Sennett–Madden,
    Philips 40175 (Serendipity, BMI)

April 18

1. **CAN'T BUY ME LOVE**
   The Beatles
   J. Lennon–P. McCartney,
   Capitol 5150 (Northern, ASCAP)

2. **TWIST AND SHOUT**
   The Beatles
   P. Medley–B. Russell, Tollie 9001
   (Mellin–Progressive, BMI)

3. **SUSPICION**
   T. Stafford
   D. Pomus–D. Daniels,
   Crusader 101 (Elvis Presley, BMI)

4. **HELLO DOLLY**
   L. Armstrong
   J. Herman, Kapp 573
   (Morris, ASCAP)

5. **DO YOU WANT TO KNOW A SECRET?**
   The Beatles
   J. Lennon–P. McCartney,
   VeeJay 587 (Metric, BMI)

6. **GLAD ALL OVER**
   The Dave Clark Five
   D. Clark–M. Smith, Epic 9656
   (Campbell Conelly, ASCAP)

7. **SHE LOVES YOU**
   The Beatles
   J. Lennon–P. McCartney,
   Swan 4152 (Gil, BMI)

8. **SHOOP SHOOP SONG**
   B. Everett
   R. Clark, VeeJay 585
   (T.M., BMI)

9. **MY GUY**
   M. Wells
   W. Robinson, Motown 1056
   (Jobete, BMI)

10. **DON'T LET THE RAIN COME DOWN (CROOKED LITTLE MAN)**
    The Serendipity Singers
    Bowers–Sennet–Madden, Philips
    40175 (Serendipity, BMI)

April 25

1. **CAN'T BUY ME LOVE**
   The Beatles
   J. Lennon–P. McCartney, Capitol
   5150 (Northern, ASCAP)

2. **DO YOU WANT TO KNOW A SECRET?**
   The Beatles
   J. Lennon–P. McCartney,
   VeeJay 587 (Metric, BMI)

3. **TWIST AND SHOUT**
   The Beatles
   P. Medley–B. Russell, Tollie 9001
   (Mellin–Progressive, BMI)

4. **SUSPICION**
   T. Stafford
   D. Pomus–D. Daniels, Crusader
   101 (Elvis Presley, BMI)

5. **HELLO DOLLY**
   L. Armstrong
   J. Herman, Kapp 573
   (Morris, ASCAP)

6. **BITS AND PIECES**
   The Dave Clark Five
   D. Clark–L. Chappell Epic 9656
   (Beechwood, BMI)

7. **SHE LOVES YOU**
   The Beatles
   J. Lennon–P. McCartney, Swan
   4152 (Gil, BMI)

8. **MY GUY**
   M. Wells
   W. Robinson, Motown 1056
   (Jobete, BMI)

9. **GLAD ALL OVER**
   The Dave Clark Five
   D. Clark–M. Smith, Epic 9656
   (Campbell Conelly, ASCAP)

10. **DON'T LET THE RAIN COME DOWN (CROOKED LITTLE MAN)**
    The Serendipity Singers
    Bowers–Sennett–Madden, Philips
    40175 (Serendipity, BMI)

May 2

1. **CAN'T BUY ME LOVE**
The Beatles
J. Lennon–P. McCartney, Capitol 5150 (Northern, ASCAP)

2. **DO YOU WANT TO KNOW A SECRET?**
The Beatles
J. Lennon–P. McCartney, VeeJay 587 (Metric, BMI)

3. **HELLO DOLLY**
L. Armstrong
J. Herman, Kapp 573 (Morris, ASCAP)

4. **BITS AND PIECES**
The Dave Clark Five
D. Clark–L. Chappell, Epic 9671 (Beechwood, BMI)

5. **MY GUY**
M. Wells
W. Robinson, Motown 1056 (Jobete, BMI)

6. **DON'T LET THE RAIN COME DOWN (CROOKED LITTLE MAN)**
The Serendipity Singers
Bowers–Sennett–Madden, Philips 40175 (Serendipity, BMI)

7. **TWIST AND SHOUT**
The Beatles
P. Medley–B. Russell, Tollie 9001 (Mellin–Progressive, BMI)

8. **SUSPICION**
T. Stafford
D. Pomus–D. Daniels, Crusader 101 (Elvis Presley, BMI)

9. **DEAD MAN'S CURVE**
Jan and Dean
B. Wilson–Berry–R. Christian–Cornfield, Liberty 55672 (Screen Gems–Columbia, BMI)

10. **RONNIE**
The Four Seaons
B. Crewe–B. Gaudio, Philips 40185 (Saturday–Gavadima, ASCAP)

May 9

1. **HELLO DOLLY**
L. Armstrong
J. Herman, Kapp 573 (Morris, ASCAP)

2. **DO YOU WANT TO KNOW A SECRET?**
The Beatles
J. Lennon–P. McCartney, VeeJay 587 (Metric, BMI)

3. **MY GUY**
M. Wells
W. Robinson, Motown 1056 (Jobete, BMI)

4. **BITS AND PIECES**
The Dave Clark Five
D. Clark–L. Chappell, Epic 9671 (Beechwood, BMI)

5. **CAN'T BUY ME LOVE**
The Beatles
J. Lennon–P. McCartney, Capitol 5150 (Northern, ASCAP)

6. **DON'T LET THE RAIN COME DOWN (CROOKED LITTLE MAN)**
The Serendipity Singers
Bowers–Sennett–Madden, Philips 40175 (Serendipity, BMI)

7. **RONNIE**
The Four Seasons
B. Crewe–B. Gaudio, Philips 40185 (Saturday–Gavadima, ASCAP)

8. **DEAD MEAN'S CURVE**
Jan and Dean
B. Wilson–Berry–R. Christian–Cornfield, Liberty 55672 (Screen Gems–Columbia, BMI)

9. **SUSPICION**
T. Stafford
D. Pomus–D. Daniels, Crusader 101 (Elvis Presley, BMI)

10. **WHITE ON WHITE**
D. Williams
L. Crane–B. Ross, United Artists 685 (Painted Desert, BMI)

May 16

1. **MY GUY**
M. Wells
W. Robinson, Motown 1056 (Jobete, BMI)

2. **HELLO DOLLY**
L. Armstrong
J. Herman, Kapp 573 (Morris, ASCAP)

3. **LOVE ME DO**
The Beatles
J. Lennon–P. McCartney, Tollie 9008 (Ardmore–Beechwood, BMI)

4. **BITS AND PIECES**
The Dave Clark Five
D. Clark–L. Chappell, Epic 9671 (Beechwood, BMI)

5. **DO YOU WANT TO KNOW A SECRET?**
The Beatles
J. Lennon–P. McCartney, VeeJay 587 (Metric, BMI)

6. **RONNIE**
The Four Seasons
B. Crewe–B. Gaudio, Philips 40185 (Saturday–Gavadima, ASCAP)

7. **DON'T LET THE RAIN COME DOWN (CROOKED LITTLE MAN)**
The Serendipity Singers
Bowers–Sennett–Madden, Philips 40175 (Serendipity, BMI)

8. **DEAD MAN'S CURVE**
Jan and Dean
B. Wilson–Berry–R. Christian–Cornfield, Liberty 55672 (Screen Gems–Columbia, BMI)

9. **WHITE ON WHITE**
D. Williams
L. Crane–B. Ross, United Artists 685 (Painted Desert, BMI)

10. **IT'S OVER**
R. Orbison
R. Orbison–Dees, Monument 837 (Acuff–Rose, BMI)

May 23

1. **MY GUY**
M. Wells
*W. Robinson, Motown 1056
(Jobete, BMI)*

2. **LOVE ME DO**
The Beatles
*J. Lennon–P. McCartney,
Tollie 9008 (Ardmore–
Beechwood, BMI)*

3. **HELLO DOLLY**
L. Armstrong
*J. Herman, Kapp 573
(Morris, ASCAP)*

4. **CHAPEL OF LOVE**
The Dixie Cups
*J. Barry–E. Greenwich–
P. Spector, Red Bird 001
(Trio, BMI)*

5. **LOVE ME WITH ALL YOUR
HEART**
The Ray Charles Singers
*H. Vaughn–C. Rigual, Command
4046 (Peer–International, BMI)*

6. **BITS AND PIECES**
The Dave Clark Five
*D. Clark–L. Chappell, Epic
9671 (Beechwood, BMI)*

7. **(JUST LIKE) ROMEO AND
JULIET**
The Reflections
*B. Hamilton–F. Gorman,
Golden World 9 (Myto, BMI)*

8. **A WORLD WITHOUT LOVE**
Peter and Gordon
*J. Lennon–P. McCartney,
Capitol 5175 (Northern, AS-
CAP)*

9. **RONNIE**
The Four Seasons
*B. Crewe–B. Gaudio, Philips
40185 (Saturday–Gavadima,
ASCAP)*

10. **IT'S OVER**
R. Orbison
*R. Orbison–Dees, Monument
837 (Acuff–Rose, BMI)*

May 30

1. **CHAPEL OF LOVE**
The Dixie Cups
*J. Barry–E. Greenwich–
P. Spector, Red Bird 001
(Trio, BMI)*

2. **LOVE ME WITH ALL YOUR
HEART**
The Ray Charles Singers
*H. Vaughn–C. Rigual,
Command 4046
(Peer–International, BMI)*

3. **LOVE ME DO**
The Beatles
*J. Lennon–P. McCartney,
Tollie 9008 (Ardmore–
Beechwood, BMI)*

4. **MY GUY**
M. Wells
*W. Robinson, Motown 1056
(Jobete, BMI)*

5. **(JUST LIKE) ROMEO AND
JULIET**
The Reflections
*B. Hamilton–F. Gorman, Golden
World 9 (Myto, BMI)*

6. **LITTLE CHILDREN**
B. J. Kramer with the
Dakotas
*M. Shuman–J. L. McFarland,
Imperial 5175 (Rumbalero, BMI)*

7. **A WORLD WITHOUT LOVE**
Peter and Gordon
*J. Lennon–P. McCartney,
Capitol 5175 (Northern, ASCAP)*

8. **HELLO DOLLY**
L. Armstrong
*J. Herman, Kapp 573
(Morris, ASCAP)*

9. **WALK ON BY**
D. Warwick
*B. Bacharach–H. David, Scepter
1274 (Blue Seas Inc., ASCAP)*

10. **IT'S OVER**
R. Orbison
*Orbison–Dees, Monument 837
(Acuff–Rose, BMI)*

June 6

1. **LOVE ME DO**
The Beatles
*J. Lennon–P. McCartney, Tollie
9008 (Ardmore–Beechwood, BMI)*

2. **CHAPEL OF LOVE**
The Dixie Cups
*J. Barry–E. Greenwich–
P. Spector, Red Bird 001
(Trio, BMI)*

3. **LOVE ME WITH ALL YOUR
HEART**
The Ray Charles Singers
*H. Vaughn–C. Rigual, Command
4046 (Peer–International, BMI)*

4. **MY GUY**
M. Wells
*W. Robinson, Motown 1056
(Jobete, BMI)*

5. **HELLO DOLLY**
L. Armstrong
*J. Herman, Kapp 573
(Morris, BMI)*

6. **A WORLD WITHOUT LOVE**
Peter and Gordon
*J. Lennon–P. McCartney,
Capitol 5175 (Northern, AS-
CAP)*

7. **WALK ON BY**
D. Warwick
*B. Bacharach–H. David, Scepter
1274 (Blue Seas Inc., ASCAP)*

8. **LITTLE CHILDREN**
B. J. Kramer with the
Dakotas
*M. Shuman–J. L. McFarland,
Imperial 5175 (Rumbalero, BMI)*

9. **(JUST LIKE) ROMEO AND
JULIET**
The Reflections
*B. Hamilton–F. Gorman, Golden
World 9 (Myto, BMI)*

10. **P.S. I LOVE YOU**
The Beatles
*J. Lennon–P. McCartney, Tollie
9008 (Beechwood, BMI)*

June 13

1. **CHAPEL OF LOVE**
The Dixie Cups
J. Barry–E. Greenwich–
P. Spector, Red Bird 001
(Trio, BMI)

2. **A WORLD WITHOUT LOVE**
Peter and Gordon
J. Lennon–P. McCartney,
Capitol 5175 (Northern, AS-
CAP)

3. **LOVE ME WITH ALL YOUR HEART**
The Ray Charles Singers
H. Vaughn–C. Rigual, Command
4046 (Peer–International, BMI)

4. **LOVE ME DO**
The Beatles
J. Lennon–P. McCartney, Tollie
9008 (Ardmore–Beechwood,
BMI)

5. **MY GUY**
M. Wells
W. Robinson, Motown 1056
(Jobete, BMI)

6. **WALK ON BY**
D. Warwick
B. Bacharach–H. David, Sceptor
1274 (Blue Seas Inc., ASCAP)

7. **LITTLE CHILDREN**
B. J. Kramer with the Dakotas
M. Shuman–J. L. McFarland,
Imperial 5175 (Rumbalero, BMI)

8. **HELLO DOLLY**
L. Armstrong
J. Herman, Kapp 573
(Morris, BMI)

9. **PEOPLE**
B. Streisand
J. Stein–B. Merrill, Columbia
42968 (Chappell, ASCAP)

10. **I GET AROUND**
The Beach Boys
B. Wilson, Capitol 5174
(Sea of Tunes, BMI)

June 20

1. **A WORLD WITHOUT LOVE**
Peter and Gordon
J. Lennon–P. McCartney, Capitol
5175 (Northern, ASCAP)

2. **CHAPEL OF LOVE**
The Dixie Cups
J. Barry–E. Greenwich–P. Spector,
Red Bird 001 (Trio, BMI)

3. **LOVE ME WITH ALL YOUR HEART**
The Ray Charles Singers
H. Vaughn–C. Rigual, Command
4046 (Peer–International, BMI)

4. **WALK ON BY**
D. Warwick
B. Bacharach–H. David, Sceptor
1274 (Blue Seas Inc., ASCAP)

5. **LOVE ME DO**
The Beatles
J. Lennon–P. McCartney, Tollie
9008
(Ardmore–Beechwood, BMI)

6. **I GET AROUND**
The Beach Boys
B. Wilson, Capitol 5174
(Sea of Tunes, BMI)

7. **MY BOY LOLLIPOP**
M. Small
J. Roberts–R. Spencer, Smash
1893 (Nom, BMI)

8. **DIANE**
The Bachelors
Rappe–Pollack, London 9639
(Miller, ASCAP)

9. **PEOPLE**
B. Streisand
J. Stein–B. Merrill, Columbia
42968 (Chappell, ASCAP)

10. **MEMPHIS**
J. Rivers
C. Berry, Imperial 66032
(Arc, BMI)

June 27

1. **I GET AROUND**
The Beach Boys
B. Wilson, Capitol 5174
(Sea of Tunes, BMI)

2. **A WORLD WITHOUT LOVE**
Peter and Gordon
J. Lennon–P. McCartney,
Capitol 5175
(Northern, ASCAP)

3. **MY BOY LOLLIPOP**
M. Small
J. Roberts–R. Spencer, Smash
1893 (Nom, BMI)

4. **MEMPHIS**
J. Rivers
C. Berry, Imperial 66032
(Arc, BMI)

5. **CHAPEL OF LOVE**
The Dixie Cups
J. Barry–E. Greenwich–
P. Spector, Red Bird 001
(Trio, BMI)

6. **PEOPLE**
B. Streisand
J. Stein–B. Merrill, Columbia
42968 (Chappell, ASCAP)

7. **LOVE ME WITH ALL YOUR HEART**
The Ray Charles Singers
H. Vaughn–C. Rigual,
Command 4046
(Peer–International, BMI)

8. **BAD TO ME**
B. J. Kramer with the Dakotas
J. Lennon–P. McCartney,
Imperial 66027 (Metric, BMI)

9. **DON'T LET THE SUN CATCH YOU CRYING**
Gerry and the Pacemakers
G. Marsden, Laurie 3251
(Pacemaker, BMI)

10. **RAG DOLL**
The Four Seasons
B. Gaudio–B. Crewe, Philips
40211
(Saturday–Gavadima, ASCAP)

1964

July 4

1. **I GET AROUND**
   The Beach Boys
   B. Wilson, Capitol 5174 (Sea of Tunes, BMI)

2. **MEMPHIS**
   J. Rivers
   C. Berry, Imperial 66032 (Arc, BMI)

3. **MY BOY LOLLIPOP**
   M. Small
   J. Roberts–R. Spencer, Smash 1893 (Nom, BMI)

4. **PEOPLE**
   B. Streisand
   J. Stein–B. Merrill, Columbia 42968 (Chappell, ASCAP)

5. **A WORLD WITHOUT LOVE**
   Peter and Gordon
   J. Lennon–P. McCartney, Capitol 5175 (Northern, ASCAP)

6. **DON'T LET THE SUN CATCH YOU CRYING**
   Gerry and the Pacemakers
   G. Marsden, Laurie 3251 (Pacemaker, BMI)

7. **RAG DOLL**
   The Four Seasons
   B. Gaudio–B. Crewe, Philips 40211 (Saturday–Gavadima, ASCAP)

8. **BAD TO ME**
   B. J. Kramer with the Dakotas
   J. Lennon–P. McCartney, Imperial 66027 (Metric, BMI)

9. **CHAPEL OF LOVE**
   The Dixie Cups
   J. Barry–E. Greenwich– P. Spector, Red Bird 001 (Trio, BMI)

10. **CAN'T YOU SEE THAT SHE'S MINE**
    The Dave Clark Five
    L. Davison–D. Clark, Epic 9692 (Beechwood, BMI)

July 11

1. **I GET AROUND**
   The Beach Boys
   B. Wilson, Capitol 5174 (Sea of Tunes, BMI)

2. **MY BOY LOLLIPOP**
   M. Small
   J. Roberts–R. Spencer, Smash 1893 (Nom, BMI)

3. **MEMPHIS**
   J. Rivers
   C. Berry, Imperial 66032 (Arc, BMI)

4. **RAG DOLL**
   The Four Seasons
   B. Gaudio–B. Crewe, Philips 40211 (Saturday–Gavadima, ASCAP)

5. **DON'T LET THE SUN CATCH YOU CRYING**
   Gerry and the Pacemakers
   G. Marsden, Laurie 3251 (Pacemaker, BMI)

6. **CAN'T YOU SEE THAT SHE'S MINE**
   The Dave Clark Five
   L. Davison–D. Clark, Epic 9692 (Beechwood, BMI)

7. **THE GIRL FROM IPANEMA**
   S. Getz/A. Gilberto
   Jobim–Gimbel–DeMoraes, Verve 10323 (Duchess, BMI)

8. **NO PARTICULAR PLACE TO GO**
   C. Berry
   C. Berry, Chess 1898 (Arc, BMI)

9. **A WORLD WITHOUT LOVE**
   Peter and Gordon
   J. Lennon–P. McCartney, Capitol 5175 (Northern, AS-CAP)

10. **PEOPLE**
    B. Streisand
    J. Stein–B. Merrill, Columbia 42968 (Chappell, ASCAP)

July 18

1. **I GET AROUND**
   The Beach Boys
   B. Wilson, Capitol 5174 (Sea of Tunes, BMI)

2. **MEMPHIS**
   J. Rivers
   C. Berry, Imperial 66032 (Arc, BMI)

3. **RAG DOLL**
   The Four Seasons
   B. Gaudio–B. Crewe, Philips 40211 (Saturday–Gavadima, ASCAP)

4. **THE GIRL FROM IPANEMA**
   S. Getz/A. Gilberto
   Jobim–Gimbel–DeMoraes, Verve 10323 (Duchess, BMI)

5. **DON'T LET THE SUN CATCH YOU CRYING**
   Gerry and the Pacemakers
   G. Marsden, Laurie 3251 (Pacemaker, BMI)

6. **DANG ME**
   R. Miller
   R. Miller, Smash 1881 (Tree, BMI)

7. **CAN'T YOU SEE THAT SHE'S MINE**
   The Dave Clark Five
   L. Davison–D. Clark, Epic 9692 (Beechwood, BMI)

8. **THE LITTLE OLD LADY (FROM PASADENA)**
   Jan and Dean
   D. Atfield–R. Christian, Liberty 55704 (Trousdale, BMI)

9. **KEEP ON PUSHING**
   The Impressions
   C. Mayfield, ABC–Paramount 10554 (Curtom, BMI)

10. **MY BOY LOLLIPOP**
    M. Small
    J. Roberts–R. Spencer, Smash 1893 (Nom, BMI)

253

1. **A HARD DAY'S NIGHT**
The Beatles
J. Lennon–P. McCartney,
Capitol 5222
(Unart–Maclen, BMI)

2. **I GET AROUND**
The Beach Boys
B. Wilson, Capitol 5174
(Sea of Tunes, BMI)

3. **RAG DOLL**
The Four Seasons
B. Gaudio–B. Crewe, Philips
40211
(Saturday–Gavadima, ASCAP)

4. **MEMPHIS**
J. Rivers
C. Berry, Imperial 66032
(Arc, BMI)

5. **THE GIRL FROM IPANEMA**
S. Getz/A. Gilberto
Jobim–Gimbel–DeMoraes, Verve
10323 (Duchess, BMI)

6. **THE LITTLE OLD LADY**
(FROM PASADENA)
Jan and Dean
D. Atfield–R. Christian,
Liberty 55704 (Trousdale, BMI)

7. **CAN'T YOU SEE THAT**
SHE'S MINE
The Dave Clark Five
L. Davison–D. Clark, Epic
9692 (Beechwood, BMI)

8. **DANG ME**
R. Miller
R. Miller, Smash 1881
(Tree, BMI)

9. **WISHIN' AND HOPIN'**
D. Springfield
B. Bacharach–H. David, Philips
40207 (Jonathan, BMI)

10. **KEEP ON PUSHING**
The Impressions
C. Mayfield,
ABC–Paramount 10554
(Curtom, BMI)

1. **A HARD DAY'S NIGHT**
The Beatles
J. Lennon–P. McCartney,
Capitol 5222
(Unart–Maclen, BMI)

2. **RAG DOLL**
The Four Seasons
B. Gaudio–B. Crewe, Philips
40211
(Saturday–Gavadima, ASCAP)

3. **THE LITTLE OLD LADY**
(FROM PASADENA)
Jan and Dean
D. Atfield–R. Christian,
Liberty 55704 (Trousdale, BMI)

4. **EVERYBODY LOVES**
SOMEBODY
D. Martin
Lane–Taylor, Reprise 0281
(Four Star Sales, BMI)

5. **WHERE DID OUR LOVE GO**
The Supremes
Holland–Dozier–Holland,
Motown 1060 (Jobete, BMI)

6. **WISHIN' AND HOPIN'**
D. Springfield
B. Bacharach–H. David, Philips
40207 (Jonathan, BMI)

7. **DANG ME**
R. Miller
R. Miller, Smash 1881
(Tree, BMI)

8. **I GET AROUND**
The Beach Boys
B. Wilson, Capitol 5174
(Sea of Tunes, BMI)

9. **MEMPHIS**
J. Rivers
C. Berry, Imperial 66032
(Arc, BMI)

10. **THE GIRL FROM IPANEMA**
S. Getz/A. Gilberto
Jobim–Gimbel–DeMoraes, Verve
10323 (Duchess, BMI)

1. **A HARD DAY'S NIGHT**
The Beatles
J. Lennon–P. McCartney,
Capitol 5222
(Unart–Maclen, BMI)

2. **RAG DOLL**
The Four Seasons
B. Gaudio–B. Crewe, Philips
40211
(Saturday–Gavadima, ASCAP)

3. **THE LITTLE OLD LADY**
(FROM PASADENA)
Jan and Dean
D. Atfield–R. Christian,
Liberty 55704 (Trousdale, BMI)

4. **EVERYBODY LOVES**
SOMEBODY
D. Martin
Lane–Taylor, Reprise 0281
(Four Star Sales, BMI)

5. **WISHIN' AND HOPIN'**
D. Springfield
B. Bacharach–H. David, Philips
40207 (Jonathan, BMI)

6. **WHERE DID OUR LOVE GO**
The Supremes
Holland–Dozier–Holland,
Motown 1060 (Jobete, BMI)

7. **HOUSE OF THE RISING**
SUN
The Animals
Price, M-G-M 13264
(Al Gallico, BMI)

8. **I GET AROUND**
The Beach Boys
B. Wilson, Capitol 5174
(Sea of Tunes, BMI)

9. **DANG ME**
R. Miller
R. Miller, Smash 1881
(Tree, BMI)

10. **UNDER THE BOARDWALK**
The Drifters
Resnick–Young, Atlantic 2237
(T.M., BMI)

1964

August 15

1. **A HARD DAY'S NIGHT**
The Beatles
J. Lennon–P. McCartney,
Capitol 5222
(Unart–Maclen, BMI)

2. **RAG DOLL**
The Four Seasons
B. Gaudio–B. Crewe, Philips
40211
(Saturday–Gavadima, ASCAP)

3. **EVERYBODY LOVES SOMEBODY**
D. Martin
Lane–Taylor, Reprise 0281
(Four Star Sales, BMI)

4. **WHERE DID OUR LOVE GO**
The Supremes
Holland–Dozier–Holland,
Motown 1060 (Jobete, BMI)

5. **WISHIN' AND HOPIN'**
D. Springfield
B. Bacharach–H. David, Philips
40207 (Jonathan, BMI)

6. **UNDER THE BOARDWALK**
The Drifters
Resnick–Young, Atlantic 2237
(T.M., BMI)

7. **HOUSE OF THE RISING SUN**
The Animals
Price, M-G-M 13264
(Al Gallico, BMI)

8. **THE LITTLE OLD LADY (FROM PASADENA)**
Jan and Dean
D. Atfield–R. Christian,
Liberty 55704 (Trousdale, BMI)

9. **I WANNE LOVE HIM SO BAD**
The Jelly Beans
J. Barry–E. Greenwich, Red Bird
10-003 (Trio, BMI)

10. **C'MON AND SWIM**
B. Freeman
Sly–Cowan, Autumn 2
(Taracrest, BMI)

August 22

1. **WHERE DID OUR LOVE GO**
The Supremes
Holland–Dozier–Holland,
Motown 1060 (Jobete, BMI)

2. **EVERYBODY LOVES SOMEBODY**
D. Martin
Lane–Taylor, Reprise 0281
(Four Star Sales, BMI)

3. **A HARD DAY'S NIGHT**
The Beatles
J. Lennon–P. McCartney,
Capitol 5222 (Unart–Maclen BMI)

4. **UNDER THE BOARDWALK**
The Drifters
Resnick–Young, Atlantic 2237
(T.M., BMI)

5. **HOUSE OF THE RISING SUN**
The Animals
Price, M-G-M 13264
(Gallice, BMI)

6. **C'MON AND SWIM**
B. Freeman
Sly–Cowan, Autumn 2
(Taracrest, BMI)

7. **BECAUSE**
The Dave Clark Five
L. Davison–D. Clark, Epic
9704 (Ivy, ASCAP)

8. **WALK-DON'T RUN '64**
The Ventures
J. Smith, Dolton 96
(Forshay, BMI)

9. **WISHIN' AND HOPIN'**
D. Springfield
B. Bacharach–H. David, Philips
40207 (Jonathan, BMI)

10. **HOW DO YOU DO IT?**
Gerry and the Pacemakers
M. Murray, Laurie 3261
(Just, BMI)

August 29

1. **WHERE DID OUR LOVE GO**
The Supremes
Holland–Dozier–Holland,
Motown 1060 (Jobete, BMI)

2. **HOUSE OF THE RISING SUN**
The Animals
Price, M-G-M 13264
(Al Gallico, BMI)

3. **EVERYBODY LOVES SOMEBODY**
D. Martin
Lane–Taylor, Reprise 0281
(Four Star Sales, BMI)

4. **A HARD DAY'S NIGHT**
The Beatles
J. Lennon–P. McCartney,
Capitol 5222
(Unart–Maclen, BMI)

5. **C'MON AND SWIM**
B. Freeman
Sly–Cowan, Autumn 2
(Taracrest, BMI)

6. **UNDER THE BOARDWALK**
The Drifters
Resnick–Young, Atlantic 2237
(T.M., BMI)

7. **BECAUSE**
The Dave Clark Five
L. Davison–D. Clark, Epic 9704
(Ivy, ASCAP)

8. **BREAD AND BUTTER**
The Newbeats
L. Parks–J. Turnbow, Hickroy
1269 (Acuff–Rose, BMI)

9. **HOW DO YOU DO IT?**
Gerry and the Pacemakers
M. Murray, Laurie 3261
(Just, BMI)

10. **WALK-DON'T RUN '64**
The Ventures
J. Smith, Dolton 96
(Forshay, BMI)

September 5

1. **WHERE DID OUR LOVE GO**
   The Supremes
   Holland–Dozier–Holland,
   Motown 1060   (Jobete, BMI)

2. **EVERYBODY LOVES SOMEBODY**
   D. Martin
   Lane–Taylor,   Reprise 0281
   (Four Star Sales, BMI)

3. **HOUSE OF THE RISING SUN**
   The Animals
   Price, M-G-M 13264
   (Al Gallico, BMI)

4. **C'MON AND SWIM**
   B. Freeman
   Sly–Cowan,   Autumn 2
   (Taracrest, BMI)

5. **BREAD AND BUTTER**
   The Newbeats
   L. Parks–J. Turnbow,   Hickory
   1269   (Acuff–Rose, BMI)

6. **HOW DO YOU DO IT?**
   Gerry and the Pacemakers
   M. Murray,   Laurie 3261
   (Just, BMI)

7. **G.T.O.**
   Ronny and the Daytonas
   J. Wilkin,   Mala 481
   (Buckhorn, BMI)

8. **BECAUSE**
   The Dave Clark Five
   L. Davison–D. Clark,   Epic
   9704   (Ivy, ASCAP)

9. **UNDER THE BOARDWALK**
   The Drifters
   Resnick–Young,   Atlantic 2237
   (T.M., BMI)

10. **A HARD DAY'S NIGHT**
    The Beatles
    J. Lennon–P. McCartney,
    Capitol 5222
    (Unart–Maclen, BMI)

256

September 12

1. **WHERE DID OUR LOVE GO**
   The Supremes
   Holland–Dozier–Holland,
   Motown 1060   (Jobete, BMI)

2. **HOUSE OF THE RISING SUN**
   The Animals
   Price, M-G-M 13264
   (Al Gallico, BMI)

3. **EVERYBODY LOVES SOMEBODY**
   D. Martin
   Lane–Taylor,   Reprise 0281
   (Four Star Sales, BMI)

4. **BECAUSE**
   The Dave Clark Five
   L. Davison–D. Clark,   Epic 9704
   (Ivy, BMI)

5. **BREAD AND BUTTER**
   The Newbeats
   L. Parks–J. Turnbow,   Hickory
   1269   (Acuff–Rose, BMI)

6. **C'MON AND SWIM**
   B. Freeman
   Sly–Cowan,   Autumn 2
   (Taracrest, BMI)

7. **G.T.O.**
   Ronny and the Daytonas
   J. Wilkin,   Mala 481
   (Buckhorn, BMI)

8. **A HARD DAY'S NIGHT**
   The Beatles
   J. Lennon–P. McCartney,
   Capitol 5222
   (Unart–Maclen, BMI)

9. **REMEMBER (WALKIN' IN THE SAND)**
   The Shangri-Las
   G. Morton,   Red Bird 10–008
   (Tender Tunes–Trio, BMI)

10. **OH, PRETTY WOMAN**
    R. Orbison
    Orbison–Dees,   Monument 851
    (Acuff–Rose, BMI)

September 19

1. **HOUSE OF THE RISING SUN**
   The Animals
   Price,   M-G-M 13264
   (Al Gallico, BMI)

2. **BREAD AND BUTTER**
   The Newbeats
   L. Parks–J. Turnbow,
   Hickory 1269   (Acuff–Rose, BMI)

3. **WHERE DID OUR LOVE GO**
   The Supremes
   Holland–Dozier–Holland,
   Motown 1060   (Jobete, BMI)

4. **OH, PRETTY WOMAN**
   R. Orbison
   Orbison–Dees,   Monument 851
   (Acuff–Rose, BMI)

5. **G.T.O.**
   Ronny and the Daytonas
   J. Wilkin,   Mala 481
   (Buckhorn, BMI)

6. **EVERYBODY LOVES SOMEBODY**
   D. Martin
   Lane–Taylor,   Reprise 0281
   (Four Star Sales, BMI)

7. **REMEMBER (WALKIN' IN THE SAND)**
   The Shangri-Las
   G. Morton,   Red Bird 10–008
   (Tender Tunes–Trio, BMI)

8. **BECAUSE**
   The Dave Clark Five
   L. Davison–D. Clark,   Epic
   9704   (Ivy, ASCAP)

9. **DO WAH DIDDY DIDDY**
   M. Mann
   J. Barry–E. Greenwich,
   Ascot 2157   (Trio, BMI)

10. **DANCING IN THE STREETS**
    Martha and the Vandellas
    Stevenson–Gaye,   Gordy 7033
    (Jobete, BMI)

1964

September 26

1. **OH, PRETTY WOMEN**
R. Orbison
*Orbison–Dees, Monument 851
(Acuff–Rose, BMI)*

2. **HOUSE OF THE RISING SUN**
The Animals
*Price, M-G-M 13264
(Al Gallico, BMI)*

3. **BREAD AND BUTTER**
The Newbeats
*L. Parks–J. Turnbow, Hickory
1269 (Acuff–Rose, BMI)*

4. **WHERE DID OUR LOVE GO**
The Supremes
*Holland–Dozier–Holland,
Motown 1060 (Jobete, BMI)*

5. **G.T.O.**
Ronny and the Daytonas
*J. Wilkin, Mala 481
(Buckhorn, BMI)*

6. **DANCING IN THE STREETS**
Martha and the Vandellas
*Stevenson–Gaye, Gordy 7033
(Jobete, BMI)*

7. **REMEMBER (WALKIN' IN THE SAND)**
The Shangri-Las
*G. Morton, Red Bird 10–008
(Tender Tunes–Trio, BMI)*

8. **DO WAH DIDDY DIDDY**
M. Mann
*J. Barry–E. Greenwich,
Ascot 2157 (Trio, BMI)*

9. **IT HURTS TO BE IN LOVE**
G. Pitney
*H. Greenfield–H. Miller,
Musicor 1040 (Screen Gems–
Columbia, BMI)*

10. **BECAUSE**
The Dave Clark Five
*L. Davison–D. Clark, Epic 9704
(Ivy, ASCAP)*

October 3

1. **OH, PRETTY WOMAN**
R. Orbison
*Orbison–Dees, Monument 851
(Acuff–Rose, BMI)*

2. **BREAD AND BUTTER**
The Newbeats
*L. Parks–J. Turnbow, Hickory
1269 (Acuff–Rose, BMI)*

3. **DANCING IN THE STREETS**
Martha and the Vandellas
*Stevenson–Gaye, Gordy 7033
(Jobete, BMI)*

4. **DO WAH DIDDY DIDDY**
M. Mann
*Barry–E. Greenwich, Ascot 2157
(Trio, BMI)*

5. **IT HURTS TO BE IN LOVE**
G. Pitney
*H. Greenfield–H. Miller,
Musicor 1040 (Screen Gems–
Columbia, BMI)*

6. **REMEMBER (WALKIN' IN THE SAND)**
The Shangri-Las
*G. Morton, Red Bird 10-008
(Tender Tunes–Trio, BMI)*

7. **HOUSE OF THE RISING SUN**
The Animals
*Price, M-G-M 13264
(Al Gallico, BMI)*

8. **G.T.O.**
Ronny and the Daytonas
*J. Wilkin, Mala 481
(Buckhorn, BMI)*

9. **WHERE DID OUR LOVE GO**
The Supremes
*Holland–Dozier–Holland,
Motown 1060 (Jobete, BMI)*

10. **SAVE IT FOR ME**
The Four Seasons
*B. Gaudio–B. Crewe, Philips
40225 (Saturday–Gavadima,
ASCAP)*

October 10

1. **OH, PRETTY WOMAN**
R. Orbison
*Orbison–Dees, Monument 851
(Acuff–Rose, BMI)*

2. **DO WAH DIDDY DIDDY**
M. Mann
*J. Barry–E. Greenwich, Ascot 2157
(Trio, BMI)*

3. **DANCING IN THE STREETS**
Martha and theVandellas
*Stevenson–Gaye, Gordy 7033
(Jobete, BMI)*

4. **BREAD AND BUTTER**
The Newbeats
*L. Parks–J. Turnbow, Hickory
1269 (Acuff–Rose, BMI)*

5. **REMEMBER (WALKIN' IN THE SAND)**
The Shangri-Las
*G. Morton, Red Bird 10–008
(Tender Tunes–Trio, BMI)*

6. **WE'LL SING IN THE SUN-SHINE**
G. Garnett
*G. Garnett, Victor 8388
(Lupercalia, ASCAP)*

7. **IT HURTS TO BE IN LOVE**
G. Pitney
*H. Greenfield–H. Miller,
Musicor 1040 (Screen Gems–
Columbia, BMI)*

8. **G.T.O.**
Ronny and the Daytonas
*J. Wilkin, Mala 481
(Buckhorn, BMI)*

9. **LAST KISS**
J. Frank Wilson and the Cavalliers
Wilson, Josie 923 (Boblo, BMI)

10. **A SUMMER SONG**
C. Stuart and J. Clyde
*Metcalfe–Noble–Stuart, World
Artists 1027 (Unart–Woart, BMI)*

257

October 17

1. **DO WAH DIDDY DIDDY**
   M. Mann
   J. Barry–E. Greenwich,
   Ascott 2157 (Trio, BMI)

2. **DANCING IN THE STREETS**
   Martha and the Vandellas
   Stevenson–Gaye, Gordy 7033
   (Jobete, BMI)

3. **OH, PRETTY WOMAN**
   R. Orbison
   Orbison–Dees, Monument 851
   (Acuff–Rose, BMI)

4. **WE'LL SING IN THE SUN-SHINE**
   G. Garnett
   G. Garnett, Victor 8388
   (Lupercalia, ASCAP)

5. **LAST KISS**
   J. Frank Wilson and the
   Cavalliers
   Wilson, Josie 923
   (Boblo, BMI)

6. **REMEMBER (WALKIN' IN THE SAND)**
   The Shangri-Las
   G. Morton, Red Bird 10–008
   (Tender Tunes–Trio, BMI)

7. **WHEN I GROW UP TO BE A MAN**
   The Beach Boys
   B. Wilson, Capitol 5245
   (Sea of Tunes, BMI)

8. **LET IT BE ME**
   J. Butler and B. Everett
   Curtis–Defano–Becaud, VeeJay
   613 (Leeds, ASCAP)

9. **A SUMMER SONG**
   C. Stuart and J. Clyde
   Metcalfe–Noble–Stuart, World
   Artists 1027 (Unart–Woart, BMI)

10. **IT HURTS TO BE IN LOVE**
    G. Pitney
    H. Greenfield–H. Miller,
    Musicor 1040 (Screen Gems–
    Columbia, BMI)

October 24

1. **LAST KISS**
   J. Frank Wilson and the
   Cavaliers
   Wilson, Josie 923
   (Boblo, BMI)

2. **DO WAH DIDDY DIDDY**
   M. Mann
   J. Barry–E. Greenwich,
   Ascot 2157 (Trio, BMI)

3. **OH, PRETTY WOMAN**
   R. Orbison
   Orbison–Dees, Monument 851
   (Acuff–Rose, BMI)

4. **DANCING IN THE STREETS**
   Martha and the Vandellas
   Stevenson–Gaye, Gordy 7033
   (Jobete, BMI)

5. **BABY LOVE**
   The Supremes
   Holland–Dozier–Holland,
   Motown 1066 (Jobete, BMI)

6. **LET IT BE ME**
   J. Butler and B. Everett
   Curtis–Defano–Becaud, VeeJay
   613 (Leeds, ASCAP)

7. **WE'LL SING IN THE SUN-SHINE**
   G. Garnett
   G. Garnett Victor 8388
   (Lupercalia, ASCAP)

8. **WHEN I GROW UP TO BE A MAN**
   The Beach Boys
   B. Wilson, Capitol 5245
   (Sea of Tunes, BMI)

9. **HAVE I THE RIGHT**
   The Honeycombs
   Blaikley, Interphon 7707
   (Duchess, BMI)

10. **A SUMMER SONG**
    C. Stuart and J. Clyde
    Metcalfe–Noble–Stuart,
    World Artists 1027
    (Unart–Woart, BMI)

October 31

1. **DO WAH DIDDY DIDDY**
   M. Mann
   J. Barry–E. Greenwich,
   Ascot 2157 (Trio, BMI)

2. **LAST KISS**
   J. Frank Wilson and the
   Cavaliers
   Wilson, Josie 923
   (Boblo, BMI)

3. **BABY LOVE**
   The Supremes
   Holland–Dozier–Holland,
   Motown 1066 (Jobete, BMI)

4. **WE'LL SING IN THE SUN-SHINE**
   G. Garnett
   G. Garnett, Victor 8388
   (Lupercalia, ASCAP)

5. **LET IT BE ME**
   J. Butler and B. Everett
   Curtis–Defano–Becaud, VeeJay
   613 (Leeds, ASCAP)

6. **DANCING IN THE STREETS**
   Martha and the Vandellas
   Stevenson–Gaye, Gordy 7033
   (Jobete, BMI)

7. **OH, PRETTY WOMAN**
   R. Orbison
   Orbison–Dees, Monument 851
   (Acuff–Rose, BMI)

8. **LITTLE HONDA**
   The Hondells
   B. Wilson, Mercury 72324
   (Sea of Tunes, BMI)

9. **HAVE I THE RIGHT**
   The Honeycombs
   Blaikley, Interphon 7707
   (Duchess, BMI)

10. **A SUMMER SONG**
    C. Stuart and J. Clyde
    Metcalfe–Noble–Stuart,
    World Artists 1027
    (Unart–Woart, BMI)

November 7

1. **DO WAH DIDDY DIDDY**
M. Mann
*J. Barry–E. Greenwich,
Ascot 2157 (Trio, BMI)*

2. **BABY LOVE**
The Supremes
*Holland–Dozier–Holland,
Motown 1066 (Jobete, BMI)*

3. **LET IT BE ME**
J. Butler and B. Everett
*Curtis–Defano–Becaud, VeeJay
613 (Leeds, ASCAP)*

4. **WE'LL SING IN THE SUN-
SHINE**
G. Garnett
*G. Garnett, Victor 8388
(Lupercalia, ASCAP)*

5. **HAVE I THE RIGHT**
The Honeycombs
*Blaikley, Interphon 7077
(Duchess, BMI)*

6. **LEADER OF THE PACK**
The Shangri-Las
*J. Barry–E. Greenwich,
Red Bird 10–014
(Tender Tunes–Trio, BMI)*

7. **CHUG-A-LUG**
R. Miller
*R. Miller, Smash 1926
(Tree, BMI)*

8. **COME A LITTLE BIT CLOSER**
Jay and the Americans
*T. Boyce–B. Hart–W. Farrell,
United Artists 759 (Picturetone,
BMI)*

9. **THE DOOR IS STILL OPEN TO
MY HEART**
D. Martin
*C. Willis, Reprise 0307
(Berkshire, BMI)*

10. **LITTLE HONDA**
The Hondells
*B. Wilson, Mercury 72324
(Sea of Tunes, BMI)*

November 14

1. **BABY LOVE**
The Supremes
*Holland–Dozier–Holland,
Motown 1066 (Jobete, BMI)*

2. **DO WAH DIDDY DIDDY**
M. Mann
*J. Barry–E. Greenwich, Ascot
2157 (Trio, BMI)*

3. **LEADER OF THE PACK**
The Shangri-Las
*J. Barry–E. Greenwich, Red Bird
10–014 (Tender Tunes–Trio,
BMI)*

4. **LET IT BE ME**
J. Butler and B. Everett
*Curtis–Defano–Becaud, VeeJay
613 (Leeds, ASCAP)*

5. **COME A LITTLE BIT CLOSER**
Jay and the Americans
*T. Boyce–B. Hart–W.
Farrell, United Artists 759
(Picturetone, BMI)*

6. **HAVE I THE RIGHT**
The Honeycombs
*Blaikley, Interphon 7707
(Duchess, BMI)*

7. **SHE'S NOT THERE**
The Zombies
*R. Argent, Parrot 9695
(Gallice, BMI)*

8. **THE DOOR IS STILL OPEN TO
MY HEART**
D. Martin
*C. Willis, Reprise 0307
(Berkshire, BMI)*

9. **RINGO**
L. Greene
*Blair, Victor 8444
(Robertson, ASCAP)*

10. **YOU REALLY GOT ME**
The Kinks
*R. Davies, Reprise 0306
(Jay-Boy, BMI)*

November 21

1. **BABY LOVE**
The Supremes
*Holland–Dozier–Holland,
Motown 1066 (Jobete, BMI)*

2. **LEADER OF THE PACK**
The Shangri-Las
*J. Barry–E. Greenwich, Red Bird
10–014 (Tender Tunes–Trio,
BMI)*

3. **SHE'S NOT THERE**
The Zombies
*R. Argent, Parrot 9695
(Gallice, BMI)*

4. **COME A LITTLE BIT CLOSER**
Jay and the Americans
*T. Boyce–B. Hart–W. Farrell,
United Artists 759 (Picturetone,
BMI)*

5. **YOU REALLY GOT ME**
The Kinks
*R. Davies, Reprise 0306
(Jay-Boy, BMI)*

6. **HAVE I THE RIGHT**
The Honeycombs
*Blaikley, Interphon 7707
(Duchess, BMI)*

7. **RINGO**
L. Greene
*Blair, Victor 8444
(Robertson, ASCAP)*

8. **LET IT BE ME**
J. Butler and B. Everett
*Curtis–Defano–Becaud, VeeJay
613 (Leeds, ASCAP)*

9. **TIME IS ON MY SIDE**
The Rolling Stones
*Meade–Norman, London 9708
(Rittenhouse–Maygar, BMI)*

10. **THE DOOR IS STILL OPEN TO
MY HEART**
D. Martin
*C.Willis, Reprise 0307
(Berkshire, BMI)*

November 28

1. **BABY LOVE**
The Supremes
Holland–Dozier–Holland,
Motown 1066 (Jobete, BMI)

2. **COME A LITTLE BIT CLOSER**
Jay and the Americans
T. Boyce–B. Hart–W. Farrell,
United Artists 759 (Picturetone,
BMI)

3. **RINGO**
L. Greene
Blair, Victor 8444
(Robertson, ASCAP)

4. **LEADER OF THE PACK**
The Shangri-Las
J. Barry–E. Greenwich,
Red Bird 10–014
(Tender Tunes–Trio, BMI)

5. **MR. LONELY**
B. Vinton
Vinton–Allen, Epic 9730
(Ripley, BMI)

6. **SHE'S NOT THERE**
The Zombies
R. Argent, Parrot 9695
(Gallice, BMI)

7. **YOU REALLY GOT ME**
The Kinks
R. Davies, Reprise 0306
(Jay–Boy, BMI)

8. **MOUNTAIN OF LOVE**
J. Rivers
H. Dorman, Imperial 66075
(Vaughn, BMI)

9. **COME SEE ABOUT ME**
The Supremes
Holland–Dozier–Holland
Motown 1068 (Jobete, BMI)

10. **TIME IS ON MY SIDE**
The Rolling Stones
Meade–Norman, London 9708
(Rittenhouse–Maygar, BMI)

December 5

1. **LEADER OF THE PACK**
The Shangri-Las
J. Barry-E. Greenwich, Red
Bird 10-014 (Tender Tunes,
Trio, BMI)

2. **MR. LONELY**
B. Vinton
Vinton–Allen, Epic 9730
(Ripley, BMI)

3. **SHE'S NOT THERE**
The Zombies
R. Argent, Parrot 9695
(Gallice, BMI)

4. **BABY LOVE**
The Supremes
Holland–Dozier–Holland,
Motown 1066 (Jobete, BMI)

5. **RINGO**
L. Greene
Blair, Victor 8444
(Robertson, ASCAP)

6. **COME SEE ABOUT ME**
The Supremes
Holland–Dozier–Holland,
Motown 1068 (Jobete, BMI)

7. **MOUNTAIN OF LOVE**
J. Rivers
H. Dorman, Imperial 66075
(Vaughn, BMI)

8. **YOU REALLY GOT ME**
The Kinks
R. Davies Reprise 0306
(Jay–Boy, BMI)

9. **TIME IS ON MY SIDE**
The Rolling Stones
Meade–Norman, London 9708
(Rittenhouse–Maygar, BMI)

10. **DANCE, DANCE, DANCE**
The Beach Boys
B. Wilson–C. Wilson, Capitol
5306 (Sea of Tunes, BMI)

December 12

1. **SHE'S NOT THERE**
The Zombies
R. Argent, Parrot 9695
(Gallice, BMI)

2. **MR. LONELY**
B. Vinton
Vinton–Allen, Epic 9730
(Ripley, BMI)

3. **I FEEL FINE**
The Beatles
J. Lennon–P. McCartney,
Capitol 5327 (Maclen, BMI)

4. **LEADER OF THE PACK**
The Shangri-Las
J. Barry–E. Greenwich,
Red Bird 10–014 (Tender Tunes,
Trio, BMI)

5. **RINGO**
L. Greene
Blair, Victor 8444
(Robertson, ASCAP)

6. **COME SEE ABOUT ME**
The Supremes
Holland–Dozier–Holland,
Motown 1068 Jobete, BMI)

7. **TIME IS ON MY SIDE**
The Rolling Stones
Meade–Norman, London 9708
(Rittenhouse–Maygar, BMI)

8. **YOU REALLY GOT ME**
The Kinks
R. Davies, Reprise 0306
(Jay–Boy, BMI)

9. **MOUNTAIN OF LOVE**
J. Rivers
H. Dorman, Imperial 66075
(Vaughn, BMI)

10. **DANCE, DANCE, DANCE**
The Beach Boys
B. Wilson–C. Wilson, Capitol
5306 (Sea of Tunes, BMI)

1964

December 18

1. **COME SEE ABOUT ME**
   The Supremes
   Holland–Dozier–Holland,
   Motown 1068   (Jobete, BMI)

2. **SHE'S NOT THERE**
   The Zombies
   R. Argent,   Parrot 9695
   (Gallice, BMI)

3. **I FEEL FINE**
   The Beatles
   J. Lennon–P. McCartney,
   Capitol 5327   (Maclen, BMI)

4. **MR. LONELY**
   B. Vinton
   Vinton–Allen,   Epic 9730
   (Ripley, BMI)

5. **TIME IS ON MY SIDE**
   The Rolling Stones
   Meade–Norman,   London 9708
   (Rittenhouse–Maygar, BMI)

6. **GOIN' OUT OF MY HEAD**
   Little Anthony
   T. Randazzo,   DCP 1119
   (South Mountain, BMI)

7. **RINGO**
   L. Greene
   Blair,   Victor 8444
   (Robertson, ASCAP)

8. **YOU REALLY GOT ME**
   The Kinks
   R. Davies,   Reprise 0306
   (Jay–Boy, BMI)

9. **I'M GONNA BE STRONG**
   G. Pitney
   B. Mann–C. Weil,   Musicor 1045
   (Screen Gems–Columbia, BMI)

10. **DANCE, DANCE, DANCE**
    The Beach Boys
    B. Wilson–C. Wilson,   Capitol
    5306   (Sea of Tunes, BMI)

December 25

1. **COME SEE ABOUT ME**
   The Supremes
   Holland–Dozier–Holland,
   Motown 1068   (Jobete, BMI)

2. **I FEEL FINE**
   The Beatles
   J. Lennon–P. McCartney,
   Capitol 5327   (Maclen, BMI)

3. **SHE'S A WOMAN**
   The Beatles
   J. Lennon–P. McCartney,
   Capitol 5327   (Maclen, BMI)

4. **MR. LONELY**
   B. Vinton
   Vinton–Allen,   Epic 9730
   (Ripley, BMI)

5. **GOIN' OUT OF MY HEAD**
   Little Anthony
   T. Randazzo   DCP 1119
   (South Mountain, BMI)

6. **SHE'S NOT THERE**
   The Zombies
   R. Argent,   Parrot 9695
   (Gallice, BMI)

7. **TIME IS ON MY SIDE**
   The Rolling Stones
   Meade–Norman,   London 9708
   (Rittenhouse–Maygar, BMI)

8. **THE JERK**
   The Larks
   Julian,   Money 106
   (Cash, BMI)

9. **RINGO**
   L. Greene
   Blair,   Victor 8444
   (Robertson, ASCAP)

10. **I'M GONNA BE STRONG**
    G. Pitney
    B. Mann–C. Weil,   Musicor 1046
    (Screen Gems–Columbia, BMI)

ROLLING STONES

In the last year and a half, the Beatles had triggered a change in rock and roll so profound that the whole style of music and music appreciation was entering a new phase. Their influence was partly in the sound of the music, although the early Beatle sound was so close to the old Buddy Holly type sound that it could hardly be called revolutionary.

Their influence was partly in the instruments they played. The drum, saxaphone, acoustical guitar, piano and bass had been the staples of the old days, but now it was the electric guitar (one lead, one rhythm), the electric bass and drums. A dash of harmonica or electric organ was used in the Beatle instrumentation, but little else.

Almost more than in their music, the revolution was in the Beatles themselves. Here were four boys—funny, fun-loving, lovable—who emerged from the working class because they loved rock and roll and played bright little songs on these simple instruments. They were amazingly amateurish when they performed, talking to each other, turning their backs on the audience. That, and the deceptively simple songs they wrote and played, made every boy sure he was a potential rock and roll musician.

In the old days, when rock and roll was scorned by our parents, stardom was the dream of the lower and working-class boys. Middle-class kids were strongly discouraged by their parents, and were told that record companies and promoters manufactured stars. But now it was acceptable for the middle class to learn the guitar, write music or at least learn to imitate well enough to play at school dances. The Beatles unknowingly were making a generation heavy with musicians instead of passive listeners and fans.

As the Beatles grew in fame they grew as musicians, From "Love Me Do" through "If I Fell" to the rich beauty of "Rubber Soul," the Beatles experimented with more intricate arrange-

1965

Think about the hate they have in Red China,
Then turn around and look at Selma Alabama,
You can leave here for four days in space,
But when you return it's the same old place
The pounding of drums
The pride and disgrace
Hate your next door neighbor
But don't forget to say grace . . .

"Eve of Destruction"
Barry McGuire

ments, subtler melodies, fuller orchestrations until they were undoubtedly the greatest masters of rock and roll technique to date. And with the international surge of adoration and imitation, many talented rock and roll fans found themselves making music—some in their hometowns, but others nationally and with big recording companies.

There was a sudden outburst of music—rock and roll and that came from the kids who felt it. The spontaneity was evident. The music was as pure and innocent as it had been in the earliest a capella days. The big difference between this music and all that had gone before was the amazing development in the performers' technique and the audiences' ability to appreciate this technique.

In a way it was odd that no one had predicted this development. All art forms in the past had gone through this basic pattern of growth. The acknowledged movement of art was from primitive, the long uphill groping of innocents, to the classical; the short-lived balance between spontaneity and technical excellence, to the baroque; the loss of freshness and preoccupation with pure technique.

The primitive period predictably is a long one, during which blind lead blind in the production of the art. Rarely at this stage is the audience aware that it is involved in an art form. The art is usually seen as a practical commodity. For example, clumsy pottery and statues were viewed this way. The primitive art is also considered lowbrow by its contemporaries because it hasn't yet been technically perfected or blessed by the critics. This progression has been observable for thousands of years, from ancient Egyptian statuary to twentieth-century jazz.

The length of the cycle has shortened through the ages as better communication has quickened exposure to art and, therefore, sped its ap-

preciation and development. Still, the proportionate lengths of the primitive, classical and baroque periods have remained about the same.

In rock and roll, the long, slow developing period lasted from around 1955 to the beginning of the Beatles. And just as Michelangelo lifted Italian art to classical perfection, the Beatles lifted rock and roll into the brief brilliance of 1964, 1965 and 1966. And they would continue like Michelangelo, whose technical excellence was so great that his style tended to become mannered.

Certainly, none of these artists—not the Beatles, Michelangelo, nor the ancients of Egypt—were aware of this progression which sprang from their innocence. This was especially true in the early stages of an art form, with its simplicity and absence of self-conscious intellectualization about the art.

In 1965 rock and roll stepped out of its simplicity and stepped squarely into its maturity. As fans, we began to study the music and to study ourselves. We became aware of the people who wrote our music instead of noticing only the performers. The new awareness could be traced directly to our respect for John Lennon and Paul McCartney, but it led us to give overdue recognition to the songwriters who had contributed greatly to rock and roll.

We discovered that the best of Motown and subsidiaries had been written by a few fantastic creators of soul: Smokey Robinson ("You Beat Me to the Punch" "My Guy," "My Girl"), Berry Gordy ("Do You Love Me?," "Quicksand"), Holland, Dozier and Holland (all the Supremes songs in 1964 and 1965, "Nowhere To Run," "I Can't Help Myself").

We found the Bob Gaudio had written "Sherry," "Big Girls Don't Cry," "Rag Doll" and "Ronnie," and certainly deserved to be considered the first season.

And we finally recognized Burt Bacharach and Hal David, who had written "Baby, It's You," "Liberty Valance," "Anyone Who Had a Heart," "Walk On By," "Wishin' and Hopin'," "What the World Needs Now," "Little Red Book," "What's New Pussycat?"—and would continue to pour out great music after rock and roll was long dead.

Bob Dylan, too, was being acknowledged for the first time by the rock and roll audience. It is hard to say if we found him or he found us, since the folkies accused him of selling out to the mindless electric rock and roll set when he recorded "Like a Rolling Stone" with more than an acoustic guitar.

While the Beatles inspired us to look back and reward our traditional songwriters, they inspired new groups to do their own songwriting. And so the new Rolling Stones and the Lovin' Spoonful wrote for themselves, as would groups like the Mamas and Papas and the Young Rascals that would spring up and dominate in this era of classical rock and roll.

We rock and roll fans were not alone in reevaluating our music. The very attractiveness of the joy in the Beatles and the new music was pulling all kinds of new people into the rock and roll camp. Jazz fans, folkies and 1940's swing lovers were all focusing on us and our music. And a year ago they had laughed us off as musical dumb-dumbs.

It was a glorious feeling. Rock and roll grew more wondrous each week. In years before we had known periods like this—music so fantastic that the whole world should have exploded into song. But this time the whole world did. If John Kennedy had turned people's attention to our generation, the Beatles had turned it to our music. Thinkers, talkers, writers . . . . everyone was analyzing rock and roll, seeing it in terms of sociology, psychology, music theory. The background music of our adolescence was being pulled into the foreground.

It was a youth world now. Adults were tuning in to all that we were doing. Everything was turned-on and go-go. Mod was the password to the future and Julie Christie was its darling. Swinging England gave us Edwardian suits, poor-boy sweaters, pants suits for women—some with bell-bottom trousers. And from France, the Courrèges look stepped back into childhood with white stockings, white boots and thigh high skirts.

The giddy infatuation with freedom, fun and future was apparant in the kicks people were getting from op art and pop art, camp, slot car racing, pop top cans, disposable paper clothing and furniture, James Bond and the Man from U.N.C.L.E.

Yet it was our generation that wanted to break away from this craziness, to disown the idiocy of *How to Stuff a Wild Bikini,* and to look around at the world and do something about all the horrors and injustices that were putting us, as Barry McGuire sang, on the eve of destruction.

College kids began to speak out against the United States fighting in Vietnam. And the public at large, still uneducated about how and why we got into Vietnam and to what extent, scorned these odd protesters as Vietniks, unwashed troublemakers.

The war had crept up on most of us. We had cared very little when we heard that the United States had sent advisers into Southeast Asia. America was too paralyzed with its fear of Russia to notice other world devleopments. Then, suddenly, the Cold War with the Russians began easing up, and the United States became aware of the two dozen new nations of the emerging Africa, of the discontent in Latin America, of the Liberation Front movements in Southeast Asia and of the hard line attitudes of Communist China.

In the panic of all these realizations the United States saw the whole "underdeveloped" world about to be snatched up by international Communism, which, to most Americans, meant international slavery. Thus, Americans supported our military interference in the Dominican Republic and worse, supported our Holy War in Asia.

We became used to hearing about escalation and search-and-destroy missions. With each newscast, people became more and more tolerant of battle stories and statistics. The widespread national feeling was that we would swoop into Vietnam and kill off the terrorists and leave this small nation safe to continue in its path of freedom and democracy.

With an attitude like this, it is easy to see why most Americans preferred to ignore the unpleasantness of protest, of teach-ins, of discussions about the legality, wisdom and honor of our interference in Vietnam.

And so they closed their eyes to Vietman and tried to concentrate on the humane accomplishments that had been made at home. Most Americans were proud of the work of President Johnson had done since late 1963. He had succeeded in carrying out President's Kennedy's dreams of civil rights legislation, tax cuts and Medicare. And he had set into motion his own War on Poverty. Head Start and the Job Corps appeared to be working. And we had just about caught up with the Russians in outer space, since both countries had men walking in space in the first half on 1965.

In New York City, the election of handsome, young, Kennedy-like Mayor John Lindsay attracted a lot of national attention. Even with the water shortage and the power blackout, the vital mayor-elect was ready to take the city in hand, and was able to generate a great deal of liberal hope. But, as we looked to this hope to avoid looking at Vietnam, we had to see that our cities faced crises that were not being dealt with fast enough or with enough money to prevent the urban nightmare that broke loose in mid-1965.

It exploded in Los Angeles, in the black ghetto of Watts where ten-thousand people took to the streets in a revolutionary uprising. It started with a minor arrest incident that triggered an outpouring of anger at white oppression, and ultimately resulted in 34 deaths, 1,032 injuries and $40 million in property damage. It was terrible to watch and know that the same thing could happen any day in any American city. And it was terrible to see the hate, both black and white, that was brought to the surface by this ugly confrontation.

With the War in Vietnam and the wars in our cities, it was becoming harder to look away to Ladybird's beautification program, to Sandy Koufax, to the comeback of round-toed shoes, to Ringo's marriage, to the new Astrodome or to LBJ's scar. Even the tragedies—the deaths of Winston Churchill, Adlai Stevenson, Albert Schweitzer, Edward R. Murrow, Nat King Cole, Sam Cooke—were tragedies we could accept as part of life. But the international bloodletting that we as Americans were getting involved in was abhorent.

Because it seemed the most disgusting to our generation, we found ourselves pulling away from our elders, drawing back from their new-found interest in us because we could not be beautiful, bright and carefree like the youth they wanted to swing with.

In 1964 we had been brought together with the older generation under the banner of "We love the Beatles." But in 1965 we were drawing apart from them under the banner "Make love, not war."

THE TOP FIFTY
1965

1. DOWNTOWN	P. Clark
2. HELP	The Beatles
3. (I CAN'T GET NO) SATISFACTION	The Rolling Stones
4. WOLLY BULLY	Sam the Sham and the Pharoahs
5. HELP ME RHONDA	The Beach Boys
6. I CAN'T HELP MYSELF	The Four Tops
7. MY GIRL	The Temptations
8. YOU WERE ON MY MIND	The We Five
9. YOU'VE LOST THAT LOVIN' FEELING	The Righteous Brothers
10. SHOTGUN	Junior Walker and the All Stars
11. CRYING IN THE CHAPEL	E. Presley
12. CAN'T YOU HEAR MY HEARTBEAT?	Herman's Hermits
13. KING OF THE ROAD	R. Miller
14. THE BIRDS AND THE BEES	J. Akens
15. HOLD ME, THRILL ME, KISS ME	M. Carter
16. CARA MIA	Jay and the Americans
17. CAST YOUR FATE TO THE WIND	Sounds Orchestral
18. YES, I'M READY	B. Mason
19. WHAT'S NEW PUSSYCAT?	T. Jones
20. LIKE A ROLLING STONE	B. Dylan
21. EVE OF DESTRUCTION	B. McGuire
22. MRS. BROWN, YOU'VE GOT A LOVELY DAUGHTER	Herman's Hermits
23. I GOT YOU BABE	Son and Cher
24. STOP!IN THE NAME OF LOVE	The Supremes
25. I'LL NEVER FIND ANOTHER YOU	The Seekers

26. NEW YORK'S A LONELY TOWN	The Tradewinds
27. LIAR, LIAR	The Castaways
28. THIS DIAMOND RING	G. Lewis and the Playboys
29. UNCHAINED MELODY	The Rightous Brothers
30. THE "IN" CROWD	Ramsey Lewis Trio
31. SILHOUETTES	Herman's Hermits
32. MR. TAMBOURINE MAN	The Byrds
33. FERRY 'CROSS THE MERSEY	Gerry and the Pacemakers
34. SEVENTH SON	J. Rivers
35. FOR YOUR LOVE	The Yardbirds
36. DOWN IN THE BOONDOCKS	B.J. Royal
37. YOU TURN ME ON	I. Whitcomb
38. PAPA'S GOT A BRAND NEW BAG	J. Brown
39. THE JOLLY GREEN GIANT	The Kingsmen
40. BABY, I'M YOURS	B. Lewis
41. I KNOW A PLACE	P. Clark
42. TICKET TO RIDE	The Beatles
43. CALIFORNIA GIRLS	The Beach Boys
44. HANG ON SLOOPY	The McCoys
45. BACK IN MY ARMS AGAIN	The Supremes
46. THE NAME GAME	S. Ellis
47. JUST ONCE IN MY LIFE	The Righteous Brothers
48. GOLDFINGER	S. Bassey
49. WHAT THE WORLD NEEDS NOW IS LOVE	J. DeShannon
50. EIGHT DAYS A WEEK	The Beatles

1. **I FEEL FINE**
The Beatles
J. Lennon–P. McCartney,
Capitol 5327   (Maclen, BMI)

2. **MR. LONELY**
B. Vinton
Vinton–Allen,   Epic 9370
(Ripley, BMI)

3. **COME SEE ABOUT ME**
The Supremes
Holland–Dozier–Holland,
Motown 1068   (Jobete, BMI)

4. **LOVE POTION NUMBER NINE**
The Searchers
J. Leiber–M. Stoller,
Kapp Winner's Circle 27
(Quintet, BMI)

5. **SHE'S A WOMAN**
The Beatles
J. Lennon–P. McCartney,
Capitol 5327   (Maclen, BMI)

6. **GOIN' OUT OF MY HEAD**
Little Anthony
T.Randazzo,   DCP 119
(South Mountain, BMI)

7. **SHE'S NOT THERE**
The Zombies
R. Argent,   Parrot 9695
(Gallice, BMI)

8. **THE JERK**
The Larks
Julian,   Money 106
(Cash, BMI)

9. **THE WEDDING**
J. Rodgers
Wood–Beach,   Mercury 72332
(Bendig–Regent, BMI)

10. **AMEN**
The Impressions
Seguire–Hardy–Schoen,   ABC
10602   (Pamco, BMI)

1. **I FEEL FINE**
The Beatles
J. Lennon–P. McCartney,
Capitol 5327   (Maclen, BMI)

2. **MR. LONELY**
B. Vinton
Vinton–Allen,   Epic 9730
(Ripley, BMI)

3. **COME SEE ABOUT ME**
The Supremes
Holland–Dozier–Holland,
Motown 1068   (Jobete, BMI)

4. **DOWNTOWN**
P. Clark
T. Hatch,   Warner Brothers
7194   (Leeds, ASCAP)

5. **LOVE POTION NUMBER NINE**
The Searchers
J. Leiber–M. Stoller
Kapp Winner's Circle 27
(Quintet, BMI)

6. **GOIN' OUT OF MY HEAD**
Little Anthony
T. Randazzo,   DCP 1119
(South Mountain, BMI)

7. **THE JERK**
The Larks
Julian,   Money 106
(Cash, BMI)

8. **YOU'VE LOST THAT LOVIN' FEELIN'**
The Righteous Brothers
Spector–Mama–Weil,   Philles
124   (Screen Gems–
Columbia, BMI)

9. **AMEN**
The Impressions
Seguire–Hardy–Schoen,   ABC
10602   (Pamco, BMI)

10. **THE WEDDING**
J. Rodgers
Wood–Beach,   Mercury 72332
(Bendig–Regent, BMI)

January 16

1. **COME SEE ABOUT ME**
The Supremes
Holland–Dozier–Holland
Motown 1068 (Jobete, BMI)

2. **LOVE POTION NUMBER NINE**
The Searchers
J. Leiber–M. Stoller,
Kapp Winner's Circle 27
(Quintet, BMI)

3. **I FEEL FINE**
The Beatles
J. Lennon–P. McCartney,
Capitol 5327 (Maclen, BMI)

4. **YOU'VE LOST THAT LOVIN' FEELIN'**
The Righteous Brothers
Spector–Mama–Weil, Philles
124 (Screen Gems–
Columbia, BMI)

5. **DOWNTOWN**
P. Clark
T. Hatch, Warner Brothers
7194 (Leeds, ASCAP)

6. **THE JERK**
The Larks
Julian, Money 106
(Cash, BMI)

7. **MR. LONELY**
B. Vinton
Vinton–Allen, Epic 9730
(Ripley, BMI)

8. **HOW SWEET IT IS (TO BE LOVED BY YOU)**
M. Gaye
Holland–Dozier–Holland, Tamla
54107 (Jobete, BMI)

9. **SHA LA LA**
M. Mann
Ludix, Ascot 2165
(Flamarlu, BMI)

10. **KEEP SEARCHIN'**
D. Shannon
D. Shannon, Amy 915 (Vicki,
McLaughlin, BMI)

January 23

1. **YOU'VE LOST THAT LOVIN' FEELIN'**
The Righteous Brothers
Spector–Mama–Weil, Philles
124 (Screen Gems–
Columbia, BMI)

2. **DOWNTOWN**
P. Clark
T. Hatch, Warner Brothers 7194
(Leeds, ASCAP)

3. **I FEEL FINE**
The Beatles
J. Lennon–P. McCartney,
Capitol 5327 (Maclen, BMI)

4. **LOVE POTION NUMBER NINE**
The Searchers
J. Leiber–M. Stoller,
Kapp Winner's Circle 27
(Quintet, BMI)

5. **THE NAME GAME**
S. Ellis
Elliston–Chase, Congress 230
(Al Gallico, BMI)

6. **COME SEE ABOUT ME**
The Supremes
Holland–Dozier–Holland,
Motown 1068 (Jobete, BMI)

7. **THE JERK**
The Larks
Julian, Money 106
(Cash, BMI)

8. **MR. LONELY**
B. Vinton
Vinton–Allen, Epic 9730
(Ripley, BMI)

9. **KEEP SEARCHIN'**
D. Shannon
D. Shannon, Amy 915
(Vicki, McLaughlin, BMI)

10. **HOW SWEET IT IS (TO BE LOVED BY YOU)**
M. Gaye
Holland–Dozier–Holland, Tamla
54107 (Jobete, BMI)

January 30

1. **DOWNTOWN**
P. Clark
T. Hatch, Warner Brothers
7194 (Leeds, ASCAP)

2. **YOU'VE LOST THAT LOVIN' FEELIN'**
The Rightous Brothers
Spector–Mama–Weil, Philles
124 (Screen Gems–
Columbia, BMI)

3. **THE NAME GAME**
S. Ellis
Elliston–Chase, Congress 230
(Al Gallico, BMI)

4. **HOLD WHAT YOU'VE GOT**
J. Tex
J. Tex, Dial 4001 (Tree, BMI)

5. **LOVE POTION NUMBER NINE**
The Searchers
J. Leiber–M. Stoller,
Kapp Winner's Circle 27
(Quintet, BMI)

6. **THIS DIAMOND RING**
G. Lewis and the Playboys
Kooper–Levine–Brass, Liberty
5576 (Sea Lark, BMI)

7. **COME SEE ABOUT ME**
The Supremes
Holland–Dozier–Holland,
Motown 1069 (Jobete, BMI)

8. **ALL DAY AND ALL OF THE NIGHT**
The Kinks
R. Davies, Reprise 0334
(Jay-Boy, BMI)

9. **KEEP SEARCHIN'**
D. Shannon
D. Shannon, Amy 915
(Vicki, McLaughlin, BMI)

10. **MR. LONELY**
B. Vinton
Vinton–Allen, Epic 9730
(Ripley, BMI)

February 6

1. **DOWNTOWN**
   P. Clark
   T. Hatch, Warner Brothers
   7194 (Leeds, ASCAP)

2. **YOU'VE LOST THAT LOVIN' FEELIN'**
   The Righteous Brothers
   Spector–Mama–Weil, Philles
   124 (Screen Gems–
   Columbia, BMI)

3. **THIS DIAMOND RING**
   G. Lewis and the Playboys
   Kooper–Levine–Brass, Liberty
   55756 (Sea Lark, BMI)

4. **HOLD WHAT YOU'VE GOT**
   J. Tex
   J. Tex, Dial 4001 (Tree, BMI)

5. **THE NAME GAME**
   S. Ellis
   Elliston–Chase, Congress 230
   (Al Gallico, BMI)

6. **LOVE POTION NUMBER NINE**
   The Searchers
   J. Leiber–M. Stoller,
   Kapp Winner's Circle 27
   (Quintet, BMI)

7. **MY GIRL**
   The Temptations
   W. Robinson, Gordy 7038
   (Jobete, BMI)

8. **ALL DAY AND ALL OF THE NIGHT**
   The Kinks
   R. Davies, Reprise 0334
   (Jay–Boy, BMI)

9. **SHAKE**
   S. Cooke
   S. Cooke, Victor 8406
   (Kags, BMI)

10. **MR. LONELY**
    B. Vinton
    Vinton–Allen, Epic 9730
    (Ripley, BMI)

270

February 13

1. **DOWNTOWN**
   P. Clark
   T. Hatch, Warner Brothers 7194
   (Leeds, ASCAP)

2. **THIS DIAMOND RING**
   G. Lewis and the Playboys
   Kooper–Levine–Brass, Liberty
   55756 (Sea Lark, BMI)

3. **YOU'VE LOST THAT LOVIN-'FEELIN'**
   The Righteous Brothers
   Spector–Mama–Weil, Philles 124
   (Screen Gems–Columbia, BMI)

4. **THE NAME GAME**
   S. Ellis
   Eliston–Chase, Congress 230
   (Al Gallico, BMI)

5. **MY GIRL**
   The Temptations
   W. Robinson, Gordy 7038
   (Jobete, BMI)

6. **THE JOLLY GREEN GIANT**
   The Kingsmen
   Easton, Wand 172
   (Burdette, BMI)

7. **I GO TO PIECES**
   Peter and Gordon
   D. Shannon, Capitol 5335
   (Vicki, BMI)

8. **HOLD WHAT YOU'VE GOT**
   J. Tex
   J. Tex, Dial 4001 (Tree, BMI)

9. **ALL DAY AND ALL OF THE NIGHT**
   The Kinks
   R. Davies, Reprise 0334
   (Jay–Boy, BMI)

10. **GIVE HIM A GREAT BIG KISS**
    The Shangri-Las
    Morton, Red Bird 10–018
    (Trio–Tender Tunes, BMI)

February 20

1. **THIS DIAMOND RING**
   G. Lewis and the Playboys
   Kooper–Levine–Brass, Liberty
   55756 (Sea Lark, BMI)

2. **DOWNTOWN**
   P. Clark
   T. Hatch,
   Warner Brothers 7174
   (Leeds, ASCAP)

3. **MY GIRL**
   The Temptations
   W. Robinson, Gordy 7038
   (Jobete, BMI)

4. **THE NAME GAME**
   S. Ellis
   Elliston–Chase, Congress 230
   (Al Gallico, BMI)

5. **YOU'VE LOST THAT LOVIN' FEELIN'**
   The Righteous Brothers
   Spector–Mama–Weil,
   Philles 124
   (Screen Gems–Columbia, BMI)

6. **THE JOLLY GREEN GIANT**
   The Kingsmen
   Easton, Wand 172
   (Burdette, BMI)

7. **I GO TO PIECES**
   Peter and Gordon
   D. Shannon, Capitol 5335
   (Vicki, BMI)

8. **HOLD WHAT YOU'VE GOT**
   J. Tex
   J. Tex, Dial 4001 (Tree, BMI)

9. **LET'S LOCK THE DOOR**
   Jay and the Americans
   Alfred–Merill,
   United Artists 805
   (Picturetone, BMI)

10. **THE BOY FROM NEW YORK CITY**
    The Ad-Libs
    Taylor, Blue Cat 102
    (Trio, BMI)

February 27

1. **MY GIRL**
The Temptations
W. Robinson, Gordy 7038
(Jobete, BMI)

2. **THIS DIAMOND RING**
G. Lewis and the Playboys
Kooper–Levine–Brass,
Liberty 55756 (Sea Lark, BMI)

3. **DOWNTOWN**
P. Clark
T. Hatch,
Warner Brothers 7174
(Leeds, ASCAP)

4. **THE JOLLY GREEN GIANT**
The Kingsmen
Easton, Wand 172
(Burdette, BMI)

5. **YOU'VE LOST THAT LOVIN' FEELIN'**
The Righteous Brothers
Spector–Mama–Weil, Philles 124
(Screen Gems–Columbia, BMI)

6. **I GO TO PIECES**
Peter and Gordon
D. Shannon, Capitol 5335
(Vicki, BMI)

7. **KING OF THE ROAD**
R. Miller
R. Miller, Smash 1965
(Tree, BMI)

8. **THE BOY FROM NEW YORK CITY**
The Ad-Libs
Taylor, Blue Cat 102
(Trio, BMI)

9. **TELL HER NO**
The Zombies
Argent, Parrot 9723
(Mainstay, BMI)

10. **THE "IN" CROWD**
D. Gray
Page, Charger 105
(American, BMI)

March 6

1. **MY GIRL**
The Temptations
W. Robinson, Gordy 7038
(Jobete, BMI)

2. **THIS DIAMOND RING**
G. Lewis and the Playboys
Kooper–Lewis–Brass, Liberty
55756 (Sea Lark, BMI)

3. **THE JOLLY GREEN GIANT**
The Kingsmen
Easton, Wand 172
(Burdette, BMI)

4. **EIGHT DAYS A WEEK**
The Beatles
J. Lennon–P. McCartney,
Capitol 5371 (Maclen, BMI)

5. **YOU'VE LOST THAT LOVIN' 'FEELIN'**
The Righteous Brothers
Spector–Mama–Weil Philles 124
(Screen Gems–Columbia, BMI)

6. **TELL HER NO**
The Zombies
Argent, Parrot 9723
(Mainstay, BMI)

7. **THE BIRDS AND THE BEES**
J. Akens
H. Newman, Era 3141
(Pattern, ASCAP)

8. **KING OF THE ROAD**
R. Miller
R. Miller, Smash 1965
(Tree, BMI)

9. **LAUGH LAUGH**
The Beau Brummels
R. Elliot, Autumn 8
(Taracrest, BMI)

10. **FERRY 'CROSS THE MERSEY**
Gerry and the Pacemakers
G. Marsden, Laurie 3284
(Unart–Pacer, BMI)

March 13

1. **MY GIRL**
The Temptations
W. Robinson, Gordy 7038
(Jobete, BMI)

2. **EIGHT DAYS A WEEK**
The Beatles
J. Lennon–P. McCartney,
Capitol 5371 (Maclen, BMI)

3. **THIS DIAMOND RING**
G. Lewis and the Playboys
Kooper–Levine–Brass, Liberty
55756
(Sea Lark, BMI)

4. **THE BIRDS AND THE BEES**
J. Akens
H. Newman, Era 3141
(Pattern, ASCAP)

5. **KING OF THE ROAD**
R. Miller
R. Miller, Smash 1965
(Tree, BMI)

6. **STOP! IN THE NAME OF LOVE**
The Supremes
Holland–Dozier–Holland,
Motown 1074 (Jobete, BMI)

7. **CAN'T YOU HEAR MY HEARTBEAT?**
Herman's Hermits
Carter–Lewis, M-G-M 13310
(South Mointain, BMI)

9. **FERRY 'CROSS THE MERSEY**
Gerry and the Pacemakers
G. Marsden, Laurie 3284
(Unart–Pacer, BMI)

10. **THE JOLLY GREEN GIANT**
The Kingsmen
Easton, Wand 172
(Burdette, BMI)

March 20

1. **EIGHT DAYS A WEEK**
The Beatles
*J. Lennon–P. McCartney, Capitol
5371 (Maclen, BMI)*

2. **STOP! IN THE NAME OF
LOVE**
The Supremes
*Holland–Dozier–Holland,
Motown 1074 (Jobete, BMI)*

3. **KING OF THE ROAD**
R. Miller
*R. Miller, Smash 1965
(Tree, BMI)*

4. **CAN'T YOU HEAR MY
HEARTBEAT?**
Herman's Hermits
*Carter–Lewis, M-G-M 13310
(Southern, ASCAP)*

5. **THE BIRDS AND THE BEES**
J. Akens
*H. Newman, Era 3141
(Pattern, ASCAP)*

6. **MY GIRL**
The Temptations
*W. Robinson, Gordy 7038
(Jobete, BMI)*

7. **FERRY 'CROSS THE
MERSEY**
Gerry and the Pacemakers
*G. Marsden, Laurie 3284
(Unart–Pacer, BMI)*

8. **GOLDFINGER**
S. Bassey
*Bricusse–Newley–Barry, United
Artists 790 (Unart, BMI)*

9. **LITTLE THINGS**
B. Goldsboro
*B. Goldsboro, United Artists 810
(Unart, BMI)*

10. **SHOTGUN**
Jr. Walker and the All-
Stars
*DeWalt, Soul 35008
(Jobete, BMI)*

March 27

1. **STOP! IN THE NAME OF
LOVE**
The Supremes
*Holland–Dozier–Holland,
Motown 1074 (Jobete, BMI)*

2. **EIGHT DAYS A WEEK**
The Beatles
*J. Lennon–P. McCartney,
Capitol 5371 (Maclen, BMI)*

3. **CAN'T YOU HEAR MY
HEARTBEAT?**
Herman's Hermits
*Carter–Lewis, M-G-M 13310
(Southern, ASCAP)*

4. **THE BIRDS AND THE BEES**
J. Akens
*H. Newman, Era 3141
(Pattern, ASCAP)*

5. **KING OF THE ROAD**
R. Miller
*R. Miller, Smash 1965
(Tree, BMI)*

6. **SHOTGUN**
Jr. Walker and the All
Stars
*DeWalt, Soul 35008
(Jobete, BMI)*

7. **FERRY 'CROSS THE
MERSEY**
Gerry and the Pacemakers
*G. Marsden, Laurie 3284
(Unart–Pacer, BMI)*

8. **GOLDFINGER**
S. Bassey
*Bricusse–Newley–Barry,
United Artists 790 (Unart, BMI)*

9. **MY GIRL**
The Temptations
*W. Robinson, Gordy 7038
(Jobete, BMI)*

10. **NEW YORK'S A LONELY
TOWN**
The Tradewinds
*Andreoli–Percia,
Red Bird 10–020 (Big Top, BMI)*

April 3

1. **STOP! IN THE NAME OF
LOVE**
The Supremes
*Holland–Dozier–Holland,
Motown 1074 (Jobete, BMI)*

2. **EIGHT DAYS A WEEK**
The Beatles
*J. Lennon–P. McCartney,
Capitol 5371 (Maclen, BMI)*

3. **CAN'T YOU HEAR MY
HEARTBEAT?**
Herman's Hermits
*Carter–Lewis, M-G-M 13310
(Southern, ASCAP)*

4. **NOWHERE TO RUN**
Martha and the
Vandellas
*Holland–Dozier–Holland,
Gordy 7039 (Jobete, BMI)*

5. **KING OF THE ROAD**
R. Miller
*R. Miller, Smash 1965
(Tree, BMI)*

6. **I'M TELLING YOU NOW**
Freddie and the Dreamers
*Tovar, Tower 125
(Miller, ASCAP)*

7. **SHOTGUN**
Jr. Walker and the All
Stars
*DeWalt, Soul 35008
(Jobete, BMI)*

8. **FERRY 'CROSS THE
MERSEY**
Gerry and the Pacemakers
*G. Marsden, Laurie 3284
(Unart–Pacer, BMI)*

9. **GOLDFINGER**
S. Bassey
*Bricusse–Newley–Barry, United
Artists 790 (Unart, BMI)*

10. **RED ROSES FOR A BLUE
LADY**
V. Dana
*Tepper-Brodsky, Dolton 304
(Mills, ASCAP)*

April 10

1. **I'M TELLING YOU NOW**
Freddie and the Dreamers
Tovar, Tower 125
(Miller, ASCAP)

2. **CAN'T YOU HEAR MY HEARTBEAT?**
Herman's Hermits
Carter–Lewis, M-G-M 13310
(Southern, ASCAP)

3. **NOWHERE TO RUN**
Martha and the Vandellas
Holland–Dozier–Holland, Gordy 7039 (Jobete, BMI)

4. **STOP! IN THE NAME OF LOVE**
The Supremes
Holland–Dozier–Holland, Motown 1074 (Jobete, BMI)

5. **KING OF THE ROAD**
R. Miller
R. Miller, Smash 1965 (Tree, BMI)

6. **SHOTGUN**
Jr. Walker and the All Stars
DeWalt, Soul 35008 (Jobete, BMI)

7. **I KNOW A PLACE**
P. Clark
T. Hatch, Warner Brothers 5612 (Duchess, BMI)

8. **GAME OF LOVE**
W. Fontana and the Mindbenders
H. Ballard, Fontana 1503 (Skidmore, ASCAP)

9. **GOLDFINGER**
S. Bassey
Bricusse–Newley–Barry, United Artists 790 (Unart, BMI)

10. **DO YOU WANNA DANCE?**
The Beach Boys
B. Freeman, Capitol 5372 (Clockus, BMI)

April 17

1. **I'M TELLING YOU NOW**
Freddie and the Dreamers
Tovar, Tower 125
(Skidmore, ASCAP)

2. **GAME OF LOVE**
W. Fontana and the Mindbenders
H. Ballard, Fontana 1503 (Skidmore, ASCAP)

3. **I KNOW A PLACE**
P. Clark
T. Hatch, Warner Brothers 5612 (Duchess, BMI)

4. **STOP! IN THE NAME OF LOVE**
The Supremes
Holland–Dozier–Holland, Motown 1074 (Jobete, BMI)

5. **CAN'T YOU HEAR MY HEARTBEAT?**
Herman's Hermits
Carter–Lewis, M-G-M 13310 (Southern, ASCAP)

6. **SHOTGUN**
Jr. Walker and the All Stars
DeWalt, Soul 355008 (Jobete, BMI)

7. **NOWHERE TO RUN**
Martha and the Vandellas
Holland–Dozier–Holland, Gordy 7039 (Jobete, BMI)

8. **THE CLAPPING SONG**
S. Ellis
L. Chase, Congress 234 (Gallico, BMI)

9. **TIRED OF WAITING FOR YOU**
The Kinks
R. Davies, Reprise 0347 (Jay-Boy, BMI)

10. **GO NOW**
The Moody Blues
Banks–Bennett, London 9726 (Trio, BMI)

April 24

1. **MRS. BROWN YOU'VE GOT A LOVELY DAUGHTER**
Herman's Hermits
T. Peacock, M-G-M 13341 (Brakenbury–Hill & Range, BMI)

2. **GAME OF LOVE**
W. Fontana and the Mindbenders
H. Ballard, Fontana 1503 (Skidmore, ASCAP)

3. **I KNOW A PLACE**
P. Clark
T. Hatch, Warner Brothers 5612 (Duchess, BMI)

4. **I'M TELLING YOU NOW**
Freddie and the Dreamers
Tovar, Tower 125
(Miller, ASCAP)

5. **TIRED OF WAITING FOR YOU**
The Kinks
R. Davies, Reprise 0347 (Jay-Boy, BMI)

6. **THE CLAPPING SONG**
S. Ellis
L. Chase, Congress 234 (Gallico, BMI)

7. **STOP! IN THE NAME OF LOVE**
The Supremes
Holland–Dozier–Holland, Motown 1074 (Jobete, BMI)

8. **NOWHERE TO RUN**
Martha and the Vandellas
Holland–Dozier–Holland, Gordy 7039 (Jobete, BMI)

9. **I'LL NEVER FIND ANOTHER YOU**
The Seekers
Springfield, Capitol 5383 (Chappell, ASCAP)

10. **SHOTGUN**
Jr. Walker and the All Stars
DeWalt, Soul 35008 (Jobete, BMI)

May 1

1. **MRS. BROWN YOU'VE GOT A LOVELY DAUGHTER**
Herman's Hermits
T. Peacock, M-G-M 13341
(Brakenbury–Hill & Range, BMI)

2. **I KNOW A PLACE**
P. Clark
T. Hatch, Warner Brothers 5612
(Duchess, BMI)

3. **GAME OF LOVE**
W. Fontana and the Mindbenders
H. Ballard, Fontana 1503
(Chappell, ASCAP)

4. **I'LL NEVER FIND ANOTHER YOU**
The Seekers
Springfield, Capitol 5383
(Chappell, ASCAP)

5. **TIRED OF WAITING FOR YOU**
The Kinks
R. Davies, Reprise 0347
(Jay-Boy, BMI)

6. **I'M TELLING YOU NOW**
Freddie and the Dreamers
Tovar, Tower 125
(Miller, ASCAP)

7. **SILHOUETTES**
Herman's Hermits
Slay–Crewe, M-G-M 13332
(Regent, BMI)

8. **COUNT ME IN**
G. Lewis and the Playboys
T. Hardin, Liberty 55778
(Skol, BMI)

9. **NOWHERE TO RUN**
Martha and the Vandellas
Holland–Dozier–Holland, Gordy 7039 (Jobete, BMI)

10. **THE LAST TIME**
The Rolling Stones
K. Richard–M. Jagger, London 9741 (Immediate, BMI)

May 8

1. **MRS. BROWN YOU'VE GOT A LOVELY DAUGHTER**
Herman's Hermits
T. Peacock, M-G-M 13341
(Brakenbury–Hill & Range, BMI)

2. **TICKET TO RIDE**
The Beatles
J. Lennon–P. McCartney,
Capitol 5407 (Maclen, BMI)

3. **COUNT ME IN**
G. Lewis and the Playboys
T. Hardin, Liberty 55778
(Skol, BMI)

4. **GAME OF LOVE**
W. Fontana and the Mindbenders
H. Ballard, Fontana 1503
(Skidmore, ASCAP)

5. **I KNOW A PLACE**
P. Clark
T. Hatch, Warner Brothers 5612 (Duchess, BMI)

6. **I'LL NEVER FIND ANOTHER YOU**
The Seekers
Springfield, Capitol 5383
(Chappell, ASCAP)

7. **SILHOUETTES**
Herman's Hermits
Slay–Crewe, M-G-M 13332
(Regent, BMI)

8. **THE LAST TIME**
The Rolling Stones
K. Richard–M. Jagger, London 9741 (Immediate, BMI)

9. **I'M TELLING YOU NOW**
Freddie and the Dreamers
Tovar, Tower 125
(Miller, ASCAP)

10. **NOWHERE TO RUN**
Martha and the Vandellas
Holland–Dozier–Holland, Gordy 7039 (Jobete, BMI)

May 15

1. **TICKET TO RIDE**
The Beatles
J. Lennon–P. McCartney,
Capitol 5407 (Maclen, BMI)

2. **COUNT ME IN**
G. Lewis and the Playboys
T. Hardin, Liberty 55778
(Skol, BMI)

3. **MRS. BROWN YOU'VE GOT A LOVELY DAUGHTER**
T. Peacock, M-G-M 13341
(Brakenbury–Hill & Range, BMI)

4. **SILHOUETTES**
Herman's Hermits
Slay–Crewe, M-G-M 13332
(Regent, BMI)

5. **HELP ME RHONDA**
The Beach Boys
B. Wilson, Capitol 5395
(Sea of Tunes, BMI)

6. **CAST YOUR FATE TO THE WIND**
Sounds Orchestral
V. Guaraldi, Parkway 942
(Friendship, BMI)

7. **I KNOW A PLACE**
P. Clark
T. Hatch, Warner Brothers 5612
(Duchess, BMI)

8. **I'LL NEVER FIND ANOTHER YOU**
The Seekers
Springfield, Capitol 5383
(Chappell, ASCAP)

9. **I'LL BE DOGGONE**
M. Gaye
Robinson–Moore–Tarplin, Tamla 54112 (Jobete, BMI)

10. **JUST ONCE IN MY LIFE**
The Righteous Brothers
G. Goffin–C. King–P. Spector, Philles 127
(Screen Gems–Columbia, BMI)

May 22

1. **TICKET TO RIDE**
The Beatles
J. Lennon–P. McCartney,
Capitol 5407 (Maclen, BMI)

2. **HELP ME RHONDA**
The Beach Boys
B. Wilson, Capitol 5395
(Sea of Tunes, BMI)

3. **COUNT ME IN**
G. Lewis and the Playboys
T. Hardin, Liberty 55778
(Skol, BMI)

4. **MRS. BROWN YOU'VE GOT A LOVELY DAUGHTER**
Herman's Hermits
T. Peacock, M-G-M 13341
(Brakenbury–Hill & Range, BMI)

5. **BACK IN MY ARMS AGAIN**
The Supremes
Holland–Dozier–Holland,
Motown 1075 (Jobete, BMI)

6. **CRYING IN THE CHAPEL**
E. Presley
Glenn, Victor 0643
(Valley, BMI)

7. **SILHOUETTES**
Herman's Hermits
Slay–Crewe, M-G-M 13332
(Regent, BMI)

8. **WOOLY BOOLY**
Sam the Sham and the Pharoahs
Samudio, M-G-M 13322
(Beckie, BMI)

9. **I'LL NEVER FIND ANOTHER YOU**
The Seekers
Springfield, Capitol 5383
(Chappell, ASCAP)

10. **JUST ONCE IN MY LIFE**
The Righteous Brothers
G. Goffin–C. King–P. Spector,
Philles 127
(Screen Gems–Columbia, BMI)

May 29

1. **HELP ME RHONDA**
The Beach Boys
B. Wilson, Capitol 5395
(Sea of Tunes, BMI)

2. **TICKET TO RIDE**
The Beatles
J. Lennon–P. McCartney,
Capitol 5407 (Maclen, BMI)

3. **WOOLY BOOLY**
Sam the Sham and the Pharoahs
Samudio, M-G-M 13322
(Beckie, BMI)

4. **MRS. BROWN YOU'VE GOT A LOVELY DAUGHTER**
Herman's Hermits
T. Peacock, M-G-M 13341
(Brakenbury–Hill & Range, BMI)

5. **BACK IN MY ARMS AGAIN**
The Supremes
Holland–Dozier–Holland,
Motown 1075 (Jobete, BMI)

6. **CRYING IN THE CHAPEL**
E. Presley
Glenn, Victor 0643
(Valley, BMI)

7. **JUST A LITTLE**
The Beau Brummels
Elliott, Autumn 10
(Taracrest, BMI)

8. **IT'S NOT UNUSUAL**
T. Jones
Mills–Reed, Parrot 9737
(Duchess, BMI)

9. **COUNT ME IN**
G. Lewis and the Playboys
T. Hardin, Liberty 55778
(Skol, BMI)

10. **I'LL NEVER FIND ANOTHER YOU**
The Seekers
Springfield, Capitol 5383
(Chappell, ASCAP)

June 5

1. **WOOLY BOOLY**
Sam the Sham and the Pharoahs
Samudio, M-G-M 13322
(Beckie, BMI)

2. **HELP ME RHONDA**
The Beach Boys
B. Wilson, Capitol 5395
(Sea of Tunes, BMI)

3. **BACK IN MY ARMS AGAIN**
The Supremes
Holland–Dozier–Holland,
Motown 1075 (Jobete, BMI)

4. **CRYING IN THE CHAPEL**
E. Presley
Glenn, Victor 0643
(Valley, BMI)

5. **MR. TAMBOURINE MAN**
The Byrds
B. Dylan, Columbia 43271
(Witmark, ASCAP)

6. **TICKET TO RIDE**
The Beatles
J. Lennon–P. McCartney, Capitol 5407 (Maclen, BMI)

7. **MRS. BROWN YOU'VE GOT A LOVELY DAUGHTER**
Herman's Hermits
T. Peacock, M-G-M 13341
(Brakenbury–Hill & Range, BMI)

8. **JUST A LITTLE**
The Beau Brummels
Elliott, Autumn 10
(Taracrest, BMI)

9. **IT'S NOT UNUSUAL**
T. Jones
Mills–Reed, Parrot 9737
(Duchess, BMI)

10. **ENGINE, ENGINE   9**
R. Miller
R. Miller, Smash 1983
(Tree, BMI)

June 12

1. **WOOLY BOOLY**
Sam the Sham and the
Pharoahs
Samudio, M-G-M 13322
(Beckie, BMI)

2. **BACK IN MY ARMS AGAIN**
The Supremes
Holland–Dozier–Holland,
Motown 1075 (Jobete, BMI)

3. **CRYING IN THE CHAPEL**
E. Presley
Glenn, Victor 0643
(Valley, BMI)

4. **I CAN'T HELP MYSELF**
The Four Tops
Holland–Dozier–Holland,
Motown 1076 (Jobete, BMI)

5. **MR. TAMBOURINE MAN**
The Byrds
B. Dylan, Columbia 43271
(Witmark, ASCAP)

6. **HELP ME RHONDA**
The Beach Boys
B. Wilson, Capitol 5395
(Sea of Tunes, BMI)

7. **TICKET TO RIDE**
The Beatles
J. Lennon–P. McCartney,
Capitol 5407 (Maclen, BMI)

8. **ENGINE, ENGINE 9**
R. Miller
R. Miller, Smash 1983
(Tree, BMI)

9. **WONDERFUL WORLD**
Herman's Hermits
S. Cooke, M-G-M 13354
(Kags, BMI)

10. **JUST A LITTLE**
The Beau Brummels
Elliott, Autumn 10
(Taracrest, BMI)

June 19

1. **MR. TAMBOURINE MAN**
The Byrds
B. Dylan, Columbia 42371
(Witmark, ASCAP)

2. **I CAN'T HELP MYSELF**
The Four Tops
Holland–Dozier–Holland,
Motown 1076 (Jobete, BMI)

3. **BACK IN MY ARMS AGAIN**
The Supremes
Holland–Dozier–Holland,
Motown 1075 (Jobete, BMI)

4. **WOOLY BOOLY**
Sam the Sham and the
Pharoahs
Samudio, M-G-M 13322
(Beckie, BMI)

5. **(I CAN'T GET NO) SATIS-
FACTION**
The Rolling Stones
M. Jagger–K. Richard, London
9766 (Immediate, BMI)

6. **CRYING IN THE CHAPEL**
E. Presley
Glenn, Victor 0643
(Valley, BMI)

7. **WONDERFUL WORLD**
Herman's Hermits
S. Cooke, M-G-M 13354
(Kags, BMI)

8. **TRUE LOVE WAYS**
Peter and Gordon
N. Petty–B. Holly, Capitol 5406
(Nor-Va-Jak, BMI)

9. **HELP ME RHONDA**
The Beach Boys
B. Wilson, Capitol 5395
(Sea of Tunes, BMI)

10. **FOR YOUR LOVE**
The Yardbirds
Gouldman, Epic 9790
(Blackwood, BMI)

June 26

1. **(I CAN'T GET NO) SATIS-
FACTION**
The Rolling Stones
M. Jagger–K. Richard, London
9766 (Immediate, BMI)

2. **MR. TAMBOURINE MAN**
The Byrds
B. Dylan, Columbia 43271
(Witmark, ASCAP)

3. **I CAN'T HELP MYSELF**
The Four Tops
Holland–Dozier–Holland,
Motown 1076 (Jobete, BMI)

4. **WOOLY BOOLY**
Sam the Sham and the
Pharoahs
Samudio, M-G-M 13322
(Beckie, BMI)

5. **WONDERFUL WORLD**
Herman's Hermits
S. Cooke, M-G-M 13354
(Kags, BMI)

6. **FOR YOUR LOVE**
The Yardbirds
Gouldman, Epic 9790
(Blackwood, BMI)

7. **HUSH, HUSH, SWEET
CHARLOTTE**
P. Page
David–DeVol, Columbia 43251
(Miller, ASCAP)

8. **CRYING IN THE CHAPEL**
E. Presley
Glenn, Victor 0643
(Valley, BMI)

9. **SEVENTH SON**
J. Rivers
T. Hardin, Imperial 66112
(Arc, BMI)

10. **HELP ME RHONDA**
The Beach Boys
B. Wilson, Capitol 5395
(Sea of Tunes, BMI)

July 3

1. **(I CAN'T GET NO) SATIS-FACTION**
The Rolling Stones
M. Jagger–K. Richard, London 9766 (Immediate, BMI)

2. **I CAN'T HELP MYSELF**
The Four Tops
Holland–Dozier–Holland, Motown 1076 (Jobete, BMI)

3. **MR. TAMBORINE MAN**
The Byrds
B. Dylan, Columbia 43271 (Witmark, ASCAP)

4. **WOOLY BOOLY**
Sam the Sham and the Pharoahs
Samudio, M-G-M 13322 (Beckie, BMI)

5. **FOR YOUR LOVE**
The Yardbirds
Gouldman, Epic 9790 (Blackwood, BMI)

6. **WONDERFUL WORLD**
Herman's Hermits
S. Cooke, M-G-M 13354 (Kags, BMI)

7. **YES, I'M READY**
B. Mason
B. Mason, Arctic 105 (Stillran–Dandelion, BMI)

8. **WHAT THE WORLD NEEDS NOW IS LOVE**
J. DeShannon
H. David–B. Bacharach, Imperial 64110 (Blue Seas–Jac, BMI)

9. **SEVENTH SON**
J. Rivers
T. Hardin, Imperial 66112 (Arc, BMI)

10. **CRYING IN THE CHAPEL**
E. Presley
Glenn, Victor 0643 (Valley, BMI)

July 10

1. **(I CAN'T GET NO) SATIS-FACTION**
The Rolling Stones
M. Jagger–K. Richard, London 9766 (Immediate, BMI)

2. **MR. TAMBOURINE MAN**
The Byrds
B. Dylan, Columbia 43271 (Witmark, ASCAP)

3. **I CAN'T HELP MYSELF**
The Four Tops
Holland–Dozier–Holland, Motown 1076 (Jobete, BMI)

4. **YES, I'M READY**
B. Mason
B. Mason, Artic 105 (Stillran–Dandelion, BMI)

5. **WHAT THE WORLD NEEDS NOW IS LOVE**
J. De Shannon
H. David–B. Bacharach, Imperial 64110 (Blue Seas–Jac, BMI)

6. **WOOLY BOOLY**
Sam the Sham and the Pharoahs
Samudio, M-G-M 13322 (Beckie, BMI)

7. **SEVENTH SON**
J. Rivers
T. Hardin, Imperial 66112 (Arc, BMI)

8. **CARA MIA**
Jay and the Americans
Tranpani–Lange, United Artists 881 (Leo Feist, ASCAP)

9. **WONDERFUL WORLD**
Herman's Hermits
S. Cooke, M-G-M 13354 (Kags, BMI)

10. **WHAT'S NEW PUSSYCAT?**
T. Jones
H. David–B. Bachrach, Parrot 9765 (United Artists, ASCAP)

July 17

1. **(I CAN'T GET NO) SATIS-FACTION**
The Rolling Stones
M. Jagger–K. Richard, London 9766 (Immediate, BMI)

2. **I CAN'T HELP MYSELF**
The Four Tops
Holland–Dozier–Holland, Motown 1076 (Jobete, BMI)

3. **CARA MIA**
Jay and the Americans
Trapani–Lange, United Artist 881 (Leo Feist, ASCAP)

4. **MR. TAMBOURINE MAN**
The Byrds
B. Dylan, Columbia 43271 (Witmark, ASCAP)

5. **YES, I'M READY**
B. Mason
B. Mason, Artic 105 (Stillran–Dandelion, BMI)

6. **WHAT THE WORLD NEEDS NOW IS LOVE**
J. DeShannon
H. David–B. Bacharach, Imperial 64110 (Blue Seas–Jac, BMI)

7. **SEVENTH SON**
J. Rivers
T. Hardin, Imperial 6612 (Arc, BMI)

8. **WOOLY BOOLY**
Sam the Sham and the Pharoahs
Samudio, M-G-M 13322 (Beckie, BMI)

9. **WHAT'S NEW PUSSYCAT?**
T. Jones
H. David–B. Bacharach, Parrot 9765 (United Artists, ASCAP)

10. **WONDERFUL WORLD**
Herman's Hermits
S. Cooke, M-G-M 13354 (Kags, BMI)

July 24

1. **(I CAN'T GET NO) SATIS-
   FACTION**
   The Rolling Stones
   *M. Jagger–K. Richard, London
   9766 (Immediate, BMI)*

2. **I'M HENRY VIII, I AM**
   Herman's Hermits
   *Murray–Weston, M-G-M 13367
   (Miller, ASCAP)*

3. **I CAN'T HELP MYSELF**
   The Four Tops
   *Holland–Dozier–Holland,
   Motown 1076 (Jobete, BMI)*

4. **CARA MIA**
   Jay and the Americans
   *Trapani–Lang, United States
   881 (Leo Feist, ASCAP)*

5. **WHAT'S NEW PUSSYCAT?**
   T. Jones
   *H. David–B. Bacharach, Parrot
   9765 (United Artists, ASCAP)*

6. **YES, I'M READY**
   B. Mason
   *B. Mason Arctic 105
   (Stillman–Dandelion, BMI)*

7. **WHAT THE WORLD
   NEEDS NOW IS LOVE**
   J. DeShannon
   *H. David–B. Bacharach,
   Imperial 64110
   (Blue Seas–Jac, BMI)*

8. **SEVENTH SON**
   *J. Rivers
   T. Hardin, Imperial 6612
   (Arc, BMI)*

9. **MR. TAMBOURINE MAN**
   The Byrds
   *B. Dylan, Columbia 43271
   (Witmark, ASCAP)*

10. **WONDERFUL WORLD**
    Herman's Hermits
    *S. Cooke, M-G-M 13354
    (Kags, BMI)*

July 31

1. **I'M HENRY VIII, I AM**
   Herman's Hermits
   *Murray–Weston, M-G-M 13367
   (Miller, ASCAP)*

2. **(I CAN'T GET NO) SATIS-
   FACTION**
   The Rolling Stones
   *M. Jagger–K. Richerd, London
   9766 (Immediate, BMI)*

3. **WHAT'S NEW PUSSYCAT?**
   T. Jones
   *H. David–B. Bacharach, Parrot
   9765 (United Artists, ASCAP)*

4. **CARA MIA**
   Jay and the Americans
   *Trapani–Lange, United Artists
   881 (Leo Feist, ASCAP)*

5. **I CAN'T HELP MYSELF**
   The Four Tops
   *Holland–Dozier–Holland,
   Motown 1076 (Jobete, BMI)*

6. **YES, I'M READY**
   B. Mason
   *B. Mason, Arctic 105
   (Stillman–Dandelion, BMI)*

7. **WHAT THE WORLD
   NEEDS NOW IS LOVE**
   J. DeShannon
   *H. David–B. Bacharach,
   Imperial 64110
   (Blue Seas–Jac, BMI)*

8. **SEVENTH SON**
   J. Rivers
   *T. Hardin, Imperial 66112
   (Arc, BMI)*

9. **LAURIE**
   D. Lee
   *M. Addington, TFC–Hall 102
   (Long–Gold Dust, BMI)*

10. **I LIKE IT LIKE THAT**
    The Dave Clark Five
    *C. Kenner, Epic 9811
    (Tune–Kel, BMI)*

August 7

1. **I'M HENRY VIII, I AM**
   Herman's Hermits
   *Murray–Weston, M-G-M 13367
   (Miller, ASCAP)*

2. **(I CAN'T GET NO) SATIS-
   FACTION**
   The Rolling Stones
   *M. Jagger–K. Richard, London
   9766 (Immediate, BMI)*

3. **I LIKE IT LIKE THAT**
   The Dave Clark Five
   *C. Kenner, Epic 9811
   (Tune–Kel, BMI)*

4. **I GOT YOU BABE**
   Sonny and Cher
   *S. Bono, Atco 6359
   (Five–West–Cotillion, BMI)*

5. **WHAT'S NEW PUSSYCAT?**
   T. Jones
   *H. David–B. Bacharach, Parrot
   9765 (United Artists, ASCAP)*

6. **DOWN IN THE BOONDOCKS**
   B. Royal
   *J. South, Columbia 43305
   (Lowery, BMI)*

7. **YES, I'M READY**
   B. Mason
   *B. Mason, Arctic 105
   (Stillman–Dandelion, BMI)*

8. **I CAN'T HELP MYSELF**
   The Four Tops
   *Holland–Dozier–Holland,
   Motown 1076 (Jobete, BMI)*

9. **CARA MIA**
   Jay and the Americans
   *Trapani–Lange, United Artists
   881 (Leo Feist, ASCAP)*

10. **DON'T JUST STAND THERE**
    P. Duke
    *B. Ross–L. Crane, United
    Artists 875 (Bernross, BMI)*

August 14

1. **I'M HENRY VIII, I AM**
   Herman's Hermits
   Murray–Weston, M-G-M
   13367 (Miller, ASCAP)

2. **I GOT YOU BABE**
   Sonny and Cher
   S. Bono, Atco 6359
   (Five–West–Cotillion, BMI)

3. **I LIKE IT LIKE THAT**
   The Dave Clark Five
   C. Kenner, Epic 9811
   (Tune–Kel, BMI)

4. **(I CAN'T GET NO) SATIS-FACTION**
   The Rolling Stones
   M. Jagger–K. Richard, London
   9766 (Immediate, BMI)

5. **WHAT'S NEW PUSSYCAT?**
   T. Jones
   H. David–B. Bacharach, Parrot
   9765 (United Artists, ASCAP)

6. **IT'S THE SAME OLD SONG**
   The Four Tops
   Holland–Dozier–Holland,
   Motown 1081 (Jobete, BMI)

7. **UNCHAINED MELODY**
   The Righteous Brothers
   H. Zert–A. North, Philles 129
   (Frank, ASCAP)

8. **CALIFORNIA GIRLS**
   The Beach Boys
   B. Wilson, Capitol 5464
   (Sea of Tunes, BMI)

9. **DOWN IN THE BOONDOCKS**
   B. Royal
   J. South, Columbia 43305
   (Lowery, BMI)

10. **DON'T JUST STAND THERE**
    P. Duke
    B. Ross–L. Crane, United
    Artists 875 (Bernross, BMI)

August 21

1. **I GOT YOU BABE**
   Sonny and Cher
   S. Bono Atco 6359
   (Five–West–Cotillion, BMI)

2. **HELP**
   The Beatles
   J. Lennon–P. McCartney,
   Capitol 5476 (Maclen, BMI)

3. **CALIFORNIA GIRLS**
   The Beach Boys
   B. Wilson Capitol 5464
   (Sea of Tunes, BMI)

4. **UNCHAINED MELODY**
   The Righteous Brothers
   H. Zert–A. North, Philles 129
   (Frank, ASCAP)

5. **IT'S THE SAME OLD SONG**
   The Four Tops
   Holland–Dozier–Holland,
   Motown 1081 (Jobete, BMI)

6. **I LIKE IT LIKE THAT**
   The Dave Clark Five
   C. Kenner, Epic 9811
   (Tune–Kel, BMI)

7. **I WANT CANDY**
   The Strangeloves
   Feldman–Goldstein–Gotteher–
   Barnes, Bang 501
   (Grand Canyon, Webb IV, BMI)

8. **(I CAN'T GET NO) SATIS-FACTION**
   The Rolling Stones
   M. Jagger.–K. Richard, London
   9766 (Immediate, BMI)

9. **DOWN IN THE BOONDOCKS**
   B. Royal
   J. South, Columbia 43305
   (Lowery, BMI)

10. **I'M HENRY VIII, I AM**
    Herman's Hermits
    Murray–Weston, M-G-M 13367
    (Miller, ASCAP)

August 28

1. **HELP**
   The Beatles
   J. Lennon–P. McCartney,
   Capitol 5476 (Maclen, BMI)

2. **CALIFORNIA GIRLS**
   The Beach Boys
   B. Wilson, Capitol 5464
   (Sea of Tunes, BMI)

3. **UNCHAINED MELODY**
   The Righteous Brothers
   H. Zert–A. North, Philles 129
   (Frank, ASCAP)

4. **LIKE A ROLLING STONE**
   B. Dylan
   B. Dylan, Columbia 43346
   (Witmark, ASCAP)

5. **IT'S THE SAME OLD SONG**
   The Four Tops
   Holland–Dozier–Holland,
   Motown 1081 (Jobete, BMI)

6. **I GOT YOU BABE**
   Sonny and Cher
   S. Bono, Atco 6359
   (Five–West–Cotillion, BMI)

7. **I LIKE IT LIKE THAT**
   The Dave Clark Five
   C. Kenner, Epic 9811
   (Tune–Kel, BMI)

8. **DOWN IN THE BOONDOCKS**
   B. Royal
   J. South, Columbia 43305
   (Lowery, BMI)

9. **PAPA'S GOT A BRAND NEW BAG**
   J. Brown
   J. Brown, King 5999
   (Lois, BMI)

10. **HOLD ME, THRILL ME, KISS ME**
    M. Carter
    Noble, Imperial 66113
    (Mills, ASCAP)

September 4

1. **HELP**
The Beatles
J. Lennon–P. McCartney,
Capitol 5476   (Maclen, BMI)

2. **LIKE A ROLLING STONE**
B. Dylan
B. Dylan,   Columbia 43346
(Witmark, ASCAP)

3. **YOU WERE ON MY MIND**
The We Five
S. Fricker,   A. and M. 770
(Witmark, ASCAP)

4. **CALIFORNIA GIRLS**
The Beach Boys
B. Wilson,   Capitol 5464
(The Sea of Tunes, BMI)

5. **UNCHAINED MELODY**
The Righteous Brothers
H. Zert–A. North,   Philles 129
(Frank, ASCAP)

6. **I GOT YOU BABE**
Sonny and Cher
S. Bono,   Atco 6359
(Five–West–Cotillion, BMI)

7. **PAPA'S GOT A BRAND NEW BAG**
J. Brown
J. Brown,   King 5999
(Lois, BMI)

8. **EVE OF DESTRUCTION**
B. McGuire
Sloane–Barri,   Dunhill 4009
(Trousdale, BMI)

9. **IT'S THE SAME OLD SONG**
The Four Tops
Holand–Dozier–Holland,
Motown 1081   (Jobete, BMI)

10. **BABY, I'M YOURS**
B. Lewis
V. McCoy,   Atlantic 2283
(Blackwood, BMI)

September 11

1. **LIKE A ROLLING STONE**
B. Dylan
B. Dylan,   Columbia 43346
(Witmark, ASCAP)

2. **HELP**
The Beatles
J. Lennon–P. McCartney,
Capitol 5476   (Maclen, BMI)

3. **YOU WERE ON MY MIND**
The We Five
S. Fricker,   A. and M. 770
(Witmark, ASCAP)

4. **EVE OF DESTRUCTION**
B. McGuire
Sloane–Barri,   Dunhill 4009
(Trousdale, BMI)

5. **UNCHAINED MELODY**
The Righteous Brothers
H. Zert–A. North,   Philles 129
(Frank, ASCAP)

6. **NOTHING BUT HEART-ACHES**
The Supremes
Holland–Dozier–Holland,
Motown 1080   (Jobete, BMI)

7. **CALIFORNIA GIRLS**
The Beach Boys
B. Wilson,   Capitol 5464
(Sea of Tunes, BMI)

8. **THE "IN" CROWD**
R. Lewis Trio
Page,   Argo 5506
(American,   BMI)

9. **I GOT YOU BABE**
Sonny and Cher
S. Bono,   Atco 6359
(Five–West–Cotillion, BMI)

10. **IT AIN'T ME BABE**
The Turtles
B. Dylan,   White Whale 222
(Witmark, ASCAP)

September 18

1. **EVE OF DESTRUCTION**
B. McGuire
Sloane–Barri,   Dunhill 4009
(Trousdale, BMI)

2. **LIKE A ROLLING STONE**
B. Dylan
B. Dylan,   Columbia 43346
(Witmark, ASCAP)

3. **HELP**
The Beatles
J. Lennon–P. McCartney,
Capitol 5476   (Maclen, BMI)

4. **HANG ON SLOOPY**
The McCoys
Russell–Farrell,   Bang 506
(Picturetone–Mellin, BMI)

5. **YOU WERE ON MY MIND**
The We Five
S. Fricker,   A. and M. 770
(Witmark, ASCAP)

6. **CATCH US IF YOU CAN**
The Dave Clark Five
D. Clark–L. Davidson,
Epic 9833   (Branston, BMI)

7. **IT AIN'T ME BABE**
The Turtles
B. Dylan,   White Whale 222
(Witmark, ASCAP)

8. **THE "IN" CROWD**
R. Lewis Trio
Page,   Argo 5506
(American, BMI)

9. **HEART FULL OF SOUL**
The Yardbirds
Gouldman,   Epic 9823
(Miller, ASCAP)

10. **I GOT YOU BABE**
Sonny and Cher
S. Bono,   Atoc 6359
(Five–West–Cotillion, BMI)

1965

September 25

1. **EVE OF DESTRUCTION**
B. McGuire
Sloane–Barri, Dunhill 4009
(Trousdale, BMI)

2. **HANG ON SLOOPY**
The McCoys
Russell–Farrell, Bang 506
(Picturestone–Mellin, BMI)

3. **CATCH US IF YOU CAN**
The Dave Clark Five
D. Clark–L. Davidson, Epic
9833 (Branston, BMI)

4. **YESTERDAY**
The Beatles
J. Lennon–P. McCartney,
Capitol 5498 (Maclen, BMI)

5. **HELP**
The Beatles
J. Lennon–P. McCartney,
Capitol 5476 (Maclen, BMI)

6. **YOU WERE ON MY MIND**
The We Five
S. Fricker, A. and M. 770
(Witmark, ASCAP)

7. **IT AIN'T ME BABE**
The Turtles
B. Dylan, White Whale 222
(Witmark, ASCAP)

8. **LIKE A ROLLING STONE**
B. Dylan
B. Dylan, Columbia 43346
(Witmark, ASCAP)

9. **HEART FULL OF SOUL**
The Yardbirds
Gouldman, Epic, 9823
(Miller, ASCAP)

10. **LAUGH AT ME**
Sonny
S. Bono, Atco 6369
(Five–West–Cotillion, BMI)

October 2

1. **HANG ON SLOOPY**
The McCoys
Russell–Farrell, Bang 506
(Picturetone-Melin, BMI)

2. **YESTERDAY**
The Beatles
J. Lennon–P. McCartney,
Capitol 5498 (Maclen, BMI)

3. **CATCH US IF YOU CAN**
The Dave Clark Five
D. Clark–L. Davidson, Epic
9833 (Branston, BMI)

4. **EVE OF DESTRUCTION**
B. McGuire
Sloane–Barri, Dunhill 4009
(Trousdale, BMI)

5. **THE "IN" CROWD**
R. Lewis Trio
Page, Argo 5506
(American, BMI)

6. **TREAT HER RIGHT**
R. Head
R. Head, Back Beat 546
(Don, BMI)

7. **BABY DON'T GO**
Sonny and Cher
S. Bono, Reprise 0392
(Mother Bertha and Ten East,
BMI)

8. **YOU'VE GOT YOUR TROUBLES**
The Fortunes
Greenaway–Cook, Press 9773
(Mills, ASCAP)

9. **YOU WERE ON MY MIND**
The We Five
S. Fricker, A. and M. 770
(Witmark, ASCAP)

10. **HELP**
The Beatles
J. Lennon–P. McCartney Capitol
5476 (Maclen, BMI)

October 9

1. **YESTERDAY**
The Beatles
J. Lennon–P. McCartney,
Capitol 5498 (Maclen, BMI)

2. **HANG ON SLOOPY**
The McCoys
Russell–Farrell, Bang 506
(Picturetone–Mellin, BMI)

3. **A LOVER'S CONCERTO**
The Toys
Linzer–Randall, Dyno Voice
209 (Saturday, BMI)

4. **EVE OF DESTRUCTION**
B. McGuire
Sloane–Barri, Dunhill 4009
(Trousdale, BMI)

5. **THE "IN" CROWD**
R. Lewis Trio
Page, Argo 5506
(American, BMI)

6. **TREAT HER RIGHT**
R. Head
R. Head, Back Best 546
(Don, BMI)

7. **YOU'VE GOT YOUR TROUBLES**
The Fortunes
Greenaway–Cook, Press 9773
(Mills, ASCAP)

8. **DO YOU BELIEVE IN MAGIC**
Lovin' Spoonful
J. Sebastian, Kama Sutra 201
(Faithful Virtue, BMI)

9. **BABY DON'T GO**
Sonny and Cher
S. Bono, Reprise 0392
(Mother Bertha and Ten East,
BMI)

10. **CATCH US IF YOU CAN**
The Dave Clark Five
D. Clark–L. Davidson,
Epic 9833 (Branston, BMI)

October 16

1. **YESTERDAY**
   The Beatles
   J. Lennon–P. McCartney,
   Capitol 5498 (Maclen, BMI)

2. **A LOVER'S CONCERTO**
   The Toys
   Linzer–Randall, Dyno Voice
   209 (Saturday, BMI)

3. **HANG ON SLOOPY**
   The McCoys
   Russell–Farrell, Bang 506
   (Picturetone–Mellin, BMI)

4. **DO YOU BELIEVE IN MAGIC**
   Lovin' Spoonful
   J. Sebastian, Kama Sutra 201
   (Faithful Virtue, BMI)

5. **EVE OF DESTRUCTION**
   B. McGuire
   Sloane–Barri, Dunhill 4009
   (Trousdale, BMI)

6. **WE GOTTA GET OUT OF THIS PLACE**
   The Animals
   Mann–Weil, M-G-M 13382
   (Screen Gems–Columbia, BMI)

7. **TREAT HER RIGHT**
   R. Head
   R. Head, Back Beat 546
   (Don, BMI)

8. **THE "IN" CROWD**
   R. Lewis Trio
   Page, Argo 5506
   (American, BMI)

9. **BABY DON'T GO**
   Sonny and Cher
   S. Bono, Reprise 0392
   (Mother Bertha and Ten East, BMI)

10. **JUST A LITTLE BIT BETTER**
    Herman's Hermits
    K. Young, M-G-M 13398
    (T. M., BMI)

October 23

1. **A LOVER'S CONCERTO**
   The Toys
   Linzer–Randall, Dyno Voice 209
   (Saturday, BMI)

2. **YESTERDAY**
   The Beatles
   J. Lennon–P. McCartney,
   Capitol 5498 (Maclen, BMI)

3. **GET OFF OF MY CLOUD**
   The Rolling Stones
   M. Jagger–K. Richard,
   London 9792 (Gideon, BMI)

4. **EVERYBODY LOVES A CLOWN**
   G. Lewis and the Playboys
   Leslie–Russell, Liberty 55818
   (Viva, BMI)

5. **EVE OF DESTRUCTION**
   B. McGuire
   Sloane–Barri, Dunhill 4009
   (Trousdale, BMI)

6. **TREAT HER RIGHT**
   R. Head
   R. Head, Back Beat 546
   (Don, BMI)

7. **HANG ON SLOOPY**
   The McCoys
   Russell–Farrell, Bang 506
   (Picturetone–Mellin , BMI)

8. **LIAR, LIAR**
   The Castaways
   Donna, Soma 1433
   (Celann, BMI)

9. **JUST A LITTLE BIT BETTER**
   Herman's Hermits
   K. Young, M-G-M 13398
   (T.M., BMI)

10. **POSITIVELY 4TH ST.**
    B. Dylan
    B. Dylan, Columbia 43389
    (Witmark, ASCAP)

October 30

1. **GET OFF OF MY CLOUD**
   The Rolling Stones
   M. Jagger–K. Richard,
   London 9792 (Gideon, BMI)

2. **A LOVER'S CONCERTO**
   The Toys
   Linzer–Randall, Dyno Voice
   209 (Saturday, BMI)

3. **YESTERDAY**
   The Beatles
   J. Lennon–P. McCartney,
   Capitol 5498 (Maclen, BMI)

4. **EVERYBODY LOVES A CLOWN**
   G. Lewis and the Playboys
   Leslie–Russell, Liberty
   55818 (Viva, BMI)

5. **EVE OF DESTRUCTION**
   B. McGuire
   Sloane–Barri, Dunhill 4009
   (Trousdale, BMI)

6. **TREAT HER RIGHT**
   R. Head
   R. Head, Back Beat 546
   (Don, BMI)

7. **POSITIVELY 4TH ST.**
   B. Dylan
   B. Dylan, Columbia 43389
   (Witmark, ASCAP)

8. **HANG ON SLOOPY**
   The McCoys
   Russell–Farrell, Bang 506
   (Picturetone–Mellin, BMI)

9. **1-2-3**
   L. Barry
   Madora–Borisoff–White, Decca
   31827 (Champion–Double
   Diamond, BMI)

10. **JUST A LITTLE BIT BETTER**
    Herman's Hermits
    K. Young, M-G-M 13398
    (T.M., BMI)

November 6

1. **GET OFF OF MY CLOUD**
The Rolling Stones
M. Jagger–K. Richard,
London 9792 (Gideon, BMI)
2. **A LOVER'S CONCERTO**
The Toys
Linzer–Randall, Dyno Voice
209 (Saturday, BMI)
3. **EVERYBODY LOVES A CLOWN**
G. Lewis and the Playboys
Leslie–Russell, Liberty 55818
(Viva, BMI)
4. **EVE OF DESTRUCTION**
B. McGuire
Sloane–Barri, Dunhill 4009
(Trousdale, BMI)
5. **YESTERDAY**
The Beatles
J. Lennon–P. McCartney, Capitol
5498 (Maclen, BMI)
6. **1-2-3**
L. Barry
Madora–Borisoff–White, Decca
31827 (Champion–Double
Diamond, BMI)
7. **POSITIVELY 4TH ST.**
B. Dylan
B. Dylan, Columbia 43389
(Witmark, ASCAP)
8. **RESCUE ME**
F. Bass
Smith–Miner, Checker 1120
(Chevis, BMI)
9. **LIAR, LIAR**
The Castaways
Donna, Soma 1433
(Celann, BMI)
10. **A TASTE OF HONEY**
H. Alpert and the Tijuana Brass
Marlow–Scott, A. and M. 775
(Songfest, ASCAP)

November 13

1. **1-2-3**
L. Barry
Madora–Borisoff–White, Decca
31827 (Champion–
Double Diamond, BMI)
2. **GET OFF OF MY CLOUD**
The Rolling Stones
M. Jagger–K. Richard,
London 9792 (Gideon, BMI)
3. **I HEAR A SYMPHONY**
The Supremes
Holland–Dozier–Holland,
Motown 1083 (Jobete, BMI)
4. **RESCUE ME**
F. Bass
Smith–Miner, Checker 1120
(Chevis, BMI)
5. **EVERYBODY LOVES A CLOWN**
G. Lewis and the Playboys
Leslie–Russell, Liberty 55818
(Viva, BMI)
6. **LET'S HANG ON**
The Four Seasons
Crewe–Linzer–Randall, Philips
40317
(Saturday–Seasons Four, BMI)
7. **LIAR, LIAR**
The Castaways
Donna, Doma 1433
(Celann, BMI)
8. **A LOVER'S CONCERTO**
The Toys
Linzer–Randall, Dyno Voice
209 (Saturday, BMI)
9. **POSITIVELY 4TH ST.**
B. Dylan
B. Dylan, Columbia 43389
(Witmark, ASCAP)
10. **A TASTE OF HONEY**
H. Alpert and the Tijuana Brass
Marlow–Scott, A. and M. 775
(Songfest, ASCAP)

November 20

1. **RESCUE ME**
R. Bass
Smith–Miner, Checker 1120
(Chevis, BMI)
2. **1-2-3**
L. Barry
Madora–Borisoff–White, Decca
31827 (Champion–
Double Diamond, BMI)
3. **GET OFF OF MY CLOUD**
The Rolling Stones
M. Jagger–K. Richard,
London 9792 (Gideon, BMI)
4. **TURN! TURN! TURN!**
The Byrds
P. Seeger, Columbia 43424
(Melody Trails, BMI)
5. **I HEAR A SYMPHONY**
The Supremes
Holland–Dozier–Holland,
Motown 1083 (Jobete, BMI)
6. **LET'S HANG ON**
The Four Seasons
Crewe–Linzer–Rnadall, Philips
40317
(Saturday–Seasons Four, BMI)
7. **A LOVER'S CONCERTO**
The Toys
Linzer–Randall, Dyno Voice
209 (Saturday, BMI)
8. **A TASTE OF HONEY**
H. Alpert and the Tijuana Brass
Marlow–Scott, A. and M. 775
(Singfest, ASCAP)
9. **LIAR, LIAR**
The Castaways
Donna, Soma 1433
(Celann, BMI)
10. **EVERYBODY'S GONE TO THE MOON**
J. King
J. King, Parrot 9774
(Mainstay, BMI)

November 27

1. **I HEAR A SYMPHONY**
The Supremes
Holland–Dozier–Holland,
Motown 1083   (Jobete, BMI)

2. **TURN! TURN! TURN!**
The Byrds
P. Seeger,   Columbia 43424
(Melody Trails, BMI)

3. **1-2-3**
L. Barry
Madora–Borisoff–White,
Decca 31827   (Champion–
Double Diamond, BMI)

4. **GET OFF OF MY CLOUD**
The Rolling Stones
M. Jagger–K. Richard,
London 9792   (Gideon, BMI)

5. **LET'S HANG ON**
The Four Seasons
Crewe–Linzer–Randall,
Philips 40317
(Saturday–Seasons Four, BMI)

6. **RESCUE ME**
F. Bass
Smith–Miner,   Checker 1120
(Chevis, BMI)

7. **A TASTE OF HONEY**
H. Alpert and the Tijuana
Brass
Marlow–Scott,   A. and M. 775
(Songfest, ASCAP)

8. **I GOT YOU (I FEEL GOOD)**
J. Brown
J. Brown,   King 6015
(Lois–Try Me, BMI)

9. **RUN, BABY, RUN**
The Newbeats
Melson–Gant,   Hickory 1332
(Acuff–Rose, BMI)

10. **EVERYONE'S GONE TO THE
MOON**
J. King
J. King,   Parrot 9774
(Mainstay, BMI)

December 4

1. **I HEAR A SYMPHONY**
The Supremes
Holland–Dozier–Holland,
Motown 1083   (Jobete, BMI)

2. **TURN! TURN! TURN!**
The Byrds
P. Seeger,   Columbia 43424
(Melody Trails, BMI)

3. **1-2-3**
L. Barry
Madora—Borisoff–White,   Decca
31827   (Champion–
Double Diamond, BMI)

4. **I GOT YOU (I FEEL GOOD)**
J. Brown
J. Brown,   King 6015
(Lois–Try Me, BMI)

5. **LET'S HANG ON**
The Four Seaons
Crewe–Linzer–Randall,   Philips
40317
(Saturday–Seasons Four, BMI)

6. **A TASTE OF HONEY**
H. Alpert and the Tijuana
Brass
Marlow–Scott,   A. and M. 775
(Songfest, ASCAP)

7. **RESCUE ME**
F. Bass
Smith–Miner,   Checker 1120
(Chevis, BMI)

8. **I CAN NEVER GO HOME
ANYMORE**
The Shangri-Las
Morton,   Red Bird 043
(Trio, BMI)

9. **OVER AND OVER**
The Dave Clark Five
R. Byrd,   Epic 9863
(Recordo, BMI)

10. **RUN, BABY, RUN**
The Newbeats
Melson–Grant,   Hickory 1332
(Acuff–Rose, BMI)

December 11

1. **TURN! TURN! TURN!**
The Byrds
P. Seeger,   Columbia 43424
(Melody Trails, BMI)

2. **I HEAR A SYMPHONY**
The Supremes
Holland–Dozier–Holland,
Motown 1083   (Jobete, BMI)

3. **I GOT YOU (I FEEL GOOD)**
J. Brown
J. Brown,   King 6015
(Lois–Try Me, BMI)

4. **LET'S HANG ON**
The Four Seasons
Crewe–Linzer–Randall,   Philips
40317
(Saturday–Seasons Four, BMI)

5. **I CAN NEVER GO HOME
ANYMORE**
The Shangri-Las
Morton,   Red Bird 043
(Trio, BMI)

6. **OVER AND OVER**
The Dave Clark Five
R. Byrd,   Epic 9863
(Recordo, BMI)

7. **A TASTE OF HONEY**
H. Alpert and the Tijuana
Brass
Marlow–Scott,   A. and M. 775
(Songfest, ASCAP)

8. **1-2-3**
L. Barry
Madora–Borisoff–White,   Decca
31827   (Champion–
Double Diamond, BMI)

9. **RESCUE ME**
F. Bass
Smith–Miner,   Checker 1120
(Chevis, BMI)

10. **ENGLAND SWINGS**
R. Miller
R. Miller,   Smash 2010
(Tree, BMI)

December 18

1. **OVER AND OVER**
The Dave Clark Five
R. Byrd, Epic 9863
(Recordo, BMI)

2. **TURN! TURN! TURN!**
The Byrds
P. Seeger, Columbia 43424
(Melody Trails, BMI)

3. **LET'S HANG ON**
The Four Seasons
Crewe–Linzer–Randall, Philips
40317
(Saturday–Seasons Four, BMI)

4. **I GOT YOU (I FEEL GOOD)**
J. Brown
J. Brown, King 6015
(Lois–Try Me, BMI)

5. **I CAN NEVER GO HOME ANYMORE**
The Shangri-Las
Morton, Red Bird 043
(Trio, BMI)

6. **MAKE THE WORLD GO AWAY**
E. Arnold
H. Cochran, Victor 8679
(Pamper, BMI)

7. **I HEAR A SYMPHONY**
The Supremes
Holland–Dozier–Holland,
Motown 1083 (Jobete, BMI)

8. **ENGLAND SWINGS**
R. Miller
R. Miller, Smash 2010
(Tree, BMI)

9. **FEVER**
The McCoys
Davenport, Bang 511
(Lois, BMI)

10. **RESCUE ME**
F. Bass
Smith–Miner, Checker 1120
(Chevis, BMI)

December 25

1. **LET'S HANG ON**
The Four Seasons
Crewe–Linzer–Randall, Philips
40317
(Saturday–Seasons Four, BMI)

2. **OVER AND OVER**
The Dave Clark Five
R. Byrd, Epic 9863
(Recordo, BMI)

3. **TURN! TURN! TURN!**
The Byrds
P. Seeger, Columbia 43424
(Melody Trails, BMI)

4. **SOUNDS OF SILENCE**
Simon and Garfunkel
P. Simon, Columbia 43396
(Eclectic, BMI)

5. **FEVER**
The McCoys
Davenport, Bang 511
(Lois, BMI)

6. **MAKE THE WORLD GO AWAY**
E. Arnold
H. Cochran, Victor 8679
(Pamper, BMI)

7. **EBB TIDE**
The Righteous Brothers
Sigman–Maxwell, Philles 130
(Robbins, ASCAP)

8. **I GOT YOU (I FEEL GOOD)**
J. Brown
J. Brown, King 6015
(Lois–Try Me, BMI)

9. **I CAN NEVER GO HOME ANYMORE**
The Shangri-Las
Morton, Red Bird 043
(Trio, BMI)

10. **ENGLAND SWINGS**
R. Miller
R. Miller, Smash 2010
(Tree, BMI)

DIANA ROSS AND THE SUPREMES

In 1966 the world was coming to a rapid boil. The war in Vietnam was getting hotter and hotter, and so was the protest movement at home. If our lack of information and our willingness to trust President Johnson had quieted our anxiety about the war in 1965, the teach-ins, the Senate hearings and the outcries of responsible leaders had shaken us into awareness of the war's horror in 1966. Now there were 380,000 Americans fighting in the faraway swamps, and there were $200 billion supporting their ill-advised involvement.

To people our age the old rationale that Communism was taking over the world looked ridiculous. We were convinced by the trouble among the Communist countries that there was no single unified Communist menace. We were also convinced by the self-burnings and protests by the Vietnamese that the regime in South Vietnam was persecuting Buddhists and suppressing free speech. And it baffled us that because the Viet Cong and North Vietnamese preferred a communist form of government the United States felt justified in attacking them.

No matter what our elders told us, we could not believe it was the great American mission to fight for any anti-Communist group, even if that group was immoral. The war was even militarily repulsive because we had been told of the French fiasco and had been warned by our own generals against a land war in Asia.

And so, more and more of our generation entered the ranks of the protesters. As the war was escalated and the draft became more of a threat to boys of our age and class, the radical protesters of 1965 were joined by the solid college students, and even a few of their parents. This isn't to say that to protest was the "in" thing. There were resolutions passed at major universities to support the war. But 1966 was a

1966

Turn off your mind, relax and
float downstream
It is not dying . . .
Lay down all thoughts; surrender to the voice
It is shining . . .
That you may see the meaning of within
It is being
That love is all, and love is everyone . . .

"Tomorrow Never Knows"
The Beatles, Revolver

turning point because "respectable" people could oppose the American involvement.

All over the country we were feeling the repercussions of the war. No one could isolate himself from its effects on the economy and the overheated racial situation. Our generation was old enough by now to feel the pressures of inflation whenever we wanted to buy a miniskirt or devise a five-dollar date. Those of us who were already married felt the economic squeeze most, especially if we wanted to borrow money or get mortgages at the new higher interest rates. Being married didn't even offer the protection of a sure draft deferment anymore.

The government, too, was feeling the money squeeze. President Johnson's War on Poverty had been a great promise to the black and poor, but it was now losing out to the war on Communism. There just wasn't enough money to support attacks on both fronts.

And as the black and the white and Puerto Rican poor realized that there would not be a revolutionary improvement in their living standards because the government preferred to escalate in Vietnam, their bitterness ignited. Riots in the Watts tradition erupted in thirty-eight American cities. The National Guard was called up in Cleveland, Chicago and San Francisco. Looting, sniping, tear gas, bayonets—it was hard to believe this was the United States and not some South American dictatorship.

The cry of Black Power rang out, terrifying the white populous and worrying the black moderates that the racial controversy was being stirred up too fast. Whites were becoming more hostile with each black step forward. The white anger about the burning and looting in the cities smoldered up against the entire Black Freedom movement. In Mississippi, James Meredith was ambushed and shot as he marched to encourage black voter registration. Even liberal whites who supported school integration and voting rights felt threatened as their cities were shaken by riot. No suburb was safe enough.

No federal program was large enough. No handout was nourishment enough for the bitter and disappointed blacks. White resentment against the demands for racial equality was infinitely greater than resentment against the Vietnam war. In fact, the same Americans who wanted to protect their way of life by opposing blacks generally believed they could protect their way of life by opposing the Communists in Vietnam.

This collection of hawk and white backlash was growing fast in 1966. And, as it grew a gorge widened between this element and our generation of doves. Unfortunately, they were old enough to vote and few of us were. Antiwar candidates were unheard of and the Republicans made sweeping advances in the gubernatorial and congressional elections. It was hard to believe how complacent we had been a few years before when everything was young and Kennedy.

It had seemed then that we were in such harmony with our parent's generation. We all had a goal of a better world, and the biggest thing we were fighting about was rock and roll. And now, rock and roll was about the only thing we had in common. With all our differences in politics and life style we were all drawn to the irresistible new kind of rock and roll. It was growing more glorious every day, and we all believed it would soar higher with each new group's contribution.

The Mamas and Papas were turning out one classic after another, and every song on their first album was worthy of a gold record. The harmony, the counterpoint, the blend of voices was so rich and so very much fun. And if the Mamas and Papas sang out with joy, then the Lovin' Spoonful, the Young Rascals, the Hollies, the Cyrkle—the whole wonderful lot of them—joined in and carried us to the heights of exhilaration. Even the Beach Boys got out of the water long enough to do their masterpiece, "Good Vibrations."

Vibrations were fantastic, but only as long as our records were spinning. If we listened to the radio, startling bulletins interrupted: "An unknown assailant murdered eight student nurses in their Chicago apartment."

"A sniper who shot and killed fourteen and injured thirty-one at the University of Texas, was identified as Charles Whitman, twenty four."

"In Mesa, Arizona, a young man entered a beauty school, forced six women and a child to lie in a circle, then shot them, killing four women and the child."

The condition of a world full of such nightmares could bring us down faster than our music could lift us up. Trouble seemed to be everywhere.

The Warren report was being doubted, and many of us came to believe something dreadful and suspicious was being covered up.

The Kennedy family was fighting with William Manchester to stop publication of his book about the dead President.

The Red Guard was shaking things up in China with the cultural revolution. DeGaulle was shaking things up in Europe by pulling out of NATO and away from the United States.

Floods in Italy were drenching the world's most precious art treasures.

In New York City, the 140-day newspaper strike killed the *Herald Tribune, Journal American* and *World Telegram and Sun,* which were forced to consolidate into the ill-fated *World Journal Tribune.* And the old Metropolitan Opera House closed down, bowing to the new Lincoln Center.

If people weren't happy with that development in music, they could surely find something that pleased them in the latest rock and roll. Solid, old-fashioned rock and roll like "96 Tears" and "Kicks" was only a tiny part of the rich, broad music of 1966. Of course there were the usual soul and folk hits, but this year, with "When a Man Loves a Woman," "Uptight," "Barefootin'" and "Land of 1000 Dances," plus the standard Motown, soul was a welcome patch of common ground between the races. And 1966 folk-rock, "Turn! Turn! Turn!" "I Am a Rock" and "If I Were a Carpenter," was mellow and more pacifist than protest. "The Ballad of the Green Berets" was the only song that specifically commented on the times, and it was apparent from its popularity that the older generation had taken an interest in buying folk-rock records.

Adults were also lured into the rock and roll market by Herb Alpert and the Tijuana Brass, who played a compromise rock and roll/big band sound and were the staple of the new over-thirty five rock and roll listeners.

Rock and roll songs, especially Lennon and McCartney and Bacharach and David compositions, were suddenly being performed by adult jazz and pop artists. Rock and roll's Butterfield Blues Band was closer to Dizzy Gillespie than to Bill Haley and the Comets. Even classical music was drawn into the rock and roll sphere. The Beatles had used a string quartet to back up "Michelle." And "Yesterday," along with "For No One" on their new "Revolver" album, was distinctly classical. The Beatles also were borrowing from Indian music, and the sitar and tabla gave "Revolver" a genuinely original and exotic appeal.

The Beatles were still the most loved and copied rock and roll group, yet they were becoming such an institution that there was a distance now between them and their fans. We couldn't identify closely with them the way we had in the beginning. They were such big stars now, and they were beginning to go separate ways as they grew rich, matured and started families. This was the last year they would do a concert tour of the United States and there would be no more Beatle movies and few television appearances. We now waited anxiously to hear each new Beatle album, knowing it would push farther and farther into the brilliance and beauty of experimental rock and roll.

In 1966, the great album we awaited was "Revolver." We had already heard "Eleanor Rigby" and "Yellow Submarine," and, from that sample, we knew the album was going to be all new, even for the Beatles. As soon as we played it, the change was apparent. The music was radically different, flavored with India, electric distortion and classical motifs. And the lyrics and ideas were a preview of a whole new kind of rock and roll.

Since "Rubber Soul," the Beatles had turned away from writing about traditional topics. All their early songs had been regular rock and roll love songs, but now in "Revolver" the only songs of romance were "Here, There and Everywhere" and "For No One." Somehow, these songs belonged back an era. Their tenderness and simplicity, sentiment and melody put them into the classical period of rock and roll. But they were the exceptions. The feel of the album was something new. It was introspective, playing with ideas of universal love, of life and of being one with all that exists. The influence of Oriental religion was clear, but what the Beatles were saying was fuzzy. Perhaps they knew something we didn't. Their earthly greed for material wealth and fame was certainly satisfied. And they had experienced something akin to universal love—universal adoration. They must have realized the irony of this vast Beatle worship when they said they were more popular than Jesus.

It seemed that disorientation had come out of their amazing success, and they were searching for reasons or meaning in a life so fickle. So they turned to India and its teachings of meditation and peace for the answer. It was a timely interest, since we were all feeling lost, with the war and the riots and the differences with our parents. Universal love seemed such a relief that we began to gravitate toward the Eastern philosophy.

In a way we were crying out to return to the simple days. It had only been a few years before when movies, TV, fashion, sports or space flights were the biggest events in the news. But this year we paid only passing attention to the movie industry's decision to start a rating code and the big conflict about nudity on the screen. Our interest in England was such that we followed the Carnaby Street craze—minis, fishnet hose, shoulder bags and, for boys, low-slung pants, wallpaper print shirts, flowered ties, turtlenecks and boots. In keeping with all this, we enjoyed *Alfie* and *Georgy Girl* and their title songs. On TV, we were briefly fascinated by Batman. But, "Holy Batmobile," it became a drag. The sports world was busy persecuting Mohammed Ali. And the New York baseball empire was in ruins as the once mighty Yankees finished in the cellar. This year Baltimore won the pennant, then beat the Dodgers in four games to win the world championship.

Beyond the world the United States sent up a rapid fire of spacecraft, but the Russians seemed to have lost interest in the space race.

But this news didn't grab us anymore. We were taking on the weight of a burdened world, and by doing so we were losing our innocence. We searched our souls for answers. Our political movement seemed so futile that groups of us began to drop out—actively to seek the simpler things. But we were to find that we couldn't go back. We had eaten the fruit of knowledge and we had to move forward from there.

Even in our music—Tommy James, Gary Lewis, the Monkees—were amusing, but too artificial and trying too hard. Now there was a new generation of teenyboppers, fighting acne, buying 45's and trying to imitate the older kids. In a way it was sad for them that we, those older kids, didn't set the playful, carefree example that had been set for us. As hard as it was to accept, those days of innocence and freedom had ended. And soon, rock and roll would, too.

The Top Fifty
1966

1. **SUNNY** B. Hebb
2. **CALIFORNIA DREAMIN'** The Mamas and Papas
3. **CHERISH** The Association
4. **MONDAY, MONDAY** The Mamas and Papas
5. **PAPERBACK WRITER** The Beatles
6. **HANKY PANKY** T. James and the Shondells
7. **WILD THING** The Troggs
8. **BUS STOP** The Hollies
9. **GOOD VIBRATIONS** The Beach Boys
10. **LAST TRAIN TO CLARKSVILLE** The Monkees
11. **WE CAN WORK IT OUT** The Beatles
12. **SOUNDS OF SILENCE** Simon and Garfunkel
13. **TURN! TURN! TURN!** The Byrds
14. **SUNSHINE SUPERMAN** Donovan
15. **96 TEARS** (?) and the Mysterians
16. **KICKS** P. Revere and the Raiders
17. **PAINT IT BLACK** The Rolling Stones
18. **RED RUBBER BALL** The Cyrkle
19. **ELUSIVE BUTTERFLY** B. Lind
20. **YOU'RE MY SOUL AND INSPIRATION** The Righteous Brothers
21. **BANG, BANG** Cher
22. **SHE'S JUST MY STYLE** G. Lewis and the Playboys
23. **FIVE O'CLOCK WORLD** The Vogues
24. **I SAW HER AGAIN LAST NIGHT** The Mamas and Papas
25. **SUMMER IN THE CITY** Lovin' Spoonful
26. **YELLOW SUBMARINE** The Beatles
27. **WINCHESTER CATHEDRAL** The New Vaudeville Band
28. **MELLOW YELLOW** Donovan
29. **THE PIED PIPER** C. St. Peters
30. **SEE YOU IN SEPTEMBER** The Happenings
31. **I AM A ROCK** Simon and Garfunkel
32. **UPTIGHT** S. Wonder
33. **THE BALLAD OF (THE GREEN BERETS)** B. Sadler
34. **DAYDREAM** Lovin' Spoonful
35. **REACH OUT I'LL BE THERE** The Four Tops
36. **YOU KEEP ME HANGIN' ON** The Supremes
37. **POOR SIDE OF TOWN** J. Rivers
38. **WHEN A MAN LOVES A WOMAN** P. Sledge
39. **GROOVY KIND OF LOVE** The Mindbenders
40. **DID YOU EVER HAVE TO MAKE UP YOUR MIND?** Lovin' Spoonful
41. **19TH NERVOUS BREAKDOWN** The Rolling Stones
42. **FLOWERS ON THE WALL** The Statler Brothers
43. **OVER AND OVER** The Dave Clark Five
44. **LIGHTIN' STRIKES** L. Christie
45. **MY WORLD IS EMPTY WITHOUT YOU** The Supremes
46. **THESE BOOTS ARE MADE FOR WALKIN'** N. Sinatra
47. **THE CHEATER** B. Kuban and the In-Men
48. **RAINY DAY WOMEN #25 AND #35** B. Dylan
49. **GOOD LOVIN'** The Young Rascals
50. **DAY TRIPPER** The Beatles

January 1

1. **WE CAN WORK IT OUT**
The Beatles
J. Lennon–P. McCartney,
Capitol 5555   (Maclen, BMI)

2. **LET'S HANG ON**
The Four Seasons
Crewe–Linzer–Randall,   Philips
40317
(Saturday–Seasons Four, BMI)

3. **TURN! TURN! TURN!**
The Byrds
P. Seeger,   Columbia 43424
(Melody Trails, BMI)

4. **SOUNDS OF SILENCE**
Simon and Garfunkel
P. Simon,   Columbia 43396
(Eclectic, BMI)

5. **EBB TIDE**
The Righteous Brothers
Sigman–Maxwell,   Philles 130
(Robbins, ASCAP)

6. **OVER AND OVER**
The Dave Clark Five
R. Byrd,   Epic 9863
(Recordo, BMI)

7. **FIVE O'CLOCK WORLD**
The Vogues
A. Reynolds,   Co. and Co. 232
(Screen Gems–Columbia, BMI)

8. **FEVER**
The McCoys
Davenport,   Bang 511
(Lois, BMI)

9. **MAKE THE WORLD GO
AWAY**
E. Arnold
H. Cochran,   Victor 8679
(Pamper, BMI)

10. **ENGLAND SWINGS**
R. Miller
R. Miller,   Smash 2010
(Tree, BMI)

January 8

1. **WE CAN WORK IT OUT**
The Beatles
J. Lennon–P. McCartney,
Capitol 5555   (Maclen, BMI)

2. **FIVE O'CLOCK WORLD**
The Vogues
A. Reynolds,   Co. and Co.
232   (Sceen Gems–
Columbia, BMI)

3. **SOUNDS OF SILENCE**
Simon and Garfunkel
P. Simon,   Columbia 43396
(Eclectic, BMI)

4. **LET'S HANG ON**
The Four Seasons
Crewe–Linzer–Randall,   Philips
40317   (Saturday–
Seasons Four, BMI)

5. **EBB TIDE**
The Righteous Brothers
Sigman–Maxwell,   Philles 130
(Robbins, ASCAP)

6. **TURN! TURN! TURN!**
The Byrds
P. Seeger,   Columbia 43424
(Melody Trails, BMI)

7. **FLOWERS ON THE WALL**
The Statler Brothers
L. Dewitt,   Columbia 43315
(Southwind, BMI)

8. **SHE'S JUST MY STYLE**
G. Lewis and the Playboys
G. Lewis,   Liberty 55846
(Viva, BMI)

9. **FEVER**
The McCoys
Davenport,   Bang 511
(Lois, BMI)

10. **AS TEARS GO BY**
The Rolling Stones
M. Jagger–K. Richard,
London 9808   (Essex, ASCAP)

1966

January 15

1. **FIVE O'CLOCK WORLD**
The Vogues
A. Reynolds, Co. and Co. 232
(Screen Gems–Columbia, BMI)

2. **WE CAN WORK IT OUT**
The Beatles
J. Lennon–P. McCartney,
Capitol 5555 (Maclen, BMI)

3. **SHE'S JUST MY STYLE**
G. Lewis and the Playboys
G. Lewis, Liberty 55846
(Viva, BMI)

4. **FLOWERS ON THE WALL**
The Statler Brothers
L. DeWitt, Columbia 43315
(Southwind, BMI)

5. **SOUNDS OF SILENCE**
Simon and Garfunkel
P. Simon, Columbia 43396
(Eclectic, BMI)

6. **DAY TRIPPER**
The Beatles
J. Lennon–P. McCartney,
Capitol 5555 (Maclen, BMI)

7. **NO MATTER WHAT SHAPE
(YOUR STOMACH'S IN)**
The T-Bones
G. Burland, Liberty 55836
(C-Near, BMI)

8. **A MUST TO AVOID**
Herman's Hermits
P. F. Sloan–S. Barri,
M-G-M 13437 (Trousdale, BMI)

9. **AS TEARS GO BY**
The Rolling Stones
M. Jagger–K. Richard,
London 9808 (Essex, ASCAP)

10. **BARBARA ANN**
The Beach Boys
Fassert, Capitol 5561
(Shoe String–Cousins, BMI)

January 22

1. **SHE'S JUST MY STYLE**
G. Lewis and the
Playboys
G. Lewis, Liberty 55846
(Viva, BMI)

2. **FIVE O'CLOCK WORLD**
The Vogues
A. Reynolds, Co.and Co.232
(Screen Gems–Columbia, BMI)

3. **WE CAN WORK IT OUT**
The Beatles
J. Lennon–P. McCartney,
Capitol 5555 (Maclen, BMI)

4. **SOUNDS OF SILENCE**
Simon and Garfunkel
P. Simon, Columbia 43396
(Eclectic, BMI)

5. **A MUST TO AVOID**
Herman's Hermits
P. F. Sloan–S. Barri,
M-G-M 13437 (Trousdale, BMI)

6. **DAY TRIPPER**
The Beatles
J. Lennon–P. McCartney, Capitol
5555 (Maclen, BMI)

7. **THE MEN IN MY LITTLE
GIRL'S LIFE**
M. Douglas
Deane–Candy–Shayne,
Epic 9876 (Jewel, ASCAP)

8. **AS TEARS GO BY**
The Rolling Stones
M. Jagger–K. Richard,
London 9808 (Essex, ASCAP)

9. **NO MATTER WHAT SHAPE
(YOUR STOMACH'S IN)**
The T-Bones
G. Burland, Liberty 55836
(C-Near, BMI)

10. **YOU DIDN'T HAVE TO BE
SO NICE**
Lovin' Spoonful
J. Sebastian, Kama Sutra 205
(Faithful Virtue, BMI)

January 29

1. **SHE'S JUST MY STYLE**
G. Lewis and the Playboys
G. Lewis, Liberty 55846
(Viva, BMI)

2. **A MUST TO AVOID**
Herman's Hermits
P. F. Sloan–S. Barri,
M-G-M 13437 (Trousdale, BMI)

3. **WE CAN WORK IT OUT**
The Beatles
J. Lennon–P. McCartney,
Capitol 5555 (Maclen, BMI)

4. **FIVE O'CLOCK WORLD**
The Vogues
A. Reynolds, Co.and Co.232
(Screen Gems–Columbia, BMI)

5. **BARBARA ANN**
The Beach Boys
Fassert, Capitol 5561
(Shoe String–Cousins, BMI)

6. **THE MEN IN MY LITTLE
GIRL'S LIFE**
M. Douglas
Deane–Candy–Shayne,
Epic 9876 (Jewel, ASCAP)

7. **AS TEARS GO BY**
The Rolling Stones
M. Jagger–K. Richard,
London 9808 (Essex, ASCAP)

8. **LIGHTNIN' STRIKES**
L. Christie
L. Sacco, M-G-M 13412
(Rambed, BMI)

9. **MY LOVE**
P. Clark
T. Hatch, Warner Brothers 5684
(Duchess, BMI)

10. **JENNY TAKE A RIDE**
M. Ryder and the Detroit
Wheels
Johnson-Tenninan, New Voices
806 (Venice–Saturday, BMI)

295

1. BARBARA ANN
The Beach Boys
Fassert,   Capitol 5561
(Shoe String–Cousins, BMI)

2. MY LOVE
P. Clark
T. Hatch,   Warner Brothers 5684
(Duchess, BMI)

3. LIGHTNIN' STRIKES
L. Christie
L. Sacco,   M-G-M 13412
(Rambed, BMI)

4. A MUST TO AVOID
Herman's Hermits
P. F. Sloan–S. Barri,
M-G-M 13437   (Trousdale, BMI)

5. WE CAN WORK IT OUT
The Beatles
J. Lennon–P. McCartney,
Capitol 5555   (Maclen, BMI)

6. SHE'S JUST MY STYLE
G. Lewis and the
Playboys
G. Lewis,   Liberty 55846
(Viva, BMI)

**7. THE MEN IN MY LITTLE
GIRL'S LIFE**
M. Douglas
Deane–Candy–Shayne,
Epic 9876   (Jewel, ASCAP)

8. JUST LIKE ME
P. Revere and the
Raiders
R. Hart–R. Dey,
Columbia 43461   (Daywin, BMI)

9. FIVE O'CLOCK WORLD
The Vogues
A. Reynolds,   Co. and Co. 232
(Screen Gems–Columbia, BMI)

10. CRYING TIME
R. Charles
B. Owens,   ABC 10739
(Bluebook, BMI)

1. LIGHTNIN' STRIKES
L. Christie
L. Sacco,   M-G-M 13412
(Rambed, BMI)

2. MY LOVE
P. Clark
T. Hatch,   Warner Brothers 5684
(Duchess, BMI)

3. BARBARA ANN
The Beach Boys
Fassert,   Capitol 5561
(Shoe String–Cousins, BMI)

**4. MY WORLD IS EMPTY
WITHOUT YOU**
The Supremes
Holland–Dozier–Holland,
Motown 1089   (Jobete, BMI)

5. JUST LIKE ME
P. Revere and the
Raiders
R. Hart–R. Dey,   Columbia
43461   (Daywin, BMI)

6. WE CAN WORK IT OUT
The Beatles
J. Lennon–P. McCartney,
Captiol 5555   (Maclen, BMI)

7. UP TIGHT
S. Wonder
Moy–Judkins, Cosby   Tamla
54124   (jobete, BMI)

8. CRYING TIME
R. Charles
B. Owens,   ABC 10739
(Bluebook, BMI)

9. DON'T MESS WITH BILL
The Marvelettes
W. Robinson,   Tamla 54126
(Jobete, BMI)

10. SHE'S JUST MY STYLE
G. Lewis and the Play-
boys
G. Lewis,   Liberty 55846
(Viva, BMI)

1. UP TIGHT
S. Wonder
Moy–Judkins, Cosby   Tamla
54124   (Jobete, BMI)

**2. MY WORLD IS EMPTY
WITHOUT YOU**
The Supremes
Holland–Dozier–Holland,   Motown
1089   (Jobete, BMI)

3. LIGHTNIN' STRIKES
L. Christie
L. Sacco,   M-G-M 13412
(Rambed, BMI)

4. MY LOVE
P. Clark
T. Hatch,   Warner Brothers 5684
(Duchess, BMI)

5. BARBARA ANN
The Beach Boys
Fasset,   Capitol 5561
(Shoe String–Cousins, BMI)

6. DON'T MESS WITH BILL
The Marvelettes
W. Robinson,   Tamla 54126
(Jobete, BMI)

**7. THE BALLAD OF THE
GREEN BERETS**
B. Sadler
B. Sadler–Moore,   Victor 8739
(Music, Music, Music, ASCAP)

8. GOING TO GO-GO
The Miracles
Robinson–Moore–Tarpin–Rogers,
Tamla 54127   (Jobete, BMI)

9. CRYING TIME
R. Charles
B. Owens,   ABC 10739
(Bluebook, BMI)

**10. THESE BOOTS ARE MADE
FOR WALKIN'**
N. Sinatra
L. Hazelwood,   Reprise 0432
(Criterion, ASCAP)

1966

February 26

1. **MY WORLD IS EMPTY WITHOUT YOU**
The Supremes
Holland–Dozier–Holland, Motown 1089 (Jobete, BMI)

2. **UP TIGHT**
S. Wonder
Moy–Judkins–Cosby Tamla 54124 (Jobete, BMI)

3. **LIGHTIN' STRIKES**
L. Christie
L. Sacco, M-G-M 13412 (Rambed, BMI)

4. **CALIFORNIA DREAMIN'**
The Mamas and Papas
J. Phillips, Dunhill 4020 (Trousdale, BMI)

5. **MY LOVE**
P. Clark
T. Hatch, Warner Brothers 5684 (Duchess, BMI)

6. **GOING TO GO-GO**
The Miracles
Robinson–Moore–Tarpin–Roger, Tamla 54127 (Jobete, BMI)

7. **THE BALLAD OF THE GREEN BERETS**
B. Sadler
B. Sadler–Moore, Victor 8739 (Music, Music, Music, ASCAP)

8. **THESE BOOTS ARE MADE FOR WALKIN'**
N. Sinatra
L. Hazelwood, Reprise 0432 (Criterion, ASCAP)

9. **WORKING MY WAY BACK TO YOU**
The Four Seasons
Linzer–Randell, Philips 40350 (Saturday–Seasons Four, BMI)

10 **LISTEN PEOPLE**
Herman's Hermits
Goulman, M-G-M 13462 (New World, ASCAP)

March 5

1. **MY WORLD IS EMPTY WITHOUT YOU**
The Supremes
Holland–Dozier–Holland, Motown 1089 (Jobete, BMI)

2. **THE BALLAD OF THE GREEN BERETS**
B. Sadler
B. Sadler–Moore, Victor 8739 (Music, Music, Music, BMI)

3. **CALIFORNIA DREAMIN'**
The Mamas and Papas
J. Phillips, Dunhill 4020 (Trousdale, BMI)

4. **THESE BOOTS ARE MADE FOR WALKIN'**
N. Sinatra
L. Hazelwood, Reprise 0432 (Criterion, ASCAP)

5. **LIGHTNIN' STRIKES**
L. Christie
L. Sacco, M-G-M 13412 (Rambed, BMI)

6. **ELUSIVE BUTTERFLY**
B. Lind
B. Lind, World–Pacific 77808 (Metric, BMI)

7. **LISTEN PEOPLE**
Herman's Hermits
Goulman, M-G-M 13462 (New Wold, ASCAP)

8. **WORKING MY WAY BACK TO YOU**
The Four Seasons
Linzer–Randall, Philips 40350 (Saturday–Seasons Four, BMI)

9. **UP TIGHT**
S. Wonder
Moy–Judkins, Cosby Tamla 54124 (Jobete, BMI)

10. **MY LOVE**
P. Clark
T. Hatch, Warner Brothers 5684 (Duchess, BMI)

March 12

1. **CALIFORNIA DREAMIN'**
The Mamas and Papas
J.Phillips, Dunhill 4020 (Trousdale, BMI)

2. **THE BALLAD OF THE GREEN BERETS**
B. Sadler
B. Sadler–Moore Victor 8739 (Music, Music, Music, ASCAP)

3. **LISTEN PEOPLE**
Herman's Hermits
Goulman, M-G-M 13462 (New World, ASCAP)

4. **THESE BOOTS ARE MADE FOR WALKIN'**
N. Sinatra
L. Hazelwood, Reprise 0432 (Criterion, ASCAP)

5. **19TH NERVOUS BREAKDOWN**
The Rolling Stones
M.Jagger–K. Richard, London 9823 (Gideon, BMI)

6. **ELUSIVE BUTTERFLY**
B. Lind
B. Lind, World–Pacific 77808 (Metric, BMI)

7. **NOWHERE MAN**
The Beatles
J. Lennon–P. McCartney, Capitol 5587 (Maclen, BMI)

8. **I FOUGHT THE LAW**
The Bobby Fuller Four
Curtis, Mustang 3014 (Acuff–Rose, BMI)

9. **WORKING MY WAY BACK TO YOU**
The Four Seasons
Linzer–Randall, Philips 40350 (Saturday–Seasons Four, BMI)

10. **LIGHTNIN' STRIKES**
L. Christie
L. Sacco, M-G-M 13412 (Rambed, BMI)

March 19

1. **19TH NERVOUS BREAKDOWN**
The Rolling Stones
M. Jagger–K. Richard,
London 9823   (Gideon, BMI)

2. **THE BALLAD OF THE GREEN BERETS**
B. Sadler
B. Sadler–Moore   Victor 8739
(Music, Music, Music, ASCAP)

3. **NOWHERE MAN**
The Beatles
J. Lennon–P. McCartney,
Capitol 5587   (Maclen, BMI)

4. **LISTEN PEOPLE**
Herman's Hermits
Goulman,   M-G-M 13462
(New World, ASCAP)

5. **DAYDREAM**
Lovin' Spoonful
J. Sebastian,   Kama Sutra 208
(Faithful Virtue, BMI)

6. **HOMEWARD BOUND**
Simon and Garfunkel
P. Simon,   Columbia 43511
(Eclectic, BMI)

7. **ELUSIVE BUTTERFLY**
B. Lind
B. Lind,   World-Pacific 77808
(Metric, BMI)

8. **I FOUGHT THE LAW**
The Bobby Fuller Four
Curtis,   Mustang 3014
(Acuff–Rose, BMI)

9. **CALIFORNIA DREAMIN'**
The Mamas and Papas
J. Phillips,   Dunhill 4020
(Trousdale, BMI)

10. **WORKING MY WAY BACK TO YOU**
The Four Seasons
Linzer–Randall,   Philips 40350
(Saturday–Seasons Four, BMI)

March 26

1. **19TH NERVOUS BREAKDOWN**
The Rolling Stones
M. Jagger–K. Richard,
London 9823   (Gideon, BMI)

2. **THE BALLAD OF THE GREEN BERETS**
B. Sadler
B. Sadler–Moore,   Victor 8739
(Music, Music, Music, ASCAP)

3. **DAYDREAM**
Lovin' Spoonful
J. Sebastian,   Kama Sutra 208
(Faithful Virtue, BMI)

4. **NOWHERE MAN**
The Beatles
J. Lennon–P. McCartney,
Capitol 5587   (Maclen, BMI)

5. **LISTEN PEOPLE**
Herman's Hermits
Goulman,   M-G-M 13462
(New World, ASCAP)

6. **HOMEWARD BOUND**
Simon and Garfunkel
P. Simon,   Columbia 43511
(Eclectic, BMI)

7. **THE CHEATER**
B. Kuban and the In-Men
Krenski,   Musicland–
USA 20,001   (M. and M., BMI)

8. **YOU'RE MY SOUL AND INSPIRATION**
The Righteous Brothers
Mann–Weil,   Verve 10383
(Screen Gems–Columbia, BMI)

9. **LOVE MAKES THE WORLD GO' ROUND**
D. Jackson
D. Jackson,   Carla 2526
(McCLaughlin, BMI)

10. **I FOUGHT THE LAW**
The Bobby Fuller Four
Curtis, Mustang 3014
(Acuff–Rose, BMI)

April 2

1. **YOU'RE MY SOUL AND INSPIRATION**
The Righteous Brothers
Mann–Weil,   Verve 10383
(Screen Gems–Columbia, BMI)

2. **19TH NERVOUS BREAKDOWN**
The Rolling Stones
M. Jagger–K. Richard,
London 9823   (Gideon, BMI)

3. **DAYDREAM**
Lovin' Spoonful
J. Sebastian,   Kama Sutra 208
(Faithful Virtue, BMI)

4. **HOMEWARD BOUND**
Simon and Garfunkel
P. Simon,   Columbia 43511
(Eclectic, BMI)

5. **THE BALLAD OF THE GREEN BERETS**
B. Sadler
B. Sadler–Moore,   Victor 8739
(Music, Music, Music, ASCAP)

6. **THE CHEATER**
B. Kuban and the In-Men
Krenski,   Musicland–
USA 20,001   (M. and M., BMI)

7. **LISTEN PEOPLE**
Herman's Hermits
Goulman,   M-G-M 13462
(New World , ASCAP)

8. **LOVE MAKES THE WORLD GO 'ROUND**
D. Jackson
D. Jackson,   Carla 2526
(McLaughlin, BMI)

9. **SURE GONNA MISS HER**
G. Lewis and the Playboys
Russell,   Liberty 55865
(Viva-Tennessee, BMI)

10. **BANG BANG**
Cher
S. Bono,   Imperial 66160
(Five–West–Cotillion, BMI)

April 9

1. YOU'RE MY SOUL AND INSPIRATION
The Righteous Brothers
Mann–Weil,   Verve 10383
(Screen Gems–Columbia, BMI)

2. BANG BANG
Cher
S. Bono,   Imperial 66160
(Five–West–Cotillion, BMI)

3. 19TH NERVOUS BREAKDOWN
The Rolling Stones
M. Jagger–K. Richard,
London 9823   (Gideon, BMI)

4. HOMEWARD BOUND
Simon and Garfunkel
P. Simon,   Columbia 43511
(Eclectic, BMI)

5. THE BALLAD OF THE GREEN BERETS
B. Sadler
B. Sadler–Moore,   Victor 8739
(Music, Music, Music, ASCAP)

6. SECRET AGENT MAN
J. Rivers
Fowler–Heller,   Imperial 66159
(Trousdale, BMI)

7. I'M SO LONESOME I COULD CRY
B. J. Thomas and the Triumphs
H. Williams,   Sceptor 12129
(Acuff–Rose, BMI)

8. SURE GONNA MISS HER
G. Lewis and the Playboys
Russell,   Liberty 55865
(Viva–Tennessee, BMI)

9. THE CHEATER
B. Kuban and the In-Men
Krenski,   Musicland–USA 20,001
(M. and M., BMI)

10. LOVE MAKES THE WORLD GO 'ROUND
D. Jackson
D. Jackson, Carla 2526
(McLaughlin, BMI)

April 16

1. BANG BANG
Cher
S. Bono,   Imperial 66160
(Five–West–Cotillion, NMI)

2. YOU'RE MY SOUL AND INSPIRATION
The Righteous Brothers
Mann–Weil,   Verve 10383
(Screen Gems–Columbia, BMI)

3. SECRET AGENT MAN
J. Rivers
Fowler–Heller,   Imperial 66159
(Trousdale, BMI)

4. TIME WON'T LET ME
The Outsiders
King–Kelley,   Capitol 5573
(Beechwood, BMI)

5. 19TH NERVOUS BREAKDOWN
The Rolling Stones
M. Jagger–K. Richard,
London 9823   (Gideon, BMI)

6. YOU BABY
The Turtles
P. F. Sloan–S. Barri,   White Whale 227   (Trousdale, BMI)

7. I'M SO LONESOME I COULD CRY
B. J. Thomas and the Triumphs
H. Williams,   Sceptor 12129
(Acuff–Rose, BMI)

8. GOOD LOVIN'
The Young Rascals
Clark–Resnick,   Atlantic 2320   (T. M., BMI)

9. KICKS
P. Revere and the Raiders
Mann–Weil,   Columbia 43356
(Screen Gems–Columbia, BMI)

10. SURE GONNA MISS HER
G. Lewis and the Playboys
Russell,   Liberty 55865
(Viva–Tennesse, BMI)

April 23

1. BANG BANG
Cher
S. Bono,   Imperial 66160
(Five–West–Cotillion, BMI)

2. YOU'RE MY SOUL AND INSPIRATION
The Righteous Brothers
Mann–Weil,   Verve 10383
(Screen Gems–Columbia, BMI)

3. MONDAY, MONDAY
The Mamas and Papas
J. Phillips,   Dunhill 4026
(Trousdale, BMI)

4. SECRET AGENT MAN
J. Rivers
Fowler–Heller,   Imperial 66159
(Trousdale, BMI)

5. SLOOP JOHN B.
The Beach Boys
B. Wilson, (Adaptation)
Capitol 5602
(New Executive, BMI)

6. TIME WON'T LET ME
The Outsiders
King–Kelley,   Capitol 5573
(Beechwood, BMI)

7. KICKS
P. Revere and the Raiders
Mann–Weil,   Columbia 43356
(Sreen Gems–Columbia, BMI)

8. GOOD LOVIN'
The Young Rascals
Clark–Resnick,   Atlantic 2320
(T. M., BMI)

9. I'M SO LONESOME I COULD CRY
B. J. Thomas and the Triumphs
H. Williams,   Scepter 12129
(Acuff–Rose, BMI)

10. YOU BABY
The Turtles
P. F. Sloan–S. Barri,   White Whale 227   (Trousdale, BMI)

1. **MONDAY, MONDAY**
The Mamas and Papas
J. Phillips,   Dunhill 4026
(Trousdale, BMI)

2. **GOOD LOVIN'**
The Young Rascals
Clark–Resnick,   Atlantic 2320
(T. M., BMI)

3. **YOU'RE MY SOUL AND INSPIRATION**
The Righteous Brothers
Mann–Weil,   Verve 10383
(Screen Gems–Columbia, BMI)

4. **SLOOP JOHN B.**
The Beach Boys
B. Wilson (Adaptation),   Capitol 5602   (New Executive, BMI)

5. **SECRET AGENT MAN**
J. Rivers
Fowler–Heller,   Imperial 66159
(Trousdale, BMI)

6. **TIME WON'T LET ME**
The Outsiders
King–Kelley,   Capitol 5573
(Beechwood, BMI)

7. **THIS OLD HEART OF MINE**
The Isley Brothers
Holland–Dozier–Holland,   Tamla 54128   (Jobete, BMI)

8. **KICKS**
P. Revere and the Raiders
Mann–Weil,   Columbia 43356
(Screen Gems–Columbia, BMI)

9. **BANG BANG**
Cher
S. Bono,   Imperial 66160
(Five–West–Cotillion, BMI)

10. **I'M SO LONESOME I COULD CRY**
B. J. Thomas and the Triumphs
H. Williams,   Scepter 12129
(Acuff–Rose, BMI)

1. **GOOD LOVIN'**
The Young Rascals
Clark–Resnick,   Atlantic 2320
(T.M., BMI)

2. **MONDAY, MONDAY**
The Mamas and Papas
J. Phillips,   Dunhill 4026
(Trousdale, BMI)

3. **SLOOP JOHN B.**
The Beach Boys
B. Wilson (adaptation),   Capitol 5602   (New Executive, BMI)

4. **RAINY DAY WOMEN #12 AND #35**
B. Dylan
B. Dylan,   Columbia 43592
(Dwarf, ASCAP)

5. **YOU'RE MY SOUL AND INSPIRATION**
The Righteous Brothers
Mann–Weil,   Verve 10383
(Screen Gems–Columbia, BMI)

6. **KICKS**
P. Revere and the Raiders
Mann–Weil,   Columbia 43356
(Screen Gems–Columbia, BMI)

7. **GLORIA**
The Shadows of Knight
V. Morrison,   Dunwich 116
(Bernice, BMI)

8. **SECRET AGENT MAN**
J. Rivers
Fowler–Heller,   Imperial 66159   (Trousdale, BMI)

9. **HOW DOES THAT GRAB YOU DARLIN'?**
N. Sinatra
L. Hazelwood,   Reprise 0641
(Criterion, ASCAP)

10. **BANG BANG**
Cher
S. Bono,   Imperial 66160
(Five–West–Cotillion, BMI)

1. **GOOD LOVIN'**
The Young Rascals
Clark–Resnick,   Atlantic 2320   (T.M., BMI)

2. **RAINY DAY WOMEN #12 AND #35**
B. Dylan
B. Dylan,   Columbia 43592
(Dwarf, ASCAP)

3. **MONDAY, MONDAY**
The Mamas and Papas
J. Phillips,   Dunhill 4026
(Trousdale, BMI)

4. **KICKS**
P. Revere and the Raiders
Mann–Weil,   Columbia 43356
(Screen Gems–Columbia, BMI)

5. **HOW DOES THAT GRAB YOU DARLIN'?**
N. Sinatra
L. Hazelwood,   Reprise 0641
(Criterion, ASCAP)

6. **SLOOP JOHN B.**
The Beach Boys
B. Wilson (adaption).   Capitol 5602   (New Executive, BMI)

7. **YOU'RE MY SOUL AND INSPIRATION**
The Righteous Brothers
Mann–Weil,   Verve 10383
(Screen Gems–Columbia, BMI)

8. **WHEN A MAN LOVES A WOMAN**
P. Sledge
Lewis–Wright,   Atlantic 2326
(Pronto–Quinuy, BMI)

9. **GLORIA**
The Shadows of Knight
V. Morrison,   Dunwich 116
(Bernice, BMI)

10. **MESSAGE TO MICHAEL**
D. Warwick
B. Bacharach–H. David,   Scepter 12133   (U.S. Songs, ASCAP)

May 21

1. **RAINY DAY WOMEN #12 AND #35**
   B. Dylan
   B. Dylan, Columbia 43592
   (Dwarf, ASCAP)

2. **WHEN A MAN LOVES A WOMAN**
   P. Sledge
   Lewis–Wright, Atlantic 2326
   (Pronto–Quinuy, BMI)

3. **GOOD LOVIN'**
   The Young Rascals
   Clark–Resnick, Atlantic 2320
   (T.M., BMI)

4. **HOW DOES THAT GRAB YOU DARLIN'?**
   N. Sinatra
   L. Hazelwood, Reprise 0641
   (Criterion, BMI)

5. **PAINT IT BLACK**
   The Rolling Stones
   M. Jagger–K. Richard,
   London 901 (Gideon, BMI)

6. **MONDAY, MONDAY**
   The Mamas and Papas
   J. Phillips, Dunhill 4026
   (Trousdale, BMI)

7. **SLOOP JOHN B.**
   The Beach Boys
   B. Wilson (adaptation), Capitol 5602 (New Executive, BMI)

8. **KICKS**
   P. Revere and the Raiders
   Mann–Weil, Columbia 43356
   (Screen Gems–Columbia, BMI)

9. **MESSAGE TO MICHAEL**
   D. Warwick
   B. Bacharach–H. David, Scepter 12133 (U.S. Songs, ASCAP)

10. **DID YOU EVER HAVE TO MAKE UP YOUR MIND?**
    Lovin' Spoonful
    J. Sebastian, Kuma Sutra 209
    (Faithful Virtue, BMI)

May 28

1. **WHEN A MAN LOVES A WOMAN**
   P. Sledge
   Lewis–Wright, Atlantic 2326
   (Pronto–Quinuy, BMI)

2. **RAINY DAY WOMEN #12 AND #35**
   B. Dylan
   B. Dylan, Columbia 43592
   (Dwarf, ASCAP)

3. **PAINT IT BLACK**
   The Rolling Stones
   M. Jagger–K. Richard,
   London 901 (Gideon, BMI)

4. **GROOVY KIND OF LOVE**
   The Mindbenders
   T. Wine–C. Bayer, Fontana 1541
   (Screen Gems–Columbia, BMI)

5. **I AM A ROCK**
   Simon and Garfunkel
   P. Simon, Columbia 43617
   (Eclectic, BMI)

6. **DID YOU EVER HAVE TO MAKE UP YOUR MIND?**
   Lovin' Spoonful
   J. Sebastian, Kama Sutra 209
   (Faithful Virtue, BMI)

7. **MONDAY, MONDAY**
   The Mamas and Papas
   J. Phillips, Dunhill 4026
   (Trousdale, BMI)

8. **GOOD LOVIN'**
   The Young Rascals
   Clark–Resnick, Atlantic 2320
   (T.M., BMI)

9. **IT'S A MAN'S MAN'S MAN'S WORLD**
   J. Brown
   J. Brown, King 6035
   (Dynatone, BMI)

10. **LOVE IS LIKE AN ITCHING IN MY HEART**
    The Supremes
    Holland–Dozier–Holland,
    Motown 1094 (Jobete, BMI)

June 4

1. **GROOVY KIND OF LOVE**
   The Mindbenders
   T. Wine–C. Bayer, Fontana 1541
   (Screen Gems–Columbia, BMI)

2. **WHEN A MAN LOVES A WOMAN**
   P. Sledge
   Lewis–Wright, Atlantic 2326
   (Pronto–Quinuy, BMI)

3. **DID YOU EVER HAVE TO MAKE UP YOUR MIND?**
   Lovin' Spoonful
   J. Sebastian, Kama Sutra 209
   (Faithful Virtue, BMI)

4. **PAINT IT BLACK**
   The Rolling Stones
   M. Jagger–K. Richard,
   London 901 (Gideon, BMI)

5. **I AM A ROCK**
   Simon and Garfunkel
   P. Simon, Columbia 43617
   (Eclectic, BMI)

6. **THE SUN AIN'T GONNA SHINE ANYMORE**
   The Walker Brothers
   B. Crewe–B. Gaudio, Smash 2032
   (Saturday–Seasons Four, BMI)

7. **MONDAY, MONDAY**
   The Mamas and Papas
   J. Phillips, Dunhill 4026
   (Trousdale, BMI)

8. **RAINY DAY WOMEN #12 AND #35**
   B. Dylan
   B. Dylan, Columbia 43592
   (Dwarf, ASCAP)

9. **STRANGERS IN THE NIGHT**
   F. Sinatra
   Singleton–Snyder–Kaempfert,
   Reprise 0470 (Champion–
   Roosevelt, BMI)

10. **IT'S A MAN'S MAN'S MAN'S WORLD**
    J. Brown
    J. Brown, King 6035
    (Dynatone, BMI)

301

June 11

1. **DID YOU EVER HAVE TO MAKE UP YOUR MIND?**
Lovin' Spoonful
J. Sebastian, Kama Sutra 209
(Faithful Virgue, BMI)

2. **I AM A ROCK**
Simon and Garfunkel
P. Simon, Columbia 43617
(Eclectic, BMI)

3. **PAINT IT BLACK**
The Rolling Stones
M. Jagger–K. Richard,
London 901 (Gideon, BMI)

4. **GROOVY KIND OF LOVE**
The Mindbenders
T. Wine–C. Bayer,
Fontana 1541
(Screen Gems–Columbia, BMI)

5. **WHEN A MAN LOVES A WOMAN**
P. Sledge
Lewis–Wright, Atlantic 2326
(Pronto–Quinuy, BMI)

6. **STRANGERS IN THE NIGHT**
F. Sinatra
Singleton–Snyder–Kaempfert,
Reprise 0470 (Champion–
Roosevelt, BMI)

7. **BAREFOOTIN'**
R. Parker
R. Parker, Nola 721
(Bonatemp, BMI)

8. **THE SUN AIN'T GONNA SHINE ANYMORE**
The Walker Brothers
B. Crewe–B. Gaudio, Smash 2032
(Saturday–Seasons Four, BMI)

9. **IT'S A MAN'S MAN'S MAN'S WORLD**
J. Brown
J. Brown, King 6035
(Dynatone, BMI)

10. **SWEET TALKIN' GUY**
The Chiffons
Morris–Greenberg–Baer–Schwartz,
Laurie 3340 (Elmwin, BMI)

June 18

1. **I AM A ROCK**
Simon and Garfunkel
P. Simon, Columbia 43617
(Eclectic, BMI)

2. **PAPERBACK WRITER**
The Beatles
J. Lennon–P. McCartney,
Capitol 5651 (Maclen, BMI)

3. **PAINT IT BLACK**
The Rolling Stones
M. Jagger–K. Richard,
London 901 (Gideon, BMI)

4. **STRANGERS IN THE NIGHT**
F. Sinatra
Singleton–Snyder–Kaempfert,
Reprise 0470 (Champion–
Roosevelt, BMI)

5. **DID YOU EVER HAVE TO MAKE UP YOUR MIND?**
Lovin' Spoonful
J. Sebastian, Kama Sutra 209
(Faithful Virtue, BMI)

6. **WHEN A MAN LOVES A WOMAN**
P. Sledge
Lewis–Wright, Atlantic 2326
(Pronto–Quinuy, BMI)

7. **GROOVY KIND OF LOVE**
The Mindbenders
T. Wine–C. Bayer, Fontana 1541
(Screen Gems–Columbia, BMI)

8. **COOL JERK**
The Capitols
Storball, Karen 1524
(McLaughlin, BMI)

9. **SWEET TALKIN' GUY**
The Chiffons
Morris–Greenberg–Baer–
Schwartz,
Laurie 3340 (Elmwin, BMI)

10. **OH, HOW HAPPY**
Shades of Blue
Hatcher, Impact 1007
(Myto, BMI)

June 25

1. **PAPERBACK WRITER**
The Beatles
J. Lennon–P. McCartney,
Capitol 5651 (Maclen, BMI)

2. **STRANGERS IN THE NIGHT**
F. Sinatra
Singleton–Snyder–Kaempfert,
Reprise 0470 (Champion–
Roosevelt, BMI)

3. **I AM A ROCK**
Simon and Garfunkel
P. Simon, Columbia 43617
(Eclectic, BMI)

4. **PAINT IT BLACK**
The Rolling Stones
M. Jagger–K. Richard,
London 901 (Gideon, BMI)

5. **COOL JERK**
The Capitols
Storball, Karen 1524
(McLaughlin, BMI)

6. **OH, HOW HAPPY**
Shades of Blue
Hatcher, Impact 1007
(Myto, BMI)

7. **YOU DON'T HAVE TO SAY YOU LOVE ME**
D. Springfield
Wickham–Napier–Bell, Philips
40317 (Robbins, ASCAP)

8. **GROOVY KIND OF LOVE**
The Mindbenders
T.Wine–C. Bayer, Fontana 1541
(Screen Gems–Columbia, BMI)

9. **DID YOU EVER HAVE TO MAKE UP YOUR MIND?**
Lovin' Spoonful
J. Sebastian, Kama Sutra 209
(Faithful Virtue, BMI)

10. **SWEET TALKIN' GUY**
The Chiffons
Morris–Greenberg–Baer–Schwartz,
Laurie 3340 (Elmwin, BMI)

1966

July 2

1. **PAPERBACK WRITER**
The Beatles
J. Lennon–P. McCartney,
Capitol 5561 (Maclen, BMI)

2. **STRANGERS IN THE NIGHT**
F. Sinatra
Singleton–Snyder–Kaempfert,
Reprise 0470 (Champion–
Roosevelt, BMI)

3. **I AM A ROCK**
Simon and Garfunkel
P. Simon, Columbia 43617
(Eclectic, BMI)

4. **WILD THING**
The Troggs
C. Taylor, Fontana 1548
(Blackwood, BMI)

5. **COOL JERK**
The Capitols
Storball, Karen 1524
(McLaughlin, BMI)

6. **YOU DON'T HAVE TO SAY YOU LOVE ME**
D. Springfield
Wickham–Napier–Bell,
Philips 40371
(Robbins, ASCAP)

7. **OH, HOW HAPPY**
Shades of Blue
Hatcher, Impact 1007
(Myto, BMI)

8. **PAINT IT BLACK**
The Rolling Stones
M. Jagger–K. Richards,
London 901 (Gideon, BMI)

9. **DID YOU EVER HAVE TO MAKE UP YOUR MIND?**
Lovin' Spoonful
J. Sebastian, Kama Sutra 209
(Faithful Virtue, BMI)

10. **SWEET TALKIN' GUY**
The Chiffons
Morris–Greenberg–Baer–
Schwartz, Laurie 3340
(Elmwin, BMI)

July 9

1. **WILD THING**
The Troggs
C. Taylor, Fontana 1548
(Blackwood, BMI)

2. **PAPERBACK WRITER**
The Beatles
J. Lennon–P. McCartney,
Capitol 5561 (Maclen, BMI)

3. **STRANGERS IN THE NIGHT**
F. Sinatra
Singleton–Snyder–Kaempfert
(Reprise 0470 (Champion–
Roosevelt, BMI)

4. **HANKY PANKY**
T. James and the
Shondells
J. Barry–E. Greenwich, Roulette
4686 (T.M., BMI)

5. **I AM A ROCK**
Simon and Garfunkel
P. Simon, Columbia 43617
(Eclectic, BMI)

6. **YOU DON'T HAVE TO SAY YOU LOVE ME**
D. Springfield
Wickham–Napier–Bell, Philips
40371 (Robbins, ASCAP)

7. **COOL JERK**
The Capitols
Storball, Karen 1524
(McLaughlin, BMI)

8. **ALONG COMES MARY**
The Association
Almer, Valiant 741
(Davon, BMI)

9. **PAINT IT BLACK**
The Rolling Stones
M. Jagger–K. Richard,
London 901 (Gideon, BMI)

10. **LITTLE GIRL**
The Syndicate of Sound
Gonzales–Baskin, Bell 640
(Duane, BMI)

July 16

1. **WILD THING**
The Troggs
C. Taylor, Fontana 1548
(Blackwood, BMI)

2. **HANKY PANKY**
T. James and the Shon-
dells
J. Barry–E. Greenwich, Roulette
4686 (T.M., BMI)

3. **STRANGERS IN THE NIGHT**
F. Sinatra
Singleton–Snyder–Kaempfert,
Reprise 0470 (Champion–
Roosevelt, BMI)

4. **THE PIED PIPER**
C. St. Peters
Kornfield–Duboff Jamie 1320
(Chardon, BMI)

5. **I SAW HER AGAIN LAST NIGHT**
The Mammas and Papas
J. Phillips–Doherty, Dunhill 4031
(Trousdale, BMI)

6. **PAPERBACK WRITER**
The Beatles
J. Lennon–P. McCartney, Capitol
5561 (Maclen, BMI)

7. **ALONG COMES MARY**
The Association
Almer, Valiant 741
(Davon, BMI)

8. **LIL' RED RIDING HOOD**
Sam the Sham and the
Pharoahs
Blackwell, M-G-M 13506
(Rose, BMI)

9. **LITTLE GIRL**
The Syndicate of Sound
Gonzales–Baskin, Bell 640
(Duane, BMI)

10. **HUNGRY**
P. Revere and the Raiders
Mann–Weil, Columbia 43678
(Screen Gems–Columbia, BMI)

1. **HANKY PANKY**
T. James and the Shon-
dells
J. Barry–E. Greenwich, Roulette
4686 (T.M., BMI)

2. **THE PIED PIPER**
C. ST. Peters
Kornfield–Duboff, Jamie 1320
(Chardon, BMI)

3. **WILD THING**
The Troggs
C. Taylor, Fontana 1548
(Blackwood, BMI)

4. **LIL' RED RIDING HOOD**
Sam the Sham and the
Pharoahs
Blackwell, M-G-M 13506
(Rose, BMI)

5. **I SAW HER AGAIN LAST**
NIGHT
The Mamas and Papas
J. Phillips–Doherty, Dunhill 4031
(Trousdale, BMI)

6. **HUNGRY**
P. Revere and the Raiders
Mann–Weil, Columbia 43678
(Screen Gems–Columbia, BMI)

7. **SWEET PEA**
T. Roe
T. Roe, ABC 10762
(Lew–Twi, BMI)

8. **ALONG COMES MARY**
The Association
Almer, Valiant 741
(Dabon, BMI)

9. **DIRTY WATER**
The Standells
Cobb, Tower 185
(Equinox, BMI)

10. **PAPERBACK WRITER**
The Beatles
J. Lennon–P. McCartney,
Capitol 5561 (Maclen, BMI)

1. **HANKY PANKY**
T. James and the Shon-
dells
J. Barry–E. Greenwich, Roulette
4686 (T.M., BMI)

2. **THE PIED PIPER**
C. St. Peters
Kornfield–Duboff, Jamie 1320
(Chardon, BMI)

3. **LIL' RED RIDING HOOD**
Sam the Sham and the
Pharoahs
Blackwell, M-G-M 13506
(Rose, BMI)

4. **I SAW HER AGAIN LAST**
NIGHT
The Mamas and Papas
J. Phillips–Doherty, Dunhill
4031 (Trousdale, BMI)

5. **WILD THING**
The Troggs
C. Taylor, Fontana 1548
(Blackwood, BMI)

6. **SWEET PEA**
T. Roe
T. Roe, ABC 10762
(Lew–Twi, BMI)

7. **SUMMER IN THE CITY**
Lovin' Spoonful
J. Sebastian–M. Sebastian–Boone,
Kama Sutra 211 (Faithful Vir-
tue, BMI)

8. **HUNGRY**
P. Revere and the Raiders
Mann–Weil, Columbia 43678
(Screen Gems–Columbia, BMI)

9. **MOTHER'S LITTLE HELPER**
The Rolling Stones
K. Richard–M. Jagger, London
902 (Gideon, BMI)

10. **PAPERBACK WRITER**
The Beatles
J. Lennon–P. McCartney,
Capitol 5561 (Maclen, BMI)

1. **HANKY PANKY**
T. James and the Shon-
dells
J. Barry–E. Greenwich, Roulette
4686 (T.M., BMI)

2. **I SAW HER AGAIN LAST**
NIGHT
The Mamas and Papas
J. Phillips–Doherty, Dunhill
4031 (Trousdale, BMI)

3. **LIL' RED RIDING HOOD**
Sam the Sham and the
Pharoahs
Blackwell, M-G-M 13506
(Rose, BMI)

4. **SUMMER IN THE CITY**
Lovin' Spoonful
J. Sebastian–M. Sebastian–Boone,
Kama Sutra 211
(Faithful Virtue, BMI)

5. **WILD THING**
The Troggs
C. Taylor, Fontana 1548
(Blackwood, BMI)

6. **SWEET PEA**
T. Roe
T. Roe, ABC 10762
(Lew–Twi, BMI)

7. **THE PIED PIPER**
C. St. Peters
Kornfield–Duboff, Jamie
1320 (Chardon, BMI)

8. **MOTHER'S LITTLE HELPER**
The Rolling Stones
K. Richard–M. Jagger,
London 902 (Gideon, BMI)

9. **HUNGRY**
P. Revere and the Raiders
Mann–Weil, Columbia 43678
(Screen Gems–Columbia, BMI)

10. **SUNNY**
B. Hebb
B. Hebb, Philips 40365
(Portable, BMI)

August 13

1. **I SAW HER AGAIN LAST NIGHT**
The Mamas and Papas
J. Phillips–Doherty,   Dunhill 4031 (Trousdale, BMI)

2. **SUMMER IN THE CITY**
Lovin' Spoonful
*J. Sebastian–M. Sebastian–Boone, Kama Sutra 211
(Faithful Virtue, BMI)*

3. **SUNNY**
B. Hebb
*B. Hebb,   Philips 40365
(Portable, BMI)*

4. **SUNSHINE SUPERMAN**
Donovan
*D. Leitch, Epic 10045
(Southern, ASCAP)*

5. **MOTHER'S LITTLE HELPER**
The Rolling Stones
*K. Richard–M. Jagger,
London 902 (Gideon, BMI)*

6. **LIL' RED RIDING HOOD**
Sam the Sham and the Pharoahs
*Blackwell,   M-G-M 13506
(Rose, BMI)*

7. **WILD THING**
The Troggs
*C. Taylor, Fontana 1548
(Blackwood, BMI)*

8. **THE PIED PIPER**
C. St. Peters
*Kornfield–Duboff,   Jamie 1320
(Chardon, BMI)*

9. **SWEET PEA**
T. Roe
*T. Roe, ABC 10762
(Lew–Twi, BMI)*

10. **SEE YOU IN SEPTEMBER**
The Happenings
*Edwards–Wayne,
B.T. Puppy 520
(Jack Gold, ASCAP)*

August 20

1. **SUMMER IN THE CITY**
Lovin' Spoonful
*J. Sebastian–M. Sebastian–Boone, Kama Sutra 211
(Faithful Virtue, BMI)*

2. **I SAW HER AGAIN LAST NIGHT**
The Mamas and Papas
J. Phillips–Doherty,   Dunhill 4031   (Trousdale, BMI)

3. **SUNNY**
B. Hebb
*B. Hebb,   Philips 40365
(Portable, BMI)*

4. **SUNSHINE SUPERMAN**
Donovan
*D. Leitch,   Epic 10045
(Southern, ASCAP)*

5. **SEE YOU IN SEPTEMBER**
The Happenings
*Edwards–Wayne,
B.T. Puppy 520
(Jack Gold, ASCAP)*

6. **I COULDN'T LIVE WITHOUT YOUR LOVE**
P. Clark
Trent–T. Hatch,   Warner Brothers 5835 (Northern, AS-CAP)

7. **MOTHER'S LITTLE HELPER**
The Rolling Stones
*K. Richard–M. Jagger,
London 902   (Gideon, BMI)*

8. **LIL' RED RIDING HOOD**
Sam the Sham and the Pharoahs
*Blackwell,   M-G-M 13506
(Rose, BMI)*

9. **YOU CAN'T HURRY LOVE**
The Supremes
*Holland–Dozier–Holland,
Motown 1097 (Jobete–Bobete, BMI)*

10. **WILD THING**
The Troggs
*C. Taylor,   Fontana 1548
(Blackwood, BMI)*

August 27

1. **SUNNY**
B. Hebb
*B. Hebb,   Philips 40365
(Portable, BMI)*

2. **SUMMER IN THE CITY**
Lovin' Spoonful
J. Sebastian–M. Sebastian–Boone, Kama Sutra 211 (Faithful Virtue, BMI)

3. **SUNSHINE SUPERMAN**
Donovan
*D. Leitch,   Epic 10045
(Southern, ASCAP)*

4. **SEE YOU IN SEPTEMBER**
The Happenings
Edwards–Wayne,   B.T. Puppy 520   (Jack Gold, ASCAP)

5. **YOU CAN'T HURRY LOVE**
The Supremes
*Holland–Dozier–Holland,
Motown 1097
(Jobete–Bobete, BMI)*

6. **YELLOW SUBMARINE**
The Beatles
*J. Lennon–P. McCartney,
Capitol 5715 (Maclen, BMI)*

7. **WORKING IN THE COAL MINE**
L. Dorsey
*A. Toussaint,   Amy 958
(Marsaint, BMI)*

8. **LAND OF 1000 DANCES**
W. Pickett
C. Kenner–A. Domino,   Atlantic 2348 (Tune-Kel-Anatole, BMI)

9. **I COULDN'T LIVE WITHOUT YOUR LOVE**
P. Clark
Trent–T. Hatch,   Warner Brothers 5835 (Northern, ASCAP)

10. **SUMMERTIME**
B. Stewart
*G. Gershwin,   Chess 1966
(Gershwin, ASCAP)*

September 3

1. **SUNSHINE SUPERMAN**
Donovan
D. Leitch, Epic 10045
(Southern, ASCAP)

2. **SEE YOU IN SEPTEMBER**
The Happenings
Edward–Wayne, B.T. Puppy 520
(Jack Gold, ASCAP)

3. **YOU CAN'T HURRY LOVE**
The Supremes
Holland–Dozier–Holland,
Motown 1097
(Jobete–Bobete, BMI)

4. **SUNNY**
B. Hebb
B. Hebb, Philips 40365
(Portable, BMI)

5. **SUMMER IN THE CITY**
Lovin' Spoonful
J. Sebastian–M. Sebastian–
Boone, Kama Sutra 211
(Faithful Virtue, BMI)

6. **WORKING IN THE COAL MINE**
L. Dorsey
A. Toussaint, Amy 958
(Marsaint, BMI)

7. **LAND OF 1000 DANCES**
W. Pickett
C. Kenner–A. Domino, Atlantic
2348 (Tune–Kel–Antole, BMI)

8. **YELLOW SUBMARINE**
The Beatles
J. Lennon–P. McCartney,
Capitol 5715 (Maclen, BMI)

9. **SUMMERTIME**
B. Stewart
G. Gershwin, Chess 1966
(Gershwin, ASCAP)

10. **BLOWIN' IN THE WIND**
S. Wonder
B. Dylan, Tamla 54136
(Witmark, ASCAP)

September 10

1. **SEE YOU IN SEPTEMBER**
The Happenings
Edwards–Wayne, B.T. Puppy 520
(Jack Gold, ASCAP)

2. **YOU CAN'T HURRY LOVE**
The Supremes
Holland–Dozier–Holland,
Motown 1097 (Jobete, BMI)

3. **YELLOW SUBMARINE**
The Beatles
J. Lennon–P. McCartney, Capitol
5175 (Maclen, BMI)

4. **SUNSHINE SUPERMAN**
Donvan
D. Leitch, Epic 10045
(Southern, ASCAP)

5. **BUS STOP**
The Hollies
G. Gouldman, Impaerial 66186
(Manken, BMI)

6. **WORKING IN THE COAL MINE**
L. Dorsey
A. Toussain, Amy 958
(Marsaint, BMI)

7. **LAND OF 1000 DANCES**
W. Pickett
C. Kenner–A. Domino, Atlantic
2348 (Tune–Kel–Anatole, BMI)

8. **SUNNY**
B. Hebb
B. Hebb, Philips 40365
(Portable, BMI)

9. **SUMMER IN THE CITY**
Lovin' Spoonful
J. Sebastian–M. Sebastian–Boone,
Kama Sutra 211
(Faithful Virtue, BMI)

10. **GUANTANAMERA**
The Sandpipers
Marti–Angula–Seeger
A. and M. 806 (Fall River, BMI)

September 17

1. **YELLOW SUBMARINE**
The Beatles
J. Lennon–P. McCartney,
Capitol 5715 (Maclen, BMI)

2. **YOU CAN'T HURRY LOVE**
The Supremes
Holland–Dozier–Holland,
Motown 1097
(Jobete–Bobete, BMI)

3. **CHERISH**
The Association
Kirkman, Valiant 747
(Beechwood, BMI)

4. **BUS STOP**
The Hollies
G. Gouldman, Imperial 66186
(Manken, BMI)

5. **GUANTANAMERA**
The Sandpipers
Marti–Angula–Seeger
A. and M. 806 (Fall River, BMI)

6. **SEE YOU IN SEPTEMBER**
The Happenings
Edwards–Wayne, B. T. Puppy 520
(Jack Gold, ASCAP)

7. **WOULDN'T IT BE NICE?**
The Beach Boys
B. Wilson-Asher, Capitol 5706
(Sea of Tunes, BMI)

8. **96 TEARS**
(?) and the Mysterians
Martinez, Cameo 428
(Arquello, BMI)

9. **REACH OUT I'LL BE THERE**
The Four Tops
Holland–Dozier–Holland,
Motown 1098 (Jobete, BMI)

10. **SUNNY**
B. Hebb
B. Hebb, Philips 40365
(Portable, BMI)

1966

September 24

1. **BUS STOP**
The Hollies
G. Gouldman, Imperial 66186
(Manken, BMI)

2. **CHERISH**
The Association
Kirkman, Valiant 747
(Beechwood, BMI)

3. **YOU CAN'T HURRY LOVE**
The Supremes
Holland–Dozier–Holland,
Motown 1097
(Jobete–Bobete, BMI)

4. **WOULDN'T IT BE NICE?**
The Beach Boys
B. Wilson–Asher, Captiol 5706
(Sea of Tunes, BMI)

5. **YELLOW SUBMARINE**
The Beatles
J. Lennon–P. McCartney,
Capitol 5715 (Maclen, BMI)

6. **96 TEARS**
(?) and the Mysterians
Martinez, Cameo 428
(Arquello, BMI)

7. **BEAUTY IS ONLY SKIN DEEP**
The Temptations
Whitfield–Holland, Gordy
7055 (Jobete, BMI)

8. **SEE YOU IN SEPTEMBER**
The Happenings
Edwards–Wayne, B. T. Puppy 520
(Jack Gold, ASCAP)

9. **REACH OUT I'LL BE THERE**
The Four Tops
Holland–Dozier–Holland,
Motown 1098 (Jobete, BMI)

10. **CHERRY, CHERRY**
N. Diamond
N. Diamond, Bang 528
(Tallyrand, BMI)

October 1

1. **CHERISH**
The Association
Kirkman, Valiant 747
(Beechwood, BMI)

2. **BEAUTY IS ONLY SKIN DEEP**
The Temptations
Whitfield–Holland, Gordy
7055 (Jobete, BMI)

3. **YOU CAN'T HURRY LOVE**
The Supremes
Holland–Dozier–Holland,
Motown 1097
(Jobete–Bobete, BMI)

4. **BUS STOP**
The Hollies
G. Gouldman, Imperial 66186
(Manken, BMI)

5. **96 TEARS**
(?) and the Mysterians
Martinez, Cameo 428
(Arquello, BMI)

6. **REACH OUT I'LL BE THERE**
The Four Tops
Holland–Dozier–Holland,
Motown 1098 (Jobete, BMI)

7. **WOULDN'T IT BE NICE?**
The Beach Boys
B. Wilson–Asher, Capitol 5706
(Sea of Tunes, BMI)

8. **CHERRY, CHERRY**
N. Diamond
N. Diamond, Bang 528
(Tallyrand, BMI)

9. **BORN A WOMAN**
S. Posey
Sharp, M-G-M 13501
(Painted Desert, BMI)

10. **LAST TRAIN TO CLARKSVILLE**
The Monkees
T. Boyce–B. Hart, Colgems
1001 (Screen Gems–Columbia,
BMI)

October 8

1. **CHERISH**
The Association
Kirkman, Valiant 747
(Beechwood, BMI)

2. **REACH OUT I'LL BE THERE**
The Four Tops
Holland–Dozier–Holland,
Motown 1098 (Jobete, BMI)

3. **96 TEARS**
(?) and the Mysterians
Martinez, Cameo 428
(Arquello, BMI)

4. **BEAUTY IS ONLY SKIN DEEP**
The Temptations
Whitfield–Holland, Gordy
7055 (Jobete, BMI)

5. **CHERRY, CHERRY**
N. Diamond
N. Diamond, Bang 528
(Tallyrand, BMI)

6. **YOU CAN'T HURRY LOVE**
The Supremes
Holland–Dozier–Holland,
Motown 1097
(Jobete–Bobete, BMI)

7. **WALK AWAY RENEE**
The Left Banke
Brown–Sansone–Calilli, Smash
2041 (Twin Tone, BMI)

8. **LAST TRAIN TO CLARKSVILLE**
The Monkees
T. Boyce–B. Hart, Colgems 1001
(Sceen Gems–Columbia, BMI)

9. **PSYCHOTIC REACTION**
Count 5
Ellner–Chaney–Atkinson–Byrne–
Michaleski,
Double Shot 104 (Hot Shot, BMI)

10. **I'VE GOT YOU UNDER MY SKIN**
The Four Seasons
C. Porter, Philips 40393
(Chappell, ASCAP)

October 15

1. **96 TEARS**
(?) and the Mysterians
Martinez, Cameo 428
(Arquello, BMI)

2. **CHERISH**
The Association
Kirkman, Valiant 747
(Beechwood, BMI)

3. **REACH OUT I'LL BE THERE**
The Four Tops
Holland–Dozier–Holland,
Motown 1098 (Jobete, BMI)

4. **LAST TRAIN TO CLARKS-
VILLE**
The Monkees
T. Boyce–B. Hart, Colgems 1001
(Screen Gems–Columbia, BMI)

5. **WALK AWAY RENEE**
The Left Banke
Brown–Sansone–Calilli,
Samsh 2041 (Twin Tone, BMI)

6. **BEAUTY IS ONLY SKIN
DEEP**
The Temptations
Whitfield–Holland, Gordy
7055 (Jobete, BMI)

7. **PSYCHOTIC REACTION**
Count 5
Ellner–Chaney–Atkinson–Byrnne
Michaleski, Double Shot 104
(Hot Shot, BMI)

8. **CHERRY, CHERRY**
N. Diamond
N. Diamond, Bang 528
(Tallyrand, BMI)

9. **WHAT BECOMES OF THE
BROKENHEARTED?**
J. Ruffin
Dean–Rise–Weatherspoon, Soul
35022 (Jobete, BMI)

10. **POOR SIDE OF TOWN**
J. Rivers
J. Rivers–Adler, Imperial 66205
(Rivers, BMI)

October 22

1. **REACH OUT I'LL BE THERE**
The Four Tops
Holland–Dozier–Holland,
Motown 1098 (Jobete, BMI)

2. **96 TEARS**
(?) and the Mysterians
Martinez, Cameo 428
(Arquello, BMI)

3. **LAST TRAIN TO
CLARKSVILLE**
The Monkees
T. Boyce–B. Hart, Colgems 1001
(Screen Gems–Columbia, BMI)

4. **WALK AWAY RENEE**
The Left Banke
Brown–Sansone–Calilli,
Smash 2041 (Twin Tone, BMI)

5. **PSYCHOTIC REACTION**
Count 5
Ellner–Chaney–Atkinson–Byrne–
Michaleski,
Double Shot 104 (Hot Shot, BMI)

6. **WHAT BECOMES OF THE
BROKENHEARTED?**
J. Ruffin
Dean–Rise–Weatherspoon,
Soul 35022 (Jobete, BMI)

7. **POOR SIDE OF TOWN**
J. Rivers
J. Rivers–Adler, Imperial 66205
(Rivers, BMI)

8. **HAVE YOU SEEN YOUR
MOTHER, BABY, STANDING
IN THE SHADOWS?**
The Rolling Stones
M. Jagger–K. Richard,
London 903 (Gideon, BMI)

9. **SEE SEE RIDER**
E. Burdon and the Animals
C. Willis, M-G-M 13582
(Leeds, ASCAP)

10. **DANDY**
Herman's Hermits
R. Davies, M-G-M 13603
(Noma, BMI)

October 29

1. **LAST TRAIN TO CLARKS-
VILLE**
The Monkees
T. Boyce–B. Hart, Colgems 1001
(Screen Gems–Columbia, BMI)

2. **96 TEARS**
(?) and the Mysterians
Martinez, Cameo 428
(Arquello, BMI)

3. **REACH OUT I'LL BE THERE**
The Four Tops
Holland–Dozier–Holland,
Motown 1098 (Jobete, BMI)

4. **POOR SIDE OF TOWN**
J. Rivers
J. Rivers–Adler, Imperial 66205
(Rivers, BMI)

5. **WALK AWAY RENEE**
The Left Banke
Brown–Sansone–Calilli,
Smash 2041 (Twin Tone, BMI)

6. **WHAT BECOMES OF THE
BROKENHEARTED?**
J. Ruffin
Dean–Rise–Weatherspoon,
Soul 34022 (Jobete, BMI)

7. **HURRAY FOR HAZEL**
T. Roe,
T. Roe, ABC 10852 (Lew-Twi,
BMI)

8. **HAVE YOU SEEN YOUR
MOTHER, BABY, STANDING
IN THE SHADOWS?**
The Rolling Stones
M. Jagger–K. Richard,
London 903 (Gideon, BMI)

9. **SEE SEE RIDER**
E. Burdon and the
Animals
C. Willis, M-G-M 13582
(Leeds, ASCAP)

10. **DANDY**
Herman's Hermits
R. Davies, M-G-M 13603
(Noma, BMI)

November 5

1. **LAST TRAIN TO CLARKS-VILLE**
The Monkees
T. Boyce–B. Hart, Colgems 1001
(Screen Gems–Columbia, BMI)

2. **HOORAY FOR HAZEL**
T. Roe
T. Roe, ABC 10852
(Lew–Twi, BMI)

3. **POOR SIDE OF TOWN**
J. Rivers
J. Rivers–Adler, Imperial 66205
(Rivers, BMI)

4. **GOOD VIBRATIONS**
The Beach Boys
B. Wilson–M. Love, Capitol 5676
(Sea of Tunes, BMI)

5. **REACH OUT I'LL BE THERE**
The Four Tops
Holland–Dozier–Holland,
Motown 1098 (Jobete, BMI)

6. **YOU KEEP ME HANGIN'ON**
The Supremes
Holland–Dozier–Holland,
Motown 1101 (Jobete, BMI)

7. **DANDY**
Herman's Hermits
R. Davies, M-G-M 13603
(Noma, BMI)

8. **96 TEARS**
(?) and the Mysterians
Martinez, Cameo 428
(Arquello, BMI)

9. **WALK AWAY RENEE**
The Left Banke
Brown–Sansone–Calilli,
Smash 2041 (Twin Tone, BMI)

10. **IF I WERE A CARPENTER**
B. Darin
T. Hardin, Atlantic 2350
(Faithful Virtue, BMI)

November 12

1. **GOOD VIBRATIONS**
The Beach Boys
B. Wilson–M. Love,
Capitol 5676 (Sea of Tunes, BMI)

2. **LAST TRAIN TO CLARKSVILLE**
The Monkees
T. Boyce–B. Hart, Colgems 1001
(Screen Gems–Columbia, BMI)

3. **POOR SIDE OF TOWN**
J. Rivers
J. Rivers–Adler, Imperial 66205
(Rivers, BMI)

4. **WINCHESTER CATHEDRAL**
The New Vaudeville Band
Stevens, Fontana 1562
(Southern, ASCAP)

5. **REACH OUT I'LL BE THERE**
The Four Tops
Holland–Dozier–Holland,
Motown 1098 (Jobete, BMI)

6. **DANDY**
Herman's Hermits
R. Davies, M-G-M 13603
(Noma, BMI)

7. **YOU KEEP ME HANGIN' ON**
The Supremes
Holland–Dozier–Holland,
Motown 1101 (Jobete, BMI)

8. **DEVIL WITH THE BLUE DRESS ON**
M. Rider and the Detroit Wheels
Stevenson–Long, New Voice 817
(Jobete–Vamico,MI)

9. **IF I WERE A CARPENTER**
B. Darin
T. Hardin, Atlantic 2350
(Faithful Virtue, BMI)

10. **I'M YOUR PUPPET**
J. Purify and B. Purify
Oldham–Penn, Bell 648
(Fame, BMI)

November 19

1. **GOOD VIBRATIONS**
The Beach Boys
B. Wilson–M. Love,
Capitol 5676 (Sea of Tunes, BMI)

2. **YOU KEEP ME HANGIN' ON**
The Supremes
Holland–Dozier–Holland,
Motown 1101 (Jobete, BMI)

3. **WINCHESTER CATHEDRAL**
The New Vaudeville Band
Stevens, Fontana 1562
(Southern, ASCAP)

4. **POOR SIDE OF TOWN**
J. Rivers
Rivers–Adler, Imperial 66205
(Rivers, BMI)

5. **LAST TRAIN TO CLARKSVILLE**
The Monkees
T. Boyce–B. Hart, Colgems 1001
(Screen Gems–Columbia, BMI)

6. **IF I WERE A CARPENTER**
B. Darin
T. Hardin, Atlantic 2350
(Faithful Virtue, BMI)

7. **DEVIL WITH THE BLUE DRESS ON**
M. Rider and the Detroit Wheels
Stevenson–Long, New Voice 817
(Jobete–Vamico, BMI)

8. **I'M YOUR PUPPET**
J. Purify and B. Purify
Oldham–Penn, Bell 648
(Fame, BMI)

9. **RAIN ON THE ROOF**
Lovin' Spoonful
J. Sebastian, Kama Sutra 216
(Faithful Virtue, BMI)

10. **MELLOW YELLOW**
Donovan
D. Leitch, Epic 10098
(Donovan Ltd., BMI)

November 26

1. YOU KEEP ME HANGIN' ON
The Supremes

Holland–Dozier–Holland,
Motown 1101   (Jobete, BMI)

2. GOOD VIBRATIONS
The Beach Boys

B. Wilson–M. Love,
Capitol 5676   (Sea of Tunes, BMI)

3. WINCHESTER CATHEDRAL
The New Vaudeville Band

Stevens,   Fontana 1562
(Southern, ASCAP)

4. I'M YOUR PUPPET
J. Purify and B. Purify

Oldham–Penn,   Bell 648
(Fame, BMI)

5. DEVIL WITH THE BLUE DRESS ON
M. Rider and the
Detroit Wheels

Stevenson–Long,   New Voice 817
(Jobete–Vamico, BMI)

6. LADY GODIVA
Peter and Gordon

Leander–Mills,   Capitol 5740
(Regent, BMI)

7. POOR SIDE OF TOWN
J. Rivers

J. Rivers–Adler,   Imperial 66025
(Rivers, BMI)

8. MELLOW YELLOW
Donovan

D. Leitch,   Epic 10098
(Donovan Ltd., BMI)

9. LAST TRAIN TO CLARKS-VILLE
The Monkees

T. Boyce–B. Hart,   Colgems 1001
(Screen Gems–Columbia, BMI)

10. RAIN ON THE ROOF
Lovin' Spoonful

J. Sebastian,   Kama Sutra 216
(Faithful Virtue, BMI)

December 3

1. WINCHESTER CATHEDRAL
The New Vaudeville Band

Stevens,   Fontana 1562
(Southern, ASCAP)

2. YOU KEEP ME HANGIN' ON
The Supremes

Holland–Dozier–Holland,
Motown 1101   (Jobete, BMI)

3. GOOD VIBRATIONS
The Beach Boys

B. Wilson–M. Love,
Capitol 5676   (Sea of Tunes, BMI)

4. MELLOW YELLOW
Donovan

D. Leitch,   Epic 10098
(Donovan Ltd., BMI)

5. I'M YOUR PUPPET
J. Purify and B. Purify

Oldham–Penn,   Bell 648
(Fame, BMI)

6. LADY GODIVA
Peter and Gordon

Leander–Mills,   Capitol 5740
(Regent, BMI)

7. DEVIL WITH THE BLUE DRESS ON
M. Rider and the Detroit
Wheels

Stevenson–Long,   New Voice 817
(Jobete–Vamico, BMI)

8. POOR SIDE OF TOWN
J. Rivers

J. Rivers–Adler,   Imperial 66025
(Rivers, BMI)

9. I'M READY FOR LOVE
Martha and the Vandellas

Holland–Dozier–Holland,
Gordy 7056   (Jobete, BMI)

10. STOP, STOP, STOP
The Hollies

Clarke–Hicks–Nash,
Imperial 66214   (Maribus, BMI)

December 10

1. MELLOW YELLOW
Donovan

D. Leitch,   Epic 10098
(Donovan Ltd., BMI)

2. WINCHESTER CATHEDRAL
The New Vaudeville Band

Stevens,   Fontana 1562
(Southern, ASCAP)

3. YOU KEEP ME HANGIN' ON
The Supremes

Holland–Dozier–Holland,
Motown 1101   (Jobete, BMI)

4. GOOD VIBRATIONS
The Beach Boys

B. Wilson–M. Love,
Capitol 5676   (Sea of Tunes, BMI)

5. BORN FREE
R. Williams

Barry,   Kapp 767
(Screen Gems–Columbia, BMI)

6. STOP, STOP, STOP
The Hollies

Clarke–Hicks–Nash,
Imperial 66214   (Maribus, BMI)

7. I'M A BELIEVER
The Monkees

N. Diamond,   Colgems 1003
(Screen Gems-Columbia, BMI)

8. DEVIL WITH THE BLUE DRESS ON
M. Rider and the Detroit
Wheels

Stevenson–Long,   New Voice 817
(Jobete–Vamico, BMI)

9. I'M READY FOR LOVE
Martha and the Vandellas

Holland–Dozier–Holland,
Gordy 7056   (Jobete, BMI)

10. THAT'S LIFE
F. Sinatra

Thompson,   Reprise 0531
(Four Star Television, ASCAP)

1966

December 17

1. **I'M A BELIEVER**
The Monkees
N. Diamond, Colgems 1003
(Screen Gems–Columbia, BMI)

2. **MELLOW YELLOW**
Donovan
D. Leitch, Epic 10098
(Donovan Ltd., BMI)

3. **WINCHESTER CATHEDRAL**
The New Vaudeville Band
Stevens, Fontana 1562
(Southern, ASCAP)

4. **GOOD VIBRATIONS**
The Beach Boys
B. Wilson–M. Love, Capitol 5676
(Sea of Tunes, BMI)

5. **THAT'S LIFE**
F. Sinatra
Thompson, Reprise 0531
(Four Star Television, ASCAP)

6. **YOU KEEP ME HANGIN' ON**
The Supremes
Holland–Dozier–Holland,
Motown 1101 (Jobete, BMI)

7. **BORN FREE**
R. Williams
Barry, Kapp 767
(Screen Gems–Columbia, BMI)

8. **SUGAR TOWN**
N. Sinatra
L. Hazelwood, Reprise 0537
(Criterion, ASCAP)

9. **A PLACE IN THE SUN**
S. Wonder
Miller–Wells, Tamla 54139
(Stein–Vamstock, ASCAP)

10. **TELL IT LIKE IT IS**
A. Neville
Davis–Diamond, Parlo 101
(Olrap, BMI)

December 24

1. **I'M A BELIEVER**
The Monkees
N. Diamond, Colgems 1003
(Screen Gems–Columbia, BMI)

2. **THAT'S LIFE**
F. Sinatra
Thompson, Reprise 0531
(Four Star Television, ASCAP)

3. **WINCHESTER CATHEDRAL**
The New Vaudeville Band
Stevens, Fontana 1562
(Southern, ASCAP)

4. **MELLOW YELLOW**
Donovan
D. Leitch, Epic 10098
(Donovan Ltd., BMI)

5. **SUGAR TOWN**
N. Sinatra
L. Hazelwood, Reprise 0537
(Criterion, ASCAP)

6. **GOOD VIBRATIONS**
The Beach Boys
B.Wilson–M. Love,
Capitol 5676
(Sea of Tunes, BMI)

7. **TELL IT LIKE IT IS**
A. Neville
G. Davis–L. Diamond,
Parlo 101 (Olrap, BMI)

8. **A PLACE IN THE SUN**
S. Wonder
Miller–Wells, Tamla 54139
(Stein–Vamstock, ASCAP)

9. **(I KNOW) I'M LOSING YOU**
The Temptations
Grant–Whitfield–Holland,
Gordy 7057 (Jobete, BMI)

10. **GOOD THING**
P. Revere and the Raiders
T. Melcher–M. Lindsay–P. Revere,
Columbia 43907 (Daywin, BMI)

December 31

1. **I'M A BELIEVER**
The Monkees
N. Diamond, Colgems 1003
(Screen Gems–Columbia, BMI)

2. **THAT'S LIFE**
F. Sinatra
Thompson, Reprise 0531
(Four Star Television, ASCAP)

3. **MELLOW YELLOW**
Donovan
D. Leitch, Epic 10098
(Donovan Ltd., BMI)

4. **WINCHESTER CATHEDRAL**
The New Vaudeville Band
Stevens, Fontana 1562
(Southern, ASCAP)

5. **SNOOPY VS. THE RED BARON**
The Royal Guardsmen
The Royal Guardsmen,
Laurie 3366 (Windsong, BMI)

6. **SUGAR TOWN**
N. Sinatra
L. Hazelwood, Reprise 0537
(Criterion, ASCAP)

7. **TELL IT LIKE IT IS**
A. Neville
G. Davis–L. Diamond,
Parlo 101 (Olrap, BMI)

8. **GOOD THING**
P. Revere and the Raiders
T. Melcher–M. Lindsay–
P. Revere,
Columbia 43907 (Daywin, BMI)

9. **A PLACE IN THE SUN**
S. Wonder
Miller–Wells, Tamla 54139
(Stein–Vamstock, ASCAP)

10. **(I KNOW) I'M LOSING YOU**
The Temptations
Grant–Whitfield–Holland
Gordy 7057 (Jobete, BMI)

THE DOORS

We should have seen it coming when "Revolver" was released, but we were too excited by the praise we were getting from fans of other kinds of music. We should have known that our music couldn't expand and absorb the influences of so many other styles of music without giving up its essence. We should have realized that the end comes to every art form when its creators dwell on their expertise. And we should have predicted how fast the end would come in this time of instant communication.

But we saw nothing. With all our introspection, our analysis, our thinking about meaning we had lost perspective on ourselves and our music. We were thinking and analyzing so much that we were losing our ability to experience. All through the years, rock and roll had been something we felt, something that got into our bodies and made us happy. We never knew why. We never asked. It was just happy, hummable magic.

And when it began to deepen musically, it began to attract a thinking audience. We began to join them in thinking analytically about rock and roll. As new recordings came out we studied them quietly, picking apart the lyrics and concentrating on bits of musicianship. Music was becoming an intellectual experience. Serious reviews were being written and serious listeners were being cultivated. "Mindless" lyrics were frowned upon and simple romantic lyrics were considered mindless.

Dancing was becoming passé. Beats were complex and subtle. In the old days, that would have been reason enough to reject a song. But now the focus was on listening. The real students of rock and roll bought only albums. Only teenyboppers or other nonthinkers perferred a stack of 45's. Because of this, the Top 40 stations began to lose touch with the new rock and roll intelligentsia. And in that new distance, rock and roll became a dead-end style of music.

1967

She (We never thought of ourselves)
is leaving (never a thought for ourselves)
Home (We struggled hard all our lives to get by)
She's leaving home after living alone
For so many years. Bye bye

"She's Leaving Home"
The Beatles, Sgt. Pepper's
Lonely Hearts Club Band

Top 40 had once been the very soul of rock and roll, but now it was beginning to lose direction. The artists that had carried rock and roll into its golden years—the Beatles, Mamas and Papas, Lovin' Spoonful, Rolling Stones, Supremes—were still turning out glorious, soaring music in 1967. And their records were still selling as singles. But their important recordings were usually albums now.

Still, it was not these groups that broadened the gap between the Top 40 and the vanguard rock and roll. But, sadly, these performers were fast becoming a part of a bygone musical era.

Soul music, too, kept its Top 40 appeal. Sam and Dave, Aretha Franklin, Brenton Wood and the regulars from Motown were a joy to listen to, to dance to. But throughout the Beatle years, white groups had edged a lot of soul out of the Top 40's so that most experimentation in soul was heard only on black radio stations. And, as for the new wave of black artists for white audiences—Jimmie Hendrix, the Chambers Brothers—their "soul was pschedelicized."

With little soul and little experimental rock and roll in the charts, the bubble gum sound was becoming the heir to the Top 40 crown. The Monkees, Tommy James, the Buckinghams, the Royal Guardsmen turned out listenable but pat versions of 1965 style rock and roll. The music they imitated had been fresh and exciting, but this music was usually lacking complexity and originality since its purpose was commercial instead of artistic. This packaged bubble gum music was pleasant enough to listen to and so it crept unnoticed into the Top 40 as thousands of twelve-year-olds ate it up. Since these little teenyboppers had taken over the 45 market, they became the ones who determined the top single hits of the day.

Those of us old enough to have weathered payola were not going to be duped into buying manufactured groups like the Monkees and Every Mother's Son. And so we turned to our FM stations and to the underground to hear something more stimulating. Until now, the more complex rock and roll grew, the more it became tantalizing. Naturally we assumed it would grow more and more intricate and more and more interesting. We were wrong. Rock and roll had reached the heights of technical excellence during the last two years. At the same time it had maintained its youthful vitality. But in 1967 the value placed on technical advance was so great that new groups were making it for technique instead of for happy listening.

If this was the general trend in rock and roll, then the Beatles were the specific force that was pulling it along. "Sergeant Pepper" was their big album of the year, and it was the most complicated album conceivable. It took four to six sessions a week for three months to record, and it was acclaimed everywhere by critics and fans of all kinds of music. It was very flattering, and it made us even surer that our music was skyrocketing into a more golden age. We didn't question the new trend in music. We listened to critics and musicians and bought the Cream and the lesser practitioners of the coming style. If we missed the fun of the old days, we felt the compensation in the intellectual merits of this music. And there was still enough good-time rock and roll around to cover the lack in the experimental style. As long as we bought Aretha Franklin, the Lovin' Spoonful *et al.,* we didn't realize that the fun was fading fast.

Rock and roll was splintering apart. It had been able to hold together when it first expanded into folk, big band, country, jazz and Indian. But now it was beginning to lose its own identity. The friendly, bright sound that had been basic to all rock and roll was only being used by the bubble

314

gum contingent. Fun was dropped completely out of the new music of the mind. It was work to play, and work to appreciate. And because of the death of that joyous, carefree spirit, the new music was no longer rock and roll.

It was the West Coast that reared up and pulled the new, deep-thinking audience completely out of the rock and roll spectrum. This time it wasn't the breezy, good-time Beach Boys of Southern California, but rather a new element with a new philosophy that had sprung from the old beatnik movement in San Francisco. This scruffy group may have been filtering out of the mainstream over the last decade, but it wasn't until 1967 that the move out of the mainstream began to have broad appeal.

In the last year or two we had seriously begun to challenge our elders' values. Their willingness to support the Vietnam war and their unwillingness to support the oppressed blacks made it hard for us to have faith in the things they held sacred. And then the sirens called from San Francisco, telling us to drop out, to stop fighting with them, to love each other and flowers and nature, and to reject the cynicism and cruelty that was eating us alive.

It sounded wonderful. Flowers, sunshine, innocence—and if recapturing childhood was too hard, there were wondrous potions to make it easy.

We had heard a lot about these drugs for about a year, and now they were becoming available all across the country. Many of us had taken Dex or diet pills to keep us awake for exams, but we never thought about that as part of the new drug scene. Now we took them to set us free. Mostly it was grass or hash and some LSD. A few prople tried other stuff but they were really on the fringe.

The local gurus told us the drugs made our minds relax, release and take in sensations we were never before capable of. And we wanted so desparately to feel new sensations. We tried meditation and sex and talking endlessly so that we could feel each other. We wanted somehow to feel joined together, and so we tried communal living and sharing everything and rejecting material wealth and material differences.

We heard often now that half the population was twenty five or under, but the fact seemed to be used more in marketing soft drinks than in dealing with protest. Berkeley had sizzled up just as 1966 was ending, and it would be a preview of things to come. But for a brief period during 1967, protest cooled and we heeded Timothy Leary and dropped out. Body paint and flower power were in Johnny Carson's monologue every night, and soon the new hippie cult was suffering from overexposure.

It was sad to see the mainstream veer west for a glimpse of Haight Ashbury. It showed how impossible it was to escape the jaded values of modern America. The area became a tourist trap, full of love-bead peddlers and bookstores that sold art nouveau posters of the Hobbit trilogy. And along with the tourists, it was invaded by sad young runaways and experienced drug users and dealers. The dreams of Gandhi, Christ and Buddha just didn't seem to stand up in the face of greed and commercialism.

The Romney–Nixon, Reagan–Rockefeller race, the purchase of Las Vegas by Howard Hughes, the death of Jayne Mansfield, the Percy–Rockefeller wedding—that was the real America. And soon we saw that flower children were as much an impossibility as a high from bananas.

There was an even greater loneliness in the under-twenty five generation when we realized our dream of peace couldn't work outside the society.

The drugs and hippie clothes were about the only things that lived on after Haight Ashbury. They were to form the basis of a new brotherhood of the young. The music, too, which had blared at the Fillmore would survive. But this was because it could grow hand in hand with commercialism despite the unselfish tone of its lyrics. In a way, those lyrics were a wailing attempt to break through the isolation we all felt. The music became more and more a telegraph of drug experiences, an outcry of disillusionment with our parents' lives, a confusion of self-analysis, self-pity and self-indulgence.

The masters of the new music were caught as tightly in the agony of the times as we were. The Beatles, the Cream, the Who, the Mothers—they had mastered the music and now they used their skills to distort, to amplify, to mock the pain and the understanding that our generation was trying to deal with.

It took a lot of skill to play this expanded new music, and few performers were musicians enough to succeed. Soon there would be batches of imitators, anxious to become rich and famous, but unable to sustain the demands of technique without giving up the spirit. Music now became an exercise in technical excellence, and when it wasn't too excellent, it leaned on over-amplification for some special personality.

The noise level itself became the emotion in the music. Perhaps this, most of all, was the thing that made the new music different from rock and roll. If rock and roll was anything, it was emotion. It was dancing and touching and, like laughter and tears, it defied intellectualization. We were captured by the bodies and eyes and smiles of the performers. And now, instead of the easy friendliness of rock and roll, we had music that kept *telling* us to touch each other, to feel, to love. But we didn't feel what the lyrics told us although we

wished we could. The flashing lights and over-amplification had a dazing effect on us in the audience. Bathed in colored light the performers' faces became a blur. The intensity of the sound put us into a sort of trance—which was really an isolating experience.

We told ourselves that we were feeling, that we were getting back to the essentials. But, like Haight Ashbury, it was all a dream.

We were not kids anymore. We were aware of the ugliness in the world and the frustration of trying to change it. We knew now that we couldn't escape by dropping out and that there was no way to regain the innocence of rock and roll. As an art it had run its course. And as an expression of our social history it was no longer representative. Some rock and roll would still be created, just as symphonies, Broadway tunes, and jazz would be written after their eras of dominance were over.

And a new generation of listeners would emerge in the next few years. Like the high school kids in 1955, we were suddenly caught between musical styles. Our taste had developed during rock and roll days, and the new rock was something we had to learn when rock and roll died. Like the new rock music, the new generation would dwell on self-analysis and would claw for the sheer joy that had been ours so easily when rock and roll was alive.

The joy of innocence and youth was over now. Simple, apolitical childhood would never be recaptured and neither would its theme—rock and roll. We were adults now, and the world we were inheriting was wracked by riot, war and human isolation. We knew we had to push ahead, and we followed Eugene McCarthy, Bobby Kennedy, Martin Luther King and Eldridge Cleaver into the great unknown of 1968. In a few years the rock and roll nostalgia would surface, but now, at least, was no time to look back.

The Top Fifty
1967

1.	GROOVIN'	The Young Rascals
2.	ODE TO BILLIE JOE	B. Gentry
3.	THE LETTER	The Box Tops
4.	LIGHT MY FIRE	The Doors
5.	I'M A BELIEVER	The Monkees
6.	WINDY	The Association
7.	RESPECT	A. Franklin
8.	TO SIR WITH LOVE	Lulu
9.	I THINK WE'RE ALONE NOW	T. James and the Shondells
10.	APPLES, PEACHES, PUMPKIN PIE	Jay and the Techniques
11.	GEORGY GIRL	The Seekers
12.	CAN'T TAKE MY EYES OFF YOU	F. Valli
13.	SOMETHIN' STUPID	N. Sinatra and F. Sinatra
14.	HAPPY TOGETHER	The Turtles
15.	EXPRESSWAY TO YOUR HEART	The Soul Survivors
16.	INCENSE AND PEPPERMINTS	The Strawberry Alarm Clock
17.	RUBY TUESDAY	The Rolling Stones
18.	GIMME LITTLE SIGN	B. Wood
19.	ALL YOU NEED IS LOVE	The Beatles
20.	KIND OF A DRAG	The Buckinghams
21.	LITTLE BIT O' SOUL	The Music Explosion
22.	SOUL MAN	Sam and Dave
23.	NEVER MY LOVE	The Association
24.	COME ON DOWN TO MY BOAT	Every Mother's Son
25.	LOVE IS HERE AND NOW YOU'RE GONE	The Supremes
26.	RELEASE ME (AND LET ME LOVE AGAIN)	E. Humperdink
27.	BROWN-EYED GIRL	V. Morrison
28.	GET ON UP	The Esquires
29.	THEN YOU CAN TELL ME GOODBYE	The Casinos
30.	COME BACK WHEN YOU GROW UP	B. Vee
31.	THE HAPPENING	The Supremes
32.	I WAS MADE TO LOVE HER	S. Wonder
33.	IT MUST BE HIM	V. Carr
34.	FOR WHAT IT'S WORTH	Buffalo Springfield
35.	SWEET SOUL MUSIC	A. Conley
36.	UP—UP AND AWAY	The Fifth Dimension
37.	I GOT RHYTHM	The Happenings
38.	YOU PRECIOUS LOVE	M. Gaye and T. Terrell
39.	ALFIE	D. Warwick
40.	THERE'S A KIND OF HUSH	Herman's Hermits
41.	I'VE BEEN LONELY TOO LONG	The Young Rascals
42.	PENNY LANE	The Beatles
43.	DON'T YOU CARE?	The Buckinghams
44.	JIMMY MACK	Martha and the Vandellas
45.	SOMEBODY TO LOVE	The Jefferson Airplane
46.	98.6	Keith
47.	YOU'RE MY EVERYTHING	The Temptations
48.	BERNADETTE	The Four Tops
49.	LET'S LIVE FOR TODAY	The Grass Roots
50.	FRIDAY ON MY MIND	The Easybeats

318

1967

January 21

1. **GOOD THING**
P. Revere and the Raiders
T. Melcher–M. Lindsay–P. Revere
Columbia 43907 (Daywin, BMI)

2. **TELL IT LIKE IT IS**
A. Neville
G. Davis–L. Diamond Parlo 101
(Olrap, BMI)

3. **SNOOPY VS. THE RED BARON**
The Royal Guardsmen
The Royal Guardsmen,
Laurie 3366 (Windsong, BMI)

4. **STANDING IN THE SHADOWS OF LOVE**
The Four Tops
Holland–Dozier–Holland,
Motown 1102 (Jobete, BMI)

5. **GEORGY GIRL**
The Seekers
Dale–Springfield, Capitol
5756 (Chappell, ASCAP)

6. **WORDS OF LOVE**
The Mamas and Papas
J. Phillips, Dunhill 4037
(Trousdale, BMI)

7. **THAT'S LIFE**
F. Sinatra
Thompson, Reprise 0531
(Four Star Television, ASCAP)

8. **NASHVILLE CATS**
Lovin' Spoonful
J. Sebastian, Kama Sutra 219
(Faithful Virtue, BMI)

9. **TELL IT TO THE RAIN**
The Four Seasons
Petrillo–Cifelli, Philips 40412
(Saturday–Seasons Four, BMI)

10. **KIND OF DRAG**
The Buckinghams
Harris, USA 860
(Maryon, ASCAP)

January 28

1. **GOOD THING**
P. Revere and the Raiders
T. Melcher–M. Lindsay–P. Revere,
Columbia 43907 (Daywin, BMI)

2. **GEORGY GIRL**
The Seekers
Dale–Springfield, Capitol
5756 (Chappell, ASCAP)

3. **TELL IT LIKE IT IS**
A. Neville
G. Davis–L. Diamond, Parlo 101
(Olrap, BMI)

4. **WORDS OF LOVE**
The Mamas and Papas
J. Phillips, Dunhill 4037
(Trousdale, BMI)

5. **SNOOPY VS. THE RED BARON**
The Royal Guardsmen
The Royal Guardsmen,
Laurie 3366 (Windsong, BMI)

6. **STANDING IN THE SHADOWS OF LOVE**
The Four Tops
Holland–Dozier–Holland,
Motown 1102 (Jobete, BMI)

7. **NASHVILLE CATS**
Lovin' Spoonful
J. Sebastian, Kama Sutra 219
(Faithful Virtue, BMI)

8. **TELL IT TO THE RAIN**
The Four Seasons
Petrillo–Cifelli, Philips 40412
(Saturday–Seasons Four, BMI)

9. **KIND OF A DRAG**
The Buckinghams
Harris, USA 860
(Maryon, ASCAP)

10. **98.6**
Keith
Powers–Fischoff, Mercury
72639 (Screen Gems–Columbia,
BMI)

February 4

1. **GEORGY GIRL**
The Seekers
Dale–Springfield, Capitol
5756 (Chappell, ASCAP)

2. **WORDS OF LOVE**
The Mamas and Papas
J. Phillips, Dunhill 4037
(Trousdale, BMI)

3. **TELL IT TO THE RAIN**
The Four Seasons
Petrillo–Cifelli, Philips
40412 (Saturday–Seasons Four,
BMI)

4. **KIND OF A DRAG**
The Buckinghams
Harris, USA 860
(Maryon, ASCAP)

5. **GOOD THING**
P. Revere and the Raiders
T. Melcher–M. Lindsay–P. Revere,
Columbia 43097 (Daywin, BMI)

6. **98.6**
Keith
Powers–Fischoff, Mercury
72639 (Screen Gems–Columbia,
BMI)

7. **NASHVILLE CATS**
Lovin' Spoonful
J. Sebastian, Kama Sutra 219
(Faithful Virtue, BMI)

8. **SNOOPY VS. THE RED BARON**
The Royal Guardsmen
The Royal Guardsmen, Laurie
3366 (Windsong, BMI)

9. **GIMME SOME LOVING**
Spencer Davis Group
S. Winwood–M. Winwood–S. Davis,
United Artists 50108
(Essex, ASCAP)

10. **THE BEAT GOES ON**
Sonny and Cher
S. Bono, Atco 6461
(Marc-Cotillion, BMI)

319

February 11

1. **KIND OF A DRAG**
   The Buckinghams
   Harris, USA 860
   (Maryon, ASCAP)

2. **RUBY TUESDAY**
   The Rolling Stones
   M. Jagger–K. Richard, London
   904 (Gideon, BMI)

3. **GEORGY GIRL**
   The Seekers
   Dale–Springfield, Capitol 5756
   (Chappell, ASCAP)

4. **TELL IT TO THE RAIN**
   The Four Seasons
   Petrillo–Cifelli, Philips 40412
   (Saturday–Seasons Four, BMI)

5. **98.6**
   Keith
   Powers–Fischoff, Mercury 72639
   (Screen Gems–Columbia, BMI)

6. **LOVE IS HERE AND NOW YOU'RE GONE**
   The Supremes
   Holland–Dozier–Holland,
   Motown 1103 (Jobete, BMI)

7. **WORDS OF LOVE**
   The Mamas and Papas
   J. Phillips, Dunhill 4037
   (Trousdale, BMI)

8. **THE BEAT GOES ON**
   Sonny and Cher
   S. Bono, Atco 6461
   (Marc–Cotillions, BMI)

9. **GIMME SOME LOVING**
   Spencer Davis Group
   S. Winwood–M. Winwood–S. Davis
   United Artists 50108
   (Essex, ASCAP)

10. **STAND BY ME**
    S. Turner
    King–J. Leiber–M. Stoller, M-G-M
    13617 (Progressive–Trio–ABT–
    Tet, BMI)

320

February 18

1. **KIND OF A DRAG**
   The Buckinghams
   Harris, USA 860
   (Maryon, ASCAP)

2. **RUBY TUESDAY**
   The Rolling Stones
   M. Jagger–K. Richard
   London 904 (Gideon, BMI)

3. **LOVE IS HERE AND NOW YOU'RE GONE**
   The Supremes
   Holland–Dozier–Holland,
   Motown 1103 (Jobete, BMI)

4. **98.6**
   Keith
   Powers–Fischoff, Mercury
   72639 (Screen Gems–
   Columbia, BMI)

5. **GEORGY GIRL**
   The Seekers
   Dale–Springfield, Capitol
   5657 (Chappell, ASCAP)

6. **TELL IT TO THE RAIN**
   The Four Seasons
   Petrillo–Cifelli, Philips 40412
   (Saturday–Seasons Four, BMI)

7. **THE BEAT GOES ON**
   Sonny and Cher
   S. Bono, Atco 6461
   (Marc–Cotillion, BMI)

8. **THEN YOU CAN TELL ME GOODBYE**
   The Casinos
   J. Loudermilk, Fraternity 977
   (Acuff–Rose, BMI)

9. **GIMME SOME LOVING**
   Spencer Davis Group
   S. Winwood–M. Winwood–S. Davis,
   United Artists 50108
   (Essex, ASCAP)

10. **STAND BY ME**
    S. Turner
    King–J. Leiber–M. Stoller, M-G-M
    13617 (Progressive–Trio–ABT–
    Tet, BMI)

February 25

1. **RUBY TUESDAY**
   The Rolling Stones
   M. Jagger–K. Richard,
   London 904 (Gideon, BMI)

2. **LOVE IS HERE AND NOW YOU'RE GONE**
   The Supremes
   Holland–Dozier–Holland,
   Motown 1103 (Jobete, BMI)

3. **KIND OF A DRAG**
   The Buckinghams
   Harris, USA 860
   (Maryon, ASCAP)

4. **THE BEAT GOES ON**
   Sonny and Cher
   S. Bono, Atco 6461
   (Marc–Cotillion, BMI)

5. **98.6**
   Keith
   Powers–Fischoff, Mercury 72639
   (Screen Gems–Columbia, BMI)

6. **THEN YOU CAN TELL ME GOODBYE**
   The Casinos
   J. Loudermilk, Fraternity 977
   (Acuff–Rose, BMI)

7. **BABY, I NEED YOUR LOVIN'**
   J. Rivers
   Holland–Dozier–Holland,
   Imperial 66227 (Jobete, BMI)

8. **GIMME SOME LOVING**
   Spencer Davis Group
   S. Winwood–M. Winwood–
   S. Davis, UA 50108
   (Essex, ASCAP)

9. **GEORGY GIRL**
   The Seekers
   Dale–Springfield, Capitol 5756
   (Chappell, ASCAP)

10. **TELL IT TO THE RAIN**
    The Four Seasons
    Petrillo–Cifelli, Philips
    40412 (Saturday–Seasons Four,
    BMI)

1967

March 4

1. **LOVE IS HERE AND NOW YOU'RE GONE**
   The Supremes
   *Holland–Dozier–Holland,
   Motown 1103 (Jobete, BMI)*

2. **RUBY TUESDAY**
   The Rolling Stones
   *M. Jagger–K. Richard
   London 904 (Gideon, BMI)*

3. **BABY, I NEED YOUR LOVIN'**
   J. Rivers
   *Holland–Dozier–Holland,
   Imperial 66227 (Jobete, BMI)*

4. **THEN YOU CAN TELL ME GOODBYE**
   The Casinos
   *J. Loudermilk, Fraternity 977
   (Acuff–Rose, BMI)*

5. **KIND OF A DRAG**
   The Buckinghams
   *Harris, USA 860
   (Maryon, ASCAP)*

6. **PENNY LANE**
   The Beatles
   *J. Lennon–P. McCartney,
   Capitol 5810 (Maclen, BMI)*

7. **THE BEAT GOES ON**
   Sonny and Cher
   *S. Bono, Atco 6461
   (Marc–Cotillion, BMI)*

8. **I HAD TOO MUCH TO DREAM (LAST NIGHT)**
   The Electric Prunes
   *Mantz–Tucker, Reprise 0532
   (Four Star Sales, BMI)*

9. **SOCK IT TO ME**
   M. Ryder and the Detroit Wheels
   *B. Crewe–Brown,
   New Voice 820
   (Saturday, BMI)*

10. **PRETTY BALLERINA**
    The Left Banke
    *Brown, Smash 2074
    (Twin Tone, BMI)*

March 11

1. **PENNY LANE**
   The Beatles
   *J. Lennon–P. McCartney,
   Capitol 5810
   (Maclen, BMI)*

2. **LOVE IS HERE AND NOW YOU'RE GONE**
   The Supremes
   *Holland–Dozier–Holland
   Motown 1103 (Jobete, BMI)*

3. **BABY, I NEED YOUR LOVIN'**
   J. Rivers
   *Holland–Dozier–Holland,
   Imperial 66227 (Jobete, BMI)*

4. **RUBY TUESDAY**
   The Rolling Stones
   *M. Jagger–K. Richard,
   London 904 (Gideon, BMI)*

5. **THEN YOU CAN TELL ME GOODBYE**
   The Casinos
   *J. Loudermilk, Fraternity 977
   (Acuff–Rose, BMI)*

6. **HAPPY TOGETHER**
   The Turtles
   *Bonner–Gordon, White Whale
   244 (Chardon, BMI)*

7. **SOCK IT TO ME**
   M. Ryder and the Detroit Wheels
   *B. Crewe–Brown,
   New Voice 820
   (Saturday, BMI)*

8. **I HAD TO MUCH TO DREAM (LAST NIGHT)**
   The Electric Prunes
   *Mantz–Tucker, Reprise 0532
   (Four Star Sales, BMI)*

9. **PRETTY BALLERINA**
   The Left Banke
   *Brown, Smash 2074
   (Twin Tone, BMI)*

10. **DEDICATED TO THE ONE I LOVE**
    The Mamas and Papas
    *Pauling–Bass–Roff, Dunhill
    4077 (Trousdale, BMI)*

March 18

1. **PENNY LANE**
   The Beatles
   *J. Lennon–P. McCartney,
   Capitol 5810 (Maclen, BMI)*

2. **BABY, I NEED YOUR LOVIN'**
   J. Rivers
   *Holland–Dozier–Holland,
   Imperial 66227 (Jobete, BMI)*

3. **HAPPY TOGETHER**
   The Turtles
   *Bonner–Gordon, White Whale
   244 (Chardon, BMI)*

4. **LOVE IS HERE AND NOW YOU'RE GONE**
   The Supremes
   *Holland–Dozier–Holland,
   Motown 1103 (Jobete, BMI)*

5. **RUBY TUESDAY**
   The Rolling Stones
   *M. Jagger–K. Richard,
   London 904 (Gideon, BMI)*

6. **SOCK IT TO ME**
   M. Ryder and the Detroit Wheels
   *B. Crewe–Brown, New Voice 820
   (Saturday, BMI)*

7. **DEDICATED TO THE ONE I LOVE**
   The Mamas and Papas
   *Pauling–Bass–Roff, Dunhill
   4077 (Trousdale, BMI)*

8. **MY CUP RUNNETH OVER**
   E. Ames
   *Morgan, Victor 9002
   (Chappell, ASCAP)*

9. **THEN YOU CAN TELL ME GOODBYE**
   The Casinos
   *J. Loudermilk, Fraternity 977
   (Acuff–Rose, BMI)*

10. **THERE'S A KIND OF A HUSH**
    Herman's Hermits
    *Reed–Stephens, M-G-M 13681
    (F.D.M., ASCAP)*

321

March 25

1. **HAPPY TOGETHER**
The Turtles
Bonner–Gordon, White Whale 244 (Chardon, BMI)

2. **PENNY LANE**
The Beatles
J. Lennon–P. McCartney, Capitol 5810 (Maclen, BMI)

3. **BABY, I NEED YOUR LOVIN'**
J. Rivers
Holland–Dozier–Holland, Imperial 66227 (Jobete, BMI)

4. **DEDICATED TO THE ONE I LOVE**
The Mamas and Papas
Pauling–Bass–Roff, Dunhill 4077 (Trousdale, BMI)

5. **FOR WHAT IT'S WORTH**
Buffalo Springfield
Stills, Atco 6459 (Ten East–Springdale, BMI)

6. **SOCK IT TO ME**
M. Ryder and the Detroit Wheels
B. Crewe–Brown, New Voice 820 (Saturday, BMI)

7. **MY CUP RUNNETH OVER**
E. Ames
Morgan, Victor 9002 (Chappell, ASCAP)

8. **RUBY TUESDAY**
The Rolling Stones
M. Jagger–K. Richard, London 904 (Gideon, BMI)

9. **LOVE IS HERE AND NOW YOU'RE GONE**
The Supremes
Holland–Dozier–Holland, Motown 1103 (Jobete, BMI)

10. **THERE'S A KIND OF A HUSH**
Herman's Hermits
Reed–Stephens, M-G-M 13681 (F.D.M., ASCAP)

April 1

1. **DEDICATED TO THE ONE I LOVE**
The Mamas and Papas
Pauling–Bass–Roff, Dunhill 4077 (Trousdale, BMI)

2. **HAPPY TOGETHER**
The Turtles
Bonner–Gordon, White Whale 244 (Chardon, BMI)

3. **THERE'S A KIND OF A HUSH**
Herman's Hermits
Reed–Stephens, M-G-M 13681 (F.D.M., ASCAP)

4. **BERNADETTE**
The Four Tops
Holland–Dozier–Holland, Motown 1104 (Jobete, BMI)

5. **FOR WHAT IT'S WORTH**
Buffalo Springfield
Stills, Atco 6459 (Ten East–Springdale, BMI)

6. **PENNY LANE**
The Beatles
J. Lennon–P. McCartney, Capitol 5810 (Maclen, BMI)

7. **THIS IS MY SONG**
P. Clark
C. Chaplin, Warner Brothers 7002 (Shawley, ASCAP)

8. **SOMETHIN' STUPID**
N. Sinatra and F. Sinatra
Parks, Reprise 0561 (Green Wood, BMI)

9. **WESTERN UNION**
The Five Americans
Rabon–Ezell–Durrill, Abnak 118 (Jetstar, BMI)

10. **I THINK WE'RE ALONE NOW**
T. James and the Shondells
R. Cordell, Roulette 4720 (Patricia, BMI)

April 8

1. **BERNADETTE**
The Four Tops
Holland–Dozier–Holland, Motown 1104 (Jobete, BMI)

2. **DEDICATED TO THE ONE I LOVE**
The Mamas and Papas
Pauling–Bass–Roff, Dunhill 4077 (Trousdale, BMI)

3. **HAPPY TOGETHER**
The Turtles
Bonner–Gordon, White Whale 244 (Chardon, BMI)

4. **SOMETHIN' STUPID**
N. Sinatra and F. Sinatra
Parks, Reprise 0561 (Green Wood, BMI)

5. **THIS IS MY SONG**
P. Clark
C. Chaplin, Warner Brothers 7002 (Shawley, ASCAP)

6. **I THINK WE'RE ALONE NOW**
T. James and the Shondells
R. Cordell, Roulette 4720 (Patricia, BMI)

7. **A LITTLE BIT YOU, A LITTLE BIT ME**
The Monkees
N. Diamond, Colgems 1004 (Screen Gems–Columbia, BMI)

8. **WESTERN UNION**
The Five Americans
Rabon–Ezell–Durrill, Abnak 118 (Jetstar, BMI)

9. **CALIFORNIA NIGHTS**
L. Gore
Liebling–Hamlisch, Mercury 72649 (Genius–Enchanted, ASCAP)

10. **STRAWBERRY FIELDS FOREVER**
The Beatles
J. Lennon–P. McCartney, Capitol 5810 (Maclen, BMI)

April 15

1. **BERNADETTE**
The Four Tops
*Holland–Dozier–Holland,
Motown 1104 (Jobete, BMI)*

2. **SOMETHIN' STUPID**
N. Sinatra and F. Sinatra
*Parks, Reprise 0561
(Green Wood, BMI)*

3. **THIS IS MY SONG**
P. Clark
*C. Chaplin, Warner Brothers
7002 (Shawley, ASCAP)*

4. **A LITTLE BIT YOU, A
LITTLE BIT ME**
The Monkees
*N. Diamond, Colgems 1004
(Screen Gems–Columbia, BMI)*

5. **I THINK WE'RE ALONE
NOW**
T. James and the
Shondells
*R. Cordell, Roulette 4720
(Patricia, BMI)*

6. **DEDICATED TO THE ONE I
LOVE**
The Mamas and Papas
*Pauling–Bass–Roff, Dunhill
4077 (Trousdale, BMI)*

7. **HAPPY TOGETHER**
The Turtles
*Bonner–Gordon, White Whale
244 (Chardon, BMI)*

8. **WESTERN UNION**
The Five Americans
*Rabon–Ezell–Durrill, Abnak
118 (Jetstar, BMI)*

9. **CALIFORNIA NIGHTS**
L. Gore
*Liebling–Hamlisch,
Mercury 72649
(Genius–Enchanted, ASCAP)*

10. **JIMMY MACK**
Martha and the Vandellas
*Holland–Dozier–Holland, Gordy
7058 (Jobete, BMI)*

April 22

1. **A LITTLE BIT YOU, A
LITTLE BIT ME**
The Monkees
*Diamond, Colgems 1004
(Screen Gems–Columbia, BMI)*

2. **SOMETHIN' STUPID**
N. Sinatra and F. Sinatra
*Parks, Reprise 0561
(Green Wood, BMI)*

3. **THIS IS MY SONG**
P. Clark
*C. Chaplin, Warner Brothers
7002 (Shawley, ASCAP)*

4. **BERNADETTE**
The Four Tops
*Holland–Dozier–Holland,
Motown 1104 (Jobete, BMI)*

5. **I THINK WE'RE ALONE NOW**
T. James and the
Shondells
*R. Cordell, Roulette 4720
(Patricia, BMI)*

6. **DEDICATED TO THE ONE I
LOVE**
The Mamas and Papas
*Pauling–Bass–Roff, Dunhill
4077 (Trousdale, BMI)*

7. **THE HAPPENING**
The Supremes
*Holland–Dozier–Holland,
Motown 1107 (Jobete, BMI)*

8. **SWEET SOUL MUSIC**
A. Conley
*Conley–Redding, Atco 6463
(Bedwal, BMI)*

9. **I NEVER LOVED A MAN THE
WAY I LOVE YOU**
A. Franklin
*Shannon, Atlantic 2386
(14th Hour, BMI)*

10. **JIMMY MACK**
Martha and the Vandellas
*Holland–Dozier–Holland Gordy
7058 (Jobete, BMI)*

April 29

1. **A LITTLE BIT YOU, A
LITTLE BIT ME**
The Monkees
*Diamond, Colgems 1004
(Screen Gems–Columbia, BMI)*

2. **SOMETHIN' STUPID**
N. Sinatra and F. Sinatra
*Parks, Reprise 0561
(Green Wood, BMI)*

3. **THE HAPPENING**
The Supremes
*Holland–Dozier–Holland,
Motown 1107 (Jobete, BMI)*

4. **SWEET SOUL MUSIC**
A. Conley
*Conley–Redding Atco 6463
(Bedwal, BMI)*

5. **THIS IS MY SONG**
P. Clark
*C. Chaplin, Warner Brothers
7002 (Shawley, ASCAP)*

6. **I THINK WE'RE ALONE NOW**
T. James and the
Shondells
*R. Cordell, Roulette 4720
(Patricia, BMI)*

7. **DON'T YOU CARE?**
The Buckinghams
*G. Beisber, Columbia 44053
(Beechwood, BMI)*

8. **BERNADETTE**
The Four Tops
*Holland–Dozier–Holland,
Motown 1104 (Jobete, BMI)*

9. **CLOSE YOUR EYES**
Peaches and Herb
*C. Willis, Date 1549
(Tideland, BMI)*

10. **I'M A MAN**
Spencer Davis Group
*J. Miller–S. Winwood, United
Artists 50144 (Essex, ASCAP)*

May 6

1. **THE HAPPENING**
   The Supremes
   Holland–Dozier–Holland,
   Motown 1107   (Jobete, BMI)

2. **SOMETHIN' STUPID**
   N. Sinatra and F. Sinatra
   Parks,   Reprise 0561
   (Green Wood, BMI)

3. **SWEET SOUL MUSIC**
   A. Conley
   A. Conley–O. Redding,
   Atco 6463   (Bedwal, BMI)

4. **A LITTLE BIT YOU, A**
   LITTLE BIT ME
   The Monkees
   N. Diamond,   Colgems 1004
   (Screen Gems–Columbia, BMI)

5. **DON'T YOU CARE?**
   The Buckinghams
   G. Beisber,   Columbia 44053
   (Beechwood, BMI)

6. **THIS IS MY SONG**
   P. Clark
   C. Chaplin,   Warner Brothers
   7002   (Shawley, ASCAP)

7. **CLOSE YOUR EYES**
   Peaches and Herb
   C. Willis,   Date 1549
   (Tideland, BMI)

8. **YOU GOT WHAT IT TAKES**
   The Dave Clark Five
   B. Gordy–R. Davis,–G. Gordy,
   Epic 10144   (Arc, BMI)

9. **I'M A MAN**
   Spencer David Group
   J. Miller–S. Winwood,   United
   Artists 50144   (Essex, ASCAP)

10. **I THINK WE'RE ALONE NOW**
    T. James and the
    Shondells
    R. Cordell,   Roulette 4720
    (Patricia, BMI)

May 13

1. **THE HAPPENING**
   The Supremes
   Holland–Dozier–Holland
   Motown 1107   (Jobete, BMI)

2. **GROOVIN'**
   The Young Rascals
   F. Cavaliere–E. Brigati,   Atlantic
   2401   (Slacsar, BMI)

3. **SWEET SOUL MUSIC**
   A. Conley
   A. Conley-O. Redding,
   Atco 6463   (Bedwal, BMI)

4. **DON'T YOU CARE?**
   The Buckinghams
   G. Beisber,   Columbia 44053
   (Beechwood, BMI)

5. **SOMETHIN' STUPID**
   N. Sinatra and F. Sinatra
   Parks,   Reprise 0561
   (Green Wood, BMI)

6. **YOU GOT WHAT IT TAKES**
   The Dave Clark Five
   B. Gordy–R. Davis–G. Gordy,
   Epic 10144   (Arc, BMI)

7. **CLOSE YOUR EYES**
   Peaches and Herb
   C. Willis,   Date 1549
   (Tideland, BMI)

8. **A LITTLE BIT YOU,**
   A LITTLE BIT ME
   The Monkees
   N. Diamond,   Colgems 1004
   (Screen Gems–Columbia, BMI)

9. **THIS IS MY SONG**
   P. Clark
   C. Chaplin,   Warner Brothers
   7002   (Shawley, ASCAP)

10. **I GOT RHYTHM**
    The Happenings
    I. Gershwin–G. Gershwin,
    B.T. Puppy 527   (New World,
    ASCAP)

May 20

1. **GROOVIN'**
   The Young Rascals
   F. Cavaliere–E. Brigati,   Atlantic
   2401   (Slacsar, BMI)

2. **THE HAPPENING**
   The Supremes
   Holland–Dozier–Holland,
   Motown 1107   (Jobete, BMI)

3. **SWEET SOUL MUSIC**
   A. Conley
   A. Conley–O. Redding,
   Atco 6463   (Bedwal, BMI)

4. **RESPECT**
   A. Franklin
   O. Redding,   Atlantic 2403
   (East–Time–Walco, BMI)

5. **RELEASE ME (AND LET**
   ME LOVE AGAIN)
   E. Humperdink
   Miller–Stevenson,   Parrot
   400011   (Four Star Sale, BMI)

6. **SOMETHIN' STUPUD**
   N. Sinatra and F. Sinatra
   Parks,   Reprise 0561
   (Green Wood, BMI)

7. **I GOT RHYTHM**
   The Happenings
   I. Gershwin–G. Gershwin,
   B. T. Puppy 527
   (New World, ASCAP)

8. **DON'T YOU CARE?**
   The Buckinghams
   G. Beisber,   Columbia 44053
   (Beechwood, BMI)

9. **YOU GOT WHAT IT TAKES**
   The Dave Clark Five
   B. Gordy–R. Davis–G. Gordy,
   Epic 10144   (Arc, BMI)

10. **CLOSE YOUR EYES**
    Peaches and Herb
    C. Willis,   Date 1549
    (Tideland, BMI)

1967

May 27

1. **RESPECT**
A. Franklin
O. Redding,   Atlantic 2403
(East–Time–Walco, BMI)

2. **GROOVIN'**
The Young Rascals
F. Cavaliere–E. Brigati,   Atlantic 2401 (Slacsar, BMI)

3. **RELEASE ME (AND LET ME LOVE AGAIN)**
E. Humperdink
Miller–Stevenson,   Parrot 400011 (Four Star Sales, BMI)

4. **I GOT RHYTHM**
The Happenings
I. Gershwin–G. Gershwin, B. T. Puppy 527 (New World, ASCAP)

5. **CREEQUE ALLEY**
The Mamas and Papas
J. Phillips–M. Gilliam, Dunhill 4083   (Trousdale, BMI)

6. **HIM OR ME—WHAT'S IT GONNA BE?**
P. Revere and the Raiders
M. Lindsay–T. Melcher, Columbia 44904   (Daywin, BMI)

7. **THE HAPPENING**
The Supremes
Holland–Dozier–Holland, Motown 1107 (Jobete, BMI)

8. **SWEET SOUL MUSIC**
A. Conley
A. Conley–O. Redding, Atco 6463 (Bedwal, BMI)

9. **GIRL, YOU'LL BE A WOMAN SOON**
N. Diamond
N. Diamond, Bang 542 (Tallyrand, BMI)

10. **SOMETHIN' STUPID**
N. Sinatra and F. Sinatra
Parks, Reprise 0561 (Green Wood, BMI)

June 3

1. **RESPECT**
A. Franklin
O. Redding,   Atlantic 2403 (East–Time–Walco, BMI)

2. **GROOVIN'**
The Young Rascals
F. Cavaliere–E. Brigati, Atlantic 2401   (Slacsar, BMI)

3. **I GOT RHYTHM**
The Happenings
I. Gershwin–G. Gershwin, B. T. Puppy 527 (New World, ASCAP)

4. **RELEASE ME —AND LET ME LOVE AGAIN)**
E. Humperdink
Miller–Stevenson,   Parrot 400011 (Four Star Sales, BMI)

5. **HIM OR ME—WHAT'S IT GONNA BE?**
P. Revere and the Raiders
M. Lindsay–T. Melcher, Columbia 44904   (Daywin, BMI)

6. **CREEQUE ALLEY**
The Mamas and Papas
J. Phillips–M. Gilliam, Dunhill 4083 (Trousdale, BMI)

7. **SOMEBODY TO LOVE**
The Jefferson Airplane
D.Slick,   Victor 9140 (Copper Penny, BMI)

8. **ALL I NEED**
The Temptations
Holland–Wilson–Taylor, Gordy 7061 (Jobete, BMI)

9. **THE HAPPENING**
The Supremes
Holland–Dozier–Holland, Motown 1107 (Jobete, BMI)

10. **SWEET SOUL MUSIC**
A. Conley
A. Conley–O. Redding,   Atco 6463 (Bedwal, BMI)

June 10

1. **GROOVIN'**
The Young Rascals
F. Cavaliere–E. Brigati, Atlantic 2401   (Slacsar, BMI)

2. **RESPECT**
A. Franklin
O. Redding,   Atlantic 2403 (East–Time–Walco, BMI)

3. **HIM OR ME—WHAT'S IT GONNA BE?**
P. Revere and the Raiders
M. Lindsay–T. Melcher, Columbia 44904 (Daywin, BMI

4. **I GOT RHYTHM**
The Happenings
I. Gershwin–G. Gershwin, B. T. Puppy 527 (New World, ASCAP)

5. **RELEASE ME (AND LET ME LOVE AGAIN)**
E. Humperdink
Miller–Stevenson, Parrot 400011 (Four Star Sales, BMI)

6. **SHE'D RATHER BE WITH ME**
The Turtles
Bonner–Gordon,   White Whale 249 (Chardon, BMI)

7. **SOMEBODY TO LOVE**
The Jefferson Airplane
D. Slick, Victor 9140 (Copper Penny, BMI)

8. **ALL I NEED**
The Temptations
Holland–Wilson–Taylor, Gordy 7061 (Jobete, BMI)

9. **FRIDAY ON MY MIND**
The Easybeats
Vanda–Young United Artists 50106 (Unart, BMI)

10. **LITTLE BIT O' SOUL**
The Music Explosion
Carter–Lewis,   Laurie 3380 (Southern, ASCAP)

June 17

1. **GROOVIN'**
The Young Rascals
F. Cavaliere–E. Brigati
Atlantic 2401   (Slacsar, BMI)

2. **RESPECT**
A. Franklin
O. Redding,   Atlantic 2403
(East–Time–Walco, BMI)

3. **SOMEBODY TO LOVE**
The Jefferson Airplane
D. Slick,   Victor 9140
(Copper Penny, BMI)

4. **SHE'D RATHER BE WITH ME**
The Turtles
Bonner–Gordon,   White Whale 249
(Chardon, BMI)

5. **LITTLE BIT O' SOUL**
The Music Explosion
Carter–Lewis,   Laurie 3380
(Southern, ASCAP)

6. **ALL I NEED**
The Temptations
Holland–Wilson–Taylor,
Gordy 7061   (Jobete, BMI)

7. **WINDY**
The Association
Friedman   Warner Brothers 7041
(Irving, BMI)

8. **HERE COMES MY BABY**
The Tremeloes
C. Stevens,   Epic 10139
(Mainstay, BMI)

9. **MIRAGE**
T. James and the Shondells
R. Cordell,   Roulette 4736
(Patricia, BMI)

10. **FRIDAY ON MY MIND**
The Easybeats
Vanda–Young,
United Artists 50106   (Unart, BMI)

June 24

1. **RESPECT**
A. Franklin
O. Redding,   Atlantic 2403
(East–Time–Walco, BMI)

2. **WINDY**
The Association
Friedman,   Warner Brothers 7041
(Irving, BMI)

3. **GROOVIN'**
The Young Rascals
F. Cavaliere–E. Brigati,
Atlantic 2401   (Slacsar, BMI)

4. **CAN'T TAKE MY EYES OFF YOU**
F. Valli
B. Crewe–B. Gaudio,
Philips 40446
(Saturday–Seasons Four, BMI)

5. **SAN FRANCISCO (BE SURE TO WEAR SOME FLOWERS IN YOUR HAIR)**
S. McKenzie
J. Phillips,   Ode 103
(Trousdale, BMI)

6. **SOMEBODY TO LOVE**
The Jefferson Airplane
D. Slick,   Victor 9140
(Copper Penny, BMI)

7. **SUNDAY WILL NEVER BE THE SAME**
Spanky and Our Gang
J. Wisner,   Mercury 72679
(Pamco, BMI)

8. **HERE COMES MY BABY**
The Tremeloes
C. Stevens,   Epic 10139
(Mainstay, BMI)

9. **LET'S LIVE FOR TODAY**
The Grass Roots
Minno–Gelber,   Dunhill 4084
(James, BMI)

10. **SHE'D RATHER BE WITH ME**
The Turtles
Bonner–Gordon,   White Whale 249   (Chardon, BMI)

July 1

1. **CAN'T TAKE MY EYES OFF YOU**
F. Valli
B. Crewe–B. Gaudio,   Philips 40446
(Saturday–Seasons Four, BMI)

2. **WINDY**
The Association
Friedman,   Warner Brothers 7041
(Irving, BMI)

3. **GROOVIN'**
The Young Rascals
F. Cavaliere–E. Brigati,
Atlantic 2041   (Slacsar, BMI)

4. **RESPECT**
A. Franklin
O. Redding,   Atlantic 2403
(East–Time–Walco, BMI)

5. **SAN FRANCISCO (BE SURE TO WEAR SOME FLOWERS IN YOUR HAIR)**
S. McKenzie
J. Phillips,   Ode 103
(Trousdale, BMI)

6. **SUNDAY WILL NEVER BE THE SAME**
Spanky and Our Gang
J. Wisner,   Mercury 72679
(Pamco, BMI)

7. **LET'S LIVE FOR TODAY**
The Grass Roots
Minno–Gelber,   Dunhill 4084
(James, BMI)

8. **COME ON DOWN TO MY BOAT**
Every Mother's Son
Farrell–Goldstein,   M-G-M 13733
(Picturetone–Goldstein, BMI)

9. **HERE COMES MY BABY**
The Tremeloes
C. Stevens,   Epic 10139
(Mainstay, BMI)

10. **DON'T SLEEP IN THE SUBWAY**
P. Clark
T. Hatch–Trent,   Warner Brothers 7049   (Duchess, BMI)

1967

July 8

1. **WINDY**
The Association
Friedman, Warner Brothers 7041
(Irving, BMI)

2. **CAN'T TAKE MY EYES OFF YOU**
F. Valli
B. Crewe–B. Gaudio, Philips 40446
(Saturday–Seasons Four, BMI)

3. **GROOVIN'**
The Young Rascals
F. Cavaliere–E. Brigati,
Atlantic 2401 (Slacsar, BMI)

4. **SAN FRANCISCO (BE SURE TO WEAR SOME FLOWERS IN YOUR HAIR)**
S. McKenzie
J. Phillips, Ode 103
(Trousdale, BMI)

5. **COME ON DOWN TO MY BOAT**
Every Mother's Son
Farrell–Goldstein, M-G-M 13733
(Picturetone–Goldstein, BMI)

6. **UP—UP AND AWAY**
The Fifth Dimension
J. Webb, Soul City 756
(Rivers, BMI)

7. **LIGHT MY FIRE**
The Doors
The Doors, Elektra 45615
(Nipper, ASCAP)

8. **A WHITER SHADE OF PALE**
Procol Harum
Brooker–Reid, Deram 7507
(Essex, ASCAP)

9. **THE TRACKS OF MY TEARS**
J. Rivers
Tarplin–Moore–Robinson,
Imperial 66244
(Jobete, BMI)

10. **DON'T SLEEP IN THE SUBWAY**
P. Clark
T. Hatch–Trent, Warner Brothers
7049 (Duchess, BMI)

July 15

1. **UP—UP AND AWAY**
The Fifth Dimension
J. Webb, Soul City 756
(Rivers, BMI)

2. **WINDY**
The Association
Friedman,
Warner Brothers 7041
(Irving, BMI)

3. **CAN'T TAKE MY EYES OFF YOU**
F. Valli
B. Crewe–B. Gaudio, Philips 4046
(Saturday–Seasons Four, BMI)

4. **LIGHT MY FIRE**
The Doors
The Doors, Elektra 45615
(Nipper, ASCAP)

5. **DON'T SLEEP IN THE SUBWAY**
P. Clark
T. Hatch–Trent, Warner Brothers
7049 (Duchess, BMI)

6. **COME ON DOWN TO MY BOAT**
Every Mother's Son
Farrell–Goldstein, M-G-M 13733
(Picturetone–Goldstein, BMI)

7. **SAN FRANCISCO (BE SURE TO WEAR SOME FLOWERS IN YOUR HAIR)**
S. McKenzie
J. Phillips, Ode 103
(Trousdale, BMI)

8. **A WHITER SHADE OF PALE**
Procol Harum
Brooker–Reid, Deram 7507
(Essex, ASCAP)

9. **GROOVIN'**
The Young Rascals
F. Cavaliere–E. Brigati,
Atlantic 2401 (Slacsar, BMI)

10. **C'MON MARIANNE**
The Four Seasons
Russell–Bloodworth, Philips 40460
(Saturday–Seasons Four, BMI)

July 22

1. **UP—UP AND AWAY**
The Fifth Dimension
J. Webb, Soul City 756
(Rivers, BMI)

2. **WINDY**
The Association
Friedman, Warner Brothers 7041
(Irving, BMI)

3. **LIGHT MY FIRE**
The Doors
The Doors Electra 45615
(Nipper, ASCAP)

4. **CAN'T TAKE MY EYES OFF YOU**
F. Valli
B. Crewe–B. Gaudio
Philips 40446
(Saturday–Seasons Four, BMI)

5. **DON'T SLEEP IN THE SUBWAY**
P. Clark
T.Hatch–Trent, Warner
Brothers 7049 (Duchess, BMI)

6. **A WHITER SHADE OF PALE**
Procol Harum
Brooker–Reid, Deram 7547
(Essex, ASCAP)

7. **I WAS MADE TO LOVE HER**
S. Wonder
Cosby–Hardaway–Wonder–Moy,
Tamala 54151 (Jobete, BMI)

8. **COME ON DOWN TO MY BOAT**
Every Mother's Son
Farrell–Goldstein, M-G-M 13733
(Picturetone–Goldstein, BMI)

9. **SAN FRANCISCO (BE SURE TO WEAR SOME FLOWERS IN YOUR HAIR)**
S. McKenzie
J. Phillips, Ode 103
(Trousdale, BMI)

10. **C'MON MARIANNE**
The Four Seasons
Russell–Bloodworth,
Philips 40460
(Saturday–Seasons Four, BMI)

July 29

1. **LIGHT MY FIRE**
The Doors
The Doors,   Elektra 45615
(Nipper, ASCAP)

2. **A WHITER SHADE OF PALE**
Procol Harum
Brooker–Reid,   Deram 7507
(Essex, ASCAP)

3. **I WAS MADE TO LOVE HER**
S. Wonder
Cosby–Hardaway–Wonder–Moy,
Tamla 54151   (Jobete, BMI)

4. **WINDY**
The Association
Friedman,   Warner Brothers 7041
(Irving, BMI)

5. **UP—UP AND AWAY**
The Fifth Dimension
J. Webb,   Soul City 756
(Rivers, BMI)

6. **CAN'T TAKE MY EYES OFF YOU**
F. Valli
B. Crewe–B. Gaudio,
Philips 40446
(Saturday–Seasons Four, BMI)

7. **WHITE RABBIT**
The Jefferson Airplane
G. Slick,   Victor 9248
(Copper Penny, BMI)

8. **MERCY, MERCY, MERCY**
The Buckinghams
G. Levy–V. Levy–Zawinul,
Columbia 44162   (Zawinul, BMI)

9. **ALL YOU NEED IS LOVE**
The Beatles
J. Lennon–P. McCartney,
Capitol 5964   (Maclen, BMI)

10. **PLEASANT VALLEY SUNDAY**
The Monkees
G. Goffin–C. King,   Colgems 1007
(Screen Gems–Columbia, BMI)

August 5

1. **ALL YOU NEED IS LOVE**
The Beatles
J. Lennon–P. McCartney,
Capitol 5964   (Maclen, BMI)

2. **LIGHT MY FIRE**
The Doors
The Doors,   Elektra 45615
(Nipper, ASCAP)

3. **I WAS MADE TO LOVE HER**
S. Wonder
Cosby–Hardaway–Wonder–Moy,
Tamla 54151   (Jobete, BMI)

4. **ODE TO BILLIE JOE**
B. Gentry
B. Gentry,   Capitol 5950
(L. Shayne, ASCAP)

5. **WINDY**
The Association
Friedman,   Warner Brothers 7041
(Irving, BMI)

6. **PLEASANT VALLEY SUNDAY**
The Monkees
G. Goffin–C. King,   Colgems 1007
(Screen Geems–Columbia, BMI)

7. **WHITE RABBIT**
The Jefferson Airplane
G. Slick,   Victor 9248
(Copper Penny, BMI)

8. **MERCY, MERCY, MERCY**
The Buckinghams
G. Levy–V. Levy–Zawinul,
Columbia 44162   (Zawinul, BMI)

9. **MORE LOVE**
S. Robinson and the Miracles
W. Robinson,   Tamla 54152
(Jobete, BMI)

10. **A GIRL LIKE YOU**
The Young Rascals
F. Cavaliere–E. Brigati,
Atlantic 2424   (Slacsar, BMI)

August 12

1. **ALL YOU NEED IS LOVE**
The Beatles
J. Lennon–P. McCartney,
Capitol 5964   (Maclen, BMI)

2. **ODE TO BILLIE JOE**
B. Gentry
B. Gentry,   Capitol 5950
(L. Shayne, ASCAP)

3. **LIGHT MY FIRE**
The Doors
The Doors,   Elektra 45615
(Nipper, ASCAP)

4. **I WAS MADE TO LOVE HER**
S. Wonder
Cosby–Hardaway–Wonder–Moy,
Tamla 54151   (Jobete, BMI)

5. **PLEASANT VALLEY SUNDAY**
The Monkees
G. Goffin–C. King,   Colgems 1007
(Screen Gems–Columbia, BMI)

6. **MERCY, MERCY, MERCY**
The Buckinghams
G. Levy–V. Levy–Zawinul,
Columbia 44162   (Zawinul, BMI)

7. **A GIRL LIKE YOU**
The Young Rascals
F. Cavaliere–E. Brigati,
Atlantic 2424   (Slacsar, BMI)

8. **MORE LOVE**
S. Robinson and the Miracles
W. Robinson,   Tamla 54152
(Jobete, BMI)

9. **CARRIE ANNE**
The Hollies
Clark–Nash–Hicks,   Epic 10180
(Jobete, BMI)

10. **BABY I LOVE YOU**
A. Franklin
R. Shannon   Atlantic 2427
(14th Hour–Pronto, BMI)

328

August 19

1. **ODE TO BILLIE JOE**
B. Gentry
B. Gentry, Capitol 5950
(L. Shayne, ASCAP)

2. **LIGHT MY FIRE**
The Doors
The Doors, Elektra 45615
(Nipper, ASCAP)

3. **ALL YOU NEED IS LOVE**
The Beatles
J. Lennon–P. McCartney.
Capitol 5964 (Maclen, BMI)

4. **PLEASANT VALLEY SUNDAY**
The Monkees
G. Goffin–C. King, Colgems 1007
(Screen Gems–Columbia, BMI)

5. **I WAS MADE TO LOVE HER**
S. Wonder
Cosby–Hardaway–Wonder–Moy,
Tamla 54151 (Jobete, BMI)

6. **A GIRL LIKE YOU**
The Young Rascals
F . Cavaliere–E. Brigati,
Atlantic 2424 (Slacsar, BMI)

7. **BABY I LOVE YOU**
A. Franklin
R. Shannon, Atlantic 2427
(14th Hour–Pronto, BMI)

8. **MORE LOVE**
S. Robinson and the
Miracles
W. Robinson, Tamla 54152
(Jobete, BMI)

9. **MERCY, MERCY, MERCY**
The Buckinghams
G. Levy–V. Levy–Zawinul,
Columbia 44162 (Zawinul, BMI)

10. **COLD SWEAT**
J. Brown and the Famous
Flames
Brown–Ellis, King 6110
(Dynatone, BMI)

August 26

1. **ODE TO BILLIE JOE**
B. Gentry
B. Gentry, Capitol 5950
(L. Shayne, ASCAP)

2. **ALL YOU NEED IS LOVE**
The Beatles
J. Lennon–P. McCartney,
Capitol 5964 (Maclen, BMI)

3. **LIGHT MY FIRE**
The Doors
The Doors, Elektra 45615
(Nipper, ASCAP)

4. **PLEASANT VALLEY SUNDAY**
The Monkees
G. Goffin–C. King, Colgems 1007
(Screen Gems–Columbia, BMI)

5. **REFLECTIONS**
D. Ross and the Supremes
Holland–Dozier–Holland,
Motown 1111 (Jobete, BMI)

6. **BABY I LOVE YOU**
A. Franklin
R. Shannon, Atlantic 2427
(14th Hour–Pronto, BMI)

7. **COLD SWEAT**
J. Brown and the Famous
Flames
Brown–Ellis, King 6110
(Dynatone, BMI)

8. **I WAS MADE TO LOVE HER**
S. Wonder
Cosby–Hardaway–Wonder–Moy
Tamla 54151 (Jobete, BMI)

9. **YOU'RE MY EVERYTHING**
The Temptations
Whitfield–Penzabene–Grant,
Gordy 7063 (Jobete, BMI)

10. **MORE LOVE**
S. Robinson and the
Miracles
W. Robinson, Tamla 54152
(Jobete, BMI)

September 2

1. **REFLECTIONS**
D. Ross and the Supremes
Holland–Dozier–Holland,
Motown 1111 (Jobete, BMI)

2. **ODE TO BILLIE JOE**
B. Gentry
B. Gentry, Capitol 5950
(L. Shayne, ASCAP)

3. **ALL YOU NEED IS LOVE**
The Beatles
J. Lennon–P. McCartney,
Capitol 5964 (Maclen, BMI)

4. **LIGHT MY FIRE**
The Doors
The Doors, Elektra 45615
(Nipper, ASCAP)

5. **COME BACK WHEN YOU GROW UP**
B. Vee
Sharp, Liberty 55964
(Painted Desert, BMI)

6. **THE LETTER**
The Box Tops
Thompson, Mala 565
(Earl Barton, BMI)

7. **BABY I LOVE YOU**
A. Franklin
R. Shannon, Atlantic 2427
(14th Hour–Pronto, BMI)

8. **COLD SWEAT**
J. Brown and the Famous
Flames
J. Brown–Ellis, King 6110
(Dynatone, BMI)

9. **YOU'RE MY EVERYTHING**
The Temptations
Whitfield–Penzabene–Grant,
Gordy 7063 (Jobete, BMI)

10. **PLEASANT VALLEY SUNDAY**
The Monkees
G. Goffin–C. King, Colgems 1007
(Screen Gems–Columbia, BMI)

September 9

1. **REFLECTIONS**
D. Ross and the Supremes
Holland–Dozier–Holland,
Motown 1111 (Jobete, BMI)

2. **COME BACK WHEN YOU GROW UP**
B. Vee
Sharp, Liberty 55964
(Painted Desert, BMI)

3. **ODE TO BILLIE JOE**
B. Gentry
B. Gentry, Capitol 5950
(L. Shayne, ASCAP)

4. **THE LETTER**
The Box Tops
Thompson, Mala 565
(Earl Barton, BMI)

5. **BABY I LOVE YOU**
A. Franklin
R. Shannon, Atlantic 2427
(14th Hour–Pronto, BMI)

6. **YOU'RE MY EVERYTHING**
The Temptations
Whitfield–Penzabene–Grant,
Gordy 7063 (Jobete, BMI)

7. **ALL YOU NEED IS LOVE**
The Beatles
J. Lennon–P. McCartney,
Capitol 5964 (Maclen, BMI)

8. **APPLE, PEACHES, PUMP-PKIN PIE**
Jay and the Techniques
Irby, Smash 2086
(Akbestal–Act Three, BMI)

9. **SAN FRANCISCAN NIGHTS**
E. Burdon and the
Animals
Burdon–Briggs–Jenkins–Weider–
McCullock, M-G-M 13769
(Sealark–Slamine, BMI)

10. **LIGHT MY FIRE**
The Doors
The Doors, Elektra 45615
(Nipper, ASCAP)

September 16

1. **THE LETTER**
The Box Tops
Thompson, Mala 565
(Earl Barton, BMI)

2. **REFLECTIONS**
D. Ross and the Supremes
Holland–Dozier–Holland,
Motown 1111 (Jobete, BMI)

3. **ODE TO BILLIE JOE**
B. Gentry
B. Gentry, Capitol 5950
(L. Shayne, ASCAP)

4. **COME BACK WHEN YOU GROW UP**
B. Vee
Sharp, Liberty 55964
(Painted Desert, BMI)

5. **APPLES, PEACHES, PUMP-KIN PIE**
Jay and the Techniques
Irby, Smash 2086
(Akbestal–Act Three, BMI)

6. **BABY I LOVE YOU**
A. Franklin
R. Shannon, Atlantic 2427
(14th Hour–Pronto, BMI)

7. **SAN FRANCISCAN NIGHTS**
E. Burdon and the
Animals
Burdon–Briggs–Jenkins–Weider
McCullock M-G-M 13769
(Sealark–Slamine, BMI)

8. **YOU'RE MY EVERYTHING**
The Temptations
Whitfield–Penzabene–Grant,
Gordy 7063 (Jobete, BMI)

9. **FUNKY BROADWAY**
W. Pickett
Christian, Atlantic 2430
(Drive In–Routeen, BMI)

10. **NEVER MY LOVE**
The Association
D. Addrisi–R. Addrisi, Warner
Brothers 7074 (Tamerlane, BMI)

Septermber 23

1. **THE LETTER**
The Box Tops
Thompson, Mala 565
(Earl Barton, BMI)

2. **COME BACK WHEN YOU GROW UP**
B. Vee
Sharp, Liberty 55964
(Painted Desert, BMI)

3. **NEVER MY LOVE**
The Association
D. Addrisi–R. Addrisi, Warner
Brothers 7074 (Tamerlane, BMI)

4. **APPLES, PEACHES, PUMP-KIN PIE**
Jay and the Techniques
Irby, Smash 2086
(Akbestal–Act Three, BMI)

5. **ODE TO BILLIE JOE**
B. Gentry
B. Gentry, Capitol 5950
(L. Shayne, ASCAP)

6. **(YOUR LOVE HAS LIFTED ME) HIGHER AND HIGHER**
J. Wilson
Jackson–Smith, Brunswick
55336 (Jalyneene–BRC, BMI)

7. **REFLECTIONS**
D. Ross and the Supremes
Holland–Dozier–Holland,
Motown 1111 (Jobete, BMI)

8. **BROWN-EYED GIRL**
V. Morrison
V. Morrison, Bang 545
(Web IV, BMI)

9. **FUNKY BROADWAY**
W. Pickett
Christian, Atlantic 2430
(Drive In–Routeen, BMI)

10. **I DIG ROCK AND ROLL MUSIC**
Peter, Paul and Mary
Stookey–Dixon–Mason Warner
Brothers 7067 (Papamar, AS-
CAP)

September 30

1. **NEVER MY LOVE**
   The Association
   D. Addrise–R. Addrisi, Warner Brothers 7074 (Tamerlane, BMI)

2. **THE LETTER**
   The Box Tops
   Thompson, Mala 565 (Earl Barton, BMI)

3. **APPLES, PEACHES, PUMPKIN PIE**
   Jay and the Techniques
   Irby, Smash 2086 (Akbestal–Act Three, BMI)

4. **COME BACK WHEN YOU GROW UP**
   B. Vee
   Sharp, Liberty 55964 (Painted Desert, BMI)

5. **(YOUR LOVE HAS LIFTED ME) HIGHER AND HIGHER**
   J. Wilson
   Jackson–Smith, Brunswick 55336 (Jobete, BMI)

6. **LITTLE OLE MAN (UPTIGHT—EVERYTHING'S ALRIGHT)**
   B. Crosby
   Moy–Judkins–Cosby, Warner Brothers 7072 (Jobete, BMI)

7. **BROWN-EYED GIRL**
   V. Morrison
   V. Morrison, Bang 545 (Web IV, BMI)

8. **HOW CAN I BE SURE?**
   The Young Rascals
   F. Cavaliere–E. Brigati, Atlantic 2438 (Slacsar, BMI)

9. **GIMME LITTLE SIGN**
   B. Wood
   Smith–Hooven–Winn, Double Shot 116 (Big Shot, ASCAP)

10. **ODE TO BILLIE JOE**
    B. Gentry
    B. Gentry, Capitol 5950 (L. Shayne, ASCAP)

October 7

1. **NEVER MY LOVE**
   The Association
   D. Addrisi–R. Addrisi, Warner Brothers 7074 (Tamerlane, BMI)

2. **THE LETTER**
   The Box Tops
   Thompson, Mala 565 (Earl Barton, BMI)

3. **LITTLE OLE MAN (UPTIGHT—EVERYTHING'S ALRIGHT**
   B. Cosby
   Moy–Judkins–Cosby, Warner Brothers 7072 (Jobete, BMI)

4. **(YOUR LOVE HAS LIFTED ME)HIGHER AND HIGHER**
   J. Wilson
   Jackson–Smith, Brunswick 55336 (Jalynne–BRC, BMI)

5. **APPLE, PEACHES, PUMPKIN PIE**
   Jay and the Techniques
   Irby, Smash 2086 (Akbestal–Act Three, BMI)

6. **BROWN-EYED GIRL**
   V. Morrison
   V. Morrison, Bang 545 (Web IV, BMI)

7. **GIMME LITTLE SIGN**
   B. Wood
   Smith–Hooven–Winn Double Shot 116 (Big Shot, ASCAP)

8. **HOW CAN I BE SURE?**
   The Young Rascals
   F. Cavaliere–E. Brigati, Atlantic 2438 (Slacsar, BMI)

9. **TO SIR WITH LOVE**
   Lulu
   Grainer–Black–London, Epic 10187 (Screen Gems–Columbia, BMI)

10. **COME BACK WHEN YOU GROW UP**
    B. Vee
    Sharp, Liberty 55964 (Painted Desert, BMI)

October 14

1. **(YOUR LOVE HAS LIFTED ME)HIGHER AND HIGHER**
   J. Wilson
   Jackson–Smith, Brunswick 55336 (Jalynne–BRC, BMI)

2. **NEVER MY LOVE**
   The Association
   D. Addrisi–R. Addrisi, Warner Brothers 7074 (Tamerlane, BMI)

3. **THE LETTER**
   The Box Tops
   Thompson, Mala 565 (Earl Barton, BMI)

4. **LITTLE OLE MAN (UPTIGHT—EVERYTHING'S ALRIGHT)**
   B. Cosby
   Moy–Judkins–Cosby, Warner Brothers 7072 (Jobete, BMI)

5. **TO SIR WITH LOVE**
   Lulu
   Grainer–Black–London, Epic 10187 (Screen Gems–Columbia, BMI)

6. **BROWN-EYED GIRL**
   V. Morrison
   V. Morrison, Bang 545 (Web IV, BMI)

7. **APPLES, PEACHES, PUMPKIN PIE**
   Jay and the Techniques
   Irby, Smash 2086 (Akbestal–Act Three, BMI)

8. **GIMME LITTLE SIGN**
   B. Wood
   Smith–Hooven–Winn, Double Shot 116 (Big Shot, ASCAP)

9. **IT MUST BE HIM**
   V. Carr
   Becaud–David–Vidalin, Liberty 44986 (Asa, ASCAP)

10. **EXPRESSWAY TO YOUR HEART**
    The Soul Survivors
    Gamble–Huff, Crimson 1010 (Double Diamond–Downstairs, BMI)

October 21

1. **TO SIR WITH LOVE**
Lulu
Grainer–Black–London, Epic 10187 (Screen Gems–Columbia, BMI)

2. **(YOUR LOVE HAS LIFTED ME) HIGHER AND HIGHER**
J. Wilson
Jackson–Smith, Brunswick 55336 (Jalynne–BRC, BMI)

3. **NEVER MY LOVE**
The Association
D. Addrisi–R. Addrisi, Warner Brothers 7074 (Tamerlane, BMI)

4. **EXPRESSWAY TO YOUR HEART**
The Soul Survivors
Gamble–Huff –Crimson 1010 (Double Diamond–Downstairs, BMI)

5. **LITTLE OLE MAN (UPTIGHT–EVERYTHING'S ALRIGHT)**
Moy–Judkins–Cosby, Warner Brothers 7072 (Jobete, BMI)

6. **IT MUST BE HIM**
V. Carr
Becaud–David–Vidalin, Liberty 55986 (Asa, ASCAP)

7. **GIMME LITTLE SIGN**
B. Wood
Smith–Hooven–Winn, Double Shot 116 (Big Shot, ASCAP)

8. **THE LETTER**
The Box Tops
Thompson, Mala 565 (Earl Barton, BMI)

9. **SOUL MAN**
Sam and Dave
Hayes–Porter, Stax 231 (East–Pronto, BMI)

10. **YOUR PRECIOUS LOVE**
M. Gaye and T. Terrell
Simpson–Ashford, Tamla 54156 (Jobete. BMI)

October 28

1. **TO SIR WITH LOVE**
Lulu
Grainer–Black–London, Epic 10187 (Screen Gems–Columbia, BMI)

2. **EXPRESSWAY TO YOUR LOVE**
The Soul Survivors
Gamble–Huff – Crimson 1010 (Double Diamond–Downstairs, BMI)

3. **GET ON UP**
The Esquires
Moorer–Sheppard–Taylor, Bunky 7750 (Hi–Mi, BMI)

4. **IT MUST BE HIM**
V. Carr
Becaud–David–Vidalin, Liberty 55986 (Asa, ASCAP)

5. **SOUL MAN**
Sam and Dave
Hayes–Porter, Stax 231 (East–Pronto, BMI)

6. **(YOUR LOVE HAS LIFTED ME) HIGHER AND HIGHER**
J. Wilson
Jackson–Smith, Brunswick 55336 (Jalynne–BRC, BMI)

7. **GIMME LITTLE SIGN**
B. Wood
Smith–Hooven–Winn, Double Shot 116 (Big Shot, ASCAP)

8. **A NATURAL WOMAN**
A. Franklin
J. Wexler–G. Goffin–C. King, Atlantic 2441 (Screen Gems Columbia, BMI)

9. **INSENCE AND PEPPER- MINTS**
The Strawberry Alarm Clock
Kornfield–Duboff, M-G-M 13810 (Akbestal-Luvlin, BMI)

10. **THE RAIN, THE PARK, AND OTHER THINGS**
The Cowsills
Kornfield–Duboff, M-G-M 13181 (Akhestal-Luvlin, BMI)

November 4

1. **SOUL MAN**
Sam and Dave
Hayes–Porter, Stax 231 (East–Pronto, BMI)

2. **GET ON UP**
The Exquires
Moorer–Sheppard–Taylor Bunky 7750 (Hi–Mi, BMI)

3. **EXPRESSWAY TO YOUR HEART**
The Soul Survivors
Gamble–Huff, Crimson 1010 (Double Diamond–Downstairs, BMI)

4. **TO SIR WITH LOVE**
Lulu
Grainer–Black–London, Epic 10187 (Screen Gems–Columbia, BMI)

5. **THE RAIN, THE PARK, AND OTHER THINGS**
The Cowsills
Kornfield–Duboff, M-G-M 13810 (Akbestal-Luvlin, BMI)

6. **A NATURAL WOMAN**
A. Franklin
J. Wexler–G. Goffin–C. King, Atlantic 2441 (Screen Gems–Columbia, BMI)

7. **INCENSE AND PEPPER- MINTS**
The Strawberry Alarm Clock
Carter–Gilbert, Uni 55018 (Claridge, ASCAP)

8. **GIMME LITTLE SIGN**
B. Wood
Smith–Hooven–Winn, Double Shot 116 (Big Shot, ASCAP)

9. **PLEASE LOVE ME FOREVER**
B. Vinton
Malone–Blanchard, Epic 10228 (Selma, BMI)

10. **I SAY A LITTLE PRAYER**
D. Warwick
B. Bacharach–H. David, Scepter 12203 (Blue Seas–Jac, ASCAP)

1967

November 11

1. **GET ON UP**
   The Esquires
   Moorer–Sheppard–Taylor, Bunky 7750 (Hi–Mi, BMI)

2. **EXPRESSWAY TO YOUR HEART**
   The Soul Survivors
   Gamble–Huff, Crimson 1010 (Double Diamond–Downstairs, BMI)

3. **THE RAIN, THE PARK, AND OTHER THINGS**
   The Cowsills
   Kornfield–Duboff, M-G-M 13810 (Akbestal–Lulvin, BMI)

4. **INCENSE AND PEPPER-MINTS**
   The Strawberry Alarm Clock
   Carter–Gilbert, Uni 44018 (Claridge, ASCAP)

5. **TO SIR WITH LOVE**
   Lulu
   Grainer–Black–London, Epic 10187 (Screen Gems–Columbia, BMI)

6. **A NATURAL WOMAN**
   A. Franklin
   J. Wexler–G. Goffin–C. King, Atlantic 2441 (Sceen Gems–Columbia, BMI)

7. **SOUL MAN**
   Sam and Dave
   Hayes–Porter, Stax 231 (East–Pronto, BMI)

8. **I SAY A LITTLE PRAYER**
   D. Warwick
   B. Bacharach–H. David, Scepter 12203 (Blue Seas–Jac, ASCAP)

9. **PLEASE LOVE ME FOREVER**
   B. Vinton
   Malone–Blanchard, Epic 10228 (Selma, BMI)

10. **I CAN SEE FOR MILES**
    The Who
    P. Townshend, Decca 32206 (Essex, ASCAP)

November 18

1. **EXPRESSWAY TO YOUR HEART**
   The Soul Survivors
   Gamble–Huff, Crimson 1010 (Double Diamond–Downstairs, BMI)

2. **GET ON UP**
   The Esquires
   Moorer–Sheppard–Taylor, Bunky 7750 (Hi–Mi, BMI)

3. **THE RAIN, THE PARK AND OTHER THINGS**
   The Cowsills
   Kornfield–Duboff, M-G-M 13810 (Akbestal–Luvlin, BMI)

4. **INCENSE AND PEPPER-MINTS**
   The Strawberry Alarm Clock
   Carter–Gilbert, Uni 55018 (Claridge, ASCAP)

5. **I SAY A LITTLE PRAYER**
   D. Warwick
   B. Bacharach–H. David, Scepter 12203 (Blue-Seas-Jac, BMI)

6. **PLEASE LOVE ME FOREVER**
   B. Vinton
   Malone–Blanchard, Epic 10228 (Selma, BMI)

7. **TO SIR WITH LOVE**
   Lulu
   Grainer–Black–London, Epic 10187 (Screen Gems–Columbia, BMI)

8. **I CAN SEE FOR MILES**
   The Who
   P. Townshend, Decca 32206 (Essex, ASCAP)

9. **A NATURAL WOMAN**
   A. Franklin
   J. Wexler–G. Goffin–C. King, Atlantic 2441 (Screen Gems–Columbia, BMI)

10. **SOUL MAN**
    Sam and Dave
    Hayes–Porter, Stax 231 (East–Pronto, BMI)

November 25

1. **THE RAIN, THE PARK, AND OTHER THINGS**
   The Cowsills
   Kornfield–Duboff, M-G-M 13810 (Akbestal–Luvlin, BMI)

2. **INCENSE AND PEPPER-MINTS**
   The Strawberry Alarm Clock
   Carter–Gilbert, Uni 55018 (Claridge, ASCAP)

3. **DAYDREAM BELIEVER**
   The Monkees
   Stewart, Colgems 1012 (Screen Gems–Columbia, BMI)

4. **GET ON UP**
   The Esquires
   Moore–Sheppard–Taylor, Bunky 7750 (Hi–Mi, BMI)

5. **EXPRESSWAY TO YOUR HEART**
   The Soul Survivors
   Gamble–Huff, Crimson 1010 (Double Diamond–Downstairs, BMI)

6. **I SAY A LITTLE PRAYER**
   D. Warwick
   B. Bacharach–H. David, Scepter 12203 (Blue-Seas-Jac, BMI)

7. **I CAN SEE FOR MILES**
   The Who
   P. Townshend, Decca 32206 (Essex, ASCAP)

8. **PLEASE LOVE ME FOREVER**
   B. Vinton
   Malone–Blanchard, Epic 10228 (Selma, BMI)

9. **I HEARD IT THROUGH THE GRAPEVINE**
   G. Knight and the Pips
   Whitfield–Strong, Soul 35039 (Jobete, BMI)

10. **I SECOND THAT EMOTION**
    S. Robinson and the Miracles
    Cleveland–W. Robinson, Tamla 54159 (Jobete, BMI)

333

December 2

1. **INCENSE AND PEPPER-MINTS**
The Strawberry Alarm Clock
Carter–Gilbert, Uni 55018 (Claridge, ASCAP)

2. **DAYDREAM BELIEVER**
The Monkees
Steward, Colgems 1012 (Screen Gems–Columbia, BMI)

3. **THE RAIN, THE PARK AND OTHER THINGS**
The Cowsills
Kornfield–Duboff, M-G-M 13810 (Akbestal–Luvlin, BMI)

4. **I SAY A LITTLE PRAYER**
D. Warwick
B. Bacharach–H. David, Scepter 12203 (Blue Seas–Jac, BMI)

5. **I HEARD IT THROUGH THE GRAPEVINE**
G. Knight and the Pips
Whitfield–Strong, Soul 35059 (Jobete, BMI)

6. **I CAN SEE FOR MILES**
The Who
P. Townshend, Decca 32206 (Essex, ASCAP)

7. **GET ON UP**
The Esquires
Moorer–Sheppard–Taylor, Bunky 7550 (Hi-Mi, BMI)

8. **HELLO GOODBYE**
The Beatles
J. Lennon–P. McCartney, Capitol 2056 (Maclen, BMI)

9. **I SECOND THAT EMOTION**
S. Robinson and the Miracles
Cleveland–W. Robinson, Tamla 54159 (Jobete, BMI)

10. **EXPRESSWAY TO YOUR HEART**
The Soul Survivors
Gamble–Huff, Crimson 1010 (Double Diamond–Downstairs, BMI)

December 9

1. **DAYDREAM BELIEVER**
The Monkees
Steward, Colgems 1012 (Screen Gems–Columbia, BMI)

2. **INCENSE AND PEPPER-MINTS**
The Strawberry Alarm Clock
Carter–Gilbert, Uni 55018 (Claridge, ASCAP)

3. **I SAY A LITTLE PRAYER**
D. Warwick
B. Bacharach–H. David, Scepter 12203 (Blue Seas–Jac, BMI)

4. **THE RAIN, THE PARK, AND OTHER THINGS**
The Cowsills
Kornfield–Duboff, M-G-M 13810 (Akbestal–Luvlin, BMI)

5. **I HEARD IT THROUGH THE GRAPEVINE**
G. Knight and the Pips
Whitfield–Strong, Soul 35059 (Jobete, BMI)

6. **HELLO GOODBYE**
The Beatles
J. Lennon–P. McCartney, Capitol 2056 (Maclen, BMI)

7. **I SECOND THAT EMOTION**
S. Robinson and the Miracles
Cleveland–W. Robinson, Tamla 54159 (Jobete, BMI)

8. **IN AND OUT OF LOVE**
D. Ross and the Supremes
Holland–Dozier–Holland, Motown 1116 (Jobete, BMI)

9. **BOOGALOO DOWN BROADWAY**
Fantastic Johnny C.
James, Soul 305 (Dandelion–James Boy, BMI)

10. **KEEP THE BALL ROLLIN'**
Jay and the Techniques
Lanzor–Randall, Smash 2124 (Screen Gems–Columbia, BMI)

December 16

1. **I HEARD IT THROUGH THE GRAPEVINE**
G. Knight and the Pips
Whitefield–Strong, Soul 35059 (Jobete, BMI)

2. **DAYDREAM BELIEVER**
The Monkees
Stewart, Colgems 1012 (Screen Gems–Columbia, BMI)

3. **HELLO GOODBYE**
The Beatles
J. Lennon–P. McCartney, Capitol 2056 (Maclen, BMI)

4. **IN AND OUT OF LOVE**
D. Ross and the Supremes
Holland–Dozier–Holland, Motown 1116 (Jobete, BMI)

5. **I SECOND THAT EMOTION**
S. Robinson and the Miracles
Cleveland–W. Robinson, Tamla 54159 (Jobete, BMI)

6. **INCENSE AND PEPPER-MINTS**
The Strawberry Alarm Clock
Carter–Gilbert, Uni 55019 (Claridge, ASCAP)

7. **I SAY A LITTLE PRAYER**
D. Warwick
B. Bacharach–H. David, Scepter 12203 (Blue Seas–Jac, BMI)

8. **KEEP THE BALL ROLLIN'**
Jay and the Techniques
Lanzor–Randall, Smash 2124 (Screen Gems–Columbia, BMI)

9. **BOOGALOO DOWN BROADWAY**
Fantastic Johnny C.
James, Soul 305 (Dandelion–James Boy, BMI)

10. **THE RAIN, THE PARK, AND OTHER THINGS**
The Cowsills
Kornfield–Duboff, M-G-M 13810 (Akbestal–Luvlin, BMI)

1967

December 23

1. **I SECOND THAT EMOTION**
S. Robinson and the
Miracles
*Cleveland–W. Robinson,   Tamla
54159   (Mobete, BMI)*

2. **I HEARD IT THROUGH THE
GRAPEVINE**
G. Knight and the Pips
*Whitfield–Strong,   Soul 35059
(Jobete, BMI)*

3. **HELLO GOODBYE**
The Beatles
*J. Lennon–P. McCartney,
Capitol 2056   (Maclen, BMI)*

4. **DAYDREAM BELIEVER**
The Monkees
*Steward,   Colgems 1012
(Screen Gems–Columbia, BMI)*

5. **WOMAN, WOMAN**
The Union Gap
*Glaser–Payne,   Columbia 44297
(Glaser, BMI)*

6. **IN AND OUT OF LOVE**
D. Ross and the Supremes
*Holland–Dozier–Holland,
Motown 1116   (Jobete, BMI)*

7. **I SAY A LITTLE PRAYER**
D. Warwick
*B. Bacharach–H. David,
Scepter 12203
(Blue Seas–Jac, BMI)*

8. **KEEP THE BALL ROLLIN'**
Jay and the Techniques
*Lanzor–Randall,   Smash 2124
(Screen Gems–Columbia, BMI)*

9. **HONEY CHILE**
M. Reeves and the Van-
dellas
*Moy–Morris,   Gordy 7067
(Jobete, BMI)*

10. **DIFFERENT DRUM**
The Stone Poneys
*M. Nesmith,   Capitol 2004
(Screen Gems–Columbia, BMI)*

December 30

1. **I SECOND THAT EMOTION**
S. Robinson and the
Miracles
*Cleveland–W. Robinson,   Tamla
54159   (Jobete, BMI)*

2. **HELLO GOODBYE**
The Beatles
*J. Lennon–P. McCartney,
Capitol 2056
(Maclen, BMI)*

3. **I HEARD IT THROUGH THE
GRAPEVINE**
G. Knight and the Pips
*Whitfield–Strong,   Soul 35059
(Jobete, BMI)*

4. **WOMAN, WOMAN**
The Union Gap
*Glaser–Payne,   Columbia 44297
(Glaser, BMI)*

5. **DAYDREAM BELIEVER**
The Monkees
*Steward,   Colgems 1012
(Screen Gems–Columbia, BMI)*

6. **DIFFERENT DRUM**
The Stone Poneys
*M. Nesmith,   Columbia 2004
(Screen Gems–Columbia, BMI)*

7. **JUDY IN DISGUISE**
J. Fred and his Playboy
Band
*Fred–Barnard,   Pulal 282
(Su–Ma, BMI)*

8. **CHAIN OF FOOLS**
A. Franklin
*D. Covay,   Atlantic 2564
(14th Hour–Pronto, BMI)*

9. **HONEY CHILE**
M. Reeves and the Van-
dellas
*Moy–Morris,   Gordy 7067
(Jobete, BMI)*

10. **BEND ME, SHAPE**
The American Breed
*English–Weiss,   Acta 811
(Helios, BMI)*

BIBLIOGRAPHY AND CREDITS

Encyclopedia Americana Yearbook. New York; Americana Corp., 1956 through 1968.

Encyclopedia Brittanica Yearbook. Chicago, London, Toronto, Geneva, Sydney, Tokyo: Encyclopedia Brittanica, Inc., 1956 through 1968.

Facts on File Yearbook. New York: Facts on File, Inc., 1956 through 1968.

Port Light. Port Washington, New York: Paul D. Schreiber High School, 1961, 1962.

Shapiro, Nat. *Popular Music: An Annotated Index of American Popular Songs,* Vol. 1, 1950–1959, Vol. 3, 1960–1964, Adrian, N. Y. 1967.

Syllabus, Northwestern University, Evanston, Ill. 1963 through 1966.

The All Time Million Seller Records, 1970 ed. Woodland Hills, Calif.: Phono-Graph Publications.

United States Copyright Office Catalogue of Copyright Entries: Music Series, 1955–1967.

World Book Yearbook. Chicago, London, Rome, Toronto, Sydney: Field Enterprises Educational Corporation, 1956 through 1968.

Billboard, Billboard Publishing Co., New York, 1955 through 1967.

Cash Box, Cash Box Publications, New York, 1955 through 1967.

Life, Time, Inc., Chicago and New York, 1955 through 1967.

Mademoiselle, Street and Smith Publications, New York, 1955 through 1967.

Saturday Evening Post, Curtis Publishing Co., Philadelphia, 1955 through 1967.

Time, Time, Inc., New York, 1955 through 1967.

American Bandstand Anniversary Show, ABC-TV, February 28, 1970.

2588 Newport Corp., Costa Mesa, California, Record library and facilities.

Album cover: Meet the Beatles, Capitol Records

Photographs by United Press International

SONG TITLE INDEX

344

ARTIST INDEX

349